LENIN THE DICTATOR

Also by Victor Sebestyen

Twelve Days: Revolution 1956
Revolution 1989: The Fall of the Soviet Empire
1946: The Making of the Modern World

LENIN THE DICTATOR

An Intimate Portrait

VICTOR SEBESTYEN

WEIDENFELD & NICOLSON

First published in Great Britain in 2017
by Weidenfeld & Nicolson

3 5 7 9 10 8 6 4 2

A CIP catalogue record for this book
is available from the British Library.

HB ISBN   978 1 47460044 6
TPB 978 1 47460045 3

Typeset by Input Data Services Ltd, Bridgwater, Somerset

Printed and bound by CPI Group (UK) Ltd, Croydon, CR0 4YY

Weidenfeld & Nicolson

The Orion Publishing Group Ltd
Carmelite House
50 Victoria Embankment
London EC4Y 0DZ

An Hachette UK Company

www.orionbooks.co.uk

In Memory of C. H.

CONTENTS

MAPS

The Russian Empire 1878–1917

BARENTS SEA

River Yenisei

N

Kureika
Monastyrskoe
Kostino

Ivychegodsk

Perm

Narym

S I B E R I A

Novaya
Uda

Krasnoyarsk

Omsk

MPIRE

al
:a

—··—·· Western border of the Russian
///////// Empire before 1914

0   500   1000 miles
0   500   1000   1500 km

Gori   St Petersburg

Gori   Moscow

WHITE SEA

NORWAY

ARCHANGEL

FINLAND

SWEDEN

OLONETS

VOLOGDA

PERM

ESTLAND

LIVLAND

PETROGRAD

NOVGOROD

Baltic Sea

KURLAND

PSKOV

TVER

YAROSLAV

KOSTROMA

VIATKA

KOVNO

VITEBSK

VLADIMIR

NIZHNY
NOVGOROD

KAZAN

UFA

GERMANY

VILNA

SMOLENSK

MOSCOW

GRODNO

MOGILEV

KALUGA

RIAZAN

SIMBIRSK

POLISH
PROVINCES

MINSK

TULA

PENZA

SAMARA

ORENBURG

OREL

CHERIGOV

TAMBOV

SARATOV

VOLHYNIA

KURSK

AUSTRIA-
HUNGARY

KIEV

POLTAVA

VORONEZH

PODOLIA

KHARKOV

BESSARABIA

KHERSON

EKATERINOSLAV

DON

ASTRAKHAN

TAURIDA

RUMANIA

KUBAN

STAVROPOL

Black Sea

TEREK

Caspian
Sea

TURKEY

TRANS-CAUCASIAN
PROVINCES

0   200 Miles

0   300 Kms

Mediterranean Sea

N

European Russia 1917

USSR 1920–36

LIST OF ILLUSTRATIONS

Vladimir Ulyanov as a baby (PA Images)
The Ulyanov family in 1879 (Sputnik/Alamy)
Alexander 'Sasha' Ulyanov (Sputnik/Topfoto)
Anna Ilyinichna (Interfoto/Alamy)
Maria Ilyinichna (Interfoto/Alamy)
Nadezhda Krupskaya, aged twenty-one (TASS Photo Chronicle
    Photas/Tass/PA Images)
Vladimir Ulyanov police mugshot (PA Images)
Yuli Martov (Jakov Vladimirovich Shteinberg/Bridgeman Images)
Leon Trotsky (Heritage Images/Getty Images)
Nadezhda Krupskaya, aged twenty-six (Sputnik/Alamy)
Inessa Armand (ITAR-TASS Photo Agency/Alamy Stock Photo)
Grigory Zinoviev (Hulton Deutsch/Getty Images)
Lev Kamenev (Granger Collection/Topfoto)
Joseph Stalin (ITAR-TASS/Topfoto)
Lenin in hiding (ITAR-TASS Photo Agency/Alamy)
Lenin in Red Square (Granger Historical Picture Archive/Alamy)
Felix Dzerzhinsky (Laski Collection/Getty Images)
Lenin's last days (ITAR-TASS/Topfoto)
Lenin in state (Interfoto/Alamy)

INTRODUCTION

On one side of Moscow's Red Square there remains a sight familiar to anyone who knew the late Soviet Union in the Communist years. Every day, long lines of people queue patiently for a ticket to visit Lenin's mausoleum, set within a huge marble plinth erected in the late 1920s. The wait can last an age; the tour itself just moments. Visitors enter a basement and walk along a bare corridor for a few metres in eerie semi-darkness, before reaching the coffin. Powerful lights illuminate the embalmed body which has been lying in this tomb on plush red velvet for nearly ninety years. There is such a crush of people that they are given a maximum of five minutes to pay their respects – or simply to gawp. A few of the visitors are foreigners. The vast majority are Russians.

It is a macabre place to go sightseeing in the twenty-first century, whoever is entombed there. But two and a half decades after the collapse of the USSR, it seems the strangest of anachronisms that Vladimir Ilyich Lenin can continue to draw such crowds. Everyone knows the havoc he wreaked; few people now believe in the faith he espoused. Yet he still commands attention – even affection – in Russia.

The present Russian leader, Vladimir Putin, has no intention of getting rid of the tomb. Rather, in 2011 he authorised vast expenditure to repair the mausoleum when there was a danger it would fall down. The Lenin Cult survives, if in an altered form. Putin's grandfather, Spiridon, was Lenin's cook after the Russian Revolution, but it is not the current President's family sentiment that has kept Lenin's remains *in situ*. The clear signal is to show historical continuity, the idea that Russia still needs – as it has always needed – a dominant, ruthless, autocratic leader, a boss, in Russian, the *Vozhd*. Lenin's tomb once symbolised an internationalist ideology, world Communism. It has since become an altar of resurgent Russian nationalism.

It is not just Lenin's body that was embalmed. His character has been 'preserved' too; his personality, his motivation and intentions,

1

have rarely been reassessed over the last generation, even in the light of a mass of new information about him since archives began opening up in the former Soviet Union. In the USSR all biographies of Lenin were hagiographies, required reading in Russian schools where children were taught to refer to the founder of the Soviet state as *Dyedushka* (grandfather) Lenin. Even the last Communist Party chief, Mikhail Gorbachev, used to call him 'a special genius' and quoted him frequently. Lenin was the pillar of Bolshevik rectitude in all ways.

In the other camp the opposite was true. The line tended to be that he may not have been as bad as Stalin, but he nonetheless created one of history's cruellest tyrannies – and a state model which at one point was copied by nearly half the world. More often than not – there are some shining exceptions – biographers were on one side or the other in an ideological divide, at a time when the Cold War mattered. Those theoretical disputes became outdated from the moment the Berlin Wall came down and the Soviet Union collapsed.

The Communist world that Lenin formed, very much in his own ascetic image, may have gone into the dustbin of history. Yet he is highly relevant today. At the end of the Cold War, neo-liberalism triumphed, along with the idea of democracy; socialism and its variants were entirely discredited. There seemed to be no alternative to the political and economic solutions offered by globalised markets. But the world looked a different place after a banking crisis and recession in 2007–08. There was a loss of confidence in much of the West in the democratic process itself. For millions of people, the certainties that two generations accepted as basic assumptions, the facts of life, were altogether less certain. Lenin would very probably have regarded the world of 2017 as being on the cusp of a revolutionary moment. He matters now not because of his flawed, bloody and murderously misguided answers, but because he was asking the same questions as we are today about similar problems.

Millions of people, and some dangerous populist leaders on the Left and Right, are doubting whether liberal democracy has been successful in creating a fair society and sustained freedom and prosperity, or can deal with gaping inequality and injustice. The phrases 'global elite', and 'the 1 per cent' are now used in a decidedly Leninist way. It is unlikely that Lenin's solutions will be adopted anywhere again. But his questions are constantly being asked today, and may be answered by equally bloody methods.

Lenin seized power in a coup, but he did not operate entirely through terror. In many ways he was a thoroughly modern political phenomenon – the kind of demagogue familiar to us in Western democracies, as well as in dictatorships. In his quest for power, he promised people anything and everything. He offered simple solutions to complex problems. He lied unashamedly. He identified a scapegoat he could later label 'enemies of the people'. He justified himself on the basis that winning meant everything: the ends justified the means. Anyone who has lived through recent elections in the supposedly sophisticated political cultures of the West might recognise him. Lenin was the godfather of what commentators a century after his time call 'post-truth politics'.

Lenin thought himself an idealist. He was not a monster, a sadist or vicious. In personal relationships he was invariably kind and behaved in the way he was brought up, like an upper-middle-class gentleman. He was not vain. He could laugh – even, occasionally, at himself. He was not cruel: unlike Stalin, Mao Zedong or Hitler he never asked about the details of his victims' deaths, savouring the moment. To him, in any case, the deaths were theoretical, mere numbers. He never donned uniforms or military-style tunics as other dictators favoured. But during his years of feuding with other revolutionaries, and then maintaining his grip on power, he never showed generosity to a defeated opponent or performed a humanitarian act unless it was politically expedient.

He built a system based on the idea that political terror against opponents was justified for a greater end. It was perfected by Stalin, but the ideas were Lenin's. He had not always been a bad man, but he did terrible things. Angelica Balabanova, one of his old comrades who admired him for many years but grew to fear and loathe him, said perceptively that Lenin's 'tragedy was that, in Goethe's phrase, he desired the good . . . but created evil'. The worst of his evils was to have left a man like Stalin in a position to lead Russia after him. That was a historic crime.

Lenin is often depicted as a rigid ideologue, a Communist fanatic, and this is true up to a point. He spouted Marxist theory constantly – 'without theory there can be no revolutionary party', he famously said. But a point he made far more often to his followers is frequently ignored

– 'theory is a guide, not Holy Writ'. When ideology clashed with opportunism, he invariably chose the tactical path above doctrinal purity. He could change his mind entirely if it advanced his goal. He was driven by emotion as much as by ideology. His thirst for revenge after his elder brother was executed for an assassination plot against the Tsar motivated Lenin as powerfully as did his belief in Marx's theory of surplus value.

He wanted power and he wanted to change the world. He retained power personally for a little over four years before failing health rendered him physically and mentally incapable. But, as he said that it would, the Bolshevik Revolution in 1917 'turned the world upside down'. Neither Russia, nor many places from Asia to South America, have since recovered.

To a biographer, though, the political is the personal, as Lenin would also sometimes say. He was a product of his time and place: a violent, tyrannical and corrupt Russia. The revolutionary state he created was less the socialist Utopia he dreamed of than a mirror-image of the Romanov autocracy. The fact that Lenin was Russian is as significant as his Marxist faith.

Lenin as a person was seldom allowed to emerge in the Cold War versions of his life. Neither side wanted him to appear human, as that would not fit neatly into their ideological baggage. He was not icy, logical and one-dimensional as he is often portrayed. He was highly emotional and flew into rages that almost crippled him.

He wrote a large number of texts about Marxist philosophy and economy, many of them unintelligible now. But he loved mountains almost as much as he loved making Revolution, and he wrote lyrically about walking in the Alps and through open countryside. He loved nature, hunting, shooting and fishing. He could identify hundreds of species of plants. His 'nature notes' and letters to his family show a part of Lenin which will surprise people who imagined him a distant and unfeeling figure.

One of the surprises while researching this book was to find that nearly all the important relationships in Lenin's life were with women. It will show another little-known side to him: Lenin in love. His wife Nadezhda – Nadya – left a sanitised and dull memoir about their life together; but, in the light of new material, and by piecing together a narrative from other sources, she emerges as far more than the house-hold drudge/secretary she is usually made out to be. Lenin would never have achieved what he did without her. For a decade he had an on-off love affair with a glamorous, intelligent and beautiful woman, Inessa Armand. Their *ménage à trois* is woven throughout nearly half this book as it is so central to Lenin's emotional life – and to Nadya's. It is a rare example of a romantic triangle in which all three protagonists appear to have behaved in a civilised fashion. The only time Lenin visibly broke down in public was at Armand's funeral, three years before his own.

Back in the days of the USSR, while on an assignment in Moscow as a journalist, I was given a private tour of the Kremlin office and rooms once occupied by Lenin. They were preserved just as they had been in his day, or so I was assured by the senior Communist Party apparatchik who showed me around. It struck me how ordinary the surroundings were, how banal, how bourgeois, and – undiplomatically – I blurted out exactly those words. Oddly, as Party hacks in those days rarely uttered heretical thoughts, he said, 'Yes, I have always wondered how he could have done such extraordinary things.' I have never forgotten the conver-sation. This is an attempt at an answer.

Victor Sebestyen, London, October 2016

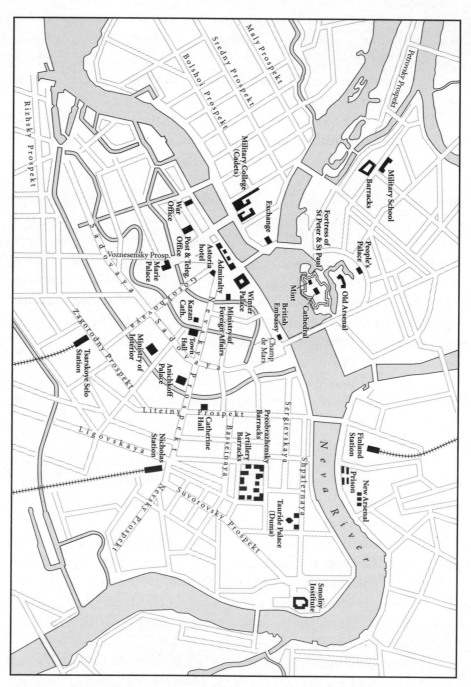

Petrograd 1917

THE COUP D'ETAT

'Insurrection is an art quite as much as war.'
    Karl Marx, *Revolution and Counter-Revolution in Germany*, 1852

'There are decades when nothing happens – and there are weeks where decades happen.'
    Vladimir Ilyich Lenin, *The Chief Tasks of Our Day*, March 1918

He was fretting about his wig, a wavy silver-grey mop which kept slipping off his shiny bald pate, threatening to spoil his disguise. Vladimir Ilyich Ulyanov – better known by the pseudonym Lenin – had struggled his entire adult life for this moment. He was on the brink of seizing absolute power in Russia and sparking a revolution that would change the world. But here he was clutching that ridiculous hairpiece, holed up in a pokey second-floor flat in a working-class suburb of Petrograd, while history was being made by others a few kilometres away in the centre of the city.

He could stand the frustration and uncertainty no longer. Lenin knew that he and his small group of fanatical socialists, the Bolsheviks, had limited popular appeal in Russia's capital, and even less in the rest of the country. Their one chance for greatness was 'to take power from the street' now, by insurrection against a weak government that could claim even less support. Timing was all, as Lenin used to say with monotonous regularity. He had declared that the coup must take place by Wednesday, 25 October 1917 or his enemies would seize *their* moment to thwart him. He was forty-seven, no longer in prime health, and if he failed his chance might never come again.

It was now the evening of Tuesday the 24th and Vladimir Ilyich had no idea if any of the plans his comrades had made for the insurrection were actually being implemented. He was a leader cut off from his

General Staff and his troops. He had appointed a 'Military Revolution-ary Committee' to work out the tactical details of the coup, but it was based on the other side of town at Bolshevik headquarters in the Smolny Institute, a grand building which had formerly been a school for daugh-ters of the nobility.

For security reasons Lenin's comrades had insisted that he stay at the safe house chosen for him in the working-class Vyborg district. Secret-ed away in the home of Margarita Fofanova, a loyal Party worker who was ordered not to allow Lenin to leave her apartment, he had spent most of the day pacing up and down the main room of the flat growing increasingly irritable. He had received hardly any visitors and heard no news of the impending uprising until around 6 p.m., when Fofanova returned and told him that there seemed no sign anywhere in the city of the Bolsheviks' shock troops, the Red Guards. 'I don't understand them,' he said. 'What on earth are they afraid of? Just ask if they have a hundred trustworthy soldiers or Red Guards with rifles. That's all I need.'

Impatient, Lenin worried that his military committee, few of whom had any fighting experience, would bungle the coup. Even worse, he imagined that his civilian comrades had, in his absence, aborted the insurrection altogether. He knew that many even in his closest circle doubted the Bolsheviks could take power, let alone keep it; some feared they would be 'hanged from lamp posts' if they tried. Lenin had imposed his will on them, as he had always found a way to do before in nearly two decades of leadership in the underground revolutionary movement. He had bullied, cajoled and finally blackmailed them by threatening to re-sign, leaving the Bolsheviks rudderless. Finally, a fortnight earlier, he had secured a majority of the senior Party figures to go along with him. But still they might change their minds and call off the uprising. Power might yet elude him.

Lenin hastily scribbled a stirring plea to his comrades. 'It is as clear as can be that delaying the uprising really would be fatal,' he wrote. 'Everything now hangs by a thread. We must not wait. We must at any price act this evening, tonight, or we may lose everything. History will not forgive delay by revolutionists who could be victorious today (and will surely be victorious today) while they risk losing all tomorrow. The government is tottering. It must be given the death blow at all costs.'

He told Fofanova to take the note to the local Vyborg Party head-quarters close by, then hand it to his wife, Nadezhda Konstantinovna Krupskaya, 'and no one else'. She would ensure that it reached the high-est Party officials.

Lenin was desperate to get to the Smolny. The leader should be lead-ing, not hiding away. But there was a warrant out for his arrest and he was in danger. He had been living underground since early July, in Finland for three months and for the last three weeks in Petrograd. At first the authorities had made half-hearted attempts to catch him. Days earlier the Bolsheviks had been warned that now the government was far more determined to track him down. Another hazard was that law and order had collapsed in Petrograd and casual violence from random criminals made parts of the city no-go areas. 'Hold-ups increased to such an extent that it was dangerous to walk down side streets,' wrote one reporter. 'On the Sadovaya [a principal street near the Finland Station] one afternoon I saw a crowd of several hundred people beat and trample to death a soldier caught stealing.'[1]

* * *

Soon after 9 p.m. Lenin's bodyguard, Eino Rakhia, appeared at the apartment. He was a Finnish Bolshevik who had become close to Lenin during many years in exile. He said that the government had ordered all the bridges across the River Neva to be raised. If that succeeded the Vyborg district would be cut off from the centre of the city and, if they could muster enough soldiers, government loyalists could take control of Petrograd quarter by quarter, cutting off Red Guard units from each other and severing communications.

'Well then, we'll go to Smolny,' Lenin said.

Rakhia warned him there was no transport and they would have to go by foot. 'It could take hours – and it's very risky.' Both were without passes that would allow them into central areas of the capital.

Lenin insisted that in that case they had better get going immediately. He found some paper and left a message for Fofanova. 'I've gone where you didn't want me to go. Goodbye. Ilyich.'

Lenin then put on his disguise – the old clothes of a labourer, a pair of spectacles and the wig that refused to stay in place even when he donned the workman's peaked cap that would become familiar in coming years.

He had shaved off his trademark reddish beard earlier in the summer. He wrapped a dirty handkerchief around his face. If anyone stopped him the plan was to say that he was suffering from toothache.

They then went out into the freezing, windy night. Lenin thought it would rain and wore galoshes over his shoes. They walked a few hundred metres but struck lucky when a near-empty tram came along. It took them several kilometres to the corner of the Petrograd Botanical Gardens, close to the Finland Station, the end of the line. In many later Soviet histories Lenin is said to have had a conversation with a tram conductress who asked him, 'Where have you come from? Don't you know there's going to be a revolution? We're going to kick the bosses out!' Lenin is supposed to have laughed heartily and explained to the woman how revolutions occur – much to the annoyance of Rakhia, who feared Lenin would give himself away.

The tram stopped by the Liteiny Bridge just before midnight. This is where the journey became more difficult and dangerous. One end of the bridge was held by Red Guards, who believed the pair were true proletarians and waved them through. The other side was still in the hands of government troops who were checking for passes. At exactly this moment a group of workers was arguing with the soldiers and the two men seized the opportunity to slip past the soldiers unnoticed.

They walked down Liteiny Prospekt – close to the Smolny – but ran into two army cadets, young officers, who asked for their identification papers. Rakhia was armed with two revolvers and reckoned that if necessary he was prepared to fight it out with them. Then he had a better idea. He whispered to Lenin, 'I can deal with those soldiers, you go on,' and Lenin moved off. Rakhia began to distract the guards by arguing with them, swaying unsteadily on his feet and slurring his words. The cadets reached for their pistols but decided to do nothing. They let them through thinking they were merely two harmless old drunks. Marxists are not supposed to believe in luck, accident or happenstance, but rather explain life through broad historical forces. Yet the second most influential Bolshevik leader in 1917, Leon Trotsky, said simply that if Lenin had been arrested, or shot, or had not been in Petrograd, 'there would have been no October Revolution'.

They reached 'great Smolny', a huge ochre-coloured Palladian building with a colonnaded façade spanning more than 150 metres. This was the 'internal arena of the Revolution'. That night it was 'bright with lights and from a distance resembled an ocean liner in the night sea'. Closer up it 'hummed like a gigantic hive'. Young Red Guards stood around outside, 'a huddled group of boys in workmen's clothes, carrying guns with bayonets, talking nervously together', warming their hands around bonfires. Lenin wasn't recognised, but his problems were not over. Both he and Rakhia had out-of-date passes – white instead of the newly valid red papers issued that morning. 'This is ridiculous, what a mess,' shouted Rakhia. 'You're refusing entry to a member of the Petrograd Soviet.' When that didn't work, Lenin started arguing with the guards too. It was only when people behind them in the queue objected to the delay, and began to push and shove, that the guards let them in. 'Lenin came in, laughing,' one man in the crowd recalled later. When he doffed his cap to the guards, the wig came off.

Lenin had never been in the building before and he had no idea where to go. For weeks the Smolny had been packed with soldiers sleeping in the corridors, revolutionary politicians plotting in its warren of 120 rooms and journalists watching the story of the Russian Revolution unfold. The stench was overpowering. 'The air was thick with cigarette smoke; the floors were covered with rubbish and everywhere there was the smell of urine. Futile signs were posted on the walls: "Comrades please preserve cleanliness".' Rakhia took Lenin, still concerned about hiding his identity, to the second floor. Here he was among as many opponents as friends.

At the top of the stairs he found Trotsky, head of the Military Revolutionary Committee, the man in charge of planning the coup. 'Vladimir Ilyich, disguised, was an odd sight,' Trotsky said later. As they greeted each other, two prominent members of an opposition socialist group eyed Lenin carefully, smiled and looked knowingly at each other. 'Dammit, they've recognised me, the scoundrels,' he muttered.

Lenin was ushered into Room 10, where the Military Revolutionary Committee had been in permanent session for days. 'We found ourselves in the presence of a little grey-haired old man, wearing a pince-nez,' recalled Vladimir Antonov-Ovseyenko, soon to become one of the Bolsheviks' most ruthless hatchet men. 'You could have taken him for a schoolmaster or a second-hand book dealer. He took off his wig . . . and then we recognised his eyes, sparkling as usual with a glint of humour. "Any news?" he asked.'

In hiding Lenin had known little about the precise details of the coup. The artist of the insurrection dealt in broad brush strokes. Now he saw maps of the city spread out on tables and he was told how the main strongpoints of Petrograd would be in Bolshevik hands by the morning. There were about 25,000 armed Red Guards available, but only a fraction of them would be needed, said Trotsky. The revolutionaries would take power without firing a shot.

Some blankets and pillows were placed in the corner of the room and Lenin and Trotsky lay down. But neither could sleep. At 2 a.m. Trotsky looked at his watch and said, 'It's begun.' Lenin replied, 'I'm dizzy. From being on the run to supreme power – that's too much,' and according to Trotsky made the sign of the Cross.*[2]

It has been an enduring myth that the Revolution was an impeccably organised operation by a group of highly disciplined conspirators who knew exactly what they were doing throughout. It is a version of events that suited both sides. Soviet historians in the following decades presented 'glorious October' as a rising of the masses, brilliantly led by the master of timing and tactics, V. I. Lenin, and his skilful, heroic lieutenants in the Bolshevik Party, who kept to a strict timetable of insurrection.

The defeated 'Whites', as they would soon be called, also held to a comforting myth: that they lost power in a precisely calibrated military takeover masterminded by an evil genius whose plans, diabolical though they were, cleverly took account of chaos on the streets of Petrograd. It would not have impressed the loyalists' supporters – or soothed their own *amour propre* – if it was put about that they were beaten by a group of plotters who very nearly botched their revolution. The Bolsheviks might easily have failed if at certain key moments they had met some slight resistance.

In reality the 'plot' was the worst-kept secret in history. Everyone in

---

* Trotsky was often asked later if he was absolutely sure that a famously militant atheist like Lenin really had crossed himself at this solemn moment. He replied that he was surprised to see it but it was hardly a thing he would forget, or invent. Trotsky was equally surprised that when Lenin said he felt dizzy he very deliberately used the German expression *'Es schwindelt'* – presumably for added emphasis.

Petrograd had heard that the Bolsheviks were preparing an imminent coup. It had been discussed in the press for the past ten days. The main right-wing newspaper *Rech* (Speech) had even revealed the date, 25 October, and the leftist *Novaya Zhizn* (New Life), run by the writer Maxim Gorky, had warned the Bolsheviks against using violence and 'shedding more blood in Russia'. The supposedly perfect clockwork timekeeping of the insurrection was so vague that nobody could tell for certain exactly when it began. At one stage the Mayor of Petrograd sent a delegation to the participants of both sides wondering if the uprising had started. He could not get an accurate answer. The Bolsheviks had little military experience. Alexander Genevsky, one of their main commanders on the ground, had been a temporary lieutenant in the Tsarist army, declared unfit after he was gassed early in the First World War. He had been asked to become a 'general' in the rebel forces. His orders were to keep the military planners at the Smolny up to date with events by ringing a number that he was told would always be available, 148–11. The few times it wasn't out of order, it was engaged. The Bolsheviks failed to master the Petrograd telephone system and had to send runners throughout the city streets. The key force of sailors from the Kronstadt naval base – reliable Bolshevik supporters – arrived in Petrograd a day late.

They won because the other side, the Provisional Government and its backers – a coalition of the centre-right, liberals and moderate socialists – were even more incompetent and divided, and because they didn't take the Bolsheviks seriously until it was too late. But mainly it was because most of the people didn't care which side won. In fact, few people realised anything significant had happened until it was all over.[3]

At the Smolny, Lenin couldn't rest during the night. He continually pored over maps and anxiously waited for news. He was short-tempered, constantly calling for more reliable information and swifter action, insisting on accelerating the revolt. 'He worked at furious speed, spitting out panting couriers and despatching aides . . . amid the buzz of telegraphs.' He was hastily preparing the statements and decrees he would make when power was assured. He moved between Room 10, where the Military Revolutionary Committee met, to Room 36, down a long corridor where the human odours mixed with the smell of boiled cabbage from the refectory on the ground floor of the building. This was where the rest of the Bolshevik leadership in the Party's Central Committee met, 'in a tiny room around a badly lit table with overcoats thrown on the floor. People were constantly knocking on the door with news.'

At one point soon after dawn the comrades began discussing the form of the new government. Lenin wondered what it should be called.

'We must not call the members ministers,' he said. 'It's a repulsive, hackneyed word.'

'Why not commissars,' Trotsky suggested, 'only there are too many commissars already. How about People's Commissars?'

'People's Commissars. I like that. And what shall we call the government?'

'The Council [Soviet] of People's Commissars.'

'That's wonderful,' exclaimed Lenin. 'It has the smell of revolution.'*

There followed a charade of modesty among the revolutionaries, who within hours would be supreme oligarchs exercising awesome power over the lives and deaths of millions.

Lenin proposed that Trotsky should be head of the government, while he himself remained leader of the Bolshevik Party. Nobody knows whether he meant it or not, but he showed little surprise when Trotsky refused. 'You know very well that a Jew can't be Premier in Russia,' he said. 'And besides you'd constantly be disagreeing with me. You're the leader. It has to be you.' The decision was unanimous.[4]

Overnight, small groups of Red Guards seized the strategic command positions of the city. They secured all the bridges across the Neva before dawn, except for the Nikolai Bridge next to the Winter Palace. Earlier they had captured the Peter and Paul Fortress, directly across the river, whose guns held a commanding view of the palace, where the Prime Minister, Alexander Kerensky, resided and the Provisional Government met. The occasional crack of gunfire could be heard, but there had been no fighting. 'It happened while the city was in deep slumber,' recorded Nikolai Sukhanov, whose eyewitness account of the Revolution remains one of the best accounts of the events. 'More like the changing of the guard than an insurrection.'

---

* Both Lenin and Trotsky had studied the French Revolution with great care and took inspiration from it. This was a deliberate echo of the Jacobins' 'Commissaires', supposedly protectors of the people. The word comes originally from the Latin commissarius, meaning the plenipotentiaries of a higher power – in this case the citizens.

At 6 a.m. the State Bank fell, an hour later the Central Telephone Exchange, the main Post Office and the Telegraph Building. By 8 a.m. the rebels had taken all the railway stations. The Bolsheviks controlled communications throughout Petrograd and had barely fired a shot. There were no casualties. In theory the government could call on the city's garrison troops, numbering some 35,000. But as Trotsky had predicted, even if the majority of the soldiers were not actively siding with the Bolsheviks, they weren't prepared to fight them either.

* * *

The timing of the insurrection was crucial to Lenin's political strategy. Since the Tsar had fallen nine months earlier power had been shared uneasily between a series of coalition governments, which had grown successively weaker, and the Soviets. In Russian the word 'soviet' means simply 'council', and they were hastily elected delegates of workers and soldiers who claimed that they had instigated and led the Revolution in February that brought down the Romanov autocracy.

Lenin had excluded the Bolsheviks from joining the government, but for the previous month they had held a small majority on the Petrograd Soviet. Lenin's plan was to overthrow the government and claim that he was acting on behalf of the Soviets. Real power would lie with him and the Bolsheviks, but keeping the Soviet on board gave him political cover and a semblance of popular support. But there was one big snag. The Congress of Soviets was due to meet that day – in the splendid white and gold ballroom of the Smolny, just below the warren of rooms where the Bolsheviks had been planning the coup. Lenin was supposed to present the takeover as a *fait accompli* when the Congress convened at noon, and declare a victory for the Revolution. However, the government still survived and the Winter Palace – symbol of power in Russia since the time of Catherine the Great – had not fallen.

Lenin had been told by his military committee that seizing the palace would be a straightforward matter, over within five or six hours. But it would take more than fifteen hours, amid a catalogue of errors that would have been farcical if the stakes had not been so high.

* * *

15

At 9 a.m. Lenin demanded the surrender of the government. He received no reply. Prime Minister Kerensky had left soon after dawn for the army headquarters in an attempt to raise some loyal troops to defeat the rebellion. The Bolsheviks had made no effort to detain him, though his escape had not been straightforward. There were thirty cars parked outside the palace but none were in working order. He couldn't even find a taxi to take him. An ensign was sent to see if he could requisition a car that would run. The British Embassy turned him down, but an official from the US Legation was persuaded to let Kerensky use his own car, a Renault, as long as it was returned.* Another officer managed to scrounge a luxurious open-topped Pierce Arrow and some fuel. Kerensky was driven around Palace Square and through the streets of Petrograd with the roof down, easily recognisable.

When the ministers met in the Malachite Room of the Winter Palace towards midday they refused to surrender and decided to hold out for as long as they could; 'doomed people, lonely and abandoned, we walked around the huge mousetrap', Pavel Malyanovich, the Minister of Justice, wrote in his diary.

Lenin was given to furious, intemperate 'rages', as his wife Nadya often said. They became more frequent as his health declined and the insomnia and headaches which had always plagued him got worse. He was in a fury much of this day as his military planners seemed to be bungling. He put off his appearance at the Congress of Soviets from midday to 3 p.m., but if he had to delay much further, his entire political strategy might fall apart. It was vital to present the coup as a complete success, a job well done.

In Room 10 of the Smolny, he barked orders to his aides and Red Guard commanders and fired off dozens of notes pleading for speedier action to take over the palace. The pleas soon turned into demands, and then threats. He paced around the room 'like a lion in a cage', recalled Nikolai Podvoisky, one of the Military Revolutionary Committee's most senior officials. 'Vladimir Ilyich scolded, he screamed. He needed the Palace at all costs. He said he was ready to shoot us.'[5]

---

* Neither the owner, US diplomat Sheldon Whitehouse, nor the driver could work out how to remove the Stars and Stripes flag from the bonnet. The loan of the car led to a formal diplomatic protest to the US government by the Bolshevik regime – the first of many over the following decades.

The ministers were holding out in the vast but gloomy symbol of Imperial Russia, which had been the Provisional Government's home since July. Much of Tsarist imperial history had been played out among the palace's 1,500 rooms, spread out over a quarter-mile-long building fronting the Neva. Kerensky had moved into the third-floor suite that had once belonged to the Emperor, with picture windows overlooking the Admiralty Spire. Most of the building was now being used as a military hospital for war wounded, with around 500 patients on this day. In the huge courtyard at the rear of the building were hundreds of horses belonging to the two companies of Cossacks charged with defending the government. Along with the Cossacks, there were 220 officer cadets from the Oranienbaum Military School, forty members of the Petrograd Garrison's bicycle squad and 200 women from the Shock Battalion of Death.* From an armed force of nine million Russians, this was all the Provisional Government could muster to protect the capital – and themselves.

The 'storming of the Winter Palace' – centrepiece of the Russian Revolution – was so sloppy that the American journalists John Reed and his wife Louise Bryant were able to stroll into the building during the afternoon without being stopped. Palace servants in their Tsarist blue uniforms took their coats as usual and some of the cadets from the Military School showed them around. On the ground floor 'at the end of the corridor was a large ornate room with gilded cornices and enormous crystal lustres', wrote Reed. 'On both sides of the parqueted floor long rows of dirty mattresses and blankets, upon which occasional soldiers were stretched out; everywhere was a litter of cigarette butts, bits of

---

* Despite their bloodcurdling title, they were mostly girls from the provinces and not at all happy to be part of the last-ditch effort to prop up the Provisional Government, which they did not support. They were marked out by their size, and with their close-cropped hair resembled young boys. The photographers who took pictures of them for the press the day before the coup noticed how small they looked compared to the Cossacks with them. They were scared – and not only of the Bolsheviks. 'At night, men knocked at our barracks and cried out with blasphemies.' When they had been ordered to the palace they were told they would be taking part in a regimental parade. They were not prepared to shoot fellow Russians. The besieging Bolsheviks were worried about their presence at the palace, too: 'People will say we shoot at Russian women,' one of them said.

bread, clothes and empty bottles with expensive French labels. Soldiers moved about in a stale atmosphere of tobacco smoke and unwashed humanity. One had a bottle of white Burgundy evidently filched from the cellars of the palace. The place was a huge barrack.'

At 3 p.m. Lenin could delay no longer. He appeared before the Congress of Soviets at the Smolny and brazenly declared a victory, though the government had not yet fallen, the ministers were not arrested, nor was the Winter Palace in Bolshevik hands. This was the first big lie of the Soviet regime. He read a statement he had prepared early that morning when he thought the coup's success was already complete.

'To the Citizens of Russia. The Provisional Government has been deposed. State power has passed into the hands of the organ of the Petrograd Soviet of Workers' and Soldiers' Deputies, the Military Revolutionary Committee, which heads the Petrograd proletariat and the garrison.

'The cause for which the people have fought – namely, the immediate offer of a democratic peace, the abolition of landed proprietorship, workers' control over production, and the establishment of Soviet power – has been secured.

'Long live the revolution of soldiers, workers and peasants!'

Declaring that the Bolsheviks had taken power was so important to his plan that he was prepared to invent it.[6]

When he returned upstairs Lenin could not contain his rage. He ordered the bombardment of the palace from the Peter and Paul Fortress, but the tragi-comedy and absurdity of the siege was only beginning. The clockwork timekeeping of the coup slipped further and further and, as the day went on, there ceased to be any deadlines at all. The Bolshevik gunners were complete incompetents. There were five heavy field-guns at the fortress, but they were museum pieces which hadn't been fired in years or cleaned in months. Some lighter training guns were found and dragged into position, but no one could find the right three-inch shells for them. Then it turned out that the guns did not have sights. In the late afternoon the commissars worked out that the original guns simply needed cleaning.

Things became more surreal for the insurgents. Even the straightforward task of raising a red lantern to the top of the fortress flagpole – the signal for the bombardment and a ground assault to begin – was beyond

18

them. No red lantern could be found. The Bolshevik commander of the fortress, Georgy Blagonravov, went out into the city to look for a suitable lamp but got lost and fell into a muddy bog. He came back, though with a purple lantern which he couldn't fix to the flagpole. The rebels abandoned any idea of giving a signal.

At 6.30 p.m. the Bolsheviks, who had been in control of the nearby naval base at Kronstadt for the last few days, ordered the battlecruisers *Aurora* and *Amur* to steam upriver and halt opposite the Winter Palace. Ten minutes later they sent an ultimatum: 'Government and troops must capitulate. This ultimatum expires at 7.10 p.m. after which we will immediately open fire.'

The ministers rejected the ultimatum. At 6.50 they sat down to dinner – borscht, steamed fish and artichokes. By this point the defenders were ready to give up and bow to the inevitable. 'The soldiers just wanted to smoke, get drunk and curse their hopeless situation,' one of their officers recalled. Most peeled off as the evening wore on. The majority of cadets went off to look for some dinner, some of the women's battalion left. The Cossacks, the only ones with any military training, stalked off 'disgusted by the Jews and wenches inside'. Fewer than 250 remained. The Red Guards could have walked in easily at any time.

The 'government' continued to pronounce edicts and reshuffle Cabinet posts; the minister left in charge by Kerensky earlier in the morning decided they had to discuss appointing a 'dictator' in Russia. Dictator of what, beyond the Malachite Room and its grand columns, ornate fireplaces and huge table vases, he never made clear. They decided to brave things out for as long as possible, arguing that when they were overthrown by force the Bolsheviks would be condemned.[7]

Most people in Petrograd did not know a revolution was happening. The banks and shops had been open all day, the trams were running. All the factories were operating as usual – the workers had no clue Lenin was about to liberate them from capitalist exploitation. That evening Chaliapin was appearing in *Don Carlos* before a full house at the Narodny Dom, and Alexei Tolstoy's *The Death of Ivan the Terrible* was playing at the Alexandrinsky Theatre. Nightclubs and concert halls were open. Prostitutes were touting for business in the side streets around Nevsky Prospekt as on any normal Wednesday evening. The restaurants were packed. John Reed and a group of other American and

British reporters were dining at the Hotel de France, close to the Palace Square. They returned to watch the Revolution after the *entrée*.

In Soviet mythology for decades to come, the Revolution was portrayed as a popular rising of the masses. Nothing could be further from the truth. Contemporary photographs show a few isolated spots around the city where a handful of Red Guards were milling about casually. There were no big crowds anywhere, no barricades, no street fighting. It is impossible to know how many people took part in the few isolated parts of the city which mattered during the insurrection. Trotsky estimated 'no more' than 25,000, but by that he meant the number of Red Guards he could have called out. The real number was far fewer – probably 10,000 at most, in a city numbering nearly two million.

There was no 'storming' of the palace, as depicted in Sergei Eisenstein's epic, cinematically brilliant but largely fictional 1927 film *October*. Many more people were employed as extras than took part in the real event.[*8]

At 9.40 p.m., at last, the signal was given to begin the bombardment with a blank shot fired from the *Aurora*, which had moored by the English Embankment opposite the palace. The ministers dropped to the floor; the entire company of the women's Shock Battalion were so scared they had to be taken to a room at the rear of the building to calm down.

Twenty minutes later the guns from the Peter and Paul Fortress began firing live ammunition. A barrage of three dozen were fired but only two hit the palace, chipping some cornices. One shell managed to miss the 1,500-room target by several hundred metres.[†] Podvoisky and Antonov-Ovseyenko, whom Lenin had threatened to shoot a few hours earlier, led a small group of sailors and Red Guards into the building and quickly realised when they began to search through the rooms that they faced almost no opposition. In the Malachite Room, 'fear gripped us like the onslaught of poisoned air', Justice Minister Malyanovich said later. 'It was clear the end was at hand.'

---

[*] And even more took part in the re-enactment of the palace seizure on the fifth anniversary of the Revolution in 1922.

[†] The explosions startled Vladimir Nabokov, the eighteen-year-old son of the Cabinet Secretary, the senior civil servant to the Provisional Government, at his home on the Morskaya, right next to the palace. He was trying to write a poem at the time.

At around 2 a.m. a little man with long, wavy red hair wearing a wide-brimmed hat and a floppy red tie bounded into the room – 'an armed mob was behind him'. He didn't look like a soldier but he shouted in a shrill, jarring voice, 'I am Antonov-Ovseyenko, a representative of the Military Revolutionary Committee. I inform all you members of the Provisional Government that you are under arrest.'

They were marched to the Peter and Paul Fortress through jostling groups of Red Guards shouting 'Run them through' and 'Chuck them in the river'. Antonov warned that anyone who tried to harm them would be shot. Throughout the day the casualty count was half a dozen dead and fewer than twenty injured, all of whom were caught in crossfire.

The Military Revolutionary Committee's problem now was controlling their own Bolshevik troops. Room after room in the palace was filled with packing cases containing some of the former Tsar's treasures, which were about to be despatched to Moscow for safekeeping. The Red Guards had different ideas. 'One man went strutting around with a bronze clock perched on his shoulder,' said Reed, who accompanied them. 'Another found a plume of ostrich feathers, which he stuck on his hat. The looting was just beginning when someone cried, "Comrades! Don't take anything! This is the property of the People! Stop. Put everything back!"' Many hands dragged the spoilers down. Damask and tapestry were snatched from the arms of those who had them; two men took away the bronze clock. Roughly and hastily the things were crammed back into the cases. Through corridors and up staircases the cry could be heard growing fainter and fainter in the distance, 'Revolutionary discipline. Property of the People.'

Others headed straight for the Tsar's wine cellar, one of the finest in the world. It contained cases of Tokays from the age of Catherine the Great and Château d'Yquem 1847, Nicholas II's favourite. 'The matter of the wine . . . became critical,' recalled Antonov. 'We sent guards from picked units. They got drunk. We posted guards from Regimental Committees. They succumbed as well. A violent bacchanalia followed.' He called the Petrograd fire brigade to flood the cellar with water, 'but the firemen . . . got drunk instead'.[9]

The real drama was happening at the Smolny. That was where the Revolution was won. The Congress of Soviets convened again at 10.30 p.m.

and there was seething anger in the smoke-filled ballroom. Lenin's hope was that the coup would be rubber-stamped, but it was denounced by many delegates. Even a few Bolsheviks objected. Lenin's opponents played right into his hands. The other socialist groups said they would 'have nothing to do with this criminal takeover' and walked out of the Soviet, never to return to any position of influence in Russia. They might have made Lenin's position difficult if they had remained a strong opposition force united against the Bolsheviks. They might even have prevented Lenin from building his dictatorship. Walking out of the chamber was a fatal mistake, as many admitted soon afterwards. 'We made the Bolsheviks masters of the situation,' said Sukhanov, an opponent of Lenin. 'By leaving the Congress we gave them a monopoly on the Soviets. Our own irrational decisions ensured Lenin's victory.'

At around 5 a.m., with the opposition about to stage their walkout into oblivion, the Bolsheviks' most spellbinding orator, the brilliant, vain and ruthless Trotsky, made one of the most famous speeches of the twentieth century. The uprising 'needs no justification', he said. 'What has happened is an insurrection, not a conspiracy . . . The masses of the people followed our banner. But what do they [pointing to the other socialists] offer us? We are told: renounce your victory, make concessions, compromise. With whom?, I ask. To those who have left us we must say: you are miserable bankrupts, your role is played out. Go where you ought to go – into the dustbin of history.'

Two hours later Lenin appeared at the Congress. Now certain of victory, and no longer in disguise, he beamed. There were no rhetorical flourishes from him. He read out the Decree on Peace he had written that morning, promising an end to the war, and the Decree on Land pledging to take over the landowners' farms. He was greeted with tumultuous applause. Some old Bolsheviks, hard men and women who never believed this moment would come, were weeping. To those who encountered him for the first time he did not seem like a revolutionary who would create a new kind of society and transform history, said John Reed. 'He was a short, stocky figure, with a big head set down on his shoulders, bald and bulging little eyes, a snubbish nose, wide generous mouth, and heavy chin. Dressed in shabby clothes, his trousers were much too long for him. Unimpressive, to be the idol of a mob . . . A strange popular leader – a leader purely by virtue of intellect; colour-less, humourless, uncompromising and detached, without picturesque idiosyncrasies – but with the power of explaining profound ideas in simple terms. And combined with shrewdness, the greatest intellectual audacity.'

Soon after the 'glorious October' Lenin said that taking power had been a simple thing, 'as easy as picking up a feather'. He was being mischie-vous, misleading. In fact it had been a long, hard road.[10]

1

A NEST OF GENTLEFOLK

'This man Lenin . . . he's not dangerous.'

Prince Georgy Lvov, the first post-imperial
Prime Minister of Russia

All of the most important relationships in Lenin's life were with wom-
en. He had very few close male friends and nearly without exception
he lost those he made, or they fell by the wayside, because of politics.
Men had to agree with him wholesale and bend to his will or be dropped
from his inner circle. As a confidant for many years in exile recalled:
'I began to separate myself from the revolutionary movement . . . and
thus completely ceased to exist for Vladimir Ilyich.' By the time he was
thirty-three the only man he addressed by the intimate Russian '*ty*'
rather than the formal '*vy*' was his younger brother Dmitry.[1]

For most of his life Lenin was surrounded by women – his mother,
sisters, his wife of a quarter of a century, Nadya; and his mistress Inessa
Armand, with whom he had a complex romantic attachment, as well
as a close working relationship that waxed and waned in intensity over
many years. During a decade and a half of exile, in various cramped
lodging houses throughout Europe, he lived in easy, friendly familiarity
with his mother-in-law, a woman of strong opinions that differed mark-
edly from his own.

Invariably, Lenin's women have been dismissed as mere drudges who
performed domestic chores for him or were allowed to handle relatively
simple and mundane political tasks. This is misleading. Lenin had more
progressive and advanced views about the role of women than most of
his male contemporaries in the revolutionary movement – though it is
true that this does not set the bar particularly high.

In many ways, Lenin the great radical was a conventional Russian bourgeois man of the late nineteenth century: hardly a feminist in the modern sense of the term. He expected the women close to him to cosset him, fuss over him and look after him, which they did. But he listened to them and took them as seriously in political matters as he did men.

His wife Nadya is frequently portrayed as little more than his secretary, an amanuensis with no opinions of her own. Yet there was much more to her than that. She was a revolutionary when she met him, had been jailed and exiled to Siberia before she married him, and she played a vital role alongside him in the underground conspiratorial network that kept the flame of revolution alive in Russia before 1917. She wrote no works on Marxism or philosophy, seldom spoke up about political tactics or policy, and rarely contradicted him, but Lenin relied on her practical skills and sound judgement. She 'ran' dozens of secret Bolshevik agents throughout the Russian empire and knew every aspect of the Party organisation. Most importantly, Nadya kept her husband's temper and fast-changing moods in check, which often demanded immense tact.

Inessa Armand was another woman whose role in his life has been misunderstood, or – in the case of the Soviet authorities after Lenin's death – deliberately ignored. For ten years until she died in 1920 they had an on-off love affair. Armand was central to his emotional life. She was also among the best-known women socialists of her generation, one of Lenin's closest aides, trusted to perform the most confidential tasks. Often she represented him at international gatherings of revolutionaries, a responsibility he delegated to very few people. She held positions by Lenin's side in Moscow after the Revolution. Frequently she disagreed with him and plainly told him so, yet they remained inseparable. Everyone who knew her – including Lenin's wife, who became her close friend in a curiously touching and devoted triangular relationship – understood how important she was to him. Yet after he died a 'cult' of Lenin was developed by his successors which encouraged worship of him as a secular icon representing the pillar of Bolshevik rectitude and she was all but written out of Soviet history books. In the five years before 1917 he wrote many more letters to Inessa Armand – on personal and political matters – than to anyone else. Their correspondence and her diaries were censored for nearly seventy years until the Communist state that Lenin founded collapsed.

Two of Lenin's sisters survived past their teens and worked with him closely in the revolutionary underground. Anna Ilyinichna Ulyanova, born in 1864, was his elder by six years; Maria was eight years younger than him. Both were repeatedly jailed or exiled during the Tsarist regime for subversive activities; they helped to smuggle underground agents and socialist literature into and out of Russia. After the Revolution they held responsible jobs in the Soviet regime. For many years in exile in Europe, one or both of them – usually Maria – shared his home, with Nadya and his mother-in-law.*

Throughout his life Lenin relied on a network of devoted women totally loyal to him – and, most of them, to his revolutionary cause. They made great sacrifices for his career and at times took enormous personal risks on his behalf: Revolution was a dangerous business. He could, and sometimes did, take their faith in him for granted. But the commitments went both ways.

Many ruthless and cynical men are sentimental about their mothers. Lenin used to say frequently to family and comrades, 'Mother . . . well, quite simply, she's a saint.' He saw her rarely for the last twenty years of her life – she died in 1916, while he was in Swiss exile – but he was a devoted, not merely a dutiful, correspondent. Wherever he was on his wanderings about Europe he wrote to her regularly. The letters were rarely about politics or his literary/journalistic work, but he reported, often in minute detail, on his domestic arrangements, his health and his travels. Many are of a 'nature notes' type about his hunting trips or excursions in the Alps, one of his great passions being walking in mountains and the untamed countryside. His letters home are invariably

---

* Lenin had two other sisters, both called Olga. The first, born in 1868, died in infancy, less than a year old. He was closest to the second Olga, born in the autumn of 1871, eighteen months younger than him. They were inseparable as children and teenagers. According to many family friends, she was the prodigy of the Ulyanov brood, intellectually and artistically gifted, the one destined for great things. She was formidably talented and creative, as well as pretty and graceful. She died from typhoid aged just nineteen. They shared rooms in St Petersburg at the time and Lenin nursed her in her final days. He was inconsolable that he couldn't save her, and for months his letters home after her death were full of guilt and gloom.

addressed to 'Darling Mother' or 'Mamoushka Dearest'. His last, a few weeks before her death, ends: 'I embrace you warmly my dearest and wish you vigour.' Lenin was petulant, ill-tempered and irascible, especially as he grew older, but his mother was the one person he never complained about to anybody, the only one to whom he always showed unqualified love.

Maria Alexandrovna Blank was born in 1835 in St Petersburg. Her father was an eccentric, a martinet and – a fact kept strictly secret by the Soviet authorities after Lenin's death – a Jew. He had been born Sril (the Yiddish form of Israel) Moiseyevich (Moses) Blank in Odessa, but while studying medicine he converted to Orthodoxy and changed his first name and patronymic to Alexander Dmitriyevich. He travelled widely in Europe after qualifying as a doctor and married the daughter of a wealthy German merchant, Anna Groschopf. She was a Protestant. Under the restrictive religious laws of Tsarist Russia, his wife was required to convert to the Orthodox faith, but she refused and brought up her six children as Lutherans.*

---

* Lenin was almost certainly unaware of his partially Jewish ancestry. His sister Anna discovered a piece of the story in her thirties when she went to Switzerland for the first time and met a family called Blank. She was told that nearly all Swiss by that name were likely to be Jews. Then she found that a silver cup – an heirloom of the Blank family that had come down to her mother – was the kind typically used in Jewish religious festivals. Soon after Lenin died Anna was asked by the Lenin Institute, established in 1924 to preserve his 'legacy', to write a definitive history of the Ulyanov family. She did a thorough job and found out details about her grandfather that were entirely new to her. She didn't mention her work to anyone outside the family for many years. But in 1932, shortly before her own death, she wrote to Stalin and revealed her findings. She went to his office in the Kremlin and handed the letter to him personally. 'It's probably no secret to you that our research on our grandfather shows that he came from a poor Jewish family,' she told him. Publishing the facts, she said, 'could help to combat anti-Semitism . . . Vladimir Ilyich always valued Jews highly and was always persuaded of their exceptional abilities'. Stalin read it carefully and responded immediately, ordering her: 'Absolutely not one word about this letter to anyone.' Stalin was himself a rabid Jew-hater and probably understood viscerally, as well as calculated politically, that it would not have helped the Bolshevik cause among Russians if it had been revealed that the founder of the Soviet state had Jewish roots. If Lenin had known, he would probably have been relaxed about the revelation. As he once told the writer Maxim Gorky, 'We do not have many intelligent people. [Russians] are a talented people. But we are lazy. A bright Russian is nearly always a Jew or a person with an admixture of Jewish blood.'

Alexander Blank began as an army surgeon, later became a police doctor and, finally, an inspector of hospitals at Zlatoust, in the vast province of Chelyabinsk in western Siberia. This gave him the civil service rank of 'state councillor', which entitled him to claim noble status. When he retired in his fifties he registered as a member of the nobility of Kazan and he bought an estate, Kokushkino, about thirty kilometres northeast of the city, with a fine manor house and forty serfs who worked the land.[2]

Maria Alexandrovna's mother died when she was three. Her father began living with his late wife's sister, Ekaterina von Essen, herself widowed. It was a shocking ménage for those days and Blank wanted to make an honest woman of his sister-in-law. He tried to marry her, but the marriage was illegal in the eyes of the Church and the couple were refused permission. Her money helped to buy the Kokushkino estate and they remained together until she died in 1863.[*]

A quiet, strong-willed, introverted woman, Lenin's mother had dark-brown hair, a slim figure and dressed elegantly, though rarely in the height of fashion. There was no kissing or embracing within the household and Maria Alexandrovna generally discouraged displays of emotion. She was the dominant figure at home, deeply respected and revered by all her children. 'She had our love and obedience,' the eldest Ulyanov daughter, Anna, recalled later. 'She never raised her voice, and almost never resorted to punishment.'[3]

She was long-suffering and always sheltered her children from the reduced circumstances they would face following family deaths and the constant attention of the secret police. She was frugal but never mean. Intelligent and well educated, she never supported – and often did not understand – her children's radical politics. She was certainly not a Marxist or a revolutionary of any kind. But she knew better than to

---

* Alexander Blank frequently scandalised middle-class opinion in ways other than his domestic arrangements. He clashed with his bosses, terrified his juniors and held highly unorthodox views about what we would today call alternative medicine. He was a great believer in 'balneology', which involved wrapping patients head to toe for several hours in wet blankets and towels. He thought that being enclosed by water was good for hygiene and killed germs. The treatment has no scientific basis – but probably killed fewer patients than regular bleeding and the use of leeches, still common practice at the time.

quarrel with her children over a political issue or ask too many questions about their illegal activities, whatever the suffering their beliefs would bring them. Few of her letters to her son Vladimir have survived, but in those she barely mentioned politics once. To Maria Alexandrovna, family came first.

At various points all of her grown-up children were jailed or exiled, on occasions several of them at once. She would always move near their prison or to a town as close as possible to their place of exile. Often she would humiliate herself pleading with officials to release one of her daughters or sons, or to treat them more leniently. Though never rich, she was comfortably off and all of them relied on her money for prolonged periods. She sent them cash, clothes, books, food parcels and never appeared to complain about being asked. Vladimir would request help more than any of her other children, though at times he received ample funds from elsewhere. For some years he awarded himself a salary from Bolshevik Party funds, but he earned little from his books and journalism. Life as a professional revolutionary could be precarious and at times he was short of ready money; well into his forties he could not have survived without regular help from his mother.

Vladimir possessed little of the serenity and patient forbearance of Maria Alexandrovna Ulyanova, but he did inherit other features of her character. 'No sooner had I come to know his mother than I discovered the secret of Vladimir Ilyich's charm,' said Ivan Baranov, a comrade from Lenin's early revolutionary years.[4]

His father's ancestry was as problematic as his mother's for Soviet historians. The last official Lenin biography published in the USSR, which appeared in the 1950s, stated that his father, Ilya Nikolayevich Ulyanov, hailed from 'poor lower-middle-class people from Astrakhan', which hides more than it tells. Lenin's paternal grandmother, Anna Alexeyevna Smirnov, was an illiterate Kalmyk woman with Central Asian roots who possessed the typical looks of her ethnic origin. Most physical descriptions of Lenin mention his 'Mongol eyes' and high cheekbones, but the Soviets systematically suppressed information about his grandparents. They would not have fitted neatly with the carefully burnished official image of the founder of Bolshevism, who had to be presented as a Great Russian through and through.*

Ilya was born in 1831 and both his parents died young. He was brought up and given a good education by his uncle Vasily, a prosperous tailor and merchant who ran a successful business in Astrakhan, a smelly fishing town along the delta where the Volga flows into the Caspian Sea. He qualified as a teacher of the sciences and taught at a series of secondary schools in provincial towns in southern Russia. He married in 1863 and taught in Nizhny Novgorod until 1869, when he was given a big promotion as Inspector of Schools in the Simbirsk Region, a job that won him the rank of a hereditary noble.

Of all the Ulyanov children, Vladimir looked the most like his father. Ilya Ulyanov had slanted eyes that flashed amber, a big domed forehead and reddish hair which he began to lose in his early twenties. Like his son he couldn't pronounce his 'r's properly and on occasions he had a hint of a lisp. He was more outgoing than his wife and enjoyed company. He was away much of the time on tours of inspection around the vast schools district under his supervision. Lenin's mother, although nominally Lutheran, seldom went to church. His father was religious and ensured that the children were brought up Orthodox in a traditional Russian manner.

He was a thoroughly decent man of liberal views, who believed in gradual reform and evolutionary change through education – the kind of well-meaning bourgeois that his son would come to despise and scorn more bitterly than he did a diehard reactionary. Ilya revered Alexander II, the 'Tsar Liberator' who emancipated the serfs in 1861 and launched a series of other modest measures to modernise the Romanov autocracy. After he was assassinated in 1881 by terrorists from the People's Will revolutionary group Ilya Ulyanov wept for days. In full-dress civil service uniform he attended the memorial service at Holy Trinity Cathedral in Simbirsk. He was a proud member of the establishment. As far as is recorded he was in contact with only one known 'subversive',

---

* Under Stalin, evidence about Lenin's Kalmyk heritage was destroyed. The truth came out by accident. The Armenian novelist Marietta Shaginyan stumbled on some surviving documents while working on her book *The Family of the Ulyanovs*, which was originally published in a small magazine in 1937 and immediately fell foul of the authorities. It wasn't reissued until 1957, after Stalin died, during a brief cultural thaw in the USSR.

the Ulyanov family doctor, Alexander Kadyan, who had been sent into internal exile by the secret police and was forced under the terms of his sentence to stay within the town. But the acquaintanceship was entirely professional.

'Our father was never a revolutionary,' Anna wrote in her short history of the family. 'In those years, being in his forties and head of the family, he wanted to protect us, his children, from that way of thinking.' Her sister Maria agreed. 'Father was totally loyal to the Tsarist regime, certainly not a revolutionary,' she told a younger comrade. 'We don't really know enough to say what his attitudes were to the radical activities of the young.'

Lenin himself never tried to conceal or fudge his roots, though the Soviets later created the myth that the founder of the world's first workers' state 'came from the people' and was from 'low social origins'. To many of those who knew him, his manner and bearing were revealing. Maxim Gorky, a convinced socialist who was born into deep poverty and really did come from the people, said that 'Vladimir Ilyich has the self-belief of a "leader", a Russian nobleman not without some of the psychological traits of that class.'[5]

2

A CHILDHOOD IDYLL

'Men make their own history, but they do not make it just as they please; they do not make it under circumstances chosen by themselves, but under circumstances directly found, and given and transmitted from the past. The tradition of all the dead generations weighs like a nightmare on the living.'

Karl Marx, *The Eighteenth Brumaire of Louis Bonaparte*, 1852

Nothing in Vladimir Ulyanov's childhood or early adolescence suggested that he would turn into one of history's great rebels. He grew up in a happy home, amid a loving family in solid, bourgeois comfort if not ostentatious wealth. He was taught – and shown by the example of his parents – the values of diligence, thrift, hard work and the importance of education.

He was born on 10 April 1870 in the small provincial town of Simbirsk, on the slow-moving River Volga 900 kilometres south-east of Moscow. Six days later he was baptised, in the Orthodox Church of St Nicholas, where the establishment upper-middle class of the town worshipped on a Sunday.

His sister Anna, six years older, recalled that at birth 'Volodya' was 'top-heavy'; he had a large head and a short, weak body. He fell over a lot and found it hard to get up, which often made him scream in frustration. 'He was very noisy, a great bawler, with combative, happy little hazel eyes,' said Anna. 'He started to walk at almost the same time as his sister Olya [Olga], who was a year and a half younger than him. She began to walk very early and without being noticed by those around her. Volodya . . . learned to walk late; and if his sister tumbled inaudibly and raised herself up independently by pressing her hands on the floor, he inevitably would bang his head and raise a desperate roar throughout the house.'

He continued to crash his head on rugs and floorboards, and his mother was for a while worried that he might be 'mentally retarded'. The midwife who delivered him said soon after his birth that 'he'll turn out either very intelligent or very stupid'. He was the most boisterous of all the Ulyanov children, 'and very demanding throughout his childhood', according to Anna.

Like many children he had a destructive streak. Whenever he was given a new toy he began to take it apart. On one birthday, the nanny, Varvara Grigoryevna Sarbatova – a retainer who stayed with the Ulyanovs for twenty years and was part of the family – gave him a present of a papier-mâché troika, complete with horses. He disappeared to play with the gift on his own. 'We began to look for him and found him behind a door. He stood there in deep concentration, twisting the legs of the horses until one by one they came off.' Despite this mistreatment of her present, Sarbatova always stood up for him. She said that all the Ulyanov children 'were gold . . . but my Voloden'ka is a diamond'.

He was the loudest and worst-behaved child in a well-ordered family. When he did misbehave, as Sarbatova would say, 'at least he owned up and didn't do things on the sly'. Except once, on a visit to his aunt in Kazan, when he accidentally broke a vase while he was alone in one of the reception rooms of the house. He denied all knowledge of the breakage and the incident was forgotten. But a few months later, back in Simbirsk, he couldn't go to sleep one night and his mother found him crying in his room. She tried to comfort him and asked what was wrong. 'I lied to Aunt Anya,' he confessed. 'I told her it wasn't me who broke that vase, when it was.'

If he was closest to his sister Olga, his childhood hero was his elder brother (by four years) Alexander, a serious, somewhat sombre youngster who with a withering look could restrain Vladimir's sometimes hot temper. 'At first Vladimir started imitating his brother and then he began consciously to curb his quick temper,' according to Anna. The two boys occupied adjoining rooms, worked together and played in the garden, walked by the Volga and often swam in its tributary, the Sviyaga. 'Whatever Vladimir was asked – what game he wanted to play, whether he would go for a walk, or wanted milk or butter with his porridge – he would usually look at Sasha before answering. The latter would purposely take his time and look at his brother, a twinkle in his eye. "I'll do as Sasha does," he would say.'[1]

Home was a substantial house on Moskva Street, towards the top of the hill, in the smart area of Simbirsk where senior civil servants, a few army officers, doctors and lawyers lived in decent, stolid style, though not in luxury.

Founded on the high bank of the Volga in 1648, Simbirsk was for a while important as a military garrison to provide defence against nomadic raids. Over the decades it became an unhurried provincial backwater. By the late nineteenth century there were 30,000 inhabitants, but as yet no railway. A few poor roads linked it with the rest of Russia, and the Volga connected Simbirsk with other, similar sleepy towns down to Astrakhan at the river's mouth nearly 1,000 kilometres to the south. In the winter, people from Simbirsk grumbled that they felt isolated, as though they were living in the middle of nowhere. On the other hand, there was natural beauty. Apple and cherry orchards covered much of the countryside for miles around. At night thousands of nightingales sang. Not much had changed in Simbirsk for a century and a half at least. It had an impressive onion-domed cathedral, two good libraries and – to some extent thanks to the liberal-minded educator Ilya Ulyanov – two excellent '*Gimnasium*' (grammar) schools. It had sizeable Chuvash and Tatar minorities, the majority of whom worked on the Volga riverboats.*

The most famous son of Simbirsk after Lenin was the novelist Ivan Goncharov, a near-contemporary, whose masterpiece *Oblomov* was much admired by the future Bolshevik leader. 'The outward appearance of my home town represented nothing but a picture of slumber and stagnation,' Goncharov wrote. 'One wants to fall asleep,

---

* After Lenin died, Simbirsk was transformed into a grandiose Leninist altar and in 1924 renamed Ulyanovsk. Much of it was flattened in the late 1920s. The church where Lenin was baptised was razed – as was a fine classical-style house where Pushkin had stayed in the early nineteenth century. The cathedral, built in memory of those from Simbirsk who died in the war of 1812, was cleared in the 1920s to make way for a monument to Lenin. The cemetery of the Pokrovsky Monastery was bulldozed to make way for a cosy square, leaving only one grave – that of Lenin's father, with its cross removed. It is still called Ulyanovsk.

looking at this calm, at the sleepy windows and lowered blinds, at the sleepy physiognomy of the people ... Over the city lay the torpidity of peace ... the calm of the generous rural and urban Russian life.'*

The Ulyanovs' comfortable two-storey wooden house had generous reception and living areas, a library full of Russian classics from Pushkin to Tolstoy, and fiction by the best foreign authors. All the children were encouraged by both parents to read widely, in a permissive way that would have shocked Ilya Ulyanov's more conservative civil service colleagues. For most of his early teens Vladimir's favourite book was Harriet Beecher Stowe's *Uncle Tom's Cabin*, an early influence on him pre-dating Marx or any of the Russian radicals. He kept the novel by his bedside for many years.

The house had a big, broad balcony overlooking a garden full of apple, plum and cherry trees and lilac bushes surrounding a well-maintained lawn. The whole family were passionate about croquet and tournaments were highly competitive. Indoors, the children, even the older ones, loved to play with toy soldiers. Vladimir always chose the American side and took the part of Abraham Lincoln, or the Union generals Grant and Sherman. His brothers Sasha and Dmitry (four years his junior) were usually Italians, and his sisters Spanish soldiers fighting Napoleon.

The game Lenin loved throughout his life, though, was chess. He was taught by his father from an early age on pieces that he had lovingly carved for his children. Ulyanov *père* was no mean player, one of the best in Simbirsk, but Vladimir was soon beating him and his older

---

* By a curious twist of fate – it was such a backwater town – Alexander Kerensky was also from Simbirsk. He attended the same school, though they did not know each other as he was eleven years younger than Lenin. In later years, he had deeply romantic memories of the town where he grew up – though he couldn't wait to get out of the place as a teenager and head to somewhere with brighter lights. He left a highly coloured account of the town where, from the summit of the hill, 'right down to the waterside stretched luxuriant apple and cherry orchards. In the spring the whole mountainside was white with fragrant blossom ... night breathed with the songs of nightingales. The fields ... during the heat of summer would be gay with the sounds of games being played, of peasants and townspeople come to mow the rich grass.'

brother regularly. He became a serious player who could give the top names in Russian chess a decent game.[*2]

Summers were spent at Kokushkino, the estate bought by Alexander Blank, which after his death was inherited by his five children. Lenin would remember Kokushkino all his life as a magical place where he had always been happy. He found peace and tranquillity there, 'where the scent of mignonette, stocks, sweet peas and tobacco plant, nasturtiums, phlox, geraniums and hollyhocks suffused the garden'.

In her memoirs Lenin's sister Anna, who became a devout Bolshevik, spoke with the authentic voice of the Russian middle classes when she talked about Kokushkino and its gracious manor house surrounded on three sides by a verandah overlooking gardens – a house at the end of a long drive and an avenue of trees. 'We began to dream about our move to Kokushkino each year and make preparations for it long in advance. We thought there was nothing better or more beautiful than Kokushkino, a little country place that is very picturesque. I think we inherited our love for Kokushkino, and our joy at seeing it again, from our mother, who had spent her best years there. The joy of country life, the open spaces were very attractive to us. Especially after the agony of our . . . prison-like high schools and the torture of the May examinations, summers at Kokushkino seemed lovely and happy beyond compare.' Vladimir bathed in the river, took boat trips and rambled in the forest to pick berries and mushrooms. He flew kites and there were picnics.[3]

The education of their children was of paramount importance for the Ulyanov parents. All of them excelled at school, but Vladimir was by far the most competitive. He had immense charm when he chose to exercise it, and as a teenager a good sense of humour. He could also be unbearably bumptious and tactless. He was exceptionally clever and let everyone else know it. Towards the end of term at the *Gimnasium*, when the marks were awarded, he would go home and call out his marks as he

---

* At school he was good enough to play 'simultaneous chess' against several opponents at once on a number of chessboards; he nearly always won all the games. His wife Nadya said later that 'Some games obsessed him to such an extent that he used to rave in his sleep.' She once heard him calling out at night, 'If he moves his knight there, I'll counter with my castle.'

passed his father's study. 'Greek – five [the top mark, naturally]; Latin – five; German – five; Algebra – five, and so on.' his sister Anna recalled. 'I can still see the scene clearly: I am sitting in my father's study and I catch the contented smile which father and mother exchange as their eyes follow the bulky little figure in uniform with the reddish hair sticking out from under his cap.' Yet the ease with which he coasted through school caused his parents some concern. Occasionally they worried that it might lead him to believe life was too easy and make him monumentally arrogant. But they didn't agonise for long.*

The curriculum was tough but narrow. There was a lot of rote learning. Almost half the classes were on the classics, and most of the rest on mathematics and the natural sciences. Under the Russian autocracy, where no politics were permitted, the rulers were scared of allowing Russian children to read some of the masterpieces of Russian literature. Very little poetry was taught. Pupils were discouraged from reading most of the great modern Russian writers – Tolstoy, Dostoyevsky, Turgenev, Pushkin, Lermontov, Gogol – because at one time or another they had all faced problems with the Tsarist censors. German, French and English were taught, but for the grammar and language. Pupils were banned from reading the European writers and thinkers of the Enlightenment and Romantic Movement – Goethe, Voltaire, Rousseau, for example. Pupils from the Simbirsk Classical *Gimnasium* were not allowed to use the main Karamzin Library in town, which had some volumes deemed too subversive for young eyes.

Discipline was harsh at the school, but Vladimir seldom complained or expressed any hint of a rebellious spirit. He found himself in trouble only once, and even then it was a minor offence, when he was overheard by a school monitor mimicking the French teacher, whom he believed was inadequate. Discipline was only slightly more relaxed at home, at least during term time. Ilya was a hard taskmaster. Strict silence was enforced during homework hours and time was set aside each day for serious reading. Offenders who broke the 'no talking' rule were sent to the 'black armchair' in Ilya's study for calm, silent reflection on misdemeanours. Once Vladimir was found asleep there.[4]

---

* The only subject at school in which the future theoretician of Marxism did not excel was Logic. Occasionally he even failed to obtain the four mark. We don't know – he never referred to it – but in later years he might have appreciated the irony.

Alexander Naumov shared Vladimir's desk at the *Gimnasium*. In most years he was silver medallist in the school, runner-up to Ulyanov, who invariably won gold. 'Vladimir Ilyich was rather short but powerfully built, with slightly hunched-up shoulders and a large head, slightly compressed at the sides . . . he had irregular and, I would say, unhandsome features: small ears, prominent cheekbones, a short, wide and slightly squashed nose, and in addition, a large mouth with yellow, widely spaced teeth. With no eyebrows on his freckled face, Ulyanov had longish, blond, soft and slightly curly hair which he combed straight back. But all these irregularities were redeemed by his high forehead, under which burned two fierce little brown eyes. His ungainly appearance was easily forgotten in conversation under the effect of these small but unusual eyes which sparkled with extraordinary intelligence and energy . . . he differed considerably from all of us. Neither in the lower forms nor later did he take part in the childish and youthful games and pranks, always keeping to himself, busy either with his studies or some other written work. Even when walking between classes, Ulyanov kept to his books, reading as he walked up and down past the windows. The only thing that he liked as a distraction was playing chess, a game in which he usually came out victorious, even when playing against several opponents simultaneously.'

Another schoolfellow described the young Lenin as 'a walking encyclopedia, extremely useful to his comrades . . . as soon as he appeared in the form, Ulyanov was immediately surrounded by his schoolmates, who asked him for a translation or a solution to a problem. He helped everybody willingly, but it seemed to me as though he nevertheless resented those who tried to live and do their schoolwork at the expense of another's labour and intellect. Ulyanov had an even and on the whole a jovial temperament, but he was extremely secretive and cool in his relations with his fellows. He had no real friends. He said "you" to everybody [children invariably spoke to each as other as "thou"] and I do not remember a single time when he would unbend and allow himself to be intimately outspoken. On the whole he commanded respect and displayed businesslike authority, but one couldn't say that he was liked, rather that he was esteemed.'[5]

At no time while he was growing up did he show any interest in politics. 'Volodya would never have concealed them . . . at that time, in short, he had no political beliefs. We were surprised that he could read and reread Turgenev several times – in the months when he was sharing a room with Sasha, who was diligently studying works of political economy.'[6]

Vladimir's idyllic childhood and teenage years were shattered, suddenly, just three months before his sixteenth birthday. His father had kept his ill health to himself, but he had been suffering from bad stomach cramps for some time and what would now be diagnosed as serious hypertension. In January 1886 he died from a stroke.

His high blood pressure was not helped by major stress in his professional life. Ilya Ulyanov had been a conscientious, model civil servant for a quarter of a century. He had supervised the opening of nearly 400 primary and secondary schools in the Simbirsk region and believed wholeheartedly that backward Russia could be modernised and thrive only through better education for all. This was a view shared by the 'Tsar Liberator' Alexander II, who initiated a series of reforms and oversaw the expansion of Russia's schools. But after he was assassinated the reforms were halted and a period of harsh reaction was established.

The autocracy felt threatened and responded in a predictably Romanov fashion. Censorship was tightened, the secret police were given sweeping new powers of arrest and detention, and political activity of practically any kind was banned. A few months after ascending to the throne the new Tsar, Alexander III, placed education in the hands of a new minister, Ivan Delyanov, whose view of schooling, as he declared on his appointment, was that 'the children of coachmen, servants, cooks, laundresses, small shopkeepers and suchlike should not be encouraged to rise above the sphere in which they were born'. The programme of opening village schools for the poor was halted; instead, a few church schools designed to prepare children for the Orthodox priesthood were established.

The new ministry gave Ulyanov awards and medals, but soon retired him. His liberal activism did not chime with the tough new regime which was determined to retreat to the past. His supporters managed to get Ulyanov's retirement deferred indefinitely and he was reinstated, but his working life was coming to an end, unhappily.

The Russian winter of 1885–6 was one of the coldest for many years and Ilya developed a bad cough. Typically he carried on working regardless, at his usual pace. On 12 January 1886 he complained to Maria Alexandrovna that he was feeling unwell, yet he still had a meeting in his study with one of his team of inspectors until about 2 p.m. Unusually, he didn't join the rest of the family for lunch. Briefly he appeared at the door of the dining room, but returned to his study. 'He looked at us as if he had come to say goodbye,' his daughter Maria recalled years later.

After lunch his wife went to find him; he was lying on a sofa shaking, unable to speak. She called a doctor and fetched the children to see their father. He was in agony, shook several times violently and died before the doctor could arrive. He was fifty-four, a year older than his son Vladimir would be when he died.

He was buried the next day and most of middle-class Simbirsk turned out at the funeral. Sasha was away studying at the University of St Petersburg and it would have taken him several days to get home. Vladimir, at fifteen, was the chief pallbearer; the others were leading dignitaries of the town.

The death of Ilya Ulyanov at a relatively early age was a terrible blow for the family. But soon another, more serious, would fall on his widow and children – a tragedy that would set Vladimir on the road to becoming the revolutionary, Lenin.[7]

3

THE HANGED MAN

'The revolutionary is a dedicated man. He has no personal interests, no private affairs, no emotions, no attachments, no property and no name. Everything in him is subordinated towards a single thought, a single passion: the Revolution.'

Sergei Nechaev, *The Revolutionary Catechism*, 1869

Late on the evening of 4 May 1887 five young men, all in their twenties, were chained and manacled in their cells at the Peter and Paul Fortress in St Petersburg, commonly known as Russia's 'Bastille'. They were marched to a steamer docked on the Neva riverside below and ferried twenty-five kilometres or so to another forbidding symbol of the power of the Tsars: the ugly and impregnable Shlisselburg Fort, built almost 200 years earlier by Peter the Great on the south-western shore of Lake Ladoga. The youths were unchained only when they were safely placed in their damp cells.

For the next three nights, unknown to the five prisoners who could hear no sound through the thick walls, carpenters were hard at work erecting gallows and gibbets in the fortress courtyard. At 3.30 a.m. on 8 May they were woken by prison guards, shackled and chained again, and told that in accordance with the sentences imposed on them at a Special Session of the State Senate held three weeks earlier they were now to be hanged. Their offence: an attempted assassination of the Tsar. Jailers said later that the five young men, all of them students at St Petersburg University, were unusually calm as they dressed and prepared themselves for death.

At around 4 a.m. they were led down stone staircases to the fortress's courtyard. Only three scaffolds had been built, so two of the young men had to wait and watch their comrades hang before they too would die.

The first to be executed were Vasily Generalov, twenty, a second-year student from a middle-class Don Cossack family, Pakhomi Andreushkin, twenty-one, a bright physics student from a well-off family in the Kuban, and Vasily Osipanov, twenty-six, son of a soldier serving in Tomsk, studying in the law faculty. All three refused the last rites, but they kissed the Cross. As black hoods were placed over their heads and they mounted the scaffold they cried as loudly and clearly as they could, 'Long Live the Narodnaya Volya'. For all of them the last word on their lips was the name of the revolutionary group they belonged to: the People's Will.

The bodies swung free for several minutes while their two comrades stood below. When they were led to the scaffold, one angrily waved away the Cross offered by the priest; he was Pyotr Shevyrev, the twenty-three-year-old son of a rich merchant from Kharkov. The other calmly kissed the Cross before going to his death, just six weeks after his twenty-first birthday. He was Alexander Ilyich Ulyanov.*[1]

Sasha's younger brother Vladimir, now seventeen, was taking a geometry exam on the day of the hanging.† Nobody was told about the executions till late the following day. His mother believed until the last moment that the death sentence would be commuted to life imprisonment at the worst.

Like the rest of his family, Vladimir had no idea that serious-minded Sasha, whose principal interest was thought to be in the natural sciences and who seemed destined for a glittering academic career, was so deeply and dangerously involved in radical politics. His mother and elder sister Anna knew that he was reading seriously on economic and political history, but not that he was involved as an activist – or that he knew any activists as friends.

High-minded Sasha was all but deified by his siblings. He had a dreamy, romantic look, a refined, delicate face and was prone to

---

* The great chemist Dmitry Mendeleyev, who created the periodic table, was briefly one of Alexander Ulyanov's teachers at St Petersburg University. He was appalled by the execution, but not altogether sympathetic to Sasha's aims. 'These accursed social questions, this needless, I believe, enthusiasm for revolution – how many great talents is it destroying?' he said after he heard about the hanging.

† Naturally he received a five.

melancholy. He was boringly well behaved, quiet and reserved even as a child. He studied so hard that he could barely be separated from his books for meals. In his last year at the *Gimnasium* he converted his bedroom into a laboratory. Out in the countryside he wanted to collect specimens of insects; he delighted in worms. There is something terribly priggish and sanctimonious about his earnestness to be seen as good. He seemed to have no sense of humour, let alone the irony possessed in abundance by his brother Vladimir. Asked by one of his sisters what was his ideal of feminine beauty, Sasha replied, po-faced, 'Oh, just like Mother.'

Vladimir worshipped Sasha as a child, but as he grew up the relationship became more complex. No criticism, not even a hint, was allowed of Sasha, but Vladimir sometimes appeared to resent the way his older brother would preach to all and sundry about what was right and good form. 'When Volodya reached that transitional age when a youngster is especially sharp and quarrelsome he was very brash and self-confident, even more so after the death of our father,' Anna wrote many years later. Alexander was unforgiving of the slightest faults, misdemeanours or irritable moods among his brothers and sisters. One day at home the two boys were playing chess. Maria Alexandrovna asked Vladimir to fetch something for her from the adjoining room. Vladimir replied petulantly that perhaps she could wait until the game was over. She asked again – and his reply was downright rude. Alexander raised his voice, something he seldom did. 'Volodya. Either you will go right now and do as Mama says or I won't play with you any more.' Sheepishly, Vladimir did as he was told.

'The different nature of the two brothers had already made its appearance in childhood,' said Anna. 'Thus they could never be close friends, notwithstanding the boundless respect and admiration which Volodya had for Sasha . . . It was absolutely clear that each had his own nature and that they were entirely different individuals.'

For his part, Sasha was cool towards Vladimir. One day a few months before his execution Anna, herself a student at St Petersburg, asked Alexander, 'How do you like our Volodya?' He replied: 'He is undoubtedly a very talented person but we don't get on very well and we are not very close. In fact we are not close at all.'[2]

*

The assassination plot was laughably amateur. The surprise was that the conspirators came as close as they did to success. Several months in the making, fifteen people were involved in the plan – a foolishly large number if one of the objects was secrecy – and it turned out that many had spoken of it with sympathisers. Yet the political police, the much-feared and supposedly omniscient Okhrana, did not know of it until a few days before the attempt, and only then through a piece of luck. One of the plotters, Vasily Generalov, was arrested on suspicion of something entirely different and found by the police with explosives equipment and some incriminating letters.

The money came from Sasha, who sold the gold medal he won from St Petersburg University for a paper he had delivered on the structure of freshwater annelid worms. It was Sasha who designed and helped build the three bombs intended to kill the Tsar as he left the Winter Palace for a service at the Alexander Nevsky Cathedral on 1 March, the sixth anniversary of the murder of Alexander II. He obtained all the necessary information from books in the university library, though whether the bombs would actually have exploded or not nobody will ever know. The main problem was obtaining the nitric acid that would detonate the device. Finally it was found and smuggled to St Petersburg from Poland.*

Alexander was arrested on Nevsky Prospekt, a few hours before the attack on the Tsar was due to take place. He had a Browning revolver in his pocket, which, unaccustomed to using guns, he had little idea how to fire. Immediately, he admitted his guilt and took sole responsibility for the plot, even though the idea had not been his, nor much of the planning.

As soon as she heard of Sasha's arrest the next day Maria Alexandrovna rushed to St Petersburg. She hoped to intervene personally to shorten what she thought then would be a prison term. She travelled by horse

---

* One of Sasha's co-conspirators would many years later play a major role in Lenin's life. The young man who bought the nitric acid to detonate the bombs was Józef Piłsudski, the Polish nationalist who in the 1920s would become the military dictator of Poland. Piłsudski wanted independence for his country from Tsarist Russia, and after the Revolution he was the hero of the Polish War of 1920 against the fledgling Soviet regime. The Poles heavily defeated and embarrassed the Soviet state – one of Lenin's biggest setbacks. In the 1880s, the young Piłsudski was sentenced to five years in exile for his part in Sasha Ulyanov's attempt to murder Alexander III. Piłsudski's brother Bronisław, who smuggled the acid, was sentenced to fifteen years' hard labour.

and wagon to the nearest train stop, 200 kilometres or so away at Syzran – alone. Vladimir was deputed to look for someone, almost anyone 're-spectable', to be a companion for her on a long, arduous journey. But he could find nobody to go out of their way to help the family of a suspected terrorist. This was a snub which stayed with him for the rest of his life.[3]

Maria Alexandrovna desperately wrote letters pleading on Sasha's behalf to everybody she thought might help, from the Tsar downwards. At first she was refused permission to see him in prison, but was finally allowed a visit. The Emperor himself intervened, and scribbled on her petition: 'It seems to me that it is desirable to allow her to see her son, so that she can convince herself what sort of person her dear little son is . . . and to show her what kind of convictions he has,' he wrote.

She saw him on 30 March. In a tearful interview, he broke down and begged her forgiveness. 'But darling Sasha, why resort to terrorism, murder? How awful.' He replied, 'What can one do, Mother, when there are no other means available?'

The trial began on 15 April, in camera, and took four days. Fifteen young men were charged. Sasha again admitted his guilt and assumed responsibility for his co-defendants' actions. At one point in the court room, according to a guard who overheard, he whispered to Generalov, 'If you need to, you can lay all the blame on me.'

Before the verdict was recorded he was allowed to read a prepared statement.

'Terror is the only form of defence, the only road individuals can take when their discontent becomes extreme,' he said. 'We . . . [students] are encouraged to develop our intellectual powers, but are not allowed to use them for the benefit of our country. Among the Russian people you can always find a dozen men or so who are so utterly devoted to their ideas and take the misfortunes of their country so much to heart that they do not consider it a sacrifice to die for their cause. There is nothing that can frighten or intimidate such people.'

Sentence was passed on 25 April. All the defendants were condemned to death. Maria Alexandrovna was again allowed to see him and she begged him to plea for a pardon. She had been told by some old friends of her husband, senior officials in the civil service, that the Tsar would be prepared to show clemency. Sasha refused: 'I am sorry Mother, but I can't do that after everything I said at the trial. It would be insincere.'

Eventually she persuaded him and he wrote a petition appealing for mercy. But it was too late.

Before the execution went ahead the Tsar took time to read the entire record of the case. He noted in the margin, at the transcript of Sasha's speech: 'This frankness . . . and honesty, is even touching!' He commuted the sentences of ten defendants but ordered Sasha's execution to go ahead. Alexander III commented in the margin of the last page of the report: 'This time God saved us! But for how long?'[4]

The death of her son was a devastating blow for Maria Alexandrovna. 'When she returned from St Petersburg afterwards, she didn't ring or knock, but came in quietly by the back door,' her daughter Maria recalled. 'The younger children crowded around her and clung to her. I thought I had seen that her hair had gone quite grey.'

Sasha and his execution were seldom mentioned among the Ulyanovs for several years afterwards – 'it was just too painful'. But the profound and immediate effect it had on Vladimir was plain. He didn't often show his feelings to outsiders and there seems to be only one contemporary record of his reaction, from a school friend who spoke to him a few days later: 'The evening was so still, as if nature itself wanted to calm and reassure us. I said so to Volodya. After a moment's silence he told me that . . . Sasha had been put to death. I was stunned. Droopingly, slouchingly, Volodya sat next to me. Under the rush of thoughts it was impossible to speak. We sat so for a long time in silence. At last he got up, and, saying nothing, we went towards the town. We walked slowly. I saw Volodya's deep grief but also had the feeling of his determination not to show it . . . Before parting I strongly grasped his hand. He looked into my eyes, responded to the handshake and quickly turned and walked home.'[5]

The Ulyanovs were shunned by bourgeois Simbirsk. The dignitaries of the town who a year or so earlier had attended the funeral of Vladimir's father no longer visited. Long-standing family friends who came to play chess with Ilya, and since his death with Vladimir, no longer called. This triggered the vitriolic, sometimes uncontrollable, loathing for liberals and 'middle class do-gooders' that he would henceforth show until his dying day. 'The bourgeois . . . they will always be traitors and cowards,' he declared with monotonous frequency from now onwards. Politics is personal – and this was personal. A young boy who rarely thought about

politics became radicalised almost overnight.* Maria Alexandrovna could bear the stares of former friends and the gossip of strangers
no longer; she decided to move the family from Simbirsk and sold the
Moskva Street house. It was bought by the town's police chief, a man of
indisputable rectitude, who nevertheless had no qualms about buying
property from associates of a terrorist.[6]

Vladimir began immersing himself in the political literature his
brother had read and a new world opened up for him. One thing still
perplexed him about his brother, though. Nearly a decade later, on the
day he met his future wife Nadezhda, the two of them were walking in
St Petersburg along the River Neva. He confided to her how bitter he
was about Sasha's execution and how much he hated the regime that
sentenced him to death. Then he said that he never imagined his brother
would become a revolutionary: 'A revolutionary doesn't give himself up
to the study of worms.'

Vladimir was now a marked man by the authorities – suspect by association with his brother and a potential troublemaker. He was set on a
collision course with the Tsarist regime.

---

* In most of the hagiographies of Lenin which appeared in the Soviet Union through
to the late 1970s there appears an entirely bogus story, designed to show that seventeen-
year-old Vladimir Ulyanov was already the revolutionary Lenin, thinking strategically.
When he was told that Sasha had been hanged he is supposed to have told his sister Maria, 'No we will not take that road . . . we will find another.' Maria was only eight at the
time and couldn't have known what he was talking about. A more credible story (but
again its veracity is uncertain) is a comment that came from one of his younger sister
Olga's tutors, Vera Kashkadanova, who claimed that Lenin said of Sasha's actions: 'It
must mean that he had to act like that; he couldn't act in any other way.'

4

THE POLICE STATE

'We Russians are slaves because we are unable to free ourselves and become citizens rather than subjects.'

Alexander Herzen, (1812–1870)

A majority of educated Russians, the intellectuals known as *intelligenty*, probably agreed with Alexander Ulyanov's sentiments, if not his actions. Even if they were not prepared to throw bombs themselves, by the late nineteenth century they would have sympathised with his frustration at being denied any voice in the way Russia was run, any stake in the country's future – 'the very term intelligentsia was a synonym for opposition', as one dissident put it.

Around 85 per cent of the Russian population were peasants, the muzhiks, who were still essentially without civil rights at all, though some advances in their legal status had been made since the abolition of serfdom in 1861. On the whole they showed no interest in politics beyond a grudging acceptance of their lot; the regime felt no need to take any notice of their thoughts whatsoever.

The small middle class and the intellectuals were different. The autocracy saw the spread of any ideas to modernise Russia along the lines of Western Europe as a direct challenge to the Romanovs' near-300-year-old dynasty. The Crown created an entire organ of state to root out 'subversion' in all its forms. As Count Sergei Witte, Prime Minister for three years under the last of the Tsars, said, 'The Russian empire . . . became a police state par excellence.'

Both the last two Russian emperors imagined that tightened repression and censorship, exile for the mildest of political opponents, and the ban – until nearly the end of the *ancien regime* – of political activity of any kind would make the monarchy safer. They could not have been more wrong. The early Romanovs – Peter the Great, Catherine II, for example – understood the nature of power and knew how to run an absolutist state. So did Lenin. The last two Tsars, through terrible judgement, incompetence and the absence of any imagination, did not. They possessed the ruthlessness, but not the efficiency or the vision. At the turn of the twentieth century, their great hope was to take Russia back to the seventeenth. It should hardly be a surprise that they didn't know how. Between them they made a series of fatal mistakes. Among the worst was to force moderate middle-class liberals, who had no real interest in revolution, to the extremes. They guaranteed the growth of a violent opposition, which they were too weak and incompetent to destroy. Students, predictably, were at the forefront of the opposition to Tsardom and the regime was constantly in a state of generational conflict with educated young people.*

Nearly 20,000 ministers, provincial governors, senior civil servants and top army officers were assassinated by revolutionary groups in the last twenty-five years of Tsarist rule. Much moderate opinion did not blame the 'terrorists', but the government. 'These ... [murders] are not melodramatic whims or romantic accidents of Russian history,' wrote the liberal Pyotr Struve, a one-time socialist, who believed in non-violent change. 'These corpses mark the logical development of a moribund autocracy ... which has stubbornly cut off, and continues to cut off, the country from all avenues of legal and gradual political development. The terrible thing for the government is not the liquidation of the Sipyagins and the von Plehves [two assassinated ministers] but the public atmosphere of resentment and indignation which the bearers of authority create and which breeds in the ranks of Russian society one "avenger" after another ... [The government] thought that it was possible to have an autocracy which introduced the police into everything, an autocracy which transformed legislation, administration, scholarship,

---

* Alexander Kerensky recalled his first days studying law at St Petersburg University in the 1890s. 'The very air of Russia seemed to be saturated with an intense desire for liberation. We became the enemies of the Autocracy almost as soon as we entered the university, and this seemed to happen naturally ... there were no arguments among the students whether the Autocracy should be fought or not ... the only argument was as to where the real truth was to be found, with the Marxists or with the *Narodniki* [the Populists].'

church, school and family into police organs ... And the police were not even able to avert a bomb ... pitiful.'[1]

Some acute foreign observers noticed that the near-daily murders created little outrage among most people against the revolutionaries; they shrugged shoulders and complained about the regime. After one particularly loathed Interior Minister was blown up by a bomb in St Petersburg, the Austrian Ambassador to Russia, Count Alois Lexa von Aehrenthal – not exactly a liberal himself – wrote: 'The most striking thing ... is the total indifference of an event that constituted a heavy blow to the principles of the government. One could hardly have expected sympathy for a minister who because of his authoritarian bent must have made many enemies. But a certain degree of human compassion or at least concern and anxiety about the immediate future would be natural. Not a trace of this is to be found ... only totally indifferent people or people so cynical that they say no other outcome was to be expected. People say that further catastrophes ... will be necessary in order to bring about a change of mind on the part of the highest authority.'[2]

Jury trials for alleged terrorists were rare in Russia and were halted altogether after the case of Vera Zasulich in 1878. The fiercely intelligent twenty-eight-year-old daughter of a penurious noble family, Zasulich, then a passionate anarchist, attempted to murder the Governor of St Petersburg, General Fyodor Trepov. She shot and wounded him after he had ordered the flogging of a radical student for refusing to salute him. In a celebrated trial, she was acquitted and hailed as a martyr. A skilful lawyer had managed to turn the proceedings into a trial of Trepov and the regime rather than of one radical defendant. Zasulich was unanimously cleared.[*3]

It was surprising how many of the terrorists were women – at a time when even the idea of Votes for Women in Western Europe or the US had barely yet become an issue of debate. That there were so many young women ready to kill and die for a political cause earned the

---

* Zasulich went into hiding immediately after the verdict when the authorities announced they would try her again, this time without a jury. She escaped from Russia and went into exile in Switzerland and later, for many years, in London. She renounced individual acts of violence and argued later they were pointless. She became a famous Marxist and will appear in this story again as a close friend of Lenin's wife Nadya, though she grew to loathe Lenin himself.

radicals some sympathy among men, in a highly patriarchal society. Sophia Perovskaya – 'a frighteningly single-minded', fanatical member of Narodnaya Volya – was the lover of Andrei Zhelyabov, who led the plot against Alexander II. She gave the signal to the bomb-throwers, who were waiting for the Tsar on the St Petersburg street where he was murdered. One of her co-conspirators described her as 'tiny, blonde, with pale-blue eyes and pink and white cheeks like a china doll . . . a beauty'. She was hanged aged twenty-seven in the last public execution in Russia on 3 April 1881, before a crowd estimated at 80,000 people. The hangman was drunk and there was no drop to the scaffold, just a wooden stool that the executioner managed in his stupor to kick away. Witnesses, horrified, said she took half an hour to die, in extreme agony.*

Vera Figner, one of the first women in Russia to train as a doctor, led a revolutionary group and planned two unsuccessful murder plots against Tsar Alexander II before her involvement in the successful attempt. She managed to evade arrest but was finally apprehended by police in the Crimea in 1883, aged thirty-one. She spent more than twenty years in jail or Siberian exile and made a speech at her trial the following year which it seems certain that Alexander Ulyanov had read and knew by heart. 'Peaceful methods have been forbidden me. We have no free press so it was impossible to think of propagating ideas through means of the printed word. If any organ of society had pointed out to me another course than violence I would have chosen it.'

Later, in exile in Switzerland, an equally passionate opponent of Lenin and Bolshevik tyranny, she recalled her life as a terrorist when 'the cult of the bomb and the gun, of murder and the scaffold, took on a magnetic charm'.[4]

Vladimir Ulyanov was heir to a long tradition of revolutionary opposition to the Tsars. After his brother's execution he steeped himself in the history of Russian radical politics, from the Decembrists' uprising onwards. These were a group of aristocratic army officers who in December 1825, following the death of Alexander I – at dinner 'between

---

* One of the saddest of all cases was the ghastly death of Maria Vetrova. Incarcerated in the Peter and Paul Fortress for subversive crimes involving the distribution of illegal literature, she was repeatedly raped by a police officer and by a prison guard. In February 1897 she poured lamp oil over herself and set herself alight.

the claret and the champagne', as Alexander Pushkin famously wrote – plotted to prevent Nicholas I succeeding to the throne. Most of them had fought in the Russian army that reached Paris a decade earlier and helped to defeat Napoleon. Having seen Western Europe, their declared aim was to build a constitutional monarchy and they dreamed of 'igniting a spark that will become a flame of liberty'.* The rebels attracted an army of 3,000 to their cause and nearly succeeded. But they were finally crushed the following year. Five of the conspirators were executed and dozens were sentenced to exile in Siberia, including members of some of the most famous noble families in Russia which were traditionally loyal to the throne, like the Trubetskoys and Volkonskys. The Tsar's Act of Indictment against the Decembrists charged them with displaying 'the insane lust for change'.

For the rest of the nineteenth century – until the overthrow of the Romanovs – Russian political history was a repeating cycle of modest reforms, followed by periods of reaction when the throne felt threatened. Up to the abdication of the last Tsar one of the principal articles in the Fundamental Laws stated, simply, 'His Majesty is an absolute monarch who is not obliged to answer for his actions to anyone in the world but has the power and the authority to govern his states and lands as a Christian sovereign, in accord with his desire and goodwill.' And the emperors meant it. Konstantin Pobedonostev, Procurator of the Holy Synod and for decades one of Russia's most senior civil servants, told Alexander III soon after his father's assassination in 1881: 'Russia has been strong thanks to Autocracy, thanks to the limitless mutual trust and the close tie between the people and the Tsar . . . we suffer quite enough from talking-shops, which simply stoke up popular passions.'[5]

The structure of the police state had been established under Nicholas I in the 1820s. He built an entire organ of government – the Third Section of the Administrative Department – to combat subversion. Essentially it was a secret service of the monarch, whose interests were seen as different from those of his subjects. Laws protecting property or the lives of other Russians were handled by a separate policing system. The Third Section, which in the 1880s became the Okhrana, had draconian

---

* When, at the start of the twentieth century, Lenin and his comrades launched their first socialist newspaper they called it *Iskra* – The Spark – as a deliberate echo of the Decembrists.

powers to detain people without trial and send them to 'administrative exile' in Siberia and the Arctic wastes at any hint of 'political crimes'. Its power and scope were unlike anything elsewhere in Europe. It became the model for the Cheka, the NKVD and the KGB in the Russia of the future – or indeed the FSB of the post-Soviet era. It invaded the lives of ordinary people. There were thousands of bureaucrats in back offices throughout the empire opening people's mail, which had been intercepted by an underworld of intelligence agents, stool pigeons and snoops. The public needed a special licence from the political police for a vast range of innocuous activities, from organising a party in a public place to opening a shop, operating any form of public transport, or reading Darwin.[6]

Again, unique to Russia, was the most rigid form of censorship in Europe which obliged all printed matter to be cleared by a censor before it was published. With direct political activity excluded and reading political matter by and large banned, 'almost all literature became a criticism of Russian life, a social commentary, one way or another'. Writers found ways to get round the censors – not always difficult; on the whole, throughout history, good authors have been cleverer than censors and this has never been truer than of the imaginative giants in Russian literature. A highly developed form of *samizdat* publishing and of distributing illegal works existed in Russia decades before the Bolshevik Revolution. Over the nineteenth century, censorship, police surveillance and prison sentences were relaxed, tightened, relaxed again and became harsher once more depending on the political climate and the sensibilities of the monarch. But over the years thousands of people were jailed or sent to Siberia simply for reading 'illegal' books. This was no longer happening in the other European empires, Austria-Hungary and Germany.

After liberating the serfs, Alexander II introduced a few other reforms: he permitted some jury trials and allowed an element of local government – the *zemstvos*, small-scale neighbourhood councils run by provincial gentry. He allowed travel into and out of Russia, which had been extremely limited. But after he was assassinated his son retreated into a paranoid absolutism. No substantial political freedoms were ever granted by the Tsars in the nineteenth century and the autocracy had no intention of conceding any. The Russian monarchy showed no ability to adapt or to modernise. The Tsars created the revolutionary movements, as one of the sharpest of the 'terrorists', Pyotr Tkachev – whom Lenin would quote often – prophetically observed in the 1860s. 'It is Russia's backwardness which is her great fortune, at least from the revolutionary point of view. In the West the social order is based on wide support of the middle class. In Russia this class [barely exists] . . . What holds things together in our country? Just the state – i.e. the police and the army. What is needed to make this state fall into fragments? Not much: two or three military defeats . . . some peasant uprisings . . . revolt in the capital.'

The Populists were the first of the revolutionary groups to gain any influence. Initially they adopted entirely peaceful means. Their conviction was that revolution would come from the peasants. So from the 1860s bands of idealistic young men and women went to the country, tried to live in communes, attempted to open first-aid centres and educate illiterate peasants in a 'back to the people' movement that would lead them to a kind of pastoral socialism. Several of the type appear in Chekhov's plays and stories. Most of them were from privileged backgrounds and were conscious of their wealth: 'our awareness of the universal truths could only have been reached at the cost of the age-old suffering of the people. We are the people's debtors – and this debt weighs down on our consciences,' as one of them said.

Almost universally these Populists from groups like Land and Liberty (Zemlya y Volya), were shunned by the peasants they were trying to help, who distrusted them because of their privilege, were wary of socialism and resented their paternalistic disruption of village life. In many cases they informed on the radicals to the police or threw them out of the neighbourhood – and in a few instances assaulted or killed them. 'Socialism bounced off the peasants like peas against a wall. They listened to our people, as they do to the village priest, respectfully but without the slightest effect on their thinking or their actions.'[7]

The next tactic was a resort to violence to destabilise the state. They still believed that revolution depended on the peasantry, and their targeted assassinations of Tsarist officials, provincial governors, police and army officers were carried out to make Russia ungovernable. From the ruins a republic of agrarian socialists would seize power and transform Russia. The biggest and most dangerous of these groups was Narodnaya

Volya, whose principal theorist and leader was the charismatic Sergei Nechaev, on whom Dostoyevsky based Verkhovensky, the nihilistic central character in *The Possessed*.

Nechaev was a charismatic leader who inspired a generation of followers with his fanaticism and asceticism. He spent ten years in jail, for long periods performing hard labour, and died a prisoner in the Peter and Paul Fortress.* His pamphlet *The Revolutionary Catechism*, banned but widely circulated, was a primer for young radicals who became the foot soldiers of the terrorist organisations. It offers a grim sort of life, but large numbers of young people were inspired by its appeal to self-sacrifice and its logic of fighting violence with violence. 'The revolutionary is a dedicated man. He has no personal interests, no private affairs, no emotions, no property, no attachments, no name. Everything in him is subordinated to one single, exclusive attachment, a single thought and a single passion: the Revolution. The revolutionary knows that in the very depths of his being, not only in words but also in deeds, he has broken all the bonds which tie him to the social order and to the civilised world with all its laws, moralities and customs and all its generally accepted conventions. He is their implacable enemy and if he continues to live with them it is only in order to destroy them more speedily. He must be prepared to destroy everyone and everything that stands in his way.'

After the murder of Alexander II the People's Will was all but wiped out by the Okhrana. But small bands of (mainly) students would form and adopt the same name, before disappearing again – such as the group to which Alexander Ulyanov belonged. Towards the end of the century the Socialist Revolutionaries (SRs) would be formed from the ruins of the Populists, a more sophisticated organisation but still with a belief that individual acts of terror would advance the Revolution.[8]

From the 1870s rival groups would be launched, inspired by an import from the West: Marxism. They gave up on the idea of a revolution emerging from the peasantry in a semi-feudal country like Russia. They believed that the Revolution would be led by the working class, the proletariat. A problem that exercised Marxist theorists – and caused

---

* Not directly for revolutionary activity. He organised the murder of a follower who disobeyed his orders and publicly disagreed with him.

endless disputes with the agrarian socialists – was that Russia was far behind Western Europe as an industrial producer and at the end of the nineteenth century had a tiny working class compared to Britain, Germany or France. Ulyanov would join the Marxists: 'I fell in love with Marx and Engels,' he told his sisters. 'Literally in love.' As Lenin he would become the most famous of all the Marxists, creator of the first state founded on Marxist principles. But he would have a complex relationship with the object of his passion. He adapted the ideas to Russian conditions in ways Marx would never have imagined. Many historians have argued that the reason Soviet-style Communism developed as it did is that Lenin tried to import a Western creed and philosophy to a backward country, as Russia was. Rather, the opposite is true. Lenin transformed a set of European ideas into a very Russian creation. His version of Marxism – its intolerance, rigidity, violence and cruelty – were forged from Lenin's experience as a nineteenth-century Russian. Lenin's Bolshevism had deep Russian roots.

5

A REVOLUTIONARY EDUCATION

'Don't be too hard on Lenin . . . I think that much of his strange behaviour can be simply explained by the fact that he totally lacks a
sense of humour.' Georgy Plekhanov (1856–1918)

Vladimir's demeanour and habits, his whole view of the world, were
transformed around the time he was eighteen. His father's death and
the violent drama of his brother's execution, soon followed by the fatal
illness of his beloved sister Olga, seemed to drain away all the cheerful-
ness, lightness of manner and good humour that had characterised his
early life. He was beginning to become the highly disciplined, tightly
contained man people would know as Lenin. He seldom talked about
his private feelings or inner life to anyone outside his family circle.
'Vladimir became grimly restrained, strict, closed up in himself, highly
focused,' as his younger brother Dmitry explained.

As expected, he won the gold medal at the Simbirsk Classical *Gimnasium* – top of his class. He should have had his pick of university places.
But the authorities were wary of him and saw him as a guilty subversive
simply by association with his brother. Attending either St Petersburg
University or Moscow, the two best in the country, were out of the
question.

It was a Kerensky who obtained a place for him at the reputable
University of Kazan. Vladimir's school principal was Fyodor Kerensky, father of Alexander. He was one of the few respectable figures in
Simbirsk society who visited the Ulyanov family and stood by them. He
wrote a glowing encomium to the university: 'Talented, invariably diligent, prompt and reliable, Ulyanov was first in all his classes, and upon
graduation was awarded the gold medal as the most meritorious pupil
in achievement, growth and conduct. There is not a single instance on

record, either in school or outside of it, of Ulyanov's invoking by either word or deed, any adverse opinion from the authorities or teachers of this school. His parents always watched carefully over the educational and moral progress of Ulyanov and since 1886, after the death of his father, the mother alone has devoted all her labour to the upbringing of her children. The guiding principles of this upbringing were religion and rational discipline. The goodly fruits of Ulyanov's upbringing were obvious in his excellent conduct.' He did notice that Vladimir kept himself to himself, but he said this deliberately to suggest that he would be unlikely to turn into a ringleader of rebellion or consort with potential troublemakers. So he wrote, 'Upon closer examination of Ulyanov's home life and character, I could not but observe in him an excessive introversion and lack of sociability even with acquaintances, and outside the school even with fellow students who were the school's pride and joy, in short an aversion to companionship. Ulyanov's mother intends to remain with him throughout his stay at university.'[1]

The family moved to Kazan, as Maria Alexandrovna pledged. But Vladimir quickly found himself in trouble. Within months, he had joined an illegal group of radicals – moderate Populists, who met at each other's homes and passed around underground literature. In December 1887 there was a wave of protests in Russian universities after a student demonstration in St Petersburg was banned; a series of arrests followed on campuses throughout the country. Some universities were closed down for several months from that winter.

In Kazan Vladimir Ulyanov was one of around 130 students who joined a peaceful student demonstration at the university. His role was minor. All he did was take part in the protest; nobody suggested he was a ringleader. He had simply been in the wrong place at the wrong time. Even the police report into the incident appeared to acknowledge that he was hardly one of the chief troublemakers. Yet he was arrested and summarily thrown out of the university on 6 December. 'During his short stay . . . he was conspicuous for his reticence, lack of attention and even rudeness. Only a day or two before the students' meeting he gave grounds for suspicion that he was fomenting trouble and that he was meditating some improper behaviour: he spent much time in the common room, talking to the less desirable students, he went home and came back again with some object the others had asked for, and in general behaved very strangely. And on 4 December he burst into the assembly hall . . . and [was] among the first to rush shouting into the corridor of the second floor, waving . . . [his] arms as though to encourage the others . . . In view of the exceptional circumstances of the Ulyanov family, such behaviour . . . gave reason to believe him fully capable of unlawful and criminal demonstrations of all kinds.' He was one of only three other students to be expelled and it was clear the police were picking on him because of who he was, not for anything he had done.[2]

He was exiled to Kokushkino and, once again, his mother and the rest of the family moved with him, on this occasion happily, as they all loved the estate. Money was tighter than it had been, but still sufficient for a middle-class lifestyle. Maria Alexandrovna was a thrifty woman who had made some modest savings and she could live comfortably on her husband's reasonably generous pension. She had made 6,000 rubles from the sale of the house in Simbirsk – ample for a decent standard of provincial living, but hardly a fortune. Ilya had left each of his children a share of his estate, some of it inherited from his brother Vasily, who had died childless. Vladimir and Dmitry, when he came of age, would get a significantly higher proportion than his daughters, as was normal in Russia.

Vladimir's mother couldn't stand waste or, as she saw it, extravagant expenditure. As a student Vladimir had taken up smoking. Maria Alexandrovna loathed the habit and at first tried to persuade him to give up on health grounds, but he wouldn't. Finally, one evening after dinner at Kokushkino, he lit a cigarette and his mother, who hardly ever raised her voice or was curt to any of her children, spoke sharply. 'Volodya, you have no income apart from the money I provide. You have no right to squander our family funds on tobacco.' He stopped smoking from that moment – and later he disapproved of other people lighting up near him.

If the authorities imagined that expelling him from university and keeping him holed up in the country would deter any revolutionary enthusiasm they were seriously misguided.[3]

His mother persuaded him to ask for permission to be readmitted to Kazan University. Reluctantly, he appealed 'To his Excellency the Minister of Education most humbly' and signed it 'Vladimir Ulyanov,

nobleman'. The minister refused. The official notification 'Not to be accepted under any circumstances' was written on his application.

Then he wrote to the Interior Ministry, again pointing out that he
was a noble by birth, asking for permission to study abroad 'in order
to support my family and to acquire a higher education'. The district
inspector of police had sent the application to the Minister of Education
with a covering note saying, 'despite his remarkable abilities, Ulyanov
cannot at present be regarded as a reliable person either as to morals or
to politics'. The minister scribbled on the application, 'Wouldn't this be
the brother of the other Ulyanov? . . . On no account should the request
be granted.'

Maria Alexandrovna was shocked that her son was denied the education she had expected for him. She went to St Petersburg and pleaded
with former colleagues of her late husband to intervene on Vladimir's
behalf but got nowhere. She wrote a begging letter to the Minister of
Education: 'It is sheer torment to look at my son and to see how fruit-
lessly pass those years of his life most suitable for a higher education.
Almost inevitably it must push him even to thoughts of suicide.'

She knew her son well enough to be assured that he had no thoughts
of killing himself. But it was typical that she would have said anything,
tried anything, to help her family. Any humiliation was worth the effort.
When she wrote to the Interior Minister asking for permission for the
family to go abroad to take the curative waters of Vichy, she was told that
there were excellent health resorts in the Caucasus. Vladimir said often
that with all the blows she had received, 'Mother's courage was a thing
to wonder at'.[4]

So he educated himself, quietly in the countryside. 'Never later in my
life, not in prison in Petersburg or in Siberia, did I read so much as in the
year after my exile to the countryside from Kazan,' he said later. 'This
was serious reading, from early morning to late at night.' Leon Trotsky
later described it 'as the crucial time that forged him as a socialist . . .
the years of stubborn work in which the future Lenin was formed'. He
pored over the socialist classics and works of philosophy, economics and
history which his brother had read so avidly.

But the work that influenced him most profoundly was a novel, *What
Is To Be Done?* by Nikolai Chernyshevsky, a man whom he idolised.
He kept a photograph of the author in his wallet throughout his life

(which he didn't of either Nadya or of Inessa Armand). Later, when he ruled Russia, a large portrait of Chernyshevsky took pride of place in his Kremlin office. He wrote a fan letter to Chernyshevsky and said once 'that I was very pained' when he never received a reply.

What Is To Be Done? was as important an influence on him as anything by Marx or Engels. Written in 1862 while Chernyshevsky was in the Peter and Paul Fortress on charges of inciting subversion, nobody could claim that it had much merit as a work of art. Not even the author himself, who admitted, without false modesty, 'I don't have the shadow of an artistic talent. I even use language badly. But that's not important . . . This reading will be useful to you . . . [as a revolutionary] and you will experience no deception, since I have warned you that you will find in my novel neither talent, nor art, only truth.'

Somehow it evaded the censors and was legally published – a bad mistake. If an autocratic regime is going to impose supposedly strict censorship, this was the book to censor. It was phenomenally successful and inspired a whole generation of radical young people like Vladimir Ulyanov, who read it five times in the summer after he was expelled from university.*

Vladimir identified strongly with the hero, Rakhmetev, who dreams of a world where poverty has ceased to exist and everyone lives in total freedom. He forsakes all pleasure in the cause of Revolution and disposes of his large private income to support impoverished students. He builds his stamina by eating raw steak, performing strenuous gymnastic exercises and physically arduous work. He does not drink and abstains from sex. Not even the wiles of a beautiful woman who professes undying love for him can steer him from his course. Selflessly, he gives her up for another man. His only real lust is for knowledge. He reads voraciously – once non-stop for eighty-two hours. Rakhmetev is known to his comrades as 'the rigorist' and has no time for anything except

---

* Nowadays it requires a superhuman effort to get through it once – as it did for this author. But Lenin always praised the book. 'Before I came to know the works of Marx and Engels . . . only Chernyshevsky wielded a dominating influence over me and it all began with *What Is To Be Done?* . . . It is his great merit that he not only showed that any correctly thinking and truly honest person must be a revolutionary, but also something more important: what a revolutionary should be like, what rules he should follow, how he should approach his goal and what means and methods he should use to achieve it.'

making revolution. He divides up the day into units of a quarter-hour for each assigned purpose. He is unswerving in his dedication, brutally honest, clinically efficient, coldly rational.

Ulyanov consciously modelled himself on Rakhmetev, as many of those who knew him well have said, including one of his earliest biographers. Nikolai Valentinov was an intimate of the Bolshevik leader in Swiss exile in the 1900s before falling out with him – partly after he dared to criticise Chernyshevsky as 'untalented' and said the book was 'crude and pretentious. Unreadable.' Lenin flared up. 'He sat up with such a start that the chair creaked under him. His face stiffened and he flushed around the cheekbones – this always happened when he was angry. "Do you realise what you are saying? How could such a monstrous and absurd idea come into your mind? To describe as crude and untalented a work of Chernyshevsky, the greatest and most talented representative of socialism before Marx . . . I declare it is impermissible to call *What Is To Be Done?* crude and untalented. Hundreds of people became revolutionary under his influence. My brother, for example, was captivated by him and so was I. He completely transformed my outlook. This book provides inspiration for a lifetime."'[5]

* * *

Unlike Rakhmetev, he took time away from books and the relentless work of an autodidact to enjoy his principal pleasures. Throughout his life Vladimir delighted in the countryside and nature. He took long walks in the woods and fields around Kokushkino, as he would later, wherever he was. He tramped up hills and mountains with relish. Increasingly over the years he would suffer from nervous exhaustion, raging headaches, insomnia and attacks of intemperate anger – the 'rages', as his wife called them. A few days in the mountain air, by the sea or amid fields would revive his spirit and restore his health. He loved the River Volga, the high banks of which he walked for mile upon mile as a child. Every April or May in exile he would write to his mother with the question, 'What is spring like this year on the Volga?'

He enjoyed the pleasures of a country squire's life. Years later he defended such an existence when he was criticised for indulging in bourgeois pursuits. 'Yes, I too used to live on a country estate which belonged to my grandfather,' he told one comrade. 'In a sense I am a scion of the landed gentry . . . I have never forgotten the pleasant aspects of life on the estate. I have forgotten neither its lime trees nor its flowers. So go on put me to death . . . I remember with pleasure how I used to loll about in haystacks, although I had not made them, how I used to eat strawberries and raspberries, although I had not planted them, and how I used to drink fresh milk, though I had not milked the cows.'*

He loved outdoor sports. That winter he sleighed and skated. He hunted – with a passion, though, as he sometimes acknowledged, with limited skill. 'He was never a hunter at heart, though he spent so many hours at the sport,' his sister Anna noted. In Kokushkino he went look-ing for game with his cousin Nikolai Veretennikov: 'In the entire course of that winter he never brought back a thing.' He was often teased about it within the family. One evening the following spring he returned to the house and said he had spotted a hare. His sisters retorted, 'I suppose it was the one you have been after all season.' He forced a laugh. In the spring and summer he fished.[6]

He was rigorous about taking physical exercise and performing gymnastics. That summer, under lime trees in the garden, he erected a horizontal bar on two posts and he practised a tough routine daily. Once he called out to his brother Dmitry with intense excitement, 'Look I have managed to balance myself at last', and showed how he could per-form the splits astride the bar.

In the autumn they were permitted to move back to Kazan. Vladimir immediately joined another band of dissident radicals, this time a Marx-ist organisation loosely connected to the newly formed Emancipation of Labour Group, most of whom lived in exile in various European cities. This was when he first read Marx. In various Soviet-era hagiographies it was said that he became converted to Marxism overnight, and his pro-fessed 'love' was a *coup de foudre*: 'I can remember as of yesterday, he was sitting at the kitchen stove, newspapers all around him, and he was

---

* Many revolutionaries whose goal was to destroy the old world could wax lyrical with nostalgia about their family estates. Vera Zasulich spent her childhood and youth on her family's idyllic manor at Byakolovo. She wrote not long before her death: 'I did not imagine that I would remember Byakolovo all my life, that I would never forget a single shrub in the front garden, not a single one of the old cupboards in the passage, that for many, many years I would dream of the silhouettes of the old trees which I used to see from the balcony.'

making violent jabbing gestures with his hands as he spoke of the new horizons opened up by Marx's ideas,' his sister Maria claimed about this supposed Damascene moment. But she romanticised. The truth is that he became convinced over time and was persuaded intellectually as well as emotionally, though his emotional attachment to Marx was always more powerful.*

Vladimir's mother became worried that if nothing was done he would go the way of Sasha and there would be another family tragedy. She looked for an alternative career path for him other than that of clandestine revolutionary, which offered no rewards of a glittering income, but the prospect of jail or the hangman's noose.[7]

* * *

Maria Alexandrovna bought a country estate and tried to turn Vladimir into a country squire. From the proceeds of the house in Simbirsk, and her share in the Kokushkino property, which was sold, she found a beautiful house outside the village of Alakayekva, fifty kilometres from Samara, with around 160 acres of prime agricultural land. She bought it from the Siberian goldmine millionaire Konstantin Sibiryakov, an interesting man with progressive social views, who wanted to introduce to Russia the kind of modern farming methods that were common in Western Europe. He owned several estates and lost money on all of them before deciding to sell – to people with liberal credentials like the Ulyanovs. The deal was handled on Maria Alexandrovna's side by Mark Elizarov, a shipping insurance official who was the admirer (later the husband) of her eldest daughter Anna.

---

* Another book that got through the Tsarist censors, who had banned such 'dangerous' books as Spinoza's *Ethics*, Hobbes's *Leviathan*, Voltaire's *Philosophy of History* and Locke's *History of European Morals*, was Marx's 674-page tome on political economy, *Capital*. One of the two censors who looked at it in March 1872 concluded: 'It is possible to state with certainty that very few people in Russia will read it, and even fewer will understand it.' The other said that it was 'a strictly scientific work' that had no relevance to Russia because it was mostly about the industrial system in Britain, which did not apply to Russia, where there wasn't 'capitalist exploitation'. Russian was the first foreign language into which *Capital* was translated – four years after it appeared in German. It quickly became popular among intellectuals hungry for a cause to believe in. Whether anyone actually read it all is dubious, but the role the book played in the destruction of the Romanovs is undoubted. Clever old censors – and clever Tsars.

Vladimir loved the gracious wooden mansion with its terraces and verandahs on three sides and he delighted in the stunning position. The estate was surrounded by woods and hills to walk in and a pond full of fish. Though he knew nothing about agriculture, he dutifully agreed to try farming, but he didn't take to it – and nor did he take to the peasants, whom he admitted he never understood. 'My mother wanted me to farm. I tried it but it would not work. Things were not going right. My relations with the muzhiks got to be abnormal,' he said later. It was his only known comment about the Alakayevka experience, though it lasted three planting seasons. He learned little about farming and showed no interest. He felt uncomfortable in the position of gentleman landowner. The peasants cheated him and his mother and the estate lost substantial sums of money. Livestock kept 'disappearing', including several cows and a horse which were stolen by their tenants. The whole experiment was a failure.*[8]

But he spent the summers voraciously reading under the linden trees. He translated *The Communist Manifesto* into Russian. He read the works of a growing number of Marxist scholars. Occasionally he went into Samara and attended clandestine revolutionary meetings. He made trips alone down the Volga on an expedition that demanded a high level of fitness. He would sail downstream for sixty kilometres, haul his boat a mile overland to the parallel river, the Usa, and travel back by boat to a point opposite where he had started. He made this journey several times.

As farming wasn't working his mother suggested another career. She persuaded him to read for the law and qualify as an advocate. He was barred from attending a university but was permitted to take the exams as an external student at St Petersburg University, and was allowed to

---

* Though there was a major upside to this rural interlude – what he called 'this back-water existence'. Soon after the Ulyanovs left Kazan in 1889, the underground reading group of Marxists he had taken part in was broken up. Most of its members were arrested and sentenced to terms of five years in jail and exile to Siberia. 'It was good fortune for me and I benefited from it,' he said years later. 'If I had stayed in Kazan at that point, I would undoubtedly have been arrested.' The estate was leased out to a rich peasant called Krushvits, of the kind the Bolsheviks would later call 'kulaks' and whom they would murder wholesale as a capitalist-exploiting class. Vladimir was for years supported by the rental income from Alakayevka until Maria Alexandrovna sold the estate in the early 1900s.

go to the capital to do so. He crammed a four-year course into twelve months and passed top of his year, obtaining the highest marks in all fourteen papers. It was a phenomenal achievement intellectually – and in one of the Russian ironies he would delight in, he got the country's most brilliant law degree while the organs of the police were keeping him under surveillance as a potential lawbreaking subversive.[9]

6

VLADIMIR ILYICH – ATTORNEY AT LAW

'Few concepts are as contemptible as that of . . . bourgeois justice.'
Lenin to Nikolai Valentinov, 1904

Vladimir's career in the law was less than glittering, not least because he hated lawyers: 'One must rule the advocate with an iron hand and keep him in a state of siege, for this intellectual scum often plays dirty,' he once told a comrade awaiting trial.

He couldn't practise immediately after qualifying. He had to get a certificate of loyalty and good character from the Interior Ministry, which he eventually obtained at the end of 1891. The Okhrana had been keeping close tabs on him in Samara, but could not see that he had done anything wrong. He found a position as an assistant barrister with a friendly and liberal-minded lawyer, Andrei Khardin, with whom he used to play chess by correspondence when he was living in Kazan three years earlier.

The two got along well, but Vladimir made very little money and was supported almost entirely by his mother. He worked on fourteen minor cases at Samara Circuit Court and lost all except one. They included defending a gang who had stolen 300 rubles from a peasant in the same village; a group of hired hands who had tried to steal grain but were caught red-handed; and one peasant who had committed four small thefts. One case might have given him some ideological satisfaction. He defended a tailor accused of blasphemy, who according to the indictment had 'cursed the Blessed Virgin, the Mother of God, the Holy Trinity and also the sovereign Lord the Emperor and his heir apparent', saying that the Emperor managed his affairs badly. The tailor asked him just before the trial whether he had any chance of getting off. 'Oh, no, none at all I am afraid.' The tailor was sentenced to a year in prison.

The case he won was a personal dispute he pursued with character-istic zeal and single-minded determination, bordering on obsession. It was a legal battle with a rich Syzran merchant, S. Arefev, about the rights to cross the Volga. In the summer of 1891 he and his soon-to-be brother-in-law in law, Mark Elizarov, hired a boatman to row them at a crossing point on the river not far from Samara. The merchant owned a steamship and claimed a monopoly on the crossing routes. He sent his steamer to block their passage and take the two young men aboard his boat. Vladimir complained: 'It makes no difference that Arefev has rented the river crossing. That's his business, not ours and it doesn't give him the right to act lawlessly on the Volga and detain people by force.'

He made a formal complaint against Arefev to the authorities, and the legal case dragged on for months at great expense in time and money. Syzran was eighty kilometres from Samara and Vladimir went twice to attend court hearings. Most young people, 'especially Russians, would have dropped the whole business out of inertia and indolence', said his brother Dmitry. But he wouldn't let go.

His mother tried to persuade him to calm down. 'Let go of this mer-chant,' she told him. 'They will postpone the case again and you'll be travelling there in vain . . . Bear in mind that they . . . [the authorities] have it in for you.' She was worried that he was too intense about things and had little sense of proportion. Nevertheless, for the third hearing he took an early-morning train and arrived just in time for vindication. To almost everyone's surprise Arefev, despite his pull as a well-to-do local dignitary, was found guilty and sentenced to a month in jail. It was the high point of Ulyanov's career as a barrister.[1]

The only political campaign he was involved in during his Samara years revealed a great deal about his methods: his rigidity, his self-assurance, use of cold logic to the point of cruelty and his strategic vision. For Ul-yanov the end always justified the means – and he kept the end in sight. He was willing to be unpopular.

Famine hit the Volga region in 1891–2, though it contained some of the best agricultural land in Russia. There had been intermittent famines in the region for centuries, but this disaster was the worst for generations. More than 400,000 people, almost all of them peasants, starved to death, or were victims of typhus and cholera. Government incompetence was held to blame by much of the middle class, even those who generally supported the Tsarist regime. The famine was reported widely in the foreign press, which brought the autocracy under international scrutiny as never before. Russia's reputation was severely damaged.

The central government did almost nothing to help the millions of starving peasants who poured into the towns begging for food. Bodies were left unburied by the roadside, hospitals couldn't cope. The novelist Lev Tolstoy launched a famine relief campaign, supported by other writers like Anton Chekhov, a trained doctor who established soup kitchens and volunteered at first aid relief centres. Large sums of money were raised, but still the supply of food was totally inadequate.

Most radical and liberal opinion saw the famine as another example of the miserable failure of a regime whose bureaucracy was too slow and inefficient to save the Russian population from starvation – and too callous to care how many died. Vladimir Ulyanov, though he had lived all his life around the worst-hit famine areas, would have nothing to do with relief or charitable work to help the dying peasants. For him the important thing was that the famine would weaken the autocracy and might further the cause of the Revolution. The thousands of people who died of hunger were simply unfortunate casualties of a war against Tsarist oppression. He argued that capitalism, by definition, hurt most people and killed many. The famine was simple proof.

He was an isolated, almost lone voice among the revolutionaries. Even his family could hardly believe his unsentimental, apparently cruel attitude. His elder sister Anna raised money for food and visited the sick to distribute medicine. His other sister, Maria, was appalled by his hard-heartedness. One of the very few times she ever allowed herself to criticise him was in a paragraph in which she compared Vladimir with his elder brother. 'Vladimir Ilyich, it seems to me, had a different nature from Alexander Ilyich. Vladimir . . . did not have the quality of self-sacrifice even though he devoted his whole life indivisibly to the cause of the working class.'

He would shrug off accusations that he was inhumane, using an inflexible logic and a cold interpretation of Marxism which Marx himself would never have countenanced. 'He conducted systematic and outspoken propaganda against the relief committees,' as Trotsky said later. Ulyanov was convinced that the end of the autocracy would be advanced if the government's incompetence and brutality were exposed. 'It's sentimentality to think that a sea of need could be emptied with the teaspoon of philanthropy,' he said. 'The famine . . . played the role of a progressive factor.'[2]

In August 1893 Vladimir moved to St Petersburg. On the recommendation of his Syzran employer, Khardin, he found a job with the successful lawyer Mikhail Volkenstein, a bluff, generous man with progressive views, who made few work demands on his young junior assistant from the provinces. Vladimir never appeared in court in the capital, though he did occasionally give advice to clients in litigation cases. His energy was taken up with making a name for himself in the revolutionary movement as a writer, journalist for obscure illegal publications, speaker at clandestine meetings and lecturer – the career he was to pursue for the next twenty years.

He settled easily into the city, as he told his mother: 'I'm in a good room, or so it seems; there are no other lodgers and the landlady has a small family; the door between my room and their drawing room is papered over, so that sounds are faint. The room is clean and bright. There is a good entrance. Since . . . it is not far from the centre (only some 15 minutes to the library) I am quite satisfied.'

But at first he made slow progress. He was a provincial among the more sophisticated St Petersburg radical set. 'His appearance . . . then was simple and modest,' Gleb Krzhizhanovsky, an old comrade who would take high positions in the Soviet regime after 1917, recalled on first meeting him. 'Short of stature, he could easily have passed unnoticed in any factory district. All you could say of his appearance was that he had a pleasant, swarthy face with a touch of the Asiatic. In a rough, country coat he could just as easily have passed himself off in a crowd of Volga peasants.' Many others would also comment on his 'Mongol' looks, with high cheekbones; 'and those eyes were unusual, piercing . . . a dark, dark brown'. He had a habit throughout his life of screwing up his eyes when he was trying to concentrate on something or someone – the result of being short-sighted, which was never diagnosed when he was a child. 'His eyes are narrow and the rapid glances beneath the eyebrows gives him an occasional squint and perhaps a look of cunning . . .

71

his hands are short and ugly,' the writer Alexander Kuprin thought. 'His eyes were dark, small and very unprepossessing,' according to Valentinov. 'His face was very mobile, capable of a whole range of changing expressions: watchful attention, thoughtfulness, mockery, biting contempt, impenetrable coldness, extreme fury. In this latter mood his eyes, to put it rather crudely, became like those of a furious wild boar.'[3]

He started losing his reddish hair young, as had his father, and most of it was gone before he was twenty-three. Once, when he was still living in Syzran, on the advice of his sister Maria he tried a quack treatment in an attempt to restore his hair. He was not entirely surprised when it failed. Alexander Potresov, who was close to him for years but like most people became estranged because of politics, met him towards the end of 1894 at a meeting in a St Petersburg suburb, in the Okhta quarter. 'Vladimir Ilyich was only young according to his identity papers. Face to face one could have taken him for at least thirty-five or forty years old. The face withered, the head almost bald except for some sparse hair around the temple, a thin reddish beard, eyes that observed one from the side, craftily, an un-youthful, coarse voice. A typical merchant from any north Russian province – there was nothing of the radical intellectual about him . . . No trace either of the service or noble family from which he came . . . It was for good reason that at the time . . . this young man in years was called "the old man" and we often joked that even as a child he must have been bald and looked old.'

There was nothing bohemian about him. He was never a dandy, but he usually dressed quite smartly within a modest budget. His suits were always pressed, his shoes clean. If he lost a button on a shirt he sewed a new one on himself. He was never slovenly or careless about appearances, as the archetype of the Russian revolutionary from the pages of, say, Conrad was supposed to be. He was extremely well ordered and tidy, nearly to the point of obsession – the adjective 'anal' as commonly used today might have been coined for him. Every morning he would dust his desk and bookshelves before he settled down to work and ensure every pencil was sharpened to a fine point and in the right place. This was a routine that he adhered to strictly, whether he was in cheap lodgings in St Petersburg, a boarding house in a provincial city in Western Europe, or in later years as the ruler of a vast empire from an office in the Kremlin.[4]

* * *

What people could see straight away, from his first days as a revolutionary 'agitator', was a single-minded man of iron discipline and unshakeable belief that he was right: 'he glowed with a force, not charm exactly, not charisma, but an intellectual energy . . . he personally identified with the cause in a way that was magnetic', said Pyotr Struve, once a socialist collaborator of Ulyanov, but later, like so many former friends, an enemy.

Ulyanov became a fluent writer who learned as a journalist to produce copy fast and efficiently. He was never a brilliant, effervescent phrasemaker like Marx or Trotsky at their best. But on his day he was clear and persuasive and he could adopt irony with great effect. He used a battering ram rather than a rapier, but in his finest work he can be powerfully convincing in his reason, logic and intellectual force, albeit often from the starting point of a fundamentally flawed premise. He wrote and published more than ten million words in his lifetime, not counting thousands of letters to family, friends and comrades. It is an astonishing output, but he made a halting start. His early articles were spiked for being too boring and dense, even for a theoretical journal of philosophical thought. His first offering was a long article he titled 'New Economic Trends in Peasant Life', a Marxist interpretation of current statistics about agricultural production in Russia. He sent it to the liberal periodical *Russian Thought* but it was rejected with a terse note saying it was not up to their rigorous standards.*

His first published piece, written in a sharper journalistic style, was 'What the Friends of the People Are', a bitter attack on the Populists, and, interestingly, on the use of terror as a tactic to bring down the autocracy such as Sasha was hanged for attempting. He no longer believed in individual acts of violence, not through principle but on practical grounds: 'We shouldn't reject terror completely as a method of struggle, but does it help attain our desired ends, or on the contrary divert from them? . . . Individual acts of terrorism create only a short-lived

---

* Almost nothing Vladimir wrote until the October Revolution was under his own name. But after his death some of his early pieces were eventually published. It is easy to see why they were rejected: it took him a while to develop a voice and readable style. He was not a natural writer.

sensation and lead in the long run to an apathy . . . and the passive waiting for another "sensation" to happen.'*

He gained an entry into the leading radical 'salon' in St Petersburg,
frequented by some of the sharpest leftist thinkers in Russia, at the home
of Stepan Radchenko. If he was slow to succeed as a journalist, he quickly built a reputation as a clever and sharp debater who could demolish
an opponent's argument with forensic skill. This was one of his great
talents. He was a hard man to argue against, as his friends and critics
acknowledged. So too did the Okhrana. Both he and the revolutionary
group he had joined, the Union of Struggle for the Emancipation of the
Working Class, were kept under surveillance. In one of the first Okhrana reports mentioning his name, in January 1894, Vladimir appears as
a speaker at a clandestine debate in St Petersburg making the Marxist
case against a Populist. The Okhrana snoop at the proceedings was impressed. 'The case for Marxism was taken over by a certain Ulyanov
(allegedly the brother of the hanged Ulyanov) who then carried out the
defence with a complete command of the subject.'5

At this point in his life, he had made almost no personal contact with
the working class in whose name he proposed to lead a revolution. For
most of the middle-class Marxists in St Petersburg drawing rooms, the
'proletariat' were theoretical. But unlike many of the other leftist *intelligenty*, he set about meeting workers and trying to understand their way
of life so he could find a voice with which to speak to them. He volunteered as a lecturer to newly literate workers interested in politics. The
talks couldn't be held at schools or factories, so lectures often took place
at the homes of wealthy supporters of radical causes. One student, Ivan
Yakovlev, recalled that on Sundays he would trudge into the centre of
the city from the poor working-class district where he lived and worked
in a factory. Vladimir taught under the pseudonym Fyodor Petrovich.

At first he would simply read to a handful of student workers from
Marx's *Capital*, which annoyed Yakovlev intensely: 'I could have read it
myself.' But over time Vladimir, who became a famously good lecturer,
learned 'how to explain socialist ideas in simple terms that related to

---

* He could nonetheless be enthused by the odd assassination. When, a few years
later, he read about the murder by a nineteen-year-old student Socialist Revolutionary, Stepan Balmashov, of the Interior Minister Dmitry Sipyagin, he calmly whistled
through his teeth and exclaimed, 'Neat job.'

Russian life'. For hours after the lecture he would talk to the students about their experience, so he could – at least vicariously – learn about the real conditions of life for workers. One Sunday Yakovlev didn't turn up and the following week Vladimir was angry with him. His student explained that he had been in an altercation with a policeman and had spent three days in jail. Vladimir told him that he was a lawyer and had Yakovlev asked he would have defended him. 'Would it have made a difference?' asked Yakovlev. 'No. The result would have been the same – but we could have had the pleasure of abusing those scoundrels.'[6]

He was also starting to progress from talk to action. When textile workers at the giant Thornton factory on the outskirts of St Petersburg went on strike for higher pay and improved conditions – in one of the first outbreaks of major industrial unrest in Russia's history – Vladimir met the strike leaders and wrote a powerful propaganda leaflet on their behalf. When he raised money for the support of the families of the scores of workers who had been arrested, the authorities began to view him as a more serious irritant. He asked permission for an extended visit to Western Europe, as a tourist and to seek treatment at a spa. Like his sisters and younger brother, he suffered from stomach and indigestion problems throughout his life. The real reason for the trip was to meet Russian radicals who were living in exile, including some of the big names in the revolutionary movement. The authorities gave their approval immediately, eager to see the back of him.

7

NADYA – A MARXIST COURTSHIP

'Thy lot is hard, a woman's lot.
A harder lot can scarce be found.' Nikolai Nekrasov (1821–1877)

On the afternoon of 13 February 1894 Vladimir attended an illegal Marxist meeting disguised as a Shrove Tuesday pancake party, at the St Petersburg home of the engineer Robert Klasson, a well-known supporter of radical causes. Most of the listeners applauded appreciatively after the guest speaker, a scientist specialising in new technological methods in industry, read out a long, discursive paper he had written, 'On Markets'. The discussion that followed was polite and uncontroversial and brief – until, typically, Vladimir brusquely laid into the scientist's talk and pointed out, in minute detail, where he had gone wrong and had shown a limited grasp of the subject. After the meeting broke up, as the group of revolutionaries were taking tea, Klasson introduced Vladimir to a shy-looking, modestly dressed twenty-four-year-old teacher of his acquaintance: Nadezhda Konstantinovna Krupskaya. She knew who he was – 'The Marxist from the Volga who had been making a name for himself in Peter'* – and was very keen to meet him. He knew nothing about her.

It was not love at first sight. She was put off by his cocksure manner, acerbic tongue and sarcasm. The conversation got round to the important work of the recently launched Committee for Illiteracy and she told him she was a great supporter of its efforts to teach working-class children how to read. Vladimir laughed – 'It seemed to me a very harsh, even cruel laugh,' she wrote later – and said, 'Well. If anyone wants to

---

* The name most inhabitants of the city called St Petersburg, and after it was renamed Petrograd well into the Soviet era.

save the Fatherland through the Committee for Illiteracy, we won't stop them.' He made it clear he didn't think it was what serious radical socialists needed to do to bring down the autocracy.

She was offended and grew nervous: 'I felt as though people could become uncomfortable under his fixed gaze.' Nevertheless, he walked her home along the Neva and she grew more at ease around him. She talked with enthusiasm about her work as a teacher in the Sunday schools established for working men in the poorer quarters of St Petersburg. He talked about the inevitability of the coming world revolution as predicted by Marx and the role he wanted to play in it. Unusually, as he seldom mentioned the subject outside his close circle, he told her about his brother and his bitter 'anger at a regime that could kill a passionate idealist who had barely reached the age of majority'. They parted at the entrance to Nadya's apartment building on better terms. But this was not the beginning of a whirlwind romance. They did not see each other again for around six months, and would face separation many more times before their work as revolutionaries together would begin.[1]

*　*　*

The name Nadezhda means 'hope' in Russian.* More than love, more than money, more than a career or personal glory, more than a faithful husband offering domestic security, Nadezhda Krupskaya hoped for a socialist revolution in Russia and the downfall of the Tsarist autocracy. She was as fanatically devoted to the cause as was Vladimir. When Nadya is described by biographers as a drudge or the skivvy to a man who often took her for granted – true, up to a point – the important thing she always said about herself is missed: that she was a passionate and intense true believer in socialism. She made many sacrifices for her demanding husband, and for the Revolution in her motherland, but there is no evidence she regretted them. Many men tell their future wives that they will change the world. Some may even believe that they will. Very few deliver.

Nadya was born on 26 February 1869 and was a year older than Ulyanov. Her father, Konstantin Ignat'evich Krupski, was an army officer from the minor nobility who had a successful career as a soldier until

---

* Vladimir, of course, means 'ruler of the world'.

he was despatched to Warsaw to help pacify Russian-occupied Poland after a pro-independence revolt had been crushed in the late 1860s. But he fell out with his superiors, who believed he was too soft on the Polish rebels.*

When Nadya, an only child, was five Krupski was cashiered from the army, with no pension, for overseeing alleged financial irregularities in regimental accounts. He appealed and won his case, but he could not get his commission back and nor could he hold down a job afterwards. He tried estate management, was a factory inspector for a brief period, and wandered around Russia looking for regular employment, with little luck. He died when Nadya was fourteen, leaving his widow and daughter in straitened circumstances. Nadya always felt a bitter personal grudge against the regime for the unjust way her father was treated.

Her mother, Elizaveta Vasilyevna Tistrova, also came from a noble, but landless and almost penniless, family. She became a teacher and made some modest earnings as an author of children's books, but at times both she and Nadya were forced to take in lodgers in their genteel but down-at-heel rooms in St Petersburg, where they settled when Nadya reached fifteen. Mother and daughter were extremely close throughout their lives. A pious Orthodox Christian, Elizaveta Vasilyevna was entirely uninterested in politics and far from being a revolutionary, though she believed sincerely in education for women – a conviction from which Nadya benefited in practical ways.

Though by no means a brilliant scholar, Nadya was highly intelligent, diligent and learned quickly. A school friend from the girls' *Gimnasium* they attended, Ariadne Tyrkova-Vil'iams, remembered her as a shy, quiet girl who didn't flirt with the boys, behaved decorously, thought with deliberation and had formed her convictions at a young age. 'Earlier than any of us, more unyieldingly than any of us, she had defined her views and set her course. She was one of those who were for ever

---

* Soviet biographers claimed that Konstantin Krupski was a revolutionary, and showed socialist solidarity with the downtrodden Poles of the Russian empire. But Nadya always denied this. He was a mild liberal by the standards of the Tsarist army of the time, but certainly not a socialist. He helped those few Russians who wanted to build some schools for Polish children, which landed him in trouble. But at no time did he express any revolutionary sympathies, according to his daughter.

committed, once they had been possessed by their thoughts or feelings.'
She 'burned with idealism', said Vil'iams.[2]

She qualified as a teacher and in 1891 found a job at an evening school
established by philanthropic factory owners for their workers. It was in
a miserably poor working-class district of St Petersburg and it opened
her eyes to the realities of life for the urban poor in Russia. She taught
basic literacy to adults, as well as history, arithmetic and Russian literature. She loved the work: 'It was my university,' she said in later years.
This was when she joined the political underground – a serious-minded
and passionately devoted young woman in search of a great cause. There
is something charmingly naïve, yet chilling, in her admission that at first
she found reading Marx tough going, but when she came to the lines
in the first volume of *Capital* 'The knell of capitalist private property
sounds. The expropriators are expropriated,' her 'heart beat so that it
could be heard'. She repeated this story many times in later years and
there's no reason to doubt her. Her view was simple and never changed:
the capitalists were, quite simply, 'the enemy'. For all her romantic idealism, 'the enemy' is a phrase she used almost as often as Vladimir did.[3]

Most of the male biographers of her husband decry her looks and describe her at best as plain, though it has to be said that few have been as
nasty as her future sister-in law Anna, who once said 'she looks like a
herring'.* Photographs of Nadya as a young woman tell a different story.
'Physically, there was much in her favour,' one (male) Russian historian
observed. 'Had she been an aristocrat, a princess involved in stylish-
ly shocking escapades, writers probably would not have called her a
rare beauty, but might have referred to her arched eyebrows, fine, high
cheekbones, and firm jaw – all conveying a sense of feminine challenge.
They might have mentioned her slightly over-full lips, presuming them
sensuous, and her intense eyes, which photographs taken at the time
[including the mugshot taken by the police] show ... As it was, she
wanted to look like the opposite of a frivolous princess, while still retaining an air of middle-class respectability. Her dress in those years was
invariably a dark, long-sleeved affair, with very little shape except for
slightly puffed-out shoulders and upper arms and a collar that pretty

---

* In later years of European exile one of Nadya's code-names in the underground was
'The Fish'.

well covered her throat. Her luxuriant hair, parted a little off the middle, was drawn straight back, both neat and austere. Far from seeming drab . . . it seems fair to guess that her conservative style was just right for [Vladimir's] taste. Here was a young woman whose obvious disdain for frivolous display bespoke her devotion to more important things.'

She showed little interest in men or anything as skittish as flirtation or a love affair. At twenty-two, soon after she started work at the school, she began seeing quite a lot of a young man, a radical engineer in the same illegal underground discussion circle that she had joined. But he suddenly left the group, saying he was wary of the level of Okhrana surveillance he was receiving. On at least one occasion she went alone to the theatre with him, which caused a row with one of her comrades. Lidia Knipovich, who was even more austere and severe than she was, 'flew at me' when she heard of the assignation, Nadya recalled years later. She said, 'When you work together, it is sufficiently silly to go to the theatre with a man.' Nadya replied sharply, 'What business is it of yours?' But afterwards Nadya turned yet more ascetic and convinced others that she wasn't interested in 'bourgeois personal relations with men'.

She was a highly practical woman. She took another job, part-time, as a copyist for the state railway administration, with the valuable perk of free travel so she could conveniently get to illegal revolutionary meetings. It was an easy, mechanical job which she recommended to others in the same position, as it left plenty of time to 'work for the cause too'. She wrote to a comrade, 'If money is needed you can get a job with some railroad. There at least you'll be able to work off the necessary number of hours and have no cares. You can be as free as a bird . . . all this pedagogy or medicine and so on absorbs people more than it should for the good of the cause.'[4]

Theoretically, men and women were supposed to be equal in Marxist circles and in the Populist cells. But the reality was altogether different. Women were allowed – encouraged – to distribute propaganda leaflets, smuggle *samizdat* literature, teach workers or peasants to read and write, open soup kitchens, shoot provincial governors and generals and nobly die on the scaffold. But they were not supposed to have ideas. The realm of writing articles in learned journals or books about ideology – broad policymaking – was strictly the domain of men. Nadya had heard the story of the 'scandal' created in 1870 by one of the earliest and cleverest of the 'radical' Russian women, Ekaterina Breshko-Breshkovskaya, who embarrassed the men in her 'discussion circle' by describing the shock and horror she caused when she 'dared to speak out against the opinion of a male comrade'. The fustiest of male-only clubs or societies in St Petersburg 'society' could not have created a more chauvinistic stir.

Nadya wanted, above all, to be of use and, as she said, she sensed she could be of great service to the cause with Vladimir Ulyanov, who 'could never have loved a woman with whose opinions he totally disagreed and who was not a comrade in his work'. They met again in the autumn of 1894 at a clandestine discussion group where he read his anti-Populist paper What the 'Friends of the People' Are, and How Do They Fight Against Social Democracy, and began to see each other regularly. He called at her apartment often, on the pretext that he was interested in the factory workers at her school, which he occasionally visited with her. Nadya knew much more about the working class than he did, and he listened to her, taking her seriously.

One other thing Nadya knew about Vladimir was that he was 'available'. He had no romantic relationships with women until he arrived in St Petersburg the year before, not even, as far as we can tell, innocent adolescent crushes. But before he met Nadya he had fallen for one of her good friends and was nursing a bruised heart. Apollinaria Yakubova was tall, auburn-haired and 'a real beauty' according to one of the comrades in the revolutionary group she and Nadya belonged to. Like Nadya she worked as a teacher in a factory Sunday school for workers and was a committed Marxist. Vladimir proposed marriage, but she rejected him in favour of Konstantin Takhtarev, a qualified doctor who would later become editor of the socialist newspaper Rabochaya Mysl (Workers' Thought). They remained friends and their paths would cross several times in the future when both couples lived in European exile.[5]

It has been described as 'a very Marxist courtship', but it did not run smoothly: politics and the secret police would intervene to separate the lovers and erect obstacles to this revolutionary romance.

8

LANGUAGE, TRUTH AND LOGIC

'In politics there is only one principle and one truth: what profits my opponent hurts me, and vice versa.'

Lenin to Angelica Balabanova, 1904

The Ulyanov style of argument and debate was formed early and did not change significantly over the next two decades. He became better at winning his point, more confident and masterful. But he was nearly always domineering, abusive, combative and often downright vicious. He battered opponents into submission with the deliberate use of violent language which he acknowledged was 'calculated to evoke hatred, aversion, contempt . . . not to convince, not to correct the mistakes of the opponent but to destroy him, to wipe him and his organisation off the face of the earth'.[1]

From his first days in the dissident salons of St Petersburg he worked out a method that marked him as different from other radical agitators; almost single-handedly he changed the language on the revolutionary Left, which followed the coarse and aggressive pattern laid down by him. For generations throughout the Communist world, harsh invective and abuse characterised political debate among so-called comrades – let alone between ideological opponents. The exchange of insults was justified on the grounds that this was how Lenin had done things. It was the Soviet way, inspired by the founder of the state, who created so much of the USSR's language, its lifestyle and political 'culture'. His successors well after the Stalin era adopted this method of derision. Communist Parties everywhere, even following the collapse of the Soviet Union in the early 1990s, learned that it made sense to play the man, not the ball – and how to do it with ruthless efficiency. It was one of the principal lessons of Leninism: 'The harshness of polemics became settled Bolshevik practice,' as one of his chief critics put it, 'and the translation of words into corresponding action, physical violence to complement verbal brutality, was no more than a logical end to the process . . . It was a manner of argument peculiarly suited to Vladimir Ilyich's personality.'

Partly, the furious sound of the debate was indeed a reflection of Vladimir's fiery and competitive temperament. But much of it was calculated and deliberate, a tactic that served him well in the endless intra-party squabbles within the revolutionary movement that would last throughout his lifetime and beyond.

Those who disagreed with him were 'scoundrels', 'philistines', 'cretins', 'filthy scum', 'whores', 'class traitors', 'silly old maids', 'windbags' (one of his favourite epithets, found frequently in his writings) and 'blockheads'. Often he would resort to the obscene, in language rarely used in the St Petersburg society of that era – his opponents were invariably 'shits' or 'cunts'. He would deliberately pile on the invective. 'He does not reply to an opponent,' recalled Moishe Olgin, a long-time comrade who saw him operate from the early days as a young revolutionary making his way in the Russian capital. 'He vivisects him. He is as keen as the edge of a razor. His mind works with an amazing acuteness. He notices every flaw in the line of argument. He disagrees with, and then he draws the most absurd conclusions from, premises unacceptable to him. At the same time he is derisive. He ridicules his opponent. He castigates him. He makes you feel that his victim is an ignoramus, a fool, a presumptuous nonentity. You are swept by the power of his apparent logic. You are overwhelmed by his intellectual passion.'[2]

His opponent would either have to deny he was a 'treacherous scoundrel' or a 'piece of shit', or simply shrug his shoulders and leave the field of battle open for Ulyanov. This was an entirely new kind of contest within the radical Left and came as a shock to the comrades. Russian intellectuals were traditionally polite and when they disagreed – which was often – they did so with courtesy. In personal relations with individuals, he nearly always behaved with impeccable manners and decency, never forgetting how well brought up he had been. But in politics, in the smoke-filled conspiratorial meeting room, he was merciless. Many others less passionate, committed and ruthlessly ambitious than him were neither prepared nor equipped to trade blow for blow and left the movement or joined rival groups where they would rarely have to meet him face to face and put up with his abuse. This is what Ulyanov wanted. He won many fights because his opponent was too exhausted or disinclined to clash with him.

It was a calculated tactic, as Vladimir Voitinsky, a future senior Soviet official and an old comrade from the turn of the century, saw clearly. 'Vladimir Ilyich was perhaps the most unemotional man I have ever met in politics. No hate, no compassion, not even irritation against his opponents. His ruthlessness in argument never stemmed from a personal grudge – each word, even each slanderous innuendo in his writings, was coldly calculating.'[3]

On the other hand, he could also use more traditional debating methods. Vladimir was brilliant at explaining his ideas in simplified, direct ways. Never a man of the people himself, he learned how to speak effectively to an audience using the force of his intellect. Maxim Gorky often heard him speak but never forgot the first time. 'His guttural "r" made him seem a poor speaker, but within a minute I was as completely engrossed as everyone else. I had never known anyone who could talk of the most intricate political questions so simply . . . no striving after eloquent phrases, but every word uttered distinctively and its meaning marvellously clear. I had not imagined him that way. I felt there was something missing in him . . . he was too plain. There was nothing of "the leader" in him. His arm was extended, with the hand slightly raised, and he seemed to weigh every word with it, and to sift out the remarks of his opponents . . . The unity, completeness, directness and strength of his speech, his whole appearance, was a veritable work of classic art; everything was there and yet there was nothing superfluous, and if there were any embellishments, they were not noticed as such, but were as natural and inevitable as two eyes in a face, or five fingers on a hand.'[4]

Leon Trotsky, who became famous as a sparkling speechmaker, agreed that at first he wasn't impressed by an Ulyanov 'performance' – but the longer he saw and listened, the more powerful the effect became. 'I see in front of me a solidly built man, a sturdy, supple figure of medium height. I hear an even-flowing, smooth voice with . . . rolling "r"s, speaking fast, almost without pauses and, at the beginning, without any particular intonation. He bends his upper body, sticks his fingers into the armholes of his waistcoat. These gestures at once swing out head and elbows. The head does not seem large . . . but what seems enormous is the forehead. He moves his arms about, neither nervously nor in an exaggerated manner. His hand is broad, with short fingers, "plebeian", strong. The speaker deals with the objections of his opponents . . . before he analyses a hostile idea he gives you to understand that it is without foundation, superficial, wrong. He pulls his arm out of his waistcoat, throws his body gently backwards . . . shrugs his thick-set shoulders either with irony or despair and stretches his arms expressively, spreading his palms and fingers. Condemnation, or derision or humiliation of the opponent always comes before refutation of his idea . . . Then begins the logical offensive. The left hand moves again towards the armhole of the waistcoat, or, more often, the trouser pocket . . . He is not out to deliver an oration, but to guide towards a conclusion; he explains, he convinces; he shames an audience; he jokes with it, tries convincing again and expounds an idea . . . There is no brilliant, crowning finale. There is no rhetorical winding up. He finishes a sentence and – full stop. Sometimes the final sentence is simply "This is all I wanted to tell you." Such an ending accords well with his whole character, but does not seem to dampen his listeners' enthusiasm.'[5]

Yet it was his aggression and menace in debate that most struck his friends and foes. One of his intimates for many years was the highly sophisticated, clever and witty Yuli Martov, to whom for a while he was probably closer than any other man – they addressed each other as '*ty*' rather than '*vy*', very rare for Vladimir. They fell out spectacularly over politics and became bitter enemies. In 1917, shortly before the Bolshevik Revolution, Martov was asked whether, even as an acknowledged atheist, he thought there might after all be life after death. 'Oh I hope not. In my opinion one earthly existence is more than enough; do you think it would be fun to continue arguing with Lenin even after death and in the hereafter listening to his gutter abuse?'[6]

9

FOREIGN PARTS

'I felt then that I had met the future chief of the Russian Revolution.
He was not only an educated Marxist – of these there were many –
but he knew what he wanted to do and how it is necessary to do it. He
smelled of the Russian land.' Pavel Axelrod in Zurich, 1895

Vladimir spent nearly half of his adult life outside Russia, though he
didn't leave his homeland until he was twenty-five. His first visit abroad
was a revolutionary 'grand tour', when he was asked by St Petersburg
Marxists to make contact with the Emancipation of Labour group of
radical exiles in Western Europe, including all the big names of the Russian dissident movement who had fled from the Tsarist regime. He left
at the end of April 1895 for a four-month trip around Austria, Switzerland, France and Germany. He was supposed to have departed earlier in
the year, but his journey was delayed after he came down with the first
of the various illnesses that would periodically afflict him over the years.
He suffered a serious bout of pneumonia that kept him in bed for weeks,
but when he recovered he was keen to go on 'an important mission for
the Revolution'.[1]

Among the first to know Vladimir was going – around the same time
as his mother and sisters were informed – was the Okhrana, whose spies
had been following him for months. Secret intelligence officials in St
Petersburg wrote about him to their most senior agent outside Russia,
Pyotr Rachkovsky, head of the Okhrana department in Paris responsible for keeping an eye on Russian political exiles in Europe. Rachkovsky
would come to know a lot about him over the coming years. 'According
to the information available to the Police Department, the above mentioned Ulyanov occupies himself with Social Democratic propaganda
among Petersburg workers,' the report on him sent to Paris said. 'The

objective of his visit is to find ways of bringing into the empire revolutionary literature as well as to establish contact between revolutionary
circles and emigrants abroad.' He had two false-bottomed and double-
lined suitcases specially made for his journey in which he planned to
smuggle back the illegal literature.

One thing he immediately discovered on his travels was that while he
thought he was good at languages, in fact he wasn't. He had swotted up
on German and English and had acquired a smattering of French from
books, but he had barely conversed with anyone in any of them. Later
he learned to be relatively fluent in three foreign languages, but when
he left Russia for the first time he was shocked by how little he knew,
particularly of German, in which he had prided himself. 'I do not understand even the simplest words – their pronunciation is unusual and
they talk so fast,' he wrote to his mother soon after stepping off a train in
Austria. 'I ask the guard on the train a question, he answers and I don't
understand him. He repeats the answer louder. I still don't understand
so he gets angry and walks away . . . In spite of this disgraceful fiasco, I
am not discouraged and continue distorting the German language with
some zeal.'[2]

His second big discovery was the magnificence of the Alps – and this
was love at first sight. Mountains invariably had a calming influence on
him and in the coming years, as Nadya said, 'Ilyich was always happiest,
most relaxed when he had mountains close to him.' From the first moment he saw one of the high Alps as his train steamed into the Austrian
Tyrol he was captivated – 'I was almost speechless.' He immediately
wrote to his mother, 'the scenery here is wonderful, extraordinary. I
am enjoying it all the time. The Alps began immediately after the little
German station I wrote to you from, then came the lakes and I could
hardly tear myself away from the window of the railway carriage.' Most
forms of mountain activity fascinated him, though he never learned to
ski. One of the reasons he would spend so many of his exile years in
Switzerland was to be close to his beloved Alps.[3]

At the end of May in the mountain village of Les Ormonts, near Les
Diablerets, Vladimir had his first encounter with the most famous of
all the Russian Marxists (until he could lay claim to that mantle himself). Georgy Valentinovich Plekhanov, fifteen years his senior, was a

venerated figure in the revolutionary movement, 'the Moses of Marxism, who brought the Ten Commandments of Socialism down from . . . [the Alpine] Mount Sinai and handed them to the youth of Russia', as Alexander Potresov put it. He was a giant of a man, nearly two metres tall, lean and always elegantly dressed, invariably in a frock coat. He wore a black pointed beard and sweeping moustaches. He had been an officer cadet in his youth and still had a military bearing. 'He's a man of colossal stature, who makes you want to shrivel up,' Vladimir said of him. Over the years they would have tempestuous quarrels which split the Russian revolutionary movement, but when they first met, according to a witness, Vladimir was almost tongue-tied. 'He was overawed in the presence of the great theoretician, the doyen of Russian Marxism.' Plekhanov, known as a prickly, vain and arrogant man, was condescending, 'but looked not without warm sympathy at the able' young man.[4]

Plekhanov was of noble birth* and after graduating from the military academy at Voronezh he studied at the Mining Institute in St Petersburg, until he was expelled in 1877 for taking part in a demonstration. Two years later, with the Okhrana on his tail, he fled Russia and had been living in exile in Switzerland ever since. His sharp and witty pamphlet *Our Differences*, written in 1885, was circulated underground and did more than anything else to popularise Marxism in Russian revolutionary circles. Vladimir called it 'a truly inspirational work' which converted many young people from Populism to Marxism, Nadya Krupskaya among them. His later book, written under the pseudonym Beltov, *On the Development of a Monist view of History*, passed the Tsarist censors on the same basis as Marx's *Capital* did: it was thought nobody would read a work with such a crushingly dull title and which seemed so esoteric. But the censors were wrong. It made his reputation as *the* theorist of Russian socialist philosophy and had a profound influence as a clearly written and straightforward primer on Marx's view that revolution was 'inevitable' as a result of the economic and social forces that drove history.

---

* The great revolutionary Plekhanov would speak with deep nostalgia until the end of his life of his large and rich family estate at Gudalovko in Tambov Province, southwestern Russia, where he was brought up. Though he returned to Russia in 1917 he was an ill man and never managed to visit the estate before he died the following year. He asked his wife Rosalia Bograd to visit it for him after his death.

Vladimir was content that his meeting with the great man was successful: he left Switzerland with letters of introduction from Plekhanov to other leading figures of the socialist movement in Europe. But the seeds of their future disagreements were sown at this visit. Plekhanov saw the vigorous Vladimir, who was becoming so well known inside Russian radical circles, as a threat – particularly after his best friend and closest associate, Pavel Axelrod, another big name in the older generation of exiled radicials, was writing letters in glowing praise of the young visitor. Axelrod invited Vladimir to spend a week at his house near Zurich and was enthused by the younger man's writing and eloquent skill in argument. He told Plekhanov that the coming young man 'has the temperament of a fighting flame'.[5]

In Paris Vladimir visited the Folies Bergère, then a decadent *fin de siècle* night club full of scantily clad dancing girls. But the high point was meeting Paul Lafargue, who could remember first-hand the Paris Commune of 1870. The Frenchman, married to Marx's daughter Laura, was a member of the Commune's leadership and Vladimir was 'filled with excitement' listening to Lafargue's stories. He would often refer to the Commune later as one of the most significant moments of modern European history – as the first attempt, however brief, at a Communist revolution. It lasted less than ten weeks before it was violently suppressed by an unholy alliance of the French Right and the Germans. Vladimir often said later that he was determined not to repeat the Commune's mistakes.

He was charmed by Paris, even though he told his mother that 'servants are very expensive . . . and have to be well fed'. Paris, he wrote, 'makes a very pleasant impression . . . broad, light streets, many boulevards and lots of greenery. The people are quite unrestrained in their manners – at first it comes as rather a surprise after one has been accustomed to the sedateness and primness of St Petersburg.' But for much of his grand tour, from the end of June 1895 onwards, he was ill with severe stomach cramps and suffering from the 'nervous exhaustion' that plagued him constantly throughout his life. The main symptoms were insomnia and crippling headaches. He went for a rest cure at a spa near Zurich, paid for by his mother. 'I have decided to take advantage of the place and get down seriously to the treatment of the problem,' he wrote to her. 'I have been at the spa several days already and don't feel too bad . . . But I have already exceeded . . . [my budget] so would ask you, Mother dearest, for another 100 rubles or so.' By the end of August, he was begging for funds again: 'Mamoushka darling can you send another 50 or 100 rubles?'[6]

* * *

Vladimir arrived back in Russia on 19 September 1895. He took various precautions, or so he had thought, on returning. He had told few people the exact date he would be arriving and he felt sure he wasn't being followed. The false-bottomed and double-lined suitcases he travelled with were now stuffed with illegal literature. When the police tapped the top of one of them he said his 'heart rapped at the throat'; nevertheless they let him and his luggage through. But the secret police kept him under close surveillance from the moment he re-entered Russia.

Vladimir was a highly secretive man and he grew to delight in the 'conspiratorial' hide and seek of the clandestine revolutionary life, the disguises and the moving to safe houses through alleyways and tunnels. It added a *frisson* of excitement to writing articles and researching in libraries.

He believed he was good at the underground life. He read up on creating codes, and how to devise false trails for the Okhrana to follow. He worked at learning conspiratorial tradecraft. Back in St Petersburg, he began to see a great deal of Nadya and she, too, under his tutelage, studied clandestine methods of communicating with other revolutionary groups. Later, she claimed that the group Vladimir led in St Petersburg was the best equipped of all the underground cells in Russia. 'Vladimir Ilyich knew all the through courtyards and was a skilled hand at giving police spies the slip. He taught us how to write in books with invisible ink, or by the dot method; how to mark secret signs, and thought out all manner of aliases. His letters were full of advice about the intricacies of underground work. He would advise about the best way of fixing paste to secrete material in the binding of books.'

He was keen to give others tradecraft advice. He wrote to Axelrod shortly after his return home from Switzerland about the best way to make invisible ink. 'It is essential to use liquid paste; not more than a teaspoonful of starch to a glass of water (and moreover, potato flour, not the ordinary flour, which is too strong). The ordinary (good) paste is only necessary for the top sheet and for coloured paper, because the paper holds well together under a press, even with the thinnest of pastes. It is a suitable method, and ought to be used.'[7]

But in truth he and his revolutionaries were amateurs compared to the Okhrana, who knew where he was most of the time, what he was writing, at which meeting he was speaking. Vladimir's big problem was not that he failed to understand the correct consistency of liquid pastes, but that, surprisingly, he was too trusting. He did not believe all the warnings he was given that he was surrounded by police informers. This was a weakness that would be repeated time and again over the next two decades. In many ways he was a good judge of character. But all too often he seemed unable to doubt the honesty of anyone whose credentials he had once accepted as a true revolutionary devoted to the cause. Several times it led him to the brink of disaster.

In the late autumn of 1895 Vladimir was one of the co-founders, among a dozen others, of the Union for the Struggle of the Working Class, the first officially Marxist revolutionary organisation in Russia (but, specifically, not a 'party') which would be loosely linked to Plekhanov's exile group. One of the other founder members, a St Petersburg dentist, was an Okhrana agent so the secret police knew almost everything about the group from the beginning, including its plans at the end of December to launch a paper, *Rabochee Delo* (The Workers' Cause).

On the night of 8 December the police raided. Vladimir was preparing copy for the first number of the publication, which included, among other 'subversive' literature, two articles by himself, 'To the Working Men and Women of the Thornton Factory' (who were threatening a strike) and 'What Are Our Masters Thinking Now?'

They swooped at a time when the paper was about to go to press and members of the editorial board were all together. Vladimir was arrested with the incriminating articles in his possession. Accompanied by two blue-uniformed policemen, he was taken by carriage, the windows curtained from public gaze, to St Petersburg's House of Preliminary Detention, where a suspect could be held for anything up to two years before a sentence was imposed – without a trial.

10

PRISON AND SIBERIA

'No one knows the kind of government he is living under who has never been in jail.' Leo Tolstoy (1828–1910)

Arrest gave Vladimir the credentials required for a revolutionary. He had written pamphlets, agitated, spoken at meetings and was the brother of a notorious 'terrorist' executed by the regime. But for social cachet a true Russian revolutionary needed time in jail and exile in the Siberian wastes to be taken seriously. It was one of the tests of commitment to the cause.

He was interrogated four times during his imprisonment in Cell 193 in the House of Preliminary Detention from December 1895 to February 1897. At no point was he physically mistreated in any way or put under any serious psychological pressure. The questioning seemed merely routine – 'a game of cat and mouse', as other detainees described the procedure.

His first formal interrogation a few days after his arrest was conducted by the prison adjutant, Alexei Dobrovolsky, and Lieutenant-Colonel Vyacheslav Klykov of the Okhrana's Special Branch. When asked if he was a member of any political party, the lawyer in him answered very precisely. 'I do not acknowledge myself guilty of belonging to the party of social democrats, or to any political party . . . I do not know anything about the existence at the present time of any anti-government party,' he told them in his first statement and repeatedly afterwards. This was strictly true. At that point a Social Democratic Party had not been formed, though he wanted to create one and talked about launching one.

He was not allowed legal representation at any time and throughout the entire process he denied all the sedition charges against him. His mother and sister Anna persuaded his notional employer, Mikhail

Volkenstein, to intervene on his behalf. The experienced and respected lawyer offered to stand substantial surety for Vladimir, but he was refused bail.[1]

He was interrogated three more times by Colonel Klykov in similar relaxed fashion. He gave nothing away. He kept himself physically and mentally fit and stayed in good humour. As he joked in letters home, 'I'm in a better position than other citizens in the Russian empire: at least I can't be arrested.' The Tsarist penal regime was far more benign for political prisoners than it would be in later years under the Soviets, when torture and summary execution were the norm.

Vladimir told his mother a few weeks after his arrest, 'my health is satisfactory. I can drink the mineral water here. It is brought in to me from a pharmacy the day I order it.' He devised a routine to get himself through imprisonment. Later, when his sister Maria and brother-in-law Mark Elizarov were arrested as subversives in February 1901, he explained his rigorous method in his usual prescriptive and bossy style. 'I particularly recommended translations to Mark, both ways, first to do a written translation from the foreign language into Russian, then from Russian back into the foreign language. My own experience taught me that this is the most rational way of learning a language. On the physical side I have strongly recommended to him . . . to do gymnastics every day, and to rub yourself down with a wet towel. In solitary confinement this is absolutely essential . . . I also advise you to arrange your work on the books you have in such a way as to vary it. I remember well that a change of reading or work – from translation to reading, from gymnastics to writing, from serious reading to fiction – helps a great deal. After dinner, for recreation in the evenings, I read fiction regularly, and never enjoyed it anywhere as much as I did in prison. The main thing is never to forget the obligatory daily gymnastics. Force yourself to go through several dozen movements of all kinds. This is very important.'[2]

He described his exercise regime and its benefits in more detail to his mother. 'They loosened my joints so that I used to get warm even on the coldest days when my cell was icy-cold, and afterwards one sleeps much better. I can recommend this, as well as a fairly easy exercise (though a ridiculous one): fifty prostrations. It is exactly what I made myself do – and I was not in the least perturbed that the warder, on peeping through the little window, would wonder in amazement why this man had suddenly grown so pious when he had not once asked to visit the prison church. But . . . [a prisoner] must not do less than fifty prostrations, without stopping, and touch the floor each time without bending the knees – write and tell Mark this.'

While in jail he began writing his first full-scale book, *The Development of Capitalism in Russia.* 'I sleep about nine hours a day and see various chapters of my future book in my sleep . . . if I had been in prison longer, I would have finished it there.' The book would be highly important because it enhanced his reputation as a radical theorist, and argued the contentious point that Russia was already well on the road to becoming an advanced industrialised country – an essential step, according to Marx, from which a proletarian revolution could triumph.

Visitors to the jail brought him money and food, clean linen and more comforts than were needed – 'Someone, for instance, brought me a frock coat, waistcoat and travelling rug,' he wrote to his mother. 'They were all immediately sent to the store room as superfluous.' His mother and Anna moved to St Petersburg from Moscow to be nearer him for visits. They sent food that accorded with the recommended diet for his delicate stomach. And after the prison doctor told him he would benefit from regular bowel clearances, they sent him an enema tube.

He asked Nadya and Apollinaria to walk together to a spot on a street corner where he could catch a glimpse of them from the prison yard. Nadya turned up at the appointed time and place as requested. Yakubova didn't show.[3]

Prisoners were allowed regular mail. Security was so lax that they easily managed to continue their conspiratorial activities inside. There was a well-established code that would let Vladimir know if a clandestine message had arrived for him in invisible ink. At 6 p.m. they brought in hot water for tea and the warders led the ordinary criminals out to the church. By this time the 'politicals' would have torn the letters into long strips. Then they would make their tea, and as soon as the warders departed they began to drop the strips into their mugs. Thus the letters would be 'developed'. In jail it was difficult to treat the letters under a flame, as was the customary method. It was Vladimir's idea to experiment with hot water. 'In order not to be discovered while writing with milk, we made little "ink pots" out of bread. These we popped into the mouth immediately we heard a rattle at the grating.' Once in a postscript to a letter to Nadya he wrote: 'Today I have eaten six ink pots.'[4]

On Wednesdays and Saturdays his sister Anna brought him books from the Library of Academic Sciences, from St Petersburg University and the Free Economic Society. Visitors were never interrogated. They could leave mail or packages at any time during the day until 5 p.m. The parcels were subjected to a cursory inspection by the Supreme Court Prosecutor or his representative, not just a prison guard. The next day they were in his cell. 'When in the corridors of the prison . . . one could hear the warders dragging heavy cases full of books, one knew that this load was meant for Vladimir Ilyich's cell,' one fellow inmate, Gleb Krzhizhanovsky, recalled.

He received a parcel twice a week throughout 1896. Almost every batch of books contained at least one volume with a letter hidden in the spine of its binding, or written in invisible ink between the lines of one of its pages, or coded by tiny markings between the lines of covering letters. The two-way traffic enabled him to keep in touch with his organisation, write strike leaflets and articles and communicate with other comrades in and out of jail.[5]

* * *

On 29 January 1897, after fourteen months in jail in St Petersburg, Vladimir was sentenced to three years' 'administrative exile' in Siberia, though at first the place where he would be sent was not decided. There was no trial and no appeal. At his mother's request he was allowed to travel at his own expense and not under police surveillance, which would make the long journey far more comfortable. He was released from jail on 13 February and permitted to stay in St Petersburg for four days before moving on. Typically, he filled those days at meetings with other revolutionaries.*

---

* Russia had been exiling political prisoners since the sixteenth century, in increasingly remote parts of the empire as its boundaries expanded. Serious offenders were sent to the hard-labour camps dotted around eastern Siberia – like Nerchinsk, where Chernyshevsky had been despatched, Omsk, where Dostoyevsky had been interned, and Sakhalin Island, off Russia's Pacific coast. The less serious 'politicals' like Vladimir were sentenced by Administrative Order and required to live in a designated place under surveillance. In 1897 there were around 300,000 exiles scattered across Siberia, roughly 5 per cent of its total population.

The first part of the journey took eleven weeks. Again he was given privileged treatment. After his mother pleaded with the authorities he was allowed to stay for a few days in Moscow to see his family. He overstayed by two days, and on 6 March he left Moscow, accompanied by his mother, his sister Anna and Mark Elizarov. His relatives left him the next day at Tula Station, returning to Moscow.

'I have left my nerves behind me,' he told his mother, but the journey was boring. 'The country is covered by the West Siberian Railway and I have just travelled throughout its entire length [around 1,400 kilometres] . . . it is astonishingly monotonous – bare, bleak steppe. No sign of life, no towns, very rarely a village or a patch of forest, and for the rest, all steppe. Snow and sky and nothing else for the whole three days.'[6]

In Krasnoyarsk, the end of the line, he had to wait while the authorities told him where he was to serve his exile.* But that was no hardship. He spent entire days in the Yudin Library, a huge collection owned by a wealthy vodka distiller and famous bibliophile. Gennady Vassilyevich Yudin, one of whose friends knew Anna Ulyanova, would give some selected prisoners on their way to exile the run of his house and the 80,000 volumes in his library.† The collection held complete sets of several periodicals dating back to the eighteenth century, which Lenin found useful for his *The Development of Capitalism in Russia*.

After five weeks, most of them spent from dawn to dusk among Yudin's books, Vladimir was told where he would serve out his exile: the small town of Shushenskoye on the River Yenisei. The news could hardly have been better: among political prisoners it was known as the 'Italy of Siberia', in the south-west of the vast region, where conditions were relatively mild. Still, it took eight days on the river steamer as far

---

* In Krasnoyarsk he had free room and board with Claudia Gavrilovna Popova, a wealthy local landowner who had sympathy with radical causes and over the years had helped hundreds of political prisoners with accommodation and food. Many recorded how kind and friendly she had been. When famine struck in 1921, under the Soviet regime, she was in her seventies. She was branded a bourgeois 'enemy of the people'. With all her money gone, she was living on handouts. When older residents petitioned the local Soviet to help her – on the basis that she had not hesitated to help victims of Tsarist repression – they turned down the request to give her extra food rations. She starved to death.

† Yudin sold his collection to the US Library of Congress in 1906 for US$150,000 – a fortune at the time. It remains the core of the Library's Russian Collection.

as the nearest big town, Minusinsk, and then a day's journey by horse and cart. He was assigned a small peasant's hut, surrounded by a vast steppe, some woods and a swamp. In the far distance, on a clear day, he could just about make out the snow-capped hills of the Sainskaya range.

He wrote to his mother soon after arriving that it was a fairly pleasant spot and gave the village a pet name. 'Shu-shu-shu is not a bad village. True, it lies in a fairly bare place, but there is a wood not far away, although much of it has been cut down. There is no way of getting to the Yenisei, but the River Shush flows close by the village and there is also a fairly big tributary of the Yenisei not far away . . . and there I shall be able to bathe. The village is surrounded by dung, which the people here do not cart to the fields but dump outside so that when you leave you have to pass through it. On the horizon lie the Sayan hills or their off-shoots. Some of them are all white and the snow on them hardly ever melts, so that there is even something artistic about them . . . you can see them when they are not hidden by clouds in the same way that you can see Mont Blanc from Geneva . . . it was not in vain that I composed a poem in Krasnoyarsk: "In Shusha, at the foot of Sayan" . . . unfortunately I have not composed more than the first line.'

Conditions were not as bad as those faced later by dissidents in the Soviet Gulag. Vladimir was even allowed to own a shotgun, a Belgian two-bore, which his brother Dmitry sent, along with plenty of cartridges. Within a month he was suggesting, not entirely in jest, that Dmitry visit him. 'We can go shooting together – if only Siberia can manage to make a sportsman out of me.'

But the Tsarist system of Siberian exile was not a holiday camp. Over the years, scores of thousands died of exhaustion in the work camps or starved to death. Prisoners were routinely beaten with the *knout* – a sort of cat o' nine tails which tore the flesh of a victim's back or thighs. In 1892, three years before Lenin was exiled, the 'Khanov Affair' received sensational coverage in *The Times* of London and the *New York Times*, which reported (accurately, as it turned out after an investigation) that gangmaster Vladimir Khanov and the overseers of convict roadbuilders on Sakhalin Island starved the inmates into cannibalism.

Perhaps the cruellest of all Tsarist punishments was reserved for wives of political prisoners, many of whom were exiled to Siberia simply for being married to a so-called 'subversive'. The Stalinist brutality in later years, when the family of a dissident was punished along with the offender, had a Russian antecedent.*

Within a month Lenin was settling down to regular hunting. He told his mother that the shooting was not bad. 'Yesterday I travelled about 12 *versts* to shoot duck and snipe. There is a lot of game, but without a dog the shooting is difficult, especially for such a poor shot as I. There were even wild goats, and in the mountains and in the taiga (30–40 *versts* from here, where the local peasants sometimes go shooting) there are squirrel, sable bear and deer.' For company he acquired a hunting dog, an Irish setter, Zhenka. He fished, he swam, he walked, in winter he skated. He played chess by correspondence with good players across the Russian empire and beyond.

The Okhrana intercepted his mail frequently, but nearly always allowed it to go through – even his correspondence with revolutionaries in Russia and exiles abroad. His frustration was not the surveillance. Mail arrived regularly but very slowly, particularly in winter. 'I received a pile of letters today from every corner of Russia and Siberia and therefore felt in a holiday mood all day,' he wrote to his mother after being without post for weeks.

He sent a barrage of requests – or rather demands – to his mother and sisters and was petulant if they were not met quickly enough. His relatives were used to the irritable tone of his complaints: 'It's a pity the books were sent so late' . . . 'you write that you will send them in a day or two' . . . 'when will these things arrive? Probably not before the end of summer . . .'. There were constant appeals for additional clothes,

---

* Invariably Jewish revolutionaries were sent to the harshest, most miserable places and many suffered from terrible neglect. Several died of disease. There were appalling tragedies among the exiled. Nikolai Fedoseyev, who founded the radical group in Kazan which Vladimir belonged to, a highly talented writer and thinker with whom he was to correspond regularly, was sent to Verkhoyansk, a ghastly hole in the Arctic far east. He drowned himself in 1898, aged twenty-seven, after a jealous fellow exile wrongly accused him of being an Okhrana double agent. Vladimir had met his lover, Maria Gofengauz, a few times. While on her way to join him in Siberia, hearing of his suicide, she killed herself – 'how terrible is this tragic story,' Vladimir said when he heard. A good friend of his, Anatoly Vaneyev, was exiled to the remote village of Turukhansk, on the edge of the Arctic Circle, where he died of pleurisy and cholera in 1899. Vladimir had repeatedly but vainly pleaded with the authorities to move him somewhere less harsh where he could receive better treatment.

cartridges for his guns and books, some kid gloves, 'my mackintosh cape which would be essential here', and some smooth black tulle for a mosquito net.*

But there was hard work too. He was near to finishing his first book and got a surprisingly lucrative publishing deal for a translation into Russian of Sidney and Beatrice Webb's classic of Fabian Socialism, *The History of Trade Unionism.* His day, thoughtfully planned to the last minute, consisted of long hours of solid work alternating with regular periods of rest, Krzhizhanovsky, in exile with him, recalled. 'In the mornings he experienced quite an extraordinary abundance of vitality and energy and he was ready for a bout of wrestling . . . and I would fall in with his mood and give him the satisfaction of pitting my strength against his. Then, after a brisk walk, we would begin our work. Special hours were set aside for writing, for the collection of statistical material, for reading philosophical and economic literature and for relaxation, when we read novels. We did receive newspapers but, of course, with a great delay and in sizeable batches. But Vladimir Ilyich devised a means of reading them in a systematic manner; he arranged them in such a way that he read one issue a day, taking into consideration the overall delay. This arrangement made him feel that he received the paper regularly, daily, though somewhat late. Whenever I tried to upset this order and maliciously picked out and read aloud news from a subsequent issue, he blocked his ears.'

On the whole he lived well in Siberia and often told his mother how fit and healthy he was. He received a basic allowance from the state which was enough to live on with reasonable comfort. He was given eight rubles a month, which does not sound much but was twice the wage of an average St Petersburg worker and more than three times the sum he paid the peasant girl he employed to clean and cook for him.

He suffered periods of melancholy and acute boredom – 'Inwardly day differs from day only because today you are reading one book, tomorrow you will be reading another; today you take a walk to the right of the village, tomorrow to the left; today you write one article, tomorrow

---

* Lenin's letters from Siberia make strange reading. They might be the letters of an indolent country squire of outdoor tastes but gentle epicurean philosophy which forbade him to take such tastes too seriously. He seemed genuinely to enjoy this quiet life, in a way he never would in his long exile abroad.

another,' he wrote to his mother. He told his sister Maria, 'At the beginning of my term . . . I decided never to touch a map either of European Russia or even the whole of Russia. It would mean too much bitterness, as I looked at all those various black spots where I could not go.'[7]

* * *

He proposed to Nadya by letter written in invisible ink. For many ardent young revolutionaries this may have seemed like the ultimate romantic gesture. But the reason was more prosaic and practical. When he wrote – between his release from jail and departure for Siberia – Nadya was herself in prison. She had been arrested for passing illegal literature and money to striking factory workers in St Petersburg and was also facing Siberian exile for three years. At first Vladimir didn't want the authorities to know his plan was for them to spend the exile years in Siberia. She accepted, also by clandestine note which he had to 'develop by dipping the note in warm water', in an offhand way that belied her strong feelings.

Nadya would be allowed to join him only if she was a 'recognised fiancée'. There were months of haggling with the authorities before they allowed her to go. The government held a high moral view of marriage and there had been a few cases of fictitious fianceés sent to radical exiles, which offended the delicate sensibilities of the Tsarist police. Vladimir's soon-to-be mother-in-law was equally determined to ensure the engagement was above board. Elizaveta Vasilyevna barely knew him – and what she knew she didn't altogether like. She was a devout Christian and he was, very publicly, an atheist; he was a revolutionary Marxist and she had no fixed views on politics. In her eyes, he might have the same sort of 'advanced' views on marriage as he seemed to hold on all other institutions in Christian civilisation. She wanted to make sure the marriage took place, so she travelled to Siberia with Nadya, ostensibly to attend the wedding. But for most of the next seventeen years Elizaveta Vasilyevna lived with them amicably. They grew fond of each other and she learned to respect him, if not all of his views.*

---

* They developed genuine affection for each other, though she often disagreed with him and stood up to him. He was not above telling terrible mother-in-law 'jokes'– one of the few kinds of jokes he told, apart from the irony he adopted so frequently. He replied to the question, 'What should be the correct punishment for bigamy?' with

Via his own mother, he sent a stream of demands for items they should bring with them – piles of books, a supply of clothes including moleskin trousers for hunting and a straw hat – 'After all, it's a Paris hat, devil take it.' When Nadya and her mother arrived on 6 May 1898, delayed several days because the water level on one stretch of the river was too low for their steamer, he was not there to greet them. He was out hunting and did not return for a few hours. The first thing Elizaveta Vasilyevna said to him was, 'Gracious, how you have spread. You look almost fat.' He told his mother, 'I found Nadezhda . . . looking not at all well. She will have to look after her health a little better here.' Often her eyes appeared to be bulging – hence the frequent 'fish' remarks about her appearance, a first symptom of the thyroid complaint, later diagnosed as Graves' Disease, from which she would suffer throughout her life.[8]

The wedding had to be in church or another religious institution, the only form of ceremony recognised as legal in Russia. It was delayed by a few days because the local priest, Father Orest, was a stickler for proper ritual, so bride and groom both needed rings. Vladimir had not bought rings and there were no jewellery shops in the middle of Siberian nowhere. Luckily another revolutionary exile in Shushenskoye, the Finnish nationalist Oskar Engberg, had been an apprentice in the jewellery trade before his arrest, and fashioned two rings from copper kopeck coins.*

* * *

The wedding eventually took place at the Peter and Paul Church in Shushenskoye on 10 July 1898. There is no record of it – either because

the not so hilarious answer, 'Two mothers-in-law.' He used to repeat it regularly to Elizaveta Vasilyevna without embarrassment and amid laughter from both. She grew to respect him and they rubbed along well during years of living together in exile. Though he hated smoking he would go out to buy her cigarettes when she needed them. And sometimes he let her beat him at cards. 'How can a brilliant man like you keep losing to an old woman like me,' she would tell him.

* Russian radicals, with their disdain for bourgeois ritual, would invariably wear their rings only for the ceremony itself and get rid of them afterwards. But Nadya kept hers, without wearing it. Not long before she died she donated it to the Central Lenin Museum in Moscow, which with typical Stalinist lack of sentiment would not display it, even in the 'Krupskaya room' of their collection. Nobody seems to know what Lenin did with his ring, but it has never been located.

the Soviets later wanted to hush up the fact that it was an Orthodox ceremony, – a slightly inconvenient truth about the Bolshevik founder – or, perhaps more likely, because many Russian church records were destroyed or went missing in the 1920s and 1930s. Neither husband nor wife ever tried to hide the circumstances of their wedding.

The newlyweds left separately and took different routes to their cottage 'so as not to attract attention', as Nadya said, though this seems an odd explanation. There was a small celebration afterwards at the Ulyanovs' home at which, equally oddly for Russia at the time, nothing stronger than tea was served.

Their relationship has perplexed biographers, of both the Left and the Right, many of whom have tried to present it as a utilitarian arrangement of convenience, a *mariage blanc*. Yet it is clear they shared a bed as well as a devotion to the Revolution.

Their 'honeymoon' was spent translating the Webbs' *History of Trade Unionism* into Russian in the mornings, working on Vladimir Ilyich's book in the afternoons, and on improving their German. It does not sound exactly romantic – and to several people their marriage seemed 'strange', held together, as one long-time comrade observed, 'not by love, affection or companionship but by commitment to the cause'. But it was obviously far more than that. They were an undemonstrative couple, though that means nothing. He never spoke about their marriage. Nadya published a volume of memoirs, a heavily doctored 'Stalinist' record written in the late 1920s and for the most part dry and turgid – though there are some surprisingly lyrical passages – in which she refers to her husband coldly and distantly as 'Ilyich' and their ascetic lives as filled only with duty and work. Her letters and shared confidences with friends tell a different story. She said many years later of their early life together in exile: 'We were young then, we were just married, we were deeply in love with each other. We were newlyweds, you know, and brought beauty to this exile. If I did not write about this in my memoirs, that does not mean that there was neither poetry nor youthful passion in our life.'[9]

Nadya wrote affectionate letters to Vladimir's family, even to Anna Ulyanova, with whom she never got on entirely well – she had heard rumours of Anna's 'herring' comment. She added long, gushing postscripts to his letters home. And they found plenty of time for each other between their work together. 'He asks me to wake him at eight in the morning or at half past seven, but my efforts are usually fruitless; he gives a couple of grunts, pulls the clothes over his head and goes to sleep again,' she remarked to his sisters. Her letters are light-hearted, cheerful and affectionate. Later she recalled their exile in Siberia as one of the happiest periods of her life.

He was the dominant figure in the relationship, but he loved her in his way. She did endless chores for him, from making fair copies of his manuscripts to tidying up and cleaning their homes. She was seldom demanding – probably one of the secrets of their companionable life together. But she could answer back and tease him, in particular about his abilities as a hunter. Time and again she wrote to his mother and sisters that he would go out for hours, dressed in leather and breeches and hunter's jacket, and return empty-handed. Once they went out for a walk from their hut. He had taken his gun but said, 'You know, if I come across anything I shan't shoot it, because I didn't bring a bag and it would be difficult to carry.' But when 'he sighted a hare he would let go at it . . . though he missed, because . . . he is apt to get too excited'. On another occasion, when he saw a flock of partridge by the roadside 'he groaned with pleasure, took aim and fired . . . but the bird simply walked away without even bothering to fly'.

She is surprised at his enthusiasm for embarking on a fishing trip and then dropping the subject later after he returned 'without so much even as a tiddler'. 'At first Volodya announced that he did not know how to gather mushrooms and did not like it, but now you cannot drag him out of the forest. He has real "mushroom fever". Next year we intend to have a vegetable garden and Volodya has already agreed to dig the seed-beds.' She told his mother that he had been delegated to buy material for a blouse for a neighbour's young daughter and instead of asking about the size asked, 'how many pounds?'.

They settled into a comfortable familiarity and an easy life in exile. They even managed to entertain. The Christmas after their wedding they expected a party of visitors. 'Almost the whole district was in town, so we saw the new year in very pleasantly at a big party . . . the main thing was the splendid mood. We mulled some wine; when it was ready we put the hands of the clock at "12" and we saw the old year out in proper style; everybody sang whatever they could and some fine toasts were pronounced – "To Mothers", "To all our friends" etc. and danced to the guitar . . . It was a real holiday. Volodya battled on the chessboard. Then we went skating.'

Twenty minutes from the cottage there was a spot she called 'the enchanted kingdom' where there was the best view of the mountains, and in the frost 'every little fish and pebble can be seen quite distinctly under the ice'. At the end of March 1899 both of them wrote a joint letter to Maria: 'Spring is in the air. The ice on the river is covered with water all the time and sparrows in the willow trees are chirping furiously; the bullocks low as they pass up and down the street and the landlady's hen under the stove clucks so loudly in the morning that she wakes everybody up.'

The Ulyanov family exerted gentle pressure on Nadya to produce an heir. But eight months after the wedding she wrote to Maria Alexandrovna: 'As far as my health is concerned I am quite well, but regarding the arrival of a "little bird" – there the situation is unfortunately bad. No little bird wants to come.'[10]

* * *

Vladimir's exile ended on 29 January 1900. But one condition of his release was that he could not live in any major city or a university town in which he might corrupt students with revolutionary ideas. He chose to settle, at least to begin with, in Pskov, 140 kilometres south-west of St Petersburg, where he could easily communicate with comrades in the capital. Nadya still had six months of her term of exile to serve and was required to stay in Ufa, a small town in western Siberia, for the duration. 'It was a great pity to have to part just as real work was commencing. But it did not even enter Vladimir Ilyich's head to remain in Ufa when there was a possibility of getting nearer to St Petersburg,' she wrote ruefully. She understood how to manage her expectations.

They left Shushenskoye on 10 February by sleigh, having packed books weighing 175 kilos into trunks. It took three weeks to get to Ufa, where he left Nadya and her mother, promising to return in June if the authorities would allow him.

Typically, he broke the rules of his 'parole' within a few days. While he was in Siberia, in the Byelorussian city of Minsk between 1 and 3 March 1898 the biggest step in the revolutionary struggle for decades had been taken – without him. The Russian Social Democratic Workers' Party was formed as the first avowedly Marxist political party in Russia. Despite endless fissiparous splits, changed names and various manifestations, this would become the Communist Party that took power in Russia and ruled the Soviet Union for seventy years. Though Vladimir was not there in person, the Party would to a large extent be formed in his image.

The idea was to unite the various groups of Marxist revolutionaries into one organisation, including for the first time the Union of Struggle in Russia with the Emancipation of Labour group connected with Plekhanov, Axelrod, Vera Zasulich and other exiles in Europe. Various shades of Marxist opinion were represented, but the principal aim of overthrowing the Romanovs and creating a socialist republic was agreed. It had a disastrous beginning. The Party was penetrated top to bottom by the secret police, who knew everything about the organisation. The launch meeting was attended by nine people; all but one was arrested within a few weeks. The second Congress, scheduled to be held in Smolensk the next year, never happened because most of the delegates were arrested on their way to it. Yet the RSDLP (as it is in English) survived and became the most influential of all the revolutionary parties in Russia, mainly thanks to the organisational flair and tactical genius of Vladimir Ulyanov.

Though he was supposed to remain in Pskov and was closely watched by the Okhrana, he managed to give his police minders the slip several times to attend meetings. He visited Moscow to see his mother and sisters. In May he wrote to the Interior Minister requesting 'most humbly as nobleman by birth VI Ulyanov' for permission to visit his wife in Ufa. When he was refused, he went anyway. Nadya had written several times with complaints that she was unwell. He sent her money for treatment and in mid-June, heavily disguised, he travelled to see her. She never spoke about the gynaecological problem from which she suffered in 1900 that might have been the reason they never had children, and Vladimir made only one reference to it. 'Nadya must still rest,' he told his mother. 'The doctor found, as she wrote to me a week ago, that her [woman's] illness requires sustained treatment and that she must rest for 4–6 weeks. I . . . [gave] her more money, as the necessary treatment will be quite expensive.'

But his luck ran out. He and an RSDLP comrade were on a train to St Petersburg – which he was specifically banned from entering – when he grew suspicious that he was being followed. They got off the train at Tsarskoe Selo, where Tsar Nicholas had his primary residence for most of the year, and took a local commuter train to the capital late that evening. First thing the next morning Vladimir was arrested in possession of two suitcases filled with subversive Party literature. 'How foolish of you to change trains there of all places,' said the Okhrana officer who picked him up. 'You must know that at Tsarskoe there is an agent behind every bush.'[11]

He pleaded innocence, but was held for a week before being released. Around 1,500 rubles that he was intending to pass on to the local Party as much-needed funds was confiscated. However, he was free. Vladimir was one of the main leaders of the new Party and, like the group in Switzerland led by Plekhanov, he was convinced that the most important thing it needed was a newspaper to popularise its message – 'a central organ that would *be* the party', as he put it – and present an authoritative political line.

But with the Okhrana constantly on his tail, and with double agents throughout Russia, a journal could not be produced at home. He begged the Interior Minister, again as 'a hereditary noble', for permission to leave Russia for Germany. At the end of July 1900 he was allowed to go – on the basis, the secret police argued, that he would be less trouble outside the country than at home. Nadya would join him abroad when her term of exile ended and she was in better health. He had decided on the name of the new paper, with its echo of the Decembrists: *Iskra* (Spark). It would be more than five years before he saw Russia again.

11

LENIN IS BORN

'The best, the most thoughtful and cultured . . . [Russian] people of
the late nineteenth century did not live in the present, which was ab-
horrent to them, but in the future, or the past.'

Nikolai Berdyaev (1874–1948)

The first time Vladimir Ulyanov used the name under which he would
become famous was in January 1901 in a letter to Georgy Plekhanov.
During his life he adopted more than a hundred pseudonyms, some of
them just once or twice. It is unclear why Lenin was the name that stuck,
but he soon began to favour it, though he used a few others off and on
for a short while afterwards. He wrote his first book under the name
N. Ilyin and a long list of articles under seemingly random initials or
partial names – K. Tulin, Karpov, L. Ul, Petrov, F. Pu, Staryk, K. T. S,
Pinyuchev. He had fake passports under several aliases, among them
Wilhelm Frei, Jakob Richter, Dr Jordan Jourdanov and Willem Meyer.
Originally the adoption of so many pseudonyms was for reasons of security, as a way to confuse the secret police.

But the Okhrana was never put off the scent for long, and often the
subterfuge caused as many problems to his own comrades as it did to
the 'enemy'.* Hiding identities, creating codes and code-names and
maintaining strict security was of course important in any conspiratorial network – and Lenin's claim to leadership was based as much on his

---

* In Russian law – under the Tsars, later under the Communists and indeed in a mod-
ified way in the post-Soviet era – everyone who arrived in a new town or city, even for
a few days, was required to register with the police. It was relatively easy for people to
assume a variety of false names. It often took time, but invariably the Okhrana would
cotton on to what was happening. Not before the new arrival had probably left town,
though. And all the spies' work did little good to protect the regime in the long run.

organisational acumen as a plotter as on his ability to inspire as speaker or with his pen. But Lenin was a highly secretive man who enjoyed the cloak-and-dagger element of the revolutionary underground. It became a habit he was unable to break, though he seldom tried very hard. Secrecy was a way of life.

Lenin never explained where the name came from, and even Nadya admitted that she had no idea of its origin. It has always been assumed that it was somehow linked with the River Lena in Siberia, but nobody can be entirely sure. If he was looking for a riverine reference the more obvious choice might well have been the Volga, where he was born and which he loved from childhood. But some years earlier Plekhanov had already taken the alias Volgin. Still, one could speculate how different history might have been if the Russian Revolution had been led by a man named Vladimir Volgin, who inspired a creed called Marxism-Volginism. From the end of 1901 he was widely known throughout the revolutionary movement, – and the espionage agencies of Europe, as Lenin, or commonly by his patronym, Ilyich, as a mark of respect.

Typically, Lenin's first letters under his new name were filled with abuse against the bourgeois and the 'liberals' who believe that 'Revolutions can be made by people who wear kid gloves'. Objectively, he argued, the liberals were on the side of the autocracy. Plekhanov was incensed by the younger man's undiplomatic intemperance. 'You turn your behind to the liberals,' he replied. 'But we [meaning the older generation of radicals] turn our face. You must tone down your remarks. There is no call now for abusing the liberals in general. This is not tactful. We must appeal from the bad to the good liberal, whatever doubts about the existence of such people there may be . . . Those whom you contemptuously refer to as liberals, property speculators etc., don't deserve to be called such. Liberalism in itself deserves respect. We must regard liberals as possible allies, but your language . . . is not at all that of an ally. Tone it down, my dear fellow!' He replied that he didn't want liberals in the Party giving the Revolution tacit support: 'The Party isn't a ladies' finishing school. Revolution is a messy business.' These were some of the first words he wrote under the pen name Lenin.[1]

* * *

Lenin settled in Munich. He took two rooms at a lodging house in the working-class suburb of Schwabing and began to make arrangements for Nadya and her mother to join him. Very few letters between Lenin and Nadya have survived, and he seldom wrote emotionally about his inner life. But in one letter dating from this period of separation, after telling her how much he missed her, he says how lonely he is and 'in the general turmoil here I live quite well, even too much so, and in spite of special, extraordinary measures for defence against the turmoil! I might almost say that I live in loneliness and on turmoil nonetheless. I dare say that in my novel situation turmoil is inevitable, unavoidable, and it would be a sin not to murmur thanks to God that I am not as nervous . . . [as other exiled revolutionaries] . . . There is much that is good along with this turmoil.'[2]

He wrote something similar to his mother, telling her his quarters were comfortable – near a park with greenery, good connections by tram to the centre of town and close to a public swimming pool, where he went every day. But in the winter of 1900–01 he described his melancholy. 'It is unpleasant without snow. I get sick of the slush; it is boring and I remember with pleasure our real Russian winter – the sledges and the clear frosty air. I am spending my first winter abroad, though it doesn't seem like winter to me. I cannot say I am pleased, though occasionally there are some fine days like those we have in a fine autumn. My life goes on as usual and fairly lonely . . . and unfortunately pretty senseless. I hope to begin my studies more systematically, but somehow I cannot manage it. Probably it will be better when the spring comes and I shall then get into my stride. Having wondered about Russia and Europe, after sitting in Shushenskoye, I long for some peaceful book work and only the strangeness of living abroad prevents me from settling down to it properly.'[3]

The couple were reunited in mid-April amid farce. In an effort to confuse the secret police, they ended up confusing each other. Nadya was travelling on a fake Bulgarian passport in the name Frau Marit-zen. Originally she was supposed to meet Lenin in Prague. She was told that a comrade would greet her at the train station, but nobody turned up. She made her way to the address he had given her. The man she met there was not Lenin but a Czech called Herr Modraczek who had no idea why she was there. He suggested that perhaps she might meet a Herr Rittmeyer in Munich, who could explain.

She took the next train to Munich. 'Wise by experience, I left my luggage at the station,' she recalled. She took a tram to Schwabing, but when she reached the address she had been directed to in Prague it turned out to be a beer hall. 'I approached the fat little German behind the bar and timidly asked for Herr Rittmeyer with a feeling that some-thing was wrong – again. "That's me," said the publican. "No, it's my husband," I muttered. And there we stood staring at each other like a couple of idiots. At last, Rittmeyer's wife came in and, glancing at me, said, "Ah . . . that must be Herr Meyer's wife. He is expecting her from Siberia. I'll take you to him."'

When she finally saw Lenin the meeting was not exactly sentimental or passionate. 'Pfui . . . Damn you. Couldn't you have written to tell me where you were?' However unharmonious the reunion, this was when their real revolutionary work together would begin.[4]

The Spark very nearly failed to ignite. Lenin had a bold vision for *Iskra*.* His plan was that it would unite Russia's disparate, loosely organised and independent Marxist 'circles' and 'study groups' into a vigorous and fast-growing Social Democratic Labour Party, built around the pa-per. Its band of 'secret agents' – Lenin's term, deliberately chosen as a counter to the Okhrana's spooks with whom they would be 'engaged in hostilities' – would smuggle the publication into Russia, across frontiers. Its writers and correspondents would be a close-knit band of profession-al conspirators, travelling around factories and workers' communities. Their duty: acquiring influence among the proletariat and binding them to the labour movement and the entire revolutionary opposition. They would provide 'socialist consciousness' to every strike and small-scale battle, linking it to a 'broader struggle'. They would teach workers to look beyond the parochial to the nationwide and international and raise the workers' vision beyond their immediate concerns. *Iskra*, as Lenin put it, 'will be the collective agitator and collective organiser . . . an enor-mous pair of bellows that would blow every spark of class struggle and popular indignation into a general conflagration'. Its editors would be

---

* The Decembrists declared that 'A Spark will start a big blaze' – the slogan on *Iskra*'s masthead.

the leaders of the Party, the General Staff and officer corps; the 'agents' its foot soldiers. The Party would lead the workers' struggle – and ultimately all other oppressed and exploited people throughout Russia and the world – to lay siege to the autocracy, storm the bastions of privilege everywhere, and go on to victory.[5]

The money to launch the paper came principally from Alexandra Kalmykova, the wife of a senior civil servant and a woman of considerable wealth in her own right. She provided 1,600 rubles with which Lenin left Russia, and soon gave him another substantial sum she had managed to raise among her friends. Eighteen months later she donated a further 2,000 rubles of her own. She had been an acquaintance of Nadya's, if not a close friend, and like her had taught Sunday school classes for workers near the Nevsky Gate area. She had plenty of money and a high social position, but, 'despised the upper-class circle' in which her riches and rank entitled her to hobnob.

She opened a successful bookshop and publishing house in a fashionable area of St Petersburg, selling cheap editions of popular books. Everyone went there – the middle-class establishment in the front of the shop and the radicals at the rear, where *samizdat* material was distributed. Kalmykova's respectability and connections protected her – up to a point. She surreptitiously sold banned radical literature and was crucial to Lenin's underground movement, gaining the not exactly original code-name 'Auntie'. Her generous fund to launch and support the newspaper acquired a code-name of its own: 'the bucket'.*

When, a short while later, the paper, and the Party, ran into money troubles they were bailed out by a generous subsidy from the textile

---

* Kalmykova's introduction to Lenin was made by Pyotr Struve, once a socialist collaborator but soon to begin a move from the radical Left towards the liberal centre. She was Struve's mistress, twenty years older than him, and in polite society referred to him as 'my adopted son' – not that anyone believed her. Like most people at one point or another Kalmykova would fall out with Lenin over politics, especially during the long-running Bolshevik/Menshevik split that was soon to engulf the revolutionary movement. She went into voluntary exile for many years but returned to Russia after 1917 and tried to rebuild their friendship, at least with Nadya. She exchanged a few cool-ish and formal letters with Lenin after the Revolution. But they never met again. Nadya on occasion understood how to use delicious irony: 'In 1922 Vladimir Ilyich had written Alexandra Mikhailovna a few lines of fervent greeting such as only he could write.'

magnate Savva Morozov, a friend of Gorky, who gave Lenin 2,000 rubles a month. Morozov was hardly a revolutionary socialist, but he was a shrewd businessman who was convinced the Romanov monarchy was doomed – and he knew how to hedge his bets. As he told Leonid Krasin, one of Lenin's staunchest lieutenants, 'these days it is necessary to be friends with one's enemies'.*

The main obstacle to launching *Iskra* was neither financial nor political. It was personal. It was important to get Plekhanov on board. He was still by far the best-known Russian radical, and an influential figure on the Left internationally. He assumed that as the older, more famous man he would be the leader of the *Iskra* group, essentially the 'Party' chief, its guiding spirit and principal strategist. 'But Lenin had other ideas,' as Alexander Potresov, one of the co-founders of the paper, remembers. He had thought Plekhanov would be a figurehead and not involve himself in *Iskra*'s day-to-day affairs, leaving him to run the paper – and the Party organisation.

The clash between them was over trivial matters, but highly dramatic. The first hint was when Lenin wrote an editorial 'mission statement' for the launch issue of the paper. Plekhanov told him high-handedly that it was a poor effort. He did not object to any of the arguments, but simply said it wasn't well written and was 'too pedestrian in tone'. Lenin was deeply hurt when Plekhanov wrote to him and said, 'This is not "written", as the French say. It is not a literary work. This does not look like anything.' Plekhanov took it away and said he would work on the article to 'elevate the tone', but returned it a few days later almost unaltered. Lenin was indignant. 'My infatuation with Plekhanov disappeared as if by magic and I felt offended and embittered to an unbelievable degree. Never, never in my life had I regarded any other man with such sincere respect and veneration, never had I stood before any man so humbly

---

* Morozov (1862–1905) was a ruthless businessman, a generous patron of the arts – he had a large collection of French Impressionist paintings – and a major philanthropist. He gave to hospitals and to schools which taught literacy to peasants and workers. He was a substantial donor to theatres, but the playwright Chekhov, who benefited from the oligarch's largesse, was no fan. When rumours began appearing that Morozov was backing Lenin financially he commented, 'Savva . . . he scurries before the Revolution like a devil before the dawn.' Morozov was prone to deep depressions. He shot himself at his villa on the Côte d'Azur in 1905.

and never before had I been so brutally kicked ... there could be no doubt that this man was bad, yes bad, inspired by petty motives of personal vanity and conceit – an insincere man.'

Lenin travelled back and forth between Munich and Plekhanov's home on the shores of Lake Geneva in a series of meetings to patch things up. After one bitter exchange Lenin, who was with another of the younger revolutionaries, Potresov, was unable to hold back his fury. 'Had we not felt such love [for Plekhanov], had we behaved towards him in a more circumspect manner, we would not have experienced such a crushing comedown, such a spiritual cold shower ... This was a most severe, an injuriously harsh lesson. The discovery struck us like a thunderbolt because up to that moment both of us had been enamoured of Plekhanov, and, as we do with our beloved, we forgave him everything, closed our eyes to his shortcomings ... Our indignation knew no bounds. Our ideal was destroyed. Two young comrades "courted" an older comrade because of their great love for him and, all of a sudden, he injects into this love an atmosphere of intrigue and makes them feel not like younger brothers, but like idiots who are being led about by the nose, like pawns that can be moved with impunity, like ineffectual careerists who must be cowed and quashed. And the enamoured youth receives a bitter lesson from the object of his love: to regard all persons without "sentimentality", to keep a stone in his sling ... Blinded by love, we had actually behaved like slaves.'[6]

When Plekhanov threatened to leave the editorial board, Lenin and his handful of backers agreed to allow the older man two votes – which they regretted almost at once, when they realised he would use every opportunity to override their wishes. At one point Lenin, exasperated, threated to break off relations after Plekhanov criticised another piece he submitted on 'The Agrarian Programme of Social Democracy'. 'I received the article with your comments,' he wrote back. 'You have a fine conception of tact with regard to your colleagues on the editorial board. You do not restrain yourself in the least in choosing the most contemptuous expressions ... I would like to know what you would say if I answered your article in the same way? If you are aiming to make our mutual work impossible – then the way you have chosen will very speedily accomplish your aim. As for our personal, apart from our working relations, you have finally spoiled them – or, more exactly, you have brought about their complete cessation.' Again the row was smoothed over, but the fractious environment took its toll.*

Lenin scored one significant victory, though. Initially it was assumed by Plekhanov and others that the paper would be produced from Switzerland, so he could keep close control over it. But it was hard to find a Swiss printer who would be prepared to risk publishing it. Germany had more advanced, sophisticated presses, a large socialist movement, and far more efficient communications with the rest of Europe. So it was agreed to publish *Iskra* from Germany, even though the editorial board consisted of Plekhanov and Axelrod in Switzerland, Zasulich in London and Lenin in Munich. He found a printer with an underground press near his rooms in Schwabing. It had a sophisticated, built-in self-destruct mechanism so that if the police raided the premises – always a possibility throughout Lenin's time in Germany – the type and the 'form' on which a page was printed would be broken up and the illegality of the content hidden.

The first issue was published on 11 December 1900 and included three pieces by Lenin. The most significant one sketched out a programme for the Party and how it should be run. It contained the essence of what would be called Leninism and the principal tactics he and his Bolsheviks would use to build support and seize power. He told workers: 'Do not merely organise yourselves into mutual aid societies, strike funds and workers' circles. Organise yourselves for a close struggle against autocratic government and against the whole of capitalist society. Without such an organisation the proletariat is not capable of rising to a conscious class struggle . . . Without such an organisation the workers' movement is condemned to impotence. The working class needs a socialist vanguard of people who shall devote to the revolution not only their spare evenings, but the whole of their lives.'[7]

---

* Not long after this incident Vera Zasulich told Lenin that 'Georgy [Plekhanov] is a greyhound. He shakes and shakes the adversary and lets him go; but you are a bulldog, you have a deadly bite.' Lenin went around telling the story and repeating the phrase 'deadly bite', obviously relishing it. Zasulich had not meant it kindly. She grew to loathe Lenin and could not bear to be in a room with him. On the other hand Lidia Dan, Yuli Martov's sister, who equally detested Lenin, described Plekhanov as 'a great man with an enormous number of petty traits'.

*   *   *

Publishing the paper and handling frayed egos was difficult enough. But distributing the publication inside Russia was a huge problem, if vital to Lenin's strategy for revolution and power in the Party. *Iskra* had to be smuggled into the country via a variety of routes, and getting copies past the customs and the secret police was an elaborate and risky game of cat and mouse.

Lenin relied to a large extent on professional smugglers, who collected bundles of copies in a number of 'safe houses' from one warehouse in Berlin. They were usually taken across the Russian border with other contraband goods, often in double-bottomed suitcases. A Russian contact would pick up the bundles and deliver them to an agent, who would then pass them to another Social Democrat from another town or province for local distribution. *Iskra* was always handed over in person, never through the post. Once in the hands of local organisations it was distributed by Party activists, pasted on walls, smuggled into factories and army barracks and on several occasions – at great risk – dropped from theatre galleries onto the audiences below.

Occasionally ordinary travellers would agree to take small consignments of the paper. The strangest, most roundabout routes were developed in haphazard ways. Once a ship's cook took delivery of copies at Marseille and travelled to the small Georgian port of Batoum. There he dumped them in the sea in waterproof packages which were fished out by local Social Democrats and taken hundreds of miles to Baku and Odessa. Other packages arrived from places as far apart as Toulon, Alexandria and Tabriz in northern Iran. One regular route was to send packages through the northern tip of Norway near the Arctic Circle, wrapped in greaseproof paper inside boxes of salted fish. Often the material was intercepted by the Russian authorities, was lost en route, or the carrier was a double agent who informed on others. One package remained unclaimed in a Stockholm warehouse for decades. Lenin estimated that only about 10 per cent of the deliveries eventually got through – just enough to make the whole enterprise worthwhile, he said.[8]

Lenin took few risks personally. The German police kept an eye on him, as did Okhrana agents in Europe. But they left him and his operation in Munich alone. His agents in Russia were often in danger. Dozens were arrested, jailed and exiled to Siberia. The *Iskra* smugglers were a varied bunch. One trusted comrade, Vladimir Smirnov, who would later become a leading official in the Soviet regime,* organised a clandestine route through Sweden and Finland using his mother, Virginiya, as one of his couriers. She often travelled into St Petersburg from her home in Helsingfors (now the Finnish capital Helsinki) with copies of the paper and highly secret lists of coded addresses of *Iskra* subscribers under her knitting. Nobody suspected her or thought to stop 'a kindly old lady who looked like a children's nanny'. The highly popular Finnish opera singer Aino Akté was a RSDLP sympathiser and a Finnish nationalist who smuggled material for the Party in her luggage when she returned from Western tours.

It is true that the penal regime in Tsarist Russia was not as harsh as the Bolshevik system would be, and the Okhrana less bloodthirsty than Lenin's Cheka. But we are dealing with degrees here, not categories. Thousands of 'subversives' died of disease, neglect and starvation in Siberian exile and jail for the 'crime' of reading or publishing banned literature, which often included nothing more radical than articles proposing mildly liberal democratic reforms in Russia that were common elsewhere in Europe. Many were executed, without a trial of any kind. In particular, the secret police were always on the lookout for illegal printing presses, which were closely guarded secrets that very few activists knew about. 'Copies' of *Iskra* could be reproduced on them, along with other material the Okhrana thought dangerous. In September 1901 a young Georgian revolutionary, Lado Ketskhoveli, acquired a sophisticated (and expensive) rotary press in Tiflis. He was arrested and the secret police tortured him mercilessly for several days to find out where the machine was located. But he wouldn't tell them. He was shot in his prison cell.[†9]

*   *   *

---

* He was married to Karin Strindberg, daughter of the Swedish playwright, and he developed wide contacts throughout the socialist parties in Scandinavia.

† Everything had a supposedly secret code-name in the revolutionary underground. The press in Tiflis was called 'Lidia' and continued operating for the next four years – an invaluable tool within the *Iskra* organisation.

The paper was aimed mainly at already converted Marxists who were reasonably well informed politically – educated workers, ideally, as Lenin saw it. There were some theoretical pieces for the intellectual readership, but it contained plenty of straightforward propaganda and news about strikes and political unrest which would not appear in any other publications. It grew popular outside Marxist circles; its influence far outweighed its meagre circulation. There were never enough copies to go around. For Lenin the important thing was for workers to know about *Iskra*. He was always encouraged when he heard that educated workers were reading from the paper to other less literate co-workers, and one group would pass their copy on to another until the worn copies fell apart.

Lenin – and later Nadya, when she reached Munich and was appointed secretary of the *Iskra* group – did most of the organisational legwork to produce the paper. He worried about every detail, from the type size of the print – he lectured contributors and other editors on why the font had to be a style that permitted maximum words on the page, however it looked – to the editorial line 'we must take to ensure the Party is organized with one voice'.

Lenin was growing increasingly dictatorial and impatient with those who disagreed with him. But he had a way of charming writers: flattery invariably did the trick, as it has always done with journalists. 'Of course he would suggest "improvements" in the work of other writers,' said Nadya. 'But he was discreet and tactful in a way that authors hardly noticed they were being corrected.' When he suggested a piece to a writer, he found a way to make it seem like the idea came from the other author, not from himself, even when in the finished article 'he had actually used Ilyich's words and turns of phrase'. Technically, he was a first-rate journalist and on occasion could be an inspired editor.

Lenin's taste for routine and order imposed itself on the rest of the staff. He spent his mornings at the library. Work on *Iskra* began immediately after lunch, when someone would fetch the post. As editor-in-chief, Lenin was allowed to read all the correspondence first and he was irritated when anyone tried to read it over his shoulder, or wandered over to a café with one of the newspapers. Nadya's job was to 'iron' the mail and look for coded messages written in milk or lemon juice or invisible ink. It was from these that he obtained news of what was going on within the Party in Russia.

Lenin was a hard taskmaster. He was angry if the decoders, even Nadya, made mistakes. Lidia Dan, one of the assistants at *Iskra* in the early days, said the whole deciphering process was 'a hazardous business because of Lenin's moods. He absolutely could not tolerate a bad decoding . . . Nor could he accept slow work or delays.'

Lenin and his wife did most of the hard graft. But *Iskra* would have possessed half the influence that it acquired on the radical Left if it had not been for Yuli Martov. Lenin was the brain of the paper, Martov its heart. The two could not have been more different, but for several years Martov was the closest male friend Lenin had. In their early thirties it seemed as though they had such a strong bond that nothing could divide them. For the last two decades of their lives the bitter enmity between them was one of the main causes of the irreconcilable split within the Russian revolutionary Left.

Julius Osipovich Tsederbaum – he was known by the sobriquet Martov as early as his days at the *Gimnasium* – was the most attractive of all the leading Russian radicals. He was born in 1873, into a middle-class Jewish family in Constantinople. His father was a commodities trader and the Turkey correspondent for two leading St Petersburg newspapers. His mother was a polished Viennese woman of the solid middle class; the atmosphere in the family was liberal, artistic, enlightened and sophisticated. They moved back to Odessa when Martov was four.

Martov, a short, stocky figure who always wore a thick bushy beard and pince-nez, was radicalised early. He abandoned the moderate liberalism of his parents and converted to Marxism in his teens. By the time he was eighteen he had already served a short prison term for distributing banned literature and was barred from going to university, but permitted to live in St Petersburg. Then, aged twenty, he was jailed again and prohibited from St Petersburg or any other university city where he might subvert young people.

He and Lenin first met in 1894; 'they just talked all evening, all night without sleeping and all the next day without a break', Martov's sister Lidia recalled. They were co-founders of the Union for the Struggle of the Working Class and were both exiled to Siberia at around the same time, though for unconnected offences. While Lenin served out his term in the 'Siberian Italy' of Shushenskoye, Martov, like most of the Jewish 'politicals', was given a far tougher time. He endured three years in the freezing north of Turukhansk, where conditions were appalling. His health suffered and he showed the first signs of the TB that would kill him before he reached fifty. Lenin appealed to the authorities to transfer him somewhere less harsh, but was ignored.*

Martov was chaotic where Lenin was controlled, a bohemian where Lenin's habits were distinctly bourgeois, and highly eccentric where Lenin was conventional. Martov was exuberant and warm, a highly popular figure with a mournful look which belied his mostly cheerful demeanour. 'He was by predilection a haunter of cafés, indifferent to comfort, perpetually arguing and gossiping,' said Potresov. He had a sparkling wit and an infectious sense of fun. Yet in many ways he was a more orthodox Marxist than Lenin, as strict in the interpretation of the prophet Marx's teachings and just as careful to guard against heretical beliefs that would water down the theory. 'He was the most intelligent man I ever met,' said Nikolai Sukhanov, the great chronicler of the Russian Revolution and a supporter of Martov. 'But he was woefully weak in action.' Another admirer described Martov as 'the Hamlet of the Russian Revolution'.

In the early days of *Iskra* they seemed like the perfect team. Martov fizzed with ideas about articles for the paper and would commission them, leaving Lenin to edit them and turn the pieces into usable copy. In the first year of *Iskra*'s existence Martov wrote more articles than Lenin. He was an original writer in his way, more imaginative and 'literary' than Lenin, but far less focused and compelling than Vladimir Ilyich when he was on form.

Earlier than most people, Martov began to see Lenin's intolerant arrogance as dangerous. Even when they were personally close he had doubts about his style and domineering personality. 'Vladimir Ilyich did not yet have, or had in a lesser measure, the confidence in his own strength – never mind in his historical calling – that was to emerge so strongly in his mature years . . . He was then in his [early twenties] . . .

---

* Adolescent though it may have been, while in London in 1902 witnesses say they saw Lenin and Martov 'drink Brudershaft' together, a German custom adopted by middle-class Russians: two men stand side by side, link arms, kiss cheeks, address each other as 'brother' and as 'thou', the Russian '*ty*'.

and he was not yet full of the scorn and distrust of people which, I believe, is what made him into a certain type of leader.' Lenin, he added, had 'no talent for friendship; he uses people too much'.

During his two years in Munich Lenin was establishing his status, as another *Iskra* editor, Potresov, put it: 'Plekhanov was esteemed, Martov was loved, but only Lenin was followed unquestioningly, as the undisputed leader. For only Lenin embodied . . . a personage of iron will, indomitable energy, combining a fanatical faith in the movement, in the cause, with as great a faith in himself. Louis XIV could say "I am the State"; so Lenin without unnecessary words invariably felt that he was the Party, that he was the will of the movement concentrated into one person. And he acted accordingly.'[10]

12

UNDERGROUND LIVES

'In an autocratic state, the more we confine the membership of the Party organisation . . . to people who are professionally engaged in revolutionary activity and who have been professionally trained in the art of combating the political police, the more difficult it will be to wipe us out.' Lenin, *What Is To Be Done?*, 1902

Lenin was frequently accused of physical cowardice, even by some of his loyal supporters. While he was safe in Western Europe, avoiding arrest and taking few risks with his own security, his underground co-conspirators and *Iskra* agents inside Russia were in constant danger. He felt no qualms about sending them on perilous missions, and when reproached he argued with calm logic that it was one thing 'for the rank and file . . . it is quite another – and a senseless thing – for the *leader* to run unnecessary risks'. When a long-standing comrade, Mikhail Silvin, told him that some revolutionary foot soldiers inside Russia were questioning his personal bravery, Lenin answered calmly, 'To allow oneself to be jailed . . . or sent to Siberian exile once is permissible; to do so for a second time would be stupid.'[1]

By the beginning of 1902 there were around a thousand 'professional revolutionaries' inside Russia acting as *Iskra* agents or engaged in other work for the RSDLP – and probably twice as many in other radical organisations or terrorist cells. They lived a hand-to-mouth existence as 'illegals' on fake identity documents, depending on the kindness of strangers and the goodwill often of people who didn't entirely agree with their aims or their ideology, but loathed the Tsarist regime even more than the idea of revolution. They moved from safe house to safe house, acquiring an instinct for knowing when they were followed. They adopted a bewildering set of code-names and aliases, the tradecraft of *konspiratsiya*, a word that in Russian means 'secrecy' rather than the English 'conspiracy'. Lenin's instructions to Party activists to maintain secrecy at all times were well known to all his operatives. 'When you are taken up with secret, conspiratorial matters, you must not speak with those with whom you normally converse, nor about the things you normally talk about, but only with those you need to talk to and only about things you need to talk about.' Those who broke the rules were invariably frozen out of the Party.

There was something comic and amateurish about the secret knocks, the disguises, the passwords and the elaborate code-names activists gave themselves – especially when one knows that the Okhrana were seldom fooled for long and had planted agents at the heart of the conspiracy. Lenin's code-name was invariably 'Starik' (the 'Old Man'); Nadya had others besides 'Fish' – she was Sablina, N. Sharko, Katya and sometimes Minoga or Maria. One of Lenin's good friends, Panteleimon Lepeshinsky, who had been in Siberian exile with him, had the aliases Lapot, Bychkov and a numerical code, 2a3b; Leonid Krasin, an engineer who would become head of the Party's 'technical committee' – in charge, among other things, of the vital printing presses – was 'The Horse', Vinter or Johanson. The Moscow Party chief and invaluably hard-working Nikolai Bauman was 'The Rook', 'The Tree', or Victor. The password used by the St Petersburg activist Cecilia Bobrovskaya to introduce herself to other revolutionaries was, 'We are the swallows of the coming spring.'

But there was nothing comic about the dangers the conspirators faced. Making revolution was a serious business. The shared risks the activists took, the passionate commitment they showed to their beliefs, forged intimate bonds of comradeship. As an ardent young Party member in St Petersburg put it: 'The constant danger of arrest, the secrecy of our meetings and the awareness that I was no longer just a grain of sand, no longer just another one of the workers, but a member of an organisation that was dangerous and threatening to the government, and to the rich – all this was new and exciting.'[2]

Life underground was intense. Elena Stasova, a clever activist who ran the most successful of all the revolutionary cells in St Petersburg and would later become one of Lenin's chief aides, was a skilled organiser and highly practical young woman. She explained what the revolutionary movement meant to her in emotional terms that would strike a powerful chord with her comrades. Stasova came from a wealthy background and a loving family. Her parents allowed her to use their country estate as a safe house for activists and a storage place for underground literature. She held illegal meetings where money was raised for *Iskra* at the Stasovas' spacious apartment in a fashionable district of St Petersburg. When Elena was arrested her parents stood bail for her. But for her and many other eager young women and men, the Party 'was our family' and dedication to the cause came before everything else, friends, parents, love. 'My life is in this, in this and only in this,' she wrote from prison after she was arrested. 'No other work can give me the strength to live. Without this work of mine I cannot live. This is the flesh of my flesh . . .'[3]

Lenin's sisters were often in trouble with the police. Anna had been arrested in St Petersburg in 1887, at the same time as her brother Alexander. She had not been involved in any way with the plot to kill the Tsar, but she was confined to the estate at Kokushkino for many months. As soon as she was free to travel again she went straight back into underground work, distributing illegal literature and organising clandestine meetings. Maria was picked up by the Okhrana in Moscow in 1899 and spent seven months in solitary confinement before serving a three-year sentence of exile in Samara. Immediately the term ended, she returned to revolutionary work as an agent for Lenin, coding letters from Russia to the *Iskra* board in Europe.

Arrests were common, as were dramatic and lucky escapes involving adventure and derring-do. None more so than the extraordinary display of cool by Lidia Gobi, daughter of the respected Professor of Botany at St Petersburg University. Gobi was a convinced Marxist who seemed more of a socialite than a socialist. Tall, elegant, well dressed, aristocratic-looking, a noted beauty, she was one of Lenin's best agents in the Russian capital and a regular courier of banned literature and secret messages throughout Russia. On a mission from the St Petersburg Party cell to Kiev she took what she thought were the correct precautions and believed she wasn't being followed to her secret meeting. Her Kiev contact handed her documents to take back to St Petersburg, when she realised she was being tailed first by one, then two and finally three Okhrana spooks who made no effort to hide the fact that they were following her. They almost reached her, near a cliff edge overlooking the River Dnieper. She looked down below, saw trees and undergrowth and, remarkably collected and brave, she wrapped the thick fur cloak she was wearing around herself, climbed onto the ledge of the cliff and allowed herself to fall. The undergrowth softened her descent and to her amazement she landed safely, uninjured, among onlookers. Totally calm, she picked herself up, apologised politely for surprising them, walked to the railway station and took the first train out of Kiev.[4]

* * *

Nadya, equally safe in Western Europe, handled day-to-day contact with the underground in Russia. She operated under the strict orders of Lenin – 'the centre', as he called wherever he was located – but she was responsible for deciphering secret letters, keeping tabs on the well-being of the Party foot soldiers inside Russia and more complex tradecraft such as developing new codes. By 1902 she 'ran' a hundred or so agents and Lenin trusted her implicitly to relay all the important information to him. 'She was at the heart of all the organisational activity,' one of the *Iskra* editors recalled later. 'It was to her that newly arrived comrades from "home" reported first; she briefed those that were leaving and sent them on their way; she established the clandestine connections and she was the one who deciphered most of the secret messages. Nearly always her room held that faint smell of paper warmed over a flame.'

The Okhrana, though, was invariably one step ahead. It had scores of officials intercepting letters and telegrams to and from Russian exiles abroad through its Department of Posts and Telegraphs – known as the *Chernyi Kabinet*, the Black Cabinet. Surveillance of mail going in and out of the main post offices of all the major cities in Russia, as well as Warsaw, Helsingfors and Tiflis, was highly efficient. The codes Lenin's agents used lacked sophistication and were invariably straightforward to break. Concealed messages inside books worked for a few weeks and occasionally months, but rarely much longer. Nadya would choose a book and in a secret letter tell agents to refer to a specific chapter, paragraph, line and letter in a word, in order to read the coded message. She picked at one point her favourite Nekrasov poems, a biography of

Spinoza and the animal fables of Ivan Krylov. The police knew that when an agent referred to an 'illness' it meant an 'arrest', a 'hospital' really meant 'prison' and an 'epidemic' was a warning that there had been a spate of arrests at a specific location.

From the safety of Munich – and later London, Geneva or Paris – Lenin was naturally aware of the risks his agents in Russia were taking and the sacrifices they made. But he was often frustrated with them, impatient if they were not delivering what he expected and downright rude about their efforts. Nadya would frequently have to tone down his furious complaints about 'incompetent' or 'dim-witted' underlings. He was in a rage, as he wrote to one comrade, that 'in nine cases out of ten all plans end in smoke . . . and the agent muddles along just anyhow. Believe me, I am literally losing all faith in . . . [smuggling] routes, plans etc. made here because I know beforehand that nothing will come of it all. It is we who have to make frantic efforts doing jobs here for lack of suitable people. In order to appoint agents, to look after them, to guide them, it is necessary to be everywhere, to rush about and see them on the job. That requires a team of practical organisers and leaders but we haven't got any, at least very few to speak of. That's the whole trouble. Looking at our practical mismanagement is often so infuriating that it robs one of the capacity for work. The consolation is that the cause is vital and despite the chaos is growing.'[5]

Nadya was worried about his state of mind. 'Those weeks and months of waiting for answers to his letters, constantly expecting the whole thing to fall through, that constant state of uncertainty and suspense were anything but congenial to his character,' she wrote. 'His letters to Russia were full of requests to write punctually, to act promptly. He did not sleep at night after receiving a letter from Russia saying that "Sonya is silent as the grave" or that "Zarin" did not join the committee in time or "We have had no contact with the old woman". I'll never forget those sleepless nights.'

She was troubled by other thoughts: that the game of hide and seek with the Okhrana was a waste of effort, drama for the sake of it. No one knew better than Nadya how amateurish so many of her husband's espionage ploys were in practice. 'All those letters about handkerchiefs [passports], brewing beer [propaganda shipments via Scandinavia], warm fur [illegal literature], and all those crude code-names for towns, beginning with the same letter – Osip for Odessa, Terenty for Tver, Petya for Poltova, Pasha for Pskov, those substitutions of women's names for men and vice versa – all this was transparent in the extreme.'*6

---

* But they did score some big successes. Twelve *Iskra* agents were arrested in Kiev in February 1902. They were held at the Lukyanokvsy Fortress in the centre of the city, supposedly under tight security, and they were due to appear in a big show trial against 'terrorists' planned for the spring. A few days before the trial was due to start they all escaped in a mass prison breakout organised right under the noses of the guards and senior Okhrana officials. This was a major propaganda coup for the Social Democrats.

13

ENGLAND, THEIR ENGLAND

'As a rule the only thing known in England about Russians is that they take lemon with their tea.' Olga Novikova (1842–1925)

Late in the morning of 14 April 1902 Lenin and Nadya disembarked at Charing Cross Station after a two-day journey from Munich. They were immediately engulfed by fog, a typical London 'pea souper' where visibility was practically zero. 'My first impression of London: hideous,' he wrote the next day to Pavel Axelrod in Geneva. He hated London, and the English, for the first few weeks while they stayed in a pokey and dirty bedsit in Sidmouth Street, in the working-class district of Somers Town.

Their first big problem was the language. 'We found that we couldn't understand a thing, nor could anyone understand us,' recalled Nadya. With the help of dictionaries they had translated the Webbs' book on trade unionism and various treatises on economics. But speaking was a different thing. Both of them had particular difficulty understanding the 'cockney' spoken by the London working classes. In time Lenin learned to like London, admire the English and became fluent in the language.[*] Neither got used to the food, though, which they both agreed was appalling: 'We found that all this ox tails, skate fried in fat and indigestible cakes were not made for Russian stomachs,' Nadya said.

They were happier when they took two small rooms on the first floor at 30 Holford Square in Clerkenwell, a respectable neighbourhood, where they were soon joined by Nadya's mother. Under the alias of a

---

[*] Not so Nadya, who never really liked 'abroad', though she lived in exile for fifteen years, and barely managed to make any non-Russian friends. She enjoyed being among other émigrés, was nowhere near as good a linguist as Lenin and often fell victim to *toska*, a peculiarly Russian strain of wistful and nostalgic longing for home.

German couple, Dr and Mrs Jakob Richter, they were lodgers of Mrs Emma Louise Yeo, a recently widowed dressmaker in her late forties, her daughter and four sons, three of whom were in the printing trade.

They had settled in comfortably when, after a fortnight, Mrs Yeo noticed that 'Mrs Richter' wore no wedding band and she threatened to turn them out. But old friends who spoke decent English came to their rescue. Lenin's erstwhile flame Apollinaria Yakubova and her doctor husband Konstantin Takhtarev, who had been living in London for some time, assured the landlady that their new lodgers were definitely married despite Nadya's ringless state. Mrs Yeo also disliked the fact that they put up curtains in their room – something respectable Londoners did not do – but she was persuaded that this was 'normal for Germans'. She softened towards him when Lenin, who throughout his life loved cats, gave her spoilt pet a warm reception. 'They were good, quiet tenants and always paid their rent on time,' Mrs Yeo's son Leonard said many years later. 'They were completely unused to English ways, but always respectful. Mrs Richter was a sweet, kind lady. He had a face alive with great intelligence but for the most part he seemed a most ordinary little man. It's amusing that such a quiet, good-natured fellow would become such a world-shaker.'*

Lenin's mother was disturbed by a letter she had received from an old family friend who visited London in November 1902, which suggested that her son's living arrangements were not entirely satisfactory. She wrote to her daughter Anna on 3 December: 'She described her small flat which has considerable drawbacks. In all they have two small rooms and one of them, that of Elizaveta Vasilyevna [who had joined them in the summer] serves both as kitchen and dining room. Water and coal . . . are both downstairs and have to be brought up; the washing-up water has to be taken outside and so on . . . they had first of all thought of looking for a larger place but Nadenka added that she and Volodya have become like cats which get used to a particular spot.'[1]

Throughout their married life Lenin and Nadya lived modestly and frugally in unostentatious if not entirely Spartan style. Nadya, with her

---

* After Lenin left London he sent her a book of scenic Geneva views with an inscription 'dedicated to the good, kind Mrs Emma Yeo'. She kept it for the rest of her life and always said that Lenin 'as a lodger had been better to deal with than many an Englishman'.

mother's help, learned the basics of housekeeping and their lodgings were always spotlessly clean. But by her own admission she was a terrible cook and never managed to improve. Fortunately Lenin was not interested in food – 'he pretty submissively ate whatever was in front of him and never complained'. Occasionally, in a gentle way, he would joke with his mother-in-law or good friends about Nadya's efforts in the kitchen. He learned how to find food stored in the larder and fend for himself, though the drawback, as she admitted to his mother, was that 'he eats out of turn, not at proper times. Whenever he comes in he starts eating.'*

But Lenin did demand privacy. He was determined, as he said, to keep himself apart from 'the squabbling mass of émigrés with nothing to do except drink and gossip' – those, as Boris Pasternak put it in *Dr Zhivago*, 'who talk, talk – in the way only Russians can talk'. He wrote to Grigory Alexinsky, an RSDLP activist he had known from St Petersburg, that 'over there, in exile, you are frightfully out of touch with Russia – and idleness and the state of mind that goes with it, a nervous, hysterical, hissing and spitting mentality, predominate . . . There is no real *live* work, or an environment for live work to speak of.' He saw no point in staying up all night debating with people he fundamentally disagreed with; it was a waste of the time he could use for valuable work. He insisted on a separate apartment, unlike many Russian revolutionaries who preferred to live in communes.

Lenin loathed the very idea of a commune – all the more so after he visited the rooms in a near-derelict house in King's Cross shared by Martov, Vera Zasulich and assorted young revolutionaries who popped in and out of the building at any time of the day or night. Tidy and ordered in his habits, he was appalled at what he found. Martov and

---

* Nadya boasted once that she might be hopeless in the kitchen, but she did know how to prepare eggs in twelve ways. However, when she was challenged it turned out they were all the same – a sort of runny scrambled – apart from the addition of something else like tomatoes, bread, an onion and so on. 'Vladimir Ilyich limited himself to the occasional wry comment about her culinary abilities,' a comrade in exile recalled. 'He would say things like he had "roasts" rather often – meaning he had overcooked boiled meat.' He invariably allowed the women in his life to monitor what he ate and for a domineering, bossy and dictatorial man he could be remarkably submissive. Often when eating out he would look at his plate and ask Nadya or, quite frequently, her mother, 'Am I allowed to eat this?'

Zasulich were notoriously messy, so he had some warning. But nothing prepared him for the chaos he encountered. Their living room was wreathed in smoke. Martov's pipe ash found its way into the sugar bowl. Zasulich's roll-your-own cigarettes settled on window sills, tables, teacups, herself, and occasionally on the person she was talking to. Her cooking methods were unorthodox even by Nadya's standards. 'I remember once how she cooked herself some meat on an oil stove, chipping off pieces to eat with a pair of scissors,' she recalled after one visit. 'Someone asked her how long the meat would take to cook. She said, "If I am hungry and in a hurry ten minutes, if not maybe three hours." She wasn't joking.'

Lenin said, 'it is impossible to live in a house where the windows and doors are never closed, where they are completely open to the street and where every passer-by considers it necessary to look in and see what you are doing. I should go mad if I had to live like Martov and Zasulich. This was not a home, but more a public thoroughfare. Martov could be with people all day. I simply can't . . . everyone has a corner in his life which should never be penetrated by anyone, and everyone should have a special room completely to himself.'

Ivan Babushkin, a young Social Democrat newly arrived from Russia after he had escaped from jail by sawing through the bars of his cell, took one look at the mess in the Martov ménage and cleaned the place up for them, saying with a sigh, 'The Russian intellectual is always dirty. He needs a servant as he is himself incapable of tidying up.'[2]

* * *

London had one big advantage for the work of destabilising the Russian empire. In Munich, the German police were beginning to take notice of Lenin's activities, prompted by the Okhrana's warnings of dangerous subversives in their midst. The British authorities were altogether more relaxed. There was a tradition of radical exiles seeking asylum in London from the 1840s onwards. Marx, Engels, Herzen, the Hungarian nationalist Lajos Kossuth and the father of Italian unification Giuseppe Mazzini had been made welcome in England, as had the anarchist writer Prince Pyotr Kropotkin, once labelled by the Tsarist regime 'the most dangerous man in Europe'. The Society of Friends of Russian Freedom, based in London, had a long list of liberal-minded and wealthy backers, who gave money to find homes for Russian émigrés after they had served time in Russian prisons and Siberian exile.

In London the police on the whole took little interest in Lenin and 'all those foreign scalliwags who congregate in Britain', as one senior officer described them. The Russian authorities would every now and then alert the Metropolitan Police Special Branch that a terrorist was about to arrive from the Continent. But as Detective Inspector Harold Brust of Scotland Yard explained, the Russians invariably exaggerated. 'A wholly false and perfectly dreadful catalogue of crimes would be tacked onto a man's record with a view to earning him disfavour with the British police . . . [We] attached not the slightest importance to what they said.'

Occasionally the police would monitor potential Russian trouble-makers, but often it was in a comic PC Plod or Buster Keaton kind of way. An officer once told Harry Pollitt, who became head of the British Communist Party in the 1920s, that at some point around 1902 as a young copper he had been ordered to hide in the Crown and Woolpack pub in St John Street, Clerkenwell, where Russian émigrés often met, and report on what was going on. According to Pollitt the report to his superiors read: 'The meeting was conducted entirely in Russian and as I know nothing of the language I was unable to report on the subjects under discussion.'[3]

The move to London had been agreed by the *Iskra* editorial board principally because it would be easier to produce the paper there. Through Martov and Nikolai Alexeyev, a Russian socialist who had lived in London for many years, Lenin was given an introduction to Harry Quelch, the editor of the British Social Democratic Party's organ *Justice*, printed at a small workshop owned by the Twentieth Century Press at 37a Clerkenwell Green, very close to his lodgings.

The building had long links with radical movements of various kinds: it had been used as a meeting place for Chartists sixty years earlier. Its small press had printed pamphlets by Marx, Engels, Wilhelm Lieb-knecht and August Bebel. Quelch, a cheerful and friendly figure, agreed to print *Iskra* and Lenin found the atmosphere congenial, though space was cramped. 'A corner was boarded off at the printing works by a thin partition that served as Lenin's editorial room,' said Potresov. 'This cor-ner contained a very small writing table, a bookshelf above it and a chair

. . . there was no room for another chair.' Lenin had happy memories of the place. When Quelch's son, Thomas, visited Moscow in 1920 and met the leader of the Soviet regime in the Kremlin, one of Lenin's first questions was: 'And how is everyone at Clerkenwell Green?'

Lenin spent afternoons at the *Iskra* 'office'. But every morning, when it opened, he would be at what he agreed was 'the richest library in the world' – the central domed Reading Room of the British Museum – where Marx had spent so much of his life. He was given a letter of introduction for a reader's ticket by Isaac Mitchell, General Secretary of the General Federation of Trade Unions, and applied saying he had come from Russia 'to study the land question'. He was issued – or rather Dr Richter LL.D was – with reader's card A72453 on 29 April.* The library was his lifeline, away from the noisy and 'squabbling émigrés who would pester me . . . in the Russian fashion at all hours'. They exhausted him and got on his highly strung nerves; 'What do you think they are here for – a holiday?' he would regularly ask.

Nadya zealously guarded his privacy. She always answered the door; he never did. When 'confronted by an intruder she stationed herself at the entrance with a "they shall not pass" expression and would intone "Vladimir Ilyich is not at home" or "he is at work". Sometimes that didn't stop the most determined characters, though, and he would have to see them,' one young visitor from Russia who repeatedly descended on them in London recalled. At times Lenin could be gregarious and welcoming, but he exerted his authority through a mixture of aloofness and good cheer, as Nikolai Valentinov remarked: 'Lenin kept everyone at arm's length. I never saw him put his hand on anyone's shoulder and nobody among his comrades would have dared, however deferentially, to do so to him.'[4]

---

* I had always thought this was an apocryphal story, yet it turns out to be true. In the 1920s the actor Miles Malleson, a left-wing Labour Party supporter, occasionally worked at the Reading Room. He became friendly with a librarian who had been at the British Museum for thirty years. The actor asked if he had known Lenin, who had read there at this time and also on several other visits to London. 'Lenin? Sorry, sir, I recall nobody by that name here.' Malleson tried a different tack, and knew that after his first visit to London Lenin returned using his real name. 'I wonder if you remember a Mr Ulyanov coming in?' The librarian remembered at once. 'Oh yes, a very charming gentleman, short with a pointed beard. A very nicely spoken man . . . do you know what became of him?'

* * *

He was determined to improve his command of English, so he placed an advertisement in *The Athenaeum* magazine: 'A Russian LL.D (and his wife) would like to exchange Russian lessons for English with an English gentleman or Lady.' Three people responded: Henry Rayment, who worked for the publisher George Bell; Mr Williams, an office clerk; and Mr Young, a worker. Over the months Lenin used all three, but his favourite was Rayment, an intelligent and educated man around the same age as he was.*

Partly to help with learning English, he and Nadya went often to the theatre – and surprisingly, Lenin became fascinated by the working-class music hall, which reached the height of its popularity in the Edwardian era. 'It is the expression of a certain satirical attitude towards generally accepted ideas, to turn them inside out, to distort them, to show the arbitrariness of the usual,' he wrote enthusiastically to Gorky after one performance in which he wrestled with the English sense of humour. 'It is a little complicated but interesting.'

Lenin took an interest in a way of life new to him and a city much bigger than St Petersburg: 'We began to look around this citadel of capitalism with some curiosity,' said Nadya. They regularly went to Speakers' Corner in Hyde Park on a Sunday, which he held up as a remarkable example of freedom in Britain. As Nadya recorded in a letter to Lenin's mother following a visit: 'One man – an atheist – tried to prove to a group of curious listeners that there was no God. We particularly liked one such speaker – he had an Irish accent which we were better able to understand. Next to him a Salvation Army officer was shouting out hysterical appeals to Almighty God, while a little way off a salesman was holding forth about the drudgery of shop assistants in the big stores.'

---

* Rayment professed himself a socialist and told Lenin that he had spoken at a few leftist meetings but was summoned by his boss and told that he had to choose between the job and the speeches. He had a wife and children so he made the obvious choice. He had travelled in Europe and lived for a while in Australia, but Lenin was surprised that he had never been to Whitechapel, in the East End of London, where large numbers of mainly Jewish émigrés from the Russian empire congregated; 'I'm puzzled that you don't know your own city,' Lenin told him. He took him around the poor neighbourhood, where Russian Jews wore long kaftans and fur hats and lived in almost closed communities – pretty much as they did in the Tsar's domains.

Lenin saw more of London than most émigrés, walking around the working-class areas and seeing ordinary life in England for himself. His favourite haunts were north of Holford Square, towards Primrose Hill and Hampstead Heath. It was a sixpenny bus ride from Clerkenwell to Highgate Cemetery, where he often went to Marx's grave and took a short walk up the hill to enjoy the panoramic vista of the whole of London below. He was as content in England as in any other bourgeois foreign country and he grew to 'appreciate the special features of English history and English life – the high development of democracy, the absence of militarism, the enormous strength of organised trade unions, the growing investment of English capital outside of England, which weakens the antagonism between the English employers and workers'.[5]

He attended leftist meetings with British socialists, and when his English was good enough he spoke to groups of British radicals.* On May Day in 1903 at the new Alexandra Palace, in north London, he made the same speech to three groups of socialists in English, Russian and German.

But Lenin's great source of joy was getting out of London and exploring the countryside. At weekends he and Nadya, sometimes with Elizaveta Vasilyevna, would take a train or bus to as remote a spot in the British Home Counties as they could find and walk in the South Downs, the Chiltern Hills or the Kentish Weald. 'Nadya and I have often been out looking for the real countryside and we have found it,' he wrote to his mother after eight weeks in England. A few months later he described one of these jaunts. 'We took sandwiches with us instead of lunch and spent the whole of one Sunday *ins Grüne* (quite unintentionally we are taking to foreign ways and arrange our outings on Sundays of all days, though that is the worst time as everywhere is crowded). We had a long walk, the air went to our heads as if we were children and afterwards I had to lie down and rest, as I did after a shooting trip in Siberia. In general we do not miss a chance to go on outings. We are the only people among the comrades here who are exploring every bit of the surrounding country. We discover various rural paths, we know all the places nearby and intend to go further afield.'[6]

---

* Lenin's command of English became reasonably good, though, as many recalled, he had a hint of an Irish brogue through his Russian accent. He said that he always found the English spoken by the Irish easier to understand.

* * *

At dawn one morning in early October 1902 a series of knocks was heard at the entrance to 30 Holford Square. A dishevelled-looking – but still strikingly handsome – young man with a mass of tousled curly brown hair, pince-nez and an air of jaunty arrogance stood at the doorstep. This was the first time that Lenin met Leon Trotsky.

'With signs and gestures – because I saw others doing so – I managed to engage a cab which took me to an address given me, probably in Zurich,' Trotsky recalled later. 'This was Vladimir Ilyich's home. I had been told in advance to knock on the door a prescribed number of times in a certain definite way. Nadezhda Konstantinovna opened the door for me. I had dragged her out of bed with my knocking. It was very early in the morning. Any sensible man, more familiar with the ordinary conventions of life, would have waited an hour or two at the station, instead of knocking at a stranger's door at the crack of dawn, but I was full of excitement. Vladimir Ilyich was still in bed and he greeted me with justifiable surprise, but kindness. It turned out he knew who I was already when I explained my pseudonym. That is how he greeted me. He said to Nadezhda Konstantinovna: "Look, Pen has arrived." She gave me tea and a makeshift breakfast while Lenin got dressed.'

Lenin had been told a lot about Trotsky, whose real name was Lev Davidovich Bronstein, born into a well-to-do Jewish farming family from Ukraine. An autodidact with a phenomenal memory and vast reserves of energy, at just twenty-two he had already gained a reputation as a dazzling journalist and polemicist (hence his pseudonym) who could write fast and fluently on literature and art, as well as about politics and Marxist philosophy. His ego and self-belief were as great – many people said greater – than his talents. So was his lifelong interest in attractive women. Trotsky's rebellion against his conservative parents was as passionate as his revulsion at the Tsar, and he had been in trouble with the police since his teens for socialist agitation against the autocracy. He had been jailed once,* had been placed in 'ad-

---

* His revolutionary name, Trotsky, had been taken from one of the prison guards he got to know in jail near Odessa.

ministrative exile' and, just a few weeks earlier, he had dramatically escaped from Siberia. He had joined the RSDLP, wrote regularly for *Iskra*, and one of his priorities after gaining his freedom was to meet Lenin.

Nadya arranged for Trotsky to stay temporarily at the nearby 'commune' occupied by Martov and Vera Zasulich. Lenin and Trotsky talked all that first day – about writing, about the future of *Iskra*, about the revolutionary struggle and the state of the Party in Russia ('lamentable and disorganised', according to the younger man).

The next day Lenin gave Trotsky a guided tour of London, with his own twist. 'I went on a long walk with Lenin . . . He showed me Westminster Abbey (from the outside) and other architectural landmarks. "That's *their* Houses of Parliament," he told me at one point. Their did not of course mean the one belonging to the English, but to the enemy.'

One Sunday Lenin took him to a socialist church – 'a social democratic gathering accompanied by the singing of pious hymns. The main speaker was a compositor who had just returned from Australia . . . his speech sounded quite revolutionary, but then the congregation stood up and began singing a hymn which began "Almighty God, put an end to all kings and all rich men". As we were leaving Lenin said to me, "The English proletariat has in itself many revolutionary and socialist elements but they are all mixed up with conservatism, with religion and prejudices; and there seems to be no way for these elements [to] come to the top."'[7]

Just when Lenin had found a new comrade whom he praised to anyone who would listen – 'How we need more such revolutionaries of such high ability, energy and promise', he told Martov – he was embroiled in another conflict with an old one. Plekhanov, behind Lenin's back, had manoeuvred the *Iskra* board into moving the newspaper's production to Geneva. Lenin had not seen the ambush coming and vehemently opposed the plan, but he lost the vote. He had no wish to live anywhere near Plekhanov. As so often when he faced political obstacles, the stress would damage his health. The headaches and insomnia which often plagued him grew worse and Nadya said he was so 'overwrought at the move from London to Switzerland that he developed a nervous illness called "holy fire" which consists of inflammation of the nerve terminals of the back and chest'.[*]

The illness was made worse by a misdiagnosis when they reached their Geneva hotel. A doctor thought Lenin had sciatica and recommended that he should use iodine over the inflamed areas, which caused agony and made him worse. He spent the first two weeks bedridden in his new Swiss home 'in terrifying pain', according to Nadya, unable to work – and utterly miserable.[8]

---

[*] The medical term for the infection was erysipelas, which in the days before antibiotics was potentially a serious disease; he was lucky to have recovered from it comparatively quickly. Even nowadays, with modern pharmacology, it can be a very unpleasant, debilitating infection from which it can take a sufferer many weeks to recover.

14

WHAT IS TO BE DONE?

'Neither in the present nor the future can the people, left to their own resources, bring into existence the social revolution. Only we revolutionaries can accomplish this . . . Social ideas are alien to the people; they belong to the social philosophy of the revolutionary minority.'

Pyotr Tkachev (1844–1886)

'A Communist who doesn't dream . . . is a bad Communist.'

Lenin to Valentinov, Geneva, 1904

The principal appeal Lenin held for his followers was not due to the strength of his indomitable will, his manifest brainpower or his brilliance as a political tactician, though all three were crucially important in his claim to be a leader. His greatest skill in his early years was his ability to inspire optimism and hope. He told his followers that they could change the world in the here and now, if they followed a set of essentially simple-to-comprehend steps and believed in a few fairly straightforward propositions. He didn't offer salvation in the afterlife but a glimpse of heaven in the immediate future – or at least the achievement of some of their goals. Marxism is supposed to be a 'scientific' philosophy which can be 'proven' empirically. But any true Communist zealot, deny it though they may, felt it emotionally, religiously, spiritually, even if those words would have stuck in the gullet of a true believer. Lenin would most definitely have denied it. But as one of his oldest comrades, Potresov, who knew him in St Petersburg in the early 1890s during his earliest revolutionary days, said, 'for Vladimir Ilyich Marxism was a not a conviction, but a religion'. Many others made the same point, at least until the 1917 Revolution.

Knowing the history of the Communist experiment in the twentieth century, it is easy to forget the fervent idealism of some of the early Russian Marxists, along with the ruthlessly ambitious and power-hungry careerists the movement attracted at the same time. Perhaps the cynics fed off the idealists in a symbiotic relationship. Or perhaps, as many historians have argued, Marxist ideology as interpreted by Lenin was itself the root cause of the disaster of Communism in practice. That suggests there was something 'inevitable' about the piles of bodies, the prison camps and the food queues left by dozens of Communist regimes over the decades after Lenin, which seems somewhat simplistic. Nothing in history is 'inevitable'.

In the 1900s nobody knew there would be a Mao or a Pol Pot or a Nicolae Ceaușescu. Lenin's appeal to mostly young people was optimistic and uplifting. With the right organisation and the right tactics, even a few revolutionaries could bring down an empire the size of Russia's and an autocratic regime as powerful as the Tsar's. 'Some few thousand nobles have ruled Russia for centuries. Why not us?' he asked.

The essence of Leninism is contained in his best-known work, *What Is To Be Done?*, inspired, as the title suggested, by Chernyshevsky. Published in 1902, just before Lenin moved to London, it had a vast impact on the radical movement and made his name as the leader-in-waiting of revolutionary socialism in Russia. It got him noticed throughout Europe as a figure on the Left. While he was in London, and later in Geneva, socialist luminaries from far and wide made their way to meet the 'coming man' among the Russian revolutionaries of the new millennium. It is a short pamphlet of 45,000 pithily written words. It is still worth reading for anybody interested in political tactics; many conservative politicians over the last hundred years have clearly read and learned things from it.

What Is To Be Done? was the bible of Lenin's Bolsheviks, the blueprint for how he would seize power and hold on to it. 'Give us an organisation of revolutionaries and we will turn Russia upside down,' he declared.

Much of it was specific to the conditions inside Russia and building a Party to defeat the Romanovs. But much had more general application. 'The essence is idealistic yet conspiratorial, optimistic yet practically based, fanatic, yet as it turned out realistic,' as one future revolutionary explained.

Lenin had no great respect for the working classes for whom he was proposing to make the revolution. 'The working class exclusively by its own efforts is able to develop only trade union consciousness,' he said. They would fall victim to 'false consciousness' and be led by the bourgeoisie, who would betray their interests. 'Modern socialist consciousness can only be brought to the working class from without and cannot be genuinely political consciousness unless the workers are trained to see all cases of tyranny, oppression and violence as abuse, no matter what class is affected . . . To bring political knowledge to the workers, the Social Democrats must go among all classes of the population, must despatch units of their army in all directions. The Social Democrat's ideal should not be a trade union secretary but a tribune of the people . . . 'This requires an organisation of people who first and foremost make revolutionary activity their profession. In a country with a despotic government, the more we restrict the membership of this organisation to those who are engaged in revolution as a profession, the more difficult it will be to catch us. It is harder to catch a dozen clever people than a hundred fools.'

There had to be a 'revolutionary vanguard' of people who could protect themselves from the police, studied Marxist ideology and mastered the arts of revolutionary conspiracy. 'Such a party could not fail' if led correctly. 'We are marching in a compact group along a precipitous and difficult path, firmly holding each other by the hand. We are surrounded on all sides by enemies and we have to advance almost constantly under their fire. We have combined, by a freely adopted decision, for the purpose of fighting the enemy, and not of retreating into the neighbouring marsh, the inhabitants of which, from the very outset, have reproached us with having separated ourselves into an exclusive group and with having chosen the path of struggle instead of the path of conciliation.'

He knew how idealistic he was being. 'My dream may run ahead of the natural march of events or may fly off at a tangent in a direction where no natural march of events will ever follow it. In the first case my dream will not have done any harm. If a man were completely deprived of the ability to dream in this way, if he could never run ahead and mentally conceive in an entire and completed picture the results of the work which his hands are only just beginning to shape, then I cannot imagine what stimulus there would be to induce men to undertake extensive and exhausting work in the sphere of art, sciences and practical endeavour

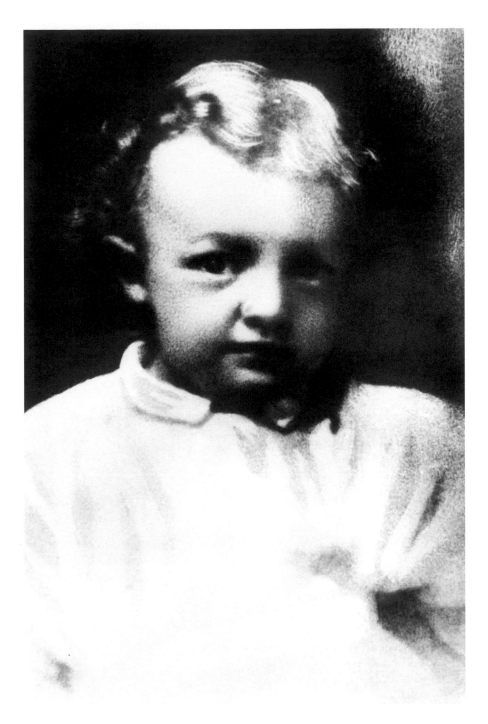

As a baby, Vladimir Ulyanov was 'top-heavy' – his head seemed too big for his body, according to his sister Anna. And 'he was very noisy, a great bawler'.

The nest of gentlefolk: the Ulyanov family in 1879. From left to right: Olga, Maria Alexandrovna (with daughter Maria on her lap), Alexander (standing), Dmitry (seated), Ilya Nikolayevich, Anna and Vladimir.

Alexander 'Sasha' Ulyanov, a
brilliant natural sciences student,
a few months before he was
hanged at the age of twenty-one.

Lenin's older sister, Anna Ilyinichna, in
her early twenties.

His other sister, Maria. Both sisters
were active revolutionaries who were
repeatedly jailed and exiled and who made
big sacrifices for Lenin's career.

Nadezhda Konstantinovna Krupskaya (Nadya) aged twenty-one, three years before she met her future husband Vladimir. 'He could never have loved a woman whose opinions he totally disagreed with and who was not a comrade in his work.'

The police 'mugshot' of Vladimir Ulyanov taken when he was arrested for the first time in 1895.

Yuli Martov (Julius Osipovich Tsederbaum), Lenin's closest male friend for many years until the two became bitter enemies and political opponents.

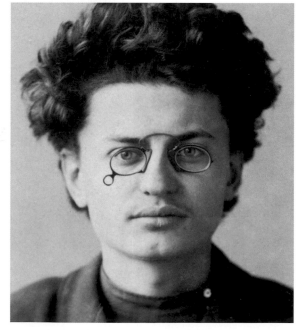

Leon Trotsky around the time he and Lenin first met in 1902, when his affectionate conspiratorial pseudonym was 'Pen'.

Nadya aged twenty-six.

Inessa Armand, Lenin's mistress. 'She seemed to be an inexhaustible spring of life . . . the fiery flame of revolution,' according to one of her comrades.

... the rift between dreams and reality causes no harm if the dreamer believes seriously in his dream, if he attentively observes life, if he compares his observations with his castles in the air and if, in general, he works conscientiously towards achieving his fantasies. If there is some connection between his dreams and life then all is well.'[1]

The organisation, of course, needed a leader and it was clear whom Lenin believed that should be. He told Valentinov: 'the right to wield the conductor's baton is given only to someone who has special leadership qualities – above all the ability to organise ... it was clear to me that he thought this right could belong only to him ... his right was asserted with such simplicity and such certainty that he might have been saying that two plus two make four. For Lenin this was a matter which required no proof. I was at first shocked by his unshakeable faith in himself ... but when I found myself in Lenin's entourage ... no one for a moment doubted his right to hold the conductor's baton and to issue orders. Adherence to [his group] seemed to imply a kind of oath of loyalty to Lenin, a vow to follow him unquestioningly.'[2]

Nadya was a constant presence and a sounding board for nearly all the important works Lenin wrote. Often she would tell him when something wasn't clear or was inelegantly phrased. Biographers who simply see her as a quiet secretary who never spoke up have misunderstood her role. 'When Lenin wrote a routine article he did it very quickly, dashing it off regardless of circumstances,' a comrade who lived close to him in Geneva in the early 1900s recalled. 'He needed only paper, ink and pen. When a more important work was in question ... he would walk up and down his room for a long time, composing the sentences which expressed his main ideas. He began to write only after whispering his ideas many times over to himself and working out the best way of putting them across. However, this solitary whispering was insufficient during the writing of certain works. He had to explain to someone ... aloud, what he was writing.'

Nadya, after Lenin's death, said: 'The bulk of Lenin's writing has been done in my presence. In Siberia, before he began to write *The Tasks of the Russian Social Democrats*, he told me everything that was to be in it. The chapters of *The Development of Capitalism in Russia*, which he regarded as particularly important, were not written down until he had expounded them to me orally. He worked out the contents of *What Is To Be Done?* by talking to himself all the time as he walked about the room. After this preliminary work . . . he recited his ideas aloud in order to polish them. Before writing it . . . [he] rehearsed to me every chapter of the pamphlet . . . He liked to do this during our walks. We used to go out of town so that no one would disturb us. He used this same method – preparation first by whispering, then by talking – to write his other works.'[3]

* * *

One of the great thought crimes in the Soviet era was to be a 'deviationist' from the truths laid down by Marx and Engels. Millions lost their lives in purges against 'deviation' during the struggles in the 1920s onwards under Stalin to maintain ideological purity and orthodoxy. The first major 'deviationist' was Lenin, who frequently turned Marxism on its head when it didn't suit his tactical purposes. The high priest and learned teacher in him was a true believer – what was the point of professing the Marxist faith if everyone among the congregation was free to interpret it as they wished? The Renaissance pope and practical politician in him could tack and weave when it was necessary, even perform a complete somersault. 'For me theory is only a hypothesis, not the Holy Scripture. It is a tool in our daily work,' he said once, mystifying his audience. 'Lenin could veer, prevaricate, intrigue and sow confusion, seeking support from the devil if it was offered,' Plekhanov noted, accurately.[4]

Marx's *Capital* came out in Russia just six years after it was first published in Hamburg, and fifteen years before it appeared in English. It was an instant success. Whether anyone read the whole of the huge book or not, let alone grasped its implications, its print run of 3,000 sold out in less than a year, while the German edition of 1,000 took five years. Marx's ideas spread rapidly among the Russian intelligentsia. His emphasis that socialist revolution could be led only by the industrial working class seemed to explain why the Populist movement of the 1870s had failed. To the Russian intelligentsia it offered hope that backward Russia would one day join the 'advanced' Western capitalist societies. It would develop along the lines Marx claimed that Western Europe had from feudalism, through a bourgeois revolution to capitalism, the stages Marx predicted would 'inevitably' lead to social-ism and then Communism.

Marxism had a particular appeal to Russian radicals entirely unsus-pected by the author himself, who had barely thought of Russia when he was writing it and hardly mentioned the country once in nearly 700 densely written pages. For many Russian intellectuals like Lenin, the idea that Marxism would bring Russia closer to the West was its main attraction. It would shine a 'path of reason, enlightenment and hope' according to Martov's fiercely intelligent sister Lidia, who had married the socialist thinker Fyodor Dan. One of the cleverest of all the Rus-sian Marxists, Pyotr Struve – though he would later abandon socialist ideas and become the kind of 'bourgeois liberal Lenin so despised' – said he and others were persuaded because it offered a 'scientific solution' to Russia's two principal problems of liberating itself from au-tocracy and developing from backward semi-feudalism: 'let us admit our lack of culture and enrol in the school of capitalism'. It appealed to Jews, not because Marx was Jewish – or, rather, a Jewish atheist – but because 'populism' and 'back to the land' ideas offered an archaic vision of peasant Russia, with its pogroms and discrimination against Jews. Marxism promised to assimilate Jews, a 'modern' and West-ern vision that preached universal human liberation based on ideas of internationalism.

A significant difference between doctrinally orthodox Marxists – Martov, for one – and the 'deviationists' was whether a primarily agrarian country such as Russia, where 90 per cent of the population were peasants and the industrial working class was growing but still tiny, was ripe for an imminent socialist revolution. This may seem an abstruse point 120 years later. But at the time it divided revolutionary Marxists as a crucial ideological issue. Lenin argued passionately that capitalism was advancing at a fast pace in Russia and the working class was growing, so it was ready for revolution. All that was needed was a push, by a Party organised efficiently, well led and centrally controlled. Others argued that Russia was not yet ready; the country had to wait for the stages of development laid out by Marx. The issue was not merely an abstract argument about the finer points of ideology. Lenin didn't want to 'wait and see'. He believed in practical action to make the Rev-olution as soon as possible. And, in any case, from the limited personal experience he had gained, he agreed wholeheartedly with Marx's own views about 'the idiocy of rural life'.

The German oracle himself was not altogether a help. He admitted that if he had to take his chances as a Russian in the vicious debates on the Left, even he might, as he put it, have 'been condemned as an indifferent, wavering Marxist'. On the whole, he stuck to his principle that there had to be an industrial revolution first and a lengthy bourgeois phase before any transition to socialism. Towards the end of his life he began to learn Russian specifically so he could look at this thorny theoretical dilemma. But he never could make up his mind about which path Russia was more likely to take.

After Marx died, Engels grew tired of getting drawn into the dispute, as he continually was by Russian comrades. In 1883 he wrote to Isaac Hourwich, the Russian economist exiled in America: 'If you have followed the writings of the Russian exiles during the last ten years, you will know yourself how the various groups among them interpret passages from Marx's writings and letters in the most contradictory ways, just as if they were texts from the classics or the New Testament. Anything I could say on the question . . . would probably be used in a similar way.'

Neither side in this doctrinal dispute would have cared to know what Marx really thought about Russians. As he wrote in a letter to Engels, 'I do not trust any Russian. As soon as a Russian worms his way in, all hell breaks loose.'

15

THE GREAT SCHISM – BOLSHEVIKS AND MENSHEVIKS

'Lenin . . . there is no other man who is so absorbed by the Revolution twenty-four hours a day, who has no other thoughts but the thought of revolution, and who, even when he sleeps, dreams of nothing but the Revolution.' Pavel Axelrod (1850–1928)

Though Lenin had loathed the idea of moving to Geneva, he tried to make the best of it. He missed his regular desk, L13, at the Reading Room of the British Museum, where he had spent so many mornings of satisfying hard work. But he acknowledged that the Swiss city had a couple of decent and well-organised libraries, one of his principal demands wherever he found himself in exile.

He and Nadya found a functional if nondescript set of rooms on two floors near a pleasant park and the lake shore in the middle-class suburb of Sécheron and settled into their new home. They were joined within a few weeks by Elizaveta Vasilyevna. A visitor who saw them at the apartment not long after they moved in, Cecilia Zelikson Bobrovskaya, an old St Petersburg acquaintance of Lenin, noted that the rooms seemed spartan. They used the packing cases for the books they had brought with them from England as makeshift dining tables. 'On the ground floor, there was a large kitchen, containing a stove on which there was constantly being heated a large enamel kettle, ready for chance visitors. Upstairs the furniture consisted of simple tables, covered with journals, manuscripts and press cuttings . . . in each room a simple iron bed covered with a blanket and two chairs. In the middle of Lenin's table a form of abacus, with which he no doubt counted the number of peasants' properties there were in Russia, or farmers with a horse, for one of his books.'[1]

They ate regularly at the nearby Café Landolt, where Russian émigrés

habitually went for cheap beer, Social Democratic gossip – and the tast-
iest sausages and sauerkraut in Geneva. Usually Lenin and Nadya had
a table to themselves, number 40 near the window. There were regular
Party meetings in a back room which had its own exit to a narrow, winding lane – in case the police came. On the whole the Russians were left
alone by the Swiss police, as they were in England. Switzerland, too, had
a long and honourable tradition of providing a safe haven for Russian
dissidents. But it was a conservative country and the authorities wanted
to make sure their guests caused no trouble.*

Martov had decamped from England some months earlier; he loathed
London, which in those days had no café culture, nowhere an intellectual could while away an entire day reading the papers and chatting with
émigrés about the finer points of dialectical materialism. 'Martov was at
our house all the time, talking with Vladimir Ilyich,' Nadya recorded.
At this time they were still good friends, but some frostiness had entered into their arguments about politics and the relationship had lost
some of its youthful ardour.[2]

The Lenins were 'at home' and offered open house to Russian visitors
on Tuesday and Thursday afternoons, a rule designed to stop comrades
dropping by at other times of the day or night. Though Lenin could be
stand-offish and aloof, he was an entertaining and generous host when
he chose to be. He liked amusing company who could banter cheerfully
and pass on funny and useful information. Valentinov, who saw a lot of
Lenin in Geneva, said that he 'delighted' in high-grade gossip. 'Lenin
disliked boring, gloomy and impassive people. He said about one [com-
rade], "He is a very good man, that is to say, he is an honest revolutionary
and useful to the Party. Unfortunately, as a person, he is as boring as an
owl – laughs perhaps once a year, and even then nobody knows why."
Lenin preferred spirited and cheerful people around him.'

In particular, he sought the company of young RSDLP activists 'from
home' who had recently arrived in Switzerland and, as Nadya put it,
'breathed of Russia'. He quizzed them incessantly about conditions in
the country and what Party members on the ground there were doing.[3]

---

* Another regular of the Landolt at this time was Benito Mussolini, who was a student in Geneva. The Russian émigrés, he wrote later in a newspaper article, formed 'a
strange, eccentric, fantastic group of nihilists and bohemians . . . the last word in fever-
ish modernity . . . their lives were orgies of strong talk and weak tea'.

He enjoyed lively evenings singing old Russian folk songs and revolutionary hymns. Panteleimon Lepeshinsky, who was in Siberian exile with him and in Switzerland, later recalled: 'Vladimir Ilyich brought into our vocal performances a quite particular passion and verve . . . though he did order us about on what we should be singing . . . He would begin in his somewhat hoarse and out-of-tune voice – what can only be described as a cross between a baritone, bass and tenor:

With courage, Comrades, we go marching
Battle will temper our souls . . .

And when it seemed to him that others did not put sufficient emphasis on the more striking passages of the song he would wave his fists energetically, tapping out the rhythm with his foot. Against all the rules of harmony . . . he would strain his vocal chords to the utmost and render the parts he liked most by pitching the notes either too high or too low.

And we shall raise over the earth
The fraternal banner of toil . . .

His voice tended to drown all the others.'[4]

He could get sentimental about music, but even then there was usually a political edge. He was moved almost to tears when, at a musical evening at his Geneva apartment, he heard a young violinist, Pyotr Krasikov, play Tchaikovsky's *Barcarolle*. Lenin said that he played the piece beautifully, with passion and feeling, but the important point was his opposition to the autocracy and his bravery: he had recently escaped from Moscow in dramatic fashion, just hours before the Okhrana were about to arrest him. Practically the only thing he had taken with him from Russia was his violin.

But Lenin couldn't afford too much sentiment. As he grew older, more ambitious and more certain of his powers, he made a deliberate effort to control his emotions and what remained of the softer side of his nature. He made a revealing comment to the writer Gorky, who recalled one evening as Lenin was listening to a sonata by Beethoven. 'I know nothing greater than the *Appassionata*. I always think with pride what marvellous things human beings can do! But I can't listen too often. It affects your nerves, makes you want to say stupid, nice things and stroke the heads of people who could create such beauty while living in this vile hell. And you mustn't stroke anyone's head – you might get your hand bitten off. You have to hit them over the head, without any mercy . . . Hm, hm, our duty is infernally hard . . .'

Welcoming and gregarious though he could be, 'Lenin's corner was a very extensive one and he allowed almost no one to penetrate it,' Valentinov said. 'There was an invisible line dividing Lenin from other comrades – and I never saw anyone crossing it.'[5]

* * *

Despite the musical evenings and comradely bonhomie in Geneva, the first major crisis of Russian Communism was threatening to split the revolutionary movement apart in a vicious conflict.

There had always been disagreements between the leading figures in the Party, and especially on the editorial board of *Iskra*. The Plekhanov/Lenin relationship was again almost at breaking point after Lenin moved to Geneva; Plekhanov loathed Trotsky; Zasulich could barely stand to be in the same room as Lenin; Potresov had contempt for Zasulich; the popular Martov tried to get on with everybody, but was becoming increasingly exasperated by Lenin's intolerance with anybody who argued with him and thought *What Is To Be Done?* was more a manual for imposing dictatorship than an illuminating guide to building socialism. It was decided to clear the air by holding the first substantial conference of Party members since the RSDLP was founded in 1898. The exiles would be there – as well as Party members working underground in Russia – and they would thrash out an agreed Party programme.

There were signs of trouble ahead from the start. The original plan was to hold the Second Congress of the Russian Social Democratic Labour Party in Brussels, starting from 30 July 1903. Forty-three delegates turned up on the first day in a flour warehouse in the centre of the city. The central window was draped with a huge red canvas bearing a slogan calling for Unity. As Plekhanov gave the opening address, rats scurried around the delegates' feet, many of whom soon began to scratch their arms and legs in evident discomfort. The Belgian police were on their trail, forcing the delegates from one drab venue to another. They were followed everywhere, from the conference rooms to the Coq d'Or inn where most of them were staying, rummaging through their luggage when they were out. The Okhrana had given the Belgian authorities a full list of 'troublemakers' and the Brussels police decided to co-operate with them. After a few days of heavy surveillance the delegates were anxious to leave Belgium as fast as possible, fearing that some of them might be sent back to Russia if they stayed much longer.

The Congress was moved to London. The last-minute change meant a lot of extra work for Lenin and Nadya. They had to find discreet meeting rooms where they wouldn't be disturbed or overheard and lodgings for the delegates, many of whom complained that they hated pubs and why weren't there any cafés – wasn't London a civilised city? One of the first meeting rooms they could find was in an anglers' club where fishing trophies decorated the walls. Others were in trade union halls and the English Club, known more familiarly as the Communist Club, which had recently opened in Fitzrovia.

The Congress reopened on 11 August, and this was when the schism within the Party was exposed in public and the words Bolshevik and Menshevik first came into use as political labels. The internecine feud would continue with venom for a decade until it was finally admitted that the differences were irreconcilable and for all practical purposes it was better to separate into two parties.

The main issues were arcane, minuscule. Lenin himself admitted that 'in substance the differences are unimportant'. They were mainly personal – Lenin now identified Martov as a potential rival leader – and only a little about what kind of revolutionary party the RSDLP would be. Lenin wanted a tightly organised, elite corps of dedicated and professional revolutionaries under a highly centralised leadership that imposed discipline on the membership. Martov had in mind a looser, more inclusive party, less under the control of the leadership, where members had significantly more of a voice.

The proximate cause of the split was of a 'how many angels can dance on a pinhead?' type. Lenin and Martov each proposed a list of membership criteria for the Party. Lenin's stated that a member was someone who 'accepted the Party programme and supports it by material means and by personal participation in one of the Party's organisations'. This was too authoritarian for Martov. After quickly looking over Lenin's resolution he told him, 'but that's dictatorship you're proposing'. Lenin replied, 'Yes, there's no other way.' Martov proposed an amendment. A member 'recognises the Party programme and supports it by material means and by regular personal assistance under the direction of one of the Party's organisations'.

Martov won the vote by twenty-eight votes to twenty-three. At this point he had the support of one of the largest groups within the Party, the organisation of Jewish socialists known as the Bund (the name means 'Union' in Yiddish). There followed a series of divisive votes on smaller matters. At one point the five Bundist delegates walked out, as did the Union of Russian Social Democrats, which had two votes in the Congress. The balance had shifted, and Lenin seized his opportunity. The next vote was on removing some members of the 'old guard' from the board of *Iskra* – Axelrod, Zasulich, Potresov, all of whom had voted with Martov. This time Lenin won the vote and, with his characteristic mastery of tactics and presentation – spin in present-day language – he branded his followers '*bolchintsvo*', the majority, and his opponents '*menchintsvo*', the minority. For the following decades, up to the Stalin era, the Russian Revolution was played out amid the rivalries of the Bolsheviks and Mensheviks.

Mayhem broke loose at the Congress. One young delegate, Alexander Shotman, was on the verge of beating another who had changed sides on one of the votes and had to be restrained by Lenin himself: 'Only fools use fists in a polemic,' Lenin told him. Axelrod brought the well-known revolutionary from Moscow Nikolai Bauman, who had supported Lenin, to tears by alluding venomously to his late mistress, who had recently died. Nadya was shocked by an altercation between the veteran Leo Deutsch, a friend of Plekhanov, and the ardently Leninist Vladimir Noskov, when the latter told the elderly man, 'You just keep your mouth shut, you old dodderer.' With each insult the atmosphere became more venomous.

Without doubt Lenin was the main cause of the bitterness. He was spoiling for a fight and he got one. He was constantly on the offensive, cajoling, hectoring and abusing delegates, then noting down their reactions and where their loyalties lay to keep for future reference. He admitted to Gleb Krzhizhanovsky, one of his oldest comrades, that his manner had been frenzied: 'I realise that I behaved and acted in a state of frightful irritation. I am quite willing to admit this fault of mine to anyone, if it can be called a fault . . . but [my behaviour] was a natural product of the atmosphere, the reactions, the interjections, the struggle.'

Krzhizhanovsky, Krasin, Potresov and several others who Lenin believed would stick with him went to the other side, though some drifted back.

But Lenin was full of excitement and seemed energised by the fray. On the final day he had a conversation with one of the other delegates which summed up his enjoyment of a political brawl. He loved the combat. His comrade had said, 'What a depressing atmosphere there has been in the Congress. All this bitter fighting, this agitation one against another . . . this uncomradely attitude.'

Lenin replied, 'No, no. What a splendid Congress . . . A free and open struggle. Opinions expressed. Tendencies revealed. Groups acquiring shape. Hands raised. A decision taken. A stage passed through. Forward! There's something I understand.'[6]

* * *

Lenin instantly understood the importance of the words Bolshevik and Menshevik. He never gave up the name for the group that followed him, or the psychological advantage it won. For long periods over the next few years the Mensheviks in fact far outnumbered the Bolsheviks, in Russia and among the revolutionaries in exile, and they were the majority in a series of future votes at various congresses and conferences. Yet they still accepted the name that Lenin had given them and they referred to themselves as Mensheviks. It was their 'brand', and Lenin knew how to exploit it. 'A name he knew was a programme, a distilled essence, more powerful in its impact upon the untutored mind than dozens of articles in learned journals,' one of his comrades said. It was foolish of the Mensheviks to allow themselves to keep that name permanently. It showed how tactically inept they were. Martov was a decent, erudite, highly clever man but a hopeless politician, no match for Lenin. If Lenin had been the minority he would have changed the name at once to something else – True Iskrists, Real Marxists, Orthodox Marxists, Revolutionary Wing of Social Democracy – anything but 'the Minority'.

The vicious mud-slinging continued after the 1903 Congress and became established practice within the Party. For Lenin, the Martovites were quite simply 'traitors', or often more colloquially 'cunts'. The Mensheviks were vilified as 'disorganisers', 'opportunists', 'Girondists', 'reformists'. The Mensheviks accused Lenin of being a 'Robespierre', a 'Jacobin', a 'terrorist', a 'despot' and – a very bad thing to be in the Marxist lexicon – a 'bureaucrat', or a 'formalist'. Martov wrote a scathing piece in *Iskra* headlined 'In Lieu of a Funeral Oration', calling Lenin 'a political corpse'. Elsewhere he said of something Lenin had written that 'reading his lines, breathing as they do a petty, at times senseless personal malice, amazing narcissism, blind and deaf unfeeling . . . endless repetition of the same old "fighting" and "scathing" little words, one becomes convinced that this is a man who is fatally condemned to slide further down the slope . . . which will take him straight to full political corruption and the shattering of Social Democracy'.

Both sides used satire and lampoon. The Mensheviks drew up a mock constitution of the All Russian Social Democratic Workers' Party, point one of which read: 'The Party is divided into those who sit and those who are sat upon.' Lepeshinsky, an amateur but talented cartoonist, produced the tale 'How the mice buried the tomcat'. Plekhanov was the 'all-wise rat' and Martov and Axelrod were the mice. The rows became deeply personal and often involved scandalous stories about sex and money. Rumours spread about Nikolai Bauman, who was 'cruel to mistresses' and beat them up with uncontrolled violence, it was said. Martyn Liadov, a fervent Bolshevik, was alleged to have spent a small fortune of Party funds in a luxurious brothel. Lenin used any dirty trick he could: he tried to win over Fyodor Dan by offering to show him a secret dossier said to contain salacious rumours about the private lives of prominent Mensheviks. The ruse failed.[7]

Lenin lost many comrades he thought he could rely on, and talented people he had admired. He parted ways with Trotsky after the 1903 Congress and they spent the next thirteen years insulting each other. Lenin invariably referred to 'the Judas Trotsky', 'that rascal', 'sordid careerist' or 'swine resounding in hollow phrases and bombast'. He wrote to one supporter after a clash: 'That's Trotsky for you! Always the same evasive cheat, posing as a leftist but *helping* the Right while he can.' Trotsky responded in kind. He told a Menshevik friend nearly a decade after the split, 'the rotten squabble, systematically inflamed by that master of such affairs, Lenin, that exploiter of any backwardness in the Russian labour movement . . . The entire Leninist edifice is built on lies and falsification and carries within it the poisonous source of its own disintegration.' Lenin, he said, 'is simply unscrupulous through and through'. His most cutting comment, as it proved to be so prophetic, was, 'when Lenin talks about the dictatorship of the proletariat . . . he means the dictatorship *over* the proletariat'.

The feud reached absurd levels. Most of the leading personalities from both sides of the divide lived cheek by jowl together in Geneva, then a small city of no more than 75,000 people. If a member of one faction saw an erstwhile comrade from the other faction, the course laid down by Lenin was to cross the road to avoid each other: 'when you see a stinking heap in your path, you don't have to touch it to know what it is. Your nose tells you it's shit and you pass by,' he said. The rival camps ate their sausages and drank coffee in separate rooms at the Café Landolt.

The dispute took a toll on Lenin. 'Often his talk on our walk consisted of vicious and abusive invective,' Valentinov said. 'When he talked about the Mensheviks, Lenin could hardly control himself. He would suddenly stop in the middle of the pavement, stick his fingers into the holes of his waistcoat (even when he was wearing an overcoat), lean back and then jump forward, letting fly at his enemies. He cared nothing for the fact that passers-by stared with some amazement at his gesticulations. These tirades of his, which were delivered with such passion . . . must undoubtedly have worn him out and used up a great deal of his reserves of energy . . . His frenzied state of rage and extreme nervous tension would be followed by exhaustion, decline of energy, listlessness and depression.'

When Lenin at this time referred to the 'enemy', he didn't mean the Tsar or the autocratic regime. He meant his old 'friend' and comrade Martov and the Mensheviks.[8]

16

PEAKS AND TROUGHS

'I don't want people with indeterminate views and shilly-shallyers. Better a small fish than a big beetle. Better two or three energetic and completely devoted men than a dozen dawdlers.'

Lenin to Nadya, 1904

Back in Switzerland, Lenin sought some calm and solace in the way he habitually did. He headed for the mountains. 'Nadya and I had a wonderful outing,' he wrote to his mother soon after returning from London. 'Down below in Geneva it was all mist and gloom but up in the mountains [about 1,200 metres] above sea level there was glorious sunshine . . . snow. And at the foot of the mountain – *la mer du brouillard*, a veritable sea of mist and clouds, concealing everything but the peak jutting up through it, and only the highest at that. Even little Salève (nearly 1,000 metres) was wrapped in mist.'

A few days later he was walking along the long chalk ridge of the Salève again, with Nadya, at one of his favourite times, to see the dawn rise. On this occasion, amid the beauty of nature which calmed his spirit, he made a political point. 'We happened to walk up with two workers, but lost sight of them when we got to the top . . . On the way down we met them again and said to them "the sunrise was very beautiful, wasn't it?" Their answer was "Unfortunately, we didn't see anything. We worked all day yesterday and we were still so very tired that we sat down for a little while, waiting for the sun to rise, but fell asleep."'[1]

It was Lenin who without a doubt had caused the split in the Revolutionary Party – and his opponents were conspiring to make him pay the price. Plekhanov had supported him in the London Congress, but almost immediately regretted it. He turned against him and made sure that Lenin was voted off the editorial board of *Iskra*, the position that had been his power base. Lenin resigned from all the organising committees of the RSDLP and was almost entirely isolated. Far fewer supporters stuck with him than he had anticipated. He lost friends, though he didn't seem to care. He shrugged when Potresov, whom he had known well from his days in St Petersburg's radical salons in the early 1890s, broke with him saying he 'could find no middle ground with Lenin. Everything boiled down to extremes – you're either with him or against him. He simplifies the human condition with a monolithic one-note nature.' Gleb Krzhizhanovsky desperately tried to engineer a reconciliation, but Lenin wouldn't hear of it. He told Lenin the split was 'futile' and asked him how he could insist that he was right when all the other Party leaders and senior comrades had deserted him. 'We implore the old man to drop his quarrel and start working for the good of the Party. We await leaflets from him, pamphlets and all kinds of advice.' What they got instead was an angry, bitter and inward-looking justification for all his actions – a polemic called *One Step Forward, Two Steps Back*, a classic of 'Leninist' belligerence and abuse at perceived enemies. 'Only naïve bumpkins can fail to see that the case of the Martovites needs to be answered with maximum pressure,' Lenin said.[2]

His self-belief and confidence were unshakeable. Splitting the Party and splitting again, going into a political wilderness, would seem a hopeless route to take for a tiny group with little popular support. But in the long term – and Lenin was always looking at the bigger picture and the longer term – the tactic paid off. In his calculation, it did not matter so much how many supporters he had. The important thing was to have a group of people, a Party, loyal to him, of disciplined and dedicated supporters who would spread the true word. 'I don't want people with indeterminate views and shilly-shallyers. Better a small fish than a big beetle. Better two or three energetic and completely devoted men than a dozen dawdlers,' he told Nadya. Those few who followed him 'hero-worshipped him in a cloying kind of way,' commented one of them who later defected from Lenin's camp, 'never doubting him. It didn't seem healthy.'*

---

* Anatoly Lunacharsky was a devout Bolshevik who venerated Lenin but could on occasion see some of his hero's faults. He said that at this time in Geneva Lenin 'worked mostly with his pen ... It seemed to me that Lenin was not the genuine revolutionary leader I had thought him to be. It began to seem as though émigré life had somewhat

* * *

Lenin's 'rages', the frantic pace and intensity with which he worked and regular political crises took their toll on his health. Throughout his life, when he was stressed he suffered from crippling headaches, stomach cramps and insomnia, which left him prostrate with nervous exhaustion.* He was on the edge of a breakdown, as Nadya knew: 'his eyes were heavy and dead-looking and his eyelids were swollen from lack of sleep . . . Sometimes when he was working from home he would move about on tiptoe in case he was disturbed by his own thoughts.' His health was made worse when in March 1904 he cycled into the back of a tramcar and suffered painful cuts to his face and bruises on his arms and legs. He walked around Geneva with bandages around his cheeks. His mother and sisters were worried about him and wrote regularly to Nadya about their concerns. He needed a holiday to restore his health and mental balance – and so did Nadya. 'At the end of June Vladimir Ilyich and I put on our rucksacks and headed, without any plan, to the mountains for a month.' They agreed not to talk about work or politics for the duration: 'Work is not a bear and we will escape to the woods,' he told her.

After a week she wrote to Maria Alexandrovna: 'We have left our work and worries behind in Geneva . . . we sleep ten hours a day and go swimming and walking. Volodya doesn't even read the newspapers properly. We took a minimum of books with us, and even those we are sending back to Geneva tomorrow, unread, while we go for a walking tour of the mountains . . . to Interlaken and then Lucerne . . . Already in a week we have recovered considerably and have begun to look healthy

---

diminished him, that the inner Party struggle against the Mensheviks had for him pushed into the background the mighty struggle against the monarchy and that he was more a journalist than a genuine leader.'

* He clearly suffered from hypertension, as his father had done: he was a stroke waiting to happen, as the arteriosclerosis in his brain established later. Around this time he visited a doctor for stomach trouble who told him that his real health problem was not in his bowels, 'it's the brain' – an accurate diagnosis no other specialist made until near the end of his life. The doctor suggested that his hectic life and schedule would prove very bad for him. It seems he did not mention this to anyone, not even Nadya.

again . . . We have been under such strain that we cannot be blamed for taking a month's holiday.'*[3]

For the first part of the holiday they were accompanied by Maria Essen, a young Bolshevik activist and one of only two members of the RSDLP Central Committee to back Lenin in the Party split. She was also a distant cousin of Lenin's mother from her Scandinavian roots. 'When walking, Lenin never seemed to get tired,' she recalled later.[†] 'I was preparing to return to Russia and as a farewell treat we decided that the three of us, Vladimir Ilyich, Nadezhda Konstantinovna and I, should go into the mountains. We took a steamer to Montreux. We visited the sombre Château of Chillon and Bonivard's cell, so beautifully described by Byron. We saw the stone to which Bonivard was chained . . . As we emerged from the dark vaults we were instantly dazzled by the bright sunshine and the overpowering scenery . . . We decided to climb to one of the peaks.' (It was the Rochers de Naye, too arduous a climb for Nadya, who stayed behind at the nearby hotel.)

'At first the climb was easy and pleasant, but the higher we went the harder it became. We left the path and climbed straight up the slope. With each step the climb became more difficult. Vladimir Ilyich strode briskly and confidently, chuckling at my efforts to keep up with him. After a while I was climbing on all fours, clutching at the snow, which

---

* Holidays were a big feature of Lenin's life. A few days in the mountains or by the sea invariably restored him, however exhausted and strained he was. Two years earlier he had had a three-week break with his mother and sister Maria at Loguivy on the Brittany coast, without Nadya. He had made all the arrangements and planned everything in advance, down to the train station at which they should leave their luggage. 'It would be good to be on the Volga in the summer,' he wrote to Maria Alexandrovna. 'Well, if I can't come to the Volga, the Volga folk can come here. There are good places here, albeit of a different kind.'

† Despite all his symptoms of an unwell man, Lenin seemed on the face of it extremely fit. He swam, skated and took regular exercise. 'He told me that every morning he stripped and did various gymnastic exercises for at least ten minutes,' Valentinov recalled. 'These included, first of all, circular movements with the arms, squatting and forward bends, with straight knees to touch the floor.' Valentinov told Lenin that he never visited the doctor and couldn't afford it. 'Lenin looked at me with disgust – I cannot find a better word – as one might look at a dirty or smelly person. "This really shows a lack of culture," he told me. "It is real backwoods behaviour. You must value and take care of your health. It is always a blessing to be physically strong and healthy, to have powers of endurance – but for the revolutionary it is a duty."'

melted in my hands, but still managing to keep up with [him] . . . At last we reached the top. A limitless panorama stretched below, an indescribable display of colours. Before us lay . . . all types of vegetation; next to us the brightness of the snow; a little lower the rich alpine meadows . . . I felt in the mood for some high literature and was about to start reciting from Shakespeare or Byron when I looked at Vladimir Ilyich. He was sitting down, deep in thought. Suddenly, he burst out, "Hm, a fine mess the Mensheviks are making for us." When we started on our walk we agreed not to talk about the Mensheviks "so as not to spoil the landscape" and as long as he was walking, he was full of fun and the joys of life, having obviously put out of his mind all thoughts of Mensheviks, or Bundists. But he had only to sit down for a minute and his mind reverted to its usual train of thought.'

After Essen left them – she was arrested a few days after she arrived in Russia – Lenin and Nadya continued their holiday around the Bernese Oberland. 'We always selected the wildest paths and got away from the heart of the mountains, far away from other human beings. We tramped for a month; each day we never knew where we would be on the morrow. By the evening we were always so tired that we sank into bed and fell asleep instantaneously . . . We had very little money with us, and existed mostly on eggs, cheese and the like, washed down with wine or spring water. We rarely sat down to a proper dinner. At one little inn, run by a Social Democrat, a worker advised us: "Don't dine with the tourists, but with the coachmen, chauffeurs and workmen. You will find it twice as cheap and twice as filling." So we took his advice.' Lenin was regularly sending cheerful letters back to his mother and Maria – 'greetings from the tramps', he wrote from Kandersteg, near Frutigen.

They ended their break at the Lac du Bré in early September. They had walked more than 400 kilometres and neither felt any guilt about taking such a long vacation. As always the fresh air and the mountains had restored his health and revived his spirit. 'It was as though the mountain streams had washed away all the cobwebs of petty intrigues,' wrote Nadya.[4]

17

AN AUTOCRACY WITHOUT AN AUTOCRAT

'What will happen to me and all of Russia? I am not prepared to be a
Tsar. I never wanted to become one. I know nothing of the business
of ruling. I don't know how to carry out the duties.'

> Nicholas II to his cousin Sergius on the day of his
> accession to the throne, 19 October 1894

The first, the original 'Communist joke' – a genre of dark humour that
became famous in the Soviet-dominated world – was the comment from
a Bolshevik commissar in 1918 suggesting that Tsar Nicholas should
have been given the highest Soviet honour, the Red Banner, for his 'services to the Revolution'.

The Tsar did as much as anyone, including Lenin, to bring about
the destruction of the Romanov dynasty and to ensure the Communist
takeover in Russia. He never gave a thought to the laws of unintend-
ed consequences. At a time when Russia needed wise and imaginative
leadership, it was landed with a ruler totally unequipped for the role. It
is no exaggeration to say that *every* major decision Nicholas II took was
wrong – from his choice of wife, Alexandra, who compounded his own
misjudgements, to his disastrous decisions on war and peace.

He never questioned his rigid belief in the principle of autocracy. In
January 1895, a few weeks after he succeeded to the throne, he told a
gathering of provincial nobles that any hopes of liberalisation politically
were 'senseless dreams' and that he had sworn it as his duty 'to maintain . . . autocracy as firmly and unflinchingly as it was preserved by my
unforgettable dead father'. He wanted to be an autocrat but didn't look
or sound like one, and he lacked the personality, the intelligence and the
strength of will to be one. He might have been a successful ceremonial
monarch. His manners were impeccable, he spoke platitudes elegantly

and he looked handsome in a uniform. But that is not how the Romanovs reigned. Though it was once calculated that by blood he was only 1/128th Russian (and the rest mainly German), by attitude and frame of mind, according to one of his longest-serving ministers, 'Our Tsar is an Oriental, one hundred per cent Byzantine.' He had a medieval belief in his divine right to rule, but no understanding of the nature of power.

He was never 'taught' kingship or anything much about administration. His principal tutor, General Grigory Danilovich, believed that 'mysterious forces emanating during the sacrament of coronation provided all the practical data required by a ruler'. His law and history tutor, Konstantin Pobedonostev, the Procurator of the Holy Synod, was not impressed by his royal charge. He once said that the main thing he could remember about Nicholas was that 'he seemed completely absorbed picking his nose'.[1]

His father Alexander III, a huge bear of a man with vast appetites for food and the bottle, treated 'Nicky' badly, giving him no role whatsoever in running his empire. When Count Sergei Witte, then the Finance Minister, suggested a minor position for Nicholas with a seat on the Trans-Siberian Committee planning the railway, the Tsar looked puzzled: 'Have you ever tried to discuss anything of consequence with His Imperial Highness the Grand Duke Tsarevich? Don't tell me you've never noticed the Grand Duke is . . . an absolute dunce.'

When Alexander died of kidney disease in November 1894, his eldest son burst into tears, not from sorrow for his father but pity for himself. Between sobs, in his father's death chamber, he cursed his fate and asked his cousin Sandro (Sergius), 'What will happen to me and all of Russia? I am not prepared to be a Tsar. I never wanted to become one. I know nothing of the business of ruling.'*

He was not a complete simpleton. He was fluent in English, German and French and had decent Italian too. It was said of him that 'he could speak several languages impeccably but had nothing intelligent or interesting to say in any of them'.† Others who knew him were more generous.

---

* Louis XVI, whose fate was so similar to that of Nicholas, said something of the same kind when he was told of his father's death: 'What a burden. And I have been taught nothing! The entire universe is about to fall on me.'
† His English was so perfect that from his early teens Alexander III got him to write his personal letters to Queen Victoria. He was an Anglophile in some ways – in particular,

'He was the best-bred person I've ever met,' said Witte. He had some fine qualities – he was dedicated to duty and hard work and was devoted to his family – 'yet his capabilities were limited by the tremendous parochialism of his education and outlook'. Even many ultra-royalists were disappointed in him. 'He understands the significance of only one fact at a time without connecting it to any others,' said Pobedonostev. 'He sticks to the unimportant . . . has a petty point of view.'[2]

Nicholas spent inordinate amounts of time on trivial matters which a junior civil servant could have handled – ordering repairs to an agricultural college for example, personally appointing provincial midwives, approving railway timetables. But as his tedious and unilluminating diaries show, he barely thought about the bigger picture and the great affairs of state. He played ministers off against each other and routinely treated them shabbily rather than trying to unify them as a team under his leadership. There were some clever and able administrators in government – Count Witte and Pyotr Stolypin stood out – but he never trusted them. At a time when a huge and still-growing empire needed efficient and creative 'technocrats', people who knew what they were doing, he relied for advice on a small coterie of reactionary courtiers.

When, a decade into his reign, he did make a big decision it was a disastrous mistake which added momentum to the revolutionary whirlwind that would topple him. He began a war with Japan for control of the South China Sea, in a bid to increase Russian power in the East. The Russians, with the customary racial superiority of European imperialists, assumed they would score a swift victory that would give them a bigger toehold in Manchuria and the Korean peninsula – after all it was, as Nicholas said, only 'yellow men, not entirely civilised' that they were taking on. But the Russian military was woefully ill-prepared and barely considered that Japan was modernising fast and had military abilities to match its imperial ambitions. Russia suffered a humiliating defeat and lost almost its entire Pacific fleet. It had to sue for peace. Nicholas felt crushed. If he had possessed the imagination, he might have realised how perilous was his hold on the throne.[3]

Historians have on the whole been rather kind to Nicholas II, mainly

he was related to their royals – but in truth he didn't like the British much, and certainly not, as he told advisers, their politics or 'civilisation'. He frequently told Prime Minister Witte that 'the English are just like the Yids', which for him was a term of abuse.

because of the grisly manner of his death and the murder of his family. But he was largely responsible for his own destruction. He was not a well-intentioned figure who was swept away by tides of history. If at the start of his reign Nicholas II had made any efforts to establish a constitutional monarchy, introduce liberal reforms and allow political activity to flourish, as elsewhere in Europe, he might have saved Russia from catastrophe – and the lives of himself and his family. He deserved his place, as the Marxists phrase it, in the dustbin of history.

* * *

In Geneva, at around 9.30 a.m. on Monday 10 January 1905, Lenin and Nadya 'were on our way to the library when we met the Lunacharskys, who were coming to see us. Lunacharsky's wife* was so excited she could not speak, only managing to wave her muff at us . . . We went to the Lepeshinsky émigré restaurant. We wanted to be together. The people gathered around there hardly spoke a word to one another, they were so excited.'†

The Russians devoured the news from St Petersburg, where the previous day an entirely peaceful protest in the centre of the city had turned into a massacre. 'We were stunned,' Nadya said. 'Hardly a word was spoken the entire morning. We began to sing the revolutionary funeral march "You Have Fallen in the Struggle" with grim-set faces. It dawned on everyone in a wave that the Revolution had begun, that the shackles of faith in the Tsar had been torn apart.'[4]

The reports from Russia were shocking. A series of strikes since the beginning of the year had closed several St Petersburg factories, though they never crippled the city or at any point looked like an insurrection. The strike leader was a charismatic priest, Father Georgy Gapon, who believed that if the Tsar was told about the harsh lives of Russian

---

* This was Anatoly Lunacharsky's first wife, Anna Malinovkaya, the sister of the Bolshevik philosopher and long-time intellectual sparring partner of Lenin, Alexander Bogdanov. Soon after the 1917 Revolution, middle-aged and in power as Commissar for Public Enlightenment, he left her for Natalya Rozenel, an actress less than half his age.

† A new café recently opened by Lenin's friends and fellow exiles in Siberia, Panteleimon and Olga Lepeshinsky, which the Bolsheviks now frequented while the Mensheviks still favoured the rear room of the nearby Landolt.

workers and was directly appealed to, he would intervene to force industrial employers to improve factory conditions and raise wages. It was hopelessly naïve, but showed the faith the public appeared to have in the Tsar. Gapon called on the strikers and their families to demonstrate on Sunday 9 January. He wrote a petition they planned to present to Nicholas. It was humble, simply put and, as things turned out, full of tragic pathos. 'SIRE: We the workers and inhabitants of St Petersburg, of various estates, our wives, our children and our aged, helpless parents, come to THEE O SIRE to seek justice and protection. We are impoverished; we are oppressed, overburdened with excessive toil, contemptuously treated . . . we are suffocating in despotism and lawlessness . . . we have no strength left and our endurance is at an end. We have reached that terrifying moment when death is better than prolongation of our unbearable suffering.'

On the Friday before the planned march Gapon was ordered to call off the demonstration or expect 'resolute measures'.* Various dignitaries – from a few liberal ministers to Maxim Gorky – urged the government to talk to the protestors. But Nicholas left St Petersburg for Tsarskoe Selo and ordered the military to disperse the crowds if they reached government buildings.

It was a beautiful winter morning with a sharp frost. The sun shone 'brilliantly from a pale-blue sky upon the white expanse of the Neva and the snow-covered roofs and streets'. The main body of the unarmed march was led by groups of women and children, 'dressed in their Sunday best'. Father Gapon was at the front of one of the columns 'wearing a long white cassock, carrying a crucifix. Directly behind him there was

---

* Gapon, as much a conman as spiritual leader or political activist, had been an Okhrana agent and became head of a semi-legal, trade union movement, created secretly by the police to challenge the socialist movements. Such was the conspiratorial, looking-glass world of Russian politics, where nothing was as it appeared. Gapon, though, went rogue and double-crossed his police handlers by inspiring the march that led to Bloody Sunday. Soon afterwards he escaped from Russia and headed to Europe, where he was given refuge in Paris by French leftists, in London by the anarchist Prince Kropotkin, and in Geneva, where Lenin met him. Lenin was interested in the priest and made overtures to recruit him to the Bolshevik cause, but Gapon threw in his lot with the Socialist Revolutionary Party instead. In early 1906 he returned to Russia and rekindled his contacts with the Okhrana, but his double role was soon discovered. In March 1906 he was murdered by the SR leaders he was planning to betray.

a big picture of the Tsar.' When the procession reached the Narva Triumphal Arch they were charged by a troop of cavalry with sabres. Most
of the marchers scattered. But some continued towards a line of infantry
– and were mown down. Gapon fell to the ground but got up, looked at
the snow turned blood-red around him and was heard to shout repeatedly, 'There is no God any longer . . . there is no Tsar.'[5]

Some demonstrators made it close to the Winter Palace. One eyewitness saw troops firing at them, 'bringing down little boys perched on
the trees in a neighbouring garden . . . A sleigh drove swiftly up the
Nevsky followed by half a dozen workmen running with bare hands and
crossing themselves, some weeping. In the sleigh sat a youth holding in
his arms a student, dead, his face one gaping wound. Three or four Cossacks came galloping up on horseback, pulled rein, looked at the sleigh,
then rode on with a jeering laugh.'

Gorky, amid the demonstration at the Troitsky Bridge, saw an officer kill one young demonstrator: 'The dragoon circled around him
and shrieking . . . waved his sabre in the air. Swooping down from his
horse, he slashed him across the face, cutting him open from the eyes
to the chin. I remember the strangely enlarged eyes of the worker and
. . . the murderer's face, blushed from the cold and excitement, his teeth
clenched in again and the hairs of his moustache standing up on his ele-
vated lip. Brandishing his shaft of steel, he let out another shriek and . . .
spat at the dead man through his teeth.'[6]

As the evening wore on the mood turned from shock to anger. British
reporter Harold Williams saw 'the faces around me and detected neither
fear nor panic . . . but hostility and hatred. I saw these looks of hatred on
every face, young and old, men and women. The Revolution was born.
The popular ideal – myth or not – of a Good Tsar, which had sustained
the regime for centuries, was suddenly destroyed.' In truth the army
had often been used over several hundred years by the Tsars to maintain
their rule, but now, in the twentieth century, it struck loyal supporters of
the regime as a barbaric excess.

It was different to former atrocities in other ways. It took place in
Russia's capital where international journalists were on the scene, and
the speed of communications meant the news was on the front pages
around the world by the next day. Foreign governments were worried
by the prospect of chaos in Russia. The American Ambassador, Robert

McCormick, reported to Washington three days later: 'The events . . . weakened if [they] did not shatter, that unswerving loyalty and deep-seated reverence which has characterised the subject of The Tsar of all the Russias. I have had evidence of this from the highest to the lowest classes and it finds expression in a letter I received . . . from Mr Heenan, our Consul in Odessa, who writes: "In all the eighteen years I have spent in Russia, I never knew the Russian public so united . . . All classes condemn the authorities and, more particularly, the Emperor. He has lost absolutely the affection of the Russian people and whatever the future for the dynasty, the Tsar will never be safe in the midst of his people." I accept Mr Heenan's view: the emperor will never be able to re-establish himself in his former unique position.'[7]

The official figure from the government put the number of dead at around 200 with 800 wounded, but the real figure was much greater – probably four times higher. In Geneva, a thousand miles from the action, Lenin was convinced that Bloody Sunday was the beginning of the end of Tsarism – and that the end would not be too far away.

* * *

Lenin had predicted an uprising against the monarchy *in theory*. A fortnight before Bloody Sunday he wrote a piece in the new socialist paper he had launched, *Vyperod* (Forward). 'A military collapse [in the Japan war] is inevitable, and with it will come a tenfold increase of unrest, discontent and rebellion . . . For that moment we must prepare with all our energy. At that moment one of these outbreaks . . . will develop into a tremendous popular movement. At that moment the proletariat will rise to take its place at the head of the insurrection.'[*8]

But when 'the moment' came Lenin was taken entirely by surprise and was woefully unprepared and ill-equipped to deal with it. So were nearly all the Marxist and Socialist Revolutionary leaders. He would call the 1905 Revolution the Dress Rehearsal, as though it had all been planned and scripted. Later, Communist rewriting of history gave

---

* No longer involved with *Iskra*, which became a Menshevik organ and did not survive much longer after the Party split, Lenin started *Vyperod* with the generous financial help of Gorky. But it was an altogether less influential paper, did not have the organised 'agents' to smuggle copies into Russia and circulated mainly among Russian émigrés in Western Europe.

Lenin's RSDLP a leading role in the events. But the Party played almost no part in the initial strikes and unrest. A mere handful of Party members were there at the demonstration on Bloody Sunday – and they were right at the back of the march, placed there almost as an afterthought.

Lenin barely uttered a word throughout the day at Lepeshinsky's nor, according to Nadya, afterwards at home. The next morning he did what he normally did: he went to the Geneva Central Library. For the next few days he read everything he could find about guerrilla warfare and military tactics in historic uprisings, particularly the 1870 Paris Commune. He wrote fiery letters to comrades in Russia demanding that armed units of revolutionaries should be formed, 'with rifles, revolvers, bombs, knives, knuckledusters, rags soaked in petrol, ropes or rope ladders, shovels for building barricades, dynamite cartridges, barbed wire, tacks against cavalry . . .'. It was totally unrealistic advice, written by a journalist not a commando, gleaned from the books he had just read, typical of an armchair general. 'Give every company short and simple bomb formulae . . . they must begin military training immediately in direct connection with practical fighting actions. Some will immediately kill a spy or blow up a police station. Others will organise an attack on a bank in order to confiscate funds for the uprising.' At no point in his life did he have any direct experience of fighting, yet that did not stop him from writing in bloodcurdling fashion as though he were a military expert.[9]

Sporadic fighting between workers and army units went on for five days in St Petersburg, and with more ferocity in Moscow, where scores of civilians were killed. Strikes continued for months amid an atmosphere of government paralysis and political crisis unknown in Russia for a century.

From the safety of Geneva, Lenin continued his calls for violence against the regime. A few weeks after Bloody Sunday he wrote an article headlined 'The arming of the people has become an immediate task'. Plekhanov, who had trained as a soldier, told Lenin plainly that 'people should not have taken up arms' – it was a mistake and it would be workers who suffered the most. Lenin replied, 'nonsense, on the contrary. They should have been more resolute, energetic and aggressive . . . those who do not prepare for armed uprising must be ruthlessly cast out of the ranks of the supporters of the Revolution and sent back to the ranks of its enemies as traitors or cowards. An oppressed class which does not strive to learn to use arms, to obtain arms, deserves to be treated as slaves.'*[10]

Lenin's cynicism was mind-boggling. At this point there was absolutely no chance that an armed uprising could succeed and he knew it. He was expecting sacrifices – possibly death – from his supporters. For a start, there were far too few of them to make any difference. In 1905 the Bolsheviks were weak inside Russia: the split had demoralised the Party. Members could not understand what the arguments were about and were desperate for the leadership, in safe overseas exile, to set aside personal differences and unite against the real enemy – the Tsarist regime.

In December 1904, just a few weeks before Bloody Sunday, Maxim Litvinov, one of Lenin's most senior lieutenants, on a clandestine visit to St Petersburg, sent a grim report back to Geneva. He said that inside Russia the Bolsheviks 'have virtually no strength . . . On the periphery, people if not everywhere against us are almost nowhere for us. The mass of Party workers continue to regard us as a handful of "disorganisers" with no support of our own. No kind of conference, let alone a secret one, will change this widely held view. I repeat, our situation is impossibly rickety and precarious . . . The [Mensheviks] are incomparably better off . . . they have thirty to forty young women from abroad, true and dedicated to the point of hysteria.' Sergei Gusev, at that time the highest-ranking Bolshevik inside Russia, said that when the 1905 Revolution began there were 215 Bolshevik members in the capital, 109 of

---

* Lenin came up with apparently harebrained military schemes from his Geneva drawing board. One dramatic moment in the 1905 Revolution was the mutiny by sailors aboard the battleship *Prince Potemkin* in the harbour at Odessa. Lenin tried to persuade a twenty-two-year-old Bolshevik student activist, with no military training, to board the ship and persuade the crew 'at whatever cost' to join the workers' revolution, bombard government buildings and help local peasants to take over nearby estates. There was no indication the sailors were interested in the Party; they simply loathed their brutal naval officers. Undeterred, Lenin insisted that 'afterwards we must get the fleet in our hands . . . the majority of the ships will rally to the crew of the *Potemkin*. But you must act boldly and resolutely.' The young man went back to the Crimea, at some risk on a fake passport, as instructed, but by the time he got there the *Potemkin* had left Odessa, and what existed of the local Party was no longer in the mood for insurrection. The next time Lenin would try to foment mutiny in the navy, in 1917, he prepared the ground more thoroughly and it was an essential part of Bolshevik victory.

whom were students. 'Only now can we understand the full disorganisa-tion of the Party,' he told Lenin. 'The St Petersburg Party is . . . helpless in the face of . . . the workers' protest. You only have to go out onto the streets to see how weak we are. And what can we do? Put out a few hun-dred leaflets, which will be unnoticed, and send out a few speakers.'

Lenin was undeterred. He kept clamouring for more action. 'It horri-fies me – I give you my word – it horrifies me, to find that there has been talk about bombs for months, yet not a single one has been made. Form fighting squads everywhere,' he told St Petersburg Bolsheviks.

A young activist who had seen much bloodshed in his home town of Kazan – a city Lenin knew well – arrived in Geneva and asked what Party members should do, as it looked like the uprising was finished. 'Well, that's simple,' said Lenin. 'Prepare for an armed rising again.' 'But Vladimir Ilyich, there's so little chance of victory.' 'Victory? That, for us, is not the point at all. What do we care about victory? We should not harbour any illusions. We are realists and let nobody imagine that we have to win. For that we are still too weak. The point is not about winning, but about giving the regime a shake and attracting the masses to our movement. The uprising is what matters. To say that because we can't win we should not stage an insurrection – that is simply the talk of cowards.'

Later in 1905, Moscow workers went on strike. Soldiers from the crack Semenovsky Guards were sent to force them back to work. They surrounded the militants in a working-class district of the city, killing dozens. Field guns shelled the area for three days, leaving hundreds dead, including eighty-six children. Lenin's comment was not to mourn the deaths. He said the important thing was that revolutionaries had fought in the streets and their defeat would teach them to hate their ene-mies: 'the one who has been whipped is worth two who have not'.[11]

* * *

There was a wave of arrests following Bloody Sunday. Gorky was picked up two days afterwards and charged with organising a conspira-torial revolution, though all he had done was witness the massacre and write about it. The multimillionaire Savva Morozov increased his sub-sidy to the Party and other industrialists also began giving money to socialist and liberal groups – 'it became fashionable to do so and if it helped their consciences, we didn't mind the help', said Leonid Krasin, the Bolsheviks' money man and technical expert who handled many of the 'donations'. He admitted it was a kind of inverted snobbery to support a cause so fundamentally inimical to their personal interests. 'At the time it was regarded as a sign of *bon ton* in . . . radical or even liberal circles to contribute money to revolutionary parties – and among those who regularly paid dues of between 5 and 25 rubles . . . [a month] were not only prominent attorneys, engineers and physicians, but also directors of banks and officials from government institutions.' A big error of the Tsar's was to make enemies of wealthy business magnates such as Morozov, Pavel Ryabushinsky and Alexander Guchkov. He thought it beneath him to deal with people in 'trade' and didn't see how important they would be. Much of the business world threw their support behind liberals who wanted Western-style reforms. One of the richest Russian industrialists of them all, Alexei Putilov, who employed 27,000 people at his vast engineering works on the outskirts of St Petersburg – and manufactured a large proportion of the weapons for the Russian army – said, 'Tsarism is lost, it is beyond hope.'[*12]

Unrest continued – in the factories and on the land, where scores of estates were burned down and their owners attacked. Many gentry landlords, or the intelligent ones, said the most significant thing about the 1905 'troubles' was that the attitudes of the peasants 'seem suddenly to have changed'. The owner of a large estate near Samara, not far from Alakayevka where Maria Alexandrovna once had an estate, said that 'instead of the previous courtesy, friendliness and humility, there was only hatred in their faces and the manner of their greetings . . . underlined their rudeness'. Another big landlord in Tula Province, one of the most agriculturally rich in Russia, noted that 'externally everything appeared to be normal. But something essential, something irreparable had happened in the people. A general feeling of fear had undermined all trust. After a lifetime of security – nobody had bothered to lock their doors and windows in the evening – the nobles concerned themselves with weapons and personally made the rounds to test their security measures.'[13]

---

* On the eve of the First World War, he predicted with some accuracy what would happen in Russia. There would be a bourgeois revolution led by moderates 'thinking they are saving Russia . . . but they will be swept away amid interminable anarchy and the revolution will be taken over by workers and peasants'.

Some émigrés returned from European exile, including Martov, Vera Zasulich and, sensationally, Trotsky, who immediately on his return from Austria in the spring threw himself into political activity, making a name for himself as a brilliant speaker and – more surprisingly – an organiser. He was the face behind the St Petersburg Soviet, which briefly flickered as a powerful symbol of opposition to the regime until it was closed down towards the end of the year.*

Many Bolsheviks tried to persuade Lenin to return to lead the Revolution from inside Russia. But instead of going to St Petersburg, he went to London to organise another Party Congress – 'a talking shop' as some Mensheviks called it – to work out a line to take on Bloody Sunday. Thirty-eight delegates turned up at the beginning of May for probably the most pointless of all the various leftist conferences before 1917. Soon after it was over the Tsar bowed to mounting pressure from the liberals – and advisers in his civil service – and granted some of the reforms he had previously maintained he never would: political parties were legalised for the first time and a kind of parliament – the Duma – was established; the Tsar relaxed censorship and there was a freer, though hardly an entirely free, press. The regime kept its hold on real power – and the Dress Rehearsal had reached its second act.

---

* This was the first use of the word 'Soviet' – which simply means 'council' in Russian – in the revolutionary context in which it became so well known: as a group of workers' representatives. Trotsky became a great draw in St Petersburg high society in 1905 as a witty orator. He described the first time he was asked to speak at a grand house. 'The butler waited for my visiting card but, woe is me, what card should a man with a cover name produce?' He received rapturous applause when he told the audience of 'nobles, bejewelled ladies and Guards officers that it was their duty to hand over the arsenals to the people'.

18

BACK HOME

'Tsarism is no longer able to suppress the Revolution; the Revolution is still unable to destroy Tsarism.' Lenin, *Novaya Zhizn*, 1905

When he thought it was safe, Lenin finally returned to Russia. One of the concessions the Tsar had made in his 17 October Manifesto on the Improvement of State Order was to grant an amnesty for some, but not all, political prisoners. Lenin thought he was taking no risks when he went back 'home' a month later, and although he was legally allowed to stay in Russia he entered on false papers under the name William Frey – old conspiratorial habits died hard. He and Nadya travelled to St Petersburg separately via Germany, Sweden and Finland. She returned ten days after him, with her mother, and after they were reunited they first stayed with a friend of Lenin's sister, Maria, and later rented an apartment on Nevsky Prospekt.

From the moment Lenin got off the train at the Finland Station on 18 November he was followed by the Okhrana, who made it obvious they were tailing him. He registered with the local police, but political work was impossible with that level of surveillance. Under the so-called new liberal dispensation Okhrana activity was in fact stepped up. Every time Lenin left the apartment he was in danger of leading the police to 'wanted' comrades or undercover operatives who were still on the run. Lenin and Nadya went underground – first in a series of safe houses in St Petersburg, and then in various small villages in Finland – on false papers. He was, successively, Dr Weber, Irvin Weyhoff and Vladimir Karpov.

It was under the alias Karpov that Lenin met Stalin for the first time, on 25 December 1905. Both attended the First All Russian Bolshevik Conference in the Finnish city Tammefors (Tampere). Stalin,

171

a Caucasian representative, was eager to grease up to Lenin and showed the 'old man' articles he had written in underground journals which supported him against the Mensheviks. Stalin was expecting to meet someone more obviously charismatic: 'I was hoping to see the mountain eagle of our Party. I was hoping to see a great man, great not only polit-ically but, if you will, physically, for in my imagination I had pictured Lenin as a giant, stately and imposing. What, then, was my disappoint-ment to see a most ordinary-looking man, below average in height, in no way, in literally no way, distinguishable from ordinary mortals. It is the accepted thing for "a great man" to come late to meetings so that the assemblage may await his appearance with bated breath; and then, just before the great man enters, the warning goes up "Hush!" "Silence!" "He's coming!" This rite does not seem to me superfluous because it cre-ates an impression, inspires respect. What then was my disappointment to learn that Lenin had arrived at the conference before the delegates, had settled himself somewhere in a corner and was unassumingly car-rying on a conversation, a most ordinary conversation, with the most ordinary delegate . . . I will not conceal that at that time this seemed to me to be rather a violation of certain essential rules.'[1]

Lenin later saw the point of Stalin and would refer to him as 'the wonderful Georgian'. But the younger man (by seven and a half years) made almost no impression on him at their first meeting. Stalin, at this time, was just one of the underground aliases of the future Soviet dicta-tor – others included Soso, Koba and Ivanovich. When they next met eighteen months later Lenin couldn't remember any of them.[*]

There was another important first meeting while Lenin was living underground. Lenin was difficult and domineering and always knew he was right. But he also knew how to lay on the charm and flatter others when it mattered. He had been corresponding with Maxim Gorky for several years. The author and playwright had been a generous donor

---

[*] Nadya loathed Stalin from very early on and told Lenin so, urging him not to trust the Georgian. Occasionally she would share her feelings with other comrades, though she naturally grew more circumspect the higher he rose in the Party and the more in-fluence he gained with Lenin. She did once complain to a trusted emigrant, the writer Viktor Shklovsky, about Stalin's coarseness and that it seemed to her that some senior Bolsheviks were selected 'at random . . . there are undesirables – like Stalin who does us dirt [will betray us]'.

to the Social Democrats and had some rich contacts who possessed fat chequebooks. They had a complex relationship which itself went through revolutionary changes. For years Lenin was the supplicant and needed Gorky's financial help and his political support: Gorky's fame as a writer and his reputation on the Left were immense. Over the years they became genuine friends, though Gorky maintained that he liked Lenin as a person but loathed him as a politician. After Lenin seized power, Gorky became a critic of the Bolsheviks, but a frequent supplicant of Lenin personally; he used to plead on behalf of other writers, artists and academics who had fallen foul of the Soviet authorities. In the week Lenin returned to Russia at the end of 1905 Gorky and his long-time mistress, the actress Maria Andreyeva, launched the first legal Bolshevik newspaper, *Novaya Zhizn* (New Life). Lenin wrote regularly for the paper, and some of his best journalism was produced in these few months, including a scathing attack on 'Nicholasha's cosmetic reforms', a call to continue the Revolution through insurrection and a piece on why the Bolsheviks should boycott the 'undemocratic Duma'.[2]

He occasionally turned up in St Petersburg incognito. It was six months before he spoke in public inside Russia at anything apart from secret Bolshevik Party meetings. When he did, on 9 May 1906, it was in front of the biggest audience of his life so far. Giving his name as 'Karpov', he appeared before 3,000 people at the St Petersburg palace of Countess Sophia Panina, the philanthropist and hostess of a well-known 'progressive' salon of mainly liberals and moderate socialists. He was 'very excited and nervous' when he began, according to Nadya. 'For a minute he stood silent, terribly pale, and it seemed as though all the blood had flowed to his heart.' But then he launched into a fiery address attacking the 'bourgeois Kadets' (a coalition of centre-right Constitutional Democrats) and the 'bogus Duma' and soon 'the excitement of the speaker was being communicated to the audience'. While he was speaking, the rumour spread throughout the Countess's ballroom that 'Karpov' was in fact the Bolshevik Lenin and he was given rapturous applause. Immediately afterwards, concerned for his security, he left the city and headed back to Finland.[3]

He made a few visits, in disguise, to see his mother, who was living in a small village outside St Petersburg. In late July he and Nadya spent a long weekend with Maria Alexandrovna and his sisters at Sablino, near the city, where there was a lake and a dramatic waterfall. 'Volodya went swimming, and we sat beneath an arbour and talked and ate,' said Anna. 'They had intended to spend the week with us but he found the newspapers so interesting on Monday morning that he and Nadya packed and left.'

* * *

The Tsar never intended to keep commitments which he said 'have been forced on me by duress'. Strikes and demonstrations continued – as did assassinations of officials by, mainly, Socialist Revolutionaries. There were around 2,500 of them in the two years after the October Manifesto.* The regime used extreme measures to suppress unrest at a time when some civil servants were claiming that the government was introducing something akin to parliamentary order. In the seven months between the Manifesto and the opening of the Duma more than 15,000 people were killed, at least 70,000 were arrested and 45,000 exiled to Siberia, though official figures put the number of dead at around 1,200. 'Terror must be met by terror,' said Nicholas.

The Tsar fired Count Witte, the liberal Prime Minister who had persuaded him to sign the October Manifesto, blaming him for the continued unrest. He was replaced by Pyotr Stolypin, a clever and able administrator, who combined the first serious economic reforms in generations – he introduced radical plans to extend private ownership of land among peasants – with stern police measures against 'subversive troublemakers'. Thousands were hanged by 'Stolypin's necktie', as it became known, after 'field courts' held in the open air condemned them to death without any proper trial. In the middle of 1906, eighty-two of Russia's eighty-seven provinces were under martial law. Uncounted numbers were taken away to exile by 'Stolypin's wagons'. Whole villages were razed to the ground – 'the Tsar went to war against his people', as the spurned Witte put it. 'It's a total Bacchanal, of arrests, searches,

---

* Lenin didn't believe in individual murders and targeting particular officials of the regime for assassination; he argued they were pointless forms of 'single combat'. He didn't argue on principle but on practical results: 'Do they help attain our desired ends – or on the contrary divert from them?' The Bolsheviks were responsible for very few assassinations, though some officials were killed at demonstrations that turned into riots.

raids,' said Stalin, who knew about such things. The Interior Minister, Pyotr Durnovo, told provincial governors: 'Arrests alone will not achieve our goals. It is impossible to judge hundreds of thousands of people. I propose to shoot the rioters and in case of resistance to burn down their homes.'

Nationalist risings in the Baltic republics, the Caucasus and Ukraine were brutally put down. There were many examples of the Tsar encouraging bloody reprisals from which even his military shied away. General Vladimir Bekman reported on 14 December 1905 that he had decided against burning the town of Tukums, in Latvia, to the ground, as other Baltic areas had been. The inhabitants had assured him they had driven the rebels out and would hand over all the weapons they possessed to him. He was short of ammunition in any case and had ordered his men not to attack. The residents had greeted his men with the usual 'bread and salt welcome', and turned over sixty-two rifles and forty-five revolvers. The Tsar read the report, underlined the general's explanations and wrote in the margin: 'This is no reason. The city should have been destroyed.' When the Tsar was given further reports about the punitive expeditions against rebellious peasants that winter, he told courtiers *'Cela me chatouille'* (this tickles me).*[4]

Years before Mussolini and Hitler's fascist thugs fought street battles with opponents after the First World War, Nicholas encouraged extremist nationalist groups to support him against democrats, liberals and socialists. He was an enthusiastic backer of the newly formed Union of the Russian People, which rallied to the support of 'Tsar, Faith and

---

* Despite the general brutality of 'these years of reaction', some prisoners were remarkably well treated. The most famous of socialist prisoners was Trotsky, arrested after the St Petersburg Soviet was broken up in early 1906. He was incarcerated in the Peter and Paul Fortress, by repute the most rigorous dungeon in the Russian empire. He recalled later that conditions were lenient. 'The cells were not locked during the day and we could take our walks all together. For hours at a time we would go into raptures over playing leapfrog. My wife came to visit me twice a week. The officials on duty winked at our exchange of letters and manuscripts. One of them, a middle-aged man, was particularly well disposed towards us. At his request I presented him with a copy of my book and my photograph with an inscription – "My daughters are all college students," he whispered to me when I gave it to him. I met him later [after the Revolution].' Trotsky managed to write most of his history of the St Petersburg Soviet in jail, and when he was released he 'felt a tinge of regret'.

Fatherland'. He invited its leaders to his palace at Tsarskoe Selo, wore its insignia on his uniforms and subsidised its newspapers. By 1906 it had 300,000 members, nearly a hundred times more than Lenin's Bolsheviks.

If at this stage Nicholas had any ideology it was anti-Semitism, a common, besetting sin throughout the Russian empire. But the Tsar's hatred of Jews was visceral, imperial in its scope and reach – from casual anti-Semitic remarks at dinner to encouraging full-scale pogroms. It ran far deeper than in a typical European aristocrat of the time and he deliberately used anti-Semitism as a way of uniting 'loyalists' to the throne. He thought it hilarious, as he told his mother, when 'a courtier amused us with funny Jewish stories – wonderfully good at imitating Jews and even his face suddenly looks Jewish'. He defined a newspaper as 'a place where some Jew or other sits . . . making it his business to stir up the passions of people against each other'.

In 1905–06 more than 3,000 Jews were slaughtered in pogroms from the Baltic states to the Crimea. Most were perpetrated by extremists calling themselves the Black Hundreds, the armed wing of the Union of the Russian People. The authorities didn't organise the pogroms, but they did nothing to stop them. The worst was at Odessa in the days immediately after the October Manifesto. More than 800 Jews were killed, 5,000 injured and 100,000 were made homeless when Jewish homes were burned down.* A few days after the slaughter in Odessa the Tsar sent a telegram to Alexander Dubrovin, the leader of the Black Hundreds. 'May you be my trusty support, serving for all and in everything as an example of lawfulness and a face of civic order.'

As is common among anti-Semites, he blamed the pogroms on the Jews themselves. He wrote to his mother on 27 October: 'The situation in Russia is still very difficult and serious. In the first days that followed the Manifesto the bad elements in the population raised their heads very high but quickly a strong reaction set in and the whole mass of the loyal

---

* An inquiry ordered by Witte, in one of his last acts as Prime Minister, established that the police armed and supplied the crowd with weapons and vodka and helped Black Hundred thugs to locate Jews. A police HQ printing press produced anti-Semitic leaflets. 'The Jews are trying to destroy Russia . . . kill them. Tear them to pieces.' When Witte called for the police chief responsible to be charged and tried the Tsar intervened to protect him.

people made themselves known. The result was understandable and what one might expect here. The people are indignant at the insolence and audacity of the revolutionaries and socialists and since nine-tenths of them are Jews all the hatred is directed against them. Hence the pogroms against the Jews. It is astonishing with what unity and how simultaneously these occurred in all cities in Russia and Siberia. In England, naturally, they write that these disorders were organised by the police. But this is . . . a fable. Not only have the Jews suffered – but also engineers, lawyers and all other kinds of bad people. What has happened in Tomsk, Simferopol, Tver and Odessa clearly shows what can happen in a storm of fury – the houses of the revolutionaries were surrounded and set on fire. Those who were not burned to death were killed as they emerged. I have received very touching telegrams from everywhere with thanks for the gift of liberty but also with clear declarations that they wish autocracy to be preserved.'[5]

The Black Hundreds often turned their attention on socialists. Many were beaten up in street brawls similar to those launched by the Nazi Brown Shirts during the 1920s.

As usual, where the violence was, Lenin wasn't. Once again his personal bravery was put in question. In his circle of confidants and the Party leadership it was axiomatic that he was too important to the Revolution to take risks with his safety. But others were more critical. 'He would never have gone onto the streets to fight on the barricades, or stand in the line of fire,' remarked Valentinov. 'Not he but other, humbler people were to do that . . . Lenin ran headlong from émigré meetings which seemed likely to end in a scuffle. His role was to "get away while the going was good" – to use his own words – meaning from any threat of danger. During his stay in Petersburg in 1905–06 he so exaggerated the danger to himself and went to such extremes in his anxiety for self-preservation that one was bound to ask whether he was not simply a man without personal courage.'

Tatiana Alexinsky, wife of one of the most senior Bolsheviks in St Petersburg, was deeply disappointed when she saw him flee from a peaceful demonstration that was suddenly attacked by Tsarist cavalry and a group of Black Hundreds in the suburbs of the city in the summer of 1906. 'I'd rather not recall the encounter. Lenin had seemed to me a legendary hero . . . assumed he was a revolutionary without fear or blemish. Not when we saw him up close . . . It wasn't his appearance that made a disagreeable impression on me . . . but his behaviour at the demonstration. When someone in the crowd, spotting some cavalry, shouted "Cossacks!" Lenin was the first to run. He jumped over a barrier. His bowler hat fell off, revealing his bare skull perspiring and glistening. He fell, got up again and continued to run away. I had a peculiar sensation. I realised there was nothing else for any of us to do . . . but still, he was the leader . . .'[6]

19

'EXPROPRIATE THE EXPROPRIATORS'

'Yes we steal . . . But we steal what has already been stolen.'
Lenin, London, May 1907

Lenin: 'In order to take power every means must be used.'
Angelica Balabanova: 'What . . . even dishonest ones?'
Lenin: 'Everything that is done in the interests of the proletarian cause is honest.'
Conversation in London, May 1907

While some critics were accusing Lenin of cowardice in the face of the enemy, other revolutionaries were branding him a 'robber', little better than a 'common thief' and a 'gangster'. If there were few serious political differences or issues of principle between the Bolsheviks and the Mensheviks, there were plenty of sharp disagreements about tactics.

The Party couldn't rely entirely on donations from millionaire magnates – Russian oligarchs of a bygone age – to finance the Revolution. Money had to be found in other ways and Lenin built what was in effect a criminal gang to steal on the Party's behalf, perhaps an original model of the Russian mafia. He didn't directly order any of the raids himself and he called them, in an echo of Marx, 'expropriations', but whatever the euphemism he chose, this was banditry. Lenin appointed Leonid Krasin head of the 'technical committee'. Krasin chose as his chief 'fixer' and right-hand man Stalin, who planned and took part in a number of 'expros', all within the Russian empire. The various gangs they employed robbed banks, stole a large sum in cash and gold from the safe aboard the steamship *Nicholas I* moored in Baku harbour and attacked post offices and state railway ticket offices. Krasin planned a major operation to print counterfeit money on a clandestine press but he couldn't find a skilful enough forger.

Martov, Plekhanov and the Mensheviks were appalled and didn't want 'to be connected to criminal acts – for obvious moral reasons and practical ones; they could have serious repercussions on any of us. We don't want to be regarded as thieves.' Lenin was contemptuous. He told Martov, 'you don't make revolution wearing kid gloves'.[1]

The dispute reached a head at the Fifth Party Congress in the spring of 1907, again in London. Originally it was to be held in Copenhagen, but the Danish authorities, after initially permitting it, changed their minds and banned the Congress from Denmark when most of the 303 delegates had already arrived. It was hastily moved to London and was fractious from the start. 'The meetings were protracted, stormy, crowded and chaotic,' said Trotsky. Angelica Balabanova, an émigré whom Lenin regarded highly and would later make the head of the Socialist International, found the whole atmosphere ghastly and was depressed 'by the all-absorbing, almost fanatical spirit of factionalism'.

Lenin had invited Gorky to attend as a special guest and when they met the day before the first session on 1 May he told the author: 'Oh, I am so glad that you have come. I have heard you enjoy a good scrap. We will have a fine old scuffle here.' He was right.* The debates were as bitter and full of vitriol as they had been at the London Congress four years earlier when the Party split had emerged. Several times the proceedings were adjourned when fist fights looked like beginning between Mensheviks and Bolsheviks. Many delegates just walked out and left, as did Gorky after a few days, complaining that 'the festive mood at the start soured quickly . . . the fury of the disputes chilled my enthusiasm'.

The most divisive issue was Lenin's 'expropriations', which Martov called 'Vladimir Ilyich's thefts . . . designed to raise money solely for the Bolsheviks for use against us'. Lenin was derisive in reply: 'When I see Social Democrats proudly and smugly declaring "We are not anarchists; we are not thieves and robbers, we are above all that" I ask myself what these people are really saying?' He challenged them with the question of what they were prepared to do for the Revolution. 'Partisan groups and "combat groups" should be free to act . . . but with the least harm to the

* Lenin was concerned that everything should be 'just so' for Gorky in London. He had booked a suite for the writer and Maria Andreyeva at the Imperial Hotel in Bloomsbury. When they checked in Lenin went up to the bedroom, inspected it carefully and found that the sheets were damp. He instructed the hotel management to place the sheets near the gas heater. 'These will have to be aired and dried. We can't have you cold and coughing.'

safety of ordinary citizens, and with the maximum harm to the personal safety of spies, the police, troops, the navy and so on and so forth . . . the authorities generally.'

He came up with convoluted and contradictory arguments to justify the robberies. At one point Maxim Litvinov, among the most intelligent of the early Bolsheviks and invariably a trusted supporter of Lenin, asked him, 'Starik, you always preach that it's right to "expropriate the expropriators". Tell me, if you met Rothschild on the street carrying a heavy purse, would you rob him yourself, threaten him with a revolver and take his purse?' Lenin laughed and replied, 'I don't think so. But if we come to power I would have no hesitation in ordering the nationalisation of Rothschild's banks and his property. But this has to be done legally . . . by the victorious people and their government. As long as the state exists – the proletarian state included – the rule of law is necessary or else everything will crumble and the most primitive instincts will be let loose.' Prophetic words.[2]

Outside the meeting hall, the Congress received the kind of attention from Fleet Street's finest that the Russian revolutionaries had never encountered before. The *Daily Mail* labelled the emigrants 'the alien menace . . . a nameless army from Russia' and called the gathering 'the Congress of Undesirables'. It calculated, more or less accurately as it turned out, that between them the delegates had served well over 650 years in jail, labour camps and Siberian exile. The *Daily Mirror* described the arrival of one delegate as 'a Princess . . . who has assassinated several provincial governors in Russia and always carries a bomb in her muff'. Photographers were keen to take pictures, and delegates turned up in fake beards and other disguises or covered their faces. A reporter who naïvely asked why they did this was told by a Bolshevik that 'the Russian police have long ears and, you see, at some point we will be going back to Russia'. Nevertheless the snappers continued to arrive every day for nearly two weeks of the Congress, most of which was held at the Anarchist Club in Jubilee Street.*

---

* The police kept a close eye on the comings and goings of the delegates. There were several bobbies standing guard outside each day and plain-clothes detectives were watching from nearby streets. At one point the anarchist Prince Kropotkin, invited as an observer by the Bolshevik leadership, recognised Edwin Woodhall, a detective who

The main problem was to find accommodation for so many delegates at the last minute. Several were forced to stay at a doss house in the East End, sharing a cramped hovel with London's drunks, vagrants, criminals and down and outs. Litvinov and Stalin stayed there for two days – at sixpence a night, in a cubicle with a mattress on hard boards – until they found somewhere more salubrious. It was an experience neither forgot.

The move to London had cost so much that the Congress almost had to be wound up early for lack of money. Some wealthy Social Democrat sympathisers suggested that the Party leaders should attend a fundraising dinner for philanthropic industrialists and bankers at the Chelsea studio of the then fashionable society portrait painter Felix Moscheles. Lenin loathed the very idea of the evening, which took place on Sunday 13 May. He described it later as 'almost unendurable . . . a stupid affair'. Neither he nor Gorky had evening clothes, but at least they managed to look relatively smart. Plekhanov, as usual, was impeccably well dressed. Lenin sat through the dinner with millionaires either side of him, barely concealing his ill grace and contempt. His English was rusty and according to audience members he was sometimes difficult to understand. So he spoke in Russian. He told the 'bourgeois and capitalists' who had gathered there that they were his 'class enemies', but nevertheless they should welcome and 'support our revolution in Russia against Tsarism' out of self-interest as well as altruism – 'you will be able to export more goods to a more cultured and free Russia'.

Most of the other Bolsheviks there, some of them in correct evening attire, struck the well-heeled diners as 'wild beasts in a zoological garden'. But one of them came away deeply impressed by Lenin. Constance Garnett, the brilliant and well-connected translator of Chekhov, Turgenev, Tolstoy and Dostoyevsky among others, recalled later that she thought the Bolshevik leader was clearly 'a man of tremendously strong character', though the other Russians at the dinner and the Congress 'were a set of self-righteous crooks'. The dinner raised barely a penny and Lenin vowed that he would never humiliate himself again

over the years of his exile in London had been detailed to follow him. They had become friendly and the Prince introduced the policeman to Lenin. 'This is the Bolshevik leader, the man they have all come to meet.'

by pleading for money from capitalists – a pledge he would break only a very few times over the following years.*

The failure of the dinner meant Lenin had to find money from somewhere to settle the mounting costs of the Congress and to raise the cash to get the delegates home. The German SDLP gave £300, but a generous benefactor unexpectedly turned up. The German-born American soap magnate and philanthropist Joseph Fels, who had lived in London for much of the 1900s, offered to help but wanted to see the Congress in action before he would hand over the large amount of £1,700 to bail out the RSDLP. He wasn't by any means a socialist, but he was highly impressed by seeing Lenin speak – 'this man has a future in Russia,' he declared – and he agreed to loan the Party the money. Lenin gave Fels a personal guarantee it would be paid back.†

The most dramatic of the 'expropriations' was masterminded by Stalin in July 1907, just a few weeks after the London Congress expressly prohibited them and Lenin pledged that he would no longer sanction them. A huge shipment of cash in a bank stagecoach was held up in broad daylight in the centre of the Georgian capital Tiflis (now Tbilisi). The plan was Stalin's and he was watching in the background while his team, led by the bandit Bolshevik Kamo (real name Simon Arshaki Ter-Petrosian), seized money destined for Russia's State Bank in the centre of the city. Fifty innocent bystanders were killed in bomb blasts and from gunshot wounds, and around fifty more were seriously injured. It was by far the biggest of the Bolshevik-inspired thefts and caused a huge stir internationally and within revolutionary parties throughout Europe, but it was one of the least lucrative. In the long run the cost was high. The State Bank was never entirely sure how much

---

* Lenin organised more enjoyable social encounters away from the Congress. He took delegates to some of his old haunts: Speakers' Corner, where the Russians were amazed that people in London could get up and say in public more or less whatever they wanted; Marx's grave in Highgate Cemetery and the British Museum, where he showed them the Elgin Marbles – 'Look at them . . . of course the museum is a hoard of colossal wealth plundered by Britain.'

† And it was – after the Revolution. Fels died in 1914, but in early 1918 Krasin went to London as Lenin's representative and among other duties he returned the £1,700, with ten years' interest, to Fels's heirs.

the robbers got away with. It thought anything between 250,000 and 340,000 rubles – an enormous sum at the time: the latter estimate was worth something over US$4 million at 2016 values. The problem was that most of the cash was in large-denomination notes, which were either marked or their serial numbers were known to the police.

Lenin publicly distanced himself from the crime. But privately he had known all about it before it happened and had approved it. As with the proceeds from other robberies, Stalin handed some of the money personally to Lenin – Kamo presented him with another cache in Geneva – and it was the Bolshevik leader who proposed the idea of using loyal Party members to cash the banknotes in various European cities. The plan backfired spectacularly: the notes were traced and within a few weeks a dozen or so Party activists were arrested, including Kamo.*

Less bloody but equally squalid and morally dubious was the Schmidt Affair. Lenin came up with a plan to swindle two teenage girls out of their inheritance – and, quite possibly, to break their hearts in the process. It is a story that shows Lenin at his most unscrupulous. While in personal financial affairs he was a pillar of rectitude and not at all greedy, in politics he was prepared to lie, steal, cheat and kill for money to further Bolshevik interests. 'Everything that is done in the interests of the proletarian cause is honest,' he told Angelica Balabanova.

Lenin's most generous financial backer, the millionaire Savva Morozov, had had a long history of depressive illness and killed himself in May 1905. Although he had left the RSDLP a sizeable legacy in his will, Lenin had his eye on a still bigger share of the magnate's fortune. Morozov bequeathed much of his money to his nephew, Nikolai Pavlovich

---

* Kamo, a Georgian like Stalin, was a highly colourful figure who frequently appeared even in staid Swiss towns wearing full Circassian costume and brandishing hand guns and sabres. Oddly, Nadya's mother – hardly a bloodthirsty radical – grew fond of him. He used to tell her stories of his dramatic escapades in the Caucasus while he was cleaning his revolvers. He was arrested in Berlin trying to cash one of the large banknotes from the robbery. He avoided prosecution by feigning insanity. He escaped from a mental hospital, returned to Russia, but was arrested again and sentenced to death, later commuted to life imprisonment. Released from jail after the Bolshevik Revolution, he ran a bandit gang in the Civil War against the Whites, but was later given relatively minor jobs in Georgia. Lenin thought he was too unstable for any senior position in the Party or state. He died in a mysterious motor accident in 1922; the suspicion was that Stalin had him killed.

Schmidt, whose family owned a profitable piano factory in Moscow. Schmidt also possessed plenty of money of his own: his father had died in 1902 and he came of age, and in control of his inheritance, in 1904 when he was twenty-one. He was also a supporter of the Social Democrats, though not specifically the Bolsheviks.

Schmidt was arrested at the end of 1905 for 'giving aid to insurgents' from his factory. He was kept without sleep for eight days, faced prolonged interrogation and threatened with summary execution. He confessed to all sorts of revolutionary activities he had nothing to do with, was thrown into a cell in Moscow's gruesome Butyrka Prison and was regularly beaten by guards. His family complained about his treatment but they were ignored. On 12 February 1907 he wrote to one of his sisters that he had suffered 'a terrible night and I fear for the next one'. The next day he was found dead. He had two wounds on his neck, cuts to his hands and severe bruises on his face. The prison authorities insisted that he had committed suicide by cutting his throat with glass after he broke the windows of his cell. But his family were convinced he was murdered. Whatever happened, the circumstances of his death at the age of twenty-three were suspicious.

When Lenin heard the young man had died, he saw an opportunity. He knew Schmidt had two younger sisters, Ekaterina, aged nineteen, and Elizaveta, seventeen, who had also shown an interest in revolutionary politics. They were now heiresses – and a highly attractive 'catch' for a gold digger with ruthless motives. Lenin recruited two handsome young Party activists to seduce and marry the girls who, swept away by romance and the excitement of helping the Revolution, would give their fortune to the Bolsheviks.

To begin with the plan went well. Ekaterina Schmidt fell in love with the dashing and smooth-talking Nikolai Andrikanis; the younger sister, Elizaveta, was swept off her feet by the good-looking but domineering and sinister bully Viktor Taratuta.* There was a dual marriage in Moscow with a guest list that included high society and the radical elite. But then a problem occurred: the course of true love did not run smoothly.

---

* There was also a younger Schmidt brother, a minor aged just fifteen. The idea was that he would be 'persuaded' by his older sisters to renounce his inheritance in favour of the Bolsheviks.

Andrikanis and his bride had second thoughts about handing over the money to Lenin. They gave a small amount to the Party but decamped to Paris and later the South of France, taking the funds with them. Lenin fulminated against this 'great betrayal', but there was little that he could do.[3]

Taratuta fulfilled his mission. Even though Elizaveta was not yet of age and the arrangement was not strictly legal, she agreed to give her share of the inheritance to the Social Democrats. Later, in Paris, the couple handed over a fortune directly to Lenin, who signed a receipt and copied a legal statement – 'I have received from Ekaterina Schmidt two hundred and seventy thousand nine hundred and eighty-four Francs', a sum that in 2016 would have been worth around US$2 million.[4]

Nadya was appalled by the scheme and disgusted by Taratuta, who she said made her flesh crawl. Lenin, as usual, simply saw the affair in utilitarian terms. He told comrades that personally the whole idea revolted him and he wouldn't have had the nerve to go through with it himself – though conscience didn't prevent him hatching the plan in the first place. He admired the 'bravado and chutzpah' of Taratuta. 'He's good in as much as he will stop at nothing,' Lenin confessed to one long-standing comrade. 'Tell me, could you go after a rich merchant lady for her money? No. I wouldn't either. I couldn't conquer myself. But Viktor [Taratuta] could . . . That's what makes him an irreplaceable person.' Later, referring to Taratuta, he said 'a scoundrel might be what we need, just because he is a scoundrel'.[*][5]

This was not the end of the Schmidt inheritance saga. Martov and the Mensheviks claimed a share of the fortune – justifiably, as the money was given to the Social Democratic Party, not just the Bolsheviks, and the Party was still technically one united structure. 'Why should we be cheated by Lenin the pimp and his accomplice Taratuta?' one of their leaders demanded. Lenin tried to keep all the money for the Bolsheviks and the row became increasingly bitter – but, in the dispute that was tearing the RSDLP apart, at least this was now something solid and substantial to quarrel about, rather than mere personal spite. Eventually Lenin agreed to let a group of three worthies, leading names from

---

[*] Lenin frequently quoted a line from Gogol's *The Government Inspector* to justify the employment of crooks, rogues, killers and ruthless rascals: 'A good household makes use even of the garbage.'

the German Social Democratic Party, arbitrate: the celebrated Marxist thinkers Karl Kautsky and Fritz Mehring and the political organiser Clara Zetkin. Lenin was ordered to hand over the money to the triumvirate, though he had taken the precaution of keeping a sizeable amount for the Bolsheviks' sole use.

For years afterwards, in his usual relentless, exhausting way, Lenin pestered the trustees to release more funds to him, writing endless letters and at one point hiring an expensive Paris lawyer. Exasperated, Kautsky couldn't stand the squabbling and quit as a trustee. 'My work is suffering from the great waste of time and energy spent on this hopeless matter,' he told Lenin. The row was never satisfactorily settled. The war intervened, when the money couldn't be disbursed, and after the Revolution the funds were no longer so necessary.[6]

Making revolution was an expensive business and while in exile Lenin always needed money. He controlled the Bolsheviks' finances personally and, secretive as ever, he told nobody exactly how it was spent, not even Nadya. He pored over accounts with immense care and itemised all expenditure in obsessive detail down to the last kopeck. In Switzerland, for example, he paid Party 'salaries' of between 200 and 600 francs a month to about a dozen members of the Bolshevik leadership, his inner circle, depending on their personal circumstances. They were not extravagant amounts but useful to ensure that families could survive. He took 350 francs a month for himself – roughly the amount, he said, of a skilled worker in Western Europe. This was topped up by regular subventions from his mother, who was also helping his sister Maria and, until he could stand on his own feet as a doctor, his younger brother Dmitry. Lenin was never rich and he did not live ostentatiously. Nor was he poor. He earned very little from his journalistic and literary efforts. But somehow he always found enough money to travel when he wanted to – on regular holidays and working trips, lecturing, researching, and attending socialist meetings throughout Europe. Now, coming up to the age of forty, he was still regularly sent money by his mother. Many émigrés lived in dire poverty. But as Nadya told her secretary towards the end of her life, they were not among them. 'They are writing about our lives now as though we were in penury. It's not true. We were never in a position of not being able to afford bread . . . there were some émigrés who had no income for two or three years and got no money from Russia. They really starved. But we were not like that. We lived simply, that's the truth.'

* * *

Lenin returned to Finland from the London Congress in early June 1907 in a state of nervous exhaustion, suffering from blinding headaches, debilitating insomnia and irritability. The 'rages' came upon him regularly and apparently from nowhere. 'The tremendous expenditure of energy demanded by every campaign that Lenin undertook, driving himself and relentlessly urging others onwards, wore him out and drained his strength,' one comrade in his clique said. 'The engine of his will refused to work beyond a certain stage of frenzied tension . . . Following an attack of his rage his energy would begin to ebb, and a reaction set in: dullness, loss of strength and fatigue which laid him out. He could neither eat nor sleep. Headaches tormented him. His face became sallow, the light died in his eyes . . . In such a state he was unrecognisable . . . Then, what was most important, not to have to see anyone, not to talk to anyone.' Gorky saw him in one of these fits of distemper and was frightened for him – 'he looked awful . . . even his tongue seemed to have turned grey'.

Nadya recognised the symptoms and she knew the remedy. She took him somewhere quiet and remote, to Styrs Udde (Stirsudden) by the Gulf of Finland. 'Here there is a pine forest, the sea, magnificent weather, in short everything is excellent,' she wrote to Lenin's mother on 28 June. 'We are bathing, cycling, Volodya plays chess, fetches water, at one time we had a craze for the English game of Donkey [a card game]. We have all put on so much weight that it's not decent to show ourselves in public,' she wrote a few days later. Lenin spent hours simply looking out over the water towards a distant lighthouse, doing nothing. 'He kept dropping off to sleep all the time. When he got to the woods he would sit down under a fir tree and fall asleep at once. The children from the neighbouring cottage called him "sleepy head".' He told his mother and sister Maria: 'The rest I am getting is marvellous, the best I have had in years. No people, nothing to do. No people and nothing to do is the best thing for me.'

Soon, however, he was on the road again, as the Bolshevik representative at the Congress of the Socialist International – an organisation originally founded by Marx – held in Stuttgart at the beginning of August. One of Lenin's great skills, as Martov noted, was 'packing Congresses'

– lobbying for votes, collecting together a caucus, elaborately planning how a debate was to be conducted, making behind-the-scenes deals. Martov, contemptuous of these political realities, meant his comment as a criticism and he used the phrase derisively. But it showed why Lenin succeeded and Martov and the Mensheviks failed. Lenin didn't only use vulgar invective or bully opponents into submission by insults. He could glad-hand other delegates, take an interest in their lives and, when he needed to, could listen: 'he could inspire followers with the personal touch'. He was pragmatic at times and could change tactics 180 degrees when it suited his case – the political arts which Martov and other leading Mensheviks regarded as beneath them, but which were so essential for a practical leader. Above all his logic was persuasive and 'everyone was impressed by his obvious brainpower'. Even Martov's sister Lidia Dan, a committed Menshevik who grew to despise Lenin's politics, saw how skilful he was. 'Lenin knew, he was convinced that he knew, the truth and that this gave him the right not only to win you over but to make you act as he wished, not because he was doing it for himself, but because he knew what was needed. Lenin had this ability to win over and command.'[7]

Lenin regarded the Stuttgart Congress as crucial because, he believed, it would establish a clear socialist line towards the war between the European powers that he was convinced would soon come and which would be, as Marx prophesied, 'the final crisis of capitalism'. Lenin was one of the principal movers behind the famous 'War resolution' in Stuttgart: 'If war threatens to break out, it is the duty of the working class and its representatives to make every effort to prevent it. Should war come, notwithstanding these efforts, it is the duty of the workers and their representatives to intervene to bring about a speedy end to the war and to take advantage of the economic and social crisis, to hasten the transformation of the capitalist society into a socialist one.' All the main leftist parties supported it, including the biggest and most influential by far – as large in terms of membership as all the other socialist parties in Europe put together – the SDLP in Germany. The same resolution was confirmed twice between 1907 and 1914, with the German socialists' support. Lenin was sure that if war began, the socialists would do all they could to persuade the masses – the men who would do the fighting – to refuse to take part.

Two famous German women revolutionaries saw Lenin in action in Stuttgart. Clara Zetkin and Rosa Luxemburg were fascinated and discussed his personality and his hold over the Bolsheviks at length. Zetkin recalled their conversation a year or so later. 'Rosa . . . who possessed an artist's eye for character, pointed him out to me with the remark: "Take a look at him. That is Lenin. Look at the self-willed, stubborn head. A real Russian peasant's head with a few faintly Asiatic lines. That man will try to overturn mountains. Perhaps he will be crushed by them. But he will never yield."'[8]

* * *

Back in Finland, 'reaction was tightening its grip – and looked as if it would drag on for years', said Nadya. The Second Duma was dissolved, which showed the regime's true commitment to parliamentary reforms. There was a fresh wave of detentions and executions and a warrant was issued for Lenin's arrest. 'Vladimir Ulyanov, alias Lenin . . . a writer on economic subjects . . . is the most dangerous and capable of all the revolutionary leaders,' the Okhrana's wanted poster declared. Technically Finland was an autonomous part of the Russian empire and dissidents had been considered safe there. But no longer. Lenin and Nadya began looking for a way back to Geneva.

Nadya and her mother could travel easily by train and boat from Helsingfors. Elizaveta Krupskaya was reluctant to go, but she was becoming increasingly frail and Nadya said, 'we couldn't leave her with no idea of who would look after her'. It was altogether harder for a man on the run like Lenin to escape. The two women went in comfort to Stockholm. At the beginning of December 1907 Lenin hid underground, shaved off his trademark beard and took on another false identity – Professor Müller, a German geologist studying limestone deposits in south-west Finland. He planned to meet them in Sweden later – but he was about to make the most physically hazardous journey of his life, through snow-covered forests and across frozen lakes, with the Okhrana on his tail.

The Bolsheviks had an established escape route from Helsingfors run by a Finnish party cell organised by the one-time head of the *Iskra* smuggling operation in Scandinavia, Vladimir Smirnov. It involved an elaborate series of trains to the port of Åbo, the former capital of Finland, and from there by steamship across the Baltic to Sweden. But the police knew about the route, were keeping close watch on it specifically for Lenin and very nearly caught up with him on a train as it approached Åbo. At one point he had to jump off the moving carriage, throwing his suitcase before him, and hope that a snowdrift would break his fall. He was lucky – because he found deep snow, and because the two Okhrana agents wouldn't risk their lives by following him. He had the address of Party contacts in Åbo and trudged for ten kilometres along an icy country road to reach the city. He arrived, freezing and hungry, at the home of local businessman Walter Borg, a Bolshevik loyalist. 'Lenin could barely feel his feet so we had to take his boots off for him.' Borg's wife Ida gave him hot milk and cognac and had to rub spirit into his hands and feet to get the circulation going.[9]

The Okhrana was keeping an eye on the port, so a new plan was formed to take a boat from Nagu (Nauvo), one of the outlying islands along the Gulf of Finland, where there was a regular steamer ferry to Stockholm. But avoiding the secret police tail involved travelling by horse-drawn cart and by foot thirty kilometres through treacherous terrain in temperatures of around 10 degrees Celsius below zero. 'No matter, I've walked further distances and in bad conditions in Siberia,' he told Party workers who warned him of the dangers of the journey. He was more concerned with the condition of his guides, a local farmer and a sailor from a village near Åbo: it was Christmas time and they were drinking large quantities of local home-brewed grog. Lenin was worried that they didn't look entirely sober. The last three kilometres were by foot across a frozen sound where the locals told Lenin he had to be extra-vigilant. But for Lenin there was no turning back. It was just after dawn on Christmas Day 1907 and a biting wind was blowing when he stepped on the ice. Legend in Finland for many years to come had it that one of the guides, the sailor Gustav Wallstens, saw Lenin cross himself and mutter a prayer before he did, though the Bolshevik leader never admitted to it. At one point as they neared the other side of the sound Lenin felt his feet give way and he feared he would slip into the sea. Wallstens reached out his hand and pulled Lenin to safety, but it was a close-run thing. He told Nadya the next day when they were reunited in Stockholm that he was convinced that he had met his end, drowned in the Finnish water. 'What a stupid way to have to die.'[10]

20

GENEVA – 'AN AWFUL HOLE'

'Life in exile and squabbling are inseparable. Living in the midst of
. . . these squabbles and scandals, this hell and ugly scum is sickening.
To watch it all is sickening, too. Émigré life is now a hundred times
worse than it was before 1905.' Lenin to Gorky, 11 April 1910

'Lenin cannot tolerate any other person with brains.'
Nikolai Bukharin (1888–1938)

On 3 January 1908 Lenin and Nadya broke their journey from Stockholm to Geneva in Berlin. The plan was to stay just one night, but after
they had dinner with Rosa Luxemburg they returned to their hotel 'feeling horribly ill'. This wasn't because Lenin and Luxemburg had bitter
disagreements at the restaurant – the brilliant German feminist and revolutionary was appalled by his 'rigid centralism . . . a socialism that has
no positive and creative spirit, but the sterile spirit of the overseer',she
told him. Both Nadya and Lenin had contracted food poisoning from
some fish. 'We both had white foam at the lips and a kind of weakness
had seized us,' Nadya said. 'A doctor had to be summoned at night . . .
[Volodya] was registered as a Finnish cook and I as an American citizen.
Therefore the chambermaid fetched an American doctor. First he examined him and said it was a very serious business. Then he looked at
me and said, "Well, you'll live." Guessing that something was not quite
right he overcharged us outrageously for the visit. We hung about . . .
[in Berlin] for an extra couple of days and then we dragged ourselves on,
half ill, to Geneva.'

They found a 'cold, cheerless' room in a boarding house and after a
day back in Switzerland Lenin told Nadya, 'I feel like I've come back to
Geneva to be buried.' A week later he wrote to Lunacharsky, 'it is devilishly sad to return to this accursed Geneva, but there's no other way

out', and the next day in a letter to his sister Maria he complained again. 'We have been hanging about in this damned Geneva for several days. It is an awful hole, but there's nothing we can do. We will get used to it.'*

Nadya said that she had never seen him so depressed. 'He had become more reserved . . . more reflective and when interrupted in reveries one seemed to catch a glint of sadness in his eyes. We found it difficult to get accustomed to life again in exile. Vladimir Ilyich spent his days in the library, but in the evenings we didn't know what to do with ourselves. We did not feel like sitting in that room . . . we longed to be among people and every evening we would go to the cinema or the theatre, although we rarely stayed to the end but left in the middle of the performance and would go wandering off. During these most difficult times . . . he sustained himself by dreaming.'[1]

He was at a low ebb, politically and personally. The crackdown against socialists continued; thousands had been killed, arrested and exiled. Lenin was beginning to realise how deeply the Okhrana had penetrated the revolutionary cells. 'Work in Russia . . . has become a spy-infested shambles,' he said. He had a grudging respect for Stolypin – 'a very smart politician who understands the need for modern economic development in Russia. He may know how to win . . . he is winning,' Lenin said. He thought Stolypin's 'carrot and stick' policy, of brutal repression against dissidents but economic reforms on the land, could 'transform Russia into a middle-class monarchy and if this continues for long it will force us to renounce any socialist agrarian plans at all . . . it is clever'.†

---

* However, years later, after the Revolution, he told an audience in St Petersburg that 'of all the places I have been in my wanderings, for convenience I would select London and Geneva as the best places to be'.

† Many historians have believed the same thing: that given time Stolypin's reforms would have worked and turned Russia into a modern bourgeois state, avoiding bloody revolution. He proposed to modernise local government and the police, improve schooling for the poor and repeal discriminatory laws against Jews and other minorities. But it is a 'counterfactual' hypothesis and seems very unlikely. The most important part of his programme was land reform, but most peasants resented the new land ownership regulations which benefited only the better-off farmers. The majority boycotted his agrarian policy to introduce small privately owned plots of land to replace the 'communes' – a system of joint land ownership that had existed for centuries. The Tsar and his royal court of arch-reactionaries grew to hate Stolypin and withdrew their support for him. Stolypin's policies were visibly failing and his relationship with the Tsar had broken down well before he was assassinated.

Lenin had a small, loyal following in exile, but the numbers had trickled to very few and he had to start building a new network almost from scratch. Stolypin's clampdown against opposition had nearly destroyed the revolutionary groups within Russia. At the high point of the 1905 uprising there was a combined membership of an estimated 140,000 – of either the Socialist Revolutionaries, the biggest single group, or the two wings of the Social Democrats; now in 1908 there were less than 7,000. Many had returned to their former lives. Thousands of Bolsheviks and Mensheviks simply gave up political activism because of the continuing bitter split within the RSDLP. 'These were days we spent more time waiting for letters from home . . . than reading or writing them,' Nadya said.[2]

With Gorky's help, Lenin managed to find the wherewithal to start another new organ, *Proletarii*, a lively, well-produced paper which published contributors from all sections of the radical movement. It was respected among émigrés, with a monthly circulation of about 10,000, but had very few readers inside Russia. Press censorship had returned, and though it was slightly less rigorous than before, Bolshevik publications were banned and there was no longer a smuggling operation as there had been for *Iskra*. 'Life returned to the way it had been in Geneva,' Nadya told Lenin's mother. He went to the library in the morning, produced journalism in the afternoon and conducted Party affairs the rest of the time. He travelled extensively around Western Europe lecturing to socialist groups. But his influence was limited. Lenin as a practical politician and by experience was a cynic. The great paradox is that by nature, as a personality, he was an optimist. It was hope and optimism that drove his belief in revolution. At this point – 'the worst year in my life,' he described it later – he admitted for the first time to doubts. 'Shall I live to see another revolution?' he asked his sister Maria in some despair.[3]

The feud with Martov and the Mensheviks continued. There were repeated efforts to heal the split, but they never came to anything. Invariably it was Lenin who made sure there would be no reconciliation 'with those scoundrel Martovites' or the 'verminous Mensheviks'. Occasionally Lenin would make a move to reach an accommodation with his opponents, but he was never trusted. As Plekhanov put it, 'Lenin desires Unity as a man desires unity with a piece of bread: he swallows it.' At one point the venerable August Bebel, a co-founder of the German Social Democratic Party, who had met Marx and was a good friend of Engels, made an effort to restore diplomatic relations between the two sides. The effort exhausted him. Exasperated, he told Lenin, 'What can one do? You are children and won't get anywhere until you grow up.' Lenin's reaction was to shrug his shoulders.[4]

A new split was opening up among Russia's Marxists, and Lenin, predictably, was the principal figure trying to widen this division too. The issue on the face of it was over an obscure and abstruse aspect of Marxist theory. But to Lenin it was again a personal matter about leadership. The row this time was within his own Bolshevik faction – a groupuscule within the group – but Lenin didn't mind how small his band of followers was as long as he had some who would do his bidding. He saw a potential rival in Alexander Bogdanov, three years younger than him, tall, burly, 'a gentle giant with a sweet nature, with a sparklingly original mind'. He had trained as a physician and studied philosophy at Moscow University. He wrote some interesting science fiction. He was drawn to Marxism and joined a radical 'reading circle' allied to the RSDLP, which was enough to get him exiled to Siberia for three years. In the Party split of 1903 he joined the Bolsheviks.

Bogdanov started developing new ideas that tried to fuse Marxism with a kind of mystic spiritualism designed to appeal to Christians and other religious people. It regarded manual labour as a religious rite and turned the masses of workers into God-like beings. Lenin thought the theory was utter hocus pocus, 'dangerous garbage', and had to be challenged 'from a philosophical, a Marxist, point of view'. More important, he was spoiling for a fight and Bogdanov had to be seen off as a potential rival for the Bolshevik leadership. Gorky was interested in Bogdanov's theories and Lunacharsky, whom Lenin liked and valued, had been converted to Bogdanov's 'God-building' notions. In reality Bogdanov was never a serious threat: as a political tactician he was as hopeless, if not more so, than Martov, and though brilliant in his way he was a dilettante, never plausible as a leader. But Lenin was taking no chances.

Gorky invited Lenin to stay for a few days in April 1908 at his villa on Capri. He told him that Bogdanov, 'an extremely talented person with a mild character', would also be there and he wanted the two of them to talk in a relaxed way and discuss their differences. Lenin was reluctant to dispute directly with Bogdanov in front of Gorky and at first he said he did not have the time to go. But when Gorky asked again he grudgingly agreed, though warning his host that 'listening to that Bogdanovite drivel makes me swear like a fishwife'. Nadya didn't wish to go and stayed behind in Geneva.[5]

Gorky and Maria Andreyeva rented the Villa Blaesus, a sprawling mansion high on a cliff on the south of the island with vistas of the Marina on one side and the famous Gardens of Augustus on the other.[*] Lenin was given a luxurious room with a magnificent sea view next to Gorky's splendid library. The writer told friends later that he was appalled by Lenin's rudeness to Bogdanov. 'Vladimir Ilyich stood before me even more firm and more inflexible than he had been at the London Congress . . . he was rather cold and in a mocking mood, stern in philosophical conversations and altogether on the alert.' Gorky wanted to help start a school on Capri that taught Bogdanov's spiritual/Marxist theories.[†] He hoped Lenin would give lectures there and contribute to a book of essays in new interpretations of Marxism that he wanted to get published. Lenin would have nothing to do with this 'total philosophical rubbish . . . this religious atheism'. He told Bogdanov and Gorky, 'Why should we be offered this type of stuff as Marxist philosophy? I'd rather let myself be hanged and quartered than take part in any publication or in any group that preaches this kind of thing.'

Marxism was a 'materialist' philosophy and to Lenin religion insulted a rational person's intelligence. 'Those who live by the labour of others are taught by religion to practise charity on earth, thus offering them a very cheap way of justifying their entire existence as exploiters, and selling them at a moderate price to well-being in heaven. Religion is opium for people. Religion is a sort of spiritual booze in which the slaves of capital drown their human image, their demand for a life more or less worthy of men.' In a letter to Gorky after his stay on Capri Lenin wrote:

---

[*] The beautiful villa, relatively newly built, was owned by the Capresan Settani family, but Gorky lived there for most of the period between mid-1906 and the end of 1909. It was later owned by the Krupp family, the German steel magnates who helped to finance the Nazi Party.

[†] Known as Machism, after the Austrian physicist and philosopher Ernst Mach who first suggested some of the ideas in the 1890s, later adapted by Bogdanov.

'Any religious idea, any idea of any God at all, even any flirtation with a God, is the most inexpressible foulness, a dangerous foulness ... Isn't God-building the worst form of self-humiliation? Everyone who sets about building up a God, or who even tolerates such an activity, humiliates himself in the worst possible way ... because he is actually engaged in self-contemplation, self-admiration. From the point of view not of the individual but of society, all God-building is the fond self-deception of the thick-witted, the philistine, the dreamy self-humiliation of the vulgar bourgeois.'[6]

There was no room for compromise with Bogdanov. On the other hand there was plenty of time for relaxation on Capri. He swam and walked and saw the sites. 'The Blue Grotto is beautiful,' he wrote to his mother, 'though it is "dramatic" in the sense that it could be scenery in a theatre. On the way here I thought about the Volga all the time. The beauty there is of a different kind; it is simpler and dearer to me.' He played chess with Bogdanov, who once managed to beat him.*

Lenin showed Gorky the other side of his nature. 'At the same time there was in Capri another Lenin – a wonderful companion and light-hearted person with a lively and inexhaustible interest in the world around him, and very gentle in his relations with people. He showed a lively interest in everything.' Most days he was on the island he would go out with the local fishermen. He would quiz them on their lives – how much they were paid, their families, their education, their beliefs. Maria Andreyeva would go with him to the nearby harbour and act as his interpreter. In his way Lenin possessed the common touch and he became friendly with two elderly brothers, Giovanni and Francesco Sparado, who taught him how to fish without a rod, by using his finger and thumb along the line to feel if a fish had taken the bait. 'Così, drin drin,' they would say, 'Like this. Understand?' When after a few attempts he landed a mullet he laughed and continually used the phrase 'drin, drin' for six days. The name seemed to stick and

---

* Gorky said that he took the loss badly and was in a foul mood afterwards. But this is the only record of Lenin being a bad loser at chess. Others said he was a perfect gentleman at the board, win or lose, and he was always happy to talk in a friendly way afterwards about the game. On this occasion it might have been more about the opponent against whom he lost.

locals on the island referred to him as 'Signor Drin Drin'.*

Gorky returned with Lenin to the mainland and together they climbed Vesuvius and visited Pompeii. Despite the author's efforts, though, he couldn't persuade Lenin to tone down his invective against Bogdanov. He spent the best part of the next year writing a long book, *Materialism and Empirio-Criticism*, lambasting Bogdanov and mounting a campaign to get him expelled from the Social Democratic Party. For Lenin, Bogdanov's religious views were heretical – and heresy had to be rooted out among his Bolsheviks.[7]

* * *

In Geneva, contacts with Bolshevik activists inside Russia were few and far between – a frustration for Lenin and especially for Nadya, who as the official 'Party Secretary' was responsible for building up networks of agents communicating with 'the Bolshevik centre'. It was a thankless task; so many had been arrested and the smuggling routes that had existed between Russia and the West before 1905 were closed down by the Okhrana. They sometimes waited weeks for any signs of clandestine mail. There were plenty of Russians in Swiss exile but few were Bolsheviks, and the hosts were tiring of their noisy, often bibulous and ever-squabbling Russian guests. Once a giant, rough-looking comrade from Georgia, Mikhail Tskhakaya, arrived at Lenin's home in suburban Geneva dressed in colourful Caucasian costume, complete with elaborate headdress, 'looking the picture of a brigand', as the terrified landlady recalled. In several Swiss cities signs appeared in lodging houses reading 'No Cats. No Dogs. No Russians.'

The émigrés formed tight communities, even though Bolsheviks, Mensheviks and SRs generally kept apart from each other. New arrivals from 'home', who had once been welcomed, were now distrusted. Nadya was the first to suspect that the Okhrana was redoubling its efforts to plant double agents inside the revolutionary movements. Two members from St Petersburg, the Komissarovs, made themselves known to her. 'The first moment, a strange feeling came over me, a kind of acute

---

* Giovanni Sparado long remembered Lenin – 'only a good man could laugh like that', he used to tell Gorky. For some years he would ask any Russians whether they knew what happened to Signor Drin Drin. 'You know . . . Signor Lenin. Has the Tsar caught up with him?'

mistrust. I could not think where this feeling came from and it soon disappeared. Katya Komissarov proved to be a very businesslike assistant, did everything quickly, accurately – and with great secrecy.' She and her husband helped to smuggle some arms into a Bolshevik cell in the Urals and knew the identities of illegal comrades, supplying them with passports. Soon afterwards the arms were confiscated and all the revolutionaries she had been in contact with were arrested as they tried to cross the frontier into Western Europe. 'All the groups [inside Russia] were riddled with informers,' Nadya admitted. 'There was not a single local organisation into which some provocateur had not crept. Every man regarded his comrade with suspicion, was on guard against those nearest to him, did not trust his neighbour.'*8

Lenin and Nadya did trust two Bolsheviks who had emigrated to the West before 1905 and became Lenin's most loyal collaborators and friends from this point on – in emigration and after the Revolution, in power. The three of them were called 'The Troika' among the other exiles. Grigory Zinoviev was probably the man closest to Lenin for the longest, and his intense, clever and pretty blonde wife Zina Lilina became one of Nadya's most intimate confidantes. Over the next nine years they were neighbours wherever exile took them, sometimes sharing a house. Born Hirsch Apfelbaum on a small farm in Ukraine, Zinoviev, thirteen years younger than Lenin, was stocky, clean-shaven, short-winded and had a high-pitched voice. He was a supreme sycophant, famously cynical, who did a lot of Lenin's dirty work for him. The Mensheviks called him 'Lenin's arms bearer', and he didn't seem to mind being mistrusted and disliked.

Angelica Balabanova, a highly moral comrade admired by Lenin for her 'innocence', hated the incessant back-stabbing among the Bolsheviks and described Zinoviev as 'simply the most despicable human being I ever met. Whenever there was an unfair factional manoeuvre to

---

* The Okhrana scored major successes against the revolutionary groups, but many observers thought the agency was highly overrated, not least by itself. The British secret agent Robert Bruce Lockhart, who worked with the Okhrana closely a few years later when he was Britain's top-ranking agent in Russia, said: 'I refuse to believe either in its efficiency or its honesty. The "dreaded" Okhrana . . . was a myth fearful more by its name than by its omniscience. It was an organisation run by bunglers and clever crooks, and in it the bunglers outnumber the brains by nine to one.'

be made or a revolutionary reputation to be undermined, Lenin would charge Zinoviev with the task.' However, he was transformed when he was on a speaking platform, from a lickspittle apparatchik into a highly effective orator – the most compelling speaker, after Lenin, among the Bolshevik leaders before the Revolution. Lenin found him useful and efficient, writing to him as 'Dear Grigory' rather than using his second name as with most of his lieutenants. Zinoviev was an Everest of pomposity, lacked any insight or anything amusing to say, but he usually did what he was told. Lenin couldn't do without him, but found him boring.

Lev Borisovich Kamenev was in many ways the most attractive of the clique around Lenin. By comparison with the others he was decent, and seemed to have a conscience and a good sense of humour. He loathed the bear-baiting that passed for debate within the Social Democrats. Married to Leon Trotsky's sister Olga, he was heavily built, richly bearded and had an avuncular look, even though he was only twenty-five when the Lenins returned to Geneva in 1908. He could tell a good anecdote, enjoyed gossip and could sometimes make Lenin laugh.* They disagreed often, but Lenin liked him – even when the rows became vicious, which they frequently did in later years. Lenin was exasperated by his 'weakness', but respected him. He was a Bolshevik by conviction, but lacked the harshness and the 'killer instinct' of the ruthless revolutionaries around him. Lunacharsky said that Kamenev 'was regarded as a comparatively gentle person, in view of his remarkable good nature. This was praise rather than a rebuke, but it is also true that compared to the others . . . he was apt to waver.'[9]

Unfortunately for Lenin and Nadya, they trusted another member of their close circle, a physician named Yakov Zhitomirsky, who had been in high positions within the Party for years. Lenin had relied on him as a 'man of confidence' who could be used for delicate tasks. He had put him on the arrangements committee of the Brussels conference in 1903, where the Bolshevik/Menshevik split began to surface. Zhitomirsky was also an Okhrana agent – known as Harting to the police in Germany, where he was a wanted man for an alleged attempted bombing in

---

* But not his brother-in-law. Trotsky couldn't bear Kamenev, despite the family relationship, and the feeling was mutual. Trotsky thought Kamenev weak and woolly.

Berlin. He moved to France, where he became a Chevalier of the Légion d'Honneur. He had been handed a 500-ruble note by Lenin – foolishly as it turned out – and he told the Okhrana that Kamo had led the bank raid in Tiflis. It was Zhitomirsky's tip-off that led to Kamo's arrest.

Now Zhitomirsky, the Russians' top agent in Switzerland, was influential in persuading Lenin to leave Geneva and move to Paris: 'in a large city there will be less spying and you'll be less of a target', he told the Bolshevik leader. According to Nadya, 'the argument was convincing to Ilyich', though he must have known that the Okhrana had a big presence in France. On 14 December 1908 they left Geneva for Paris. 'We hope that a large city will cheer us up a little,' he told his mother the day before he left. 'We are sick of sitting in this provincial backwater. Life is so dull in this petit-bourgeois town.'

Zhitomirsky informed the Okhrana Paris office exactly when Lenin would be arriving in the French capital and where he would be staying.[10]

21

INESSA – LENIN IN LOVE

'I can see her now coming out of Lenin's apartment. She seemed to be an inexhaustible spring of life. She was the fiery flame of revolution – and the red feather in her hat was like the tongue of that flame.'

Grigory Kotov

She was by far the most glamorous of all the Russian émigrés in the radical circles of Paris. A sophisticated, chic thirty-five-year-old with a slim figure, chestnut hair and bright-green eyes, she was exuberant, highly intelligent, witty and invariably wore a smile on her face. Inessa Armand was altogether different, more striking and vibrant, more overtly sexy, than the run-of-the-mill Olgas and Tatianas who frequented the Bolshevik cafés and bistros of the Avenue d'Orléans. Even her French-sounding name had a hint of the exotic. She could talk as easily about the latest couture fashions as she did about Marx's theory of surplus value – and fluently, in four languages. She dressed elegantly, always with a Parisian hat, and played the piano beautifully. She cut a dash like no other among the comrades of the Left Bank; Party members described her as 'ever cheerful' and spoke of her 'happy dynamism'. Nadya said that when she arrived 'all of us became very attached to Inessa . . . she always appeared to be in good spirits . . . she seemed to radiate warmth'. Another observed that 'Inessa by her own admission did everything in life with passion – revolutionary politics and romance.'[1]

She first met Lenin towards the end of May 1909 at the Café Aux Manilleurs on the Avenue d'Orléans in the *quartier* around Montparnasse where the leftists in Paris congregated. She had gone to a socialist meeting with an old émigré friend, Elena Stasova, and heard him speak for the first time. She knew him by reputation and had read his books.

She had joined the Bolshevik faction of the RSDLP. She admired him as an intellectual and was enthused by his talk that evening, but he didn't initially attract her as a man. 'I loved you but I wasn't "in love" with you then . . . I was a little in awe of you,' she admitted to him later. She said she was surprised by his odd manner of meeting people, caused by his short-sightedness, when he would look eyeball to eyeball with an interlocutor and then screw up one of his eyes into a squint. Their relationship took time to develop.

It was more than eighteen months before a love affair started, though they saw each other often at Paris cafés and Party meetings. Over that period she had become an ardent Bolshevik – none would be more loyal to him over the next decade – and he had begun to entrust her with increasingly important political work. She interpreted for him in French, a language in which he was never comfortable, and sometimes in English. Quickly he could see she was intelligent enough, and agile enough in debate, to represent him at a series of meetings in France and elsewhere in Europe. He made her head of the Bolsheviks' International Bureau. She was the Bolshevik representative to the French Socialist Party, a big responsibility at the time, as so many Russian Party members were living in France.* Inessa had an incisive mind, she was beautiful, she was exciting, she was an experienced woman of the world who had few bourgeois hang-ups about female sexuality – and Lenin was smitten. Charles Rappaport, an English socialist living in Paris who saw them together frequently in Paris cafés, said that Lenin 'with his little Mongol eyes was mesmerised by Inessa . . . he couldn't stop looking at her'.[2]

There had barely been a hint of scandal surrounding Lenin and other women before he fell for Inessa. When he returned to Russia after the 1905 Revolution he occasionally met up with Elizabeth de K, a young, blonde society hostess with moderate leftist views who had allowed him to use her large apartment in St Petersburg for clandestine meetings. Sometimes when the meetings were over he would stay to talk; once she played the piano for him – his favourite piece, Beethoven's Pathétique Sonata. But they were never lovers, as she repeatedly stressed. Lenin

---

* Lenin asked her to translate into French the speech he made at the funeral of Paul Lafargue and his wife, in 1911, which he considered highly important – Laura Lafargue was Marx's daughter.

tried to convert her to Marxism but failed, and after that he seemed to lose interest in her. 'There were days when I wasn't sure whether he was a man or machine,' she told an acquaintance later.[*3]

By contrast with Inessa, the years had not been kind to Lenin's forty-year-old wife. She looked much older than her age. Lidia Dan, Martov's engaging sister who loathed Lenin but was fond of Nadya, said that even if she had been no great beauty 'her plainness was illuminated by her charm . . . her good nature'. Now she was frumpy and had let herself go. She had put on a lot of weight and she showed other disturbing symptoms of the thyroid complaint she had been suffering from for some years, which would soon be diagnosed as Graves' Disease: her eyes bulged and her neck swelled. But she had made no effort with her appearance, either because she thought it was too bourgeois a thing to concern herself with or because she was in such low spirits. 'The Paris years', she said later, 'were the most trying of our time in exile.'

She always wore the same black dress in winter and a lighter one in summer; the only concession she made to fashion was occasionally to change the trimming on her hat, another long-time friend, Clara Zetkin, recalled. 'She looked like a tired-out wife of a worker forever worrying whether she would manage to get everything done that she had intended.' The Okhrana agent who kept a watch on her in Paris was perhaps a shade harsh, but fairly objective when in one of his reports he described her as 'only around forty but with medium-brown hair, stoops, grey eyes, small nose, thin lips. Dressed always slovenly.'[4]

Throughout their marriage there were periods when Nadya and Lenin shared a bed, and others when they slept separately. During a large part of their Paris years, as friends such as the ever-loyal Bolshevik Lidia Fotieva, who later became Lenin's secretary in the Kremlin, said, Nadya

---

* After the Revolution, some émigré White officers forged a cache of letters which suggested that this fleeting *tendresse* was a torrid affair, but it was an amateurish hoax. Another fiction was the claim – again from White sources in the early 1920s – that while in exile in Paris Lenin frequented a brothel, where he was a loudmouth drunk who talked about women. A Russian émigré painter apparently used to accompany the Bolshevik leader, 'and we shared our women . . . Lenin was very gay and very good-natured but in matters of love he was absolutely voracious.' This has the ring of absolute untruth. Even in the unlikely event that he had visited such an establishment, he would surely have been careful never to have been found out.

was sleeping in her mother's room. In September 1911, a few months after Lenin and Inessa became lovers, Inessa moved into an apartment a few doors along the street from them in the Rue Marie-Rose.

Elisabeth Inès Armand was born on 8 May 1874, though over the years a few other dates were given by her or her family and comrades to confuse police and immigration authorities in various European countries. She was born in Paris, but barely lived there until she returned as a Bolshevik activist in her thirties.

Her mother, Nathalie Wild, was partly English, partly Scottish, partly French and partly Russian. She made a modest living as an actress and a singing teacher in Lyon and later in Paris. Inessa's father was Théodore Pécheux d'Herbenville, a moderately successful French opera singer who often worked under the stage name Théodore Stephane. The couple married soon after Inessa was born, so technically Inessa had been illegitimate; they split up when Inessa was five and her father died soon afterwards.

Nathalie was left with three young daughters to look after – Inessa was the middle of the trio – and they were almost penniless. To ease the financial burden, when Inessa was six her mother's sister Sophie took her to live with her in Russia – the French quarter of Moscow was thriving at that time. Her aunt became a music tutor to the Armand family of rich Franco-Russian textile manufacturers, who employed more than 1,200 workers at a factory in Moscow. Inessa spent a great deal of time with the Armand children at their estate near the village of Pushkino, thirty kilometres north-east of the city.

The eldest Armand son, Alexander Evgenevich, five years older than Inessa, fell in love with her and when she was nineteen they married, at a big society wedding attended by the Moscow business elite. Inessa settled down to what appeared to be a normal, privileged upper-middle-class life. Alexander was a thoroughly decent man of liberal views, generous, a loving husband. She gave birth to four children, two boys and two girls, in eight years. She seemed content, but something was missing in her life, she told friends. She needed a cause to strive for and something to believe in. She began a course of serious reading: the classics of philosophy, history and political economy, unusual subjects for a well-to-do woman of her environment and upbringing.

She became a convinced, passionate feminist. She joined the Moscow Society for Improving the Lot of Women, which among other good works tried to rehabilitate prostitutes. Inessa at this stage was a great admirer of Tolstoy. One of the other members of her group had the idea of writing to the esteemed writer and asking what he thought could be done about the social problem of prostitution, which was destroying the lives of so many Russian women. He had expertise in this area: as a young man he had been a famously enthusiastic customer of courtesans – and, just as famously afterwards, he had 'reformed' and become a moral arbiter of the nation's conscience. He replied: 'Nothing will come of your work. It was thus before Moses, it was thus after Moses. Thus it was, thus it will be.' Inessa was disgusted and gave up on Tolstoy. She became interested in socialism. Lenin's bulky and prolix *The Development of Capitalism in Russia* was on her reading list and she said later that it was one of the books that converted her to Marxism.

Her internal life was going through a revolution too. If she seemed to be living in harmony with her husband, she had started a love affair with another man – Alexander's younger brother Vladimir. He was just seventeen, newly enrolled as a student at Moscow University; she was twenty-eight, the mother of four young children. In 1903 she left her husband for her brother-in-law, taking the children with her.

Alexander continued to maintain Inessa and the children generously. He supported her various causes, bailed her out when she was in trouble with the police and jailed; twice in the future he would help her to escape from prison and exile. He looked after the children when she was unable to and he always kept a home open for her in Pushkino, and a flat in Moscow. He was always a friend, the most tolerant of husbands and a compassionate father. He later took a mistress himself, but admitted that he had always been in love with Inessa, however erratic her behaviour appeared to be. He was never a revolutionary, though he never complained about Inessa's political life and understood her total commitment to the cause.

The lovers left Russia for a tour of Italy, France and Switzerland – paid for by Alexander – where she became pregnant with Vladimir's child. Back in Russia she bore a son, André, and grew even more active in politics. Alexander had managed to keep the secret police off her trail, with a mixture of persuasion and bribery. But eventually the Okhrana caught up with her. She was arrested for running a library of illegal books. Despite being a mother of five young children, including a baby, she was jailed in a notoriously harsh prison and then sentenced to exile in the frozen north, at a godforsaken place near Archangel.

Vladimir, who was also deeply implicated in subversive politics, followed her, but he became seriously ill with tuberculosis. He went to the South of France for treatment. However he was too far gone with the disease and there was no cure to be found. At the beginning of 1909 she escaped from exile, hid briefly in St Petersburg, and with her husband's help managed, after a dramatic journey across frozen lakes in Finland, to reach Vladimir in Nice. Two weeks after the lovers were reunited, he died in her arms.

Heartbroken and unable to return to Russia, she sent for her children to join her. She enrolled at the New University in Brussels, which had started teaching one of the most highly regarded economics courses in Europe, though she managed to do most of her reading and written work in Paris. She completed a three-year course in eighteen months and qualified with merit. She settled into the émigré underground world, in her case quite comfortably on her husband's money, started making a new life for herself, and found a new love – Lenin.[5]

Lenin said that 'most of the émigrés went to seed as soon as they arrived in Paris. Only the strongest survived. The rest were destroyed by petty feuds, domestic quarrels, poverty – and alcohol.' Lenin survived, but he never liked Paris, despite the presence in his life there of Inessa. He had wanted to get out of the 'backwater' of Geneva and looked forward to living in a big city. But typically, as soon as he got to one he began complaining. 'God, Paris is a rotten hole,' he told his sister Anna after a few days in France – the word 'hole' being one of his favourite terms of abuse about a place; at various times in his voluminous letters he calls Paris, Geneva, London, Berlin, Zurich, Berne and Moscow 'a hole'. He wrote to his mother after a few weeks, 'I can't understand what on earth made us go to Paris. I have still not been able to adapt myself.'

For a start it was then one of the most expensive cities in Europe. The cost of living was far higher than in Switzerland, which at that time, with no banking industry and no manufacturing base, was a poor country,

cheap to live in. At first Lenin and Nadya moved into the most extravagant and ornate apartment that they ever took during their marriage
– four big rooms in an elegant building next to the Parc Montsouris.
There was a room each for Nadya's mother and for his sister Maria,
who lived with them for a few months. By Lenin and Nadya's standards
it was luxurious. There were gilt mirrors above marble mantelpieces,
chandeliers, parquet floors. Nadya loathed it and felt uncomfortable.
'He . . . [Volodya] took only a very remote part in the efforts we were
making to fix up our new quarters,' she told his mother. 'He had more
important things to do. The contempt with which the concierge looked
upon our white deal table, common chairs and stools was worth seeing.
In our "parlour" we had only a couple of chairs and a small table. It was
not at all cosy.'

Prices were exorbitant, she said. A visitor from Russia who arrived
for tea asked her what the cost of goose and veal was in the city, and
her reply was not in her usual mild manner. 'During our time in Paris,
we didn't eat either. Had he interested himself in the price of horsemeat and lettuce I could have helped him.' Maria Alexandrovna sent
food parcels from Russia, along with money, to tide them over. They
received delicacies that reminded them of home, including his favourite
fish: smoked sturgeon fillets, Russian salmon, caviar. He thanked her
profusely. 'We are greatly enjoying these little dainties and thinking of
the Volga as we eat them.'[6]

After six months they moved to more modest accommodation of the
kind they were used to: two rooms and a kitchen/dining room on the
second floor of a classic Paris apartment building, in a quiet street off
the Boulevard Montparnasse. It was sparsely furnished but scrupulous-
ly clean and well ordered, and as usual they lived in simple bourgeois
style, set apart from the other émigrés. Ilya Ehrenburg, then a young
student but a skilled reporter who would become one of the best-known
journalists in the Soviet Union, 'was struck by how neat everything was
in the apartment. The books were ordered in the shelves. Lenin's desk
was tidy.' His lodgings were not like those of the other exile Russian
revolutionaries he had seen, and nor was Lenin himself, who was usually neatly dressed. 'He wore a dark suit with a stiff white collar. And
looked very respectable.' Madame Rue, the concierge, said – not entirely perceptively – that they 'must have led bleak lives. Imagine . . . they

did not have any human weaknesses. Monsieur Ulyanov neither drank nor smoked. He went out to the library or to a meeting and that was all.'

Lenin seldom moved in the bohemian world of 1900s Paris, where artists like Chagall, Juan Gris, Diego Rivera, Vlaminck, Soutine, Modigliani* and Léger all worked in a golden period for painting – and drank at the Café Rotonde, near St Germain des Prés. Once he played chess with the Belgian poet and artist Guillaume Apollinaire.

On the whole he found it difficult to get down to serious literary work in Paris; he wrote no important book there, and though he churned out journalism at his usual furious rate, little of it was memorable. He hated the Bibliothèque Nationale – 'inferior in every way to the British Museum . . . now that is a wonderful institution, the best library in the world to work in'. By contrast, the Paris library closed for two hours at lunchtime; the staff were 'rude and unhelpful' and the books he had asked for took an age to arrive from the stacks. 'He complained about the Bibliothèque all the time,' said Nadya.[7]

Both of them developed a great interest in that very French hobby of the time, cycling. Lenin was obsessed with cleaning the bikes and making sure they were well oiled, the tyres pumped full of air, and they would take off regularly to the Paris *bois*, to Fontainebleau, St Germain-en-Laye and, Nadya's favourite, the Forêt de Meudon. Lenin would sometimes go much further, getting up at the crack of dawn and returning late at night, having cycled for seventy or so kilometres.

He was in a state of fury when one afternoon he found his precious bicycle – bought for him by his mother – had been stolen. He used to leave it in the basement of a building near the library and paid the concierge ten centimes a day. When he discovered it had disappeared she shrugged her shoulders and said he had been paying to leave the bicycle there, not for her to watch out for it. 'He railed against the library, against concierges – against Paris.'[†]

---

* Although he did meet Modigliani once. The artist set fire to a paper Lenin was reading – accidentally or not is unclear – and Lenin had to put out the flame. The artists who occasionally went to hear him speak regarded him as a 'cranky extremist' according to the English landscape painter and later famous war artist Christopher Nevinson.

† He bought a replacement bicycle but that, too, came to an unfortunate end. Lenin had become fascinated by airplanes: Louis Blériot's first crossing of the English Channel was in 1909, seven months or so after he arrived in Paris. He regularly went to see

The endless 'fetid squabbling', he said, was 'unbearable' – though he was one of the most determined and loudest squabblers of them all. 'Life was full of turmoil in Paris . . . Our people, Party members, would sit in cafés until late at night . . . drinking,' Nadya said. 'The conflict within the Bolshevik faction was nerve-wracking . . . Often V. I. used to come home very late, fired up . . . Once after a heated debate late at night I hardly recognised him when he returned. His face was drawn and he could hardly speak.' Anna Ulyanova visited from Russia six months after they arrived in Paris and said her brother 'was grey in colour, and looked drawn and gaunt'. He was suffering from crippling headaches and insomnia.[8]

Fearing, again, that he might be on the edge of collapse, Nadya took him away for a long break. For nearly six weeks they went to a comfortable *pension* in the small village of Bon-Bon, in the Seine-et-Marne area seventy kilometres south-east of Paris. 'He didn't work at all, and we tried hard to refrain from talking about Party matters,' Nadya told his mother. 'We went for walks every day and . . . went cycling in the Clarmont Forest close by.' They relaxed in a way they seldom did – they were brought breakfast in bed each morning by a young girl who remembered him years later 'as that very polite, very kind Russian gentleman who taught me how to ride a bicycle'. He wrote to Zinoviev that 'after three weeks I am beginning to come round'.*

Lenin's holidays were vital to his health and the balance of his mind. Occasionally a few people in his circle raised their eyebrows when he was *hors de combat* for so long, but he gave a logical and sensible defence

---

air displays, a big popular attraction at the time. He was cycling back from a display at Juvisy-sur-Orge, twenty kilometres from Paris, when a car collided with his bike, just outside the airfield. He was barely injured – just a few cuts and bruises – but his cycle was a write-off. 'People were very kind and helped me take the number and volunteered as witnesses,' he told his sister Maria. 'I have found out who the owner of the car is (he is a viscount, devil take him!) and now I have taken him to court.' Lenin won the case and got enough compensation to buy a replacement bicycle.

* The one thing Nadya had against this holiday was the other people at the *pension*, with whom they shared a *table d'hôte* dinner. She could be a terrific Bolshevik snob and she thought them 'so bourgeois . . . They were all mediocre characters, though very good at talking about their own comforts. Of course such a large dose of mediocrity was rather boring. It was a good thing that we were able to keep aloof from them and live according to our own lights.'

of them – naturally with a political twist. And he criticised other Party members for not taking enough rest and recuperation when they were needed. 'Revolutionaries must be strong and remain healthy,' he said. A revolutionary's health 'is official, public property . . . To go on being ill and undermining your working capacity is something quite intolerable in every respect.'

Apart from his own, the one person's health he was deeply concerned about was his mother's. By the summer of 1910 he hadn't seen her for nearly five years and she was coming up to seventy-five. He heard from his sisters that Maria Alexandrovna was looking old and feeling weak. She was reluctant to leave Russia, but he eventually persuaded her to go on a family holiday he organised in Stockholm. Typically, when she first saw him she was worried about how thin he looked, not her own ailments. He broke the holiday for one evening when he made a speech to Swedish socialists. It was the first time she had seen him appear in public. 'He spoke well, so impressively and skilfully . . . but why does he exert himself so much, why does he speak so loudly? That is harmful. He is not looking after himself.' She gave him a plaid blanket for the winter which he used regularly.*

When she returned home Lenin accompanied her to the quay, but he couldn't board the Russian steamer – he might have been arrested. 'This was the last time he saw his mother and he had a premonition of that as his eyes followed the departing ship,' said Nadya. His sister Maria recalled, 'I shall never forget the expression on his face as he stood there looking at Mother. How much pain there was on his face.'[9]

On one of his bicycle rides outside Paris in early 1911 Lenin passed through Longjumeau, in the Yvette Valley, eighteen kilometres from the city. On the edge of the village he spotted an abandoned workshop and some outhouses, which he realised would be the perfect home for a project he had been planning for some time: he wanted to open a school for working-class Party members from inside Russia, whom he could train in the theory of Marxism and the practice of conspiracy. After their education he would send them back home as the vanguard

---

* The plaid blanket was on his bed when he died, and it was in his coffin with him.

of the movement to mount the insurrection which would spark revolution throughout the world. He rented the buildings immediately, hired contractors to turn them into usable lecture rooms, set up the curriculum, selected eighteen young activists as the first students to make their way secretly to France – and he chose a loyal, reliable and efficient Bolshevik to launch the school and run it. He appointed Inessa.

The school was conceived as Lenin's answer to the summer courses Gorky had started in Capri run by Bogdanov, who, at Lenin's instigation, had been expelled from the Party at the end of 1909. Inessa put her heart and soul into making it a success. The school opened in spring 1911 and Lenin gave the first lecture – on the *Communist Manifesto*. He gave thirty others over the next couple of months, on economics, organising a political party, and the theory of socialism. Inessa administered the school and lectured on economics and feminism; Zinoviev and Kamenev occasionally gave lessons on culture. Nadya was a regular lecturer on running an illegal newspaper and organising a network of clandestine agents. As the weather improved Lenin 'does his work out in the open, he rides his bicycle a great deal, he goes bathing and is altogether pleased with country life', Nadya wrote to his mother. 'He is extremely fond of excursions that begin at six or seven in the morning until late at night.'

The best evidence is that it was around the time the school opened that Lenin and Inessa became lovers. In a frank letter to him later – she was the only woman outside his family with whom he corresponded using the intimate address *ty* – she says again that at first, 'I was terribly scared to see you'. But she goes on: 'The desire to see you was there but it seemed better to drop dead on the spot than to come into your presence; and when, for some reason, you popped into NK's [Nadya's] room I instantly lost control and behaved like a fool. Only in Longjumeau . . . (and later) did I get used to you. I so much loved not only to listen to you but also to look at you as you spoke. First, your face is so lively . . . and second, it was convenient to watch because you didn't notice at the time. I loved you but I wasn't "in love" . . . But then I did fall in love with you.'

There was nothing bohemian about the affair; it was all very discreet. The senior Bolsheviks around Lenin in Paris knew about it, but it was very seldom gossiped about.* Predictably, the Okhrana and the French police were well aware of the relationship. Both report several times about her – using her alias 'Popoff, Sophie' – clearly as 'la maîtresse de Lenine'. One says she had been sent to Paris 'par son amant, Lenine'. This would not have been to embarrass Lenin; at that time it would have been assumed that a revolutionary leader living in Paris probably had a lover. It was just routine intelligence work.[10]

Nadya certainly knew, as did her mother. Elizaveta Krupskaya noticed how 'animated Lenin was when he was talking with Elizaveta and she didn't like it'. This was a time when Nadya was writing her gloomiest letters home to Lenin's family. She didn't mention Inessa and didn't sound jealous, only desperately sad. 'I'm in a state of utter melancholy . . . time now seems just to be frittered away,' she wrote to Maria Alexandrovna. Explaining a delay in writing to her sister-in-law Maria, she finally told her: 'I was in no fit state to write . . . we are just jogging along.'

At no point did she behave like a betrayed wife or show her true feelings. According to Alexandra Kollontai, who was in a position to know, Nadya was definitely *au courant* with what was happening. She told a close comrade later, after the Revolution when she was appointed Soviet Ambassador to Norway, that 'Nadya offered to leave him and let him go off with Inessa, but he told her to stay.'[11]

Perhaps Lenin simply wanted to have his cake and eat it. Inessa didn't seem to mind a conventional *ménage à trois*, which, she told him, 'would not cause pain to anyone'. Or perhaps he realised that, however exciting and passionate their love affair may have been, Inessa was altogether 'higher-maintenance' than Nadya. She was more emotionally demanding, manipulative, and had five children who came first for her. Besides, as he saw, the two women in his life were genuinely becoming good

---

* Many people have speculated that the rival to Inessa in the 'most glamorous woman Bolshevik' stakes, Alexandra Kollontai, based her story *A Great Love* (published first in 1923 when Lenin but not Inessa was still alive) on this romance. It's about a Russian revolutionary (Senya) who wears a cloth cap and has a sick wife (Aniuta) who has a love affair with a beautiful and wealthy fellow revolutionary (Natasha) who happens to be a very good linguist. But equally the story could have been autobiographical. Kollontai was herself a rich revolutionary, fluent in several languages, who had numerous love affairs with other revolutionaries.

friends. 'Life always seemed more cheerful when Inessa was around, more cosy, gayer,' Nadya said. 'There was so much that was good in Paris in my relations with Nadya,' Inessa told Lenin. 'I became close to her.' She even managed to charm Nadya's sometimes stern and irascible mother. 'Inessa spent a long time talking to her; they would often chat and smoke together . . . Mother became closely attached to her.'

Very few people seemed to have a bad word to say against Inessa in the pre-Revolution years. 'I can see her now coming out of Lenin's. She seemed to be an inexhaustible spring of ife. She was the fiery flame of revolution – and the red feather in her hat was like the tongue of that flame,' said Grigory Kotov, a Russian émigré in Paris. 'She was . . . the kind of person . . . [who was] ready to share with her comrades her last crust,' said another. Angelica Balabanova was almost alone in detesting her as 'the perfect – almost passive – executrix of Lenin's orders . . . she was so saturated with the master's authority and infallibility that the possibility of any divergence was inconceivable to her. She was the prototype . . . Bolshevik of rigid, unconditional obedience . . . I didn't warm to Inessa. She was pedantic, one hundred per cent a Bolshevik . . . in the way she thought and spoke. She spoke a number of languages fluently, and in all of them repeated Lenin verbatim.'

Nadya was patient and determined to make the best of it. She may have been jealous, but she saw her main task as Lenin's helpmate, ensuring his peace of mind. If that meant giving Inessa warmth and friendship, it probably seemed like another sacrifice she was prepared to make for the Revolution.[12]

22

BETRAYALS

'That man . . . he fooled us all for years. I never saw through that scoundrel. What a swine!' Lenin to Zinoviev, 1917

Lenin's ability to tack and weave politically, to change direction when he thought it opportune, was a constant source of surprise to Bolsheviks who were less tactically flexible than him. He was a fanatic, an ideologue, but in pursuit of power he was a pragmatist – 'theory is vital in our work, but it is not Holy Writ', he told his supporters, most of whom believed that is exactly what Marxist theory was supposed to be. 'A Marxist must recognise living life and take notice of reality . . . not cling to the theory. Theory is grey, but green is the eternal tree of life.' When circumstances changed, Lenin changed.

Despite the assassination of Stolypin in September 1911, the regime believed that its brutal crackdown on dissent had defeated the revolutionaries.* Scores of thousands had been jailed or executed and now there was a modest effort by the government make some gestures at reform. In moves reminiscent of Charles I's conflicts with Parliament before the Civil War in seventeenth-century England, the Tsar had prorogued two Dumas which he thought challenged his royal prerogatives.

---

* There has never been proof, but the best evidence suggests that the assassination at the Kiev Opera House was in fact organised by Stolypin's enemies within the government and the royal court, though the Tsar himself was definitely not involved. The man who pulled the trigger, Dmitry Bogrov, a twenty-four-year-old lawyer from a well-off Kievan family, was a Socialist Revolutionary, but he was given the means to commit the murder by senior figures in the Interior Ministry. And it was the police who got him a hard-to-obtain ticket to the opera that evening for the performance of Rimsky-Korsakov's *The Legend of Tsar Saltan*. Earlier in the day he had begged the police for a ticket. It was a terrorist act – but the terrorists seem to have been government officials.

He established a third with tight voting restrictions that guaranteed a conservative, pro-monarchy majority.

Lenin had boycotted the Dumas since 1905 and insisted the Bolsheviks should have nothing to do with them. He attacked Social Democrats, mainly Mensheviks, who wanted to compromise with the Tsar's parliamentary reforms as naïve. Making deals with 'bourgeois democrats' and 'soft liberals' was a treacherous road for revolutionaries, he argued. Then in May 1912 he changed his mind, put up Bolsheviks for seats in the forthcoming Fourth Duma elections and wrote several articles in favour of parliaments in general and Nicholas II's Duma system in particular. In *Nevskaya Zvezda* (The New Star), a legal paper in Russia, he contradicted the line he had taken for years: 'Where representative institutions don't exist, there is *much more* deception [Lenin's italics], political lying and fraudulent trickery of all kinds . . . the greater the degree of political liberty in a country and the more stable and democratic its representative institutions, the easier it is for the mass of the people to find its bearings in the fight between the parties and to *learn politics*.' A short while later he declared that 'not a single socialist renounces democracy . . . unless he decides that questions of political freedom are of no consequence, in which case he ceases to be a socialist . . . Whoever wants to approach socialism by any other path than that of political democracy will inevitably arrive at absurd and reactionary conclusions both economic and political.'[1]

It is unlikely he meant any of this: there would be no 'democratic institutions' in the state Lenin built and little talk about democracy. But as a political tactic it seemed perfectly timed: in one move it wrong-footed the Mensheviks, the liberals and the Tsarist regime; it made Lenin seem reasonable and constructive, and it brought the Bolsheviks new members at a time when they were sorely needed. Elena Stasova, Lenin's most senior agent in St Petersburg, wrote around this time telling him that the Party had been 'almost destroyed' and there were probably no more than 800 loyal Bolsheviks in the capital, and perhaps the same number again in all of Russia. The organisation, she said, 'is cut to ribbons. There are no solid regional centres. The local organisations are cut off from one another and in the majority of cases, everywhere, there are only workers in them; the professionals [professional revolutionaries] have long since vanished. There are no secret addresses [safe houses] anywhere, nor any such conspiratorial practices.'

Lenin's about-face on parliaments appeared to be a clever ploy and increased his reputation within the revolutionary movement as a master tactician. It seemed like a good idea at the time. But it was one of his biggest mistakes; it led to a bitter personal blow and caused serious damage to the Party as a whole.

Lenin chose as the leader of the Bolshevik group of seven in the Duma – in effect the chief of the Party in Russia – a thirty-four-year-old Russified Pole named Roman Malinovsky. For a while Malinovsky was one of his favourites, a trusted confidant, the young man he was planning to turn into one of the stars of the Revolution.

Lenin admired him mainly because he was working-class, originally from peasant stock, but also because he was vigorous, super-intelligent, had a powerful charm, was an eloquent speaker – Nadya said that he had 'a beautiful voice' – and was a natural leader. He didn't mind that Malinovsky could also be boorish, rude, a heavy drinker and displayed violent mood swings. 'At last, for the first time, we have an *outstanding* worker, a real leader representing us,' Lenin said of him. 'The results may not be visible immediately, but they are bound to be outstanding.'[2]

A tailor turned metalworker, Malinovsky had been arrested three times and eventually jailed from 1899 to 1902 for 'robbery with breaking and entering'. There was also a charge outstanding of attempted rape. The police noted on his file that he was a heavy spender and his wages were never sufficient for his expensive tastes.

Soon after coming out of prison he got a job as a metal-turner and joined the Metalworkers' Union. He was recruited into the Social Democratic Party. He was also recruited by the Okhrana as a spy and agent provocateur. Partly he was motivated by straightforward greed; partly the secret police threatened to reactivate the attempted rape charge.

At first he was simply receiving a few small amounts of cash to supplement his wages. But as he rose in the labour organisation he became more important to the Okhrana. He betrayed the real names of agents, codes and the addresses of safe houses. For three years from 1906 he was head of the union, careful to steer a steady course between the Bolsheviks and Mensheviks. He became central to the regime's main policy in dealing with the Social Democrats: keeping the party divided and fighting among themselves. Part of the strategy was to build up Lenin, who was still vehemently against healing the Party split with the Mensheviks.

Soon Malinovsky was no longer a casual piece-rate informant but on a retainer from the Okhrana with a regular salary of 100 rubles a month plus expenses, considerably more than the average wages of a metalworker. He had a code-name, Portnoi (tailor). 'Malinovsky was given the order to do as much as possible to deepen the split in the Party,' Police Director Sergei Beletsky said. 'The whole purpose of my direction is summed up in this: to give no possibility of the Party uniting. I worked on the principle of *divide et impera*.'[3]

He was also ordered to 'come out' as a Bolshevik and to take the first opportunity to get acquainted with Lenin. The Bolshevik leader was so taken with him when they met for the first time in January 1912 at the Party Congress in Prague that Malinovsky was promoted to membership of the Central Committee – high leadership – and persuaded to stand as a deputy in the Duma.

The secret police were equally pleased with their protégé. He was given a personal telephone hotline to Okhrana headquarters. Meetings with police chief Beletsky were held at private rooms in the most fashionable restaurants. He was taken to meet the Assistant Minister of Justice, the chief of the Okhrana and the Governor General of Moscow.

Both the Bolsheviks and the regime did what they could to ensure his easy election. The police arrested all his most popular rivals to smoothe his way, and he was given a certificate of good repute to clear his criminal record. The police showed their appreciation by raising Malinovsky's retainer to 5,000 rubles a month, with bonuses for particularly valuable information – by far the highest amount that any of their spies had received.*

---

* The Okhrana was not as omniscient or efficient as it was often made out to be. In fiction, spies have traditionally been brilliant 'masterminds'. Less so in fact. On the whole, barring some remarkable exceptions, spies have been quite dim. But one thing the Okhrana was good at was recruiting double agents and provocateurs. Around the same time that Malinovsky began his double life, Yevno Azef, the leader of the Socialist Revolutionaries, the biggest terrorist organisation in Russia, behind hundreds of assassinations of government officials, had been an Okhrana agent. About to be unmasked by his comrades, he escaped to Germany in the nick of time. He died in Berlin in 1918, of natural causes.

Malinovsky was earning his money. He knew all the senior Bolsheviks in Russia and betrayed many of them, including Yakov Sverdlov, who became one of the most important Bolshevik leaders after the Revolution. In February 1913 Lenin sent Sverdlov on a secret mission to St Petersburg from Swiss exile. He was staying in the capital at the home of a Bolshevik sympathiser but was arrested when he was moving from there 'to a safer place'. Very few others apart from Malinovsky would have known the details. A month later, Stalin was picked up by the police at a concert given to raise money for Bolshevik members of the Duma. He had asked Malinovsky if it was safe to go and was told 'Yes for sure.' Both were sent to Siberia, where they remained until February 1917.[*]

Lenin had a blind spot about Malinovsky. Some people had warned him that the young man was untrustworthy, but he wouldn't listen. Nikolai Bukharin was arrested in Tula in 1911, the day after he saw Malinovsky. He wrote to Lenin with his suspicions, but Lenin was furious that his trusted confidant was being slandered. After escaping from Siberian exile, Bukharin went to see Lenin and told him personally that he was convinced Malinovsky was a double agent. Lenin thought he was jealous. 'Vladimir Ilyich thought it utterly impossible for Malinovsky to have been an agent provocateur,' Nadya said. 'The rumours . . . [about him] came from Menshevik circles . . . Only once did a doubt flash across his mind.' They were taking a walk after an evening with the Zinovievs. 'All of a sudden he stopped on the little bridge we were crossing and said: "It may be true . . ." and his face expressed anxiety. "What are you talking about, it's nonsense," I answered. Ilyich calmed down and began to abuse the Mensheviks . . . He had no further doubts on the question.'

Lenin said simply that at the time he did not believe the allegations, not just because of their provenance, but 'if Malinovsky was a

---

[*] Sverdlov was Stalin's most bitter enemy – even more so than Trotsky would famously become – and the antipathy began when they were exiled together at Kureiko, a remote hamlet in the frozen wastes of Siberia, just inside the Arctic Circle. After a while, Sverdlov could hardly bear to be anywhere near the Georgian. 'A comrade is with me but we know each other too well,' he wrote to a friend. He didn't name 'the comrade' but it was definitely Stalin. 'Saddest of all in exile or prison conditions . . . a man bares himself and all his petty aspects are revealed. The worst thing is that all the trivialities of . . . [a person's] life are seen.'

provocateur, the Okhrana would not gain from that as much as our Party did'. It seems a rationalisation, hardly likely, given the damage Malinovsky caused, but Lenin sincerely believed it.[4]

The Okhrana's top agent was becoming too difficult to control and his police handlers were tiring of him. He made incendiary speeches in the Duma designed to keep Bolshevik suspicions at bay, but the police thought they were damaging to the regime. They paid him off with 6,000 rubles and gave him a ticket out of Russia.

Lenin couldn't understand why Malinovsky resigned from the Duma in May 1914, seemingly at the height of his authority, leaving the Bolshevik ranks inside Russia in disarray. At first he was angry. But then he was persuaded that Malinovsky had suffered a nervous breakdown and he was mollified. The truth was that Malinovsky feared his double life would be exposed.

Lenin continued to believe in him until the secret police files were opened after the Tsar abdicated and the Okhrana was abolished. For a ruthless, intensely secretive man, whose life was bound up in conspiratorial plotting, Lenin could be naïvely trusting. He hardly ever spoke about Malinovsky after the truth about him emerged, though he did admit to Zinoviev in the summer of 1917, 'that bastard, that man Malinovsky. He fooled us all for years. I never saw through that scoundrel. What a swine!'*[5]

Another millionaire turned up at just the right time to boost the Bolsheviks' fortunes. Press censorship was relaxed in spring 1912 and as the Bolsheviks had decided to take part in the Duma elections they were allowed, for the first time, to publish a legal newspaper. Lenin was excited and he saw it as a big opportunity to attract a mass membership for the Party. He had high ambitions. He wanted to produce a daily paper, full

---

* Malinovsky was thrown out of the Party in 1914, but not because he was a traitor – those charges were never proved against him in a 'court of inquiry' chaired in 1914 by Lenin. He was reprimanded for abandoning his position at the Duma. He chose to return to Russia from Germany after the war. He was tried secretly and maintained throughout that Lenin knew he was working for the Okhrana, but that was certainly untrue. He was sentenced to death but believed that if he could talk to Lenin he would be pardoned or the sentence would be commuted to a prison term. Lenin would not listen to him or intervene and Malinovsky was shot in November 1918.

of news as well as propaganda, relying on correspondents from around Russia, but with him as the guiding spirit, a chief editor *in absentia*. Though the Bolsheviks were partially legalised, there was still a warrant out for his arrest and he couldn't return to Russia. Lenin had the format of the paper worked out. He had chosen a title – *Pravda* (Truth); he selected a team of journalists to staff it and contribute to it. All he lacked was enough money to produce the publication. The vital funds came from a gift by Viktor Tikhomirov, who had just inherited a fortune following the death of his father, a Kazan merchant. He had been a member of a group of radical intellectuals meeting secretly in Kazan, but when he moved to St Petersburg after the 1905 uprising he joined the Social Democrats, was convinced by Lenin's *What Is To Be Done?* and became a Bolshevik. Tikhomirov donated Lenin 100,000 rubles – a huge sum – to launch what would become one of the most famous, or rather notorious, newspapers in the world.

On Lenin's orders *Pravda* tried carefully to remain on the right side of the law, occasionally overstepping it, when an issue would be confiscated. It had a print run of 60,000 and on most days sold out within a few hours. Of the many newspapers that began appearing at this time, representing practically all shades of opinion, it was one of the most professionally produced. Despite regular harassment from the regime it survived a range of crises. It was banned nine times – only to reappear the next day, with a slightly different title. The new name would always have the word '*Pravda*' in it. So when the regime closed one paper down, a new incarnation would appear – Workers' Truth, Daily Truth, Evening Truth, Truth of Labour, The Way of Truth, Proletarian Truth, and so on. The job of editor was not the safest, though the paper was supposed to be legal. In its first thirty-eight issues *Pravda* had a succession of thirty-six editors, all of whom were arrested. Between them they spent forty-seven months in jail. By the time the regime finally banned it soon after the First World War began, 636 issues of *Pravda* had appeared and Lenin had written voluminously for the paper – 280 pieces under his byline, many more unsigned. He concerned himself with every aspect of the paper, from the 'Party line' to advice on typography. There is no evidence he was an expert on fonts and type sizes, but he wrote to one of the editors, Vladimir Karpinsky, telling him he could squeeze more material into two pages if the paper changed to the smaller *brevier* script and fitted a more compact masthead into the corner of a page; 'then there could be room provided for another two articles'.[6]

Nadya told Lenin's sisters that 'he became another person after the first number of *Pravda* appeared'. He added a postscript: 'now at last there is real *live* work to do'. But he couldn't be closely enough involved with *Pravda* from Paris; he had to get nearer to Russia. He chose to move to Krakow, just ten kilometres from the Russian border. 'No matter how provincial and barbarous this town of ours may be, by and large I am better off here than in Paris,' he told his mother in mid-June 1912, soon after arriving. It turned out to be one of his favourite cities in Europe.

* * *

Traditionally, England, Switzerland and France were the destinations of choice for Russian émigrés. The Austrian part of Poland was a new departure, but there was a lot to recommend it and 'in so many ways it is much more convenient than Paris', thought Nadya. 'Whereas the French police assisted the Russian police in every possible way, the Poles . . . were hostile to the whole Russian government. In Krakow we could be sure that our letters would not be intercepted and that no one would spy on the newcomers.'

When Gorky wrote asking him why he was in 'bourgeois' Austria he said it was convenient: 'the frontier is close by and we make good use of it. It's much nearer to Petersburg. We get the papers from there on the third day. It's become far easier to write for [them] from here. Co-operation and communication with them goes much easier. There is less squabbling here, which is an advantage.'[7]

They rented a house with the Zinovievs in Zwierzyniec, a well-to-do suburb close to the River Vistula and a forest. 'The streets were unpaved and exceedingly muddy,' Nadya told Lenin's mother. 'But five kilometres away there's Las Wolski, a beautiful wood which we frequent on our bicycles.' Further in the distance were the foothills of a range of peaks. They were smaller than Lenin's beloved Alps, but he felt happy that mountains were nearby. 'Volodya is quite jolly in Poland,' Nadya said.

In later years Lenin often spoke with delight about a mountain jaunt he took with a Krakow friend, Sergei Bagoczki. They set off one day to climb the serene Babya mountain, a well-known Tatra attraction. The tour to take was to walk halfway up in the afternoon, spend the night at a hut, and see the peak at dawn. But on the day they picked the weather was changeable. They left their bicycles at the foot of the mountain and set off along a sloping path. 'We soon reached woods,' recounted Bagoczki. 'It was getting darker. Unfortunately, we had left our torches with our bicycles. The path zigzagged up . . . but it disappeared. We started looking for the path in all directions, but in vain. It was dark, we moved slowly, stumbling against bushes and stumps. There was the danger that we might have to spend the night in the woods. Suddenly a light twinkled . . . and we could see the windows of a hut.' They stayed the night and asked the hut watchman to wake them at 4 a.m. 'Through my sleep I heard Vladimir Ilyich's voice: "It's already seven and we were not roused. We missed the sunrise." We called the watchman. "But gentlemen, look through the window . . . such mist that nothing can be seen two steps from you. I thought you'd better sleep." . . . He said there would be no change before tomorrow. So our enterprise was doomed to failure. We could not wait till the next day because Vladimir Ilyich had to be in Krakow in the evening. Our fiasco did not discourage him. "On my first free day I shall come again," he said. Hardly two weeks passed by and we went . . . the watchman greeted us as old friends and promised to wake us early, no matter about the weather. Four o'clock came; there was mist but not as thick as it had been last time . . . We reached the top but the mist persisted. We could see no more than a few yards ahead. We decided to wait and have breakfast . . . after half an hour the mist began to lift . . . in front of us a wonderful view was unveiling. In the distance, lit up by the bright rays of the sun, the long range of the Tatra peaks as if suspended in the air; below, everything wrapped in fog, like a blanket of thick foam. Vladimir Ilyich was glowing: "You see our efforts were not in vain," he said.'[8]

Galicia was dirt-poor but recognisable to Lenin as 'almost Russia', he told his mother, 'it reminds me of home'. The peasants were similar to those he saw on market days in Simbirsk or Kazan: 'there are bent-nosed women in colourful dresses . . . just like Russia'. The Jewish quarter, Kazimierz, looked like a *shtetl* in any of the western regions of the Tsar's empire – like Russian-occupied Poland just a few kilometres away. 'Each of us secretly thought about Russia,' Nadya said. 'We all had a strong desire to go . . . We avoided speaking about this, but all of us secretly thought about it. Krakow . . . was only semi-exile.'[9]

23

A LOVE TRIANGLE –
TWO INTO THREE WILL GO

'Vladimir Ilyich could never have loved a woman with whose opinions he totally disagreed and who was not a comrade in his work.'

Nadezhda Krupskaya, *Memoirs* (1930)

'I am an invalid and tire very easily,' Nadya wrote to Lenin's mother on 3 May 1913 from Krakow. Ten days later Lenin told Maria Alexandrovna that he was 'seriously worried about N's health . . . she is getting no better'. She was suffering from heart palpitations, she had fainting spells, her neck bulged, her eyes swelled and she had crippling headaches. She could walk no further than a few hundred metres before she was exhausted. She looked in her sixties, not forty-four. Lenin consulted several 'comrade doctors', Bolshevik émigrés in Poland, but none was sure what was wrong with her beyond diagnosing an endocrine problem of some kind. His brother Dmitry, a physician with a practice in Crimea, consulted the latest medical research in Europe. Diagnosing from a distance, he assured Lenin that whatever was wrong, an operation would be unnecessary and might make her condition worse – a great relief to Nadya, who was terrified of surgery.*

Finally Lenin took her to see one of the top neurologists in Poland,

---

* Lenin often criticised 'comrade doctors' and generally advised his friends, including many Bolshevik activists, not to trust them. When he heard that Gorky was being treated for an illness by an erstwhile Party member, he wrote suggesting – not in jest – that he should consult someone else. 'The news that a Bolshevik is treating you, by a new method, even if he is only a former Bolshevik, upsets me . . . God save you from doctor comrades in general and doctor Bolsheviks in particular. But really in ninety-nine cases out of a hundred doctor comrades are asses . . . I assure you, except in trivial cases, one should be treated *only* by men of first-class reputation.'

Dr Jan Landau, from the University of Krakow. 'It has been discovered that I have thyroid trouble,' she wrote to her sister-in-law Maria. 'The doctor has frightened me and every day I go to the clinic for electrical treatment [a form of electroconvulsive therapy]. That takes three hours and afterwards I wander about half the day like a lunatic. They feed me bromides, which make me very sick.'[1]

The treatment wasn't working and Lenin looked about for other cures. His Polish friend Bagoczki, a neurologist, recommended that Nadya should see a Swiss surgeon and endocrinologist, Professor Theodore Kocher, who had won the Nobel Prize for medicine in 1909 for pioneering work on the pathology, physiology and treatment of the thyroid gland. Bagoczki advised that the professor would probably suggest surgery, but Nadya didn't want an operation so they decided that some peace and quiet during the summer would help. They went to the Tatra Mountains and rented a large bungalow with a pretty terrace in the tiny hamlet of Biały Dunajec, near the village of Poronin, 700 metres above sea level. The house was surrounded by a forest, the foothills of mountains and a stream; 'the air is wonderful and the view of the mountains beautiful,' Nadya said. Lenin also loved 'our rural life. We get up early and go to bed at almost the same time as the cocks and hens,' he told his mother. 'Poronin is almost Russian: thatched roofs and poverty, the women and children barefoot. The men go around wearing the "*gurali*" costume [a traditional Polish folk dress]: white cloth trousers and white cloth half cloaks, half jackets.'

It was a country idyll, but Nadya's health was getting no better; her heart palpitations and dizzy spells were becoming more frequent. Lenin finally persuaded her to see Professor Kocher at his clinic in Berne. He diagnosed Graves' Disease, also known as Basedow's Disease or toxic goitre, and recommended an operation to cut out half of Nadya's thyroid gland. It was new, highly complex and potentially dangerous surgery, but Kocher had performed over two thousand similar operations. She conquered her terror and agreed to go through with the procedure.[2]

Kocher's fees were extremely high but Lenin had no qualms about consulting the best available doctors, for himself and for Nadya, whatever the cost. With his mother ailing, for once he didn't want to bother her for help in paying the professor's bill, though he was comfortable about asking the Party for the money. He thought it was entirely reasonable that the Bolsheviks should look after vital assets such as important

Party workers like Nadya. He wrote to the editors of *Pravda*, asking them for a contribution towards the operation. 'I beg you not to be late,' he wrote on 10 June. The paper agreed to help, though the money took time to come through. A few days later he wrote again with more urgency: 'My wife is going to have an operation. The money is badly needed.'

Lenin and Nadya arrived in Berne on 12 June. But Kocher was a bit of a diva and in such high demand that he had a full waiting list. When they were told that they would have to be patient, wait their turn, and hang around in Berne at considerable expense, Lenin was furious. 'There was a great row with Kocher – a capricious character,' he wrote to Kamenev. 'He's a celebrity and likes to be begged.'[3]

There were several delays over the following weeks, but the operation went ahead on 10 July. Three days later Lenin wrote to his mother: 'At last they operated on Nadya on Wednesday. The operation evidently went off successfully, for yesterday [Friday] she already looked fairly well and she began to drink and eat with pleasure. The operation was apparently rather difficult. For about three hours they tortured her without an anaesthetic, but she bore it heroically. On Thursday she was very ill – high temperature and delirium – and I was thoroughly frightened. Yesterday, however, things were obviously better.'*

Nadya stayed in hospital to convalesce for a fortnight after the operation. Lenin took the opportunity, in between caring for his wife, to perform some political tasks. 'While I was in hospital,' she said laconically, 'Vladimir Ilyich lectured in Geneva, Lausanne, Zurich and Berne on the problems of national minorities.'[4]

Lenin was not a man with a highly developed conscience. But just before moving to Krakow he ended the physical side of his affair with Inessa – or at least he tried to. They went for a few days to Arcachon, in southwest France, and he told her that he couldn't continue hurting Nadya. Inessa was angry and unhappy and said that she didn't think their relationship 'was causing hurt to anyone else', but Lenin insisted that he was finding 'managing' the affair too difficult. The evidence from her

---

* In the long term, though, the surgery was only a partial success. The immediate symptoms disappeared for a while after Lenin and Nadya returned to Poland following the operation. But they would recur throughout her life, sometimes causing her acute pain and discomfort.

letters suggests, though, that it continued, on and off, for some years.

His relationship with Inessa was central to Lenin's emotional life, and highly important to him professionally. From 1912 onwards he wrote to her frequently; discounting brief postcards, of which there are many, around 150 letters survive. It is certain that he wrote several more which have disappeared or were destroyed. At one point in 1914 Lenin asked her to return all his letters to her: 'Sending them by registered mail is not convenient; a registered letter can easily be opened by friends . . . and so on . . . Please bring all the letters, come yourself, and we will talk about it.'* Their letters mix the personal and the political, moving from one to the other almost seamlessly, and show how intimate was their bond. They also reveal a tempestuous relationship in which the lovers clearly had flaming rows. Inessa was passionate, but could be demanding and difficult. It is easy to see why Lenin fell for her – and why he didn't want to live with her.

Inessa and her five children followed them to Krakow within six months, taking an apartment in the same street. The three of them spent a lot of time together – 'V. I. would write a speech and make it in front of us, Inessa would transcribe it,' Nadya wrote to Maria Ulyanova. She said elsewhere: 'For hours we would walk along the leaf-strewn forest lanes. Usually we were in a threesome, V. I., Inessa and I . . . sometimes we would sit on a sunny slope covered with shrubs. He would sketch outlines of his speeches, getting the text right, while I learned Italian . . . Inessa would be sewing a skirt or enjoying the warmth of the sun.' Inessa played the piano well, and despite Lenin's claim that he couldn't listen to too much Beethoven because 'it makes you go too soft', she often played him the *Appassionata* Sonata.[5]

Lenin and Nadya became close to Inessa's children, particularly the younger ones. Nadya grew to love Inessa's two daughters, Inna and Varvara, and the affection was returned. Whether it was an – unnamed – gynaecological condition that arose after her Siberian exile, which required two months' treatment, or her thyroid problems which had

---

* Almost all the correspondence was censored by the Soviet authorities after Lenin died. Apart from a very few letters that were entirely mundane about trivial Bolshevik Party affairs, none appeared until after the collapse of the USSR in 1991, and many turned up only some years after that. It seems likely that Lenin destroyed some of the letters she returned, but nobody knows for sure.

probably existed undiagnosed for years, Nadya and Lenin had no children. She rarely mentioned any disappointment, but every now and then a hint of regret would appear. She wrote sometimes about the pain of other women who were childless. She might well have been thinking of herself when she said of her great friend, the perennially single Vera Zasulich that she 'had an enormous need for a family. One had only to see how lovingly she played with Dimka's [Lenin's younger brother Dmitry] fair-haired little boy.'

Lenin liked children too, up to a point. He was fond of the Zinovievs' son Stepan, born in 1909. In Krakow Lenin often carried him around on his shoulders and played with him affectionately, even wrestling with the boy on the floor. 'Sometimes, Vladimir Ilyich and Styopka knocked everything about in the room,' his mother Zina Lilina wrote later. 'When it became very noisy I would try to stop them, but he insisted "don't interfere, we're playing".' Once, as they were walking along a street in Krakow, he sighed, looked sad and told Zina, 'It's a pity we haven't got a Styopka like that.'*6

Separating Inessa and Lenin's personal relationship from the political was never easy. The two were bound up together. He trusted her implicitly to perform tasks large and small that he would not have given to anyone else. Lenin had such self-belief that he rarely thought anybody could perform better than him at anything that required political judgement and skill. But he acknowledged once that Inessa did. He persuaded her to represent him at a conference in Brussels that required considerable tact and *nous*. Famous figures in international socialism would be there like Karl Kautsky, Martov, Rosa Luxemburg and Plekhanov; she was reluctant, and apprehensive, about appearing as Vladimir Ilyich's

---

* Later Lenin was close to his sister Anna and Mark Elizarov's adopted son Gora – a child prodigy whom the couple had heard about in 1911 when they were living in Saratov. His real name was Georgy Lozgachev, and aged just six he had taught himself to read Russian, and from bibles, Church Slavonic and a smattering of Hebrew. Anna Ulyanova and her husband offered to adopt him and give him a better education and his natural parents agreed. Lenin in his last years grew to love him. Other accounts differ about Lenin's fondness for children, though. Panteleimon Lepeshinsky, who knew him well from exile in Siberia and émigré life in Geneva, recalled that Lenin had found it deeply annoying to look after his young daughter, Olga, 'because she teased him about being bald'.

voice. Eventually, after he practically begged her to go, she relented and, from many accounts, she performed remarkably, always keeping her temper and remaining diplomatic. He wrote to her afterwards: 'You have rendered a very great service to our Party. I am especially thankful because you replaced me . . . you handled the thing much better than I could have done . . . I would probably have gone up in the air, would have called them scoundrels. And that's what they were trying to provoke. You carried it off calmly. I greet you a thousand times.'[7]

After three months in Krakow Lenin sent her on a dangerous and foolhardy mission back to Russia, where she was a wanted woman. Her task was to make contact with a Bolshevik cell in St Petersburg which Lenin hadn't heard from in a long time. She went disguised as an old peasant woman with false ID in the name Fransiska Yankevich. From the moment she crossed the border into Russia the Okhrana followed her. She found the comrades she was told to look for. But the whole St Petersburg Party was so compromised by double agents that she was betrayed, arrested and jailed.

Her husband got her out of prison. He paid her bail of 5,500 rubles and helped her escape back to Poland. She left her youngest children with him in Moscow, and from September 1913 took a room in the Kamenevs' home, close to Lenin's, returning to the familiar routine in the ménage. 'Our entire Krakow group were drawn close to Inessa . . . we lived together in a small and friendly circle.'

Out of the blue, in December she surprised everybody and suddenly left Krakow and returned to Paris. It is unclear exactly why, though it seems likely that after another short trip away together in Switzerland Lenin again decided to end the affair. Perhaps he felt guilty about Nadya, who was still recovering from her operation. Inessa was deeply hurt and depressed. Soon after she reached Paris she wrote to him, making no effort to hide her feelings or the nature of their relationship.

'Sunday morning . . .
My dear,
    Here I am in Ville Lumière and my first impression is one of disgust. Everything about the place grates – the grey of the streets, the overdressed women, the accidentally overheard conversations, even the French language . . . It was sad that Arosa was so temporary, somehow

transitory. Arosa was so close to Krakow, while Paris is, well, so final.* We have parted, parted, you and I, my dear! And it is so painful. I know, I just feel you won't be coming here. As I gazed at the familiar places I realised all too clearly, as never before, what a large place you occupied in my life, here in Paris, so that all our activity here is tied by a thousand threads to the thought of you. I wasn't at all in love with you then, though even then I did love you. Even now I would manage without the kisses, if only I could see you, to talk with you occasionally would be such a joy – and it couldn't cause pain to anyone. Why did I have to give that up? You ask me if I am angry that it was you who "carried out" the separation. No, I don't think you did it for yourself. There was much that was good in Paris in my relations with NK [Nadya Konstantinovna]. In one of our last conversations she told me I had become dear and close to her only recently.'[8]

She dates the rest of the letter Sunday evening and most of it is about Party affairs and politics:

'When you write to me about business matters, give me some indication of what the KZO [the Committee of Russian Social Democrats Abroad] may talk about and what they may not.

'Well, my dear, that's enough for today. I want to send this off. There was no letter from you yesterday! I'm rather afraid my letters are not reaching you – I sent three letters (this is the fourth) and a telegram. Is it possible you haven't received them? I get the most unlikely ideas thinking about it. I've also written to NK, to your brother and to Zina [Lilina, Zinoviev's wife]. Has nobody received anything? I send you a big kiss.

Your Inessa.[9]'

He wrote to her making it equally clear how important to him their affair was – and what she meant to him: 'Dear friend . . . Your latest letters were so full of sadness and evoked such gloomy thoughts in me and aroused such feelings of guilt, that I can't come to my senses.'

---

* Arosa, a Swiss Alpine resort, is where it seems Inessa and Lenin spent a few days in autumn 1913. It is clear that they were both in Switzerland at the same time, though it is not entirely established that they were together. The best evidence suggests they were.

24

CATASTROPHE – THE WORLD AT WAR

'A war between Austria and Russia would be a very useful thing for the Revolution, but it is not likely that Franz Josef and Nikolasha will give us that pleasure.' Lenin to Gorky, 25 January 1913

'Tsarism is a hundred times worse than Kaiserism . . . From the point of view of the working class and the toiling masses of Russia, the lesser evil would be the defeat of the Tsarist monarchy and its army.'
Lenin to Alexander Shlyapnikov, 17 October 1914

Lenin had been predicting a world war between the major powers for a dozen years after 1900. 'War is coming . . . waged for the division of colonies, a struggle for markets and for the freedom to loot foreign territories. Thieves will fall out.' Five years before the war began he said, 'war is inevitable. The capitalist world has reached a stage of putrefaction. People are already beginning to poison themselves with the drugs of nationalism and chauvinism. I think we shall soon see a general European war . . . and the working class will not be able to find the strength to avert the carnage . . . they are not sufficiently organised or class-conscious to do so . . . and in a war it is the workers who will suffer terribly. But it is the workers' enemies who will weaken each other. The workers will pay a heavy price, but in the end they will gain.'[1]

As the years went on he changed his mind and ruled out an imminent conflict – though he wasn't alone there: very few people at the time saw the war coming. Lenin thought the great powers could avoid a war in the short to medium term. In November 1912 he wrote to his mother and his sister Maria: 'There is much talk about war here as you can see from the papers. If war does break out, I shall probably have to go to Vienna, or perhaps the town where we last met [a coded meaning, he was referring to Stockholm, but I do not believe there will be a war.' A month

231

later he told Gorky: 'There will probably not be a war and we shall stay here for the time being, taking advantage of the Poles' desperate hatred of Tsarism.' He was confident in his judgement, as always. If he thought war was imminent between Austria and Russia he wouldn't have stayed in Galicia, where he was bound to be considered a citizen of an enemy nation when fighting broke out. Clearly he had thought of moving from Austrian Poland to Scandinavia; but he reckoned the Swedes or the Danes might have been pressured to extradite him to Russia. It was a serious miscalculation to stay in Poronin, which soon led to personal and political problems. First, he was arrested, jailed and for a short period genuinely believed he might be lynched as a spy. Second, when the opportunity came to return to Russia, the only way he could get there was to seek help from Germany, opening himself up to treason charges.[2]

When war did begin he miscalculated again. He was sure that the German Social Democratic Party – the oldest in the world and the biggest, the party which most Marxists believed would spark and lead the world revolution – would vote against the war in the German parliament. 'They cannot support an imperialist and dynastic war . . . they are not such rascals,' he told Zinoviev a few days before the German socialists, carried on a wave of nationalism, voted to grant the government as much money as it needed to pursue the conflict. The equivalent parties in France, Austria and Britain did the same and Lenin was furious. 'They have betrayed socialism . . . From this moment I cannot call myself a Social Democrat. I am a Communist.'*

Early in the afternoon of 7 August 1914, six days after the Austrians declared war on Russia, the police arrived to search Lenin's house in Poronin. A hysterical 'spy mania' swept through Galicia, even in the remote region of the Tatra foothills where Lenin, Nadya and the Zinovievs had removed themselves for the summer. Previously they had been popular among the locals. Now the neighbourhood Catholic priest stirred up the villagers to be wary of the 'Muscovite gang' amid them. In one sermon he warned that the Russians might try to poison the water wells. One villager told a gendarme that he had spotted Lenin seated on

---

* And he meant it. One of the first things Lenin did when he seized power in Russia was to change the name of the RSDLP to the Communist Party.

the top of a hill 'writing in a notebook – just like a spy would be doing'. The servant girl Nadya had hired to clean the house had been gossiping about them in the village. She was fired and given a train ticket to go and see her family in Krakow.

Lenin was far too complacent about the threat of arrest. He had not even bothered trying to hide an old Browning pistol – unloaded – before the police went through his possessions. They also found notebooks full of densely written statistics and figures, research material for an article he was writing about grain production in Russian farming communes. The police confiscated them as suspected evidence of espionage. Lenin was told to appear early the next morning at the police station in the nearby town, Nowy Targ, 'for questioning'. Over the course of the day he, Nadya, Zinoviev and his friends saw that the danger was potential-ly serious. He found a local doctor who was prepared to stand bail for him. He wrote to government officials and the chief of police in Krakow, using his real name, which he did very rarely. He made plain that he was a bitter enemy of the Russian regime. 'The local police at Nowy Targ suspect me of espionage. I lived in Krakow for two years ... I personally gave information about myself to the commissary of police in Zwierzyniec ... [the area where he lived]. I am an emigrant, a Social Democrat. Please wire Poronin and Mayor of Nowy Targ to avoid mis-understandings ... V. I. Ulyanov.'

When he arrived the next morning at the Nowy Targ police head-quarters there was a menacing-looking crowd outside to catch a glimpse of 'the Russian spy'.

He was put in jail with an assortment of petty thieves, drunks and vagrants. This was the fourth time he had been in prison so the con-ditions did not disturb him. He quickly impressed the other inmates. Though he couldn't speak Polish and wasn't qualified as a lawyer in the Habsburg lands, he tried to help them with their cases – he was 'popu-lar, and a real bull of a fellow', one of his cellmates recalled later.

There were increased demands for his release, including requests to the local police from officials in Krakow. But the Nowy Targ gendarmes resisted the pressure and Lenin languished in a provincial jail.[*]

---

[*] The main support for him locally came from Galician Jews, who saw in Lenin an im-portant enemy of the Tsar. He had become friendly with the owner of the general store, Mendel Singer, who raised money for his legal defence. They retained the services of a

Zinoviev and other Bolshevik activists in Galicia advised Nadya to seek the help of Victor Adler, the veteran leader of the Austrian socialists, whom Lenin had met a few times at various conferences over the years, and the distinguished Social Democrat member of the Austrian parliament, Hermann Diamand. Adler, a venerable figure on the European Left, had profound disagreements with Lenin, who was far too extreme for his liking; but he went to see the Interior Minister in Vienna, Karl, Baron Heinold, and argued that releasing the Bolshevik leader would be in Austria's best interests. 'Ulyanov is no ordinary Russian citizen and certainly no spy. He is a determined opponent of Tsarism and a man who has devoted his whole life to the struggle against the Russian government. If he appeared in Russia they would arrest him straight away.' 'But are you sure,' the minister asked, 'that this Ulyanov is an enemy of the Tsarist government?' 'Oh yes,' Adler replied, 'a more implacable enemy even than your Excellency. He was an enemy of Tsarism when Your Excellency was its friend. He is its enemy now. And he will be its enemy when Your Excellency may again be its friend.'

Lenin was released on 19 August after eleven days in jail and allowed to pass through Austria to Switzerland. He and Nadya, with an increasingly frail Elizaveta Krupskaya, decided against settling in Geneva for a third time and opted for Berne. As usual, within days he was calling his new base 'a hole'. He told his sister Maria, 'It's a dull little town, but better than Galicia and the best there is now. Never mind, we'll adjust ourselves.'[3]

*   *   *

To the Tsar, and especially to the Empress, 1913 seemed the high point of their reign. It was the 300th anniversary of the rule of the Romanov dynasty and eager crowds greeted the royal couple as they toured the country. The Jubilee celebrations fooled those willing to be fooled about the permanence of the monarchy and the popularity of the ruler: 'Now you can see for yourself what cowards those state ministers are . . . [who]

---

respected local attorney, Dr Bernard Cohen, and gave the money to Nadya. In spring 1918 Singer was surprised to receive a letter with a Moscow postmark. 'Please accept my apologies for leaving without paying you in 1914, owing to certain difficult circumstances. The money is enclosed.' In 1920 Lenin sent a couple of Soviet officials to locate documents and books he and Nadya had left in Poland. They found a stash of Lenin's papers carefully stored away in Singer's attic.

constantly frighten the Emperor with threats of revolution and here, you can see for yourself, we need merely to show ourselves and at once their hearts are ours,' Empress Alexandra wrote to one of her ladies-in-waiting towards the end of the year. The Tsar had been told that in fact the crowds were nowhere near as big or as enthusiastic as the court had expected; the Okhrana reported many disturbances and anti-regime outbursts at Jubilee events. But the Emperor and his court believed the anniversary had shored up the monarchy.*

Foreigners were equally convinced. A note from the British Foreign Office to the Cabinet in the summer of 1913 said confidently that 'nothing could exceed the affection and devotion to the person of the Emperor displayed by the population wherever His Majesty appeared. There is no doubt that in this strong attachment of the masses to the person of the Emperor lies the great strength of the Russian autocracy.' In February 1913 *The Times* of London had carried a special edition on the anniversary in Russia and predicted that 'no hope seems too confident or too bright' for Tsar Nicholas and his country.[4]

Just when he imagined he was at the zenith of his dynasty's power, the Emperor made the most catastrophic of all his poor decisions – the mistake that as much as anything cost him his throne and his life. The war was a disaster for Russia far greater than for any of the other combatant nations. As Lenin acknowledged, if not for the war, 'Russia might have gone on living for years, maybe decades, without a revolution against the capitalists.'

Even some historians who have little sympathy with Tsar Nicholas have argued there was little he could have done to prevent war in August 1914, that the rush towards a conflict had a momentum of its own. This seems simplistic. Surely the point of an autocracy – or at least one that functions properly – is that the autocrat is responsible, at the time and in history, for his decisions. Nicholas had an alternative. He could have decided not to go to war, saved his life and his country from a century-long catastrophe.

---

* The celebrations required very heavy policing and the army provided most of it. In some places the royal couple were due to tour, crowds were often banned in case they turned into anti-government demonstrations. In St Petersburg there were soldiers everywhere. 'The city was literally turned into an armed camp,' said the Chief of the Corps of Gendarmes. The autocrat was unsafe in his own capital.

Many of his advisers warned against war. Count Sergei Witte told the Tsar that Russia 'cannot afford to risk defeat because the army is the mainstay of the regime and may well be needed to preserve order at home'. He was thanked – and told to stop being so negative. Witte then told Maurice Paléologue, the French Ambassador to Russia, that a war between Russia and the Triple Alliance of Germany, Austria-Hungary and Turkey would be 'madness for us . . . it can only have disastrous results'.

In February 1914 the Interior Minister, Pyotr Durnovo, an extreme right-winger who as Police Director had ordered the destruction of entire villages after the 1905 Revolution, wrote a prescient memorandum to Nicholas warning that Russia and the monarchy were too weak to withstand a long war of attrition that would be likely in a conflict with Germany. He predicted with remarkable accuracy what was likely to happen: 'The trouble will start with the blaming of the government for all disasters. In the legislative institutions a bitter campaign against the government will begin, followed by revolutionary agitation throughout the country, with socialist slogans, capable of arousing and rallying the masses, beginning with the division of the land and succeeded by a division of all valuables and property. The defeated army, having lost its most dependable men, and carried away by the tide of the primitive peasant desire for land, will find itself too demoralised to serve as a bulwark of law and order. The legislative institutions and the intellectual opposition parties, lacking real authority in the eyes of the people, will be powerless to stem the popular tide, aroused by themselves, and Russia will be flung into hopeless anarchy; the issue of which cannot be foreseen.' The Tsar's favourite mystic, Grigory Rasputin, whom the Tsarina trusted more than anyone as 'Our Friend, sent from God', warned against war and predicted that if a conflict with Germany broke out, 'it will be the end for all of you'. Even he was ignored.[5]

In Russia the war started on a wave of patriotic fervour, as it did in all the belligerent countries. The Tsar was wildly cheered from the Winter Palace balcony when the declaration of war was made in St Petersburg, whose name had been changed to Petrograd to make it sound less German. The pan-Slavic nationalists and jingoistic press had for long been clamouring for battle. They were convinced it would be short, 'over by

Christmas', and end in victory – with Russia in control of the Balkans and having achieved the long-cherished Romanov ambition of seizing Constantinople from the Turks.

The opening offensives went well for the Russians. They quickly took swathes of Galicia from Austria-Hungary. But the moment they came up against the well-trained, professional German army sent to reinforce its Austrian ally they were entirely outmatched and suffered defeat after defeat. They lost an entire army corps at the Masurian Lakes, more than 120,000 men killed and wounded. The Battle of Tannenberg, just four weeks after the start of the war, was one of the worst ever defeats in Russian history: the entire 2nd Army was wiped out, with casualties of over 160,000. The winning general, Paul von Hindenburg, said later that 'we had to remove the mounds of enemy corpses from before our trenches in order to get a clear field of fire against fresh assaulting Russian waves. Imagination may try to reconstruct the figure of their losses, but an accurate calculation will remain for ever a vain thing.' The defeated general, Alexander Samsonov, went into the woods behind his command post and shot himself. Within three months the Russians had lost any real chance of waging an offensive war and were fighting to survive.[6]

Lenin was not a military man, but he acutely described the Russian army as 'a beautiful apple rotten at the core'. In the nineteenth century the Russian empire had expanded eastwards and southwards in the Caucasus; it had performed well in the Balkan Wars in the 1900s, less so against the British and French in the Crimea and poorly against the Japanese in 1904–05. Its tactics had barely changed since the time of Napoleon; the army was entirely unprepared for a war of attrition.

Russian casualties were staggering, far greater than anyone expected, and there were so few reserves that the army was soon forced to send untrained men from the second levy to the Front. By the end of October 1914 Russia had lost 1.2 million men, killed, wounded or missing, a high proportion of whom were trained junior officers and professional NCOs. The commander of the 8th Army, General Alexei Brusilov, who would later become supreme army commander, said that the Battle of Przemyśl that October was the last in which he commanded 'an army that had been properly taught and trained before the war . . . After hardly three months of war the greater part of our regular, professional officers and trained men had vanished, leaving only skeleton forces which had to be hastily filled with men wretchedly instructed who were sent to me from the depots . . . From that period onwards, the professional character of our forces disappeared . . . many could not even load their rifles. Such people could not really be considered soldiers at all . . . the regular army vanished, replaced by an army of ignoramuses.' The reserves in the rear were the men who 'were the breeding ground for mass desertion, discontent and finally mutiny which created the Revolution'. These were the men who would become Lenin's willing accomplices.[7]

The army ran out of equipment quicker than it ran out of soldiers. There were 6.5 million men under arms in October 1914, and only 4.6 million rifles issued. When war broke out the entire Russian army had just 679 motor cars and two motorised ambulances. Equipment, including heavy artillery, senior officers and wounded soldiers, was moved around from the railheads on peasant carts over muddy roads. The primitive state of communications was at the root of the military disaster. Along Russia's long Western Front there were just twenty-five telephones and a few Morse coding machines, and telegraph communications constantly broke down. Commanders and their aides had to move around on horseback to find out what was happening at the Front – rather as in the days described in *War and Peace*.

Industry was not producing enough ammunition, including shells for heavy guns, partly because the Tsar and the court nobility objected to business people making too much money from war. The generals thought there would be enough for the short war they were assured of and made no contingencies for weapons manufacture after a few months of combat. Many battalions had no ammunition after just a few weeks of fighting. By mid-October 1914 some soldiers were ordered to limit themselves to firing just ten rounds a day during battle. In many cases, when German heavy artillery bombarded their trenches Russian gunners were forbidden to return fire. At the Battle of Przemyśl Russian troops charged the Germans practically with their bare hands, and when they were mown down unarmed troops in the rear would fill the gaps, with orders to take the weapons from the fallen men. 'They were flung into the firing line armed with a bayonet in one hand and a kind of bomb/grenade in the other.'

Morale sank quickly, which the Bolsheviks used to their advantage.

Brusilov said that after the professional soldiers had been wiped out in the first weeks of the conflict, most of his reserves could see little further than their village or province and had no idea why the war was being fought. 'The new drafts arriving from the interior of Russia had not the slightest notion of what the war had to do with them,' he said.[8]

Vast numbers of Russian soldiers preferred being taken prisoner to fighting. In the first year of the war four and a half times as many Russians were captured than were killed in action – 1.2 million to 270,000. In the British army that number was reversed, with the dead outnumbering POWs by around five to one. As the war progressed Russian prisoners outnumbered the dead by sixteen to one. 'Threatening signs of growing demoralisation are becoming more and more evident,' General Alexei Polivanov, Minister of War, told the Tsar a little more than six months into the conflict. Some of the top commanders knew that a disaster was in the making, but could do nothing about it.[9]

In Swiss exile, Lenin saw the unpopularity of the war as a great opportunity to spread Bolshevism in the Russian army. But he was fighting battles of his own. For him the war that really mattered was not in the trenches and battlefields of Galicia and western Ukraine. He was more or less indifferent to the bloody conflicts in which millions of young working-class men were being butchered. Lenin's war was for the leadership of the revolutionary movement.

25

IN THE WILDERNESS

'How laughable and disappointing. Look at my fate. One fighting campaign after another – against political stupidities, banalities, opportunism . . . It has been like this since 1893. And so has the hatred of the vulgar people in payment. But I still would not exchange this fate for "peace" with the philistines and vulgarisers.'

Lenin to Inessa Armand, 5 December 1916

Lenin settled down to Swiss exile again, though he was bored by Berne and, worse to his mind, it had no decent libraries. He was studying Hegel's dialectics to get a firmer philosophical grasp of Marxism, Aristotle (in the original Greek), and trying to write a major book, which would eventually appear as *Imperialism: The Highest Stage of Capitalism*. But he lacked much of the material he needed and he became deeply frustrated.

Life returned to the way it had been before the war. They found a small apartment on the outskirts of town, near some charming woods. 'Across the road lived Inessa, five minutes' walk away the Zinovievs'. We would wander . . . the three of us for hours along the forest paths,' Nadya recalled. *Pravda* had been closed down early in September 1914 as it came out (under Lenin's direction) firmly against the war, but he produced a copious amount of journalism elsewhere. He lectured tirelessly in Switzerland and occasionally France. And, as always, he feuded bitterly with opponents in the revolutionary movement – the real enemy, as he saw things. Though he had some fame on the European Left, he was almost unknown in his own country outside the revolutionary movement. Even the reading public in Russia was not particularly interested in him. Two years before the war began a St Petersburg publisher, Mikhail Kedrov, brought out three volumes of his collected works. There were only 200 subscriptions. He had produced a print run of 3,000 but fewer than half were sold within a year and the rest were remaindered as waste paper.

In the first years of the war, and as he reached middle age – he was now in his mid-forties – Lenin was becoming increasingly impatient, irascible and difficult to deal with. As usual when he was under stress, he was plagued by insomnia, bad headaches and stomach cramps. The intemperate 'rages' described by Nadya occurred with more frequency. He quarrelled with almost everybody, even his sister Anna, one of the very few times there were cross words within his family. After a letter from him in the autumn of 1915 complaining harshly about something she had written along the lines that the war was going badly, Anna, deeply hurt, replied, 'Volodya . . . I feel I am being terrorised by you . . . to the point that I am scared of making any incautious expressions.' She had always supported him, worked for him ceaselessly and happily performed whatever task he had asked of her, yet he muttered to Nadya and close comrades that his sister had 'never made sense in politics in any case'. Anna heard of his remarks and suggested that perhaps her brother 'can't control himself'. They made up soon afterwards, but the incident showed the febrile state he was in.[1]

It was only with his ménage of Nadya and Inessa that he could reveal his true feelings. 'Watching him closely . . . he had become more re-served, more reflective, and when interrupted in reveries . . . one caught a glint of sadness in his eyes,' said Nadya. He wasn't on the whole prone to self-pity, but he could be mournful in his letters to Inessa. 'How I weary of this fetid back-parlour of revolutionary politics,' he told her. 'I am tired of meetings; my nerves are weak; my head aches; I am abso-lutely exhausted.'

The endless internal battles wore him down, even though he admit-ted, at least to Inessa, that often he was the cause of them. He could unburden himself like this only to her: 'Oh, how these "little matters of business" are mere fakes of the real business, surrogates of the busi-ness, a real obstacle to the business in the way that I see the fuss, the trouble, the little matters – and how I am tied up with them inextri-cably and for ever! . . . That's a sign that I am lazy and tired and in a poor humour. Generally I like my profession – and yet I almost hate it.' He treated each slight, each disagreement or small setback as a person-al insult. During the war he was removed from the editorial board of the German Social Democratic magazine *Vorborte* he raged in a letter to Inessa: 'Anyone who forgives such things in politics is a donkey or a scoundrel – impudent, insolent, stupid – and I shall never forgive . . . [them]. For such things you punch a man's face or turn away. To grant equality to little pigs and fools – never. But of course all this is *entre nous* and I can't write otherwise when I am speaking frankly, though perhaps the bad language might pass.'[2]

The death of Nadya's mother was a blow to their comfortable, if dull, life in Berne. Elizaveta Vasilyevna had been ailing for some time; she had shrunk to a dangerously small size and low weight, and had been suffering from dementia for several years. In early spring 1915 she came down with influenza, and was too weak to recover. On the night of 20 March she died, in her sleep, with Nadya beside her, aged seventy-five. She had wanted to return to Russia to die but it was impractical. 'We had no one there to look after her,' Nadya said. She and her son-in-law had quarrelled occasionally, but had lived together on generally good terms for nearly twenty years.

Nadya asked for her mother's body to be cremated, then a relatively novel practice and legalised in Switzerland only at the turn of the century. 'Vladimir Ilyich and I sat in the cemetery and after two hours they brought us a metal jug still warm with her ashes and they showed us where to bury them,' she told a friend.*[3]

A month later, deep in mourning, Nadya suffered a painful, recurring outbreak of the toxic goitre, Graves' Disease, which was supposed to have been cured by surgery two years earlier. The symptoms were

---

* Elizaveta Vasilyevna did eventually find her way back to Russia. On 21 February 1969, in the Brezhnev years, the Soviet government arranged for her ashes to be taken to Leningrad, as it was then called, where she was born. White propaganda in the Civil War put about an altogether different account of Lenin's mother-in-law's death, which was widely believed by some people. The story went like this. During her final illness Nadya sat up with her mother night after night. On 20 March, exhausted, she asked Lenin to relieve her for a few hours, 'but don't fail to wake me if Mother needs me'. Lenin sat with a book, while Elizaveta peacefully died during the night. The next morning Nadya was mortified and asked him why he had not woken her as he had promised. 'But I acted strictly in accordance with your instructions,' he is said to have replied. 'You wanted to be woken in case your mother needed you . . . [she died] so simply and logically did not need you any more.' This account is a popular anti-Communist myth, entirely fabricated. Nadya's account that she was with her mother is the truth.

familiar: heart palpitations, a swollen neck and luridly bulging eyes. She looked and felt awful. Doctors told her she must go on a rest cure and though she loved the Alps, she wrote to her friend Alexandra Kollontai, in exile in Scandinavia, for an alternative recommendation. 'I must go to the mountains . . . between 1,100 and 1,300 metres. Do you know if there are such mountains in Sweden or Norway? I'd be glad to get out of Switzerland; it's a sort of sleepy backwater here. Ask someone please if there are such mountains . . . and if living there is cheap.' But they could not reach Scandinavia. Geography was against them. How different might the history of the Revolution have been if Lenin had managed to find exile during the war in Norway or Sweden? He would not have had to make a pact with the Germans that almost destroyed his reputation in his homeland, and might have cost him his life as an alleged traitor.[4]

The quaint revolutionary threesome settled for the Alps instead and went on regular breaks to the Bernese Oberland. On one trip during the war, Lenin, Nadya and Inessa were gone for nearly four months to a resort at Sörenberg, between Berne and Lucerne. One visitor remembered watching Lenin working in the garden of the guest house where they were staying, while Inessa played the piano in the living room. He would stay in touch with Zinoviev and other revolutionaries with a phone call every morning at 8.30 a.m. In the afternoons they walked, usually the three of them. They would 'return in the evening with bouquets of rhododendrons and wild flowers and baskets of mushrooms. We were comfortable there . . . all around us there were woods and high mountains – and there was even snow on the peak of the Rothorn. Mail arrived with Swiss punctuality. We discovered that even in such an out of the way village it was possible to obtain free of charge any book from the Berne or Zurich Public Library.' Once Lenin was spotted swimming in the nude in the River Kleine Emme.[5]

Nadya regained her health amid the mountains. But then came another family bereavement. Lenin knew he would almost certainly never see his mother again, but when she died on 25 July 1916 aged eighty-one following a series of illnesses, he was distraught. Maria Alexandrovna had been a constant in his life, though he had seen little of her in the previous twenty years. He was miserable that he couldn't have been there at her death, or go to her funeral at the Lutheran section of Volkovo Cemetery in Petrograd. The pallbearers were his brother-in-law Mark Elizarov and

Vladimir Bonch-Bruevich, a family friend and staunch Bolshevik who became Lenin's personal secretary when he returned to Russia.

Lenin's uncompromising stance against the war seemed like a risky mistake to many of his loyal supporters. Party activists, particularly in Russia during the early euphoria over the war, believed it made the Bolsheviks look extreme and unpatriotic. Support drifted away and 'the consequences are very serious for us', a loyalist from Petrograd warned Lenin. Even Inessa, who loathed German and Austrian imperialism, didn't agree with Lenin about the war – and frequently told him so.

Lenin was unapologetic. In the short term he accepted that the Bolsheviks would pay a price. But strategically Lenin was right. In the long run his consistent line against the war was a crucial factor in helping him seize power – and keep hold of it. When the mood changed in Russia and war-weariness started growing, support for the Bolsheviks increased. Lenin could plausibly argue that as he had always been against the conflict, he and the Bolsheviks could bring peace. It was the main promise to the people in 1917.

Lenin's line was simple. He wanted his country to lose the war; defeat would be a spark to revolution. 'Tsarism is a hundred times worse than Kaiserism,' he told Alexander Shlyapnikov, one of the leading Bolsheviks in Scandinavia, who ensured that the statement was smuggled from Sweden into Russia. 'From the point of view of the working class and the toiling masses of Russia, the lesser evil would be the defeat of the Tsarist monarchy and its army.' He wasn't a pacifist – far from it. 'That sort of talk about peace is for clergymen and philistines.' He wanted to turn the war between nations into a class war against the capitalist oppressors. 'The entire essence of our work (persistent, systematic, maybe of long duration) must be to turn the national war into a civil war. When this will happen . . . isn't clear. We have to let the moment ripen – force it to ripen . . . but we are duty-bound to work, for as long as it takes, in this direction.'

The following month he made the same point to Alexandra Kollontai in Sweden. 'Turning the present imperialist war into civil war is the only proper proletarian slogan.' The socialist movement, he added, would benefit from the war; it would be 'purged' by the conflict. 'The European war has done a great service to international socialism in that it has clearly revealed the whole state of rottenness, baseness and swinery of the opportunists . . . thus giving a magnificent incentive towards cleaning up the workers' movement and ridding it of the filth which has accumulated during the scores of peaceful years.'[6]

The Left, including the Social Democrats, split into three groups with different positions on the war. The Defencists supported their own countries 'in defence of the Fatherland'. The Internationalists were neutral and maintained what had been the traditional socialist argument that workers shouldn't be killing each other for the benefit of the capitalists. The Defeatists wanted their own country beaten as the lesser of two evils because 'victory' would strengthen their own capitalist regimes and delay the Revolution. Lenin was the arch-'defeatist', but would also support the Internationalists when compromise with them made tactical sense.

Throughout the war he was in bitter conflict with the Defencists – 'vermin who have betrayed socialism', he called them. His opponents were mostly the usual suspects – Mensheviks and 'bourgeois liberals dressed up as socialists'. The chief traitor was Georgy Plekhanov, who said at the start of the war that 'if I wasn't old and sick I would be a volunteer and join the army. To run through the German comrades with a bayonet would give me great pleasure.' Lenin wrote a terse reply: 'It must be the primary task of Social Democrats in each country to combat their own nation's chauvinism.' They were hardly ever in direct communication again, though they argued incessantly in the press throughout the war.

There were repeated efforts to unite the Left, but it proved impossible. There could be no compromise between Lenin, Plekhanov and the German Social Democrats. At one key conference in September 1915, at a Swiss mountain resort, Trotsky (an Internationalist) drafted what became known as the rousing anti-war Zimmerwald Manifesto – 'Working Men and Women! Mothers and Fathers! Widows and Orphans! Wounded and Crippled! To all who are suffering from the war, or as a consequence of the war, we cry out over the frontiers, over the smoking battlefields, over the devastated cities and hamlets: WORKERS OF THE WORLD UNITE.' Lenin supported it, but it was defeated by a combination of the Mensheviks and the Germans. Lenin was not surprised. He had never taken the conference seriously anyway, knowing he would be defeated. He spent much of it outside the meeting room playing with the dogs of the owner of the Zimmerwald Hotel, where the proceedings took place. At Kiental, another Alpine resort, seven months later Lenin was defeated again and there was no outright condemnation of the war. But the Manifesto became the Bolsheviks' battle cry.

Lenin wrote scores of articles about the politics of the war, and what it would mean for the Left. But he barely mentioned the human dimension of the conflict, the industrial scale of the slaughter taking place. He argued that the outcome of each individual battle did not matter. Declaring a victory at any given moment for one side or the other, 'for one set of thieves, against another group of thieves', was irrelevant. That it was Europe's working class who did most of the dying was a bloody reality about which he seemed to care little. Martov was a pacifist, neutral in the war, and he was fighting his own internecine battles with Lenin, but he was right when he told a group of friends that Lenin 'wasn't interested in . . . peace or war. The only thing that interests him is the Revolution. And the only real revolution for him is the one in which the Bolsheviks have seized power.'[7]

Inessa and Lenin had tempestuous rows, which always mixed the personal and the political. During a conversation in Berne soon after the war broke out he told her that he had close friendships and respect for only 'two or three women during my life' – clearly implying, though not saying explicitly, that she was one of them. He heard nothing more about the comment for several days, but then out of the blue received an indignant letter back accusing him of 'extreme arrogance' by saying he knew only two or three women who deserved respect. Lenin was affronted and wouldn't let the matter drop. He told her she had wilfully misunderstood his point. 'Never, never have I written that I value only three women. Never! What I wrote is that my unconditional friendship, absolute respect and trust are dedicated to only two or three women. This is a completely different thing.'[8]

Soon afterwards they had another serious disagreement which clearly crossed the line between socialist theory and their own relationship – on the issue of 'free love'. Following a long discussion about love and marriage with her daughters Inna and Varvara early in 1915, Inessa began work on a pamphlet she wanted to write about women's rights under the law – marriage, divorce, love and sex in the new age of revolution. She wrote a synopsis, which she was anxious to show Lenin, assuming he would be as enthusiastic about the subject matter as she was and would give her encouragement. Instead the response she received was cold, harsh, rude and pedantic – like a lecture on Marx he might have given at Berne Rathaus, rather than to a woman with whom he had been on intimate terms. Her synopsis covered a range of feminist topics, but he picked up on only one area – her call for women to have 'freedom of love'. Freud would no doubt have as much to say as Marx about why he concentrated on this subject, but his thoughtless comments wounded Inessa deeply. The free love demand, he told her dogmatically, was politically incorrect – a bourgeois concept, not a proletarian one; 'you should consider the *objective logic* of class relations in matters of love'. Besides, a self-interested and 'immoral pursuit of love at any cost' would result in promiscuity and adultery.

Inessa was understandably enraged, both by the point he was making and his tactless way of putting it. It was prudish, unimaginative and entirely ignored her own position. Had Inessa not left her husband for love? Did he not love her, adulterously? She replied that the issue had nothing to do with class relations and he was 'confusing freedom of love . . . with freedom of adultery. Surely even a fleeting passion is . . . more poetic and pure than kisses without love between a husband and wife.'

Lenin still didn't see her point and defended himself as though the matter was entirely academic, as though they had not conducted a love affair, and he wasn't still living with his wife. 'Kisses without love between vulgar spouses are *filthy*. I agree. These need to be contrasted . . . with what? It would seem: kisses with love. But you contrast a fleeting (why a fleeting?) passion (why not love?) – and it comes out logically as if kisses without love . . . are contrasted to marital kisses without love.' Weren't both reprehensible?*[8]

---

* Nadya was much more prudish than Lenin and never believed in the kind of 'free love' advocated by Inessa and, more notoriously, by Alexandra Kollontai. Nadya liked Kollontai and they became good friends, but she admitted that she was 'deeply shocked' by Kollontai's famous comment that when women's emancipation arrived and there was equality between the sexes, for women making love would be 'no more

They agreed to disagree – a rare event with Lenin – but the exchange clearly left Inessa dissatisfied. For a while she cut herself off from Lenin and Nadya, was slow in replying to his letters and displayed increasing independence. There was no mistaking his need for her when she wasn't near him, in this lover's apology. 'Dear friend, . . . Apparently the lack of reply to several of my latest letters indicates – in connection with something else – a certain changed mood, a decision, your situation. At the end of your last letter a word was repeated twice. I went and checked. Nothing. I don't know what to think, whether you are offended by something or were too distracted . . . I'm afraid to ask, as I know you don't like questions, and so I've decided to think that you don't like being questioned and that's that. So I'm sorry . . . '[9]

The Germans were keeping as close an eye on Lenin as were the Okhrana. Lenin knew German spies were following him and he was careful to avoid obvious contact with any Germans or their agents while he was in exile. If it became known back home in Russia that he was consorting with anyone representing the Triple Alliance – but particularly a German – it would severely damage his reputation and harm the Bolsheviks. He was on the lookout for provocateurs and kept his distance from newcomers. In Berne he regularly met Karl Moor, a Swiss banker and Social Democrat who helped finance the Bolsheviks. Lenin began to be suspicious of him when Moor wanted to introduce him to other leftists whom Lenin didn't know. He wrote to trusted Swiss radicals and asked them to check Moor out. 'What is Moor like? Has it been completely and absolutely proved that he is honest? Has he had any recent direct or indirect hobnobbing with German Social Imperialists [Lenin's new term for pro-war Social Democrats] . . . I urge you to check him very carefully – with documentary evidence if you can. There must be

significant than sipping a glass of water', as it was, she argued, for most men. Nadya was bourgeois middle class when it came to sexual matters, and treated marriage – her own and those of others – with much more reverence than other feminists in her radical set. She never expressed approval for any alternative to monogamy, and certainly never flirted with another man after she married Lenin. His comment on Kollontai's 'glass of water' remark was typical Lenin: 'Yes of course everyone has needs. But who would choose to drink from a puddle?'

no room for the shadow of doubt or rumour.' Moor passed the test and Lenin was satisfied.*

But through guile, secrecy and elaborate subterfuge – all things Lenin enjoyed immensely – he maintained some links with Germany that proved vital to the success of the Revolution. If it had not been for an obese, louche, corrupt multi-millionaire socialist called Alexander Helphand – usually known by the code-name Parvus – Lenin might never have seized power in Russia. Of all the scoundrels, crooks, charlatans, murderers and ruthless cynics – as well as idealists, clever thinkers and subtle politicians – who appear in these pages, Parvus was the most curious and grotesque.

Born in 1867 near Minsk, the son of a Jewish artisan, Helphand/Parvus went to school in Odessa and university in Berne, where he obtained a doctorate in philosophy. He returned to Russia and became a successful journalist and public speaker; he was 'scintillatingly quick-witted, with a paradox nearly always on his lips'. In a series of articles in 1904 he forecast, almost exactly as it happened, Russia's defeat in the war against Japan, and the revolutionary opportunity at home. He could be a serious thinker. The idea of 'permanent revolution', the central theory of what would become Trotskyism, was developed by him. He played a prominent part in the 1905 Revolution, along with Trotsky, with whom he was close politically and personally. But they drifted apart. They were arrested, separately, towards the end of 1905 and exiled to Siberia. Both escaped, Parvus to Germany, where he made a fortune in various businesses – from publishing to selling chemicals, pharmaceuticals and condoms to the German army. Parvus loved political plotting, 'being in the know' and at the centre of events; but he loved money rather more.

Briefly he became Gorky's agent and represented his literary interests in Germany, at a time when *The Lower Depths* was playing to full houses. According to Gorky, Parvus took 20 per cent of the profits for himself, and agreed to give a quarter to Gorky and the rest to

---

* Moor was an odd fish. He was very wealthy but a genuine radical – and, in fact, also a double agent for German military intelligence. He never betrayed Lenin, however, who admired his intelligence and his useful gossip about Swiss politics. Strangely, after the Revolution, though his role as a German agent was exposed, he moved to Soviet Russia and kept in occasional contact with Lenin.

the German Social Democratic Party. Parvus amassed more than 100,000 marks, but instead of handing Gorky his share he wrote to him frankly, explaining that he had spent it all on a luxurious trip to Italy with a female companion. Gorky replied good-humouredly that 'it must have been a very pleasant holiday'. Yet he still complained to the German Social Democrats. A 'court' comprising Party heavyweights Kautsky, Bebel and Zetkin 'condemned Helphand morally' and he left Germany for Constantinople, where he became a political adviser to the 'Young Turk' movement which wanted to modernise the Ottoman empire. He made another vast fortune in trade with the Turkish military.

As a young man he had been handsome and svelte, but he grew hideously obese. 'His stomach vibrated like a sack of grain,' one of his good friends remarked. 'He was a massive, gigantic figure . . . broad, bull-like face with its high forehead, tiny nose and carefully trimmed beard, and a flabby double chin, behind which his neck completely disappeared. The small lovely eyes were deeply embedded in fat. His short legs were barely strong enough to support his body, and when he was standing up or walking he seemed to use his arms to maintain himself on an even keel.'

He saw the war as an opportunity to make a vast amount of money – but also to further revolution in Russia. Despite his champagne breakfasts and series of young mistresses which shocked the puritan comrades, he believed that revolution was bound to come to Russia, and he wanted to be the man to speed up the process. He was convinced 'that the interests of the German government are identical with those of the Russian revolutionaries. The Russian Social Democrats can achieve their aims only with the destruction of Tsarism. On the other hand, Germany would not be completely successful if it were not possible to kindle a major revolution in Russia.' In March 1915 he wrote an eighteen-page memorandum which he presented to the German Foreign Ministry detailing how Russia could be destabilised from within by groups of revolutionaries, who would organise a series of army mutinies, strikes and acts of sabotage. The German government was convinced the plan could work and gave Parvus a million marks – the equivalent of more than US$4 million in 2016 – to bring about revolution in Russia. Parvus moved his business operations to Copenhagen, where he could appear more neutral and operate more freely.*

He went to Berne in May 1915 with the sole intention of meeting Lenin and offering him a large amount of money to help the Bolsheviks. He wouldn't be the only recipient of the German largesse: many other radical groups, the Mensheviks and the Socialist Revolutionaries among them, would be offered cash too. But Lenin was key to the plan. As Parvus told Arthur Zimmermann, the German Foreign Minister, Lenin was 'much more raving mad' than the other revolutionaries and the most vociferous against the war.

Parvus arrived in Switzerland with his latest paramour, Ekaterina Groman, and took a suite in the most expensive hotel in Berne. One evening he entered a restaurant where Russian émigrés habitually met and went straight to a table where Lenin, Nadya, Inessa and a group of Bolsheviks were dining. Lenin knew a great deal about Parvus but they had never met. They had a brief conversation, and the two of them left the restaurant. Lenin took Parvus to his apartment where they talked alone for several hours. Lenin told nobody details of the meeting. All Helphand said, later, was that he tried to convince Lenin that the Bolsheviks couldn't win without German help. Lenin distrusted Parvus on sight. If it ever got out publicly that he had accepted funds from 'this dissipated man' his political career could be finished. He turned down any deal – 'Parvus ate without salt,' Lenin maintained, meaning he got nothing out of the meeting. But he kept a line of contact open to 'that fat man' through one of his most trusted and useful lieutenants, Yakov Fürstenberg, also known as Ganetsky Hanecki or Borel, who lived in Copenhagen and took a job with Parvus.† It suited Lenin politically to disassociate himself from Parvus, but he genuinely

---

* Rosa Luxemburg, beacon of socialist purity, despised him. Helphand, she sneered, was 'first to make a fortune during a war in which millions of proletarians are being killed, and then sit in the safety of Klampenborg in Denmark and run from there a limited company for the exploitation of . . . two national proletariats – for this "superior" revolutionary role we have little understanding'.

† Lenin also turned down work writing for the socialist paper which Parvus had established, *Die Glocke* (The Bell), which was a tub-thumping pro-war journal campaigning for German victory. He described it as 'an organ of renegades and dirty lackeys . . . a cesspool of German nationalism . . . not a single honest thought, not a single serious argument, not a single straightforward article could be found'.

hated him – everything from his appearance to his extravagant lifestyle and his hypocrisy. No money went from Parvus to the Bolsheviks until Lenin returned to Russia in 1917. Later he would be altogether less fastidious.[10]

26

THE LAST EXILE

'How could this obstinate little man . . . Lenin ever have become so important?' Stefan Zweig, *The Tide of Fortune*, 1927

At the beginning of 1917 Nadya and Lenin had never been so poor. They were no longer receiving money from Russia following his mother's death. Rich donors to the Bolsheviks had dried up; there was no access to the tainted funds from the Schmidt inheritance and Lenin was earning a pittance from writing and lecturing. He was still awarding himself the same Party 'salary' as before, but it wasn't a great deal for two to live on. Nadya was taking work copying and teaching Russian to private students but they were few and far between. She was left a small legacy of 4,000 rubles from an aunt – her mother's sister, who had been a teacher in Novocherkassk, a small town near Rostov. An Austrian banker transferred the money from Galicia, but took a 50 per cent commission. Unlike her husband, Nadya seldom complained about money, but she wrote to her sister-in-law Maria: 'We shall soon be coming to the end of our former means of subsistence and the question of earning a living will be serious. It is difficult to find anything here. I will have to think of a literary income.* I don't want this side of our affairs to be Volodya's worry alone. He works so hard as it is. The question of an income worries him greatly.'[1]

Soon afterwards Lenin told Maria the same thing. 'I must say I need an income. Otherwise I shall simply perish. Truly! The fiendishly high cost of living – there is nothing to live on. Money must be squeezed out

---

* Nadya was negotiating a commission with a publisher to write a popular pedagogical dictionary about child development and teaching methods. But no deal was ever finalised before she and Lenin returned to Russia.

forcibly somehow. Shlyapnikov must speak about this to Gorky himself, if this isn't too awkward . . . and to the publisher of *Letopis* [a left-wing magazine] to whom two of my articles have been sent . . . let them pay immediately – and as much as possible. If this is not arranged I shall not be able to hold out. Of this I am sure. This is *very, very* serious.' Lenin was wont to whinge about money, even when his mother was alive and sending him subventions. But he had seldom written in such desperate terms before. He was not utterly penurious in the way many other Russian émigrés were – 'I never had to worry about bread . . . that never happened in my life,' he admitted. But he faced unaccustomed hardships.

They had moved to Zurich in March 1916, into the most modest of all their various homes in the long years of exile. 'We were reduced to . . . the very lower depths of the town,' as Nadya admitted.[2]

At first they rented one room in a boarding house in the ancient, down-at-heel centre of Zurich. They took their meals at a small eating house close by, run by a middle-aged blonde woman, Frau Perlog. It was dark and dirty and 'smelled more like a mouldy cellar than a restaurant', but, typically, Lenin made a political point and said he liked how 'plebeian' it was, and was delighted to be 'frequenting a place where they used chipped cups for tea'. They shared the dining room with a prostitute known as Red Maria – a reference to the colour of her curly hair rather than her politics. She told Lenin and Nadya her troubles, explaining that she was resorting to her profession to support her ageing mother and younger siblings. Her Austrian lover had been taken away from her by the war, which she said 'was nothing but robbery of men, a dirty trick . . . by the rich'. Frau Perlog would echo the sentiment. She told Lenin that she didn't understand why the soldiers didn't just shoot their officers and go home. Lenin smiled and agreed.

After a few weeks they moved to a small room on the second floor of a five-storey building, 14 Spiegelgasse, in the medieval centre of Zurich overlooking a courtyard 'that often smelled of a nearby sausage factory'.* The apartment was sublet to them by a cobbler, Titus Kammerer, who ran his business from the ground floor of the building next door. It

---

* It was the building next door to the boarding house where the playwright Georg Büchner wrote *Woyzeck*.

was a miserable and dark room, but they got used to it, despite the poor heating in the winter and the overpowering smells in the summer. There was one table to eat and work on, a couple of chairs and two single iron bedsteads. Kammerer recalled that Lenin and Nadya 'lived in a very plain way . . . but he seemed like a good fellow . . . with a neck like a bull . . . she was a good soul but she didn't look well much of the time. She would have been a good hausfrau, but she had her mind always on other work.'

They ate very simply and the meals were rarely improved by Nadya's extraordinary capacity to burn the potatoes or oatmeal they invariably ate for lunch. Lenin would look at Herr Kammerer and joke, 'There! You see we live in grand style.' They ate meat as a special treat on Sundays. Frau Kammerer gave Nadya the first cookery lessons of her life, showing her how she could prepare simple, cheap but nourishing meals in her own tiny room.[3]

As usual, Lenin would stick to a routine. Each morning he would be at the Central Library at Zähringerplatz by 9 a.m. and come home for lunch. He returned to the library for two hours, and then read the papers at either the Café Adler or the Café Odeon on the Limmatquai by the lake. He held meetings of his small Bolshevik faction in a back room of the Zur Eintracht, another café in the old city. One or two evenings a week he would give lectures on socialism. As always they would take regular exercise. On Thursdays, when the Zurich Central Library closed at lunchtime, he and Nadya would walk up the 700-metre-high Zürichberg, 'take a chocolate snack and find a favourite spot in the thick of the woods where there were no crowds'. In fine weather they would remain until evening. At weekends they would go for long walks by the lake shore.

In six months Lenin completed one of his longest and most interesting books, *Imperialism: The Highest Stage of Capitalism*. Much is dated, but some of his ideas had resonance now: 'Capitalism . . . is no longer the progressive force described by Marx'; the free market era 'has been followed by a new one in which production is concentrated in vast syndicates and trusts which aim at monopoly control'. Giant multinational technology companies 'freeze out other competition to forestall independent technological innovation'. Financial control 'has passed from the industrialists themselves to a handful of banking conglomerates – the creation of a banking oligarchy'.

There were few territories left for rising powers like the US to exploit. They had no alternative but to resort to militarisation and war. 'National independence movements . . . will have to be crushed in an endless cycle to maintain their markets. This movement for national independence threatens . . . capital in its most valuable and promising fields of exploitation, and capital can maintain its dominance only by continually increasing its military forces.' These were points made as much on the Right as the Left in 2017 – especially the dangers to the economy of a 'banking oligarchy' and the monopoly aims of the technology corporations.

* * *

Zinoviev was in Zurich, Inessa split her time between Berne, Zurich and occasional visits to Paris, and as war-weariness grew, a trickle of Mensheviks and 'Defencists' drifted towards Lenin. But the numbers were small. The Swiss police barely took any notice of the Bolsheviks, though the Russian and German spies continued to follow him closely: 'they knew what he was reading, what he was writing, what he had for breakfast', as Zinoviev put it.* Nadya and Lenin hardly ever met anyone outside a tight-knit group of Russian émigrés, though Zurich was teeming with exiles from various European countries waiting out the war. Occasionally he met the great Austrian writer Stefan Zweig, an anti-war pacifist, at the Café Odéon, where Bolsheviks frequently congregated – the Mensheviks favoured the Adler. Zweig was not impressed, wondering in later years 'how could this obstinate little man . . . Lenin ever have become so important?'.[4]

Lenin did not despair: 'Reaction is triumphant at the moment . . . but our day will come,' he told Inessa in a letter in the new year of 1917. He was not sure when, though he didn't appear to think it would be

---

* The local authorities seemed more concerned with the group of Dadaist poets and artists who had congregated in Zurich during the war. The avant-garde painter and early film-maker Hans Richter said the police believed 'we were capable of perpetrating some new enormity at any moment to shock the provincial sensibilities of the Swiss. All the quiet and studious Russians were doing, in an unostentatious little way, was planning a world revolution.'

imminent. At the end of 1916 he had applied for a further year's extension on his residence permit to stay in Switzerland and, with his application, had to send proof that he had; a bank account (he had, it contained 100 francs credit). He wrote to Inessa about his latest plan – to establish a small publishing company to produce a series of pamphlets about the tasks for the Left in Europe while the war dragged on. A few days later he wrote to her again, and clearly the fall of the Romanovs and returning to Russia was not at the forefront of his mind. He was convinced, for some reason – he never explained why – that the Western powers were about to invade Switzerland and was concerned about Party funds. 'If Switzerland is drawn into the war, the French will occupy Geneva immediately. To be in Geneva then is to be in France – is to be in touch with Russia. I am therefore thinking of turning the Party's funds to you, for you to keep on your person, sewn up in a special little bag.' Nothing came of the plan, but at one point he genuinely imagined that Inessa would walk around Switzerland for the duration of the war with the Bolshevik money chest secreted about her clothes. For a highly clever man who would soon be in charge of one of the most powerful empires the world had seen, Lenin had some bizarre ideas.[5]

At the Zurich Volkshaus on 22 January 1917 he spoke on the lessons of the 1905 Revolution to a group of Swiss students and young workers. 'The coming years, precisely because of this predatory war, will lead to popular risings by the working class . . . and these upheavals will lead to the victory of socialism. We of the older generation may not live to see the decisive battles of this coming revolution. But I can express the confident hope that the youth, which is working so splendidly in the socialist movement, will be fortunate enough not only to fight but to win this revolution.' He was asked by the young Romanian leftist Valeriu Marcu when he thought that a revolution in Russia might begin. He answered, 'Perhaps in two, perhaps in five, at the latest in ten years.' Revolution had been his main thought every day for the last two decades, but when it finally came just a few weeks later, he was totally unprepared for it and as surprised as anyone.

27

REVOLUTION – PART ONE

'And over Russia I see a quiet far-spreading fire consume all.'
Alexander Blok (1880–1921)

'We danced the Last Tango on the rim of trenches filled with forgotten corpses.' Vasily Shulgin (1878–1976)

In Petrograd, the well-off were partying like there was no tomorrow – which, for so many of them, there wouldn't be. This was at the tail end of the so-called 'Silver Age' in Russian culture, an extraordinary flowering of art, literature, music, design and science. Amid the raw creative energy of the revolutionary moment writers like Alexander Blok and Nikolai Gumilev wrote their finest poetry, and Wassily Kandinsky, Marc Chagall and Kazimir Malevich were producing remarkable paintings. The great tenor Fyodor Chaliapin was at the height of his powers; Sergei Diaghilev's *Ballets Russes* amazed audiences throughout Europe. Sergei Rachmaninov, Igor Stravinsky and Sergei Prokofiev were in varying ways revolutionising music. Russian scientists like the chemist Dmitry Mendeleyev and the pioneer of modern psychological research Ivan Pavlov were winning Nobel Prizes. But the reverse side of the coin was a 'senseless ennui', as the writer Dmitry Merezhovsky put it, and a pervasive air of impending doom. In a famous poem Anna Akhmatova captured the spirit:

We are all winners, we are all whores
How sad we are together.

The epic, thoughtless scale of the bacchanal, the drinking and promiscuity, went beyond decadence. It was part hysteria, part statement of hopelessness. 'To what state have the Romanovs brought us? To the fifth act of a tragedy played in a brothel,' said Merezhovsky, whose politics were of the Right. His wife Zinaida Gippius, a fine poet, wrote in her diary, 'Russia is a very large lunatic asylum. If you visit an asylum on an open day you may not realise you are in one. It looks normal enough but the inmates are all mad.'[1]

Vodka had been banned since the start of the war, though wine and liqueurs were not, which didn't lead to harmony between the classes.* The poor resorted to home-made or black-market hooch to drown their sorrows; the rich binged on vast quantities of wine and champagne. Huge fortunes were gambled away overnight, while food shortages hit average families and inflation rocketed. The price of most foods, including the Russian staple, bread, rose 500 per cent between summer 1914 and January 1917. Inflation in medicines was higher still: a kilo of aspirin cost two rubles in 1914, by the end of 1916 it was 200. The price of quinine rose from four rubles a kilo to 400. Speculation and crude profiteering were rife. There had been long queues outside food shops since the autumn of 1915 and they were getting longer as the war went on. Camps with beds had been established outside some big bakeries and butchers. In January 1917 an average working woman in St Petersburg would put in a ten-hour shift – and spend forty hours a week queuing for food.

Shows of vulgar excess during wartime shocked foreigners and the middle classes at home. Sir Samuel Hoare, the British intelligence chief in Petrograd, grew to hate the Russian upper classes: 'their wealth and the lavish use they made of it dazzled me after the austere conditions of wartime England'. One guest at an extravagant reception given in Petrograd for a visiting Japanese prince reported 'too much glare, silver and plate, food and music, too many flowers and servants'. The suicide rate in Russia tripled during the war years – an epidemic that affected mainly young people under twenty-eight.

There was sexual licence on a previously unprecedented scale, and

---

* A foolish prohibition which left a giant black hole in the budget. The sale of vodka was a state monopoly and the scale so large that the tax brought in nearly 20 per cent of the state's income. To make up for the loss the government had to borrow yet more, adding to the already enormous debts caused by the war, and also to print money which fuelled inflation. Though rarely mentioned, the vodka ban was a big factor in the fall of the Tsarist regime; and seventy years later, when the last Soviet leader, Mikhail Gorbachev, tried to prohibit alcohol, the result was similar. It helped to bankrupt the USSR and played a major part in the collapse of the Soviet Union.

among the rich, divorce – rare until around 1910 – became common. The millionairess Madame Zimin played bridge every Sunday at her palatial Petrograd apartment with her 'three husbands – two ex and one real'. Alexander Blok chased women frenetically, and his actress wife Lyuba was only slightly less promiscuous. 'I have had a hundred women – 200 – 300 (maybe more?),' he wrote. 'But really only two: one is Lyuba; the other – all the rest.'[2]

Morale in the army had sunk. Five million soldiers had been killed, wounded or taken prisoner by the end of 1916. They were deserting in droves. The President of the Duma, Mikhail Rodzianko, told friends that 'the symptoms of the army's disintegration could already be felt in the second year of the war . . . Reinforcements from reserve battalions were arriving at the Front with a quarter of the men having deserted . . . sometimes echelons bound for the Front would halt because they had nothing left but officers and subalterns. Everyone else had scattered.' Officers overstayed their leave, often by many weeks, and spent their time at the gambling halls and smart restaurants. 'Hotels thronged with officers who should be at the Front. There is no disgrace in being a shirker or in finding a sinecure at the rear.'[3]

The soldiers were increasingly weary of the war. This was the recruiting ground for the Bolsheviks and other radical groups. By tradition there had always been a large garrison of troops in Petrograd, principally in case they were needed to quell potential revolt. Senior generals were worried that far too many soldiers were crammed into the city – more than 250,000 of them – and many 'were looking dangerous and menacing', as one general said. 'It is putting kindling wood next to a powder keg.' He noted that 4,000 men from the crack Preobrazhensky Regiment were shoehorned into barracks built for 1,200. 'If God does not spare Russia a revolution . . . it will be started not by the people but the army.'[4]

Predictions of imminent revolution were on the lips of everyone in the intelligentsia, among Russia's upper classes and the more acute foreigners. 'More and more every day the signs of trouble multiplied – and yet nothing was done to avoid the inevitable crisis,' Meriel Buchanan, the daughter of Sir George Buchanan, the British Ambassador to Russia, confided in her diary. The British Field Marshal Sir Henry Wilson, formerly Chief of the Imperial General Staff, spent most of January and early February 1917 in Petrograd, Moscow and the Eastern Front as head of an Allied mission looking at how the other Entente powers could aid Russia. He reported to London that 'opinion prevails . . . [here] that the Emperor and Empress were a danger to the country and would very likely be assassinated'. His diary entry for 16 February reads: 'It seems as certain as anything can be that the Emperor and Empress are riding for a fall. Everyone – officers, merchants, ladies – talk openly of the absolute necessity of doing away with them.'* There was a more sanguine view from the British Cabinet Minister Lord Milner, visiting Russia separately around the same time. He told his ministerial colleagues at the beginning of February that 'I have formed the opinion that there is a great deal of exaggeration in the talk about revolution'.⁵

The Okhrana was aware of the public mood and repeatedly sent warnings to the highest levels of the government. A report to the Interior Minister, Alexander Protopopov, in October 1916 stated in stark terms that it wasn't the revolutionary groups the regime should be worried about: 'it is the people'. The agent said that 'now anger is not directed against the government generally but against the Tsar'. The report told the minister, if he didn't already know, that invariably Alexandra was called 'the German woman' and scandalous sex rumours were rife about the relationship between her and Grigory Rasputin 'which are extremely damaging to the government'. It did not matter whether the stories were true – they certainly were not – but they were widely believed. The country was on a precipice 'beside which 1905 was child's play. The alarming mood grows stronger by the day. It penetrates through all levels of the population and there is the very strong threat of great turbulence, brought about . . . principally by economic factors, hunger and the unequal distribution of food and the monstrous price increases

---

* The Field Marshal had heard of the last audience with the Tsar given to Sir George Buchanan early in January 1917. The ambassador told him that there was now a barrier between him and his people and that if Russia was still united as a nation it was in opposing his present policy . . . 'Your Majesty, if I may be permitted to say so, has but one safe course . . . namely, to break down the barrier that separates you from your people and to regain their confidence.' The Emperor, who was significantly shorter than the languid and elegant Buchanan, drew himself up to his fullest height and replied coldly, 'Do you mean that *I* am to regain the confidence of my people or that they are to regain *my* confidence?'

in articles of prime necessity. Until now this discontent has had an economic basis and has not been connected with a political movement. But it only needs something concrete and specific to take on a political expression. If bread becomes more scarce this will touch off the strongest kind of disorders . . . and endless street riots.'

A few weeks later an Okhrana report from agents who had infiltrated front-line troops and reserves warned army chiefs that if 'there is a revolution it would be supported by two-thirds of . . . active soldiers'.

On 5 January 1917 the Petrograd Okhrana was reporting to the Interior Ministry that there were plots to topple the Tsar by members of the royal family and senior centre-right figures in the Duma, who argued that 'we have to save the monarchy from the monarch'. It said that 'the mood in the capital had taken on an exceptionally threatening character. The wildest rumours are circulating in society that the government intends to take various reactionary steps . . . the population openly, on the streets, in the streetcars, in the theatres and in shops, expect some sort of extraordinary action, a crisis, initiated by one side or another.'[6]

At their decadent, wild parties the intelligentsia knew things could not continue as they had. 'We know something is coming,' Zinaida Gippius said. 'But will it be "the Revolution", or some monstrosity with an unknown name?'[7]

In Zurich, early on the afternoon of 2 March, Lenin was preparing to return to the Central Library after lunch with Nadya. She was washing the dishes, he was putting on his coat, when they heard footsteps running up the stairs to their room. Breathless, the young Polish Bolshevik Party member Mieczysław Bronsky blurted out: 'Haven't you heard the news? There has been a revolution in Russia.' Lenin at first didn't believe him. 'We've heard this sort of rumour before. It might be German propaganda.' But all three went to the Bellevue Platz on the lake shore, where the newspapers could be read on wall posters. The news was confirmed by the *Neue Zürcher Zeitung*, the *Züricher Post* and some foreign papers, though the reports from Petrograd provided few details. Lenin knew that there had been a wholesale mutiny in the army, a Provisional Government had taken power in Russia and there were riots on the streets of the capital and in Moscow. It wasn't clear at that stage that the Tsar had abdicated. As in 1905 Lenin was entirely unprepared for the news, though he grasped the significance of the events straight away.

The first person he contacted was Inessa, who was staying for a few days at a health resort in Clarens, near Montreux. He wrote to her from a nearby café: 'We are in a state of great agitation today. I am *beside myself* that I cannot go to Scandinavia. I will *never forgive myself* [Lenin's italics] for not risking the journey in 1915 . . . Russia must have been on the brink of revolution for days . . . I am so excited.'[8]

Then he worked out a political line to adopt. He had not expected the fall of the *ancien regime* so soon but, as he repeatedly said, 'revolutionaries don't wait for a revolution . . . they make the revolution'. This might be his only opportunity for power – and he was determined to seize it. Immediately he outlined how the Bolsheviks should deal with the new rulers in Russia. Within a few hours of hearing about the Revolution he wired Alexandra Kollontai in Norway, the most senior Bolshevik in Scandinavia. 'These are our tactics. 1) No trust or support for the new government. 2) Alexander Kerensky is especially suspect. 3) Arm the proletariat as the only guarantee of their protection. 4) Immediate elections to the Petrograd City Council. 5) Make no rapprochement of any kind with other parties. Telegraph this to Petrograd.' Essentially this was the policy that he would pursue until his coup brought him to power seven months later: no compromises; no recognition of 'the government that supports an imperialist war'; no deals with other socialist parties, especially the Mensheviks. It seemed extreme to most of his supporters in exile and in Russia, out of step with the mood of the times. But he was right and they were wrong. Lenin's reputation as a master of timing and as a super-skilful tactician, his understanding of the nature of power, would rest on how he would act over the next few months.[9]

This time, unlike in 1905, he was desperate to return to Russia as quickly as possible, but he faced great obstacles. How could he get there? 'From the moment the news of the Revolution came . . . he didn't sleep at night and all sorts of incredible plans were being made: we could go by airplane! But such things could be thought of only in the delirium of the night. One had only to speak of it to realise how impractical they were,' said Nadya.

One idea was to get a forged Swedish passport, easy enough to obtain. But Lenin could speak no Swedish. 'Nadya, surely I could learn a few words easily enough?' 'Don't be ridiculous. You will fall asleep at some point and see Mensheviks everywhere in your dreams, start swearing and shout "scoundrels" or something and give the whole game away.'

Plans were becoming more and more absurd. He wrote to Ganetsky in Stockholm: 'It is impossible to wait any longer. All hopes of a legal journey are vain. Find a Swede who looks like me. But as I know no Swedish he will have to be a deaf mute. In any event I will send the photograph.' He told Vyacheslav Karpinsky, the chief Bolshevik in Geneva, to 'take out papers in your name for travelling through France, the Netherlands and England, which I will use. I will travel on them through Holland and England and then on to Russia. I will put on a wig, go to the consulate in Berne with your papers, but wearing the wig, and they can photograph me.' Adopting that ruse, it is unlikely he would have got out of Switzerland. [10]

A group of revolutionaries were discussing their plight at a café a few days after the Revolution. One respected Bolshevik, Olga Ravich, Zinoviev's first wife and a brave woman who had been arrested and jailed for trying to pass one of the 500-ruble notes that had been stolen from the Tiflis bank robbery, said that she could marry a Swiss man, get a passport and travel through Germany to Russia. 'A brilliant idea,' Lenin replied, 'but not of much use to me.'*

He continued to explore the idea of going by way of England, though it was a remote and risky proposition. He telephoned Inessa at Clarens and asked her to go to London on his behalf and find out from the British government whether they would grant him passage. She refused to go: she was feeling unwell and the chances of success were so slim that she didn't see the point of trying. That evening he wrote her an angry letter. 'I must say I am keenly disappointed. In my opinion everybody these days should have a single thought: to get to Russia as fast as possible. I was certain you would rush off to England, as only there could you find out how to get through and how great the risk is.' A few days later he wrote again. 'My nerves naturally are overstrung . . . No wonder! To just sit here on tenterhooks . . .'[11]

*

* But he was amused by the idea. He suggested she should find 'a convenient old man for the purpose' and recommended Pavel Axelrod, a long-time Menshevik enemy of his who, though a naturalised Swiss and a widower, was aged sixty-seven. Ravich – in her early thirties – declined the suggestion.

The Revolution had begun almost exactly as the Okhrana warnings had predicted. The 1916–17 winter in Russia was the coldest of the century so far, a significant and often underrated factor in what was about to happen. Temperatures in Petrograd throughout the end of January and most of February averaged minus 15 degrees Celsius. Transport links to the cities, including the railways, were almost at a standstill and no grain or other food supplies were getting to Petrograd or Moscow. The capital's mayor, A. P. Balk, reported on 19 February that in the previous week the city had received just 5,000 *poods* of flour (an ancient Russian measure of weight, amounting to around 16 kilograms) compared to the usual 30,000 *poods* and the city's bakers were allowed to use only 35,000 *poods* of flour rather than the normal 90,000. Thousands of women – and it *was* mostly women – were queuing all night for bread. Then on 23 February the Arctic weather broke 'and the temperatures were an almost balmy 5 degrees'. That is when a wave of strikes and demonstrations in Petrograd began – 130,000 or so people on the 23rd, International Women's Day, more than 180,000 the following day. By the afternoon of the first big street protests people were no longer shouting 'We want bread' and 'We are hungry' but 'Down with the Tsar', 'Give us peace' and 'Damn the German woman'. The police couldn't contain the crowds, and the troops refused to fire on civilians. Mobs lynched police – they stoned the Chief of the Petrograd Gendarmerie to death – and began to take over government buildings. They 'liberated' the Peter and Paul Fortress and released the few prisoners inside, most of whom had been arrested only in the previous few days. Much of the city was in the hands of the protestors.*

The Tsar was no longer in the capital, nor at Tsarskoe Selo, but at his military headquarters at Mogilev, near the Front. In another of his disastrous list of errors he had eighteen months earlier taken personal command of the army – against the advice of all his ministers and his Imperial General Staff. It meant that when things went wrong he couldn't blame his field commanders but took responsibility for the conduct of

---

* That didn't deter Princess Catherine Radziwill from holding on 25 February the *soirée* that all Petrograd society had been talking about for weeks. In his diary Maurice Paléologue, the French Ambassador, said that her brilliantly lit palace on Fadanka and the opulence of the evening brought to mind Paris in 1789.

the war himself.* He had been told of the street demonstrations, but did not grasp how serious they were and believed the usual methods against riot in the capital – sending in the troops – would work. Alexandra wrote complacently, telling him, 'this is a hooligan movement. Young people run and shout that there is no bread, simply to create excitement, along with workers who prevent others from working. If the weather were still very cold they would probably all stay home. But all this will pass and become calm . . .'[12]

He chose to ignore the more realistic warnings given by the President of the Duma, Rodzianko: 'Situation serious. In the capital anarchy. Government paralysed. Transport of food and fuel completely disorganised. Public disaffection growing. On the streets chaotic shooting. It is essential at once to entrust a person enjoying country's confidence with the formation of a new government. There should be no delay. All delay is death.' Having heard nothing, a few hours later he sent another cable. 'Situation deteriorating. Imperative to take immediate steps for tomorrow will be too late. The last hour has struck, decisive as the fate of the Fatherland and dynasty.' The Tsar's only reaction was to glance at the telegram and turn to his chief aide, the addled seventy-nine-year-old, heavily bewhiskered courtier Count Vladimir Fredericks, and say, 'that fat fellow Rodzianko has again written to me all kinds of nonsense. I shan't even bother to answer.'[13]

Nicholas sent a fateful order to General Sergei Khabalov, commander of the Petrograd Military District: 'I order you to use whatever force is necessary to stop tomorrow the disorders in the capital, which are unacceptable at this difficult time of war with Germany and Austria.'

Khabalov said later that he was dismayed by the Tsar's instructions. He knew, if Nicholas didn't, that the troops wouldn't obey orders. The

---

* His officers pleaded with the Tsar not to appoint himself army commander, but Nicholas argued that his presence would improve morale and if the troops would not fight for Russia, they would for him. How wrong he was. General Brusilov, in command at the Front, said the decision was a terrible misjudgement. 'Everyone knew that Nicholas understood next to nothing about military matters and, although the word "Tsar" still had a magical power over the troops, he utterly lacked the charisma to bring the magic to life. Faced with a group of soldiers, he was nervous and didn't know what to say.' The Council of Ministers, which rarely criticised the Tsar, was unanimous in opposition. 'The decision you have taken threatens Russia, You and Your dynasty with the gravest consequences.'

Revolution was sparked by bread riots but it succeeded because every regiment in the Petrograd guard – the smart regiments that for centuries had been fiercely loyal to the Romanovs – mutinied. It was the famous Guards of the Preobrazhensky, Volinsky, Pavlovsky and Litovsky, known as the Tsar's praetorians, who decided the fate of the Emperor.

A day and a half after the Tsar's order the Petrograd Chief of Police described the scenes in the capital in his last report to the Interior Minister. 'At six in the morning the telephone rang. The city prefect told me that an NCO in the Volinsky Regiment of the Guard named Kirpichnikov had just killed his superior officer . . . the assassin had disappeared and the attitude of the regiment was threatening . . . [to other officers]. I now saw how far anarchy had spread and infected the barracks. A short while later the Prefect called again with more bad news. Brigadier-General Dobrovsky, commander of a battalion of sappers in the Guards, had been killed by his men. The events moved vast. The Volinsky troops . . . chased almost all its officers out of the barracks. These mutineers joined the Preobrazhensky regiment, whose barracks were near their own. They succeeded in capturing the arsenal on the Liteiny Bridge. Soldiers were dashing about the streets armed with guns. A raging crowd invaded the Prison of Preliminary Confinement and opened the cells. Soon it was the same in all the city's prisons. The police stations were taken by the mob. Policemen who were not able to change into mufti were torn to pieces. Fires finished off the rest.'

Historians have often said that it had been a generally peaceful uprising. This is a popular myth that has gained authority largely because the February Revolution was genuinely supported by the vast majority of people. But it was violent. Far more people were killed in February than would die in the Bolshevik coup in October – 1,433 in Petrograd and around 3,000 in Moscow, where armed gangs roamed the streets for several days. The October coup was almost bloodless by comparison.[14]

After ordering the troops to suppress the demonstrations, the Tsar prorogued the Duma. Again, his instinct when in trouble was to ban politics. But the Duma politicians refused to go quietly and when the following morning members entered the Tauride Palace,* there was

---

* The enormous palace had originally been built by the statesman and soldier Prince

nobody to enforce the Emperor's will. With no government, anarchy on the streets, the army in open mutiny and mobs throughout the city shouting 'Death to the Tsar', they filled the power vacuum, or tried to, with a 'Temporary Committee of the State Duma'. First, the Duma established a Provisional Government led by an elderly liberal, Prince Georgy Lvov, who quickly formed a coalition comprising some Kadets – the centre-right Constitutional Democrats – other liberals and moderate socialists, like Alexander Kerensky, who would be in charge until elections to a Constituent Assembly. Second, it had to decide what to do about the Tsar. They agreed unanimously that Nicholas had to go, but the royalists wanted him to abdicate in favour of his son Alexei, and retain a constitutional monarchy. They were swung around against the Romanovs and the idea of monarchy by the liberals and leftists – 'it is not only unacceptable, but also utopian, given the general hatred of the monarchy among the mass of the people'. They agreed, with the Kadets' blessing, that they would force the Tsar to abdicate in favour of his brother Michael, who gave his word to them that the following day he would dissolve the Romanovs' claim to the throne.

It was only when the top army officers advised Nicholas to abdicate – in particular his Chief of Staff, General Mikhail Alexeyev – that he agreed to go. He said his son was too ill to be Tsar 'and I can't bear to be parted from him'. The dignity of his departure and his gentlemanly bearing should not mask how hopeless Nicholas II had been as a ruler, and in what a terrible state he was leaving his country. The Duma had despatched two right-wing politicians, Alexander Guchkov and Vasily Shulgin, to extract the abdication proclamation. The Tsar was returning to Petrograd from his military headquarters in the imperial railway carriage. They met him at a remote station near Pskov at 9.45 p.m. on 1 March. The Tsar 'was absolutely calm, almost impenetrable,' Guchkov recalled. 'I even wondered whether we were dealing with a normal person. One might allow oneself some show of emotion on the occasion, but nothing of the sort.' A few words were drafted on a page. 'We hand over the succession to Our Beloved Brother the Grand Duke Michael Alexandrovich and bless him on his succession.' Fredericks placed the

Grigory Potemkin, Catherine the Great's lover (and, some say, secret husband). It was home to the Duma (in the right wing of the building as it faced the River Neva) and, since the Revolution, to the Petrograd Soviet (which met in the left wing).

document on the royal writing desk. 'Then, bowing his head for a few moments, he dipped his pen and . . . for the last time appended his signature as Tsar of All the Russias to the writ of Abdication.' Nicholas admitted later he was seething with anger and deep in pain, but as one of his aides said soon afterwards, the extraordinary event was as matter-of-fact 'as if he were turning over command of a cavalry regiment'.[15]

The radical groups had played virtually no part in the Revolution, as Sergei Mstislavsky, a leading Socialist Revolutionary activist in Petrograd, acknowledged. 'We SRs were fast asleep, like the Foolish Virgins in the Gospel,' he said in a somewhat inappropriate analogy. 'The truth of the matter is that outside of the small factions of the revolutionaries . . . slewing in our own juices, the socialist parties were completely bankrupt.' The Bolsheviks had reluctantly joined the street demonstrations, but had not led them. 'We didn't think this was going to be a revolution, so went along with the protests with a heavy heart, thinking they would be brutally suppressed by the Tsar,' said Vladimir Kayurov, one of the leaders of the Party underground in Russia. The highest-ranking Bolshevik in Petrograd at the time, Shlyapnikov, who reached Petrograd soon after the Revolution, admitted later that in February 1917 the Bolsheviks were weak, with a maximum of 3,000 members in Russia, and almost entirely broke. In the previous two months, he said, a paltry 1,117 rubles and fifty kopecks had gone into Party funds. The Petrograd Bolsheviks couldn't afford to send agitators to the provinces and they had relied on activists visiting relatives or going out of the city on regular work assignments.[16]

The Revolution had been entirely spontaneous, an outpouring of anger – a classic example of a popular revolt against an incompetent and bankrupt regime. The Tsar's secret police had beaten the Bolsheviks and other revolutionary groups; but they had forgotten about the people. The British journalist Arthur Ransome began his 3 March despatch for the *Daily News*: 'Let there be no mistake . . . This was not an organised revolution. It will be impossible to make a statue in memory of its organiser, unless that statue represents a simple Russian peasant soldier.'*

---

* Ransome's adventure stories written later, when he produced a number of novels, were nowhere near as exciting as his life. He was a gifted reporter and wrote vivid despatches from the front line of Russia's revolutions. A left-winger, but not from his

For the first few days it seemed as though 'a miracle has occurred and we may expect more miracles', as Alexander Blok wrote to his mother. There was a giddy sense of freedom – but also of foreboding. 'There is the extraordinary feeling that nothing is forbidden, that anything can happen.' After 300 years in absolute power the Romanov dynasty had collapsed in a matter of days 'like a train crash in the night, like a bridge crumbling beneath your feet, like a house falling down'.

writings a Communist, he was certainly a British spy and very possibly a double agent. He left his first wife back in England and ran off with Evgenia Shelepina, Trotsky's trusted secretary. It is still not entirely clear, as some of his biographers claim, whether he seduced her to work for British intelligence, or vice versa. Or indeed neither.

28

THE SEALED TRAIN

'The Germans turned upon Russia the most grisly of all weapons. They transported Lenin in a sealed train like a plague bacillus from Switzerland into Russia.'

Winston Churchill, *The World Crisis*, Volume Two, 1929

The idea originally came from Lenin's former friend turned bitter enemy, Yuli Martov. He had been languishing in Swiss exile for the last ten years with his group of supporters, all equally desperate to return to revolutionary Russia.

On the evening of 6 March 1917 a large gathering of leftist émigrés met at the Zur Eintracht café to discuss how they could get home. It was rare for Bolsheviks, Mensheviks and SRs to be in the same room together, but on this exceptional occasion the feuding habit was broken. One German socialist who was there said that, at the start of the meeting, he had 'never seen Lenin so excited and furious'. He could barely stay in his seat, paced up and down the hall 'like a bundle of nervous energy' and repeatedly said, 'We must go at all costs, even if we go through hell.'

The suggestion of going through Germany was made by Martov early in the meeting. The Provisional Government in Petrograd had freed all political prisoners. Perhaps, he said, they could broker a deal whereby the Russians would repatriate some German and Austrian prisoners in return for a guarantee of safe passage through Germany for the Russian exiles stuck in Switzerland?

Lenin immediately looked interested and, for once, told Martov that he was on to an 'excellent idea'. But the Bolshevik leader was far too impatient to negotiate through the government under Prince Lvov, which he described as 'ten capitalists and one hostage to democracy'. It would take far too long and be altogether too cumbersome. Nor did he want to deal with the new Petrograd Soviet of Workers' and Soldiers' Deputies, which had quickly established itself as a rival power base in Russia's capital. As usual, Lenin was determined to operate in secrecy. He told a Bolshevik aide, 'we ought to get busy on Martov's excellent plan . . . only we cannot go about it directly. They would suspect us . . . Non-party Russians and Russian patriots should appeal to the Swiss ministers with a request that negotiations be started with representatives of the Swiss government in Berne. We cannot participate directly or indirectly. Our participation would ruin everything. But the plan itself is very good and very correct.'[1]

Secrecy was vital to Lenin: 'I personally can't make any moves unless very special measures have been taken,' he told Inessa. He recruited the Swiss socialist Robert Grimm, editor of the radical *Berner Tagwacht*, to negotiate on his behalf – discreetly. He didn't trust Grimm, 'a detestable centrist', he told a group of comrades. But Grimm could be useful and he was well connected with the Swiss government and socialists throughout Europe. At the same time, Lenin opened a second front and started other confidential talks with someone he found equally loathsome: through his trusted lieutenant in Scandinavia, Ganetsky, he made contact with Helphand, the shadowy Parvus. Lenin had refused any 'tainted' Kaiser's money when Parvus had offered it two years earlier. Now he could no longer afford such scruples. He was prepared to make a deal with the Germans if the terms were right.[2]

From the German point of view, investing in Lenin seemed an entirely justifiable tactic of war and a risk worth taking – though they, too, had an interest in keeping the agreement secret from their own people, and if possible from the Western Allies. General Erich Ludendorff, as Quartermaster-General one of the two most senior commanders in the German army, admitted that he had no idea who Lenin was before the February Revolution in Petrograd – and didn't have any understanding of Lenin's politics or of Marxism. It was mumbo jumbo to him. But if Lenin could help to destabilise Russia, wooing him onto their side made military sense. It became a yet more tempting aim now: in February 1917 the German High Command was certain that the US would imminently enter the war on the Allies' side (which they did on 6 April). It was important to avoid continuing to fight on two fronts. Ludendorff said later that 'having once sent Lenin to Russia, our government had a special responsibility. From the war's point of view, his journey was justified. Russia had to be beaten.' General Max Hoffmann, Germany's commander of the armies against Russia, was equally candid. 'In the same way that I hurled grenades into enemy trenches and released poison gas against our opponents so do I have the right to use propaganda against our enemies.'[3]

Once Helphand/Parvus was convinced that Lenin was serious about a deal, he persuaded the German Ambassador to Denmark, Count Ulrich von Brockdorff-Rantzau, to approach Berlin with the idea of helping Lenin reach Petrograd. He predicted, with remarkable prescience, that if Lenin returned to Russia he would topple the Provisional Government, take power in an armed uprising and promptly conclude a separate peace. He said that Lenin had such a 'lust for power' that he would certainly agree to accept German help to reach his homeland.

The ambassador cabled the German Foreign Ministry at once. 'We must now definitely try to create the utmost chaos in Russia. To this end we must avoid any traceable interference in the course of the Russian Revolution. But we must secretly do all that we can to aggravate the differences between the moderate and the extreme parties . . . since we are interested in the victory of the latter. For another upheaval will then be inevitable, and will take forms that will shake the Russian state to its foundations. Support by us to the extreme elements in Russia is preferable, because in this way the work is done more thoroughly and achieves its results more quickly. According to all forecasts we may count on the disintegration being so far advanced in three months or so that military intervention by us will guarantee the collapse of Russian strength.' It was an optimistic forecast but the German Foreign Minister, Arthur Zimmermann, agreed that it was in German interests 'that the radical wing of the Russian Revolution should prevail'. Kaiser Wilhelm was personally told the general outline of the idea and approved of it.[4]

Lenin rejected the Germans' first proposal. The plan was that Lenin and Zinoviev should be escorted through Germany to Russia by a German businessman, Georg Sklarz, who had already made arrangements to pay their train fares and was on his way to Switzerland to meet them. Before he arrived, Lenin scotched the idea as too compromising politically. He did not care about the morality of any deal; he wanted 'deniability' if it was ever claimed that he was in Germany's pocket. Sklarz immediately returned to Berlin.

Lenin heard nothing from the Germans for a few days; he was beside himself with anger and fear that he would never get out of Switzerland. He told Inessa that he wasn't prepared to risk taking a ship from France to Scandinavia 'and getting sunk by a U-boat', which had happened a few days earlier to the steamer *Zara*, with a few Russian émigrés on board. 'But this is torture for us,' he complained. 'What if *no passage whatever* is allowed either by Germany or England? This is possible!'[5]

Grimm was getting nowhere in the other set of negotiations with the German representatives in Berne. On 20 March Lenin, exasperated by the slow pace of the talks, replaced him and appointed another go-between, Fritz Platten, the Secretary of the Swiss Socialist Party. It was he who finally struck a deal with the German Ambassador to Berne, Count Gisbert von Romberg. Lenin had a list of demands. He insisted that he would buy all the tickets 'at normal tariffs' – a group of Swiss socialists had raised a substantial amount of money for the journey – and that the returning exiles must travel in a carriage that would 'enjoy extra-territorial rights' (which explains the idea that the train was 'sealed'). As far as possible 'the journey shall be made without stops and on a through train. No passports will be checked.' They would not leave the carriage for the entire duration of the journey, and they would talk to nobody apart from each other. Romberg remarked snootily that it was 'unusual for travellers to propose conditions to the government of the country through which they intended to travel'. But he forwarded a text of the agreement to Berlin. The Germans had demands too. They insisted that everyone who went on the journey signed a declaration that they understood the terms of the deal and accepted full responsibility for whatever reception greeted them in Russia. It was not impossible that they would be immediately arrested and tried for treason. Lenin agreed the terms on behalf of the Bolsheviks. As usual, even if they had doubts, his followers would do as 'the old man' told them.

Within two days von Romberg told Platten that the Foreign Ministry in Berlin had approved the plan and would soon send a train carriage to the Swiss border to meet them. There would be space for sixty passengers.[6]

*

The agreement did not remain a secret for long. The story leaked to re-porters in Zurich and spread quickly throughout the émigré cafés where journalists, writers and artists talked of little else. The left-wing press was outraged and could scarcely believe that Lenin, the most radical of all the revolutionaries, would strike a deal with ultra-right-wing German militarists and imperialists. When the first rumours spread, 'pandemo-nium broke out in the Plauen Café in Zurich' (the main meeting places for intellectuals in the city), wrote the leftist journalist J. Ley, who spent most of the day there. 'Arthur Grumbach, the famous correspondent for *l'Humanité*, and Otto Pohl of the Viennese *Arbeiterzeitung* were beside themselves with anger.' Stefan Zweig loudly expressed his disapproval of Lenin, and the pacifist French writer Romain Rolland, who had won the Nobel Prize two years earlier, was apoplectic with fury. 'He thought it very wrong of Lenin to enter into an agreement with Ludendorff . . . and was worried about the repercussions this would have with the inter-national peace movement.' Rolland at one point reached into his jacket pocket and showed Zweig a telegram he had received from Lenin asking him to see him off at the train station. He declined. James Joyce, who heard the news later in the day, commented, 'it sounds just like the Tro-jan horse to me. I suppose Ludendorff must be pretty desperate.'[7]

Lenin never felt he had to justify his actions. To him, accepting help from the Germans – and, as became clear later, large amounts of their money too – would have seemed rational and reasonable. Lenin by this time in his life had ceased thinking in conventional moral terms and would have felt it entirely acceptable to take help from anyone if it would bring forward the socialist revolution, first in Russia – and then throughout the world.[8]

He seldom talked about the 'sealed train' and defended his actions in writing only once. 'Nobody asked the Germans for help . . . but there was a coincidence of interests. We would have been fools not to take ad-vantage of it,' he said. But he knew it didn't look good, which is why he was careful to cover his tracks and keep well away from direct personal involvement in the financial nuts and bolts – especially any murky de-tails that could be traced back to Parvus.

The British knew about Lenin's negotiations with the Germans be-fore the sealed train deal was agreed, well before the news was leaked to the press. The government considered an idea to counter the Germans by bribing Lenin to campaign for Russia to stay in the war. Clearly they didn't know their man or understand the stakes Lenin was playing for. Lord Milner passed on a note to Prime Minister David Lloyd George from the intelligence services suggesting a possible approach to the Bolshevik leader. Milner's covering letter said: 'Even Lenin could be got by bribery . . . anything can be done in Russia, Turkey or Greece by bribery . . . the enclosed note is well worth your personal perusal.' Lloyd George didn't pursue the idea.[9]

After the details were finalised, things moved rapidly. 'We had just two hours to pack and . . . [clear out] our whole household,' Nadya recalled. 'We had to settle our accounts with the landlady, return books to the library and so on.'

There was no time, she lamented, to collect her mother's ashes from the crematorium and take them to Russia to bury them in Petrograd, as Nadya knew Elizaveta Vasilyevna would have wanted. They had to leave them behind in Switzerland.

Herr Kammerer was in Spiegelgasse to wish them goodbye. He told Lenin that he hoped 'that in Russia you won't have to work as hard as you have done here in Zurich'. Lenin 'replied with a classic understatement and said, "I think, Herr Kammerer, that in Petrograd I shall have even more work."' The landlord hoped that he and Nadya would find some good accommodation in Petrograd. Lenin said he was sure he would find somewhere comfortable, 'but I don't know that it will be as peaceful as it has been here with you'.

When they left their last place of exile Nadya and Lenin had barely anything to show for sixteen years of life in Western Europe. He walked from the lodgings with a knapsack on his back containing some prized books, papers and documents, a battered suitcase with a few clothes and some bedding. They left a few possessions with the Kammerers, but as Nadya described to friends later, their baggage consisted of 'a basket of household items, a basket of books, a box full of newspaper clippings and another of archival material . . . and a Swedish kerosene stove'. The last item was for making tea on the train journey.[10]

At around 11 a.m. on Monday 27 March Lenin and Nadya were joined by a party of thirty others for a lunch at the Zähringer Hof Hotel in the centre of Zurich. When he drew up the names of passengers

making the journey and handed them to Fritz Platten, Lenin placed Inessa's at the top of the list.* Most of the Bolshevik clique close to him
who were still in Switzerland were there, including Zinoviev and his
wife and nine-year-old son Stepan, Olga Ravich, who had found other
means of reaching Russia than marrying an elderly Swiss gentleman,
Anatoly Lunacharsky, and Karl Radek, a Polish Bolshevik who was
technically a deserter from the Austro-Hungarian army and therefore
potentially taking a great risk when he boarded the train.

Lenin read out a pugnacious 'Farewell Address to Swiss Workers'. He
repeated his standard call for 'civil war' throughout Europe by workers
against their rulers. 'We are not pacifists . . . We are opposed to imperialist wars over the division of the capitalists' spoils . . . but we have
always considered it absurd for the proletariat to disavow revolutionary
wars that may prove necessary in the interests of socialism.' But he was
less upbeat addressing his own group of Bolsheviks privately, some of
whom were already celebrating – far too prematurely for Lenin's liking.
'Single-handed, the Russian proletariat cannot bring the socialist revolution to a *victorious* conclusion,' he warned. Then at 2.30 p.m. the party
moved off to Zurich's Hauptbahnhof.

There was mayhem at the station. The party of revolutionary Russians was greeted by an angry crowd waiting to see them off. Some were
shouting 'Traitors', 'German spies', 'Pigs' and 'Frauds'; others carried
placards declaring 'Shame for taking the Kaiser's gold'. Amid the general hostility, a few well-wishers turned up. Siegfried Bloch, a young
Swiss acquaintance, managed to get near Lenin and say, 'We hope that
we shall see you back among us again.' Lenin laughed and replied, 'Well
. . . that would not be a good political sign.'

At the platform for the local train heading to the Swiss-German border at Schaffhausen Lenin stood alone for a while, looking nervous and

---

* Almost no contemporary accounts mention Inessa's presence on the train and the
Soviets later clumsily tried to censor the fact that she was there. Official histories in
the Soviet Union until the 1970s did not mention her on the passenger list. Though
the 'sealed train' idea had originally been Martov's, he declined to go with Lenin. He
wanted to wait until he had received a formal invitation to return from the Petrograd
Soviet and an assurance that he would be allowed back into Russia. It was a slow and
cumbersome process. He got there a month later. Plekhanov had returned a week earlier, through France and England, and received a hero's welcome in Petrograd.

awkward, checking his watch every few seconds. Lunacharsky was famous for his tendency to exaggerate and romanticise, but he could at
times be perceptive. He said at that moment Lenin looked like a man
who was thinking, 'At last, at last the thing for which I was created is
happening.' Lenin climbed up into the carriage, and as he was finding
his seat Radek asked him how he was feeling. Lenin whistled and said,
'In six months' time we shall either be swinging from gallows, or we
shall be in power.'

There was a scuffle when the German revolutionary journalist Oscar
Blum broke through the crowd and tried to get on the train to join the
Russians. He was physically thrown off it by Lenin personally, who was
convinced the interloper was a police spy.

At 3.10 precisely, amid catcalls and boos from the crowd lining the
platform, the train slowly steamed out of the station. A seven-day journey lay ahead before Lenin would reach home.[11]

The 'sealed train' was waiting at Gottmadingen, a tiny station on the
German side of the border. It comprised a locomotive, a green carriage
of three second-class compartments and five third-class compartments
of hard wooden seats, with a baggage van at the rear. There was a lavatory at each end of the carriage, but no sleeping car. Two German officers
accompanied them all the way through Germany to the Baltic port of
Sassnitz. They took the compartment at the rear, and before the train
moved one of them drew a chalk mark along one side of the corridor
which established where the 'German' side of the train began. The
rule was that not a word would be exchanged between the German soldiers and the Russians. Three of the carriage's four doors were locked.
According to the agreement, at no point were their passports or any documents checked. They were merely counted through into Germany.

Lenin and Nadya demanded their own second-class compartment,
so that he could have privacy to get down to work straight away. He was
making revisions to a pamphlet that he had begun writing and nearly
completed, which would become known as *The April Theses* – one of
the most dramatic of his 'deviations' from Marxist orthodoxy, which
became required reading in Soviet schools after Lenin's death. In little
more than 10,000 words Lenin completely overturned Marx's teaching that every society must go through a 'bourgeois' capitalist period

as a first stage before there could be a socialist revolution. He declared that backward, mainly agrarian peasant Russia could leap through the industrial, capitalist phase of development and spark a socialist revolution that all of Europe would soon copy. And he outlined more or less exactly how the Bolsheviks would seize power in Russia and institute a 'dictatorship of the proletariat'. It was heady stuff, and, as he said, complicated to write. He was finding it hard to concentrate on the train.

Sharing a long railway journey in close proximity to Lenin must have been agony for the other passengers. He was a severe martinet at the best of times, but on this journey, with the risks so great and the potential rewards so high, his agitation and frequent explosions of nervous energy were in a heightened state. The excitement and drama of being with him at a moment when history was being made was one thing. But he was bossy and a bully, and enduring his constant whingeing complaints would have been quite another.

The train left Gottmadingen soon after 10 p.m. Within an hour Lenin was telling Nadya that he couldn't bear the noise coming from the next-door compartment and it was impossible to work under these conditions – 'it's simply unendurable'. There was loud laughter and general high spirits in the adjoining compartment. He could hear the high-pitched squeaky giggle of Ravich and the bass baritone of the short, hirsute and erudite Pole Radek – 'a little revolutionary goblin, a brilliant mimic, full of wit and amusing paradox' – telling a series of jokes. Lenin recognised that Radek could be useful as a popular journalist and rabble-rouser, but he always thought him 'an insufferable fool'. He told Nadya he would put up with the noise no more, marched next door, took Ravich by the arm and bundled her to a quieter compartment along the corridor. Some of the comrades tried to protest; Lenin simply ignored them.

Next, he was irritated by the fug of tobacco smoke that had quickly filled almost the whole of the carriage. Lenin instituted a smoking ban on the train and would permit it only in the two lavatories. Predictably a long queue formed, and there were noisy, acrimonious quarrels between the passengers – most revolutionary Russians of that era tended to be chain-smokers. Lenin improvised a socially just answer: he got some paper and carefully cut it into strips for use as 'tickets', one set for smoking, the other for normal lavatory use. Lenin, naturally, was the ticket-master. This was the earliest known example of a Lenin-inspired,

Communist-run rationing system: imposed from above, no objections permitted, causing maximum sullen dissatisfaction to many.[12]

It was a long, slow journey. The train seldom went above forty kilometres an hour, but the Germans kept their side of the bargain. At one point they held up a military train with the Crown Prince Wilhelm on board to give Lenin priority. Nonetheless the party was delayed for nearly twenty hours in Berlin – an agonising wait during which they were not allowed out of the carriage. They were running short of food. Many of the Russians had brought some provisions with them – bread, cheese, chocolate – but supplies had long gone and no one could go out to buy any food.* At one point a group of German Social Democrats tried to meet the Russians and talk with Lenin. They had reached the carriage steps, but were told that if they tried to get any further they would be thrown off the train. It took another day to arrive at Sassnitz. Lenin, according to Nadya, had barely looked out of the window the entire journey to see for himself the conditions of wartime Germany. He concentrated on rewriting his *Theses*.

By the time the party reached the tiny port, at around 6 p.m., they had missed the last ferry across the Baltic to Trelleborg. They had to remain in the sealed carriage for an extra uncomfortable night. When they crossed next morning, the day was freezing cold and the sea was rough. Everyone was violently seasick apart from Radek, Zinoviev and Lenin, who spent the entire five hours pacing the deck, looking anxious. He had worked out, while writing the *April Theses*, his strategy for bringing down the Provisional Government in Petrograd, but would he get the chance? At one point he asked Zinoviev, 'Will we be arrested as soon as we reach Russia?' Zinoviev had no answer.[13]

---

* There has been much speculation about why the train was held up for so long in Berlin. The obvious answer is that during the war the entire German railway system was severely congested – it was devoted to ensuring that troops and equipment were moved efficiently, and many trains were delayed. But various historians have claimed that the real reason was to enable Lenin to hold a secret meeting with German officials. It has been said that he met high-ranking generals and ministers overnight at the German Foreign Ministry at Wilhelmstrasse, and was handed millions of marks in gold. There is no evidence that this meeting ever took place and it seems highly unlikely. The Germans certainly gave money to the Bolsheviks, but did so using subtler methods and go-betweens. And Lenin, surely, would never have risked meeting German officials, having gone to such lengths to keep German help 'deniable'.

Ganetsky met them on the quayside early on the Friday evening and had to hurry them to catch the train to Malmö, which was scheduled to depart in fifteen minutes. About an hour later the Social Democrats of Malmö greeted the hungry émigrés with a smorgasbord, which the Russians – even Lenin – 'annihilated with incredible speed . . . they seemed like a band of barbarians', according to one of the restaurant staff. Late that night they took an overnight sleeper train to Stockholm.

The sealed train story and the wanderings of the 'exotic' Russian radicals became big news in Sweden. For the first time anywhere there was a picture of Lenin in a newspaper and Sweden's quality daily *Politiken* carried a profile of the man who promised a revolution in Russia and, once in power, an end to the war. He was fêted wherever he went in Stockholm. He was met at the train by Carl Lindhagen, mayor of the city, who gave him breakfast, and there was a lunchtime reception for him laid on at the Hotel Regina by Swedish socialists.

He refused to give any interviews, but he wrote a press release explaining why he had agreed to travel through Germany: he wasn't 'helped' by the Germans, it was simply a travel arrangement, he claimed. He categorically denied that he or the Bolsheviks had accepted any German money.

Parvus had travelled from Copenhagen and asked to meet him, but Lenin refused point-blank. He made sure there were two Bolshevik witnesses in his party who heard the refusal and could report it later

Cut off from news for five days, Lenin read the papers carefully. He 'flew into a fury', recalled one of his party, when he read proof that Malinovsky had been a double agent. The Provisional Government had abolished the Okhrana and, selectively, opened its files, which established incontrovertibly that Malinovsky had been paid vast sums as a police informer. 'How could that bastard have fooled us for so long?' he asked Nadya rhetorically.

He had a full day of meetings with socialist politicians and Bolshevik exiles in Scandinavia, but he found time for some shopping. Reluctantly, he was persuaded by Radek and Nadya to buy new clothes. 'I am not going to Petrograd to open a gentleman's outfitter,' he complained. But he was persuaded that the man returning to take power in Russia should look the part. The coat and suit he was travelling in were threadbare, the only footwear he had with him were hobnail boots which had been made for him by Herr Kammerer in Zurich, and his derby hat was out of shape. 'He looked like a workman on a Sunday excursion in unsettled weather,' one of the Swedes who met him said.

Accompanied by Radek to the most upmarket department store in Stockholm, Bergström's, he bought a smart new suit and some decent black shoes. 'Most likely it was the decent appearance of our stolid Swedish comrades that was evoking in us a passionate desire for Ilyich to resemble a human being,' said Radek. Lenin also bought a bowler hat, and an entirely new item he had never worn before – a dark-grey work-man's peaked cap. It would soon become his trademark headwear.[14]

Shortly after 6.30 that evening Lenin's group met to take the overnight train to Finland, on the last leg of the journey to the Russian empire. A hundred or so people were at the station to see them off and this time they were armed with bouquets of flowers and baskets of fruit, not the brickbats and abuse they had encountered in Zurich. 'Lenin was the centre of everyone's attention,' one of the Swedes who was there that evening said. He was smiling and beaming, waving from the carriage window as the train departed.

The British had a chance to prevent Lenin entering Russia and thought hard about taking the opportunity. They considered exerting pressure on neutral Sweden to refuse him an exit visa and detain him at the border. The British Minister in Stockholm, Sir Esmé Howard, wrote later: 'For a hectic moment the Allied Ministers discussed whether they could, naturally with the help of the Swedish authorities, hold up the arch-revolutionary on his way through. But the plan seemed impossible. It looked as if it might make the problem worse . . . so far had the Revolution gone in Russia by that time that it seemed wiser to let things take their course rather than interfere.'[15]

But the British Foreign Office did wire Kerensky, then Minister of Justice in the Provisional Government, wondering whether 'a mistake had not been made in permitting Lenin to return'. They received a speedy reply insisting that Russia's new government 'rested on a democratic foundation . . . Lenin's group should be allowed to enter'. It was the British who controlled the out-of-the-way border crossing point towards which Lenin was heading: Tornio, in a bleak area of swampy marshland which, for many hundreds of years, history had passed by.

Now it was a busy railhead and the principal supply route that the Western Allies used to send vital war materiel and military advisers to Russia. The area was teeming with British troops, traders making dubious business deals – and spies from various countries.

The railway journey from Stockholm took two days on a circuitous route around the Gulf of Bothnia. But at least Lenin and Nadya had a couchette-style sleeping compartment, which they shared with Inessa and a young Bolshevik from Georgia, David Suliasvili. Lenin couldn't sleep. He was in a highly anxious state, still wrestling with his *April Theses* and apprehensive that the British would not let him cross the border, or, if he was allowed through, worried that the Provisional Government would arrest him as soon as he entered Finland. And he was furious with the latest news of what the Bolsheviks in Petrograd had been up to without him to lead them. He had got hold of some Russian newspapers and had read the last few issues of *Pravda*. The Bolsheviks' paper had been legalised the first day after the February Revolution and jointly edited by Kamenev and Stalin, who were freed from exile at the same time. Lenin flew into 'one of his rages' and stayed that way for most of the journey according to Nadya, when he saw that the paper – on behalf of the Party – had argued that the war should continue. 'Those idiots may ruin everything,' he said. It took him several hours to calm down.[16]

The most pressing concern was getting into Russia. The end of the railway line on the Swedish side was Haparanda. Lenin's party had to get off the train and transfer to a horse-drawn sleigh, two by two, for the last kilometre and a half across a frozen river to Tornio. Lenin waved a red scarf tied around an alpenstock as his sledge reached the border post, which, as he had suspected, was manned by British troops who had been alerted that a dangerous revolutionary was on his way. The soldiers' orders were to let them through, but to give them a grilling, and an uncomfortable, humiliating time.

A young British control officer, Harry Gruner, was one of the MI5 team on duty. On a freezing night, he detained them at the post for hours while they were strip-searched one by one. Zinoviev's wife Zina never forgot the humiliation. 'We were undressed to the skin,' she recalled. 'My son and I were forced to take off our stockings . . . All our documents, as well as children's books and toys my son had brought with us, were taken.' Lenin was searched and interrogated. Quite what information an inexperienced young intelligence officer thought he could obtain from a man like Lenin remains a mystery. The whole party's belongings were meticulously searched; eventually Gruner had no alternative except to wave them through. For years afterwards he was teased by his colleagues for letting 'Lenin, the most dangerous man in the world, free'. They would say to him, 'You're a bright lad, locking the stable door after the horse was out, or rather in.'*

The tension eased the moment they crossed the border. Lenin was smiling and beamed as he entered the third-class carriage on a Finnish train that had been despatched to Tornio by Shlyapnikov. As the train pulled away he stood up, raised his right hand, clenched his fist and addressed his companions. 'We are on home territory now. We will show them we are the worthy masters of the future.' [17]

---

* The writer William Gerhardie, a colleague, suggested – only half facetiously – that Gruner alone may have held the responsibility for having brought about the Bolshevik Revolution. 'Were he a Japanese he would have committed hara-kiri.'

29

TO THE FINLAND STATION

'People who imagined that they had made a revolution always saw next day that they did not know what they had been doing, and that the revolution which they made was nothing like the one they had wanted to make.' Friedrich Engels (1820–1895)

'Everything is so terribly good and so Russian,' Nadya enthused to one of her fellow travellers as the train sped through the familiar birch forests, lakes and small towns of Finland – Tammefors, Kuokkala, Terijoki, all places she and Lenin knew well. For more than six hours they were in a 'shabby, uncomfortable compartment' with wooden slat seats, but they were happy – 'almost home, our faces were glued to the windows'. They shared a carriage with a contingent of Russian soldiers and Lenin began lecturing them about the 'predatory' war and how a socialist revolution would bring peace – 'as he argued the merits of "defeatism", the soldiers gaped at the strange philosopher with open mouths'. It was Easter Monday, 3 April, by the Gregorian calendar and many of the passengers were eating *paska*, the traditional Russian Easter cake, which most of the exiles hadn't tasted in many years.

In late-afternoon drizzle they reached the railway junction of Riihimäki, and changed trains for the main Helsingfors–Petrograd line. They still had one final obstacle in front of them before they were truly 'home'. In an hour or so they would be reaching the frontier into Russia proper and it was still possible that the Provisional Government would have the Bolshevik émigrés arrested. It seemed less likely now, but Lenin was still nervous and 'clearly looked under strain', remarked Radek.[1]

But instead of government soldiers or police, Lenin was greeted at the border town of Beloostrov at about 9 p.m. by a welcoming committee of scores of cheering locals and some high-ranking Bolsheviks. His sister Maria had come from Petrograd to meet him. Shlyapnikov, Lev Kamenev and Fyodor Raskolnikov, a young officer from the Kronstadt naval base who had mutinied in the Revolution and was the leading Bolshevik agitator in the navy, had joined her. Alexandra Kollontai presented Lenin with a bouquet of sodden and wilting flowers. She was supposed to give a speech but – strange for her, she was usually a highly accomplished speaker – she was nervous, became tongue-tied and froze. Instead, she planted a kiss on his cheek; Lenin drew back and looked startled.

While passport and customs officials checked the returning émigrés' documents, a big red flag and revolutionary bunting decorated Locomotive 293 of the Finnish State Railway. It would be a short hop of an hour or so before the train reached Petrograd. Lenin might have used the time to reflect on an extraordinary, dramatic week in his life and think with satisfaction that he had not been marched off to jail. Or he might have tried to relax. Instead he sought out Kamenev and began berating him for the articles he had been publishing in *Pravda* which appeared to show Bolshevik support for the war. 'What idiocy,' he said. Kamenev looked pale and apprehensive when Lenin drew attention to one particular piece in which he had written: 'The slogan "Down with the War" is absolutely impractical. When army stands against army, it would be the most stupid policy to propose that one of them should lay down arms and disperse . . . that would not be a policy of peace, but of slavery. As long as the German army obeys the orders of the Kaiser, the Russian soldier must stand firmly at his post, answering bullet with bullet, shell for shell.' Lenin told Kamenev 'that when we read that rubbish we really swore at you. It's nonsense. Our priority is ending the war . . . whatever it takes.'[2]

It was typical of Lenin that the first thing he did on returning home after ten years in exile was to abuse one of his lieutenants for being politically out of line.

In Petrograd the Bolsheviks organised a fanfare welcome for Lenin. In later years citizens in Communist states became used to big orchestrated ceremonies and mass rallies on the high days and holidays of socialist rule – May Day, for example, and the anniversary of the October Revolution. They were a major part of the Soviet way of life. Even when some Communist regimes proved to be useless at organising virtually everything else, they could always mount a good parade. This, the return of Lenin, the Leader across the water, was the prototype and the early Bolsheviks were determined to get it right. All day, from early morning, Party activists had been touring the barracks and working-class districts of Petrograd putting up posters: 'Lenin arrives today. Meet him.' The factories were closed for Easter, it was a public holiday, and many people may have been tempted by a false rumour going around the city that anyone who turned up would receive free beer. Nonetheless it was strange that so many people went to the Finland Station at a late hour, in the freezing cold, to welcome him – especially as so few people had any idea what Lenin looked like. His picture had never appeared in a Russian paper, not even *Pravda*.

But from 9.30 p.m., on a bitterly cold and damp night, thousands turned up at the unprepossessing Finland Station, a dull-looking provincial building at the time rather than the great hub of international travel fit for a modern capital. 'The throng in front of the station blocked the whole square, making movement almost impossible and scarcely letting trams through,' recorded Nikolai Sukhanov, a leading Petrograd Menshevik whose irrepressible energy and great contacts made him a superb historian of the Revolution. There was a regimental band playing music in the 'imperial waiting room' and three armoured cars were mounted on the concourse. Giant red flags were draped around the station. For dramatic effect, the Bolsheviks had persuaded the garrison at the Peter and Paul Fortress to loan them a giant mounted searchlight which had been switched on at dusk and gave the whole scene spectacular lighting.

Lenin's train drew in at 11.10 p.m. An honour guard from the Kronstadt naval base wearing their red and blue uniforms and caps with red pompoms were ready to greet the dignitary. The band struck up the 'Marseillaise', not knowing yet how to play the 'Internationale'. But at first few of the sailors and soldiers – or the workers and assorted curious onlookers milling about the station – recognised the stocky man in a threadbare coat, pointed beard and bowler hat who stepped down to the platform. When after a few moments word spread about which of the returning exiles was Lenin, a chorus of cheers rose, but it was a delayed reaction. Nadya said later that all Lenin 'really wanted was a cup of tea'. But the excitement of the occasion got to him.

He was formally welcomed by Nikolai Chkheidze, the Menshevik Chairman of the Petrograd Soviet, but Lenin pointedly ignored him. Neither could stand the other. Lenin thought the Menshevik 'a loathsome opportunist'; his rival regarded Lenin as a dangerous extremist and 'a mischief maker'. Chkheidze made a rambling speech about the need for co-operation between socialists. Lenin fidgeted with the lapel of his coat and looked bored throughout. At some point he had changed headgear, discarding his bowler hat and donning the peaked cap he had bought in Stockholm.

He climbed onto a chair one of the soldiers had found for him, began speaking and disregarded everything the moderate Chkheidze had just said. This was no time for compromise and diplomatic phrases, he declared. It was time to move towards building a socialist state. 'The piratical imperialist war is the beginning of civil war throughout Europe . . . The hour is not far distant when the people will turn their arms against capitalist exploiters. The worldwide revolution has already dawned. Germany is seething . . . Any day now the whole of European capitalism may crash. I still don't know if you have faith in all the promises of the Provisional Government. What I know for certain, though, is that when they make sweet promises, you are being deceived in the same way that the entire Russian population is being deceived. The people need peace. The people need bread and land. They give you war and hunger – and the landowners still have all the land. Sailors, comrades, we have to fight for a socialist revolution, fight to the end. Long live the worldwide socialist revolution.' Most of the crowd cheered enthusiastically, but Sukhanov heard a small group of soldiers complaining angrily. 'Ought to stick a bayonet into a man like that,' muttered one of them. 'If he came down here we'd show him. Must be a German,' said another.

It was nearly midnight before Lenin managed to leave the station. A group of sailors lifted him atop an armoured car, and with its headlights blazing raced him through the Petrograd streets to Bolshevik Party headquarters.[3]

Someone with a fine sense of irony in the Provisional Government had assigned the Bolsheviks the lavish Kshesinskaya Mansion as their base. The talented ballerina Mathilde Kshesinskaya had been Nicholas II's mistress before he married and was crowned Tsar. Since then she had made do with a succession of Grand Dukes, including her present admirer, the Emperor's cousin Grand Duke Andrei Vladimirovich. The Tsar had given her an enormous neo-classical villa in the centre of the city and she had decorated it in the height of Russian bling of that era – velvet curtains, frescoed ceilings, chandeliers in the shape of swans, huge mirrors and plenty of gilt. Most of the furniture had been removed when the government commandeered the mansion 'in the name of the Revolution' and replaced it with functional chairs and some ugly plain tables. But, as Shlyapnikov acknowledged, it was still an incongruous meeting place for radicals. 'It would have been better for the exercise of Kshesinskaya's profession than for the transaction of Bolshevik Party business – it was full of bathrooms, pools and suchlike,' he said. Trotsky hated the mansion. He said that even when scores of Bolshevik workers and soldiers were inside, it smelled 'like the satin nest of a court ballerina'.[*4]

Lenin hadn't slept for two days on the last leg of his journey. He was, as Nadya said, too nervous, but adrenaline must have kept him going. He took supper of tea and sandwiches with sixty of the leading Petrograd Bolsheviks and some hangers-on. At around 1 a.m., in the vast ground-floor reception room, he stood at the marble fireplace with its gilded blackamoor supports and launched into a two-hour-long speech arguing the case for the Soviets to seize power immediately. It was an extraordinary performance – a clear, unyielding statement of Bolshevik aims in which the idea of compromise and negotiation did not feature once. Peasants should seize land in the countryside without waiting for permission, he said; armed workers should patrol the streets and mete out 'revolutionary justice' against the exploiting class; Russian troops should bring about peace by fraternising with German soldiers at the Front. 'We don't need a bourgeois democracy. We don't need a parliamentary republic. We don't need any government except by the Soviets of the Workers', Soldiers' and Peasants' Deputies.'

---

* After the Bolshevik Revolution Mathilde Kshesinskaya met Shlyapnikov to plead for her possessions back. She tried every trick in the book, including tears, but the ascetic revolutionary was adamant. She lost almost everything, including her mansion and a suitcase of jewellery the Tsar had given her. But she was allowed to leave Russia and went to her house in Cap d'Antibes, which had also been a gift from Nicholas. She eventually married her Grand Duke Andrei.

The Menshevik Sukhanov has left the only record of Lenin's appearance that night. He said he was impressed, if appalled. 'I shall never forget that thunder-like speech which startled and amazed not only me, a heretic who had accidentally dropped in, but all the true believers as well. I am certain that no one had expected anything of the sort.' The speech lacked wit or pathos, it was simplistic, 'but Lenin had a way of hammering, hammering and hammering ideas into the heads of his audience until he took them captive. I felt as though I had been beaten about the head with flails.'

The applause was rapturous and soon followed by enthusiastic singing of revolutionary songs. Lenin looked entirely exhausted when he finished, but it was nearly dawn before he managed to get away.[5]

30

THE INTERREGNUM

'The Revolution was made in the streets, the Government in the salons.' Nikolai Sukhanov (1882–1940)

'And someone, falling on the map,
Does not sleep in his dreams.
There came a Bonaparte
In my country.'

> Marina Tsvetaeva, on Alexander Kerensky, *The Swans'*
> *Encampment*, July 1917

Lenin finally got some sleep. He left the singing Bolsheviks at the Kshesinskaya Mansion and was taken in a commandeered car to his sister Anna's apartment on Shirokaya Street, in a prosperous, middle-class district of Petrograd, where he lived for two months after his return. In the morning he and Nadya truly realised their exile had reached an end. 'When we were alone . . . we looked about the room,' said Nadya. 'It was a typical city apartment. We sensed instantly that in reality we were now in Peter and that all those Parises, Genevas, Bernes and Zurichs were already genuinely in the past.'

This was the first time he met his nephew Gora, now twelve, whom Anna and Mark Elizarov had adopted six years earlier. They would form a close bond, and instantly they were playing together in a relaxed way. At one point they were wrestling energetically and making a racket in the flat. His sister was cross: 'Volodya! Now that you've completely tormented him, leave the poor boy alone. Look . . . you've broken the table.'

His first venture out of the apartment that morning was to visit his mother and sister Olga's grave at the Volkovo Cemetery. Vladimir

Bonch-Bruevich, his old family friend and loyal Bolshevik function-
ary, who had carried Maria Alexandrovna's casket at her funeral nine
months previously, drove him but discreetly kept his distance when
Lenin went to the graveside, with its simple headstone. 'Always calm,
always in complete control of himself, Vladimir Ilyich never, especially
in the presence of other people, disclosed the depth and intimacy of his
feelings. But all of us knew how tender and affectionate he felt towards
his mother, and knowing this we realised that the path leading to the little mound on the Volkovo Cemetery was one of the most difficult roads
he trod.'[1]

With no more time for sentiment, Lenin returned to politics. Word of
his incendiary speech the previous night had spread. Even his closest
supporters were mystified by his tactics and extremism, his call for insurrection and demand for revolution now. His optimism – 'if we push
. . . we are bound to win', he had said – seemed to many in his clique like
a rash, utopian dream. Mid-morning on the day after he arrived in Petrograd he attended a joint meeting of Bolsheviks and Mensheviks at the
magnificent Tauride Palace. He was greeted by catcalls and boos from
both sides. One leading Bolshevik from Lenin's home region of the Volga, Pavel Lebedev, told him plainly they were 'perplexed, most of us are
. . . I think it can only be explained, Comrade Lenin, by your prolonged
lack of contact with Russian life'. Others were far less polite. 'What you
have been saying sounds like the ravings of a madman,' the Menshevik Boris Bogdanov, one of the leaders of the Soviet, shouted at him.
'It's obscene to listen to this claptrap.' Ivan Goldenberg, who had once
been on the Bolshevik Central Committee and had known Lenin well,
said that preaching civil war was 'dangerous nonsense, but of course it is
useless to talk of unity with someone whose watchword is schism. Your
programme means insurrection, which will lead us . . . to anarchy. These
are tactics which echo something old – primitive anarchism.'[2]

When the uproar died down Lenin was calm, and repeated the
same unyielding points he had made the previous night, which would
soon be published in Petrograd as *The April Theses*. 'There must be no
compromise with the Provisional Government, which cannot in any
case survive. All power must go to the Soviets,' he declared. The war
had to end at once; the army, the police and the civil service had to be

abolished; the banks and the 'commanding heights' of the economy nationalised. Everything had to be destroyed before it would be rebuilt under socialism.

Ministers in the Provisional Government were congratulating themselves that they had been clever to allow Lenin back into the country, convinced that his extremism had made life easier for them. The Socialist Revolutionary leader Viktor Chernov, Minister of Agriculture, said Lenin's ideas were so radical and 'raving' that 'the Bolsheviks' dangers will be limited and localised'. Prince Lvov, the Prime Minister, told Vladimir Nabokov (father of the novelist), his closest aide and Chief Secretary to the Cabinet, 'Don't worry about Lenin. The man is not dangerous – and, besides, we can arrest him whenever we want.' That Tuesday evening after Lenin's arrival, the Foreign Minister, Pavel Milyukov, leader of the Kadets and a highly regarded historian before he went into liberal politics, confidently told friends over dinner that the Bolshevik chief's ideas 'are entirely unacceptable . . . Now he's in Russia, he will learn better.' Though Lenin had been back in the country for less than twenty-four hours, the minister was writing him off. 'Lenin is a completely lost man.'[3]

Overnight the Revolution had brought political freedoms never before known in Russia – and hardly ever since. People could say, write and read what they wanted, something they could not do a year later – nor their great-grandchildren a hundred years later. Within days, scores of newspapers representing all shades of opinion began appearing on the streets of Petrograd, Moscow and other cities. But along with those freedoms came anarchy, violence and a breakdown in law and order which the government was unable to prevent. Immediately after the Revolution there was wild rejoicing at the fall of the Romanov monarchy. Statues of historic Tsars were torn down and imperial emblems like the double-headed eagle were destroyed amid a series of spontaneous celebrations throughout the country. They were particularly joyful in the empire beyond Russia, from Warsaw to Tiflis, where many people hoped the Revolution would soon lead to national independence. Everywhere, a republic was an overwhelmingly popular cause. Lurid, semi-pornographic, anti-monarchist pamphlets with titles like *The Secrets of the Romanovs*, *The Night Orgies of Rasputin* and *The German*

Woman's Evil Lies were instant sell-outs. All the institutions of the former regime were under attack.

But celebration had quickly given way to something darker: a quest for revenge, which Lenin and the Bolsheviks were quick to exploit, but which other socialists were convinced would destroy the ideals they had been struggling for over many decades. 'Lynch-law, the destruction of houses and shops, jeering and attacks on public officials and strangers, unauthorised arrests, seizures and beatings-up for no reason – all are recorded every day,' one enthusiastic revolutionary acknowledged apprehensively within a fortnight of the February Revolution.

Gorky had supported the 1905 insurrection and the overthrow of the Tsar but loathed the heedless 'destruction of the mob . . . an anarchic wave of plebeian violence and revenge . . . [has] brought the country to a new dark age of barbaric chaos', he said. Other intellectuals were appalled that all symbols of the old order and all traces of the past Russian civilisation were being wiped out: national monuments, old buildings, libraries, works of art. 'This is the struggle of culture against anarchy,' Gorky said in a pessimistic piece in his newspaper, *Novaya Zhizn*. And he wrote to his wife Ekaterina about his beloved Petrograd: 'This is no longer a capital; it is a cesspit. No one works; the streets are filthy; there are piles of stinking rubbish in the courtyards. It hurts me to say how bad things have become. There is growing idleness and cowardice in the people and all those base and criminal instincts . . . it seems are destroying Russia.'[4]

Not everyone agreed. Alexander Blok believed that violence would be 'cleansing', a cathartic but necessary way of healing centuries-old wounds. Trotsky saw the violent mood as predictable, understandable and justifiable. 'It is natural that people unaccustomed to revolution and its psychology, or those who have previously only experienced in the realm of ideas that which has unfolded . . . may view with sorrow, if not disgust, the anarchic wildness and violence which appeared on the surface of the revolutionary events. Yet in that riotous anarchy, even in its most negative manifestations, when the soldier, yesterday's slave, all of a sudden found himself in a first-class railway carriage and tore out the velvet facings to make himself foot cloths, even in such an act of vandalism the awakening of personality was expressed. That downtrodden, persecuted Russian peasant, who was struck in the face and subjected to the vilest curses, found himself, for perhaps the first time in his life, in a first-class carriage and saw the velvet cushions, while on his feet he had stinking rags, and he tore up the velvet, saying that he too had the right to a piece of good silk or velvet.' Lenin was determined to stoke up this desire for revenge and destruction, convinced it would help sweep him to power.[5]

From the start, there was a fatal weakness in the political arrangement immediately after the February Revolution. Two rival seats of power were established – a recipe for chaos. The Duma set up the Provisional Government of Prince Lvov, which, supposedly, was a seamless transition from the Tsarist regime. But on day one the government recognised the Soviet of Soldiers', Workers' and Peasants' Deputies as a partner and accepted that all government measures had to be approved by the Soviet before they were put into effect. The Soviets were hastily elected representatives from factories, army regiments and land communes, chosen within days of the Revolution, usually without a secret ballot. The Petrograd Soviet was more than 600-strong. They were not representative or in any modern sense democratic. But nor was the Duma which appointed the coalition government; that was a gerrymandered so-called parliament rigged by the Tsar and based on a minuscule electorate of property owners. They were frequently at loggerheads over the next few months and both tried to claim a bogus legitimacy. It has often been said, glibly, that the Provisional Government had power without authority and the Soviets had authority without power. But in fact both lacked power or authority. Lenin was able to expose this weakness time and again over the following months to make the system appear unworkable. As one of his supporters remarked, 'for sheer political incompetence and well-meaning ineptitude, history has few more striking examples' than the interregnum between the fall of the Tsar and the Bolshevik coup.

The Soviets seemed anything but traditional chambers of parliament. 'Anyone who wants gets up and says whatever he likes,' one member of the Petrograd Soviet based in the Tauride Palace said after just a couple of weeks of work. 'At first . . . deputies were sitting on chairs and benches . . . and tables. In the hall stood people of every description, creating confusion and disruption. Then the crowds of standing people became so dense that it was difficult to move about in the hall. A few hours later the chairs had completely vanished . . . and people dripping with sweat stood tightly squeezed together. The next day, or the day after, the tables too had vanished, except for the chairman's, and the Assembly looked like a mass meeting.'[6]

Over the following weeks things became increasingly chaotic, with more Soviets being formed in cities and provinces throughout the country. In the capital's Soviet, 'issues had to be resolved under the pressure of an extraordinary mass of delegates and petition-bearers from the Petrograd garrison, from the Front, from the backwaters of Russia', the moderate Vladimir Stankevich recalled. Many delegates were barely literate. 'The most important decisions were often reached by completely accidental majorities. There was no time to think matters over, everything was done in haste, after many sleepless nights, in confusion. Everyone was physically exhausted. No sleep. Endless meetings. The lack of proper food; people lived on bread and tea.'

The Duma was equally a madhouse: 'members were motivated by one single characteristic: their fear of the masses – and who could blame them'. In particular they were scared of the soldiers, whose mutiny had brought down the Tsar, and whose anger could turn on them. Three weeks after the Revolution the Minister of War, Guchkov, who had witnessed the Emperor's abdication, wrote to the head of the Russian army and Chief of the General Staff, General Alexeyev, telling him that 'the government has no real power and its orders are executed only in as much as this is permitted by the Soviet, which holds in its hands the most important elements of actual power, such as troops, railroads, postal and telegraph services . . . the Provisional Government exists only while it is permitted by the Soviet'. Lenin saw quickly how he could exploit this power vacuum. After just a few days back in Russia he was telling loyal supporters: 'Very soon the government will not be in a position to preserve itself.' Many still thought he was raving-mad.[7]

Vladimir Nabokov, the most senior civil servant in Russia, could see how weak and ineffective Prince Lvov had turned out to be. 'I do not recall a single occasion when . . . [he] used a tone of authority or spoke decisively and definitively. He was the very embodiment of passivity.' A decent, well-meaning liberal, now aged fifty-six, Lvov was entirely out of his depth in the revolutionary times of 1917. He was a rich landlord from the old nobility, with long experience of the *zemstvo* movement of local government and a great believer in modest, evolutionary reforms. He had played a significant role in financing hundreds of hospitals, schools and agricultural colleges for peasants. After the serfs were emancipated in the 1860s, Lvov gave peasants on his estates land in a gesture more generous than almost any landlord in the country. He was a kind man, but ineffective. One of his close allies, Alexander Bublikov, a powerful figure in the Duma, liked him – in fact almost everyone liked him – but he became exasperated by Lvov's 'permanent look of dismay and his constant efforts to be nice to everyone . . . he was a walking symbol of the impotence of the Provisional Government'. One of his old friends said he would always remember his air of 'solemn *ennui*'.*

His good intentions led to woeful misjudgements about revolutionary Russia. He used to speak about the 'soul of the Russian people . . . which by its very nature is a universal, democratic soul', and he told Nabokov, who looked sceptical, that once the peasantry was freed from the yoke of Tsarist tyranny they would learn to rule themselves in the liberal, democratic spirit of Western Europe and the United States, which he admired hugely. Government colleagues were amazed by the immensity of his indecision. When faced with a series of thorny problems his habit was invariably to wait and see. One minister recalled how he would say, 'Gentlemen, we must be patient. We must have faith in the good sense, statesmanship and loyalty of the Russian people' – and then move on to other business.[8]

Lvov was completely overshadowed by a charismatic younger man who took over from him as Prime Minister early in the summer and came to be identified with all that was wrong with the Provisional Government: Alexander Kerensky. Aged thirty-six, but looking much younger, his face was deathly pale, almost sallow, and he possessed a 'nervous, febrile manner, fragile in appearance, with a frantic intensity that made him seem to be permanently in pain'. He had bright-green eyes, slightly narrow, and many people who knew him described how he tended to move

---

* Even as a young man he displayed world-weariness. On a visit to Niagara Falls, his companion waxed lyrical about the splendour of the view. Lvov replied, 'Really, now, what of it? A river flows and drops. That's all.'

his limbs jerkily in energetic bursts. The code-name in his Okhrana file was 'Speedy'.

Unlike Lenin, who came to loathe provincial Simbirsk, Kerensky wrote often that as a youth he had been happy there amid 'the breath-less songs of nightingales'. But he couldn't wait to get out. He obtained a decent law degree at St Petersburg University and like so many stu-dents became involved in radical politics. But he was never seduced by Marxism – he said he hated 'its austere completeness and orderly logic, borrowed from abroad' – or by revolutionary terrorism. He joined the moderate workers' group the Trudoviks, and later, when the war broke out, the Socialist Revolutionaries.

He was jailed for four months in the Kresty Prison during the 1905 Revolution, where his health broke down. After his release he was a public defender in a number of high-profile political cases. He became famous for dramatic pleas for clemency against capital sentences. He was elected to the Duma in 1912 and quickly came to be celebrated for highly emotional theatrical speeches which 'left him drained . . . his whole body would tremble, sweat poured down his pale cheeks'. He was admired by the galleries, if not by the more traditional Duma members. Early in life he had wanted to be an actor, until persuaded to take up a more stable profession, but his speeches, particularly during the war when he had a remarkable gift for rousing troops, were big set-piece oc-casions, occasionally accompanied by fainting fits.* These were partly genuine. He was an ill man for much of his life: he suffered from serious lung and kidney complaints. But they were perfectly timed.

He turned into an extraordinary orator who could mesmerise crowds. A Kerensky performance 'resembled the passage of a cyclone. Crowds gathered for hours to catch a glimpse of him. His path was everywhere strewn with flowers. Soldiers ran for miles after his motor car, trying to shake his hand or kiss the hem of his garment. At his meetings in great halls . . . audiences worked themselves up into paroxysms of enthusi-asm and adoration. After a speech, the platform where he had appeared would be littered with watches, rings, bracelets, military medals and banknotes, sacrificed by admirers for the common cause.'[9]

---

* One of Kerensky's teachers watching him play the lead part, Khlestakov, in a school production of Gogol's The Government Inspector wrote acidly that 'the figure of this lovable lady-killer and . . . conman might have been created for him'.

But Kerensky was not all show. He could be brave. He denounced anti-Semitism wherever he saw it – amid court circles or in the lower ranks of the army. Once he went to Kuzhi, a small town near the Front in western Ukraine, where Jews were being lynched for allegedly (but entirely wrongly) helping German troops, and pleaded with soldiers and local soldiers to stop their 'barbarous and counter-productive' actions. His intervention prevented what might have turned into a far bloodier pogrom. Personally he was invariably kind. He didn't know Lenin but recognised his sister Anna on a steamer on the Volga, just before the war started in July 1914. The two got talking and, apparently, he said to her, 'Look now, you'll see Vladimir soon.' 'Why do you say that?,' she asked. 'The war will change everything in Russia,' he said enthusiastically. 'And your brother will be able to return.'*

Kerensky was the only declared socialist in the first Provisional Government and the only one who was a member of both the Duma and the Petrograd Soviet. But he was a socialist in name only, more, as one of his friends said, 'a perpetual student radical'. He never ventured out on the streets during the nine months of the Provisional Government. He scurried between the Right and Left wings of the Tauride Palace trying to make himself useful, or at least plausible, to both. In the Duma he always wore a perfectly pressed morning coat with a starched dress shirt and collar. When he made fiery speeches in the Soviet he ripped off the collar and took off his coat to appear more proletarian. He was not a revolutionary, but, as Trotsky put it, 'a man who merely hung around the Revolution'.†

He presented himself after February 1917 as 'the undisputed leader of the people' and for a while his popularity was enormous. He was the favourite of the liberal intelligentsia, and also the sections of the army which wanted to continue the war. He was convinced of his own greatness, and convinced a few others too. Zinaida Gippius wrote in her

---

* This story comes from friends of Kerensky, but has corroboration from Lenin acquaintances, though not directly from Anna Ulyanova or her family.

† In the winter of 1916 he was critically ill after an operation to remove a tubercular kidney. He was close to death for a month. While he was convalescing he started an affair with Lilya Baranovskaya, a cousin and close friend of his wife Olga, who had left her army officer husband. For many months, between the two revolutions, they all lived together, with their various children.

diary: 'there is only one name that unites everybody – and that is . . . Kerensky. We loved him. There was something alive, something birdlike and childish in him. He is the right man in the right place.'[10]

Lenin loathed him as the type of bourgeois liberal for whom he had nothing but contempt, even though Kerensky's father had so generously tried to help his family. From the first day after the February Revolution, Lenin identified him as the most implacable foe of the Bolsheviks and the greatest threat to him personally. That is why he reserved his greatest abuse for him. He described Kerensky as 'that flabby windbag', and 'no more than a balalaika on which they . . . [the other Provisional Government ministers] play, in order to deceive the workers'. Kerensky proclaiming socialism was an insult to real socialists. 'One should push such people up against the wall, and if they still don't give in, trample them in the mud.'

31

'PEACE, LAND AND BREAD'

'We know from experience that great affairs have only been achieved in our time by those who have not striven to keep their word, once given, and were able, when necessary, to twist others round their fingers.' Niccolò Machiavelli, *The Prince*, 1532

The public Lenin adopted a highly populist style of politics that would be recognisable – and imitated by many a rabble-rouser – a hundred years later, even in long-established, sophisticated democracies. He offered simple solutions to complex problems. He lied unashamedly. He was never a sparkling orator, as Kerensky and Trotsky were in their varying ways. But he was brilliant at presenting a case in direct, straightforward language that anyone could understand, and explaining how the world could be changed if only people would listen to him and his Bolsheviks. Economic injustice and semi-feudalism had held Russia back for centuries? His answer was simple: 'All the people have to do is expropriate a thousand banking and industrial big-shots . . . and break the resistance of a few dozen millionaires,' he said. The people were hungry for land? Simple. 'The peasants must seize the estates from their former landowner masters. They must be masters now.' Workers may not understand how to run industries? Lenin had a solution: 'Arrest a score or two of capitalists, keep them in the same condition as Nicholas Romanov now lives, and they will disclose to you all the clues and secrets of their enrichment.' Lenin knew that a revolutionary state would need experts, professionals in various fields, to keep functioning. But he argued that people had heard too much from experts. 'Any worker will master any ministry in a few days; no special skill is needed . . . and it isn't necessary to know the techniques of the work, that's the job of a bureaucrat and we can compel them to do the work just as they are compelled to work now.'[1]

With brazen cynicism he would promise people everything and anything. He promised peasants land – though he didn't believe in handing the estates to peasants; he wanted to nationalise the land on which peasants would work on big state-owned collective farms. He said workers should run their factories. But he didn't actually believe in workers controlling their enterprises, or his other pledge of establishing co-operatives managed by trade unions. He aimed to centralise control of labour under the leadership of his Party. When the Provisional Government delayed the Constituent Assembly elections it had originally planned for early September, Lenin attacked it for 'betraying' democracy. Of course, he didn't believe in 'bourgeois democracy' – free elections between competing political parties, and there would be none for seventy years in the state which he created. He told his lieutenants that in their propaganda it was important to keep things simple. 'We must talk about peace, land and bread, these things. Then we will shine like a beacon in the darkness.' He defended what he knew were lies on the basis that he rationalised most things: the end – socialist revolution – justified the means.[2]

Day after day for the first three months after Lenin returned to Russia he spoke at scores of meetings and became a popular draw. He was clear, logical, direct, sincere, apparently honest and persuasive. He was not a powerful physical presence, 'but people could sense there was something remarkable about him', as Gorky, who grew to despise the way he conducted politics that spring, acknowledged. Most importantly, he sounded optimistic, upbeat, positive, and offered his listeners hope. He smiled and laughed a lot during this period. He was visibly enjoying the Revolution. Some people who knew him before the war, though, including many who spent time in exile with him, noted a marked change in his demeanour. 'How he had aged,' remarked Roman Gul, an old Social Democrat comrade who saw a lot of him in Switzerland. 'Lenin's whole appearance had altered. And not only that. There was none of his old geniality, his friendliness or comradely humour in his relations with other people. The new Lenin that arrived was cynical and rude, a conspirator against everyone and everything, determined to launch his drive for power.'

This was the first time Lenin had spoken to large groups of workers. His experience up to now had been at small meetings of Party activists and conferences of socialists – intellectuals mainly – who were in broad agreement with him. But he found he had developed a voice that could reach ordinary workers. It did not happen immediately, though, and he had to work hard at simplifying his message. Initially, by his own admission, he became 'very nervous in front of crowds'. At his first big meeting a few days after arriving at the Finland Station he was terrified he would freeze entirely. He was sharing a platform with Alexandra Kollontai; before they went onstage his face turned pale and, as he confessed, he 'was scared and asked her to make the speech'. Kollontai was astonished that he seemed to lack confidence and did what she could to boost him, telling him that of course he could do it superbly, there was nothing to be apprehensive about speaking to large numbers. He mounted the platform, delivered the speech, received rousing applause, and never admitted to stage fright again.

The society hostess Countess Irina Skariatina told friends that despite her first instincts of shock and outrage, she was impressed by Lenin. 'I have been there twice . . . He is bald, terribly ugly, wears a crumpled old brown suit, speaks without any oratorical power, more like a college professor calmly delivering his daily lecture . . . Yet what he says drives the people crazy. No, positively it is not the way this man speaks but what he says that electrifies his listeners more than any other orator I have ever heard.'

He wrote incessantly – forty-eight pieces in *Pravda* during May alone, though some were only a few hundred words long. It was a phenomenal work rate, but he and other politicians were satisfying a hunger for politics entirely unknown in Russia. A new word was coined in the language in the spring of 1917: *mittingovanie*, meaning attending political meetings. 'Day and night, across the country, a continuous disorderly meeting went on from February until the autumn,' said the writer Konstantin Paukovsky, who had also seen life at the Front and knew how soldiers were being politicised. In Petrograd the weeks following the February Revolution were 'a festival of liberation', wrote the American reporter Albert Rhys Williams. 'You cannot buy a hat or a packet of cigarettes without being enticed into a political discussion . . . The servants and house porters demand advice on which party to vote for in the local elections for the Soviet. Every wall is placarded with notices of meetings, lectures . . . and announcements, not only in Russian, but in

Polish, Lithuanian, Yiddish . . . Two men argue at a street corner and at once one is surrounded by an excited crowd. Even at concerts now the music is diluted with political speeches by well-known orators. Nevsky Prospekt has become a kind of *Quartier Latin*. Book hawkers line the pavement.' John Reed said simply that for months 'in Petrograd every street corner was a public tribune'.[3]

* * *

The Provisional Government drifted from crisis to crisis and always looked unstable. It survived a series of street demonstrations at the end of April which the Bolsheviks had not initiated, but which they led enthusiastically. There were more than 150,000 people on one march, many holding placards demanding 'Down with the government', but it never got out of police control. Lenin's opponents on the Right, as well as Mensheviks and SRs, accused him of attempting to lead a putsch. He denied it categorically – and at this point he was being honest. The Bolsheviks had made no plans to topple the government and were in no way ready to mount a coup. 'The matter might have been different if we saw that the masses . . . [on the demonstrations] had swung sharply in our direction,' he told Zinoviev and Kamenev later. 'But that did not happen. We prepared a peaceful demonstration but some comrades, it is true, went too far . . . The slogan "Down with the Provisional Government" is adventurist. We cannot overthrow the government at this time. We wanted only a peaceful reconnaissance of our enemies' forces.'[4]

There were four coalitions in eight and a half months, and seven major Cabinet reshuffles. None could ensure law and order, maintain a grip on the army or control inflation, which grew exponentially. The government was in no position to borrow any more from the West; its credit was worthless, so its answer was to print more money. The Treasury printing works outside Petrograd could barely keep pace: it did not have enough 'guillotines' to cut the sheets of notes from the presses, so in many cases bank customers cut off individual notes themselves. Average industrial wages trebled in the three months after February, but had fallen in real purchasing power by two-thirds.

The army was a sullen mass, defeated and depressed. Soldiers believed, with some justice, that it was their mutiny which had turned the Revolution and brought down the old regime. Government ministers feared the troops could do the same to them. Immediately after the Revolution the soldiers made a series of demands to bring 'democracy' to the army and a guarantee that they would not be prosecuted for any refusal to obey orders during the February uprising.

The deal they reached handed Lenin enormous influence within the army and was a major factor in helping the Bolsheviks to gain enough support among soldiers and sailors to seize power a few months later. Order Number One, as it was called, had a profound effect in the armed forces. It made the army answerable to the Petrograd Soviet, not the Provisional Government; troops and sailors would elect their own committees, which would send delegates to the Soviet. Soldiers were 'citizens', not subject to martial laws. The committees would control the weapons, 'which shall in no cases be surrendered to their superior officers'. They would no longer have to salute officers when they were off-duty; officers were banned from striking the men, as they habitually did in the Tsarist army. Officers had to address their men with the formal '*vy*' rather than '*ty*'. Soldiers addressed their officers as 'Mr General' or 'Mr Colonel' rather than 'Your Honour' or 'Your Excellency'. Lenin despatched a large number of recruiting sergeants into the barracks, and soldiers were joining the Bolsheviks. He stepped up his campaign for a separate peace with the Germans to end the war.

'This is the end of the army,' declared the clever and influential right-wing politician Vasily Shulgin when he heard about Order Number One. But the army was already dead. More than a million and a quarter men had already deserted: around 10,000 a day left their regiments in April and May. 'All discipline has vanished in the army,' the French Ambassador, Maurice Paléologue, reported to Paris. 'Officers are being insulted . . . and if they complain are massacred . . . Deserters are wandering over Russia, filling the stations, storming the carriages and paralysing the transport links, both military and civil. Soldiers positively swarm at big junctions. A train arrives: the soldiers make the passengers get out, take their places and compel the stationmaster to switch the train's destination to wherever they demand. It may be a train full of troops for the Front. The men get out at some station, hold a meeting, confer with each other for an hour or two, and wind up by demanding to be taken back to their starting point.'

Colonel Alfred Knox, the British Military Attaché to Petrograd, was incredulous about the state of the Russian forces. At the end of April he and a group of other British officers visited the Northern Front, 'where units have been turned into political debating societies . . . and parleying takes place daily with the enemy, who laughs at the credulity of the Russian soldier. On the home front, in rural Russia, prisoners of war had been freed by the peasants and were working on landlords' estates while in Moscow German and Austrian officers walked about freely . . . surely there has never been another country at war in which the POWs declared a strike for better pay and conditions in life.'

The government had ceased counting the number of deserters, and even if they caught up with some of them, 'What could we do?' wondered General Klembovsky, an aide to the chiefs of staff at army headquarters. 'The death sentence? You can't hang whole divisions. Courts martial? But then half the army will be in Siberia. You don't frighten soldiers with the threat of imprisonment or hard labour. "What of it. We will be back in five years – with a whole skin," they say.'[5]

Troops had become radicalised, but not necessarily in the way Lenin wanted. General Brusilov, who would be appointed Army Commander-in-Chief in the summer of 1917, said later that 'the soldiers wanted one thing: peace – so they could go home . . . [to their villages], rob the landowners and live freely without paying taxes or recognising any authority. Soldiers veered towards Bolshevism because they believed it was their programme. They did not have the slightest idea of what Communism was, or what the Socialist International meant, but they imagined themselves at home, living without laws or landowners. The anarchistic "freedom" is what they called Bolshevism.'

The writer Ivan Bunin spent the first part of 1917 in a village on the Volga and kept a diary of the period. He was a vitriolic anti-Bolshevik, but he agreed with Lenin about the war. The peasants were simply fed up with the conflict and 'realised, as their masters should have, that victory was impossible . . . The people don't want to fight. They are tired of the war and they don't understand what we are fighting for. The war isn't their business. They grow more furious by the day.'

Lenin's critics were appalled by his determination to stir up class hatreds for his political ends. But to him, socialism *was* class war; and the accompanying violence was inevitable. As he so often said, 'No great question . . . has yet been resolved in history other than by force.' Chaos in Russia, he told close comrades, should be welcomed on the basis that 'what's bad for them, the bourgeois government, is good for us'. But even some of his admirers were shocked by the crude, mob-rousing populism he displayed in the spring and summer of 1917, such as the slogan he used in most speeches, 'Loot the looters'. The passionate socialist Gorky was in despair. 'Every day my anxiety grows,' he wrote to his wife on 14 June. 'The crazy politics of Lenin will soon lead to a civil war.'[6]

The Civil War was already happening on the land, which was engulfed in chaos. The Provisional Government's writ never ran throughout much of provincial Russia, where law and order had entirely broken down. Hundreds of large estates throughout Russia were seized by peasants who evicted, brutalised and in many cases murdered their landowners. It was a process that began well before the Bolshevik seizure of power, almost immediately after the February Revolution. The 'marches on the manors' were a spontaneous movement to force the landowners to hand over the estates to their tenants – in most cases, formerly their serfs. In the past the squire was protected by the army, which for centuries had put down peasant and serf unrest using harsh measures. But now, since the Revolution, the soldiers were often the leaders and instigators of the violence and in many parts of the country the police force no longer existed. The squire was now on his own.

Fury against the estate owners had been an abiding tradition among the muzhiks. Deep within the commune – the *mir* – under serfdom was the belief that land should not be privately owned by the gentry who never worked on it, but only by those who ploughed the fields and tended the livestock. 'We are yours, but the land is ours,' the saying went. The accepted belief was that one day the Tsar would divide up the land anew and hand over the estates to peasant farmers in an entirely different dispensation. The Tsar was gone, but now, many thought, was the chance for the great redivision of the land that would bring justice for the peasantry.

From the early summer, mostly in areas with the best agricultural land, assemblies of peasants would meet in villages and vote to confiscate the squire's domains. Groups of men – there were some women, but

307

mostly it was men with guns, pitchforks and hoes – would head for the manor, demand to see the landlord and evict the whole family, usually with just a few hours' notice. Often the deed was accompanied by grisly violence, justified as payback for the brutality of the Stolypin period of 1905–07, when thousands of peasants were killed by soldiers acting on behalf of the gentry landowners. There were many examples similar to that which took place in June 1917 at the fine manor house of Bor Polianshcina near Saratov. A mob led by a group of army deserters hacked the aged Prince Vladimir Saburov to death with axes as retribution for the role his son had played as local 'land captain' in 1906, when twelve peasants had been hanged in front of their wives and children. After the bloody murder they burned down the house, where there had been one of the finest private libraries in Europe. They marched on Tolstoy's manor at Yasnaya Polyana, 200 kilometres south of Moscow, though the great novelist had idolised the Russian peasantry and always campaigned for their rights. His aged and semi-blind widow Sophia pleaded for help from the Provisional Government but none came. She and her daughters packed her books and boxes in one room and stood guard with a revolver and an axe. On the night the mob came to the manor all the lights were off and they assumed the house had already been looted, so they passed on to another estate nearby.

Prince Lvov was powerless to restore order in the countryside, and from his reaction it is not entirely clear he wanted to. He shrugged his shoulders and said in blasé fashion that he 'entirely understood . . . the revolution on the land'. He told ministers over lunch in early June that it was 'the revenge of the serfs as a result – and I say this as a landowner – of our original sin. If only Russia had been blessed with a real landed aristocracy, like that in England, which had the decency to treat . . . [peasants] like human beings rather than dogs. Then things here might have been different.'[7]

At the end of May a newly created All Russian Assembly of Peasants, a self-appointed group of delegates from local land assemblies, declared that all the property seizures that had been carried out so far were legal, and all their so-called 'laws' were legitimate. Lenin supported the Assembly, on the basis that he would promise the peasants anything to gain their backing. But it was a charade. He had a low opinion of Russia's muzhiks, whom he regarded as barbaric and semi-feudal. Nevertheless he would go along with the assemblies – for now. As the Bolshevik leader in Nizhny Novgorod said, barely disguising his contempt, 'the local peasantry has . . . a fixed opinion that all civil laws have lost their force . . . [since February] and that all legal relations ought now to be regulated by peasant organisations'.

Prince Boris Vyazemsky refused to accept the verdict of one of these assemblies that he must hand over Lotarevo, his family estate in the fertile Tambov 'black earth' province, with its beautiful manor house, stud farm and hospital. His brother Dmitry had been among the most brutal of the army officers who had hanged hundreds of peasants in the troubles of 1906, and the entire family had been resented since. When a mob came to evict him with sticks and clubs in the summer of 1917 a village elder said that though they respected him personally they wanted to finish for good with the Vyazemskys and 'take the land that rightfully belongs to us'. The prince wouldn't leave the estate in his own carriage. The peasants formed a kangaroo court and ordered him to be sent to the Front. He had barely got to the nearest railway station before another mob of army deserters and peasants ran him through with bayonets. When he was dead they cut off his head.

The peasants had made their revolution – before Lenin would later unmake it for them and impose his own version of what a revolution should be.[8]

32

THE SPOILS OF WAR

'Lenin is a man of great capacities, but the abnormal conditions of underground life have dwarfed and stunted them most gruesomely. He could say of himself, "I know not where I am going, but I am going there with determination." Lenin's devotion to the revolutionary cause permeates his entire being. But to him . . . there is no difference between personal policy and the interests of the Party . . . of socialism. Lenin possesses an outstanding mind, but it is a mind of a single dimension. He is an absolutely honest man, but with a one-track mind . . . and consequently a man with a stunted moral sensitivity.'
Viktor Chernov, Lenin profile in *Delo Naroda* (The People's Cause),
April 1917

Lenin and Kerensky never spoke to each other. But once they did speak *at* each other, when they both appeared at the first All Russian Congress of Soviets on 17 June.* The main hall of the Naval Cadet College on Vasilyevsky Island was full to bursting, but the Bolsheviks were vastly outnumbered. There were about 900 SRs and Mensheviks, and 105 Bolsheviks. It was a dramatic occasion that nearly backfired against Lenin, but he was smart enough on his feet to save the day.

---

* Soon after Lenin returned to Russia Kerensky wanted to meet him. He thought it might help the Provisional Government gain support from the Left, but he never understood his enemy. The Cabinet Secretary, Vladimir Nabokov, noted that ministers barely mentioned Lenin, either at official meetings or privately. So he was surprised 'when I heard Kerensky saying he would like to meet Lenin and have a chat with him. In reply to the puzzled questions that followed . . . he explained that the Bolshevik leader was "living in a completely isolated atmosphere, he knows nothing and sees everything through the lens of his own fantasies, and he has no one to help him get his bearings on what's going on".' Perhaps Kerensky was in truth talking about himself? In any case, Lenin refused to meet him.

At one point in the morning session the leading Menshevik from Georgia, Irakli Tsereteli, said that politics in Russia was gridlocked and no party could form a functioning, plausible government on their own or was ready to assume power. Lenin rose, cleared his throat and said: 'Yes there *is* such a party. We, the Bolsheviks, are prepared. No party should refuse this and our Party certainly doesn't. It is ready to take over full power at any moment.' A few Bolsheviks cheered him in a lukewarm way. But most of the hall burst into laughter and began jeering him. He looked unfazed and stayed on his feet. When the noise in the hall died down, but still to some barracking, he carried on. 'You can laugh all you want to, but unlike others we have a programme in relation to the economic crisis. Look at what you are doing by continuing the war,' he said, pointing a scornful finger at Kerensky and other ministers. 'Capitalists with 800 per cent war profits are walking about the country just as before. Why don't you publish the figures of their profits, arrest some fifty of them and keep them locked up for a bit, even if you keep them under the same luxurious conditions as you keep Nicholas Romanov. You talk about peace without annexations and contributions. Put that into practice in our own country . . . You talk to us about an advance on the Front. We are not against war in principle. We are only against a capitalist war for capitalist ends, and until the entire government and the bourgeoisie is ousted, your type of socialists are the mere tools of those who have brought this disaster upon the world.'*

There was a hush in the hall and Kerensky rose to reply. He was now Minister of War and he wore a brown military tunic and gaiters, though he had never been in the military. He had his arm in a sling around his neck, though he had no wound or injury that anybody knew about. 'His face was pale with nervous tension, and his eyes blazed like fiery beads,' as one observer near him recalled. He began in quiet, measured tones.

'Our duty is to strengthen our new-won freedom so that our comrades who have come back from exile in Siberia shall not go back there,

---

* The British journalist Morgan Philips Price, who later became a Labour MP, reporting the event for the leftish magazine *Common Sense*, was the only foreign correspondent covering the Congress. He wasn't overly impressed by Lenin, 'a short man with a round head, small, pig-like eyes and close-cropped hair . . . One sat spellbound at his command of language and the passion of his denunciation but when it was all over one felt inclined to scratch one's head and ask what it was all about.'

so that *that* comrade [pointing a finger at Lenin] who has been living comfortably all this time in Switzerland shall not have to fly back there again. He proposes to us a new and wonderful recipe for our revolution; we are to arrest a handful of Russian capitalists. Comrades, I am not a Marxist. But I think I understand socialism better than brother Lenin, and I know that Karl Marx never proposed such methods of Oriental despotism.'

As he continued, 'his face flushed and his voice harsher with excitement', he became more melodramatic, as was his usual rhetorical style. 'You tell us that you fear reaction. You say you want to strengthen our new freedom, and yet you propose to lead us the way of France in 1792. How did it end in France after 1792? It ended in the fall of the Republic and the rise of a dictator. The problem for the Russian socialist parties is to prevent such an end as occurred in France . . . instead of reconstruction, you clamour for more destruction. Out of the chaos that you wish to make will arise a dictator.' He paused and dramatically walked across the room towards the group of Bolsheviks around Lenin. 'I will not be the dictator that you are trying to create. Who will?' And then he turned his back on Lenin, who sat there smiling, calmly stroking his chin. It was a rousing performance.[*][1]

Lenin was full of optimism, partly because he was convinced his message was getting through, but mostly because he had a vast new source of funds at his disposal. Bolshevik Party membership was growing. From a maximum of around 23,000 at the beginning of March it had reached 200,000 by July. More importantly, the Bolsheviks had quickly established a thriving newspaper empire, by far the largest of any other political organisation in the country. *Pravda* was legalised at the end of February. By mid-April it was printing – and selling – 85,000 copies a day in Petrograd. There were provincial editions of the paper and versions for different nationalities which appeared in, among other languages, Georgian, Latvian, Polish, Armenian and Yiddish. Large editions were produced for soldiers – *Soldatskavie Pravda* for front-line

---

* According to Kerensky's memoirs, never a reliable record of events but as melodramatic as his speeches, Lenin 'picked up his briefcase, with his head bent . . . and strode out of the hall almost unnoticed'. But this was wishful thinking on his part. Lenin remained seated and stayed in the hall longer than Kerensky did.

troops had a daily print run of 70,000 – and a special edition for sailors. Suddenly the Bolsheviks were able to afford a brand-new, expensive, state-of-the-art printing press, and had the money for large stocks of newsprint, a distribution system involving substantial numbers of people, and they found competent journalists to produce readable, in some cases brilliant, copy. Altogether, by the beginning of July they were producing forty-one publications with a circulation of nearly 350,000. 'It was an extraordinary feat of organisation' to get the papers up and running so quickly, said Trotsky, and it made a huge propaganda impact for the Bolsheviks. People who had barely heard of them before now knew where they stood – certainly on the issue of the war.

The operation was masterminded by Lenin, but could not have happened without large amounts of money from the Germans, as part of the deal which included the 'sealed train' journey. It is certain that Lenin knew all the details, though he didn't handle the arrangements personally, and there is no paper trail linking him directly to the transactions. It was some time after the Soviet Union collapsed in 1991 before any of the evidence came to light; the Communist Party had carefully buried the proof for more than seventy years. Even now the details are sketchy. Nobody knows for sure how much was funnelled from Germany to the Bolsheviks between February 1917 until at least March 1918. The German Social Democrat Edward Bernstein was one of the first to make allegations publicly. But he was well known as a long-standing enemy of Lenin and he admitted that he could prove nothing from his 'undoubtedly reliable sources'. Also, he claimed that the amount the Germans gave Lenin was fantastical – 'as much as fifty million gold marks' he said, worth around US$100 million now. Whatever the true figure, it was nowhere near as much as that, though it was certainly a large sum.

Rumours began circulating about Germany financing the Bolsheviks soon after Lenin returned to Russia. They were always denied. When the Provisional Government began investigating the allegations in April, with the intention of charging him with spying for an enemy country, they came up with partial information but no solid proof and made the mistake of trying to invent some of the evidence instead.*

---

* The US government sent Edgar Sisson, the former editor of *Cosmopolitan* magazine and at this point the head of the American Committee on Public Information, to investigate the Provisional Government's allegations against Lenin. His report, 'The

The Germans admitted later that they backed the Bolsheviks financially, without saying by how much. They congratulated themselves
on a successful strategy when the Bolsheviks took power. The German
Foreign Minister, Richard von Kühlmann, was almost inclined to boast:
'The disruption of the Entente . . . constitutes the most important war
aim of our diplomacy,' he told government colleagues. 'Russia was the
weakest link in the enemy chain. Our task has been to loosen it and,
when possible, to remove it. This was the purpose of our "subversive"
activity in Russia [with revolutionary groups] . . . It was not until the
Bolsheviks had received from us a steady flow of funds through various channels and under different labels, that they were in a position
to build up their organ, *Pravda*, to conduct energetic propaganda and
appreciably to extend the narrow base of their Party . . . It is entirely in
our interests.'[2]

The German money was channelled through Helphand/Parvus,
who was in regular, direct communication with Lenin's chief factotum
in Scandinavia Ganetsky. It was deposited into Scandinavian banks and
Ganetsky transferred it to one of his relatives, Evgenia Mavrikovna Sumenson, who seemed on the surface to be a respectable, well-dressed
middle-class woman of a certain age, but was a trusted and long-serving
Bolshevik agent. She opened several accounts in Russian banks, though
even a hundred years later only a couple of them have been traced. In the
spring of 1917 records show there were a million rubles in the Bank of
Siberia in Sumenson's name and around the same amount again in the
Azov Don Bank. She would hand it to another operative in the Bolshevik
underground, Mechislav Kozlovsky, who would distribute it to *Pravda*
and its offshoot publications, as well as for other propaganda purposes.
'I gave him money whenever he asked for it, without ever taking any

German Bolshevik Conspiracy', which came out in 1918, was clear that plenty of money had changed hands, but had doubts about some of the government's evidence or
whether it would stand up as proof of espionage. One of America's best-known Russia
scholars and diplomats, George Kennan, later American Ambassador to Moscow, author of the Cold War policy of 'containment' of the USSR and no friend of Bolshevism,
dismissed most of the government's evidence as fake. 'The state of affairs suggested in
the main body of the documents is of such historical implausibility that the question
might be asked whether they should not be declared generally fraudulent . . . at every
hand one finds serious discrepancies between circumstances suggested by the documents and known historical fact.'

receipts, as I was under the impression that he was Ganetsky's deputy,'
Sumenson said later.

Sumenson was arrested by the Provisional Government's intelligence
services on 8 July and confessed to her side of the transactions, but kept
the name of Lenin out of the affair. Lenin simply lied and claimed he
had no financial links with Ganetsky of any kind and had no idea of a
connection between Ganetsky and Parvus.[*]

Once in power Lenin was quick to cover his tracks. The new regime
after the Revolution destroyed all the evidence they could find when
officials went through Provisional Government papers. Lenin and Trotsky certainly knew about the cover-up, and more than likely ordered
it. They were determined to leave no traces, but at least one surviving
note suggests they were careless. Fyodor Zalkind and Evgeny Polivanov, two functionaries from the Foreign Commissariat under Trotsky,
reported that they had located some 'relevant material which has been
confiscated'. They wrote to Lenin that 'in the Ministry of Justice
archives from the files of the so-called "treason" of Comrades Lenin,
Zinoviev, Kollontai and others, we have removed German Imperial
Bank order number 27433, dated 2 March 1917, authorising payment of
monies'. They say they 'examined all the books of the New Bank of
Stockholm . . . there appeared an order 2,704 from the Imperial German
Bank' which they also removed. The documents surfaced seventy years
later.[3]

A big war chest from Germany was a great boost to Bolshevik fortunes. But the incompetence of Lenin's opponents was a bigger factor
– and he was quick to seize the opportunities they repeatedly gave him.

---

* Parvus wrote to the Provisional Government investigators denying any involvement
– in his best grandiloquent manner which convinced nobody. 'You lunatics . . . Why do
you worry about whether I have given money to Lenin? Lenin and others have never
demanded or received any money from me either as a loan or a gift. But I have given
them – and many others – something much more effective than money, or dynamite. I
am one of those men who have given spiritual nourishment to the revolutionary determination of the Russian proletariat . . .' When in power Lenin refused any contact with
Parvus and barred him from Russia when he asked to return in 1918. 'Absolutely not,'
Lenin told Bonch-Bruevich, his private secretary. 'The Revolution must not be tainted
by people like him.'

33

A DESPERATE GAMBLE

'I know of cases where soldiers in regiments which had promised to go on the attack after hearing a speech by Kerensky ... change their minds and refuse to attack when the time for action came.'
General Anton Denikin, army commander on the Western Front,
June 1917

'Those who make revolutions by halves are simply digging their own graves.' François-René de Chateaubriand (1768–1848)

The writer W. Somerset Maugham, who freelanced from time to time as a British intelligence agent, spent the spring and summer of 1917 in Petrograd. His mission: to do all he could to keep Russia in the war and ensure that Germany would have to continue fighting on two Fronts. 'I was exhilarated by the responsibility of my position,' Maugham wrote later. 'I went as a private agent, who could be disavowed if necessary, with instructions to get in touch with parties hostile to the government ... to prevent the Bolsheviks from seizing power.' Maugham boasted that he had 'unlimited money at my disposal', but when he suggested giving £50,000 to the Mensheviks and SRs, most of whom still supported the war, the British Foreign Office baulked at the sum and the risky nature of the enterprise. As the Germans were giving Lenin and the Bolsheviks the equivalent of millions this seems somewhat short-sighted and penny-pinching, but it is doubtful that Maugham's plan could in any case have succeeded.

The Allies' policy of exerting maximum pressure on war-weary Russia to continue fighting was a boon to Lenin. He told comrades throughout May and June that the one thing he really feared was that the Provisional Government would do 'the sensible thing', steal Bolshevik policy and seek a separate peace with Germany. 'It would cut the ground from under our feet,' he told Trotsky. At one point in May he thought it would happen, but he didn't grasp the argument of the other ministers in the government, some of whom believed that if Russia could hold out for a little longer, the Western Allies would win the war for them and Russia would benefit.

Publicly the Western Allies welcomed the February Revolution. The US President, Woodrow Wilson, said that 'a new and liberal government in Russia, replacing the tyrannical and corrupt' Tsar was a desirable partner for America. 'Now Russia's forbidding autocracy has been shaken off and the great, generous Russian people have been added to the forces that are fighting for freedom . . . for justice and for peace . . . here is a fit partner for a League of Honour.' When Lenin heard of the President's speech he muttered, 'what a hypocrite and windbag'.

The British Prime Minister, David Lloyd George, sent a message to Prince Lvov two days after the Revolution: 'We believe the Revolution, whereby the Russian people have placed their destinies on the sure foundation of freedom, is the greatest service they have yet made to the cause for which the Allied peoples have been fighting since August 1914.'

But behind the public utterances the Western leaders were seriously worried that the Provisional Government would cave in to pressure from the Left and sue for a separate peace with Germany. The British sent spies like Somerset Maugham and Robert Bruce Lockhart – as did the French and the Americans – to meddle covertly in Russia's politics, and diplomats were more openly trying to stiffen the Provisional Government's resolve. The Allied interference led directly to a military disaster which hastened the second 1917 Revolution and helped bring about the outcome they least wanted: Bolsheviks in power and Russia's withdrawal from the war.[1]

The Minister of War, Kerensky, and the Kadet members of the government wanted to show Russia's commitment to the war effort. They persuaded the top brass in the army to lay plans for a summer offensive – a big push that would drive the Germans and Austrians out of Ukraine, much of which had been occupied for two years. Before it began, the Army Chief of Staff, Brusilov, warned Kerensky of his growing doubts. Dozens of mutinies had already taken place even in supposedly loyal and well-trained units, and thousands of soldiers were refusing to move up to the Front. As many as three-quarters of the troops might desert, he told Kerensky – 'But he paid not the slightest attention to my words.'

The offensive was a desperate gamble, with odds stacked against the Russians. On 16 June it started with a two-day heavy artillery bombardment of German trenches in north-west Ukraine. Two days later the troops moved forward and at first the German lines were broken – a 'Triumph for Liberty' was heralded in the patriotic newspapers. But the advance stalled on the third day; the Germans regrouped and counter-attacked. The Russians fled in panic. The supply lines were stretched and many units were without weapons or ammunition. But the main reason the offensive failed was that the men refused to fight. In one night alone, a crack battalion of the 11th Army arrested 12,000 deserters near the Ukrainian town of Volochinsk. There were hundreds of cases of men shooting their officers before running away. The Russians lost nearly 200,000 men killed or wounded and millions of square miles of territory in a few weeks. Baron Alexei Budberg, from a famous noble family, was a colonel in one of the front-line regiments and anything but a typical, reactionary, old-school officer. He said that even before this point the army 'no longer existed as a military organisation . . . eighty per cent of the soldiers, officers and men would have agreed with the slogan "Down with the War". It's terrible as an officer to give an order without any confidence – often without the slightest hope – that it will be carried out.' The failed offensive was a fatal blow for the Provisional Government and the authority of its leaders – and a big propaganda coup for Lenin, who stepped up the Bolshevik campaign against Kerensky, who despite the disastrous military defeat became Prime Minister in early July.[2]

Kerensky thought about an armistice with Germany soon after he became Premier, but he ruled it out. He argued that it would make him 'responsible for national humiliation'.*

---

* In 1931 the British-Canadian press magnate Lord Beaverbrook, lunching with Kerensky in London, asked him whether the Bolsheviks could have been stopped if the Provisional Government had sought a peace deal with the Germans. 'Of course,' he replied. 'We should be in Moscow now.' A surprised Beaverbrook asked why on earth he hadn't done so. 'We were too naïve,' Kerensky replied.

But although the Western Allies knew the pressure he was under they did not make things easier for him. They offered him no more loans to ease Russia's economic plight, no reinforcements and little extra war materiel. In diplomatic terms they bullied the Provisional Government into continuing the war – a woefully short-sighted policy. The British Ambassador, Sir George Buchanan, reported back to London in July: 'I saw Kerensky this morning. I told him that though I was one of the few who had not abandoned all hope of Russia being able to pull herself to- gether, I could not assume responsibility for sending favourable reports . . . [home] unless he could give me satisfactory assurances regarding the maintenance of order in the rear as well as on the food and trans- port questions. I told him that what preoccupies me most was that the Socialist [not the Communist] members of the Government are afraid of making the army a really efficient fighting force lest it might one day be used against the Revolution . . . I could not conceal how painful it was to watch what was going on in Petrograd. While British soldiers were shedding their blood for Russia, Russian soldiers were loafing in the streets, fishing in the rivers and riding on the trams and German agents are everywhere.'

Once, after Kerensky had been hectored by both Buchanan and by David Francis, the American Ambassador, he met Somerset Maugham and tried to explain the government's predicament: 'I will not be able to keep the army in the trenches. I don't see how we can go on. Of course I don't say that to the people. I always say that we shall continue whatever happens, but unless I have something to tell my army, it's impossible.' The ice-cool espionage agent showed little sympathy.*

---

* Some of the agents were dubious about their mission. Bruce Lockhart told his bosses that they were pursuing a futile policy. 'The Allies were blinded in their desire to pro- long the military collaboration of Russia at all costs,' he wrote. 'They entirely failed to see what was possible and what was not . . . they were simply playing into Lenin's hands and estranging Kerensky from the Russian people.'

34

THE JULY DAYS

'This is when they are going to shoot us. It would be the most advantageous time for them.' Lenin to Trotsky, 4 July 1917

'A revolution is impossible without a revolutionary situation; furthermore, not every revolutionary situation leads to revolution.'
Lenin, *The Collapse of The Second International*, 1915

By midsummer Nadya could see all the signs of overwork, strain and nervous exhaustion in her husband which had so often brought him near to collapse. He was sleeping badly and 'suffering from terrible headaches, his face was white and his eyes showed great fatigue'. He was buoyed by the excitement of the revolutionary moment – 'at last it is real work we are doing', he told comrades. But the relentless speaking and non-stop journalism, quite apart from leading a fractious political party like the Bolsheviks, was taking its toll. In Swiss exile regular walking in the mountains, or swimming in lakes and rivers, kept him fit and had relaxed him. But since he returned to Russia he had taken almost no exercise and eaten poorly. After one speech, recalled Nadya, 'when he arrived home, he was not excited and happy but tired out, exhausted. Even our walks were of no help and didn't go well. Once we went out to Yelagin Island [a popular local beauty spot, with woods and a lake], but it was so crowded there that we couldn't really stroll as we liked. Then we took up the habit of walking the empty streets of the Petrograd side.' These were close to Anna and Mark Elizarov's apartment where they were still staying, but the gentle city walks were not enough to re-energise Lenin. 'He looked terrible at this time,' another comrade said. 'His face was sallow. His tongue was grey.' Inessa had gone to Moscow a few days after arriving in Russia to be with her children, in particular her son André who was suffering from suspected tuberculosis. At least once, and possibly more while she was in Petrograd, she met Lenin at his sister's apartment, as is clear from his note to her – 'My dearest friend . . . With us life is unchanged from what you saw here yourself. There is no end to the exhaustion . . .'*

Nadya knew the cure: a break as far away from stress or work as was possible. She despatched Lenin, with his sister Maria, for a few days to a remote spot on the Finnish coast where he could rest and recuperate. But before he went, there were serious political decisions to be made. The Bolsheviks had called for a series of demonstrations in Petrograd for late June and early July to protest against the war and to exert maximum pressure on the shaky Provisional Government. On 20 June Lenin told his closest lieutenants at a hastily convened late-night meeting of the Bolshevik Central Committee that the idea was to 'probe and see what develops', but not to let the protests get out of hand. 'We must be specifically careful not to give way to a provocation. One false move on our part could wreck everything. Even if we were now able to seize power we're in no position to hold it . . . in the Soviets of both capitals [Petrograd and Moscow] not to speak of the others elsewhere in the country, we are in an insignificant minority. This is a basic fact . . . Events should not be anticipated. Time is on our side.' A week later he met his close circle again and said that the demonstrations should go ahead, but 'we must handle ourselves with care'.

With his sister Maria Lenin left Petrograd on 29 June for the dacha owned by Vladimir Bonch-Bruevich and his wife Vera, a doctor, in the small fishing village of Nevyola on the Karelian Isthmus. Nadya stayed behind in the city. He sat on the verandah for long periods looking out at the sky and the countryside, bleak but in its way beautiful. He went for long walks. He read English novels and chatted to his sister. He bathed in a nearby lake, causing a great deal of anxiety to Bonch-Bruevich, a genial, paunchy, ginger-bearded giant of a man who looked more like a gentleman stockbroker or lawyer than a dangerous revolutionary. 'Vladimir Ilyich was a strong swimmer but he liked venturing too far out . . . we kept warning him it could be dangerous; the cold currents

---

* Lenin was now more careful about how they should write to each other. He gave her precise instructions in two successive letters. She should address hers to his sister Maria at the *Pravda* offices and mark the letters 'For V. I.'. And he gave her the names of two emissaries they could use – 'our entirely trusted comrades'.

might create whirlpools. We said people had drowned nearby in this lake not long ago. "Well, I promise I won't drown," he said. Then he just laughed and disappeared under the water.' The break had its usual effect and restored his energy.[1]

There are still those who claim it was a 'diplomatic holiday', conveniently timed so that Lenin could distance himself from what was happening in Petrograd. The demonstrations turned violent and there were bloody clashes in the streets. The city was in chaos and even some Bolsheviks and their sympathisers thought an attempted coup was taking place. Sergo Ordzhonikidze, a leading Party organiser and at that time a close friend of Stalin – he would later become the leader of the Bolsheviks in Georgia – said he believed the demonstrations were 'the first serious attempt to finish with the power of the Provisional Government'. Others were not so sure, including most of the Menshevik leadership and the Provisional Government's chief intelligence official, Boris Nikitin, who admitted that it was more of a 'muddle than a plot'.

Even now the only thing that is clear about the July Days, as they were called, is that there was nothing planned or organised about them. It is highly unlikely that Lenin would have authorised a putsch if he was not in Petrograd to oversee it. He had dreamed of a revolution for most of his life, had written about little else for the last twenty-five years, had made himself an expert on 'the art' of insurrection. Surely, if this was the central moment of his life, Lenin wouldn't have left things so much to chance. It seems entirely out of character.

On the other hand, the Bolsheviks had called for the demonstrations and it was always probable that they could get out of control. They appeared to want their cake and eat it. When the rioting began while Lenin was 'on vacation', the leadership left in Petrograd panicked, had no idea what to do and lost their nerve.

Some military units – the 1st Rifle Brigade and a large contingent of sailors from the Kronstadt naval base – mutinied, pledged loyalty to the Bolsheviks and wanted to storm the Tauride Palace to topple the government and the Duma. For several hours on 3 July they were in control of Petrograd and could easily have marched into the Tauride and the Winter Palace if they had wanted to. The Bolshevik leadership dithered and never gave the order.

Later in the day troops loyal to the government fought back. Around 300 people – soldiers and civilians – died in street battles. Petrograd was in total confusion. Nobody knew who was in charge of the government; Kerensky was in Kiev following a series of fiery speeches to troops on the Ukraine Front. Angry soldiers from both sides were patrolling the streets, where isolated rioting continued all day. Sailors and troops backing the Bolsheviks couldn't understand why the Party bosses hadn't seized power when it looked as though it was theirs: 'Take the power, you son of a bitch, when it is offered,' a soldier shouted in Trotsky's direction late that afternoon.[2]

In Nevyola at 6 a.m. on Wednesday 4 July Lenin was woken by a frantic knock at the door of the Bonch-Bruevichs' wooden cottage. It was a nervous-looking Maximilian Savelev, an editorial board director on *Pravda*, who had been sent by the rest of the Bolshevik leadership to beg Lenin to return to Petrograd at once. 'The demonstrations have got totally out of hand and violent, there's chaos in the city.' Lenin flew into one of his rages. 'What are they doing? They will bring the whole cause to perdition,' he said. Bonch-Bruevich had come to the door and Lenin told him, 'this is absolutely the wrong time. We will have to do something quickly. It cannot work. We cannot seize power now.'

He raced to the nearest railway station, Mustamäki, to take the first Petrograd train. Some of the passengers had heard the news and were blaming 'those damned Bolsheviks' or 'that Lenin fellow' for the riots, though nobody recognised him. At this point barely anyone in Russia – even long-standing Bolsheviks – knew what Lenin looked like. He found some of the morning papers on the train. They did not make comfortable reading. The Menshevik *Rabochaya Gazeta* (Workers' Daily) called it 'a stab in the back for the Revolution'. The Socialist Revolutionary *Delo Naroda* said the riots would lead to civil war. The Kadets' paper, *Rech*, simply came out with the headline 'Anarchy'. Lenin was furious when he saw a blank white page in *Pravda*. He later discovered that a piece scheduled to appear counselling caution was pulled at the last minute because the Bolshevik leadership had no idea what political line to take.

At the Finland Station Lenin took a horse-drawn cab to the Kshesinskaya Mansion. Isolated shooting was continuing in parts of the city. He rushed to the third-floor meeting room where most of the Bolshevik Party Central Committee had gathered, along with leaders of the Kronstadt sailors. He didn't greet any of them. He just looked at them and growled, angrily, 'You should all be thrashed for this.' Then he began searching for a face-saving way out for himself and the Bolsheviks. The mutineers were still in control of parts of Petrograd, and thousands of demonstrators were outside the mansion waiting for him to speak. He gave a mealy-mouthed, lacklustre performance, calling off the demonstrations – 'we always wanted this to be peaceful, with no violence'. But at the same time he tried to hedge his bets. The Bolshevik call 'to give power to the Soviets will win one day, despite the zigzags of history, but maybe not today', he said. Sukhanov, who was standing at the front of the throng, called it 'a most ambiguous display'. The crowd was perplexed. A small group of soldiers and workers marched towards the Tauride Palace, but were halted by pro-government troops from the Izmailovsky Regiment and a detachment of Cossack cavalry. The immediate threat was over and Kerensky was on his way back to Petrograd from the Front. Lenin always maintained that there was no plot to overthrow the government at that point – 'it was a little more than a demonstration, but a lot less than an insurrection', he said later. But this was the low point in Lenin's push for power.[3]

Back inside the mansion, Lenin's temper had abated. He was calmer and told the comrades that they had to prepare for a backlash by the government – 'a period of reaction' – and 'we will have to learn from the fiasco which will damage us'. He decided the Bolsheviks must give up on large street demonstrations, which would never bring them victory but merely make them unpopular and appear anarchic. They needed to organise more effectively in factories and in barracks to form armed groups loyal to the Bolshevik cause, and more specifically to its central leadership. These were the 'Red Guards' who would lead an uprising when the time was right.

In the riots that day none of the Bolsheviks had any idea what was happening in the city. 'Give me an exact account of your strength?' Lenin challenged his comrades. 'Name the units which would definitely follow us? Who is against us? Have the Neva bridges been accounted for?' No one could give him any answers. He said that when the Bolsheviks made a serious attempt at seizing power it had to be organised efficiently and ruthlessly, not left to chance and a mob. They had to establish a 'military revolutionary body that can plan' an insurrection with precision.[4]

More immediately they had to look after their own safety and prepare for a counterstrike by Provisional Government forces. Lenin said he would go underground and stay in hiding until he was safe. 'This is when they are going to shoot us. It would be the most advantageous time for them,' he told Trotsky.* That night he spent with Nadya at a safe house on the Petrograd side of the city, near Anna and Mark Elizarov's apartment.

* * *

The next day the sensationalist, right-wing, pro-government newspaper *Zhivoe Slovo* (Living Word) accused Lenin of being an enemy agent and the Bolsheviks of receiving vast amounts of money from the Germans. 'Horrors! Petrograd was yesterday almost seized by the Germans,' its lead item began. If the story was true in essence the details were almost entirely fabricated, but they were widely believed.

That evening Kerensky ordered the arrest of Lenin and his chief lieutenants on charges of 'high treason and organising an armed uprising'. The Bolshevik leader went deeper underground. He stayed in five different Petrograd addresses over the following five days, sometimes changing places twice a day. Early on 6 July armed militiamen raided the Elizarovs' flat. Nadya yelled, 'Gendarmes! Just like the old regime' as they barged in. Lenin wasn't there but they arrested his brother-in-law, a tall, heavily built man who could not have resembled Lenin less.

---

* At this stage Trotsky had not officially joined the Bolsheviks, but had met Lenin several times since he returned to Russia and the pair had made their peace. He had parted ways with the Mensheviks some years ago and been what he called a 'freelance revolutionary' showing loyalty to no side. But now he saw a real prospect for power and realised an alliance with Lenin was the only way to achieve it. He was willing to be led – if not to obey slavishly. He recognised that Lenin was a doer, not just 'one of those revolutionaries who talks, talks, talks'. From this moment he threw in his lot with Lenin and the Bolsheviks enthusiastically. He brought several hundred of his own supporters with him, including some who would reach high positions in the Soviet regime after 1917.

But they had no idea what Lenin looked like so they picked up Elizarov just in case, despite his protests.[*]

The army raided the Kshesinskaya Mansion, but no senior Bolsheviks were there. All had fled. They commandeered the building for government use and threw all the Party members out. Simultaneously the police swooped on the *Pravda* offices, where they missed Lenin by only a few minutes. They ransacked the place on government orders, ripping out the telephones and ruining the ready-to print manuscripts. They destroyed the expensive, nearly new rotary presses and broke up the linotype machines.

Some of the names on the government's 'wanted' list were already under lock and key. Trotsky had voluntarily given himself up. Kamenev was identified at a roadblock trying to leave the city by car. Alexandra Kollontai was arrested in her apartment. Lenin was put up for a day and night in an affluent part of Petrograd at the apartment of a skilled worker and a trusted Bolshevik activist, Sergei Alliluyev. He had taken the room which was usually occupied by Stalin when he was staying in the city.[†]

That afternoon Lenin, Nadya and Zinoviev were in the apartment along with the remnants of the Bolshevik leadership who were not facing arrest. Feelers had been put out by Lenin to members of the Petrograd Soviet that if he gave himself up to them, would they guarantee his safety? They said they could not promise anything as the government was determined to bring him to trial. Nevertheless he suddenly looked at Nadya and told her, 'I have decided that Grigory and I will turn ourselves in and appear for trial. We must say goodbye. We may never see each other again.' They embraced briefly – one of the very few moments of tenderness they ever displayed in public. Then she returned to the Elizarovs' apartment.[5]

Immediately Nadya left there was a quick formal meeting – that is, minutes were taken – of five other Bolshevik Central Committee

---

[*] He was released later that evening when he was identified to prison authorities as 'definitely not Lenin'.

[†] The next-door room belonged to Sergei and Olga Alliluyev's sixteen-year-old daughter Nadezhda, who a short while later married Stalin (and committed suicide in 1932). She remembered little about this first encounter with the Bolshevik leader except the noise from the adjoining room – 'a scraping of the pen day and night'.

members, including Stalin, Sverdlov and Elena Stasova, which counter-manded Lenin's decision. They persuaded him that it was too dangerous to give himself up, there would never be a fair trial and his safety was too important for the cause. It was Stasova whose argument was the most influential. She said that there was a rumour spreading throughout the city, and in the Soviet, that the government had unearthed documents proving that Lenin had been a spy for the Okhrana. He forced a wry smile and made the kind of tactical retreat for which he was famous. 'You're right, I can't do it. It will be all right for the others. They will go to jail for a while and then be released. But I'll swing.' He made the argument simply in a statement issued the following day. 'There is no guarantee of a just trial in Russia at the moment . . . to give oneself up to the authorities would be to yield to counter-revolutionaries to whom these charges against us are simply part of a small skirmish in the civil war.'

Once again he faced charges among his own supporters of cowardice. 'Many members of the Soviet were outraged,' said Sukhanov, includ-ing several Bolsheviks who expressed 'an unqualified resentment and condemnation of Lenin from the political and moral point of view. The flight of the shepherd could not but deliver a heavy blow to the sheep . . . what kind of general abandons the army, his comrades, and seeks per-sonal safety in flight?' There was no death penalty at the time, or prison with hard labour. 'Lenin risked absolutely nothing but imprisonment and he might have had as much freedom of action in jail as in hiding . . . the others carried on working and writing and came out of jail after a few weeks with martyrs' haloes.'

But Lenin genuinely feared death if he stayed in Petrograd. He wrote to Kamenev that afternoon, worried about the notes he had written for a book he had been working on. '*Entre nous*, if I am done in, please make sure to publish my blue notebook *Marxism and the State*.' This wasn't paranoia, but an accurate judgement of his value to the Bolsheviks. Trot-sky was clear. 'If they [the Provisional Government] had managed to arrest him it is likely they would have dealt with him in the manner the German army officers dealt with Rosa Luxemburg,' he wrote later.* 'In

---

* Luxemburg was the inspiration for the Berlin socialist uprising in June 1919, which survived for a few weeks before it was suppressed by the German army. She was mur-dered in grisly fashion and her body thrown into the Landwehr Canal.

that case it is very probable there wouldn't have been a Bolshevik Rev-olution.' A bitter ideological enemy, the American Ambassador, David Francis, made the same point and had continually advised the gov-ernment to arrest Lenin. 'Had the Provisional Government arraigned Lenin . . . tried and executed . . . him Russia would not have been com-pelled to go through another revolution, would have been spared the reign of terror and the loss from famine and murder of millions of her sons and daughters,' he wrote later.

On the run, Lenin decided instead to go further into hiding and find as safe a place as he could in Finland, 'almost Russia', where it would be far more difficult for the government agencies to track him. He changed his suit for more ordinary clothes, and, with Stalin's help, he shaved his moustache and beard. 'That's good now,' he said after examining himself in the mirror. 'I look like a Finnish peasant and there's hard-ly anyone who would recognise me.' This was the start of another of Lenin's urgent escapes from Russia. Few of his fellow Bolsheviks would know where he was or set eyes on him for the next three months.[6]

35

ON THE RUN

'When there's the State there's no freedom; when there's freedom
there will be no State.' Lenin, *The State and Revolution*, 1917

Shortly before 11 p.m. on 9 July Lenin, with Grigory Zinoviev, left the
apartment where they had been hidden by Alliluyev. The plan for their
escape was placed in the hands of the veteran Bolshevik metalworker
Nikolai Yemelyanov, who owned a small hut by the Gulf of Finland
thirty kilometres from the city centre, where they would be safe – at
least for the time being. But getting there without hindrance was worrying the two men on the run. Lenin was in a highly nervous state – 'he
was in a desperate mood', Yemelyanov recalled.

The Finland Station was heavily policed so they decided to go by foot
from Alliluyev's home in central Petrograd to the suburban railway station of Novaya Derevnya, where they could catch a train on the small
branch line to Sestroretsk. Walking was thought safer than taking a car
or a taxi; vehicles were regularly being stopped by patrols.

Lenin wouldn't stand on the platform for fear of being recognised.
The three of them hid under a line of waiting goods wagons. When their
train was about to depart at around 1 a.m. they clambered onto the last
freight coach. Lenin insisted on sitting on the steps and clinging to a
handrail, in case he had to jump off in a hurry. 'But it's dangerous, you
might fall,' Yemelyanov said. 'Don't worry, I'm good at holding on,' he
replied.

At one station a group of soldiers noticed Lenin and two of them
moved to ask what was going on – but they had been drinking heavily
and decided instead to return to their hooch bottle. After forty nervous
minutes, near the end of the line, the three of them got out at Razliv, and
walked the kilometre and a half to Yemelyanov's hut, where they were

to sleep in a hayloft which their host's two adolescent sons had prepared for the distinguished Bolshevik visitors.

Zinoviev wrote a lyrical account of their stay in the barn. 'Cool nights marked with stars; the smell of cut hay . . . smoke from a small fire where venison simmered in a small pot. We go to bed early . . . It is cold. We cover ourselves with an old blanket . . . but it is narrow and each of us tries to leave the larger part to the other . . . Sometimes I cannot sleep for a long time, lying there in absolute silence. I can hear the beating of Ilyich's heart. We are sleeping pressed closely against each other . . .'

Lenin delighted rather less in the interlude. He always thought of himself as a man apart from his followers and cannot have enjoyed sharing a bed of hay with Zinoviev. He complained about the midges – 'the insatiable mosquitoes gave no respite' – he complained that he wasn't getting enough information from Petrograd, and he was concerned about security. The hut was surrounded by other houses and was close to a campsite crowded with summer holidaymakers. It was near a lane used by many people throughout the day. There was a 200,000-ruble price on his head and he could be spotted by chance, despite his disguise. The newspapers had rightly reported that he had left Petrograd and had gone underground. Lenin insisted they had to move somewhere safer. Yemelyanov located another hiding place – a small thatched hut three kilometres away, in a clearing deep in a forest by a lake. Only a few peasants lived anywhere nearby. For the next three weeks this was where the coming Bolshevik Revolution would be planned.[1]

Lenin liked this more secluded second hiding place. He and Zinoviev made tea or cooked potatoes in a tin kettle suspended on forked sticks over a small fire. In the heat of the day they swam in the lake and in the long evening twilights Lenin fished for carp and bream. Via a circuitous route to avoid being followed by police spies, messengers from Petrograd came at least once a day, rowing the last part of the journey across the lake. Nadya came for the day once, changing trains several times to lose the men trailing her.

On a writing pad by the fire he furiously wrote articles for the Party press and he got down to serious work on *The State and Revolution*, a study of the ideal of Communism that he wanted to build. There was no need for 'bourgeois democracy' or the State, he argued. After the

Revolution, when the proletariat was free, the working class would govern themselves: that is when the State, as Engels had said, would 'wither away'. The book's best-known *aperçu* is neatly phrased: 'When there's the State there's no freedom; when there's freedom there will be no State.' For a while it was considered one of Lenin's most significant works, full of insights about the promised land to come. However, as time went on, under his successors, the book understandably went out of fashion and was seldom quoted in the Soviet Union, where the State resolutely refused to wither away but became ever stronger, more centralised and more vicious. It has a depressingly hollow ring when read a century later, though it has value as a kind of utopian dream: 'We do not know when . . . [the State] will wither away, but we know it will.'[2]

The rural idyll could not last. Zinoviev had a narrow escape one day when he went out hunting for game in a clearing among the woods. He was discovered by a forester who grew suspicious and asked him who he was and where he came from. He played dumb and pretended he was a Finnish peasant who didn't speak Russian. Then word got through from Bolsheviks in Petrograd that the police believed Lenin was hiding somewhere around the Gulf of Finland. Lenin decided he had to get further away, into Finland proper. Zinoviev was less worried that he might be hanged and decided to return incognito to Petrograd.

Lenin needed a fake passport to cross the Russian–Finnish 'administrative border'. It would be the last of the innumerable false identity documents that he used in his life as a conspirator; this time he was a machine operator by the name of Konstantin Petrovich Ivanov. There is a curious photograph of him without a beard, the only one in existence, in which he appears a decidedly unimposing figure, shorn of all authority, entirely unrecognisable as the man who led the world's first Communist revolution.

The hastily devised plan was for both of them to leave on 8 August, with Yemelyanov and two new courier-guides, the Finnish Bolsheviks Eino Rahkia and Alexander Shotman. It involved a ten-kilometre walk eastwards through the forest from the lake to the tiny railway station at Levashevo, back towards Petrograd. From there, Zinoviev would head to the capital. Lenin would move on north to Finland, at first staying in the village of Udelnaya with a Bolshevik supporter, Emil Kalske, and then crossing the border posing as a stoker on a railway locomotive. It seemed to Lenin a well-laid plan. It turned into a disaster and he was lucky to escape in one piece – or jail.

First they got lost in the woods. Yemelyanov was a local and supposed to know his way, but he took an unfamiliar short-cut and soon he had to admit he had no idea where he was. To make matters worse, as dusk descended they were being choked by smoke: in a nearby clearing a local farmer had been burning a peat bog. They stumbled around in the forest as darkness fell, ravenous with hunger. Shotman had packed just three small cucumbers for the five of them on the entire journey. When they came to a stream they couldn't find a bridge and they had to wade across waist-deep. Finally, by a stroke of luck, they saw the flicker of a lantern. It was a tiny railway station, but not Levashevo, though at least it was on the same Petrograd–Finland line. Tired, hungry and wet, they had to wait hours in darkness for a train. Lenin was furious with Yemelyanov and Shotman for the hopeless disorganisation of the escape plan. It was putting the entire Revolution at risk. 'Lenin's nerves were on edge. He cursed us with extreme savagery,' Shotman recalled. 'Surely we ought to have obtained a detailed map of the area? Why hadn't we studied the route and so on? We also caught it over the "reconnoitering"; why did it only seem to be the right station? Why didn't we know precisely?'[3]

Things became increasingly muddled. The station they had happened upon, Dibuny, was under guard by a corps of army cadets. Lenin and Zinoviev hid in a ditch and, as the train finally arrived, at around 1 a.m., the 'guides' went to look around. One of the soldiers grew suspicious of Yemelyanov, whom he didn't believe was a local. He was placed under arrest. Another cadet thought there was something odd about Shot-man's behaviour. While they were being interrogated, the other three slipped past the distracted guards and into one of the compartments at the rear of the train. It had not been part of any plan, but a piece of luck. Eventually they got to Udelnaya, many hours late.

The next day Zinoviev returned to Petrograd. Lenin changed into stoker's overalls and in the evening mounted the engine cab of Loco-motive 293, driven by Hugo Jalava, heading across the border to the seaside town of Terijoki. His mood had lifted, though he still had the tricky matter to negotiate of crossing into Finland. Jalava had been told that Lenin was a journalist writing a piece about steam trains. He didn't altogether believe the story but allowed Lenin on board anyway and noted that his passenger seemed to enjoy 'keeping himself busy feeding wood into the furnace . . . clambering between logs'.

At the border post at Beloostrov, where four months earlier Lenin had been given a hero's welcome when he returned to Russia, there were more militiamen on the station platform than usual. The government still believed that Lenin was hiding somewhere in Finland. The train halted for more than twenty minutes as passports were checked, but the soldiers didn't look in the locomotive cab.

Lenin stayed for two days with Rahkia's relatives in a small village near Terijoki, but he felt isolated. He was determined to reach Helsingfors, where he could establish good communications with Bolsheviks in Petrograd – and, as he thought, he would be close enough for him to direct the Party.

He stayed in a series of safe houses organised by Shotman. Apart from the short periods when he was on the move, under a variety of disguises, he never stepped outside onto the streets. One night he was billeted at the home of the veteran Finnish socialist Karl Willik, during which, he later told Nadya, he reread Jules Michelet's vivid, beautifully written account of the Terror during the French Revolution. He often saw the Jacobins as an inspiration for the Bolsheviks.* But for most of his time in the Finnish capital Shotman put him up with one of his close friends, Gustav Rovio, an ardent Bolshevik who also happened to be the Helsingfors police chief. There was a price on Lenin's head, but he was hiding in the safest place in the city. 'Our people will laugh their heads off when I go back to Petrograd and tell comrades where I lodged Lenin . . . No one from Kerensky's people will have thought of looking for Vladimir Ilyich there, with a policeman.'[4]

* * *

The hate campaign against Lenin and the 'traitor Bolsheviks' reached a crescendo in August. Newspapers loyal to the government were running

---

* 'The example of the Jacobins is instructive,' he wrote in *The State and Revolution*, 'but the Jacobins of the twentieth century would not set about guillotining the capitalists; following a good model is not the same as copying it. It would be enough to arrest 50–100 magnates and queens of bank capital, the main knights of treasury-fraud and bank pillage; it would be enough to arrest them for a few weeks so as to uncover their dirty deeds . . . to show all the exploited people who really needs the war.'

salacious stories claiming that when he had been in Petrograd he had moved into Kshesinskaya's ornate boudoir, where the Bolsheviks held decadent orgies. Cartoons depicted Lenin on the gallows (though one of the first things the Provisional Government had done was to abolish the death penalty). In the press he was public enemy number one. But in reality the police were only going through the motions of searching for him; most of the 800 or so 'subversives' arrested after the July riots were freed within a few weeks. Kerensky was far less worried about Lenin than by threats from the Right. The Kadets, some monarchists and reactionary newspapers were demanding 'an end to anarchy' and he feared a counter-revolution led by the army.

Kerensky possessed no real power. His government was just about surviving day to day. He was in many ways a decent man, unable to control the great sweep of events unfolding in Russia. But his real weakness was vanity: the appearance of power went to his head. When he became premier, he signalled that he was aiming to sideline the Petrograd Soviet by moving it to the Smolny Institute. The government returned to the traditional seat of administration, the Winter Palace. Much of the Petrograd literary world still adored Kerensky – people like Stanislavsky, Marina Tsvetaeva, Dmitry Merezhovsky and Zinaida Gippius. He began to live in the Winter Palace and took over the suite of Alexander III. He slept in the late Tsar's bed and moved his mistress in with him. He had a picture taken of himself behind Alexander's immense desk, which he sent to admirers. He had Nicholas II's billiard table, which had been in a packing case since the abdication, placed back in one of the state rooms. He kept a retinue of servants as large as the Tsar's. When he came and went the flag on the palace roof was raised and lowered, as it had been for Nicholas.

Kerensky believed that the Right was planning a coup against the Provisional Government and to install as dictator the popular General Lavr Kornilov, a genuine war hero from the early days of the fighting in 1914–15 and, since the February Revolution, commander of the Petrograd Military District. There are various interpretations of the Kornilov Affair even decades later; many still hold to the view the Soviet historians had for generations that the general had ambitions to be a dictator. It is clear, though, that Kornilov was never planning to topple the government, but wanted to force Kerensky to act more firmly against the Bolsheviks and to bypass the Soviet – 'a council of rats and dogs', as he called it. Yet Kerensky saw him as a serious rival. Kornilov, a wiry, forty-seven-year-old Cossack, was politically naïve and not the most intelligent of operators: 'he has the heart of a lion, but the brains of a sheep', according to his former commander, General Alexeyev. He had surrounded himself with a group of pro-monarchy advisers and oddball charlatans who were using him in their own power play. When in mid-August Kornilov made a series of political demands to toughen Kerensky against the Left, the Prime Minister seized his opportunity and plotted the general's downfall. He accused Kornilov of mounting a coup attempt, fabricated the evidence to 'prove' it, and ordered the general's arrest on treason charges. Foolishly, Kornilov reacted by declaring martial law and sending troops to Petrograd to 'support the government and stiffen its resolve'. Kerensky appealed to the Left – the Bolsheviks, Mensheviks and SRs – for help and the Bolsheviks enthusiastically answered the call.

The so called Kornilov 'coup' was over without a shot being fired; loyal troops found the general, arrested and jailed him. But Bolshevik mythmaking for the next seven decades claimed that they had been the decisive factor in defeating a serious attempt to take over the government. They had sent a few Red Guards to mount a defence of the Winter Palace if need be. They manned some roadblocks. That was the extent of their militant action. Yet the Kornilov Affair turned into a propaganda victory for Lenin, who the Bolsheviks spun it to appear that had 'halted' a counter-revolution and the return of the Tsar. It was yet another disaster for Kerensky. Now he was totally isolated. The Right and moderate liberals didn't trust him. They saw him as weak. Lenin was biding his time for the opportunity to overthrow him.

Lenin was becoming increasingly frustrated that he was stuck in Helsingfors, while the 'revolutionary moment is ripening in Russia', as he told Kamenev. He was maintaining contact two or three times a day with secret couriers from Petrograd. The Bolsheviks had organised a safe route that was never given away to Kerensky's intelligence agents. He was seeing the papers on the morning they were published. Yet Lenin felt isolated and impatient that he was not in Petrograd to dictate events.

In Petrograd, each coalition the Provisional Government formed was weaker than the last, the food queues were getting longer, and crime on the streets was an epidemic – 'government has come to a standstill at the top and locally', said Sukhanov. Inflation was climbing dangerously. The government was printing money at an unprecedented rate – 429 million paper rubles in April, 729 million in June, 1.1 billion in July. Prices of some basic foodstuffs had quadrupled between February and September. More than 500 factories in Petrograd and Moscow had closed down and over 100,000 workers had lost their jobs in the capital since February. A series of strikes were called for the end of September. Desertions from the army had 'become a headlong escape by soldiers from the Front', as Brusilov put it.

Lenin was not as isolated as he was made to appear. Bolshevik Party membership had risen to more than 350,000. On 1 September the Bolsheviks, for the first time, won a small majority on the Petrograd and Moscow Soviets. 'This is a big advance and will mean a lot . . . the masses are listening to us,' he told Shotman, who was one of his regular liaison men from the Party headquarters in Petrograd.

Kerensky was nominally in charge of the government and he made a good show of holding power. But after the Kornilov Affair even some of his long-standing admirers among the intelligentsia began to despair of him. 'Kerensky continues to fall and already the Bolsheviks are masters in the Soviet. Trotsky is chairman,' Zinaida Gippius wrote in her diary. 'Exactly when the slaughter, the cannonades, the uprising, the pogrom in Petersburg will start is still not certain. But it will come.'

From mid-September Lenin became convinced that the time to strike against the government would be soon and if the Bolsheviks missed their chance another may not come again for years, when he would no longer be alive to see it. He still believed Kerensky could make a peace deal with the Germans – or move the government to Moscow, far from the Front and the army garrisons. Either would have made mounting a Bolshevik insurrection more difficult.

From his Finnish hideout he wrote a series of ever more desperate letters to the comrades in Petrograd, demanding insurrection now. On 12 September: 'We must at once begin to plan the practical details of a second revolution. The majorities . . . [on the Soviets] show that people are with us if we immediately promise bread, peace and land.'

The next day he was more shrill. 'There is no reason to wait for events such as the Congress of Soviets [scheduled for 25 October]. To wait is lunacy for the Congress will do nothing. It cannot do anything. First, we must beat Kerensky, then convene the Congress. As Marx said, insurrection is an art . . . It would be naïve to wait for a formal majority for the Bolsheviks. No revolution ever waits for *that*. History will never forgive us if we do not take power now.'

The other Bolsheviks in the leadership 'were aghast, stunned', said Bukharin. They decided to burn every copy of the letters – except one;* officially all they did was 'note Comrade Lenin's views'. Since July, in Lenin's absence, the rest of the Party leadership had been following a more conciliatory line. They had even taken part in joint meetings with Kerensky's aides to work out legislation for the Constituent Assembly elections planned for November and December. If the government or the Kadets obtained evidence that Lenin was planning an imminent coup they could destroy the Bolsheviks.

The next few weeks showed Lenin's great skills as a leader. If anything disproves the Marxist idea that it is not individuals who make history but broad social and economic forces it is Lenin's revolution. He dragged his reluctant and frightened comrades with him towards an uprising most of them did not want. He used a mixture of guile, logic, bluster, threats and calm persuasion to impose his will on them. 'The rest of the leadership has blunted the growing Revolution by playing spillikins . . . they're miserable traitors to the proletarian cause,' he told Nadya. Without Lenin driving them, most of the others would have been content just talking about revolution, said Trotsky.

He tried one more time with another 'letter from afar', as he called it. 'The Bolsheviks are *guaranteed* victory in an uprising . . . if we *suddenly* strike from three points: Peter [Petrograd], Moscow and the Baltic Fleet. We have the technical capability and the armed support. If we seize the Winter Palace, the General Staff, the telephone exchanges, the railway stations . . . it is ninety-nine per cent certain that we will win with few losses . . . it is my profound belief that if we wait and let the present moment pass, we shall *ruin* the Revolution [Lenin's italics].'

He told comrades in the leadership that if they didn't approve his

---

* None of the letters surfaced until 1925, the year after Lenin's death.

plan he would resign from the Central Committee and take his ideas 'to the membership'. That threat made them think again: 'another leader at that time was inconceivable, for us and the membership'. At the same time he demanded that they let him go back to Petrograd so he could lead them in person. They refused. His safety was too important. But they allowed him to move to a closer hiding place, in Vyborg, a small town still in Finland, but only ninety kilometres from Petrograd.[5]

36

REVOLUTION – PART TWO

'Lenin didn't give a damn what anyone else thought.'
Nikolai Bukharin (1888–1938)

'I tell you what to do with people such as Lenin. We shoot them.'
Colonel Alfred Knox, British Military Attaché to Petrograd,
21 October 1917

With Lenin in hiding for three months, Trotsky's was the public face of the Bolsheviks, though technically he had only just become a Party member. He was far better known than Lenin inside Russia and hugely enjoyed the limelight: 'While Lenin needed an office, Trotsky needed a stage,' it was said. After his release from jail in mid-August, Trotsky appeared several nights a week to full houses at the enormous Cirque Moderne on the outskirts of Petrograd, which seated 2,500 people. He fascinated and terrified the middle classes; he was 'the very incarnation of the revolutionary . . . his huge forehead surmounted by great masses of black wavy hair . . . lips heavy and protruding . . . he was all tempera-ment, an individual artist'. He caused a sensation.

He had a sharp, somewhat rasping, high-pitched voice. But on his day he was a brilliant performer – funny, direct, imaginative and inspiring.[*] Sukhanov, a Menshevik who went out of curiosity, was among listeners at Trotsky's first appearance after coming out of prison. 'The mood was

---

[*] Despite nearly a decade and a half of mutual mistrust and hostility, Lenin relied heavily on Trotsky in the weeks running up to the Revolution – and afterwards. They were never personally close but both acknowledged that politically there were few differences between them. Trotsky said that he found it difficult 'to surrender to Lenin's Party' until he saw that Lenin's was the only plausible path to power. Angelica Balabanova, who hated Trotsky, once asked Lenin what had kept them apart from 1903 to 1917. 'Now don't you know? Ambition, ambition, ambition.' He meant Trotsky's ambition, not of course his own.

one of excitement throughout the hall. The hush of the audience indicated expectation. They [were] mainly soldiers and workers, though the crowd consisted of a few bourgeois, male and female. Trotsky at once began to heat up the atmosphere ... He depicted with extraordinary force the suffering of soldiers in the trenches ... Trotsky knew what he was doing. Soviet power, he said, was destined not only to put an end to the suffering of the soldiers at the Front. It would provide land and stop internal disorder. "The Soviet government will give everything the country has to the poor and to the soldiers. You, bourgeois," he would point to the well-dressed people in pricier seats. "You own two coats? Give one to the soldier freezing in the trenches. You have warm boots? Stay at home. Your boots are needed by a worker." The mood around me verged on ecstasy. It seemed that the mob would at any moment spontaneously burst into some kind of religious hymn. "We will defend the cause of the workers and peasants to the last drop of our blood," he said. "Who is in favour?" The crowd ... raised its hands as one. I saw the uplifted hands and burning eyes of men, women, adolescents, workers, soldiers, peasants. They agreed. They vowed. I watched this truly grandiose spectacle with an unusually heavy heart.'[1]

Lenin was determined to force the pace and reach Petrograd as soon as possible. He argued that 'the leader should be where the great issues are decided'. But his comrades again refused permission. Shotman reported their decision and was the butt of Lenin's anger. 'I will not leave it at that, I assure you. The traitors ... they have not heard the last of this.'

First he had to find a way out of the Finnish capital. He went with the police chief Rovio to a theatrical costumier to find a bespoke wig made to measure for him. But he was told that could take weeks and he needed a disguise immediately. There was only one 'ready to wear' hairpiece that fitted him, a grey one that made the forty-seven-year-old revolutionary look like a sixty-seven-year-old retired office worker. At first the shopkeeper didn't want to sell it as it made Lenin look so uninspiring; eventually he gave in and Lenin took it. On 30 September he left for Vyborg, lodging with some friends of Rovio. His guide was Eino Rakhia, whom Lenin liked from his dramatic July journey to the Finnish capital. From Vyborg he would make secret plans for getting to Petrograd – without his comrades' approval. He bought another wig, acquired a jacket with a dog collar and black hat, and disguised himself now as a Lutheran pastor from Finland. He took the afternoon Petrograd train on 7 October. This time he crossed the border without incident on travel documents he had used before. He never left Russia again.

Few people knew he was back in the city: Nadya, Yakov Sverdlov, the Party Secretary, Lenin's sisters and Anna Ulyanova's friend Margarita Fofanova, who had agreed to put him up in her apartment near the Finland Station. The next day the rest of the leadership found out he had returned and were insisting on an immediate meeting. At first several of the inner circle of the Party were reluctant. But Lenin bullied them into agreeing to meet in two days' time, late at night.

He was not an easy house guest, according to Fofanova. 'He told me to obtain every day, not later than 8.30 in the morning, all the Petrograd newspapers, including the bourgeois ones. Exact times were laid down very firmly for breakfast and lunch –"it will be difficult in the first week; everything will fall on you", he told me.' He was right. Lenin did not leave the apartment for the first three days. Nadya visited him daily, careful not to be followed. He continually raged against his comrades: 'they are wavering, with dread of the struggle for power'.[2]

At 10 p.m. on Wednesday 10 October, still in his disguise as a priest, Lenin arrived at a smart Petrograd apartment block, 32 Karpovka, overlooking the river. He knew the third-floor flat he was about to visit would be safe: it was the home of the prominent Menshevik journalist and strong critic of the Bolshevik leader Nikolai Sukhanov; this was the last place Kerensky's spies would think to look. Sukhanov's wife, though, Galina Flaxerman, was a loyal Bolshevik and had suggested to her husband, affectionately, that perhaps that night he should sleep somewhere near his office, as he occasionally did, rather than make the tiresome nine-kilometre journey at night when the tram service was unreliable.[*]

History can be dramatic and full of exciting, rousing action on battlefields and barricades – and sometimes it can be made in committee meetings. There were twenty-one Bolshevik Central Committee

---

[*] Later, Sukhanov saw the joke that one of the most important meetings in Russian history took place at his apartment while he was elsewhere, sleeping. It was very likely one of the biggest stories ever missed by a journalist so close to the event. 'Oh, the novel jokes of the merry muse of history,' he said when he realised.

members, but only twelve sat at the round table beneath a single lamp in Sukhanov's living room where the decision was made to trigger the Russian Revolution. It was a minority of an already small minority.

Lenin spoke for an hour and repeated his demands that a coup should be mounted immediately. He was impatient and constantly on the verge of anger, but as Trotsky said later, 'he was obviously restraining himself'.

Occasionally he banged his fist on the table to emphasise a point. 'Since the beginning of September there has been a certain indifference to the idea of insurrection,' he began. Then he outlined clearly and in detail why 'we must seize power now and not wait for the Soviets, or any Congresses . . . The time is right now and the moment of decision has arrived. The masses are tired of words and resolutions. The majority are now with us. The success of the Russian and the world revolution depends on two or three days' struggle.'

The argument ran on for seven and a half hours. Occasionally there was a short break when Flaxerman made tea or served spicy sausages, and to give the taker of the minutes, a young office clerk named Varvara Yakovleva, a break. At midnight the lights went out, as was usual in Petrograd at that time; the current was on for just a few hours a day. They continued by the light of an oil lamp and candles.*

Lenin had convinced most of the doubters. Originally Trotsky had wanted to wait until after the Congress of Soviets – which he chaired – had met. But Lenin persuaded him that would be too late. 'By that time the Congress will be up and running and it is difficult for a large, organised body of people to take swift, decisive action. We must act on the 25th, the day the Congress meets, so that we may say to it "Here is the power! What are you going to do with it?"'

Only Lenin's oldest comrades, Kamenev and Zinoviev, held out. They were against a coup on principle and for practical reasons. 'There is no demand by the people for an uprising,' said Kamenev. There was everything to be gained by 'waiting a few weeks for the Constituent

---

* The eleven others around the table were the trade unionist Andrei Bubnov, Felix Dzerzhinsky, who later became the feared head of the Cheka intelligence agency, Kamenev, Kollontai, Georgy Lomov, the Bolshevik chief in Moscow, Grigory Sokolnikov, joint editor of *Pravda*, Stalin, Sverdlov, Trotsky, Moisei Uritsky, who would become another Soviet spy chief, and Zinoviev.

Assembly where we have an excellent chance of winning a big legal majority. Comrade Lenin's plan means to stake on one card the fate not only of our Party, but the fate of the Russian and world revolution.' Zinoviev agreed and said simply that if they failed, 'we will all be shot'.

Almost at dawn a vote was taken. It went Lenin's way ten to two, with only Zinoviev and Kamenev voting against. Lenin reached across the table and picked up a pencil. There was no paper so – famously – he scrawled on a child's exercise book the biggest decision the Bolsheviks took: 'Recognising that an armed uprising is inevitable and the time perfectly ripe, the Central Committee proposes to all the organisations of the Party to act accordingly and to discuss and decide from this point of view all the practical questions.'[3]

The decision did not remain a secret. Kamenev and Zinoviev went public with their opposition. Within days they distributed to Party members in Petrograd an address that stated: 'Before history, before the international proletariat, before the Russian Revolution and the Russian working class, we have no right to stake the whole future at the present moment upon the card of armed insurrection.'

Together they wrote a blistering letter in Gorky's paper *Novaya Zhizn*, though it was signed only by Kamenev. 'Not only Zinoviev and I, but also a number of practical comrades, think that to take the initiative in an armed insurrection at the present moment . . . is an inadmissible step ruinous to the proletariat and the Revolution. To stake everything on insurrection in the coming days would be an act of despair. And our party is too strong, it has too great a future before us, to take such a step.'

Lenin was furious and called them 'traitors'. A cardinal rule among conspirators was supposed to be secrecy, and here were two leading, long-standing cadres 'swindling their comrades with endless slanderous lies . . . this is worse than strike-breaking'. He wanted them thrown out of the Party: 'From now on I no longer consider them comrades.'

Trotsky agreed, but then he seldom supported anything his brother-in-law, Kamenev, did. Stalin recommended a milder reaction – a reprimand, as long as they promised to say no more. Finally Lenin calmed down and left their punishment as a ticking-off.

All of Petrograd was talking about an imminent coup. *Novaya Zhizn* speculated on the date, predicting, almost correctly, 20 October.

Kerensky was as out of touch and complacent as the Tsar had been and actively welcomed the insurrection attempt. He told the British Ambassador, Buchanan, a few days before the uprising, 'all I want them to do is act . . . then I will crush them'. On 20 October he told Nabokov that if and when the insurrection began, it would 'be like July again . . . I am prepared to offer prayers for a rebellion. I have greater forces than necessary. They will be utterly defeated.' On 21 October, after speaking to the Prime Minister, the American Ambassador Francis cabled the State Department. 'Beginning to think the Bolsheviks will make no demonstrations; if so shall regret as believe sentiment is turning against them and . . . [now] opportune moment for giving them wholesome lesson.' Some leading personalities on the far Right relished a coup. The steel and metals industrialist Stepan Liazonov – 'The Russian Rockefeller' in the popular press – told John Reed that a Bolshevik insurrection would not last a day. 'The government would declare a state of siege . . . the military commanders can deal with those gentlemen without legal formalities.'

So the government made no effort to prevent the coup. They arrested no Bolsheviks. They didn't try to seize the Smolny Institute. They didn't reinforce the defences of the Neva bridges or any communications centres. They didn't believe the Bolsheviks could win.*

Trotsky, officially named head of the Bolsheviks' Military Revolutionary Committee on 12 October, made little secret about what it was up to. One of the first things it did was to issue a 'mission statement' – rather strange for a conspiratorial revolutionary group about to plot a putsch. 'In the interests of the defence of the Revolution and its conquests against attacks by counter-revolution, commissars have been appointed by us in military units and at strategic points in the capital and its environs. Commissars as representatives of the Soviet are inviolable. Opposition to the commissars is opposition to the Soviet of

---

* At this point there was a last-gasp effort by some ministers to explore the possibility of looking for a separate peace with Germany – which might, even at this stage, have saved the Provisional Government. On 20 October the Minister for War, General Alexander Verkhovsky, told Kerensky that the army was 'unfit to fight' and recommended that the best way of counteracting the Bolsheviks would be to at least begin talks with the Germans – 'and cut the ground from under the extremists'. Kerensky dismissed the idea – and fired Verkhovsky.

Workers' and Soldiers' Deputies. The Soviet has taken all measures to protect revolutionary order against attacks by counter-revolutionaries.'

On 21 October he made one of his most dramatic appearances at the Cirque Moderne. He whipped up the audience into a near-frenzy. After a fiery speech he demanded: 'If you support us without hesitation . . . and want to bring the Revolution to victory, if you give the cause all your strength . . . let us all swear our allegiance to the Revolution. If you support this sacred oath we are making then raise your hands.' The entire audience rose and shouted, 'We swear.'

Kerensky was now loathed by the people who had idolised him a few months earlier. On 24 October, the eve of the Revolution, Zinaida Gippius wrote in her diary: 'Nobody wants the Bolsheviks. But nobody is prepared to fight for Kerensky either.'[5]

37

POWER – AT LAST

'Whoever has experienced the power and the unrestrained ability to humiliate another human being automatically loses his own sensations. Tyranny is a habit. It has its own organic life; it develops finally into a disease . . . blood and power intoxicate.'

Fyodor Dostoyevsky, *The House of the Dead*, 1862

'First we must seize power. Then we decide what to do with it.'

Lenin to Trotsky, 24 October 1917

From the first moment, Sovnarkom – the name for the Council of People's Commissars which Lenin thought 'smelled like revolution' – felt insecure. Lenin knew that power could slip away at any time, which explains so much of the seventy-four-year history of the Soviet State. From 25 October 1917, having achieved power illegitimately, Lenin's only real concern for the rest of his life was keeping it – an obsession he passed down to his successors. Throughout its existence the Soviet Union identified itself with the founder of the State, alive or dead. The regime he created was largely shaped by his personality: secretive, suspicious, intolerant, ascetic, intemperate. Few of the more decent parts of his character found their way into the public sphere of his Soviet Union.

Throughout his life as a revolutionary Lenin was absorbed in the study of one subject above all others: the nature of power, how it is grasped and used, how it changes those who possess it and those who don't. He wanted power for its own sake, as egotists do. But he genuinely believed that he was going to use it to improve the lives of the majority of people. It is how he justified the lies, the deceit and terror that followed: everything was acceptable in pursuit of the socialist dream. As Angelica Balabanova, who respected him and admired him but grew to fear and loathe him, put it, Lenin's 'tragedy was that, in Goethe's phrase, he desired the good . . . but created evil'.

He wasn't interested in the trappings of power and didn't enjoy them. His aim was to impose his ideas and personality on others; to bend people to his will. He disliked ostentatious display and lived modestly with Nadya in dull, bourgeois style. Gorky once said that this simplicity, in such a dictatorial man, was an example of Lenin's 'narcissism'. Martov thought likewise, though at the same time he often said 'there was no vanity in Lenin' – a paradox apparent in few powerful men.

Lenin did not want power for luxury, money or sex. Inessa was his only known romantic interest outside marriage. He enjoyed power, but he didn't enjoy violence personally. He was not a sadist. He never wore anything resembling a military uniform, as so many dictators favoured. He was usually in a shabby suit and tie. He knew the Bolsheviks would use terror and accepted it, always justifying it as necessary. But he never witnessed an execution and had no interest in hearing about one. He saw only three dead bodies in his life: his father, his sister Olga and his mother-in-law. To Lenin, the blood he would spill was largely theoretical.

Nobody in Petrograd believed the Bolsheviks would survive for long. It was a 'government of journalists and pamphleteers', who had no idea how to run an administration, according to the journalists on one liberal newspaper. A witty headline in another paper on the morning after the coup described the Bolsheviks as 'Caliphs for an hour'. The leading Menshevik, Tsereteli, gave them 'no more than three days'. Gorky, who had been out on the streets the day before, watching the Revolution with a heavy heart, said Lenin would last two weeks at the most, though he soon revised that opinion. Vladimir Nabokov, out of a job when the government was overthrown but not under arrest like the ministers he had worked for, 'refused to believe for one minute in the strength of the Bolshevik regime . . . expect its early demise'. Zinaida Gippius said, 'this government by a bunch of swindlers can't last long'. Some foreign embassies were rashly telling their governments the same. An aide to the British Ambassador cabled the Foreign Office within a few days that 'it can be taken for granted that the Bolshevik Government is already on its last legs'. The American Ambassador, having told the State Department that a Bolshevik coup would never happen, now called the takeover 'a disgusting thing' and assured Washington that the Bolsheviks would soon be ousted.[1]

Some of the senior Bolsheviks felt no more confident. Bonch-Bruevich said they lived 'sitting on suitcases', so they could flee at any moment. Lunacharsky wrote to his wife just four days after his appointment as People's Commissar for Enlightenment, a grandiloquent title chosen by himself to cover the portfolios of education and culture: 'Things are so unstable. Every time I break off from a letter I don't know if it will be my last. I could at any moment be thrown into jail.' The ever-practical Sverdlov had laid his hands on more than 100,000 gold rubles, some jewels and seven false passports – including one for himself, Lenin and other leading Bolsheviks – which he had placed in a fireproof safe in case they were forced to make a quick getaway. Nadya told comrades, in candour, that Lenin's fear was that 'power may slip away from his fingers . . . and for that reason was determined not to be too lenient'.[2]

That explained one of his first actions as Chairman of Sovnarkom, on the afternoon after the coup. Just as dawn broke following his appearance at the Smolny, when he knew the Winter Palace had been seized and Petrograd was in Bolshevik hands, he went to Bonch-Bruevich's apartment to try to get some rest. He could sleep for no more than two or three hours and soon returned to the Smolny, which would be the seat of power in Russia for the next five months. In Lenin's few hours' absence Kamenev had been in charge, as temporary Sovnarkom Chairman. He had decreed an end to capital punishment for troops at the Front, which the Kerensky government had reintroduced in the summer. Lenin's reaction was predictable – and Kamenev told comrades later that he had predicted it, but announced the decree anyway. Lenin sought out Kamenev and said, 'Nonsense. How stupid. This would be a serious mistake, an unpardonable weakness. How can you make a revolution without firing squads? If you believe that we can win without executions . . . to get our way, you are under a naïve delusion. What other means of repression do we have? You don't understand the serious difficulties we are going to encounter.' According to Trotsky, he proposed rescinding the decree straight away, but 'someone said it would create a bad impression on the first day of the Revolution so he thought for a moment and said "yes . . . it would be better simply to resort to a firing squad when it becomes obvious there is no other way, but not to shout about it" and the matter was quietly dropped'. From his first few hours as leader of Russia he laid the ground for rule by terror. 'Many times a day, from the start, he would say things like, Well, what sort of dictatorship is this, show it to me,' said Trotsky. 'Vladimir Ilyich was under no illusions.'

On day two he began to censor the press and threatened to close down opposition newspapers. As the Romanovs had done, so would the Bolsheviks. A few weeks earlier, on 15 September, in one of the Party papers, *Rabochii Put* (The Workers' Path), Lenin called censorship 'feudal . . . Asiatic' and praised a free press 'as much more democratic in principle than any alternative'. He promised 'incomparably more press freedom' if the Bolsheviks had their way. On 27 October Lenin wrote a Decree on the Press which established a system of censorship run by his Party apparatchiks. 'Any organ of the press may be . . . [closed down] for inciting resistance to the Decrees of Sovnarkom . . . or if found to be sowing confusion by means of obviously defamatory distortion of the facts.' The measures were supposed to be 'temporary' against 'clear counter-revolutionaries . . . emergency measures must be taken to stop the torrent of filth and slander against the new authority. As soon as the new order has been firmly established all administrative measures affecting the press will be lifted and the press will be granted full freedom.'

The State would take over ownership of the presses and all the newsprint. The new government would allot the resources 'equitably'. Political parties would be given a share and any groups of citizens would be guaranteed access to a nationalised printing plant if they were able to collect a given number of signatures for a newspaper of their own. 'This will provide real freedom of the press for all and not just for the rich. It will act for the people's enlightenment and not for their stultification and deception.' When there were murmurs of dissent among his clique he said, 'there's a unanimous chorus from those jackals. Aren't we going to bridle this rabble? The bourgeois press is a weapon no less dangerous than bombs or guns aimed at us. Why should we place it in their hands?' Around the same time he shocked Emma Goldman by telling her that 'free speech is a bourgeois prejudice, a soothing plaster for social ills. In the workers' republic, economic well-being talks louder than speech.'[3]

From 28 October Kadet papers were closed down. Red Guards smashed some of their presses and linotype machines and confiscated the others. A few editors and prominent journalists were arrested. The best-selling SR newspaper *Volya Naroda* (The People's Will) was shut down. It appeared the next day with a new masthead as *Volya*, and the following day, after the editor was jailed, as *Narod* – just as used to happen in banned newspapers during Tsarist times. When it finally died its farewell editorial echoed Marx: 'History repeats itself . . .'

When the socialist paper *Den* (Day) was banned it turned into an evening publication Night, then Midnight, then Darkest Night. The opposition press was driven underground.

Some press criticism was permitted – reluctantly and for a short while. Gorky wouldn't be silenced. Day after day until his newspaper was closed down the following summer, he warned with prescience in his column 'Untimely Thoughts' about the Bolsheviks' intentions. Immediately after the Press Decree he wrote: 'Lenin and Trotsky do not have the slightest idea of the meaning of freedom or the Rights of Man. They and their fellow travellers are already intoxicated by the foul poison of power, as they show by their disgraceful attitude to free speech, to the person, and to all rights for which the democracy struggled . . . The working class cannot fail to understand that Lenin is only performing a certain experiment on their skin and on their blood . . . Lenin is not an omnipotent magician but a cold-blooded trickster, who spares neither the honour nor the lives of the proletariat.'

A few days later: 'Lenin is one of those people who possess a quite exceptional strength of character . . . he is a man of many gifts and he has all the qualities of a "leader" – especially the complete lack of morality essential for such a role, and the aristocrat's contempt for the masses. Life in all its complexity is unknown to Lenin. He does not know the masses. He has never lived among them, but he found out from books how to raise the masses onto their hind legs, how to enrage their instincts easily. To Lenin, the working class is like iron ore to a metalworker. Is it possible, given present circumstances, to cast a socialist state out of this ore? Evidently not. But why not try? What does Lenin risk if his experiment fails? . . . I am mistrustful of Russians in power – recently slaves themselves, they will become unbridled despots as soon as they have the chance to be their neighbours' masters.'[4]

Lenin did not hide his ambition to close down the opposition press. A few weeks after the coup, at a meeting of the Petrograd Soviet, he

complained about press criticism and a Menshevik stood up and heckled to loud applause: 'What do you mean, criticism. Which papers?
Where? You've closed them all.'

'No not yet,' Lenin replied. 'But we soon will.'

The Old Left was shattered. The venerable father of Russian Marxism,
Georgy Plekhanov, now sixty-one and in poor health, had broken with
Lenin years ago but was horrified that his erstwhile comrade had tak-
en power for himself and his Party, sidelining other socialists. The day
after the coup he wrote an open letter to the Petrograd working class
saying that the Bolshevik 'revolution is the greatest historic calamity,
which will turn back the clock from all the gains made in Russia since
February'. The next day soldiers and sailors burst into his Petrograd
apartment when he was taking tea with his wife, Rozalia Markovna.
A soldier drew a pistol and pressed it towards his chest, demanding,
'You, scum, hand over your weapons. We are going to search. If we find
any we'll shoot you on the spot.' Plekhanov drew himself up to his full
184cm height and replied, 'You will probably do it anyway. Go on . . .
but I haven't got any weapons.' They roughed up the apartment and
left him unharmed, but Plekhanov went into hiding.* A week after the
Revolution Vera Zasulich, sixty-eight, told a comrade in despair: 'I feel
as though everything I struggled for, everything that was so dear to me
my entire life, has crumbled to dust.'[5]

Kerensky fled to the Front and tried to raise an army to recapture the
capital and return in triumph. But most of the army refused to support
him and all he could muster were a few hundred Cossacks under the 3rd
Cavalry commander General Pyotr Krasnov. On 28 October they captured Gatchina, forty-five kilometres south of Petrograd, a strategic base
from which they could seize the city. Lenin was seriously worried that
they would march on Petrograd and he would be toppled after just three

---

* He was admitted, secretly under an assumed name, to a clinic in Petrograd and
later fled to Finland, where he died in a village near Terijoki on 30 May 1918. He was
soon rehabilitated politically, though. During the Soviet years his attacks on Lenin and
the Bolsheviks were censored, but his philosophical works on Marxism were admired
– even by Lenin – and were taught in schools as a compulsory subject up until the collapse of the USSR.

days. At around midday he went to the Petrograd military headquarters and took personal command of the defence. He closely questioned every order given by members of his Military Revolutionary Committee, most of them, apart from Trotsky, ex-soldiers. So haphazard had been the coup – even though it had succeeded – that he distrusted all the information given to him.

He got on to the Hughes wire, an early prototype of a telex machine, which he had never used before. He didn't announce his name or title. The conversations showed how uneasy and tense he was.

First he contacted Alexander Sheinman, Chairman of the Helsingfors Soviet. 'Can you move the greatest possible number of destroyers and other warships to Petrograd at once?' he asked. Sheinman said he would have to ask the Baltic Fleet commander as he didn't know. 'This is a naval matter. What's the news in Petrograd?'

'The news is that Kerensky's troops are on the move and have taken Gatchina . . . it is imperative that we have the strongest reinforcements as soon as possible.'

'Anything else?'

He received a typical Lenin answer. 'Instead of your question "Anything else?" I expected to hear you say you were ready to set out immediately and fight.'

Sheinman: 'It seems to me useless to repeat that. We have made our decision and . . . everything will be done.'

Lenin: 'Have you stocks of rifles and plenty of ammunition to help us?'

Then Ivan Mikhailov, head of the Helsingfors Soviet's military section, came on the line. 'How many men do you need?'

'As many as possible but only loyal men who are ready to fight.'

He was promised 5,000 within twenty-four hours – 'and they are ready to fight'.

'Can you provide food for them?'

'Yes. We have plenty of provisions. We also have thirty-five machine guns. We can send them and their gun crews without any detriment to our position here, and a few field guns.'

'On behalf of the Government of the Republic I urgently request you to begin sending these forces immediately. Are you aware a new government has been formed? What is the attitude of your Soviet to it?'

'Yes, we heard from the newspapers. People here are enthusiastic about power passing into the hands of the Soviets.'

'I take it the forces will start off immediately.'

Finally Nikolai Izmailov, the Baltic Fleet representative on the Soviet, came on the line. He said he would despatch the battleship *Republic* and two destroyers. They should arrive in Petrograd within eighteen hours. Lenin said he wanted the vessel in the Ship Canal as close to the shore as possible. Izmailov, who had been a naval officer, told Lenin impatiently that the ship couldn't be anchored near the shore and in any case 'its guns have a range of twenty-five *versts* . . . In short, let the sailors and their commanders handle this.'

Lenin asked for all available stocks of rifles and ammunition. 'Goodbye, good luck,' he said.

'Goodbye. Will you tell me to whom I was speaking?'

'Lenin.'

'Goodbye . . . We are setting everything in motion now.'

Lenin did not seem relieved by this news and wasn't convinced the reinforcements would arrive.

He had a big problem persuading the Petrograd garrison soldiers to move against Kerensky's forces. Later that evening Nikolai Podvoisky, the former army officer who had played a major part in planning the coup, had an uncomfortable meeting with Lenin. 'The Volinsky and other trusted regiments are simply refusing to leave . . . we can't get a single army unit to go,' he explained.

'Then you must get them out,' Lenin replied. 'They must go this very moment, at whatever the cost.'

'But there's nothing we can do with the regiments.'

According to Podvoisky, 'Lenin went into a terrible rage. His features became unrecognisable. He fixed his eyes on mine and, without raising his voice, though he seemed to be shouting, he said, "You will answer personally to the Central Committee if the regiments don't leave the city immediately. Do you hear me? At this very moment."'

Podvoisky managed to raise a few men, but only after he told them what Lenin would most likely do to them if they were determined to stay in barracks.[6]

If Krasnov's few Cossacks had moved quickly on the city from Gatchina that day they might have taken power back for Kerensky. But they were as unwilling to fight as the garrison troops were. Trotsky – as much as Lenin – played a part in defending the city. He said that if troops were going to be unreliable, the Bolsheviks would arm workers. Throughout the day he toured factories making impassioned speeches urging workers to 'turn Petrograd into a fortress'. At the Soviet that evening he called on everyone to march to the Front to save the Revolution. A rough voice interrupted him: 'Why aren't you there yourself with the Red Guards?' He replied, dramatically, 'I'm going now' – and left the platform. It was exactly the right revolutionary gesture, as John Reed, who was there, described it. But there was no need for the garrison troops, the battleships from the Baltic Fleet or a workers' militia.

It was bribery and deception that saved the Bolsheviks from defeat. On 30 October Kerensky's forces reached the heights of Pulkovo, twenty-five kilometres outside Petrograd. There had been no major battles, only a few small skirmishes in heavy rain. Late that night Pavel Dybenko, a dashing former naval officer and now Navy Commissar in the new regime, was smuggled into their camp and negotiated a deal promising the Cossacks safe passage to the Don and autonomy over their part of the steppe. They saw no reason to fight for Kerensky and surrendered to the Bolsheviks, who kept their side of the bargain and let them go. Trotsky arrived on the scene late at night on 31 October and agreed the terms of the agreement.* At 2 a.m. he despatched a cable to Lenin: 'This night . . . will go down in history. The attempt to move counter-revolutionary troops against the capital of the Revolution has been decisively repulsed. Kerensky is retreating; we are advancing. All the country from now on will be convinced that the power of the Soviets is no ephemeral thing, but a fact. There will be no return to the past. Before us are struggles, obstacles and sacrifices. But the road is clear and victory is certain.'†[7]

---

* But the Don Cossacks were cheated of their 'independence' not long afterwards. Despite the promises they were subsumed into the highly centralised USSR, as eventually were all the so-called autonomous regions.

† Kerensky remained in hiding inside Russia or in Finland throughout the Civil War that followed, hoping for a triumphal return to Petrograd. Eventually he accepted it would be unlikely to happen and left for Berlin in 1922, and subsequently Paris – the route taken by hundreds of thousands of Russian émigrés. When France fell to the Germans in 1940 he left for the US. He lived in New York, making a good income on the speaking circuit. Then he went to California and joined the Hoover Institution. He died in 1970 aged eighty-nine.

*

Late on the afternoon of 29 October the new People's Commissar for Social Welfare, Alexandra Kollontai, arrived at her ministry in a grand neo-classical building in Kazan Street. She was greeted by a picket line of office workers. An elderly footman in full livery refused to let her in, telling her he had no idea who she was. She told him her title and demanded to see the most senior official in the building. The footman said that petitioners were allowed in only between 1 and 3 p.m. and as it was now past 5 she had better leave and return another day. When she tried to force her way through, he slammed the door in her face. She returned early the following morning with an escort of soldiers, but she found a picket line outside and the building inside almost empty. The entire civil service which had worked for the Tsarist regime and the Provisional Government had gone on strike in mass protest against the new government. Only the cooks, cleaners, doormen, porters and support staff were working as normal.

Kollontai went down to the picket line and threatened to arrest them all unless one of them found the keys to her office safe. As she had feared, the safe was empty; her predecessor, the Kadet Countess Sophia Panina, had taken the ministerial funds with her and refused to pay any of the money back until told to do so by the Constituent Assembly due to be elected the following month.*

On the same day Shlyapnikov, Commissar for Labour (and Kollontai's former lover), tried to enter his office. The janitor told him that only some of the cleaners were in the building, everyone else was on strike. He went back to the Smolny, where Bolshevik Party officials and clerks

---

* The two women had known each other since childhood – and loathed each other, though the Countess did acknowledge once that Kollontai 'dressed very well – for a revolutionary'. Panina, in whose palace Lenin had in 1906 caused a sensation as a speaker, was arrested and charged with embezzling 93,000 rubles from the ministry/ commissariat. On Lenin's orders, in early December she appeared in the first Soviet 'show trial' before a Revolutionary Tribunal. The proceedings were a farce, with the verdict decided by the Bolshevik Party and Sovnarkom – as would become so familiar in the Soviet years. She was ordered to pay back the money, refused and was jailed in the Peter and Paul Fortress. She was released only when some of her rich friends raised the cash to bail her out. She was allowed to leave Petrograd and joined the Whites in the Civil War, escaping to Germany and then to the US. She died in New York in 1956, aged eighty-four.

were still working. He tried to recruit some staff from one of the commissariats, so he could set up an office. A mid-level civil servant came to see him: 'Well you won't find one – certainly not for you. What, a trade unionist all your life and now you are recruiting blackleg scabs. You should be ashamed.'

It was nearly two weeks before Trotsky tried going to his assigned office as Foreign Affairs Commissar. He turned up smartly dressed early on the morning of 9 November at the grand General Staff building opposite the Winter Palace. Some curious officials who wanted to see the famous revolutionary leader went to meet him, as one recalled. 'The new "minister" arrived and said, "I am Trotsky, the Commissar." He was greeted with ironic laughter. To this he paid no attention at all and just told all of us to get to work. We left – but to our homes, with the intention of not returning to our offices while Trotsky was head of the ministry.' Trotsky took it in his stride. As he told a friend when he returned in good humour to the Smolny later that morning, what foreign relations would the Bolsheviks need anyway? 'All I'll do is issue a few revolutionary proclamations to the foreigners and then shut up shop.' He had gone to the commissariat only for one purpose: to find copies of the so-called 'secret treaties' that the Tsarist government had signed with the Allies to enter the war. He couldn't find them and was told that a secretary in the Provisional Government had taken them the day before the Revolution.[*8]

Lenin called the strikes 'sabotage . . . nothing but blackmail' and issued repeated orders for the civil servants to return to work. He was not too concerned about most of them, though. He knew that for the time being the Revolution could live without officials from the Foreign or Welfare Commissariats. But it needed money immediately. If the Bolsheviks couldn't pay supporters, buy supplies or requisition food there was no way it could survive for any length of time. Lenin told Vyacheslav Menzhinsky – who was given the job of Finance Commissar largely because years earlier he had briefly worked as a lowly bank clerk – 'without money we are helpless. The wages of railway workers, telegraph workers and the like have to be paid.'

---

* They turned up later and when Trotsky published them, as we will see, it caused a major diplomatic incident.

They had to return to bank robbery in order to get it. On the first day after the Revolution Lenin personally, and Sovnarkom formally, asked the head of the National Bank, Ivan Shipov, to release ten million rubles to the government. He refused, saying it would be illegal. He didn't recognise the Bolshevik regime or the Soviet as a legitimate government; the National Bank employees had joined the civil servants' strike. Three days later Lenin demanded the money again and once more was turned down. Couriers sent from the Smolny with drafts signed by the commissars were rejected and soon Sovnarkom would be starved of funds. And starved of anyone who knew how the banking system worked. 'There were some people among us who understood . . . from books and manuals,' one Party worker admitted. 'But there was not a single . . . [person] who knew the technical procedures of the Russian State Bank.'

On 7 November Menzhinsky, accompanied by a squad of Red Guards and a small detachment of soldiers, arrived at the bank, which was deserted apart from Shipov and a few of his closest aides. They were given an ultimatum. Unless the cash was forthcoming in twenty minutes all 'white-collar' employees above the position of clerk would lose their jobs and their pensions and all men of military age would be drafted into the army and sent to the Front. They still held firm. Shipov was placed under guard and locked up in the Smolny, in Menzhinsky's room. The commissar had to share with his deputy.

Lenin was furious with Menzhinsky and three days later ordered the Deputy Commissar, Nikolai Gorbunov, and the newly appointed State Bank Commissar, Nikolai Osinsky, to 'go and take the money, at least five million, and don't dare come back without it'.

Red Guards surrounded the bank while the two Bolsheviks entered the building and ordered junior clerks, at gunpoint, to open the vaults. Five million rubles were hastily stuffed into sacks – as in a heist movie. Gorbunov and Osinsky carried the bags over their shoulders, got into a waiting armoured car and took them directly to Lenin's office. He was not there; the pair transferred the money into red velvet bags and kept guard over the swag. Osinsky was holding a cocked revolver throughout the procedure. When he returned, Lenin was beaming. The bags were put in an old wardrobe in an adjoining office and a sentry stood permanent guard. This was the first Soviet Treasury.[9]

38

THE MAN IN CHARGE

'There was nothing in Lenin's personal appearance to suggest even faintly a resemblance to the super-man . . . he looked at first glance more like a provincial grocer than a leader. Yet in those steely eyes there was something that arrested attention, something in that quizzing, half-contemptuous, half-smiling look which spoke of boundless self-confidence and conscious superiority.'

Robert Bruce Lockhart, meeting Lenin, spring 1918

'The fact that all his . . . [Lenin's] powers and energies are concentrated upon one thing makes it easy for him to appear extraordinary in the eyes of the masses and become a leader, in the same way that those who really concentrate on God become saints and those who live only for money become millionaires.' Ignazio Silone (1900–1978)

Almost every evening until the following new year Lenin and Nadya went for a walk – as had been their routine in exile. 'Nobody knew his face at that time, so we would often stroll around the Smolny,' she said. It took several weeks for his beard to grow back and even people who might have recognised him were confused. Petrograd was a lawless place in the first months of Bolshevik rule and random crimes were commonplace. But Lenin never needed intervention by the one bodyguard who followed a discreet distance behind him.*

Lenin and Nadya were given a two-room apartment, with a kitchen,

---

* But he was the victim of crime within a few days of the Bolshevik coup. His first official car, a luxurious and beautiful Turcat Méry which had been made in 1915 for the Tsar, was stolen when it was parked outside the Smolny. A group of firemen took it and planned to sell it for a large sum to a private buyer in Finland. Stepan Gil, who had been one of Nicholas II's chauffeurs but became a loyal Bolshevik and Lenin's driver, led a search for it and found it before the car left Petrograd.

on the first floor of the Smolny. It was comfortable, if far from luxurious. For Lenin the important thing was its security: it backed onto a corridor leading to a courtyard through which he could flee quickly if necessary – and he told Nadya it might be necessary at any point. Nobody was allowed to enter without a special pass signed by Lenin. Nadya liked the accommodation and enjoyed her time at the Smolny. 'Our room had once been occupied by an upper-class lady. It had a partition screen on one side of which stood the bed . . . one had to enter via the washroom.'

For years Nadya had worked for him as his secretary and she held a position as a Party official as well as personal confidante. Now he had all the help he needed. The change was difficult for her and, as she told friends, she desperately needed some work to be useful. Lunacharsky gave her a job as one of his deputy commissars. Her one regret was that she was no longer there to look after Lenin, and to watch out for his health. He ate badly – grazed on food, 'living from hand to mouth' and not taking enough care. 'He was in a neglected condition. Zheltyshev [Yuri, his bodyguard] fetched him lunch – bread, which was laid down as his ration. Sometimes Maria Ilyinichna [Lenin's sister] brought him food of some sort from her home, but I wasn't at home a lot of the time and there was no concern for his diet.' Predictably, he was soon complaining about stomach pains, indigestion and insomnia.[1]

'Each session of the Sovnarkom represented improvisation on a grand scale,' Trotsky told one of his chief aides after a few days as Foreign Affairs Commissar. 'Everything was in its beginning . . . everything had to be built anew. There is no use looking for precedents because history hasn't supplied any.' Lenin repeatedly said, 'we have to destroy everything . . . everything, to create the new' and at first the regime appeared like an extension of the revolutionary underground, where conspirators met, holed in the corner, while a couple of armed plotters kept watch for police spies. Despite the efforts of a secretary to impose some semblance of solemnity, 'we could not help feeling that we were attending another sitting of a . . . revolutionary committee', said one long-time Party activist who sat in on a few early sessions. 'For years we had belonged to various underground organisations. All the commissars remained seated in their topcoats or greatcoats . . . [in case they had to escape in a hurry] . . . many wore the forbidding leather jacket.'[2]

Soon Lenin's sense of order prevailed and meetings were much more structured. He was obsessive about secrecy and the big, difficult, more squalid decisions were often taken by a small clique of his trusted lieutenants – at the beginning he relied most on Sverdlov and Trotsky – who were careful to leave no paper trail. But Lenin was fussily insistent that the bulk of the formal Sovnarkom business must be conducted as he instructed. Meetings usually began at around 5 p.m., often lasted six or seven hours with barely a break, and for the first month Lenin was present at every one.

Meetings were in a surprisingly small and dingy room on the third floor, 'dark even on sunny days', recalled one regular visitor. 'Light struggled to get through, and it was difficult to draw the curtains. A few armchairs rested against the walls. The furniture was ill assorted, gathered from various places around the building. A worn, faded carpet covered the floor. It was like the reception room of a provincial lawyer.'

Lenin loathed anyone being late and instituted a system of fines for unpunctuality. Typically, he wrote the rules himself. Any commissar or official who was late by up to half an hour was fined five rubles, which rose to ten for anyone late by an hour. 'Only People's Commissars who give proper notice and reasons for being late will be excused the fine.' He instituted similar regulations for all government bodies. 'Lateness by ten minutes for a meeting without good reason will incur a reprimand; a second offence, loss of one day's pay; a third time a public reprimand in the press . . . Anyone more than fifteen minutes late will incur a reprimand in the press or compulsory labour on days off.'

He limited time for speakers rigorously, referring to a pocket watch he kept on a green-baize table in front of him. Most of the commissars had been writers, agitators, trade union organisers, 'conspirators'. Very few knew anything about administration and Lenin's claim that 'any worker can learn how to run a ministry in a few days' was immediately put to the test. He realised that of course it was nonsense. As Trotsky admitted, often the commissars knew next to nothing about complex subjects. 'The discussion was always concise. The speaker . . . had no more than five to ten minutes and yet Lenin, somehow gropingly, always found the right line along which to steer the debate. When there was a meeting at which many people were present, among them specialists or people unknown to Lenin, he resorted to his favourite gesture: he would put his right hand over his forehead and eyes and look through between his stretched fingers. Thus, playing peek-a-boo, he observed the speaker and the participants very intently and attentively and saw exactly what he needed to see. He would watch a speaker from under his hand, as if he were feeling him out and weighing every word; it was a special look of interrogation. He kept one eye on the watch . . . and would occasionally remind the orator that time was up.'

He took notes throughout, or wrote them furiously to be handed to a speaker requesting information or making an observation. Often they were angry complaints if he saw anyone whispering at meetings or appearing not to be concentrating hard enough. He fired off a message to one of his favourites, Lidia Fotieva, his loyal and efficient personal secretary for many years, when he saw her talking to one of the stenographers. 'If you're going to chatter, I swear I will throw you out.' On another occasion a couple of weeks later he couldn't spot her when he wanted her to find something for him. 'I'm giving you a reprimand. You are not to *sleep* but to organise things so that *everyone* can easily locate you [his italics] and always [underlined three times] when it is to do with me.' He was extremely fond of using italics and underlinings for emphasis.

Lenin was given a small private office on the first floor of the building, along the corridor from his apartment – Kollontai thought it was 'cramped . . . a desk was shoved tight against a wall under a single lamp, and there was little space'. By the second day after the Revolution he became infuriated that so many people he didn't know, including those with no urgent business, barged in without knocking or being announced. In pencil he drafted instructions to the chief doorman of the building with his own hand: 'Admit members of the "Cabinet" if the attendant recognises them; if not, demand to see their identification. All others must write their names and purpose of their visit in no more than two words on a piece of paper. The attendant must bring that piece of paper to the Chairman [Lenin] without whose permission nobody is allowed into the office. If the office is empty, keep the door open so one of the secretaries can answer the telephone. If someone is in the chairman's room, always keep the door closed.'[3]

Appointments to responsible posts were haphazard, often given to totally inexperienced people for political reasons and to those who happened to be in the right place at the right time. One day, during the stand-off between the new regime and the State Bank, a relatively minor Bolshevik activist, Mikhail Peskovsky, was chatting to the Finance Commissar Menzhinsky, an old colleague. He casually mentioned that he had been a student in London some years earlier and one of his subjects for a few months, among other things, had been finance. 'Menzhinsky looked at me and said, "Well, in that case we must appoint you as Director of the State Bank." I was frightened and told him that I had no desire for that position, it was not my job and I wouldn't suit it. Menzhinsky . . . asked me to wait and he left the room. After a while he came back with a piece of paper. Under the signature of Ilyich my appointment to the position was confirmed and I asked Menzhinsky to revoke the appointment but he remained unmoved.'*

Nikolai Gorbunov, twenty-five, who for many years held the key position of Secretary of Sovnarkom and was a personal assistant to Lenin, had a similar experience. An engineer by training, he had caught the eye of Vladimir Bonch-Bruevich, head of Lenin's private office. BB, as he was called, asked him into the Smolny at the beginning of November – 'and I was taken to see Lenin, who told me I was given the job'. He had no experience of any administrative work, 'and to start with I was given no instructions about what my duties were. I had not the slightest idea about the work, or secretarial duties in general. I couldn't type, but somehow I confiscated a typewriter, on which I managed to bang out documents using two fingers, as for a long time no typists could be found.' On one occasion he had to take detailed minutes of a Sovnarkom meeting, having no shorthand of any kind. Lenin was 'a stern taskmaster . . . he let very little slip and was extremely demanding. He used to say "work in my secretariat is real drudgery – no rest, no holidays" and he was right.' But Lenin did take a close interest in those who worked near to him. He told his staff this wasn't 'softness' on his part. It was colder, more calculating than that. 'Those of you who work at Smolny are State material . . . valuable State property.'[4]

Lenin showed his own inexperience. In general he was shrewd about appointing talented and efficient people for the top positions, whom he

---

* Eventually he managed to persuade senior comrades that he really wasn't up to the task and he returned to obscurity in another commissariat, but he was famous for a day or two.

picked on ability as well as political *nous* and status in the Party. But he didn't always know what the jobs entailed. Adolph Joffe, one of the cleverest of the early revolutionaries, whom Lenin appointed to the key position of Ambassador to Germany – and later a roving diplomat for the Soviets – was surprised by a conversation with Lenin at the Smolny a few days after the Revolution, as he explained in a letter to his good friend Trotsky. 'The day after Leonid Krasin was named Transport Commissar, a post for which despite his many great qualities he is entirely unsuited, I was leaving Petrograd. I went to see Vladimir Ilyich before I went. He asked me when I was leaving and I told him I didn't know exactly when the train was departing. "Call up Krasin," he said. In his view the Transport Commissar was supposed to know the entire railway timetable, even if he had only been in the job a day and had never had anything to do with the railways before. It was the same with everything else.'[5]

Lenin, though, was smart to pick Yakov Sverdlov as the man to oversee the apparatus of government, technically with the title of Chairman of the Central Committee Executive. He was a brilliant organiser, ruthlessly efficient, notoriously unsentimental and a fast learner. Aged thirty-two, he had served seven years in the Tsar's jails or in Siberian exile, during which time he voraciously read everything he could lay his hands on. He possessed a photographic memory accompanied by exhaustive curiosity. Short, wiry, with dark good looks, he had a mop of thick black hair, piercing hazel eyes, a goatee beard and pince-nez. He habitually wore the commissar's leather coat, but often added something raffish of his own – a floppy Bohemian black cravat. He had a deep, booming voice which some people found attractive, others, when he was in a dark mood, terrifying. 'He was like a diamond,' according to Lunacharsky, that had been 'chosen for its absolute hardness to be the axis of some delicate, perpetually revolving piece of mechanism'. If Lenin was the mastermind of the Revolution, the theoretician, and Trotsky its showman and orator, Sverdlov was its chief operating officer. Lenin said, simply, 'Sverdlov . . . he is indispensable . . . it would take six men to replace him.'[6]

During his first few days as Russia's leader Lenin ruled by decree. Dozens of them came from the Smolny in a flurry, most written by

Lenin himself. Apart from the Decree on the Press, there were decrees on Peace, which promised a swift end to the war, on Land, which set out a vast agrarian reform that gave peasants rights to own and run estates, and on Workers' Rights, which assured 'freedom from capitalist exploitation' and control over factories. A separate decree guaranteed an eight-hour working day – something for which the trade unions had been struggling for decades. All the nations of the Russian empire, from Armenia to the Baltic states and Poland, were given the right to independence. Women were ensured equal rights in work, marriage and over family property. Russians were assured freedom of religion. Under the old regime the Orthodox Church was the established religion, many others had been banned, and there were still ecclesiastical courts which had considerable power. Decrees nationalised the banks and major industries.

When Lenin wasn't chairing meetings he was furiously writing these decrees, many of which read as though they had been dashed off with little thought. Others were merely 'exercises in propaganda, not government', as one of Lenin's old comrades charged with implementing them admitted. From the start, the decrees showed two characteristic aspects of his rule that stood out: a dictatorial tone, and the way Lenin could be sidetracked by small things. The man who often thought in a grand historical sweep and believed he was starting a world revolution could be obsessed by trivia. For example, when it was touch and go whether his revolution would survive, food stocks were running out in Petrograd and Russia was still at war, he spent hours on a subject close to his heart, but still a matter that could have been handled by a mid-level official. He wrote in his own spindly hand a Decree on Libraries; its hectoring tone was typical: '1. The Public Library [formerly the Imperial Library] must immediately arrange the exchange of books with *all* the libraries in Petrograd and the provinces and also with foreign libraries (Finland, Sweden etc.). 2. No charge must be made for sending books from one library to another. 3. The reading room in the Library must be open every day, not excluding Sundays and holidays, from 8 a.m. to 11 p.m. This is the procedure in private libraries and reading rooms used by the *rich* in civilised countries. 4. An appropriate number of employees must be immediately transferred to the Public Library from the Commissariat of Enlightenment . . . and employing the services of women more widely, since the men are being drafted into the army . . . nine-tenths of the present personnel in the ministry being engaged in work which is not only useless but harmful . . . ' He goes on for a further few clauses in a similar fashion.[7]

The frenetic pace of the decrees was partly Lenin's determination to move forward with speed. But the main reason was prompted by insecurity: if his regime didn't survive he wanted the evidence of his decrees to remind history of the things he intended to achieve. The decrees were agreed by Sovnarkom, but hardly even discussed by the Soviets in whose name he had taken power. Quickly the Soviet became the rubber-stamp body it would remain for the next seven decades – 'a sorry parody of a revolutionary parliament'.

A few Bolsheviks rebelled, but Lenin saw them off. A week after the Revolution Kamenev and Zinoviev attempted to bounce Lenin into agreeing to a coalition government with other socialist parties – the Mensheviks and Socialist Revolutionaries. It seems scarcely conceivable that, having worked closely with Lenin for the last fifteen years, only now did they suddenly realise that he really did intend to create a one-party state. More likely, they thought Lenin would be swept aside and they could take leadership of the Bolsheviks when he was gone.

On 4 November they threatened to resign from the government, and when Lenin called their bluff they walked out of Sovnarkom and the Central Committee of the Party with three other commissars, Nikolai Milutin, Viktor Nogin and Alexei Rykov. They went public – a heinous offence in Lenin's eyes. 'We believe that only the formation of all the Soviet parties will be able to consolidate the results of the heroic struggle of the working class and the Revolution,' they wrote in *Izvestia*, the paper controlled by the Soviet. 'There is only one alternative to this: the maintenance of an exclusively Bolshevik government run by means of political terror. We cannot and do not want to go this way . . . we cannot assume responsibility for this fatal policy, pursued in opposition to the will of the majority of workers and soldiers, which . . . would lead to the establishment of an irresponsible regime and to the destruction of the Revolution and the country.' Lenin called them 'traitors and deserters . . . two of whom even before the insurrection acted as strike-breakers'. But he did not worry; they did not represent a significant split in the Party or a threat to himself. He let them go into isolation, temporarily.

Sure enough, within weeks they submitted and returned to the fold.

First to slither back, predictably, was Zinoviev, who told Lenin, with weasel words: 'We prefer to make mistakes together with millions of workers and soldiers and to die together with them rather than to stand apart at this decisive, historic moment.'

Lenin wasn't a dictator at this point, and would face considerable opposition and monumental challenges in the next few years, but, as Trotsky put it, 'from the moment the Provisional Government was deposed, Lenin acted in matters large and small as the government'.[8]

39

THE SWORD AND SHIELD

'In every revolutionary there is a hidden gendarme.'

Gustave Flaubert, *Sentimental Education*, 1869

A secret decree written by Lenin set up the Cheka, the main building block for the Soviet police state. There were numerous name changes over the years – the GPU, GPRU, NKVD, MGB and finally, in its best-known incarnation, the KGB. Whatever it was called, its tasks remained the same: to protect the Party and its leadership from any perceived threat of subversion, and to dispense 'revolutionary justice'.* It was, in Lenin's words, 'the Party's sword and shield', and the two images formed its emblem. Most operatives called themselves Chekists, up to the day it was disbanded in the 1990s. The Russian President a hundred years after the Revolution, Vladimir Putin, a long-serving KGB officer until the collapse of the USSR, used to say he had been a Chekist. So did thousands of people who worked for the imitation agencies the Cheka spawned throughout the Communist world – the East German Stasi or the Securitate in Nicolae Ceauşescu's Romania.†

It was set up on 7 December 1917 as the Extraordinary Commission (Chrezhvychnaya Komissiya) for Combating Counter-Revolution, Speculation and Sabotage. Officially the Cheka was supposed to work hand in hand with a separate commission established three days earlier to combat the 'wine pogroms' – people who were looting the cellars of the Tsar and the rich who had either been arrested or fled Petrograd.

---

* As he said he would, Lenin – unilaterally – changed the Party's name in March 1918 from the Social Democratic and Labour Party, which despite all the various splits it had been since 1895, to the Russian Communist Party (Bolshevik).
† The present-day FSB, Russia's much-feared replacement of the KGB, retains the sword and shield motif as its 'logo'.

'Attempts to break into wine cellars, liquor stores, warehouses, shops and private homes will be broken up by machine gun fire without any warning.' But the Cheka's remit was always intended to be wider.

In Lenin's words, the Cheka's job was to 'investigate and liquidate all attempts or actions connected with counter-revolution or sabotage, no matter from whom they come, throughout Russia'. But its functions and powers were not made public until the mid-1920s, and from the first it operated outside the law under top-secret protocols with virtually no political accountability. The Soviet had no control and neither, over the years, did Sovnarkom. It answered only to Lenin.

Soon the Cheka became the most feared of the State 'organs', and its chief the most hated man in Russia. Lenin said the Cheka needed 'a staunch proletarian Jacobin' in charge, though the forty-year-old 'ruthless, cold, shy and deeply puritanical' Felix Dzerzhinsky wasn't exactly a proletarian. He came from a wealthy landed Polish family which, like Lenin's, had a claim to nobility. He was referred to as 'Iron Felix' or 'the Iron Count'.

Born in Vilna, he went to one of Poland's best *Gimnasia* schools before being expelled in his teens for persistently speaking Polish to classmates – a seriously seditious activity under the Tsars. He loathed the Romanov regime and the Russian bourgeoisie with a deep hatred that never left him. For Dzerzhinsky, the Revolution was personal. He was a founder member of the first Marxist revolutionary group in Poland and almost immediately afterwards was arrested, aged twenty. He was tortured and kept in solitary confinement for a year. He spent two periods of exile in Siberia, but managed to escape both times. Soon after he married fellow RSDLP member Zofia Muszkat she was arrested for smuggling subversive literature; he was left alone with a baby son. In 1912 he was arrested again and this time was treated with extreme brutality. He was beaten regularly and held for long periods in manacles – his wrists and ankles were permanently scarred. He was released from jail when the Tsar fell.

He moved awkwardly – 'slender and haggard, with long dark wavy hair, a face abnormally thin and angular, he had a jutting moustache and a satanic pointed beard', as one Sovnarkom colleague described him. 'He had very correct manners and in speech he was quiet . . . formidably focused . . . without a single ray of humour in his character.'

He was grimly fanatical and entirely incorruptible. Józef Piłsudski, the future military dictator of Poland, remembered Dzerzhinsky from schooldays as 'tormented . . . but he was a person who did not know how to tell a lie'. A comrade who knew him well loathed his prudish asceticism: 'he couldn't understand or tolerate moral weakness in others'. He didn't always know where to find it, though. Under his nose, but not to his knowledge, for more than two years the organisation that was supposed to combat profiteering and 'speculation' became one of the country's biggest speculators. Warehouses were full of goods taken from the 'bourgeois' as State property but sold to officials or friends of officials. 'They looked for counter-revolutionaries, but took the valuables,' the saying went.[1]

Dzerzhinsky at first tried to turn down the Cheka post and told Lenin he was not qualified for it. Lenin attempted persuasion, and when that didn't work ordered him to take the job. The Bolshevik leader soon knew he had made a wise choice, from his point of view. Dzerzhinsky was utterly loyal, but not a lackey. He was prepared at times to argue with Lenin, though they agreed on the big things, in particular on the need for vigilance to save the Revolution and terror against enemies, perceived or real.

At the meeting in which the Cheka was established Dzerzhinsky was clear about his task 'to fight a merciless war against all enemies of the Revolution. We need to send to that front – the most dangerous and cruel of fronts – determined, hard and dedicated comrades ready to do anything in defence of the Revolution. I do not seek forms of justice. We are not in need of justice. It is war now – face to face, a fight to the finish. Life or death.'

At first the Cheka had fewer than forty staff, based in a ramshackle office on the fourth floor of a scruffy building on Gorokhovaya, not far from Nevsky Prospekt. Dzerzhinsky kept what files the Cheka possessed in his briefcase and placed a notice on a wall close to the door: 'Death to the Bourgeoisie'.* Within three months there were 600 staff,

---

* The Russian secret police will for ever be identified with the building the Cheka moved into the following March in Moscow – the former headquarters of the Lloyd's Insurance Company at 22 Lubyanka, an address that would very soon become one of the most feared prisons in the world. It was – and is – a vast building occupying practically an entire city block. Dzerzhinsky told colleagues that one of the main reasons he

excluding its own blue-uniformed security troops, which numbered around 300 by the spring of 1918. Originally, according to Lenin's decree, 'the Commission will carry out only a preliminary investigation in so far as this is necessary for preventive purposes'. But almost immediately it went far beyond these powers and, without legal authorisation, moved from investigation to execution. The Cheka could easily do so because it had Lenin's protection, and virtually nobody knew what its powers were. Its officials could make them up as they went along. Soon, it was a state within the State.

Dzerzhinsky became in many ways Lenin's right hand, as close to him in the early days of the Red regime as Sverdlov and Trotsky. Accurate figures are still hard to come by as to how many people were murdered by the Cheka immediately after the October Revolution. Dzerzhinsky reported 884 executions to Sovnarkom between December 1917 and June 1918, but it is certain there were far more.*

Lenin kept a close eye on the Cheka and always defended it. When in its early days critics in the Bolshevik leadership were concerned that it was behaving like a law unto itself, he said, 'without such an institution the workers' regime could not exist'. There were efforts by some commissars after the Revolution to limit its powers, but he would always ensure the Cheka was accountable only to him, and his successors did the same. He told Dzerzhinsky a few months after the Cheka was established: 'What astonishes me is that so few [critics] are able to estimate the work of the Cheka broadly . . . You must act firmly, quickly and loyally. When I place its achievements beside its mistakes the latter sink into insignificance . . . For us the important consideration is that the Cheka has made the dictatorship of the proletariat a living reality

chose it was the vast size of the cellar space, where noise could easily be muffled. And so it proved. The slogan about the bourgeoisie was later written in bigger lettering in the interrogation rooms when the Cheka moved to Moscow.

* Including Lenin's first cousin, Viktor Ardashev, who was arrested and shot by the Cheka in Ekaterinburg in January 1918. The killer was almost certainly Yakov Yurovsky, one of the men who murdered the Tsar and his family a few months later. Lenin found out about Ardashev's murder only when he asked an aide to send greetings to his cousin but was told that he had been executed. He liked Ardashev, with whom as a child he had spent summers in Kokushkino, though it is unlikely the affection was returned. He had been a well-known Kadet, a lawyer who had helped to organise the civil service strike in Ekaterinburg.

. . . its work is priceless. There is only one way to free the masses and that is to crush the exploiters. This is the task of the Cheka, and for this it deserves the gratitude of the proletariat.'

The Cheka was more ruthless than the Okhrana, but it is a question of degree and not a category difference. In many ways they were a mirror image of each other. The Okhrana had operated as a private police force of the Crown, the Tsar's sword and shield. The Cheka's role was similar and so were its techniques. Most of the early Bolsheviks had long experience of the Okhrana's methods and the Cheka copied many of them, such as infiltrating opposition groups, using agents provocateurs and recruiting double agents. While the Red Army would later enrol former Tsarist officers in its ranks, the Cheka did not do the same with former Okhrana agents. Dzerzhinsky, Lenin, Sverdlov and Stalin all argued that they simply couldn't be trusted. The Cheka had to start from scratch and learn how to organise an espionage agency. Marx and Engels had left no blueprint; the Okhrana had.

Lenin was interested in the technical details of its operations. It was he, in a note to Dzerzhinsky soon after the Cheka was set up, who suggested that 'it would be useful to carry out arrests at *night*'. The knock at the door in the small hours became the classic modus operandi of 'the organs' throughout the Communist years.[2]

40

WAR AND PEACE

'Without peace, and soon, the Revolution cannot survive.'

Lenin to Trotsky, 7 November 1917

The war had not ended. Lenin knew he had to deliver on his promises of peace to avoid the fate of Kerensky. He was prepared to make peace at almost any price.

His first tactic – on the day of the Revolution – was to appeal for a general peace between all the belligerent nations. He demanded an immediate conference to end the conflict: 'We have thrown down a challenge to the imperialist plunderers of all countries,' he said. He never expected his call to work, and predictably all sides rejected the proposal out of hand.

Next, Lenin sued for a separate, temporary truce with Germany, and he tried to play for time. He genuinely believed that his revolution would spark immediate uprisings in Western Europe and advance the world revolution – an article of faith among Bolsheviks. With each small-scale army mutiny or strike in Germany, Britain and France he expected an insurrection among workers, inspired by the Bolsheviks, that would bring down their governments. All he had to do was wait – and encourage the workers of the world to unite. Trotsky as Foreign Commissar was making daily speeches calling 'on workers everywhere to rise up against their masters and stop the war'.

Russia's separate peace with Germany caused the first collision between the Western powers and Lenin's regime – the original Cold War with the Soviets. 'Disgusting!' the American Ambassador David Francis wired back to Washington. Two days later he reported to the State Department: 'I have a strong suspicion that Lenin and Trotsky are working in the interests of Germany; but whether that is correct or not, their success will unquestionably result in Germany's gain.' He wrote in his diary the day after the Revolution, 'of course we could not, and I would not, recognise any ministry of which Lenin is Premier and Trotsky Minister of Foreign Affairs'.* President Woodrow Wilson was more emollient and said he hoped 'we may be privileged to assist the people of Russia to attain their hopes of liberty and ordered peace'. But he added that the 'government in Petrograd was established by force and not recognised by the Russian people. It cannot of course be recognised . . . [by the US] particularly if it pursues a separate peace with Germany.'

Robert Cecil, the second-ranking minister in the Foreign Office, said: 'The actions of the extremists in Petrograd would be a breach of the agreements between us . . . it would put them practically outside the pale of the ordinary councils of Europe. There is no intention of recognising such a government.' The French were equally adamant. 'What? Talk with Lenin . . . after he has broken the treaties with us? After abandoning us in the middle of war? Never . . .' said Gustave Hervé, one of the leading socialist politicians in the country. The French Foreign Minister, Stéphen Pichon, pointed out that 'whatever Lenin does, we shall carry on fighting'.†

There were advisers in all the Allied countries who told the governments that the best way of dealing with the new regime was to negotiate

---

* Francis, en route back to Washington a few weeks after the Revolution, was one of the guests at a lunch given by George V at Buckingham Palace. The King asked him what should be done about Russia and the Bolsheviks and he replied, 'We should topple Lenin.' The King said, 'Well . . . I agree, but your President doesn't seem to think so.'

† Unofficially, though, all the Allied governments despatched agents to talk with the Bolshevik regime in an effort to persuade Lenin and Trotsky to stay in the war. Britain used Robert Bruce Lockhart as a go-between, the Americans sent Raymond Robins under the guise of Chairman of the American Red Cross Committee, but in reality Woodrow Wilson's secret conduit to the Bolsheviks with a direct line to Lenin, who spoke to him often and admired him – 'an honest and decent man . . . I always liked him,' he said later. The French used the spy Captain Jacques Sadoul, who blunted the purpose of his mission when it turned out that he was a fanatical Communist and fervent Lenin supporter. The British, as has been proven beyond doubt, did more than spy on the Bolsheviks and try to influence them. Various secret agents plotted with opposition groups to bring down Lenin's regime because it was making peace with Germany (see Giles Milton's excellent *Russian Roulette* and Robert Service's *Spies and Commissars*).

with Lenin. Bruce Lockhart advised the British government to do so and there were members of the Cabinet who wanted to talk with the Bolsheviks. But it is unlikely that this would have succeeded; Lenin needed to end Russia's war as his first priority, and soon it became politically impossible for the Western governments to deal with the Bolsheviks.

Separate peace talks were bad enough. But the Allies were appalled and embarrassed when Trotsky published the 'secret' treaties the Tsar had signed with Britain and France before the war began. They showed deals were made to divide the post-war spoils when Germany was defeated: the Middle East would be carved up, Russia would get Constantinople – the dream of the Romanovs for three centuries – and France would get Alsace-Lorraine back. For Lenin these proved that the war was 'an imperialist adventure all about colonies and plunder'. For the Allies the revelations put a stop to any agreement with the Bolshevik leader.*

The British Prime Minister, Lloyd George, said he had wanted to talk to Lenin – but not after the treaties were leaked. Afterwards, he admitted, 'the difficulties ... in persuading certain members of the government to have any dealings with Petrograd which would involve recognition of the Bolsheviks were considerably enhanced'.[1]

The Russian–German peace talks began on 1 December at the grim and ugly town of Brest-Litovsk, in what was then Byelorussia (now Belarus) on the border with Poland. It had been repeatedly shelled by both sides during the war and much of it was destroyed. The daily sessions, in a military fort, were extraordinary – 'worthy of some great historical painter', as one of the Russian delegates recalled. On the Central Powers' side, 'black-coated, much be-ribboned, exquisitely polite old-style gentlemen in morning coats', most of them a count or a baron, at the very least a 'von'. On the other side sat scruffy revolutionary Communists, many of whom had recently come out of jail or Siberian exile and spent their lives fighting the aristocratic order.

Prince Max von Baden recalled the formal opening dinner: 'My

---

* Kerensky knew these treaties were potentially explosive. When he became Prime Minister in the summer of 1917 and saw them for the first time he ordered officials to 'hide them'. That is why Trotsky couldn't immediately find them when he became Foreign Commissar and had to send a team of trustworthy agents to search for them.

cousin Prince Ernst von Hohenlohe was placed next to Madame [Anastasia] Bitsenko, who had qualified for her place in the talks by killing a minister. On 5 December 1905 she had assassinated the general, and former War Minister, Viktor Sakharov.'

General Max Hoffman, commander of the German army on the Eastern Front, left an entertaining personal account. 'I shall never forget that first dinner with the Russians. I sat between [Adolph] Joffe and [Grigory] Sokolnikov [editor of *Pravda* and from March 1918 Finance Commissar]. Opposite me sat a worker who was obviously amazed by the large amount of silverware on the table. He tried to catch this and that on his plate with various bits of cutlery but he used the fork exclusively for the purpose of cleaning his teeth. Directly opposite me . . . sat Madame Bitsenko and directly opposite her a peasant, [Roman] Stashkov, a thorough Russian phenomenon with long grey locks and a huge beard. The orderly couldn't hide a smile when he asked Stashkov whether he wanted red or white wine with one course. "Which is the stronger?" he asked.'*

Lenin's tactics were to string out the talks for as long as possible – and he knew just the man who could obfuscate for ages. At first Joffe led the Russian delegation. After a few days he was replaced by Trotsky. Nobody could make longer speeches going nowhere than Trotsky. Lenin told him before departing to Brest: 'We need someone to do the delaying . . . and you will do it better than anybody. String out the talks until there is a revolution in Germany – or as long as possible.'

---

* Stashkov was only there by accident, according to Joffe. The leaders of the delegation realised at the last minute that there was no peasant representative with them among the workers and soldiers and Party apparatchiks. This was typical of the Bolsheviks' mentality – but potentially embarrassing for the 'Workers' and Peasants" regime. As they were driving from the Smolny to the Warsaw Station, Joffe and Kamenev suddenly saw an old man in a typical peasant's coat carrying a pack on his back. Kamenev ordered the car to stop, got out and asked the old man where he was going. 'To the station, *barin*, I mean *tovarisch* [comrade].' 'Get in,' said Kamenev. 'We'll give you a lift.' At first the peasant was delighted, but then he realised they were not heading to the Nikolaevsky Station, where trains left for central Russia and his home village. He asked the two Bolsheviks to let him out, but Kamenev said, 'there's no need for you to go to your village . . . come with us to make peace with the Germans'. He had no idea where Brest-Litovsk was, or what was happening there. But when he was offered some remuneration he agreed to go. That is how he became a delegate and 'plenipotentiary representative of the Russian peasantry' at the talks.

Trotsky went and, master of blather as he was, talked endlessly. For one whole day he gave a long lecture to the assorted German and Austrian diplomats on the first volume of Marx's *Capital*. On another he went through every clause in a potential treaty in German and Russian insisting upon two separate interpreters, doubling the time involved. The Germans were getting bored and suspicious, though the elaborate dinners and social events went on. Trotsky reported at one point in mid-December that he thought 'time might be running out at the talks' and, in a postscript, asked Lenin whether he should wear evening dress at one of the receptions. 'Go in a petticoat if you want to, only get us peace.'

The Germans tired of the Russians' delaying tactics and just before Christmas offered a peace on their terms. They insisted on keeping the lands they had occupied: Poland, Lithuania, Courland and most of Western Ukraine. At the end of December Trotsky sought an adjournment and went back to Petrograd for talks with Lenin and the other commissars.

The peace deal with Germany was the first big test of Lenin's position as leader of the Revolution. It opened a split within the Party that almost toppled him and might have destroyed the Bolshevik regime after just a few weeks. Lenin wanted to accept the German terms. But he wasn't – yet – a dictator within his own Party and to begin with he was in a minority. He had to fight hard to get his way. At first most of the comrades refused to approve an abject, humiliating peace. The opposition against him was led by Bukharin, but included Kamenev, Kollontai and Dzerzhinsky. Only Stalin and Zinoviev were entirely behind him. Inessa was living in Moscow but had a high position on the Soviet there and sent him messages begging him to think again before making 'a disgraceful peace'. They wanted to fight a 'revolutionary war' against Germany which they argued was the likeliest way of sparking an uprising in Western Europe. 'We must look at the socialist republic from the international point of view,' Bukharin said at a dramatic meeting of the Bolshevik Central Committee on 11 January 1918. 'Let the Germans strike, let them advance another hundred kilometres, what interests us is how it affects the international movement.'

Lenin said the idea of a revolutionary war was 'suicidal' and hopelessly naïve. The army was 'zero as a fighting force. It barely exists. We might not last more than a few days. I'm prepared to yield territory to the present victor to gain time, obtain a breathing space. That's what this is all about and only that. Signing a treaty in defeat is a way of gathering strength. If we were to wage a revolutionary war, as Bukharin wants, it would be the best way of getting rid of us right now. For us, as well as from the international point of view, the preservation of the Soviet republic stands above all else.'

He said there was no point in risking the Revolution on the possibility of an uprising in Germany, which he was beginning to doubt was imminent. 'Germany is only just pregnant with revolution, while we have already given birth to a completely healthy child.' He did not persuade the others.

Trotsky came up with a different formula that sounds nonsensical but was accepted by the others. His tactic was to play for yet more time under the attractive-sounding slogan 'Neither war nor peace'. He would return to the talks, declare the war at an end, but refuse to sign 'an annexationist peace'. If the Germans invaded, which Russia couldn't prevent in any case, it would appear to the world that the Germans were committing an act of aggression against a 'peaceable country'.

Lenin told him that the issue was the survival of the Revolution. 'We can restore the balance of the Party later,' he said. 'We can save the Revolution only by signing the peace terms. Better a split than being overthrown . . . Let's admit your plan is accepted and we refuse to sign the peace treaty. The Germans attack at once. What will you do then?' 'We will sign the peace terms under bayonets,' Trotsky said. 'Then the picture will be clear to the workers of the world.' Lenin called Trotsky's idea 'international showmanship' but he had to go along with it, knowing it would fail. As Nadya said later, Lenin was in 'a shattered state', in constant rages, hardly sleeping, looking ill and seriously worried that his dreams for the socialist Revolution would be wrecked by his own comrades' stupidity.

The Germans had decided that they would countenance no more delays. While the talks were adjourned, back in Berlin army chief Ludendorff asked Hoffmann, 'Tell me, is it really possible to negotiate with these people?' Hoffmann said, 'Yes, for now. Your Excellency needs troops on the Western Front and this is the quickest way to get them.'

Trotsky returned to Brest-Litovsk and tried playing for time again with his 'Neither war nor peace' tactic. After a few days Hoffmann had had enough. 'This time the Comrades will simply have to swallow what's put before them,' he said in his diary. On 9 February he told Trotsky that if the deal was not signed by the next day, the Germans would invade Russia. When the time expired Trotsky declared the Russians were 'leaving the war' but refused to sign a peace treaty – a new concept in diplomacy. There was a silence. The Germans seemed not to understand and had no idea what to make of it. Eventually Hoffman stood up and loudly but simply declared, 'Unerhört' (unheard of).

A week later the Germans announced they would resume hostilities against Russia on 18 February. Even then most of the Bolshevik leadership refused to agree the peace terms. Lenin's motion at Sovnarkom to sign immediately was defeated by six votes to five.

Five days later the Germans issued a final ultimatum: the Russians were given until 7 a.m. on 24 February to accept the terms or face an overwhelming invasion. Lenin told his comrades: 'We must sign. If you don't, you are signing the death warrant of Soviet power within three weeks.' He threatened to resign as head of the government and from the Bolshevik Party altogether – a tactic he had used before. Nobody was prepared to call his bluff.

Within three days the Germans advanced and captured more territory than in the previous three years of the war. Lenin thought that they would march on Petrograd.*

There were three more meetings on 18 February. Lenin made a final appeal: 'I understand our impulse is to resist this shameful, robber peace. Our reason will tell us in our calmer moments the plain truth: Russia can offer no resistance, we are exhausted after three years of war. There may be people who will be willing to fight in a great cause. But they are romantics who would sacrifice themselves without any prospects of real advantage. Wars are not won nowadays with enthusiasm.' Trotsky finally swung round to Lenin's position and turned the vote seven to four Lenin's way. But there was anger against him. At a broader

---

* This was when he decided that if he survived in power he would move the capital to Moscow as soon as he could.

party meeting four days later Lenin was greeted by shouts of 'Traitor' and 'German spy' even among his closest comrades. The debate was heated and tempers were short. At one point Karl Radek rose from his seat and shouted at Lenin, 'If we had five hundred courageous men in Petrograd we would put you in prison.'

Lenin smiled and answered wearily: 'Some people may indeed go to prison after this but if you will calculate the probabilities you will see that it is much more likely that I will send you rather than you send me.'

At midnight on 23 February Lenin personally sent the telegram to Berlin accepting the peace terms. By then the Germans had made much tougher demands. The Russians should have accepted the deal offered in December. Now, as Lenin told his 'Cabinet', the peace was even more of a 'partition, enslavement, humiliation'. Apart from the territory they had already lost they were forced to give up the Baltic states, Finland and nearly all Ukraine to the Central Powers and the ports of Kars, Andalan and Batum to the Turks – 1.8 million square kilometres, sixty-two million people, around 32 per cent of its best agricultural land, 54 per cent of its industry and 89 per cent of its coalmines.

Already facing an enormous economic disaster, they had to pay a huge 'indemnity'. Around 120 million gold rubles were shipped to Germany. The price of peace was high.

The treaty was eventually signed on 3 March. None of the Bolshevik leaders wanted to put their names to such a 'shameful peace'. Trotsky moved himself out of contention by resigning as Commissar for Foreign Affairs. Joffe flatly refused, as did the new Foreign Affairs Commissar, Georgy Chicherin. Sokolnikov proposed Zinoviev should go and Zinoviev proposed Sokolnikov, who first said he wouldn't do it, but then was ordered to go by Lenin. He signed, as he would say later, with self-disgust.[2]

41

THE ONE-PARTY STATE

'Nobody has ever been made happier by force.'

Vladimir Medem (1879–1923)

'I am mistrustful of Russians in power – recently slaves themselves, they will become unbridled despots as soon as they have the chance to be their neighbours' masters.'

Maxim Gorky, *Novaya Zhizn*, 13 November 1917

Russia's first freely elected parliament – the Constituent Assembly – survived for about twelve hours. There would not be another for nearly seventy-five years.

The introduction of a representative democracy was the single biggest promise made by the Provisional Government after the Tsar was overthrown. Originally the date for the elections was set for September; then it was pushed back to October and finally to mid-November. Polling would be staggered over two weeks because of the size of the country and the huge logistical task of counting the votes.

Each time the elections were postponed the Bolsheviks complained that the government intended to 'strangle democracy' and was planning to cheat people of the 'free parliament they have struggled for'. But Lenin in power had no intention of allowing a free parliament. He may on occasions in the past have written in praise of elections. But he didn't believe in 'bourgeois democracy' on principle and certainly not in practice for a revolutionary state. The dictatorship of the proletariat and the authority of the Soviet were 'not only a higher form of democracy . . . [but] the only form of democracy'.[1]

On the first day after the coup, within hours of seizing power, Lenin wanted to postpone the elections indefinitely. 'We have to put them off,' he told his circle of comrades. 'They may cost the Revolution its head.

We must have the chance to renew the electoral lists. On our own side the candidate lists are of no use whatsoever. They include a lot of intellectuals who got on by accident whereas we need workers or peasants.' And he didn't want the right-wing parties to be allowed to stand at all. 'We have to make the Kadets illegal.'

Virtually his entire entourage opposed him – not only the usual suspects, but hardliners like Dzerzhinsky and Sverdlov, as well as occasional waverers such as Stalin was in those days. Sverdlov said simply, 'We can't, it's the wrong time . . . it would look very bad.' At first Lenin was not convinced. 'Why isn't it a good moment?' he asked. 'That's nonsense . . . rubbish. What if the Assembly turns out to be a Menshevik-Kadet-SR one? Will that be good for us? It is a mistake, an obvious mistake . . . We have already won power . . . now we will have to win it all over again, probably by military measures.' Reluctantly, though, he caved in and allowed the elections to go ahead.

Immediately he regretted it. Lenin knew the Bolsheviks would not do well. But they did even worse than he expected and won fewer than ten million votes, around 24 per cent of the total, which made a nonsense of the claim that they were supported by the masses. The Socialist Revolutionaries won by far the most votes – 39 per cent, though their success was complicated because they split into two before the campaign began. It was seldom clear to voters during the campaign whether a candidate was a 'Right' SR, which was opposed to the Bolsheviks, or a 'Left' SR, which was friendlier to them and at the beginning of December became the only coalition partner allied to Lenin's Party. The Mensheviks got only 3 per cent of the vote and the Kadets 5.

Lenin delayed the opening of the Assembly, while he plotted ways of abolishing it altogether. He calculated that most people didn't care about it. Intellectuals were interested, he said, but the majority of workers and peasants were concerned about peace and bread – the food shortages were becoming as serious as a year ago when the Tsar was toppled.

Lenin prepared his strategy first with a decree firing the neutral electoral commissioners, whose job was to oversee practical arrangements for running the Assembly, and putting the Bolshevik Party hack Uritsky in their place.

On 27 November, the day the Assembly was supposed to have met for the first time, Lenin issued a decree banning the Kadet Party. He declared its members 'enemies of the people' and Red Guards arrested every prominent Kadet they could find – dozens of people, many of whom had just been elected to the Assembly. When opponents objected that this wasn't legal he responded: 'It is senseless even to discuss the question of legality . . . The Kadet Party, brandishing the weapon of democracy . . . constitutes the general staff of the civil war against the exploited class.' Meanwhile Trotsky warned bluntly what was likely to happen. 'We are not about to share power with anybody. If we stop halfway it wouldn't be a revolution but an abortion . . . a false historical delivery.'[2]

Lenin could put off the day no longer. On 5 January 1918 the Assembly gathered at the Tauride Palace. Petrograd was 'in a state of siege' from early in the morning. The government had declared martial law and flooded the city with troops and Red Guards. Demonstrations had been banned, but at noon around 40,000 workers, students and civil servants defied the order and began to march the two kilometres from Mars Field to the Tauride Palace on a bitterly cold and snowy day. When they reached Liteiny Prospekt, Red Guards, hidden from rooftops, opened fire. The protestors scattered and two huge banners they had been carrying – 'All Power to the Assembly' – lay trampled in the slush. At least ten people were killed and seventy seriously wounded.

Tempers were frayed when the chamber filled and proceedings started at 4 p.m. Many of the Assembly members had been at the demonstration outside, which had been dispersed by machine-gun fire – the first time troops had shot at an unarmed crowd since the February Revolution. There were armed guards scattered throughout the hall and several of the deputies had weapons with them too. Carl Lindhagen, the Mayor of Stockholm, who met Lenin nine months earlier during the 'sealed train' journey, in Petrograd as an observer, said, 'It's going to be a Wild West show today . . . everyone's carrying a gun.' Lenin had arrived an hour or so earlier – by the back door, surrounded by bodyguards. He was watching from a mezzanine box where government ministers used to sit during sessions of the Tsarist Duma. He affected a nonchalant and bored manner which, as one of his clique said, belied his inner nerves. He chatted with a couple of American journalists in a relaxed way, asking one of them, Albert Rhys Williams, how he was getting on learning Russian. 'I'm finding it difficult, the words are so long,' the reporter said. 'Well you should do it as I learned languages: get to know the nouns first, then the verbs and leave the grammar to the last.' At one point a little later he pretended to be asleep, with his hands over his eyes. But he was alert. The SR leader Viktor Chernov was elected to the Assembly chair and made a long, grandiloquent speech denouncing the Revolution. The Bolsheviks were vastly outnumbered but heckled and jeered him throughout.[3]

After he had finished, the serious business began. Sverdlov proposed a Bolshevik motion calling on the Assembly automatically to ratify Sovnarkom decrees as a rubber-stamp body – beginning with Decrees on the Rights of Workers, the nationalisation of the banks, and a Decree on Compulsory Labour 'to destroy the class of parasites'.

It was defeated by a big margin and the Bolsheviks walked out – 'We won't stay in this counter-revolutionary body,' said the leader of the Kronstadt sailors, Raskolnikov. There was an adjournment and Lenin then gave the order to dissolve the Assembly: 'the situation is now clear and we can get rid of them', he said. But he ordered the Red Guards not to use violence. He said that when the deputies left later that night the palace should be locked up and nobody was to be allowed back in the next day.

When delegates filled the chamber again at 11.30 p.m. the speeches became longer and duller: 'one sailor, sitting in . . . a box cursed Tsereteli in a monotone and raised his rifle at him. Another amused himself by sighting Chernov along his gun barrel, grinning,' recalled Reed. Lenin left around 1 a.m., thinking it unnecessary to witness the end of Russia's brief experiment with democracy.

At around 4 a.m. the Navy Commissar Dybenko ordered the commander of the Red Guards, Anatoly Zheleznyakov, to empty the chamber. He approached Chernov on the podium, tapped him on the shoulder and said, 'Everybody here should leave the chamber now because the guards are tired.' Chernov told him that 'We are also tired but that cannot interrupt our work which all Russia is watching.' The guards, most of whom were drunk, began fingering their weapons menacingly and turning the lights off one by one. At 4.40 a.m. on 6 January all the delegates filed out and the gates of the palace were locked behind them. When they began to return to the Tauride the next afternoon the way was barred by soldiers and a decree was posted on the palace gates dissolving the Assembly.

Lenin told Trotsky later that 'yes it was a risk, a big risk, not to put off the Assembly. But in the end it was for the best. Dispersing it . . . means the full and open liquidation of formal democracy in the name of the revolutionary dictatorship. It will serve as a good lesson. The people wanted to convene the Assembly so we convened it. But the people at once sensed that this Assembly represented . . . [a return to the past] so now we have carried out the will of the people.'

A few days later Vladimir Medem, one of the leaders of the Jewish Bund, told a friend, a delegate to the Assembly, that 'there are many impatient people who think that without the Constituent Assembly it will be easier and quicker to make everyone happy. But nobody has ever been made happier by force.'[4]

Lenin was right about his strategy, though. There was little significant support outside the intelligentsia for the Assembly, no big demonstrations, no strikes, no mutinies in the army. 'There was apathy among the soldiers and workers . . . Lenin judged correctly,' said one of his Sovnarkom comrades.

Just after dawn on 6 January, a few hours after the Assembly was closed down, two sailors from the Baltic Fleet cruiser *Seagull* walked into the Mariinsky Hospital in Petrograd. They burst straight into the room where, under armed guard, two former Provisional Government ministers were sleeping, strangled them and shot them to make sure they were dead. Then the killers calmly walked out into Liteiny Avenue without anyone stopping them.

The ministers, a well-known physician, Andrei Shingarev, and the Professor of Constitutional Law at Petrograd University, Fyodor Kokoshkin – both leading Kadets – had been transferred to the hospital only the previous day. Since their arrest immediately after the Bolshevik coup, they had been held in the Peter and Paul Fortress. But both reported feeling unwell and were moved to the hospital supposedly under tight security.

When Lenin was told about the murders later that morning he summoned the Commissar for Justice, Isaac Steinberg. 'This is a serious matter and it has to be investigated urgently and properly . . . not skated over.' Steinberg was a Left SR and belonged to the junior partner in the Sovnarkom, but had spent years in exile in Siberia under the Tsarist regime as a Populist agitator. He was a highly respected lawyer. He immediately set up an investigation, which Lenin said he supported wholeheartedly.

To begin with the investigation proceeded normally. The head of the Baltic Fleet said he would co-operate and Dybenko announced with solemnity at a Sovnarkom meeting: 'I shall write a strong appeal to the sailors not to do such things again and we will say we are going to bring the culprits to justice.' Then he paused and the tone changed. 'But of course they will only regard the affair as an act of political terror.' That, according to the Justice Commissar, was when he realised that under the Bolsheviks the phrase 'political terror' would justify a wide range of crimes.

Steinberg insisted on continuing with the investigation and believed the killers had been identified. 'Naturally, they should be arrested,' he told Lenin. But it was not so simple. 'Do you want us to go against the sailors? That might be tricky.' 'Yes,' said Steinberg. 'If we don't now it will be more difficult to rein in the violence and quench the thirst for blood later. This was murder, not political terror.'

Lenin shrugged his shoulders. 'Really? I don't think the people are interested in such matters. Ask any worker or peasant. They won't have heard of Dr Shingarev.' Steinberg said he could only go after the guilty sailors 'if I can have a detachment of Red Guards to surround their barracks and take them'. He wasn't given the men and the killers were never arrested.*[5]

The wave of crime and anarchy spreading through Petrograd and other major cities was a dilemma for Lenin. He had witnessed some of it himself on New Year's Day, just after he returned from a Christmas break in Finland with Nadya. Early in the afternoon, as Lenin was driven from a speaking engagement back to Smolny, random shots were fired at his car. Fritz Platten, the Swiss socialist who helped to organise the 'sealed

---

* The only person charged in connection with the murders was the commandant of the Red Guards at the hospital, Stepan Basov, who appeared before a Revolutionary Tribunal a few weeks later. He claimed that the killing was justified because 'at least it means there are two less bourgeois mouths to feed'. He was given a telling-off.

train' through Germany, was on a short visit and was in the car with him. When he heard the shots he covered himself over Lenin's body to protect the Bolshevik leader. Platten received a slight glancing wound on his hand; Lenin was unharmed. But there were several bullet holes along one side of the vehicle. Nobody knew Lenin was in the car so it was not an assassination attempt, just random violence. But it showed how lawless Russia had become over the last year. The chaos had to be controlled.

On the other hand, Lenin was himself encouraging much of the violence for political reasons – as people's revenge against the bourgeois for 'centuries of gross inequality' and as 'revolutionary justice against the exploiters'. At first his rhetoric had considerable appeal: wasn't this what the Revolution was all about, to abolish privilege? The settling of accounts with the bourgeoisie, in Dzerzhinsky's favourite phrase, began before the Cheka took control of the terror.

The apartments of the rich were robbed and vandalised, they were attacked on the streets, they were routinely abused. People took revenge into their own hands, and Lenin egged them on. In mid-December 1917 he had declared that those who 'hoarded' food or wealth were 'enemies of the people', and in typically vicious language called for 'a war to the death against the rich, the idlers and parasites . . . [citizens must] cleanse the Russian land of all vermin, of scoundrel fleas, the bedbug rich . . . in one place they can jail a dozen rich men, a dozen scoundrels, half a dozen workers who shirk on the job . . . in another place they will be out to work on cleaning latrines. In a third they will be given yellow tickets [as prostitutes were given] after a term in prison, so that everyone knows they are harmful and an eye can be kept on them. In a fourth, one out of every ten idlers will be shot. The more variety the better . . . for only practice can devise the best methods of struggle.'

Soon, Bolshevik agitators whipped up random mobs into action. 'Wrest from the bourgeoisie the millions taken from the masses and cunningly turned into silken undergarments, furs, carpets, gold, furniture and paintings . . . we will take them and give them to the proletariat and then force the bourgeoisie to work for their rations,' urged a Party apparatchik in Ekaterinburg in December 1917. The rich were branded 'former people', awarded far lower rations, and were placed at the back of the queues for bread. Some scions of great aristocratic families starved to death. Middle-class families were made to share their homes with the poor and often ended up with the smaller rooms in a larger apartment – 'a revolution in domestic life, a new world, where the servants and masters literally changed places'. The revenge notion was justified by Trotsky in a robust, if chilling, way: 'For centuries our fathers and grandfathers have been cleaning up the dirt and filth of the ruling classes, but now we will make them clean up our dirt. We must make life so uncomfortable for them that they will lose the desire to remain bourgeois.'

One of Lenin's decrees codified Bolshevik ideas of 'revolutionary justice'. At a stroke he abolished the existing legal system, though he kept the Tsarist principle that there was one system of justice for normal crimes against property and separate laws for crimes against the State. He established 'People's Courts' for common criminals – essentially ad hoc mob trials in which twelve 'elected' judges, most of them barely literate, would rule less on the facts of a case than with the use, in Lenin's words, of 'revolutionary conscience'. Lenin's hatred of the law and lawyers shone through in this decree. 'The Court proceedings were not evidence-based, the procedures were more or less made up as they went along. There were cases of some people being convicted on "denunciations" by people involved in long-term family feuds, and some of women denouncing their unfaithful husbands,' said Steinberg. 'The sentences fitted the mood of the crowd, which freely voiced its opinions from the gallery.'

Lenin's other new creation was borrowed from the French Revolution – the Revolutionary Tribunal. They dealt with crimes against the State and were popular for a year or so but were phased out over time. Public trials were replaced by closed ten-minute hearings by a 'troika' of Party members operated by the Cheka.

Lenin had a very simple, straightforward and at least honest argument in favour of this system of so-called justice: his system was far superior, practically and morally, because it operated in the interests of the exploited classes – which justified everything. 'For us there does not, and cannot, exist the old system of morality and "humanity" invented by the bourgeoisie for the purpose of oppressing and exploiting the "lower classes". Our morality is new, our humanity is absolute, for it rests on the ideal of destroying all oppression and coercion. To us, all is permitted, for we are the first in the world to raise the sword not in the name of enslaving or oppressing anyone, but in the name of freeing all from bondage ... Blood? Let there be blood, if it alone can turn the grey-white-and-black banner of the old piratical world to a scarlet hue, for only the complete and final death of that old world will save us from the return of the old jackals.'[6]

When he was tackled head-on about the amount of bloodshed he had unleashed, he was unapologetic. The American journalist Lincoln Steffens asked him, 'Will the Red Terror and the killing continue?' Lenin replied: 'Do you mean to tell me that these men who have just organised the slaughter of seventeen million men in a purposeless war are concerned over the few thousand killed in our revolution, which has a conscious aim – to avoid the necessity of future wars? But never mind ... I don't deny the terror, don't minimise the evils of revolution. They occur. They must be counted on.'

On 21 February 1918 Lenin issued a decree, 'The Socialist Fatherland in Danger' – written in his familiar literary style – which allowed Red Guards to 'shoot on the spot ... enemy agents, profiteers, marauders, hooligans and counter-revolutionary agitators'. When he read it the Justice Commissar, Steinberg, went to see Lenin and protested that such harsh measures would 'destroy the Revolution'. Lenin replied: 'On the contrary ... do you really believe that we can be victorious without the very cruellest revolutionary terror?' 'Then why do we bother with a Commissariat of Justice at all? Let's call it frankly the Commissariat for Social Extermination and be done with it.' Lenin's face lit up, according to Steinberg, and he said: 'Well put. That's exactly what it should be; but we can't say that.'

* * *

Amid the strictest secrecy, overnight on 10–11 March, two government trains left Moskovsky Station in Petrograd bound for Moscow. The first carried Lenin, Nadya, Maria Ulyanova, Sverdlov, Dzerzhinsky and Stalin, accompanied by forty-three typists, secretaries, bodyguards and telephonists. The second train, an hour or so behind, contained the rest of the Bolshevik leadership with an assortment of Party hacks and civil servants, along with two carriages full of files and documents. They were moving the entire Soviet government to Russia's second city and the historic capital pre-dating the time of Peter the Great.

The move was Lenin's personal decision, and many of his close clique didn't like it. In fact Lenin didn't like it. He hardly knew Moscow, but what he did know he detested. He had never lived there or stayed for longer than a few days at a time. His early letters in the 1890s are full of references to Moscow as 'a foul city', a 'filthy hole', and in one, 'a nightmare ... sickening'. But Lenin realised that the Brest-Litovsk agreements gave Russia no guarantees and the Germans could break them at any time. At one point before the treaty was signed they had just about reached Pskov, only 150 kilometres from Petrograd, a few days' march away. 'The peace we have come to is unstable,' he told comrades. 'The breathing space we have achieved can be broken any day ... There's no doubt that our international situation is so critical that we must strain every nerve to survive for as long as possible until the Western revolution matures, a revolution that is maturing much more slowly than we expected and wanted.'

Most of the old Bolsheviks saw Petrograd as a Western city in the European tradition and regarded Moscow with its onion-domed churches as the capital of Orthodoxy and Old Russia – semi-Asiatic. Moving there seemed to many a step backwards and suggested a separation from the European roots of socialism: 'Moscow, with its medieval walls and its countless gilded cupolas, was an utter paradox as a fortress of the revolutionary dictatorship,' said Trotsky. Others in the Bolshevik leadership remarked that moving away seemed 'cowardly' and would look like a moral defeat. The Bolsheviks should consider 'the glorious spirit of the Smolny'. Lenin dismissed their arguments. When the government moved, power and authority would move with it. 'If the Germans in one big swoop overrun Petersburg [he nearly always referred to it by that name, or Peter] – and all of us – then the Revolution perishes. If the government is in Moscow, then the fall of Petersburg will be a grievous blow, but only a blow. If we stay ... we are increasing the military danger. If we leave for Moscow, the temptation for the Germans to take Petersburg is much smaller. What is the advantage for them in taking a hungry and revolutionary city? ... Why do you prattle about the symbolic importance of Smolny? The Smolny is what it is because we are in it. When we are all in the Kremlin, all your symbolism will be in the Kremlin.'

Moscow was in a dreadful state when Lenin and his comrades

arrived. If the coup in Petrograd had been generally peaceful, there had been serious fighting for six days in Moscow between Red Guards and troops loyal to Kerensky. Around a thousand fighters from both sides and civilians caught in the crossfire were killed before Kerensky's men surrendered. There was still rubble lying on many streets and some of the city's finest old buildings – including St Basil's Cathedral – had been severely damaged. The stucco in many of the palaces was studded with bullet holes.

When Lenin and Nadya arrived they stayed for five days in a two-room suite at the National Hotel, just off Red Square, whose one-time grandeur even then had somewhat faded. They were spotted by a reporter 'sitting in the lobby surrounded by rags and tatters of baggage and bedding rolled up in a blanket, a battered trunk, parcels of books, and every kind of basket'. The next day one of the guards at the Trinity Gate of the Kremlin refused at first to allow Lenin through because he had never seen a picture of him and didn't recognise him.

The Kremlin itself had been sorely neglected since the Tsar fell. Some of the buildings were falling to pieces; horse manure filled the courtyards and the place stank. Lenin's first order was to replace the music on the clock at the Spassky Gate, which was still playing 'God Save the Tsar'. It was changed to the 'Internationale'.

Lenin and Nadya were temporarily given a functional but far from cosy two-room apartment at the magnificent Cavalry Corpus of the Great Kremlin Palace, where some of the other Bolshevik magnates were also staying. Most of the Tsar's servants were still there and stayed on.* Five weeks later, as the Kremlin was being refurbished, they moved into a comfortable but simple three-room apartment, plus a maid's room, on the first floor of the main government building, which remained their Moscow home. Many of the other comrades were given far more luxurious billets in the Kremlin or in grand buildings nearby.

Lenin was infuriated that the renovations on the flat were slow. He wrote a typical angry note, with an implied threat, to the deputy head of public property after the work had been going on for longer than a

---

* Including one old retainer, a waiter, Stupishin, from the days of Alexander III, who one evening served Lenin and Trotsky on the finest imperial crockery. He made sure, trying to hide a smile, that the gilded double-headed eagle symbol faced each diner at the table, though all they had to eat was vegetable soup and buckwheat porridge.

month. 'I should very much like to have the name and address of the person you entrusted to complete the work on the apartment. It's dragging on inordinately and the person guilty of such unbelievable delays must be found.'

Back in Moscow, he began to see Inessa regularly. She was given a senior official position – head of the Women's section of the Party Central Committee. But her position of influence was not connected to the jobs she held or her titles. Everyone close to Lenin knew about her place in his life. A special closed-circuit telephone system was set up in Moscow so that Party officials could communicate without going through the normal operator. On Lenin's orders Inessa's apartment was one of the first to be connected to it. He called her regularly on the phone. Hers was one of the few numbers – 31436 – in his personal address book. She visited the Kremlin and occasionally he visited her in her apartment not far from the Kremlin – at 3/14 Arbat, apartment 12, corner of Denezhny and Glazovsky. He took down the address in his own hand.

The move was supposed to be temporary. Zinoviev declared the following day: 'We are convinced that the change in capital will not last long and that the difficult conditions dictating its necessity will pass.' But the Communist magnates grew to enjoy their new living conditions and palatial Kremlin surroundings, and soon there was no more talk about a return to Petrograd.[7]

42

THE BATTLE FOR GRAIN

'If the rich farmers persist in sucking the people's blood, we will turn them over to the people themselves. If we find too many obstacles in dealing out justice to these traitors, the conspirators, the profiteers, then we will let the people deal with them.'

Maximilien Robespierre, 1792

Much of Russia was hungry – and Lenin had to find someone to blame. From the first he thought that scapegoating the farmers would be the most efficient way to feed the country, whatever misery and bloodshed would be inflicted on Russia's thousands of villages. The Bolsheviks didn't create the immediate food crisis; the dislocation of the war, a transport system that had completely broken down and poor harvests were among the causes. But Lenin's punitive policies of compulsion and brutal terror in the countryside made things a great deal worse.

Lenin needed an enemy. So he invented a new class of Russian – kulaks, or rich peasants – whom he claimed were hoarding grain and deliberately starving the rest of the country, particularly the cities.* In reality there were very few rich peasants in Russia – a small number owned any substantial amount of land, some were moneylenders to other peasants, a few possessed more than one horse, cow or a plough. Fewer than 2 per cent of peasant households employed anybody out-side their own family. Lenin's campaign against kulaks was an extension of the class war he was waging in the cities. Rigorous Marxists always suspected rural life and the peasantry – a 'backward class', still semi-feudal – which stood in the way of the inevitable historical development

---

* The word *kulak* means, literally, 'fist' and refers to 'tight-fisted' people. So it was an easy transfer to suggest 'profiteers' and exploiters.

towards socialism, according to the German oracle himself. Most of the Bolsheviks were from the urban intelligentsia, which generally despised the muzhiks for being part of superstitious, illiterate Old Russia. The Bolsheviks suspected, perhaps rightly, that the peasantry would never support them. So they were coerced, bullied and eventually terrorised into obedience. Originally those identified as kulaks were mostly the village elders or the leaders of the communes. Or they were the most successful, imaginative or hardest-working farmers. Before the Revolution Lenin had promised that peasants would be given land seized from the major landowners – the nobles, big industrialists and the Church. There was little talk of that after the coup.

Food shortages worsened during 1918 and affected the cities hardest, partly because the transport system was so poor that distribution was a huge problem, and partly because of inflation. Money quickly became worthless following the Revolution and farmers refused to be paid in cash. The mint, which had employed around 3,000 people in 1917, had a staff of 13,500 a year later: 'printing money was the only growth industry', said Sukhanov, not entirely in jest. Within a year the number of rubles in circulation rose from 60 billion to 225 billion. An entire parallel system of payment in kind and barter was created. Some strict Bolsheviks, experimenting with supposedly socialist economic theories, thought inflation a good thing because it would destroy the reliance of the economy on money. Lenin disagreed and realised what it would do to the value of everything, but like so many leaders throughout history he was powerless to deal with inflation once it had taken hold.

Millions of people were leaving the cities in the hope that there would be more food in the country, which for a while there was. Petrograd lost two-thirds of its population within eighteen months. 'This is a dying city,' Gorky wrote to his wife. 'Everyone is leaving, by foot, by horse, by train. Dead horses are lying in the streets; dogs eat them.' Quickly, people were eating them too, in a country where, unlike in France at the time, horsemeat was by no means a delicacy. Russian exile Emma Goldman, who went back to Petrograd in 1918 after living in America for nearly twenty years, compared the 'gaiety and vivacity and brilliance' of the city with her return, when 'it was almost in ruins as if a hurricane had swept over it. The houses looked like broken old tombs upon neglected and forgotten cemeteries . . . the people walked about like living corpses;

the shortage of food and fuel was slowly sapping the city . . . emaciated and frost-bitten men, women and children were being whipped by the common lash, the search for a piece of bread . . . it was a heart-rending sight by day, an oppressive weight at night. It haunted me, this awful oppressive silence broken by occasional shots.'

Zinaida Gippius said most of her friends, the 'former people', had 'distended stomachs . . . by the spring of 1919 practically all of them had become unrecognisable'. Some of the intellectuals were 'on the books . . . working for the Bolsheviks as minor clerks. They are given just enough to die of hunger but slowly. People with swollen bellies were advised to eat their potatoes unpeeled, but by the spring there were no potatoes . . . they had vanished, as had the potato-skin flat cakes.'[1]

Lenin never tried to pretend there was no crisis. 'We shall perish and ruin the whole Revolution if we do not conquer famine in the next few months,' he wrote to Shlyapnikov in early June 1918. 'The time before the new harvest is the most difficult and critical period for us.' He was well aware of conditions in Petrograd when he told Trotsky three months after the government moved that 'the city is in a catastrophic condition. There is no bread. The population is given the remaining potato and flour crusts . . . Petrograd is on the verge of perishing from starvation.'

Lenin's answer to the food crisis was increased compulsion and terror. He launched 'a battle for grain' with a bloodcurdling speech in early summer 1918 blaming the kulaks and the 'profiteers' for hunger in Russia. 'The kulaks are the rabid foes of the Soviet government . . . these bloodsuckers have grown rich on the hunger of the people. These spiders have grown fat out of the workers. These leeches have sucked the blood of the working people and grown richer as the workers in the cities have starved. Ruthless war on the kulaks! Death to all of them.'

First he set a fixed rate the government would pay for corn and other grains at mid-1916 prices – absurdly low as inflation had increased at least sevenfold in the last year and a half. When peasants refused to sell at that price, hid their stock and seeds, or threatened to replant crops that weren't covered by fixed prices, he used force. A decree written by Lenin on 13 May set up the Food Commissariat, which established a system of grain requisitions 'using armed detachments of workers and Red Guards . . . we will conduct a merciless war'.

The decree was clear about what the regime would do and why. 'The peasant bourgeoisie, having accumulated in their cash boxes enormous money which they extorted from the State during the war, remains stubbornly resistant to the groans of the starving workers and poor peasants . . . they will not bring their grain to the collection points, threatening to force the government to raise prices again, so that they can sell their grain at fabulous prices to speculators . . . the greedy stubbornness of the village kulaks and rich peasants must be brought to an end. Only one way remains: to answer the violence of the grain owners against the poor with violence against the grain hoarders. Not one *pood* of grain should remain in the hands of the peasants beyond the amount required for sowing of their fields and feeding their families until the next harvest.'[2]

Requisition brigades, as they were called, were sent to more than 20,000 villages within the first two months of the decree. Usually they consisted of seventy-five men, armed with two or three machine guns, who would surround a village and demand that peasants hand over a set yield of grain decided by the local Bolshevik Party headquarters. 'Speculators who are caught red-handed not delivering the required amount of grain and can be convicted on clear evidence will be executed on the spot,' Lenin's decree declared. Often the brigades acted with extreme brutality, routinely torturing suspects until the 'right' amount of grain was found. One Bolshevik official who saw a brigade sweep through a village in the 'black earth' region of southern Russia was shocked. 'The measures of extraction are reminiscent of a medieval inquisition. They make the peasants strip and kneel on the ground, whip or beat them, sometimes kill them.' Lenin personally suggested an added twist on the 'class war in the villages'. He said that when punishments were inflicted, the brigades 'should call upon at least six witnesses who must be picked from the poor population of the neighbourhood'. There were cases of the brigades holding twenty or thirty villagers ransom until the amount of grain they demanded was handed over. Originally Lenin had insisted that all peasants should hand over grain by name and anyone who failed to do so would 'be shot on the spot'. But the Food Commissar, Alexander Tsyurupa, and Trotsky baulked at the idea and it had to be slightly watered down to say that a peasant 'who failed to deliver to properly designated rail stations and shipping points should be declared an enemy of the people'.

Even Dzerzhinsky warned against the harshness of the 'battle for grain' and told Lenin that it would damage the Bolsheviks' reputation with rural Russia, 'perhaps for a generation', but Lenin took little notice. Rather, he demanded harsher action. On 23 August he wrote to the Bolshevik chiefs in Penza Province: 'Comrades, the kulak uprising in your five districts must be crushed without pity. The interests of the whole Revolution demand it, for the final and decisive battle with the kulaks everywhere is now engaged. An example must be made. 1) Hang (and I mean hang, so the people can see) not less than 100 known kulaks, rich men, bloodsuckers. 2) Publish their names. 3) Identify hostages . . . Do this so that for hundreds of miles around the people can see, tremble, know and cry: they are killing and will go on killing the bloodsucking kulaks. Cable that you have received this and carried out [instructions]. Lenin.

PS Find tougher people.'

A few days later, on the 29th, he cabled again to express 'extreme indignation that absolutely nothing definite has been received from you about what serious measures have been taken to suppress the kulaks mercilessly and to confiscate their grain in the five districts run by you. Your inaction is criminal.'

At least 3,700 people were killed, probably many more, in the first year of food requisitions. Entire villages were burned down, or the seed supply used for planting the next year's crop was confiscated leaving the peasants destitute. Tsyurupa, a ruthless old Bolshevik and hardly a soft touch, once said that 'the food brigades emulate the methods of the Tsarist police'. He was advised by Lenin to toughen up. The 'battle for grain' was justified because it would pacify rural Russia and 'this is the meaning of the dictatorship of the proletariat', he said.

Lenin wanted to issue another decree declaring that 'in every grain-producing district twenty-five or thirty hostages should be taken from among the rich, who will answer with their lives for the collection and loading of all surpluses'. Tsyurupa replied that he disapproved of hostage-taking. At the next Cabinet meeting Lenin demanded to know why he had not reported how he was intending to comply with the orders about hostages. Tsyurupa seemed uncomfortable and murmured that he did not know how to organise it. Lenin looked straight at him and said, simply, 'Energetically.' He then sent the commissar a note, explaining what he meant. 'I am not suggesting that hostages be *taken*, but that they be *appointed* by name from each district. The object of appointing them is that, being rich, just as they are responsible for their contribution, so they are responsible with their lives for the immediate collection and loading of grain surpluses.'

Stalin was posted to Tsaritsyn (later renamed Stalingrad, and then Volgograd) in June 1918 to secure food supplies. He purged the city of anyone suspected of being a counter-revolutionary. It wasn't tough enough for Lenin, who ordered him to be yet more ruthless – 'be merciless', he cabled. Stalin replied swiftly: 'Be assured our hand will not tremble.'*

But the ruthless war was having little effect on Russia's supply. In the first year requisitions yielded little extra grain. Even by the government's official figures the food brigades collected only about 570,000 tons – from a total harvest yield of forty-nine million tons. Lenin later wound down the food brigades and, for a while, his rhetoric against the peasants softened. He tried a different tactic to get them on his side. But campaigns against kulaks and forcing farmers at gunpoint to produce for the State became a feature of Soviet life for decades to come.[3]

The food requisitions prompted the first major rebellion against the Soviet regime. The Socialist Revolutionaries had split in two after the Bolshevik coup; the 'Lefts' became junior partners in Lenin's regime, with a few Sovnarkom seats and high positions in the Cheka. The 'Rights', like the Mensheviks, never accepted the new government.

The Lefts soon realised they had made a mistake and from March 1918 began to separate themselves from the coalition. Then in early July they tried to bring down the government with a coup attempt of their own, which came close to succeeding.

The Lefts were led by Maria Spiridonova, who after the February Revolution had emerged a heroine from eleven years in jail. She was the only woman leader of a political party in Russia's history and could claim broad support in rural Russia where the SRs, heirs of the Populist tradition of agrarian socialism, were strongly represented in the villages.

---

* Vyacheslav Molotov, for years a loyal lickspittle of both Lenin and Stalin, had no hesitation in saying towards the end of his life (in the 1970s) that both leaders were 'hard men . . . harsh and stern. But without a doubt Lenin was harsher.'

The SRs had received twenty million more votes than the Bolsheviks in the Constituent Assembly elections.

Spiridonova, thirty-four, had been horribly maltreated in prison. She had been raped several times by guards, who repeatedly extinguished cigarettes on her bare arms. She was painfully thin, had long dark hair which, unusually for the time, hung loose below her shoulders, and intense blue eyes. Men often used the word 'hysteric' in their descriptions of her, but she was fiercely intelligent, a mesmeric, passionate speaker and had no fear. She was ruthless in her way and not opposed to violence – she had, after all, murdered a policeman when she was twenty-one. But she was bitterly opposed to Lenin, whom she met only once. She refused to accept the 'humiliating' Brest-Litovsk peace, which she said shamed the whole of Russia.

It was the Bolsheviks' war against the villages that prompted the Left SRs to action. She told followers that her whole life had been devoted to the welfare of peasants: the security official she had shot in January 1906 in Tambov Province, Gavril Luzhenovsky, had been in charge of the brutal suppression of a peasants' revolt. Lenin, she declared, was almost as bad as Luzhenovsky had been. 'I accuse you, Lenin, of betraying the peasants, of making use of them for your own ends. To you . . . they are dung, only manure. Our other differences are only temporary, but on the peasant question we are prepared to give battle. When the peasants are humiliated, oppressed and crushed, you will find me holding the same pistol which once forced me to defend . . . [them].'[4]

The first shot in the Lefts' rebellion was fired on 20 June in Petrograd. A Socialist Revolutionary terrorist killed the head of the city's propaganda and agitation section, V. Volodarsky (his Party soubriquet; his real name was Moisei Goldstein). Lenin was in a rage – less with the SRs than with the Party chief in Petrograd, Zinoviev. A group of Bolshevik factory workers planned to attack the SR headquarters in the city. Zinoviev had prevented them. He received a typical cable from Lenin the next day. 'Disgraceful! This is im-per-missible [underlined twice]. The workers were right. I protest that you should be meddling with the completely correct revolutionary initiative of the masses. The terrorists will take us for milksops. It is necessary to encourage the energy and mass character of the terror against counter-revolutionaries and especially in

Petrograd, whose example will be decisive.' The SRs in Petrograd were attacked, though Volodarsky's killer was not immediately found.

Two weeks later the Lefts responded, directed by Spiridonova. On 6 July one group murdered the German Ambassador to Moscow, Count Wilhelm Mirbach, the only diplomatic representative from any major country in Russia. The object was to kill the Brest-Litovsk Treaty as well as the count, give the Bolsheviks a diplomatic headache and, possibly, prompt the Germans to begin a fresh war against Russia. It was a clumsy operation by the twenty-year-old Cheka agent Yakov Blumkin, who initially missed the ambassador from point-blank range, and managed to hit him only by luck on the third attempt when he was in fact aiming at one of Mirbach's aides. He escaped after exploding a hand-made bomb.*

Another group of 'terrorists' took Dzerzhinsky hostage – so much for the sword and shield's own security arrangements – and locked him up in the SRs' headquarters in the palatial Morozov Mansion, along with other Bolshevik officials like the President of the Moscow Soviet, Pyotr Smidovich. A third detachment took over Moscow's Central Post Office and sent two cables to telegraph offices, provincial Bolshevik headquarters and government agencies throughout the country. One reported the assassination of Mirbach; another said there had been a government takeover and ordered them to stop all telegrams signed by Lenin, Trotsky and Sverdlov.

The Bolsheviks had few reliable troops or Red Guards in Moscow at the time and Lenin knew that General Mikhail Muravyov, a former Tsarist officer turned Bolshevik, commander of the Red forces in

---

* All kinds of conspiracy theories surfaced at the time and for many years later that Lenin orchestrated the Mirbach murder. The ambassador was sending reports back to Berlin, which Soviet spies knew about, saying that the Bolsheviks would not last long and the Revolution had already proved a failure: 'Lenin is finished,' he wrote in a letter to the Kaiser in mid-June. The conspiracy version was given credence by the fact that later the assassin, Blumkin, remained in the Cheka, was given membership of the Communist Party and rose in its ranks. However, it is hard to see how Lenin could have gained from killing the ambassador. The Germans might have been enraged enough to invade Russia again and at this point it was not at all certain that they wouldn't win the war in the West. Why deliberately antagonise them? No evidence has surfaced in nearly a hundred years that has established Lenin had anything to do with the murder, and plenty to suggest it made life more difficult.

Ukraine, had changed sides again and joined the SRs.

The Spiridonova coup might have succeeded if the Lefts really wanted power, or if they had allied with the Mensheviks and joined forces with the Right SRs. But 'we were never really serious, we wanted to make a show more than make a real revolution. We never really wanted to bring down the government,' Steinberg, one of the leaders of the revolt, said later. It was 'less a coup d'état and more a coup de théâtre', said another.

Trotsky was put in charge of suppressing the uprising. He co-opted a corps of 700 Latvian troops to storm Spiridonova's headquarters, retake the Post Office and free the prisoners. Sporadic fighting went on for a few hours. In the Kremlin at around midnight Lenin was seriously worried and 'the atmosphere was like the front in a theatre of war', said the commander of the defending troops, General Jukums Vatsetis. He kept being asked by Lenin, 'Comrade, can we hold out till morning?'

But by 9 a.m. 'the crisis was over', Trotsky reported. The leading SRs gave themselves up and were arrested. Around 200 were executed in the next weeks and 600 jailed. Muravyov either committed suicide or was shot trying to escape after he was arrested – depending on which version of his death, SR or Bolshevik, you believe. Spiridonova was treated comparatively leniently, considering how ruthlessly the Soviets usually dealt with their enemies. She was jailed for a year, was freed, but then sent to a psychiatric hospital. She was released in early 1921 on condition that she never took any part in politics again. She kept to the bargain.[*5]

---

* She couldn't survive Stalin's Great Purge though. She was arrested in 1937, sent to the Gulag and was executed in 1941.

43

REGICIDE

'The decision . . . [to kill the Romanovs] was not only expedient but necessary. It showed everyone that we would continue to fight, stopping at nothing. It was needed not only to frighten, horrify and instil a sense of hopelessness in the enemy but to shake up our own ranks, to show that there was no retreating, that ahead lay either total victory or total doom.' Leon Trotsky, 1935

'In England and France they executed their kings some centuries ago, but we were late with ours.' Lenin, 1919

The grisly deed was not performed as the English had arranged for the death of Charles I or the French for Louis XVI. There was no trial, however cursory or stage-managed. There was no public execution to give it a semblance of judicial and State authority. The monarch was allowed no opportunity to perform his final act with regal dignity. Tsar Nicholas II and his immediate family were butchered in secret by a group of thugs, some of them drunk, in a squalid basement, their remains were burned and thrown down a mineshaft – and then the men who ordered the murder lied about it.

There is no paper trail proving that Lenin gave the orders to kill the Tsar. It is unlikely that he would ever have signed such a warrant, and even if he had, he would surely have covered his tracks most carefully. If any evidence had existed, the Soviet magnates who succeeded him would have destroyed it. But there is no doubt that Lenin gave the order – almost certainly verbally to his then second-in-command, Sverdlov, and probably at a meeting in the Kremlin on 12 July 1918. The timing and details were left to others – Sverdlov and his henchmen – but the decision to kill all the Romanovs and to do so in secret was Lenin's. It is likely that apart from Lenin and Sverdlov, most of the Red magnates

401

did not know the murders had taken place until two days after they had happened.

At around 4 p.m. on 18 July members of the Sovnarkom gathered for their routine meeting in the room adjoining Lenin's private office on the third floor of the Great Kremlin Palace. Lenin was in the chair, but before the commissars got down to the agenda they heard a prepared statement from Sverdlov. 'After a White Guard attempt to abduct the Romanov family, on the night of 16 July the Ekaterinburg Soviet had ordered the execution of Nicholas Romanov. The rest of the family have been evacuated to a safe place.' There was little reaction among the thirty-three Communist officials sitting around the table. Sverdlov then urged comrades to approve the decision taken by the local Communists. There was silence.

Lenin was writing a note to Foreign Commissar Chicherin, but broke off and asked, 'Any questions for Comrade Sverdlov?' Only one comrade raised his voice to speak, though the name was not recorded in the minutes. 'And the family was taken away?' it asked. No reply was recorded.

Lenin paused for a moment and then asked, 'What decision should we take?' But it needed no discussion. They approved the action taken by the comrades in Ekaterinburg. The brief minute reads that 'Comrade Sverdlov's report was received and noted.' They then went on with the rest of the agenda of twenty items which included the reorganisation of the Red Cross, a draft Decree on Health Protection and a report on collecting government statistics. Lenin looked around the table again and said, 'We shall now proceed to read the Draft Decree from the Health Commissariat, article by article.'

The official government newspaper *Izvestia* reported the next day that 'the former Emperor Romanov has been executed . . . the wife and son of Nicholas Romanov have been sent to a safe place'. The lie was believed even by some commissars for several days. Trotsky was not in Moscow until a week after the meeting and recorded in his diary his conversation with Sverdlov when he arrived at the Kremlin. Sverdlov told him about the Tsar 'almost in passing', according to Trotsky.

'And where is the family?'

'The family along with him?'

'All?'

'Yes all,' Sverdlov replied.

'Why . . . who decided the matter?'

'We decided it here. Ilyich thought that we shouldn't leave the Whites a live banner to rally around, especially under the present circumstances.'[1]

The Tsar had been guaranteed safety under the Provisional Government – 'He must not be made a martyr,' said Kerensky, who visited him several times at Tsarskoe Selo, where he remained for a few weeks after he abdicated. 'He seemed to be genuinely enjoying his new manner of life . . . as though the shackles of a heavy burden had been lifted from his shoulders,' Kerensky added, though we know from his diary how miserable Nicholas really was – if not at that stage scared for his family's safety. At first the Provisional Government believed the former Tsar and Empress would seek refuge in Britain. But, having originally said the Romanovs were welcome, his cousin King George V shabbily changed his mind. He thought it would be a highly unpopular move and reflect badly on him, so he reneged on his commitment with weasel words and let Lloyd George – who was happy to allow the Romanovs to go to Britain – take the blame.

The Romanovs were moved to the Siberian town of Tobolsk in the spring of 1917. Kerensky believed they might be attacked and harmed if they remained near Petrograd. They lived in comfort in the former governor's mansion, 'with some favourite courtiers, six chambermaids, two valets and three cooks, a wine steward and two pet spaniels'.

Lenin first discussed what to do with the royal family a few days after the coup, in early November 1917, but came to no firm decision. Most of the comrades wanted the former Tsar to face trial and voted on several Sovnarkom resolutions to bring him to court. They proposed no legal action against the rest of the family. Trotsky was especially keen on a great show trial like Louis XVI's, with him, theatrically, as the chief prosecutor, taking the centre-stage role of Saint-Just. Lenin played along with the idea, but prevaricated. All the time he and Sverdlov had known the fate they envisaged for the Emperor; it was a question of how and when his execution would take place and whether Nicholas alone would die. Lenin had no conscience about regicide. To him, the Tsar was a 'very particular class enemy' and the Romanovs were a '300-year-old disgrace'. His dilemma was fear of what the Germans and Kaiser Wilhelm would do if the Bolsheviks murdered his close cousins. He wasn't at all worried about popular opinion inside Russia. He was sure that few people cared what happened to the Tsar and his family.

There was a tussle between Bolsheviks in two regions as to who should have the 'revolutionary honour' of dealing with Nicholas. Sverdlov made sure that his old friend from Siberian exile, Filipp Goloshchekin, head of the Urals Soviet and Communist chieftain in Ekaterinburg, would get the nod. Lenin agreed. Goloshchekin, forty-two, had been jailed for two years in the forbidding fortress of Schlüsselberg (where Sasha Ulyanov had been executed) and met Lenin in exile in Paris. Sverdlov described his friend as 'cold . . . very energetic', and Lenin thought him 'useful and efficient'.

The former Emperor and his family were moved to Ekaterinburg in June 1918. They lived in a generously proportioned neo-classical building, the Ipatiev House, but the living conditions were no longer good.

Goloshchekin wanted the Tsar murdered, so that he could claim credit. Lenin wanted to wait. But time was now pressing and Lenin could put off a decision no longer. Ekaterinburg was surrounded by an army of troops from a Czech legion at war with Austria-Hungary. These were soldiers who were supposed to be crossing Russia so they could return to Western Europe by ship from the Far East, but who had begun to fight against the Bolsheviks. If they captured the town they could free the Tsar, so Goloshchekin told Sverdlov they had to act fast.* He went to Moscow to get final authorisation to kill the entire family – which was given after that 12 July meeting in the Kremlin.

Goloshchekin had already picked the man who would be in charge of doing the dirty business: Yakov Yurovsky, whom he had appointed commandant of Ipatiev House.†2

---

* They took Ekaterinburg a week after the Tsar's murder.

† Sverdlov survived Nicholas II by only a few months. He died in the great Influenza epidemic in March 1919. All kinds of rumours spread later that he was in fact killed on order of Lenin, but no real motive has ever emerged. Sverdlov had not challenged Lenin in any way and had he lived he would very likely have been Lenin's natural successor. Another fascinating 'what if' in history, is what might have happened in Soviet Russia if Sverdlov and not his great enemy Stalin had emerged as leader after Lenin's death.

*

A tall, well-built forty-year-old 'with a shock of black wavy hair, dapper and cultured, with a well-trimmed Van Dyck beard', Yurovsky was a highly intelligent, puritanical Bolshevik, burning with bitterness against the bourgeoisie and particularly the royal family. One of ten children, he had been brought up in extreme poverty and had faced discrimination because of his Jewish roots which he blamed directly on the Romanovs and the Russian aristocracy. He thirsted for revenge and as a leading figure in the local Cheka he was in a position to exact plenty of it. Goloshchekin knew his man and believed Yurovsky would 'do an efficient job'. He left the practical details in Yurovsky's hands.

Yurovsky had selected an execution squad days earlier, and the method.* He had toured the area close to town and found the best spot to cremate the bodies of the eleven victims and inter the ashes – an abandoned mineshaft near the village of Koptyaki, twelve kilometres from Ekaterinburg.

At 1.30 a.m. on 16 July, Yurovsky woke Dr Evgeny Botkin, the loyal family physician who had been part of the Tsar's retinue for many years, and told him to rouse the others. He said there was 'unrest in the city and [out of] concern for their safety they would be moved' to the basement. The explanation was convincing, as they had heard shooting for the last few nights from their rooms.

It took the prisoners half an hour to wash and dress. At around 2 a.m., in semi-darkness, they descended the steep, narrow staircase. Yurovsky led the way. Next came Nicholas, with the Tsarevich Alexis

---

* There are four names other than Yurovsky who were officially recorded. His deputy commandant, Grigory Nikutin, whom the former Empress thought 'handsome and decent', Cheka official Pyotr Ermakov, well known as an alcoholic, Pavel Medvedev, a welder from a local factory, and a mechanic, Mikhail Kudrin. But recently more files have been opened and we know the identities of four others who took part: Alexei Kabanov, a soldier at one of the machine-gun posts outside the Ipatiev House, Viktor Netrebin, a nervous seventeen-year-old Cheka novice, Stepan Vaganov, a frequent drinking partner of Ermakov, and the Latvian soldier Jan Tsel'ms. For many years the legend among the Whites had it that the murder squad were mostly 'Jews, Letts and Hungarians'. In fact a Lettish group had originally agreed to take part when they thought the Tsar would be killed, but when they were told the whole family would be slaughtered they refused to kill the young girls and women. Apart from one, the killers were all Russian, and all gentiles – Yurovsky's parents were converted Jews.

in his arms. Both wore military shirts and caps. Then came the former Empress, holding her pet King Charles spaniel, Jemmy, followed by her four daughters and then Botkin. The maid Demidova carried two large pillows, in one of which she had concealed a box containing jewellery. Behind them came the valet, Trup, and the cook, Kharitonov. According to Pavel Medvedev, who wrote a detailed account, the 'family appeared calm as if expecting no danger'.

They were taken, through a courtyard, to a basement room at the opposite end of the house, which had previously been occupied by the guards, five metres wide and six metres long. It had one small oval-shaped window, barred with a grille. All furniture had been removed. None of the prisoners knew that the execution squad was in an adjoining room.

Alexandra asked why there were no chairs and two were brought in. Nicholas placed his son on one of them; Alexandra sat in the other. The rest were told to line up against one of the walls. There they waited for a few minutes before Yurovsky re-entered with the executioners.

As he described it some years later, 'I told the Romanovs that "in view of the fact that their relatives continued their offensive against Soviet Russia, the Executive Committee of the Urals Soviet had decided to shoot them". Nicholas turned his back to . . . [us] and faced his family. Then, as if collecting himself, he turned round, asking, "What? What?" I rapidly repeated what I had said and ordered the detachment to prepare. Its members had previously been told whom to shoot and to aim directly at the heart to avoid too much blood and to end it all more quickly. Nicholas said no more. He turned again towards his family. The others shouted some incoherent exclamations. All this lasted a few seconds. Then the shooting started. It went on for two or three minutes. I shot Nicholas on the spot. The Empress barely had time to cross herself before she was shot. She died instantly. Elsewhere in the room there was bloody carnage as the guards lost control and shot wildly. The shots ricocheted from the walls to the floor and around the room like hailstones. Alexis fell off the chair, shot in the leg, still alive. Kharitonov sat down and died.'

The guards made a complete mess of their job. Six of the victims were still alive when the salvo of shooting stopped. Alexis lay in a pool of blood, moaning. Yurovsky finished him off with two bullets to the head.

Demidova offered some resistance with her pillows. But she went down, bayoneted to death. 'When one of the girls was stabbed, the bayonet would not go through the corset,' Yurovsky said. The whole 'procedure', as he called it, took more than twenty minutes. A trained firing squad would have finished the task in seconds.

Medvedev recalled the scene: 'They had several gunshot wounds on various parts of their bodies; their faces were covered with blood; their clothes too were blood-soaked.'

The executioners brought sheets from an adjoining room, and after stripping the corpses of valuables – which they pocketed – carried them, dripping with blood, on improvised stretchers across the lower floor to a Fiat truck waiting at the main gate. The vehicle's engines had been running from the moment the Romanovs had been woken, in an attempt to mask the noise of the shooting. They piled the corpses on top of each other.

Yurovsky was ruthless, a cold-hearted killer, but he had moral qualms about the theft of 'people's property'. He demanded, under threat of death, the return of loot stolen from the bodies. He confiscated a gold watch, a cigarette case encrusted with diamonds and some other items.

Medvedev was in charge of the clean-up operation. Guards brought mops, pails of water and sand to remove the bloodstains. One of them described the scene: 'The room was filled with something like a mist of gunpowder . . . there were bullet holes on the walls and the floor . . . especially many on one wall . . . puddles of blood on the floor. There were also pools of blood in other rooms they had to cross to get to the courtyard . . . leading to the gate.'

The detail drove to the 'burial ground' Yurovsky had chosen. When they began to undress the corpses they found yet more treasure. The 'girls and women wore some kind of corset . . . filled with jewels embedded inside'. Alexandra had worn a pearl belt made of several necklaces sewn into linen. Yurovsky put the jewels in a bag – the diamonds alone weighed more than eight kilos. The bodies were burned and lowered into the mine.

Yurovsky was worried that the shaft would be too shallow to conceal the remains of the Romanovs for long. He searched a broader area and found some deeper mines a few kilometres along the road towards Moscow. The following night he and a group of Cheka officials returned with some petrol and sulphuric acid. They dug up the bodies, placed them on a truck and drove them to their new resting place, a shallow grave nearby. Acid was poured over them and the grave was covered with earth and brushwood.*[3]

Lenin was a great admirer of the People's Will leader and author of the *Revolutionary Catechism* Sergei Nechaev. Before the Revolution he occasionally reminded his clique of Nechaev's views on regicide. He once told Vladimir Bonch-Bruevich: 'People have completely forgotten that Nechaev possessed a special talent as an organiser, an ability to establish particular skills in illegal work . . . It's enough to recall his precise reply to the question, who should be killed in the royal family? He said "the whole *ektenia*" [the entire list of Romanovs read out in a traditional Orthodox service]. So who should be killed? The entire house of Romanov . . . That was pure genius.'

Yet when Lenin had ordered 'the whole *ektenia*' killed he lied about it – worried, principally, about international reaction. The Soviets tried for years to maintain the fiction that the murders at Ekaterinburg were ordered by the local Soviet; they stuck to the story that the rest of the family died in haphazard circumstances during the Civil War, that their deaths were collateral damage.†

---

* The following night, 120 kilometres away at Alapaevsk, the former Tsarina's sister, Grand Duchess Ella, who had become a nun, her companion Sister Barbara, Grand Duke Sergei and five other Romanovs were murdered – again at the hands of the Urals Cheka – in even ghastlier fashion. They were taken at the dead of night by cart to a forest and forced to walk to the mouth of a disused mine. They were beaten with rifle butts and, one by one, thrown down the shaft into a waterlogged pit. Sergei died quickly – he had somehow managed to struggle to the surface and was shot in the head. The others were left to starve to death.

† Adolph Joffe, Russian Ambassador to Germany in the summer of 1918, was certain that Lenin knew all along what the fate of the Romanovs would be. He wrote in his uncompleted memoirs: 'I was in Berlin when . . . [they] were executed. I was officially informed only of Nicholas II's execution. I knew nothing about . . . [the family] and thought they were still alive. When representatives of Wilhelm II and the brother of the former Empress, the Duke of Hesse-Darmstadt, and other princes came to see me and asked about the fate of Alexandra Feodorovna and her children, I always told them what I believed. But I began to have doubts; I had been hearing various rumours. Despite all the queries I sent to Moscow, I could get no sense out of them. Finally when Dzerzhinsky was in Berlin incognito, en route to Switzerland, I made him tell me the

Even if the truth had come out it may not have made much difference in Russia, so inured were the people becoming to violent death, and so unpopular were the Romanovs. The British spy Robert Bruce Lockhart wrote in his diary: 'the population of Moscow received the news . . . [of the ex-Tsar's death] with amazing indifference. Their apathy towards everything except their own fate was complete, yet symptomatic of the extraordinary times in which we are living.'

The former Tsarist Prime Minister Vladimir Kokovtsov was riding in a tram in Petrograd on the day the news was announced. 'There was no sign of grief or sympathy among the people,' he said. 'The report of the Tsar's death was met with smirks, mockery and base comments. Some passengers said "high time".'[4]

truth . . . He told me that Vladimir Ilyich had said I must be told nothing. According to Dzerzhinsky, Lenin had said, "Better if Joffe knows nothing. It'll be easier for him to lie to them there in Berlin."'

44

THE ASSASSINS' BULLETS

'Is the end near? If it is, tell me straight so that I don't leave matters pending.' Lenin to Dr Vladimir Rozanov, 30 August 1918

'Revolution devours its children mercilessly.'

Alexander Herzen (1812–1870)

Just after 10 a.m. on 30 August 1918 Moisei Uritsky, head of the Petrograd Cheka, was leaving his office at the Internal Affairs Commissariat at Palace Square. As he reached the pavement outside the building and was about to step into his car, a shot rang out. Uritsky slumped to the ground in a pool of blood – 'a bullet hole where his left eye had been', according to one witness.

There was an exchange of gunfire between Uritsky's bodyguards and a young man wearing a military cadet uniform, but he got away on a bicycle. Meanwhile Uritsky was rushed to the nearest hospital, where he died within a few minutes of arrival.*

Lenin heard about the assassination an hour after it happened. He liked Uritsky, a long-standing Bolshevik who had been at the crucial meeting in October the previous year which decided to mount the Bolshevik coup. He said the loss would be a severe blow to the Revolution. Lenin was told that the immediate response would be tightened security by the Cheka and Red Guards at government and Communist Party buildings. He had a brief meeting at noon with his sister Maria, who pleaded with him not to leave the Kremlin that day. He replied that he

---

* The assassin was soon identified as Leonid Kannegisser, twenty-two, who was arrested a day later, horribly tortured to discover if he had accomplices, and, when it was found he had none, shot. He was a supporter of the SRs but had not acted with their knowledge. He was a talented poet – a friend of the writer Sergei Esenin and of Marina Tsvetaeva – and his poems were published posthumously in Paris in the 1920s.

had a speaking engagement planned for later that day at the Michelson factory, an engineering plant in a working-class district of Moscow, and he wanted to honour it. He had a brief lunch with Bukharin, who also said it would be foolish to go anywhere in Moscow that day and advised him to stay put in the Kremlin.

Lenin had a pile of correspondence to work through – including a cable he sent to Trotsky in Sviyazhsk, Tatarstan, one of the fronts in the Civil War that was raging across swathes of Russia. Lenin told him he must use 'extreme measures' against soldiers who showed lack of vigour and 'strength' on the battlefield. 'They should be told that from now on we are applying the model of the French Revolution . . . and they will be put on trial and even shot.'[1]

At 5 p.m. he was driven to the factory and spoke for about thirty-five minutes. It was a typical performance. 'The Revolution was not brought into being so that landlords can return to their properties,' he said. 'Those parasites who sucked the blood of the people for so long must know that neither liberty nor equality will give them back their lost wealth, which will go safely into the hands of the workers. Wherever the bourgeoisie rule they give nothing to the toiling masses . . . Take America . . . the freest country, they say. There they have a democratic republic. And what is the result? A handful of millionaires and billionaires insolently dominate and the entire nation is in bondage. Wherever so-called "democrats" rule you find plain, straightforward theft. Our way is superior. We have only one choice: victory or death.'

The applause was enthusiastic and he smiled as he waved goodbye. He marched towards the exit where his car was waiting and paused briefly to speak to a group of women who were politely asking about the problems of food supply.

Suddenly three crisp, loud shots were heard. The crowd around the factory gate scattered. Lenin was lying on the ground, blood seeping through his white shirt and dark jacket. His driver and bodyguard, Stepan Gil, bent down over him to see if he was still breathing. Lenin's eyes were open and he was conscious.

One man from the factory committee ran up to Gil and realised the wounded man was Lenin. He told Gil, 'You must take him to the nearest hospital. It's not far.' But Gil said, 'No, I will take him home.' Lenin must have heard and he whispered, 'Home, home'. The two men lifted him into the car and Gil drove at breakneck speed through the Moscow streets to the Kremlin.

When they arrived, Lenin refused help. He put his jacket on by himself and climbed the three floors of stairs to his apartment. His sister Maria opened the door in a state of alarm. Lenin was bleeding profusely, looked in great pain but said, 'I've been shot and slightly wounded, just in the arm.'

There were no surgeons on hand but two medically qualified people were quickly found in the Kremlin just metres away from Lenin's apartment: Vera Velichkina, Bonch-Bruevich's wife, and Vera Krestinskaya, who was married to the senior Party apparatchik Nikolai Krestinsky, examined him, and made him comfortable until surgeons arrived. Velichkina injected him with morphine. Nadya was still at her office in the Enlightenment Commissariat and a car had been sent to bring her back to the Kremlin.

Within half an hour Professors Vladimir Rozanov and Vladimir Mints, distinguished hospital specialists, had cleaned his wounds. They found that one bullet had gone through his neck from left to right, missing his aorta by a fraction of a centimetre and, having pierced his lung, lodged in his neck above the clavicle. Another bullet was in his left shoulder. The third shot had gone harmlessly through the jacket Lenin was wearing. The first was the most serious because it affected his breathing. The surgeons demanded oxygen tanks, gauze, more bandages, dressing and other equipment which was nowhere to be found in the Kremlin. Officials had to rush out and find supplies from a pharmacy on the main Moscow shopping street, Tverskaya, close by. The surgeons decided to leave the bullets inside Lenin's body.

When Nadya returned home she first encountered Sverdlov, who looked worried and grave. All he said was, 'We are making the arrangements for Ilyich.' She took that to mean he thought Lenin was dying and when she reached the bedroom, which by now resembled an operating theatre, she was grief-stricken.

Lenin's arms were raised on a hoist, he was still conscious and he could see the extent of his injuries. 'Is the end near?' he asked Rozanov. 'If it is, tell me straight so that I don't leave matters pending.' The

Grigory Zinoviev (Hirsch Apfelbaum), Lenin's most loyal sidekick and lickspittle in their exile years. Later, after the Revolution, he became head of the
Communist International.

Lev Kamenev (Leon Rozenfeld) spent many years in European exile with Lenin. Lenin was contemptuous about his 'weakness' but enjoyed his jokes and gossip.

A young Joseph Stalin – 'the wonderful Georgian', as Lenin once described him – around 1907, when he organised a great bank robbery in Tiflis to finance the Bolshevik Party.

Lenin in hiding in Finland, three weeks before the October Revolution, disguised as a Finnish worker, the only extant picture of him as an adult without his trademark beard.

Lenin in Red Square addressing the soldiers and Communist Party activists on the first anniversary of the October Revolution, 1918.

Felix Dzerzhinsky (centre), head of the Cheka, 'the sword and shield' of the Communist Party. 'Iron Felix', fanatical, ruthless, ice-cold and ascetic, was the most hated and feared man in Russia after 1917.

For the last nine months of his life, Lenin could hardly speak more than a handful of words or walk, and was confined to a wheelchair most of the time. His decline was kept a strict state secret for months.

The Afterlife. While Lenin lay in state, his successors, against his family's wishes, made the decision to embalm his body – 'for ever if we can,' said Dzerzhinsky – and place him on public display. He still draws huge crowds every year.

surgeons reassured him the injuries would not be fatal. But he did not seem convinced.

When he saw Nadya he looked at her for a few seconds in silence and then said, 'You've come. You must be tired. Go and lie down.' She said later 'that the words he said were irrelevant . . . his eyes said something different: "this is the end". I went out of the room so as not to upset him.'

The first person he sent for after Nadya was Inessa, who rushed to his side at once. She brought her youngest daughter Varvara, then sixteen, with her. Nadya took the girl off to look around the Kremlin and then some family photographs, 'leaving her mother alone with Lenin for a long time', according to one of the other Kremlin wives.

Immediately after the visit, Inessa wrote to her eldest daughter, Inna, dating the note 'from my bed in the middle of the night'. She said she was writing in haste and a state of excitement and that the murder attempt and near-death experience 'has reunited us and brought us even closer together'.[*2]

The suspect was apprehended immediately. Workers from the Michelson factory held her at gunpoint until Cheka officers came and arrested her. She was Fanny Kaplan (born Fanya Yefimovna Roitman), twenty-eight, the daughter of a schoolteacher in Volhynia Province. She had been involved in radical politics from her teenage years, first in an anarchist group when she was arrested in 1906 for trying to assassinate a Tsarist official. She bungled the attempt and was wounded from the blast of her own home-made bomb. She was sentenced to 'eternal hard labour'. She was sent first to a tough prison at Maltsev, where she was frequently caned in public – a routine punishment at the time – then to Orel in central Russia and finally to the notorious Akatua silver-mining camp in eastern Siberia, where conditions were so harsh that hundreds of inmates died. She developed serious problems with her sight and was partially blind in one eye. She was released after the February Revolution

---

* There was one other wounded victim, Maria Popova, one of the women who was talking to Lenin after his speech at the factory. She remembered chatting with him. She said, 'I told him "they've given permission to buy flour, but they haven't lifted the roadblocks", and Lenin replied, "according to the decree they can't lift the roadblocks. We must struggle." Then there was a shot and I fell.'

and went to live in Crimea. In prison she had ditched anarchism and become a Socialist Revolutionary. After eleven years as a convict she was as dedicated and fanatical as the day she had been arrested as an eighteen-year-old.

Kaplan must have known what would be in store for her when she was arrested. She was taken to the Lubyanka, where she was briefly held in the same cell as the British intelligence agent Robert Bruce Lockhart, whom the Cheka arrested on suspicion (wrongly) of involvement in the plot, and two other British spies. He watched the guards push her into the cell. 'She was dressed in black. Her hair was black, and her eyes, set in a fixed stare, had great black rings under them. Her face was colourless. She might have been any age between 20 and 35. Doubtless the Bolsheviks hoped that she would give us a sign of recognition. Her composure was unnatural. She went to the window and, leaning her chin upon her hand, looked out into the daylight. And there she remained, motionless, speechless, apparently resigned to her fate, until . . . the sentries came and took her away.'

She was moved to another cell after a few hours; two days later she was taken to the Kremlin and placed in solitary confinement in a room directly below Sverdlov's.

She was interrogated repeatedly by two deputy heads of the Cheka, Yakov Peters and Nikolai Skrypnik, the Commissar for Justice, Dmitry Kursky, and the head of Moscow's Revolutionary Tribunal, Stanislav Dyakanov.

Her interrogators were convinced she was part of a broader conspiracy by the Socialist Revolutionaries, whose coup attempt had been foiled just a few weeks earlier. But Kaplan never broke and maintained throughout that she had acted on her own, which the best evidence suggests seems to have been the case.

With total calm she told them repeatedly: 'I don't belong to any party.'

'Why did you shoot at Comrade Lenin?'

'I regard him as a traitor. The longer he lives the further he'll push back the idea of socialism. For dozens of years.'

'Who sent you to commit the crime?'

'I committed the attempt on my own behalf.'

They asked her about her connection with the SRs and to name names of other Party members that she knew. She said she had encountered many while she was in prison but none had anything to do with her attempt to murder Lenin.

'How did you feel about the October Revolution?'

'I was in Kharkov, in hospital, when it took place. I didn't like it. I viewed it negatively. I was for the Constituent Assembly and I still am.'

'So why did you shoot at Lenin? Who sent you to do it?'

'I made up my own mind to shoot Lenin a long time ago. I was the one who shot him. I decided to . . . [do it] back in February. The idea matured in my mind in Simferopol [in the Crimea] and since that time I have been preparing it.'

Many people over the decades have doubted whether the murder attempt was the work of a lone gunwoman, especially someone with such extremely poor eyesight as Kaplan. According to some theories there was another woman shooter from an SR assassination team in the vicinity – not on a 'grassy knoll', but lurking near the Michelson factory gates, who approached Lenin unseen. Kaplan willingly accepted the blame while the real killer escaped. Others say the Cheka knew someone else had fired the shots but were happy to scapegoat Kaplan, as a prelude to a major crackdown of terror against any opposition.* Yet no hard evidence has surfaced that anyone else was involved and Kaplan's Browning pistol was found at the scene of the crime; three shots had been fired. One rogue SR said the real culprit was another 'terrorist' named Lidia Konopleva but she was never traced and there's no proof that she was near the scene of the crime. Kaplan did have close links with Socialist Revolutionary activists, but she was not connected to any terrorist 'combat cell'.[3]

By this stage Lenin had become used to being shot at. There had been the incident on New Year's Day in Petrograd, and in Moscow random violence on the streets was rampant. Law and order had almost broken down. Just three weeks earlier Lenin's car had been fired at three times in one day. In the morning a group of youths – who turned out to be Bolsheviks – shot at his car from a side street; Lenin got out and rounded on them: 'You mustn't just casually fire at people from a street corner

---

* See the work of Robert Service, a scholar I respect vastly, who is convinced Kaplan could not have fired the shots because of her eyesight and general mental confusion.

without seeing who you are shooting at.' In the afternoon his car was halted by an unofficial roadblock of armed workers, who fired shots in the air, demanded to see his documents and wouldn't believe he was *the* Lenin. They let him go, but the workers were later arrested. In the evening he was shot at again from a street corner not far from the Kremlin by an unidentified man, who missed.[*]

None of those were attempts on his life, just a normal day in downtown Moscow in the summer of 1918. The Kaplan incident was different – a direct attack on Lenin and the regime.

Late in the evening of 3 September the commandant of the Kremlin guard, Pavel Malkov, was summoned to the Lubyanka and told by one of Dzerzhinsky's aides, Varlam Avanesov, that it had been decided to sentence Kaplan to death and that he, Malkov, was to carry out the order. 'The execution of any human being, especially a woman, was no easy thing. It was a heavy responsibility. But I had never been ordered to carry out a more just sentence than this,' he said later. 'I asked Avanesov, "When?" and he replied, "Today, immediately." No one commuted the death sentence on Kaplan. It was duly carried out and it was I who carried it out.'

Shortly before the execution he was told to report to Sverdlov, who went through the details with him. Malkov's instructions were to shoot Kaplan in the back of the neck – the classic Bolshevik method – in a garage in one of the Kremlin courtyards, with a car engine running to

---

[*] A few months later he was held up at gunpoint again. On 19 January 1919 he was visiting Nadya, who was convalescing in Sokolniki, in the northern outskirts of Moscow, following another painful attack of Graves' Disease. On the way, his car was halted by six armed men. The bandits ordered him out of the car, demanded his wallet and took the Browning pistol he carried in his coat. His sister Maria, accompanying him, was searched too and blurted out, 'How dare you search us. Don't you know who we are? Don't you recognise Lenin? You have no right to do this.' 'We have every right,' the bandit leader replied. Lenin's chauffeur, Stepan Gil, tried to intervene but Lenin told him to stand down. The bandits took the car and drove off, leaving Lenin and his entourage to walk to the nearest Party headquarters for help. They were refused admission – the bandits had taken his identity papers and the officials didn't believe he was *the* Lenin. Eventually a call was put through to Dzerzhinsky, who recognised his voice and asked if there was a political motive for the incident. 'No, definitely not. Otherwise they would have finished me off.'

muffle the noise, 'and her remains must be destroyed without trace', ordered Sverdlov. She was shot at 4 a.m. on 4 September. The execution was witnessed by one person – a slightly odd choice by the Cheka officials: the 'proletarian poet' Demyan Bedny was there, said Sverdlov, for the purpose of 'revolutionary inspiration'.

Lenin did not interfere in the decision. Malkov wrote an account of the execution nearly forty years later. 'A charming fable existed that Kaplan was supposed to have remained alive and that at the last minute Vladimir Ilyich had asked for Kaplan's life to be spared. There are stories from so-called eyewitnesses that she was seen in a camp on Solovki Island or Kolyma, in 1932 or 1938, to show that Lenin was a kindly fellow who generously forgave his enemies their evil deeds. But nobody annulled Kaplan's death sentence. These were nothing more than stories.'[4]

By the time of Kaplan's execution the Bolsheviks had begun an orgy of revenge violence throughout the major cities and towns of Russia – Red Terror on a vast scale. Rumours spread immediately in Moscow and Petrograd that Lenin was dead and for some days the regime was thrown into panic. The doctors were issuing three-hourly bulletins on Lenin's health, but although they were accurate they were widely disbelieved. Dr Rozanov said that 'Vladimir Ilyich has been lucky. If the bullet had landed one millimetre in either direction, he would already be dead.' There had been a serious haemorrhage into Lenin's chest cavity and there was a chance of an infection, but he was healing well. Five doctors were treating him around the clock and within two days he was declared to be out of danger.

Well before then, though, the Communist magnates had launched a series of brutal reprisals. At 11 p.m. on 30 August, a few hours after the shooting, Sverdlov wrote a decree warning opponents what was about to happen: 'A few hours ago a villainous attempt was made on the life of Comrade Lenin. The working class will respond to attempts on the lives of its leaders by still further consolidating its forces and by merciless mass terror against all the enemies of the Revolution.'

The Cheka was unleashed. In Petrograd 500 prisoners – Zinoviev referred to them as 'hostages' – were immediately 'executed as a result of the terror proclaimed after the murder attempt on Vladimir Ilyich and the killing of Uritsky'. The following month there were 300 more. For-mer Tsarist officials and Socialist Revolutionaries were shot in public. In Nizhny Novgorod, forty-one people were executed the afternoon af-ter Lenin was shot. Their names were published and the local Cheka warned that 'to every murder of a Communist or an attempt at such a murder we shall reply by shooting bourgeois hostages'. In Kronstadt the sailors had held around 400 prisoners in a fortress for several months. The next morning there were no more prisoners: all had been killed.

The same was happening throughout the country. Sverdlov, now acting as head of the government, was receiving constant messages from com-missars who had been despatched to the provinces. Stalin, in Tsaritsyn overseeing the war against the kulaks, cabled Moscow two days after the assassination attempt, reporting on dozens of arrests and executions: 'Having heard of the wicked attempt of capitalist hirelings on the life of the greatest revolutionary, the leader of the proletariat . . . we answer this base attack with the organisation of systematic mass terror against the bourgeoisie and its agents.' Altogether 6,185 death sentences were issued in the two months after Lenin was shot, but it is likely that many more people were killed. 'We must put an end once and for all to the papist-Quaker babble about the sanctity of human life,' Trotsky said, justifying the terror.

From now on there were practically no restraints on the Cheka. The message was that they could do more or less what they wished. At a cabaret-circus in Moscow, an off-duty group of Chekists attended the clown act Bim-Bom, a duo of circus comics who had been highly pop-ular since the turn of the century with a mixture of slapstick farce and political satire. Everybody in Moscow went, from the well-off to work-ers. At one point during the show the Chekists, who had all had a drink or two, went on stage and began hectoring the clowns for their 'counter-revolutionary' and insulting material. The audience thought it was all part of the act – until one of the Chekists pulled out his revolver and shot dead the clown known as 'Bom'.* The incident prompted protest; the deputy head of the Cheka, Yakov Peters, investigated but took no action

---

* He was Iwan Radsunski, mainstay of the act, who over the years worked with several 'Bims' – at this point Mieczsław Stanewieski.

against the killers, who he said were merely showing a little too much
zealous revolutionary vigilance.

* * *

The murder attempt was the beginning of the 'Lenin cult', the exaggerated praise and semi-religious worship that characterised leadership in
the Communist world for the following decades – perfected later by Stalin, Mao Zedong and Kim Il-Sung but originating in the days after the
threat to Lenin's life. Three days after the shooting Zinoviev made an
absurd speech that set the tone: 'Lenin is the greatest leader ever known
by humanity, the apostle of the socialist Revolution,' he gushed. Supposedly an atheist, he compared Lenin to Jesus Christ and said he was
'leader by the Grace of God' – as Orthodox priests had referred to the
Tsars. Trotsky rushed back from the Front and at the Moscow Soviet
called Lenin 'the greatest human being of our revolutionary epoch, our
new age . . . the loss of Lenin would be devastating to the Revolution'.
The papers were full of special editions with extravagant and often fictitious material about Lenin's heroism and personality. It was the first
time the Soviet press had written at any length about Lenin the person.[5]

Lenin recovered and was back at his desk within three weeks.[*] He
took occasional exercise and walked around the Kremlin precincts with
his left arm in a sling. Against his express orders he was filmed by a
camera crew organised by Bonch-Bruevich. There were still rumours
in Moscow that he had been killed and buried; Bonch-Bruevich and

---

[*] Visitors while he was convalescing included Maxim Gorky, who was still writing
newspaper articles regularly attacking the Revolution and Lenin personally. The Bolshevik leader wanted to see him. Gorky recalled: 'I called on him when he was still
unable to use his arm freely and could hardly move his perforated neck. In answer to
my words of indignation he spoke unwillingly, as though it was something that bored
him. "It was only a scuffle. What can be done about it? Everyone acts in the only way
they know how."' Angelica Balabanova recalled him a few days after the shooting, 'sitting on a balcony in the sun . . . I was overcome by emotion and embraced him silently.
Only when I was leaving did he refer to what had happened . . . When we spoke, he
seemed relieved that others decided Kaplan's fate. He said, "The Central Committee
will decide what to do with her." But when he said this he must have known Kaplan was
already dead.' Nadya, though, 'was deeply affected by the thought of revolutionaries
condemning other revolutionaries to death . . . when we were alone afterwards she wept
bitterly when she spoke of this'. One makes of that what one will, but Balabanova is
usually a reliable source.

Sverdlov wanted to prove he was alive. 'Was that a camera I saw on a rooftop?' Lenin asked one day. 'I thought I told you there were to be no photographs?' 'Yes, Vladimir Ilyich,' Bonch-Bruevich admitted, 'they are filming. This is the only way we can show for sure that you are still with us. It will do a lot to help us.' Lenin was furious for a while, but was mollified. 'Well, you're probably right but I still don't like it.' On Stalin's prompting, Lenin's security detail was trebled in size and when he left the Kremlin three identical cars departed from the gates at the same time, so no potential assassin knew which of the vehicles was Lenin's.

Leonid Krasin, one of Lenin's oldest comrades, wrote sagely to his wife on 7 September that 'as it happens, the attempt to kill Lenin has made him much more popular than he was. One hears . . . people who are far from having any sympathy with the Bolsheviks, saying that it would have been a disaster if he had succumbed to his wounds, as it was thought at first that he might. And they are right . . . in the midst of all this chaos and confusion, he is the backbone of the new body politic, the main support on which everything rests.' Many people who may have loathed him were saying the same sort of thing.[6]

45

THE SIMPLE LIFE

'In Lenin there was that combination in one person of self-castigation, which is the essence of all real asceticism, with the castigation of other people.' Pyotr Struve (1870–1944)

While many of the other Kremlin magnates were soon enjoying the trappings of power, Lenin and Nadya lived fairly modestly. Their domestic arrangements were similar to the way they had existed in exile – unostentatious, though now they did have a maid/cleaner, Olymprada Zharalova, who had previously worked at an iron foundry in the Urals. Soon after they moved to Moscow, Lenin's sister Maria began to live with them.* There were two cats, and occasionally a stray came to visit. Lenin loved cats and it was invariably he who left food and water out for them; Nadya and Maria often forgot.

They seldom ate at the Kremlin restaurant, where top Communist Party officials were provided with decent meals at a time of tight rationing and hunger in Moscow. The Kremlin is a vast precinct, almost a small city within the city, comprising myriad streets and office buildings where 3,500 people worked within six months of the move from Petrograd. Nadya was often seen trudging along the pavements with black bread under her arm and a tureen of soup. Lenin put in a punishing seventeen hours almost every day, but he did try to return to the apartment for lunch – as he had done in Geneva or Zurich.

Occasionally they entertained. When Clara Zetkin called a few months after the attempt on Lenin's life she found 'Nadya and Lenin's sister at supper, which I was immediately and heartily asked to share. It

---

* She continued to live with Nadya – though in a different Kremlin apartment – after Lenin died, and until their own deaths.

was a simple meal: tea, black bread, butter, cheese. Later the sister tried to find "something sweet" for the "guest of honour" and discovered a rare jar of preserve.' The modesty and simplicity were partly for political reasons: Lenin knew that his lifestyle would become known, and he wanted to convey to others that his outwardly puritanical ways should be those of all good Communists. But mainly it was genuine; it was the way he had always lived and the way he liked. He loathed the big, boozy, seven-course dinners with endless vodka toasts and macho storytelling that became the norm among Communist chieftains. He never went.[1]

His one luxury was the guest house in Gorki, twenty kilometres south-west of Moscow, where Lenin first went to convalesce from his wounds after he was shot. He started using it regularly – 'it's just like a little Switzerland, peaceful,' he said – and in his last two years lived there more or less permanently. It was called a 'dacha', or cottage, but it was far bigger and more comfortable than anywhere they had lived before, a gracious manor house fronted by six white columns, with a gaudy interior full of plate glass and chandeliers. It had once been owned by Savva Morozov, but was taken over by the Tsarist regime to entertain State guests and inherited by the Bolsheviks. In an area known as 'the little hills', it was surrounded by fir and silver birch trees, a beautiful garden, and had a verandah with stunning views. Both Lenin and Nadya grew to love it, though at first she said it was 'so new and strange to us . . . we had never lived anywhere like it, so used as we were to humble dwellings . . . we felt exquisitely embarrassed. We found the smallest of the rooms to live in.'

At Gorki, there were four bodyguards on permanent duty and a staff of three others, including a cook, Spiridon Putin, whose grandson Vladimir would decades later also become the leader of Russia.[2]

Most of the other Communist magnates lived far more lavishly. Lenin had envisaged his 'vanguard' of revolutionaries as an austere, almost monastic order, enduring hardship for the cause. But quickly, as Joffe said, it had become a privileged caste. The Communists had removed themselves from the people.

The pampered lifestyle of the Bolshevik elite – and the corruption that went along with it – began early. Within a few weeks of the coup Lenin was sent a report from the Workers' Section of the Smolny Institute, citadel of the October Revolution, telling him that while Petrograd was going hungry, corrupt Bolshevik officials at the Smolny were selling food by the lorry-load to black marketeers at fantastical prices. 'The hungry workers see the well-dressed tsarinas of the Soviet Party bosses coming out with packets of food and being driven away in their cars,' the report said. 'They say it's just the same as it was in the old days with the Romanovs and their fraüleins . . . They are afraid to complain to Zinoviev [Party boss in Petrograd] since he is surrounded by henchmen with revolvers who threaten the workers when they ask too many questions.' Lenin was furious, though not entirely surprised. He put a stop to the immediate scandal but similar cases were constantly occurring. Lenin was always concerned that corruption – and bureaucracy – might eat into the soul of the Party, but he couldn't, or wouldn't, do anything significant about the problem.

The privileges for Communist apparatchiks started innocuously enough. Regular meals for comrades who worked devotedly for the Revolution at low wages and great sacrifice seemed a reasonable price to pay for loyalty. In early 1918, when food shortages were extreme throughout Russia, Lenin supported a plan to open a restaurant just for Bolshevik activists in Petrograd, on the grounds that you can't make revolution on an empty stomach: 'The workers will understand the necessity of it,' he said.

Some purists thought that Party officials should be more rigorous than the rest of the population about keeping to the same rations as everyone else. They were countermanded by Lenin. 'The heroics of personal self-sacrifice, which is their basic position, are, especially in the present conditions, profoundly petty bourgeois,' he said. 'The working class cannot march in the vanguard of the Revolution without its activists, its organisers. The activists have to be cared for and at the present time . . . must be supported physically.'[3]

The workers might have understood, had the privileges remained at a few decent meals. But the system quickly extended into a range of perks for the Communist elite based on seniority, length of membership, and loyalty. It was a system that had nothing to do with Marxism, but mirrored the complex *chin* system of the Tsarist civil service, with its minutely graded table of ranks which awarded benefits in a highly rigid manner. The Communist *Nomenklatura* system likewise protected the best jobs for Party members. Within two years, 4,000 Bolsheviks and their families were living in the Kremlin and the hotels commandeered by the Party, the Metropol and the National, both by Red Square.

There were 2,000 domestic staff employed by Communist officials within a year of the move to Moscow, and a complex of special shops, a spa, a hairdresser, and restaurants with cooks trained in France. In Petrograd senior Party officials lived in the luxurious Hotel Astoria, recently restored to its former glory of Tsarist times. 'Grishka' Zinoviev lived in a spacious apartment in town, but a suite was always available for his use, as was an assortment of young mistresses.

Soon after Stalin was appointed Commissar for State Control in 1919, the highly influential job that would give him immense power over State appointments and the entire business of government, Lenin ordered him to look at corruption in high places generally, and more specifically 'to carry out an ultra-secret inspection of the Smolny offices' without Zinoviev or other Petrograd officials knowing about it. Stalin didn't often say no to Lenin but on this occasion he refused the order, claiming that spying on comrades would undermine the work of the Party and was against Bolshevik spirit. The reason, of course, was that he didn't want to be loathed by other comrades as the man who would begin to take their privileges away. That was not how he would rise to the top.[4]

Lenin was by no means given the most luxurious of the dachas. Other senior magnates were allotted finer and bigger ones. Trotsky for a while had one of the grandest houses in the region, Arkhangelskay, once owned by Princess Yusupov. Stalin's formerly belonged to an oil millionaire.

Within a few months of the Revolution Gorky was writing to his wife that 'only the commissars lead a pleasant life these days. They steal as much as they can from the ordinary people in order to pay for their courtesans and their unsocialist luxuries.' Lenin didn't have either, but he knew that many of his leading comrades did. Complaints were frequently made by the old-school Bolsheviks, the true believers in a Party whose ranks were increasingly filled with careerists.

A comrade whom Lenin had known for many years wrote to him from Tula in early 1919 with an 'it wasn't like that in my day' message: 'We have cut ourselves off from the masses and made it difficult to attract them. The old comradely spirit in the Party has died completely. It has been replaced by a new one-man rule in which the Party boss runs everything. Bribe-taking has become universal; without it our Communist comrades would simply not survive.' Lenin ignored several similar warnings.

Joffe – one of the uncorrupted officials – returned from Berlin to a job in the Foreign Commissariat and was shocked. He wrote to his great friend Trotsky, 'there is enormous inequality and one's material position largely depends on one's post in the Party; you'll agree this is a dangerous situation. I have been told, for example, that . . . Old Bolsheviks are terrified of being kicked out mainly because they would lose their right to reside in the National Hotel and other privileges connected with this. The old Party spirit has disappeared, the spirit of revolutionary selflessness and comradely devotion.' He coined a new word for the careerist breed of new Communists, which Trotsky would steal and later use often: 'radishes – Red on the outside, White inside'.

Lenin's private office was as unshowy, spartan almost, as his living quarters a little way along the corridor in the Kremlin's main government building. It was a smallish room of no more than eighteen square metres with a worn brown carpet and a potted plant in one corner. It was simply furnished. Every item – left by the Tsar – was functional, except an old clock which fell behind between three and fifteen minutes a day. Constant repairs did not help, yet Lenin insisted it stay: 'another clock would be no different', he said, mysteriously. 'It was the kind of room that might belong to the headmaster of a provincial school,' said one regular visitor.

Lenin allowed no curtains in his office and the blinds were never lowered. His secretary Lidia Fotieva, thirty-six when the government moved to Moscow, said, 'it was as though he felt cramped and stifled in a room cut off from the outside world by lowered blinds'. The temperature had to be kept at 14 degrees Celsius exactly, 'and if it was raised as much as one degree he could not bear it'.*

---

* He sometimes ostentatiously deprived himself of comforts. One day in the freezing winter of 1918 the moulting sheepskin mat put under his desk to keep his feet warm was replaced by a fine polar bear skin. He protested – loudly – and demanded the old mat be returned. 'It's a luxury I don't need . . . altogether unnecessary in a ruined country like this.'

He had three telephones on his desk. The pens and pencils were neatly ordered and sharpened to a stiletto point. There was an inkstand with two small hanging lamps. Pride of place on the desk was a strange statue of an ape sitting on a pile of books staring at an oversized human skull, representing Darwin's theory of evolution.

There were no personal photographs or pictures of family. On the wall opposite his desk hung a large picture of Marx. Next to it on the left was a map of Russia and to the left of that a bronze plaque of Stepan Khalturin, a revolutionary who was executed in 1881 for assassinating a Tsarist general, Fyodor Strelnikov. Lenin said he wasn't commemorating the deed but the 'sheer courage of the young man'. There was a portrait of Chernyshevsky on one wall. He had long hated smoking, but after the attempt on his life he banned it anywhere near him. There was a large 'No Smoking' sign in his office and the adjoining conference room.

Lenin disliked soft, padded chairs. He sat at his desk on a plain wooden chair with a wicker seat and back. There was a chandelier lamp from the ceiling and he never left the office without switching off the light. Every day he tore a page from a wall calendar. In one corner of the office there was a small table laden with maps and atlases, which he enjoyed studying. There were around 2,000 books and dictionaries in several bookcases of his office; he told his secretaries to guard against books being appropriated by visitors. In some volumes he wrote 'Lenin's copy'. Fotieva once said that 'in general, Vladimir Ilyich liked customary, unchanging surroundings. It was as though in this quiet of the room and of things that were always the same and always in the same places he found rest from the rich, varied events of his life.' In other words, which an ultra-loyal and long-standing Bolshevik would never have used, he was deeply conservative, fussy and extremely difficult to work for.

Lenin still adopted many secretive, conspiratorial ways of old. He frequently sent letters and messages to people in Moscow by bicycle courier and told a secretary not to despatch the packet without finding out if the recipient would be there to receive it. 'Seal the letter in an envelope and if necessary sew it and seal it with wax . . . Be sure to write "To Be Opened By Nobody Else" and warn the messenger that the addressee must sign a receipt.' The receipt had to be shown to Lenin. Once one of his letters was delayed and he sent an angry note to Gorbunov, the Executive Secretary of the Sovnarkom: 'Yesterday I discovered that an urgent document I gave Fotieva was forwarded "ordinary" and was several hours late; had I not intervened again it would have been delayed for days. If it happens again I shall resort to severe punishment and dismissals.' On several occasions he threatened to 'arrest on the spot' assistants who didn't live up to his perfectionist standards.

On the other hand Fotieva said that most of the time he was kind in personal matters and good-humoured: 'I think it can be said he worked jovially . . . with a great deal of laughter.' This was something often said about Lenin, which is not always easy to square with his demanding, difficult, domineering and ruthless persona. His sense of irony was acute, often at the expense of someone else. But some of his stern critics noted a broader sense of humour, even occasional silliness. Gorky often remarked that 'Lenin loved to laugh . . . and when he laughed it was with his whole body. On occasions he was overcome with laughter and would laugh sometimes until he cried. He could give to his short characteristic exclamation "hm, hm" an infinite number of modifications, from biting sarcasm to noncommittal doubt. Often in his hm, hm one caught the sound of the keen humour which a sharp-sighted man experiences who sees clearly through the stupidities of life.'

Sometimes he could do things which surprised his closest aides, as Fotieva recalled. 'Once, after a delegation from Bokhara in Central Asia had left at an hour when he usually went home for dinner, the door between his office and the conference room was locked on the inside. Assuming that it had been locked by a Cheka employee who guarded another door, and concerned because Lenin had left instructions for us to carry out, we banged desperately on the door. After several minutes it was opened by a smiling Vladimir Ilyich. He was dressed in Bokharan national costume which the delegation had just given him and he had taken it into his head to try it on.' Sadly no picture of this exists.[6]

Lenin's petulant rages over minor matters became more pronounced after the failed attempt on his life. Nadya was around less often to tame the furies, and few people were strong enough to stand up to him the more powerful he became. He could sometimes lose all perspective and waste time on trivia when Russia and his regime were facing great crises.

In the summer of 1918 he became obsessed with removing Tsarist statues and busts in public places and replacing them with figures from the Enlightenment and socialism – Danton, Darwin, Engels, Herzen and many more. In July 1918, while the battle for grain was raging and on the day he gave instructions to proceed with the murder of the Tsar and his family, he sent a note to Anatoly Lunacharsky in the middle of a Sovnarkom meeting asking if he had recently spoken with Vasily Vinogradov, the official responsible as head of the Statues Commission. 'Not yet,' replied Lunacharsky.

A note came back: 'When are you going [to Petrograd, to discuss various issues] . . . the day, the hour?'.

'Tomorrow at midnight.'

'Telephone Vinogradov and give him an immediate appointment.'

Then, also at the meeting, he wrote a note to Fotieva telling her to call Vinogradov to make an appointment for Lunacharsky. This was happening during a discussion about the Russian food crisis. He wouldn't let the matter drop.

Three weeks later there were more notes on the subject to the Commissar for Enlightenment. 'There's still no outdoor bust of Marx anywhere. I am astonished and outraged that this has not been done. I am reprimanding you and scold you for this criminal negligence. I demand the names of those others responsible so that they can be put on trial. Shame on the saboteurs and loafers.'

His temper could be phenomenal and out of all proportion. In the autumn of 1918 a lift in the Kremlin was out of action for three days. He might have got an assistant to ring up a maintenance team to ask what was going on. But Lenin sent an extraordinary note in his own hand to the commandant of the Kremlin: 'This is the height of disgrace. There are people suffering from heart disease for whom climbing the stairs is harmful and dangerous. I have pointed out a thousand times that this lift must be kept in order and that one person should be responsible for it. I strongly reprimand you and charge you to establish the identity of those guilty of not giving due warning . . . [that the lift wouldn't work].* Let me have a list of the people responsible for the lift once again and the penalties imposed on them.'

He wasted his time on tasks he might have expected others to perform,

---

* In Communist Party speak a reprimand wasn't just a word. Every member had a written Party record which would count towards future jobs and Party positions. A formal reprimand from the leader was a big black mark.

as Trotsky noted. 'Lenin's way of dealing personally with many things cost a great expenditure of energy. Often he would write letters himself, address the envelopes by hand and stick them down.'

Lenin's preferred method for dealing with many administrative problems was to threaten to 'line up and shoot' someone. But few threats were quite as absurd and disproportionate as this, even if it was mostly a petulant outburst. When Stalin was in Tsaritsyn organising revolutionary justice against the kulaks there were problems with his field telephone. Lenin cabled him: 'Threaten to shoot the idiot who is in charge of telecommunications and does not know how to give you a better amplifier and how to get a decent working telephone connection.'

Lenin was taking almost no exercise, he was eating badly, he was working under extreme pressure around the clock and he had been very nearly killed. When, in the past, the 'rages' came upon him or when he suffered from headaches and insomnia, Nadya's answer was to drag him away on holiday. It was no longer so easy. He could go to Gorki for a few days but work weighed heavily there too 'and he couldn't rest properly', she said. Occasionally, though, he could get away for a day or two to hunt.

One of his regular companions was Nikolai Krylenko, a Justice Commissariat official who would later become Chief Prosecutor of the Soviet Union and make rousing performances at Stalinist show trials.* On one of their first outings, near Smolensk in autumn 1918, 'we chased white partridge and black grouse', Lenin wrote to his sister Anna. 'The best thing about it was that for two whole days there wasn't a single telephone call . . . not a single message, not a single question for me to answer.'

They hunted fox – an altogether different sport in Russia than in Britain, or many other countries. In Russia the fox is shot. The idea is to force the animal into a circle from which there is only one exit, where the hunter is waiting. 'The fox came straight at Lenin, who at first did not spot him because the animal's red coat was covered with snow from the spruce trees,' Krylenko recalled. 'When he did see the fox he was transfixed . . . stared and stared and didn't shoot . . . the fox just stood there, still, for a moment before heading off like lightning. "Why didn't you

---

* Until he was 'purged' himself in 1938 and executed, hours after his last court appearance.

429

shoot?" I asked. "Well . . . he was so beautiful and pretty," he replied.'

Sometimes he would hunt just for a Sunday, with Jan Rudzutak, a Latvian bodyguard who later rose to the Soviet Politburo under Stalin. Rudzutak would wake Lenin, 'who was already in his felt boots, a black horse leather jacket and leather trousers, with a packet of sandwiches and a small tin box filled with pieces of sugar for tea'. Once, after an entirely unsuccessful day's sport – more often than not his bag was still empty; power had not made him a better shot – their sleigh broke down forty kilometres from Moscow. They had to walk two and a half kilometres to the nearest railway station, an exhausting journey through snowdrifts.

A hunting trip with Krylenko in late 1919 gave him a health warning. Following another unsuccessful day's sport, they journeyed twenty-five kilometres in a peasant car and stayed two nights in a hayloft. He allowed nobody to serve him tea or food and got it all himself – 'he never complained, though he was clearly fatigued'. The next morning he complained of a bad headache and a few hours later, after wading through a swamp, he slumped down on a tree stump and was unable to move. He said he had 'pins and needles'.[7]

Occasionally Lenin and Nadya went to the theatre in Moscow, but more often than not they left after the first act. 'We went a few times to the Moscow Art Theatre,' said Nadya. 'Once we saw . . . a play about a riverboat disaster on the Mississippi and Ilyich for once liked it immensely . . . We wanted to go to the theatre the next night and they were playing Gorky's *The Lower Depths*. It irritated him . . . After that we gave up going for a while . . . the last time we went we saw Dickens's *The Cricket on the Hearth* . . . he was already bored halfway through the first act. Dickens's middle-class sentimentality got on his nerves and he walked out in the middle of the next act.'

On the whole Lenin's taste in literature, and all art, was highly conservative and utilitarian. He had read for pleasure in adolescence and early adulthood, but rarely after that. For a well-educated, intellectually sophisticated and intelligent man of that era he was surprisingly poorly read – certainly compared to, say, the omnivorous readers Stalin, Trotsky, Bukharin and Lunacharsky among his Bolshevik clique. He knew little about painting or any of the visual arts. He enjoyed music

– particularly Beethoven's piano sonatas and, surprisingly, Wagner – but he seldom listened in case, as he had told Gorky, it would make him go 'soft'.

Lunacharsky described his tastes euphemistically as 'orthodox'. In many ways Lenin was a philistine. 'Throughout his life he had little time to devote to any systematic study of art and always considered himself ignorant on these matters. Since he hated all dilettantism, which was alien to his nature, he disliked to express himself on the subject of the arts. Nonetheless he had very definite tastes: he liked Russian classics, realism in literature and painting.'

Lenin was bewildered by most modern art and literature and was appalled by the idea that the search for the new should destroy the old. He once told Clara Zetkin 'that it took courage for me to admit I am a barbarian in these matters because I neither understand nor enjoy the work of Futurists, Imagists, Cubists, Formalists – and other ists'.

Typically, he had decided opinions, and like most dogmatic people was not much interested in finding out about the things he didn't understand. His curiosity about the arts stopped when he was around twenty-five. His first great love was Turgenev. Lenin carried around a volume of his collected works wherever he was in exile and reread him time and again. He enjoyed the poems of Nekrasov, who wrote beautifully about nature, if at times the work was dripping with sentimentality, as Lenin occasionally admitted.[8]

Usually he judged writers less on artistic merit than on their politics.[*] Lenin acknowledged that Tolstoy was a 'giant' but he loathed the Tolstoyan world view, with its mysticism and pacifism. 'The contradictions in Tolstoy . . . are glaring. On the one hand, we have the great artist, the genius who has not only drawn incomparable pictures of Russian life but has made first-class contributions to world literature. On the other hand, we have the landlord obsessed with Christ. On the one hand, the remarkably powerful, forthright and sincere protest against social falsehood and hypocrisy; on the other the jaded, hysterical sniveller called the Russian intellectual, who publicly beats his breast and wails, "I am a bad, wicked man, but I am practising moral self-perfection; I don't eat meat any more, I now eat rice cutlets." On the one hand, his merciless

---

[*] The exception being Turgenev, whom he loved 'despite the fact that he was a liberal'.

criticism of capitalist exploitation. On the other, the crackpot preaching of submission . . . Tolstoy could not possibly understand either the
working-class movement and its role in the struggle for socialism, or the
Russian Revolution.'*

He hated Dostoyevsky as 'grossly, dangerously reactionary' and
'totally vile', though he admitted his genius and 'vivid images of reality'. Once he described *The House of the Dead* as 'an unsurpassed
achievement because it so remarkably describes not only a Siberian penal colony, but also the whole Russian people living under the
Tsars'.

Lenin loathed most contemporary Russian writing. He was contemptuous of Alexander Blok, whose long poem *The Twelve* published in the
spring of 1918, compared Lenin (not unfavourably) with Jesus and the
Bolsheviks with the Apostles.[†] But Lenin reserved special contempt for
the Futurist poet Vladimir Mayakovsky, whose work became hugely
popular in the early Soviet years, much of it – though by no means all –
in praise of Lenin and the Communists.

He reacted with fury when he heard that the State Publishing House
was printing 5,000 copies of Mayakovsky's *150,000,000* and Lunacharsky was supporting its publication. 'Aren't you ashamed about
voting for this?' he wrote to Lunacharsky. 'It is nonsense, stupidity,
double-eyed pretentious rubbish and affectation. I believe such things
should be published one time out of ten, and *not more than* 1,500 copies

---

* Lenin loathed the portrait of Novodorov in Tolstoy's last novel *Resurrection* (1899),
half idealistic dreamer and half ruthless opportunist revolutionary who has a lot of
Lenin about him. 'The whole of Novodorov's revolutionary activity, though he could
explain it very eloquently and very convincingly, appeared to be founded on nothing
but ambition and the desire for supremacy. But, devoid of these moral and aesthetic
qualities which call forth doubts and hesitations, he very soon acquired a position in
the revolutionary world which satisfied him – that of leader of a Party. Having once
chosen a direction, he never doubted or hesitated, and therefore was certain that he
never made a mistake . . . His self-assurance was so great that it either repelled people
or made them submit to him. And as he carried out his activity among very young people who mistook his boundless self-assurance for depth and wisdom, the majority did
submit to him, and he had great success in revolutionary circles.' How perceptive and
prescient.

† Blok soon became disillusioned by the Revolution, though, and within three years
asked for permission to leave Russia. After long delays it was granted, but his health
was failing and he died in 1921 before he could emigrate.

for libraries and cranks. You should be flogged for your Futurism.' Lunacharsky wrote back saying he didn't like the poem himself but other influential critics did, 'and when Mayakovsky reads in public he is a great success among workers'.

Lenin was not mollified. He wrote to Lunacharsky's deputy, the historian Mikhail Pokrovsky, asking him to intervene. 'Again I am asking you to help in the struggle against Futurism etc. Cannot this be stopped? Let's agree to publish these Futurists twice a year and *in not more than 1,500 copies*. Can't any reliable anti-Futurists be found?' He told Gorky that Mayakovsky 'shouts, invents words, and doesn't go anywhere . . . it's incomprehensible, difficult to read, disconnected, drivel. Is he talented? Very talented even? Hmmm. We shall see.'

At a reception once he was fulminating against the Futurists and Symbolists in general and Mayakovsky in particular when Nadya interrupted him. 'How many times have I told you, Volodya, that you should get Mayakovsky's books . . . then you would understand him too. You just can't get down to it.'

He reacted similarly to modern painting and sculpture. An art student, Mikhail Gorlovsky, accompanied Lenin around an exhibition and heard his thoughts on abstract painting. 'We all belonged to the avant garde and naturally approved of constructivism only. Among the pictures at this exhibition there was one detested artist whom we all contemptuously called "the dauber". But he remained undeterred and went on with his realistic pictures. It was just this work that gave Lenin pleasure. "This, you see, is clear to me. I understand this, so do you, and so do the workers and everybody else. But explain to me what do I see in your pictures? In all these pictures [painted by you] I cannot find either eyes nor noses," he said.'[9]

Lenin had fixed opinions about what art was for in the socialist world. 'Why turn away from real beauty, and discard it for good and all, just because it is "old"? Why worship the new as the god to be obeyed, just because it is "new"? That is nonsense, sheer nonsense,' he told an old comrade two years after seizing power. 'Art belongs to the people. It must have its roots in the broad mass of workers. It must be understood and loved by them. It must be rooted in and grow with their thoughts and feelings and desires. It must arouse and develop the artist in them.

Are we to give cake and sugar to a minority, when the mass of workers and peasants still lack black bread?'

In the early Soviet years, before 'socialist realism' became the prescribed genre in literature, painting, film and even music, the first big new thing in the arts under Communism was 'Prolekult', proletarian culture. The idea was that art would reflect the experience of people in the workplace, and many artists went to factories to produce work collectively in teams rather than individually. 'The "I" of bourgeois culture would yield to the "we" of the new world,' as Lunacharsky said. Large amounts of money were spent on projects like building an orchestra from the sound of clanking factory machinery, and replacing old paintings in museums with often abstract new pieces produced in working conditions by a team of labourers and artists together. This was the first 'cultural revolution' under Communism, which aimed to destroy everything old and start anew. 'It's time for bullets to pepper museums,' said Mayakovsky. 'In the name of our tomorrow, we shall burn Raphael,' wrote another Prolekult propagandist.*

The brain behind Prolekult and the organiser of its grand projects was Lenin's old sparring partner Alexander Bogdanov, who had argued with him in the 1900s about religion and now wanted to reinvent culture. On a large budget, given to him by his old friend Lunacharsky.

Lenin loathed Prolekult for aesthetic and political reasons. He believed that even if socialism destroyed capitalism it had to build on its foundations – a principle as important culturally as it was socially and economically. And he believed that most of the Prolekult 'artists' were poseurs and fakes. But he had to tread warily. He did not interfere with Bogdanov's little empire for a while and allowed it funds as long as it remained clearly an artistic movement. But then Bogdanov and Lunacharsky made a mistake politically. Late in 1919 they over-reached and demanded autonomy for Prolekult as a branch of Soviet society with equal importance to the Communist Party. That is when Lenin stepped in, took away the money, demanded that Prolekult be subsumed within a minor Party body, and banned it from operating within State museums and factories. It went out of fashion. 'Prolekult as an institution is

---

* Operas were produced in rewritten versions. *Tosca* became 'The Battle for the Commune' and Glinka's *A Life for the Tsar* was transformed into 'The Hammer and Sickle'.

a nonsense,' he said. 'One can become a Communist only by enriching one's experience and memory with the knowledge of all the wealth that mankind has produced.'*

To begin with Lenin was more lenient towards books than newspapers. Censorship was established immediately after the Revolution but was mild for the first three years. The State Publishing House, Gosizdat, was founded by Lenin in December 1918 and took a monopoly on book publishing. The following year it had a monopoly on paper production; three years later, on the sale of all books. All manuscripts had to go to a preliminary censor, as they had done in Tsarist times. For the first few years, before Lenin became ill, censorship operated with a light hand. But within a few years some of Russia's best writers had left: Ivan Bunin, Marina Tsvetaeva, Alexei Tolstoy, Boris Zaytsev, Vyacheslav Ivanov. Eventually Gorky left.† When Evgeny Zamyatin, author of the brilliant dystopian novel *We*, emigrated he said: 'Russian literature will only have one future – its past.'

Libraries, the institution beloved by Lenin, the places where he had spent so much of his life, came under attack. From the start of 1920 Nadya's job at the Enlightenment Commissariat was to purge 'unacceptable' books from Russia's public libraries – 'an act of intellectual vampirism', Gorky called it. She held the job until Lenin died. She performed the task with her customary zeal – and she had his blessing. Works by ninety-four authors including Kant, Descartes, William James, Schopenhauer, Pyotr Kropotkin and Ernst Mach were removed. 'This tree of unknowledge was planted by Nadezhda Krupskaya under Lenin, with his direction and advice,' acknowledged the chairman of the Central Libraries Commission later.

---

* At one point, however, when Lunacharsky asked for additional funds for the Bolshoi Opera, Lenin furiously refused. 'What, money for that landlord art? Absolutely no. Instead we should close it down altogether. Workers don't want to go there.' For a short while he followed through with the idea of closing the Bolshoi, but was persuaded out of it and ultimately approved Lunacharsky's budget increase. His initial reaction showed his true opinion, however.

† Though he had an extremely complex relationship not only with Lenin but with the Soviet state. He returned a few years later under Stalin.

46

REDS AND WHITES

'Soviet authority is organised civil war.' Leon Trotsky, July 1919

'White Guards . . . the last dream of the old world.'

Marina Tsvetaeva, July 1919

Lenin said that the Civil War in Russia began on 25 October 1917. 'Of course there will be attempts to overthrow us,' he told his closest comrades at about the same time the Winter Palace fell to the Bolsheviks that evening. He was not a military man, he had no experience of warfare; he had never worn a uniform. But it turned out that he had a good understanding of strategy, he was shrewd at picking efficient generals, he was a ruthless commander-in-chief, and, importantly, he possessed the gift of luck.

Lenin never went to the Front, he did not make stirring speeches to the troops, but he was in charge of military and political strategy. He made the major decisions and allowed his staff officers to work out the details. He pored over maps with his military aides, fired off dozens of encouraging or hectoring telegrams a day, worked around the clock, but left the soldiers to win his war, along with the trusted man he chose to command them: Leon Trotsky.

Above all, Lenin was lucky in his enemy. In contrast to the Bolsheviks' unified leadership, the 'Whites' were fragmented; there were three main armies separated by thousands of miles. Even when they managed to communicate over such vast distances, their leaders often loathed each other and had strong disagreements about strategy and tactics. There were all kinds of practical and military reasons the Whites lost the war: they controlled a smaller population to recruit from, and their problems with communications were insuperable. But the main reason ran deeper. The Whites were stuck in the past – they were 'the last dream of the old world', as the poet Marina Tsvetaeva, one of their passionate devotees, put it. Most Russians – and the minority groups in the empire, from Finland to the Caucasus – may have loathed and feared the Bolsheviks, but they did not want a return to the past. 'We didn't put forward a single new idea,' acknowledged Vasily Shulgin, one of their leaders, in the summer of 1919. And when, after two and a half years, with three million dead from war, disease and hunger, they were defeated, most acknowledged why. 'Their old regime psychology prevented the Whites from facing the new world the revolutions had created,' Pyotr Struve, one of Lenin's old friends turned enemies, said. 'They conducted themselves as though nothing had happened whereas in reality the whole world around them had collapsed and in order to defeat the enemy they themselves had to undergo a rebirth. Nothing so hindered the White movement as this condition of psychologically staying put . . . in circumstances that ceased to exist. Men with this *ancien regime* mentality were immersed in this raging sea of revolutionary anarchy and could not find their bearings. In the revolutionary storm that struck Russia in 1917 even out-and-out restorationists had to turn revolutionaries in the psychological sense, because in a revolution only revolutionaries can find their way.'[1]

The immediate task for Lenin was to build an armed force from the ruins left after defeat by the Germans. He put Trotsky in charge of creating the Red Army, which quickly became an effective fighting unit – or at least, effective enough to beat off the Whites. For orthodox Marxists the very idea of a standing army was anathema: armies had existed to oppress the working class and forestall revolution. But Trotsky realised the Bolsheviks couldn't rely on a ragbag assortment of former private soldiers who had just been beaten in a war, and untrained factory workers like the Red Guards – 'vagabond, unstable elements' as he described them. They needed a proficient unit fast. He saw that the only way was to use Tsarist officers with experience to establish a new army and train the men as soon as possible, and then to lead them. Many Bolsheviks in the existing army, and Party members, objected, first that 'class enemies' were being given special treatment ahead of their own people, and second that the Tsarist officers would betray the regime given half the chance. But Lenin backed Trotsky wholeheartedly. Disloyal officers were 'not as dangerous to the Revolution as the loss of whole regiments through the incompetence of semi-educated Communist commanders who couldn't even read a map', argued Trotsky. Lenin agreed with him.

The Red Army was formed by the Tsarist officer corps. More than 8,000 volunteered immediately after the Revolution, including around fifty generals. They were mostly career army men who would serve a civilian government, whatever its politics. Many had joined up before the Brest-Litovsk Treaty was signed, when it looked as though the Germans might sweep through Russia, and they acted from patriotism. Others wanted to be on the winning side, and bet on the Bolsheviks.

Increasing numbers volunteered when they could see the Red Army was turning into a professional outfit. But the regime needed many more; Trotsky and Lenin resorted to force to press-gang them, and terror threats to keep them loyal. Altogether more than 50,000 Tsarist officers joined the Reds in the Civil War, including doctors, vets and engineers – most of them because their families were held hostage if they didn't. They were told they would be watched by a commissar and if they did anything suspicious they would be shot and/or their families would be arrested. Only those who had relatives in Russia were recruited. Trotsky's 'Special Order Number 30' of September 1918 stated: 'Let the turncoats realise that they are at the same time betraying their own . . . fathers, mothers, sisters, brothers, wives and children.'

He told one of his trusted Bolshevik commanders how to keep the officers in line. 'In case of dubious . . . [activity] put tough commissars over them with revolvers in hand. Give senior commanders the choice: Victory or Death. Don't take your eyes off unreliable commanders. In the event of desertion by a member of the command staff, the commissar pays with his head.'

Trotsky was a harsh disciplinarian. He issued death sentences for 'unjustified retreat' and 'panic-mongering', and Lenin backed him. When other commissars objected to Trotsky's orders to execute a commissar and commander for withdrawing their troops during a siege of a strategic town, Lenin immediately took his side. He wrote a note in red ink on a blank sheet of paper that bore the Sovnarkom seal. It read: 'Comrades: Knowing the strict character of Comrade Trotsky's orders, I am so convinced, so absolutely convinced, of the correctness, expediency and necessity for the success of the cause . . . that I unreservedly endorse this order. Lenin.' He told Trotsky as he was signing it: 'I will give you as many blanks as you want.'

Like Lenin, Trotsky had no military experience and had been a journalist, a pamphleteer, before the Revolution brought him power. But he was decisive, got things done by cutting through red tape and had a clear, logical mind. He was loathed by many Party members for his arrogance and hauteur, his perfectly pressed uniforms and his swagger. But nobody could deny his energy or his showmanship. He criss-crossed Russia in his special train equipped with a printing press, telegraph machines, an orchestra and a film crew and gave electrifying performances to rally often jaded and unwilling troops. He was the Red Army's persuader-in-chief.[2]

The Whites had some competent military leaders, but they quarrelled with each other. Some wanted the monarchy back, most wanted to re-turn the estates to the pre-1917 landlords, a few wanted a Western-style democracy. None wanted independence for the nations within the Rus-sian empire, which was what Lenin was promising – along with land for the peasants and more power for the workers. He didn't mean the pledges, but any lie was justified for the Revolution. 'We can tell the Ukrainians and Latvians anything . . . We have to be tactful at this stage, be careful,' he told Kamenev. 'We can always get . . . [these countries] back later.' The Whites were offering very little and increasingly they found it hard to recruit soldiers. Like the Reds, they had to conscript, used press gangs and resorted to terror.

The three White armies never managed to join forces; the Reds al-ways found ways to cut them off from each other. They all claimed victories, but each was short-lived. There were no fixed fronts for most of the war. It was guerrilla fighting for much of the time between small units, not major armies on battlefields. Some towns and cities changed hands five or six times within two years.

The best of the generals was Anton Denikin, forty-five at the time of the Bolshevik Revolution, head of the Voluntary Army in the south of Russia – the first of the White units to be formed.* He was lowly

---

* Originally it was commanded by Lavr Kornilov, who soon after the October Rev-olution escaped from jail at the Bykhov Monastery, with a group of his entourage of officers. But he was killed in action in April 1918.

born for an Imperial Staff officer, the son of a Polish seamstress and a liberated Russian serf. 'He had irrepressible charm,' acknowledged one of his rivals, 'a tendency to stoutness, a large bald head bordered by trimmed greying hair, a pointed beard and a twirled moustache ... his often stubborn look dissolved into a natural smile and infectious laughter.' His diary shows him to have been extremely bright and imaginative. He understood what was wrong with the White movement and his army, most of whom were more interested in loot than in the war. 'I cannot do anything with my army, I am glad if it simply carries out my orders,' he told Major-General Herbert Holman, head of the British mission to his unit. 'In some areas we control, justice serves as a pretext for personal vendettas and ... is a system of organised lynch law.' He added that sometimes his men, mostly the Cossacks, could not manoeuvre at any speed 'because they are laden down by so much booty'.

In the east, the White forces were commanded by forty-three-year-old Alexander Kolchak, the youngest rear-admiral in the Tsarist navy and an Arctic explorer often called 'Kolchak of the Pole'. Two metres tall, clean-shaven, he was an ill-humoured martinet – 'a man of extraordinary valour and patriotism, but like a big, sick child ... a slave to the idea of serving Russia but irritable and impetuous. He lives in a world of mirages and borrowed ideas.' He styled himself, a shade optimistically, Supreme Ruler of Eastern Russia and Siberia, but one of the observers at Kolchak's 'capital', Omsk, reported that 'in the army there was disintegration, at the headquarters illiteracy and hare-brained schemes, in the government moral decay, panic and graft'. In Omsk, Kolchak lived with his twenty-something mistress while his wife was in exile in Paris with their son. According to his chief aide-de-camp Kolchak's favourite reading, which he kept by his side, was the anti-Semitic *Protocols of the Elders of Zion*. There was desertion from both armies on a massive scale – more than a million in 1918 alone from the Red Army, and four million overall during the war. But about 80 per cent of Kolchak's conscripted peasant army deserted, by far the highest proportion of any unit in the conflict from either side. Eventually, in January 1920, he was betrayed by his own side, who handed him over to the Bolsheviks to face a firing squad.

The 3rd Army in the north-west was the smallest, led by Nikolai

Yudenich, fifty-five, son of a minor court official. During most of the First World War he was commander of Russian forces against the Turks – 'a man of 157 centimetres, weighing 127 kilos, his body was shaped like a coupe, with unnoticeable legs'. He was probably the most liberal politically of the three and accepted Russia should be a free democratic republic. Neither of the other two had any higher opinion of democracy than Lenin did: Denikin described the Constituent Assembly as 'something from the time when Russia was insane'.

None of them recognised independence claims by any of the nations within the empire; all agreed that Russia was 'whole and indivisible'. Kolchak was pressed by Britain, the US and France to pledge independence to Finland and Estonia. He refused. 'History would never forgive me if I give up what Peter the Great won.' The Baltic states and Finland stayed neutral in the Civil War – a great help to the Bolsheviks.[3]

The Western Allies bankrolled the Whites with large amounts of money and arms – and lied about it. They supported the Whites' side, but so half-heartedly that their intervention made no difference. They had no clear policy on how to deal with Lenin's new regime, and no conviction.

They felt entirely justified in doing *something*. The Brest-Litovsk peace had broken treaties with Britain and France. The Germans had moved regiments that were based in the east to the Western Front. The Bolsheviks had seized foreign assets, including dozens of companies owned by American companies, from Singer Sewing Machines to mining interests. They had confiscated individual Westerners' property. They were refusing to pay loans taken out by the Tsarist government. They were threatening to spread revolution everywhere, with campaigns of propaganda and subversion. They were seen as dangerous, but the Allies could not agree on what to do about them.

Within weeks of the October Revolution the British had decided they would help the Whites. 'It is of particular importance to us, even if we cannot ultimately prevent it, to delay as long as possible, the establishment of . . . [Bolshevik] authority,' Lord Milner told Prime Minister Lloyd George. 'Civil War [in Russia] or even the continuance of chaos and disorder would be an advantage for us.'

The British had a few thousand troops in the ports of Archangel and

Murmansk in northern Russia, who had been there since the start of the First World War to supply the Russian military and to help as advisers. After the Bolshevik coup they remained for most of the Civil War, occasionally skirmishing with the Red Army, but now supplying Kolchak and Denikin. Officially they claimed they were neutral and denied they were helping the Whites, but they were fooling nobody, certainly not Lenin. The British were by far the biggest financial backers of the Whites. Altogether they gave them more than £100 million, a vast sum at the time, and sent several spies to help mount plots to undermine the Bolshevik government.

The Americans lied too, principally to hide the truth from their own people, rather than to deceive the Russians. The US Secretary of State, Robert Lansing, was a passionate anti-Communist, a Cold Warrior before the term was invented. 'Bolshevism is the most hideous and monstrous thing that the human mind has ever conceived,' he said. 'It finds its adherents among the criminal, the depraved and the mentally unfit.' He wanted to help the Whites, but secretly and semi-legally. American law forbade the government granting loans to independent armies or mercenaries. Lansing wrote to Walter Page, American Ambassador to Britain, on 13 December 1917 with a scheme to get around the US Congress: 'The only practicable course seems to be for the British and French governments to finance the . . . enterprise, in so far as it is necessary, and for this Government to loan them the money to do so. In that way we could comply with the statute and at the same time strengthen armed opposition to the Bolsheviks.'[4]

But the American President and Lloyd George were reluctant to commit themselves too far while there was still a war to win against Germany. And when the First World War was over, it was too late. They approved money for the Whites, and they encouraged the Czech Brigade to fight the Bolsheviks, whose original whose mission was supposed to be crossing Russia eastwards on its way back to Europe, to fight the Austrians. The Americans were not prepared to go further. One of the hypotheticals of history is: how would Russia have progressed if the Whites had won the Civil War? But the Allies were never prepared to fight a full-scale war against the Bolsheviks – the only way a White victory could have been achieved.

*

There was savage barbarity on both sides, partly because neither Red nor White could depend on the loyalty of the people under their control. For the most part the civilian population, mostly peasants, had a 'plague on both your houses' view. They hated the Bolshevik grain requisitions and the war against the kulaks, but the Whites never accepted that there had been a revolution on the land and wanted to turn the clock back and restore the estates to the old landowners. Both sides were forcing civilians to join their armies, but the peasants didn't want to fight. Millions voted with their feet and deserted, risking death and hard labour sentences if they were caught.

Lenin followed events anxiously from his map room in the Kremlin. 'If we don't conquer the Urals by next winter [1919] we will lose the Revolution I'm sure,' he told Zinoviev, and he wrote frequently in a similar worried tone. He deluged commanders and provincial Communist Party bosses with directives and telegrams designed to motivate or terrify. When things went well he would occasionally celebrate. Simbirsk was captured by the Reds while he was convalescing after being shot by Kaplan. 'The seizure of Simbirsk, my home town, is the most health-giving and best bandage for my wounds,' he told Trotsky on 10 September 1918. 'I felt an unprecedented surge of courage and strength.'

But on the whole the cables were fearful, violent and demanded an ever-increasing use of terror. They make the grimmest of reading. The word 'shoot' was one he used casually. In September 1918 he told the Party boss in Saratov 'temporarily to appoint your own army commanders and shoot conspirators and waverers without asking anyone or idiotic red tape'. A few days later he wrote to the leaders of the Soviet in the Caucasus: 'if there is an offensive in Baku [where there were big oil refineries] . . . make preparations to burn Baku down *totally*'. When Kazan was besieged a month later he cabled Trotsky: 'There must be no question of taking pity on the town and putting matters off any longer . . . merciless annihilation is what is vital once it is established that Kazan is enclosed in an iron ring.' He ordered a commander that 'the taking of hostages from the bourgeoisie and from officers' families must be stepped up in view of the increased instances of treason'. Another was told a few days later: 'It would be a disgrace to fail to punish by shooting, absence from duty and evasion of mobilisation orders.' There were scores in a similar tone.[5]

Lenin faced a series of skirmishes inside his own Cabinet which were to develop into a major split in the Communist Party after he was gone. Immediately after the Revolution Lenin quickly saw how Trotsky and Stalin loathed each other; their rivalry soon burst into the open in the Civil War. Lenin's tactic was to play them off against each other.

Their mutual feelings were clear from the first Sovnarkom meeting at the Smolny immediately after the coup. Both of them had arrived early and behind a wooden partition overheard 'a conversation of a rather tender nature' between Pavel Dybenko and Alexandra Kollontai, almost twenty years his senior, who had recently started an affair which had become the gossip of the Bolshevik Party. Stalin and Trotsky looked at each other, surprised. Stalin was amused but Trotsky, not exactly prudish in his own behaviour, was shocked. As Trotsky later recounted, the Georgian, 'with a kind of unexpected jauntiness and pointing his shoulder towards the partition, said smirking, "That's him, with Kollontai, with Kollontai."' Trotsky was offended. 'That's their affair,' he snapped. 'Stalin sensed he had made a mistake . . . His gesture and laughter seemed out of place and unendurably vulgar, especially on that occasion and in that place . . . he never again tried to engage me in conversation of a personal nature. Stalin's face changed. His yellow eyes flashed with the glint of malice.'

The first sign of major friction came when Stalin was despatched to Tsaritsyn in June 1918 to supervise the campaign against the kulaks in the southern Russian region. It was a Party post and technically he wasn't supposed to interfere directly in the Red Army, Trotsky's sphere. But within days he wrote to Lenin complaining that in Tsaritsyn, an important army base, there was 'a bacchanal of profiteering'. He demanded military powers to deal with the 'disaster' of the Southern Front so he could be more rigorous about appointments. 'If Trotsky will thoughtlessly hand out credentials right, left and centre . . . you may be sure that within a month everything here in the north Caucasus region will be lost to us indefinitely.' He wanted authority to dismiss commanders, 'and the absence of a piece of paper from Trotsky won't stop me'. When Trotsky heard, he was enraged. 'I categorically insist on Stalin's recall,' he cabled the Kremlin. Lenin patched up the quarrel for a while. But it flared up regularly. At one point a few months later Stalin tried to get the Communist Party's Central Committee to dismiss Trotsky as head of the Red Army. He lost and Trotsky was given a vote of confidence. It was a temporary blow to Stalin, and Lenin attempted again to make peace.

Another time Trotsky complained that Stalin had been drinking wine from the Tsar's Kremlin cellars. Stalin was summoned by Lenin to a triangular showdown. 'If the rumour got around at the Front that there was drinking at the Kremlin it will make a bad impression.' Stalin tried to laugh off the matter. 'How can we Caucasians get along without a bit of wine?' he protested. Lenin on this occasion backed Stalin. 'You see, the Georgian cannot do without an occasional glass of wine.' That ended the discussion and, as Trotsky said later, 'I capitulated without a struggle.' Lenin knew that the squabbling between the two rivals would one day scar the Party he founded, but he did nothing to settle the issue once and for all. Lenin believed he needed them both.[6]

At one point in the late summer of 1919 Denikin's Volunteer Army was 350 kilometres from Moscow. But that was the high point of their success. They were overstretched, could not maintain their supply lines, and when they faced a counter-attack they were forced to retreat. To supporters such as Marina Tsvetaeva the Whites were the 'youth and glory of Russia', the only real hope of defeating the Bolsheviks.* But to most Russians they seemed as savage as the Bolsheviks. Their defeat was political as well as military; they never received enough support to

---

* She wrote a series of haunting poems, *The Swans' Encampment*, about the Civil War and the struggle against the Bolsheviks. One was called simply 'White Guards' and embodied all she genuinely believed they stood for:
White Guards, Gordian Knot
Of Russian Valour.
White Guards, white mushrooms
Of the Russian folksong.
White Guards, white stars
Not to be crossed from the sky.
White Guards, black nails
In the Ribs of the Antichrist.

defeat a regime that was ably, if ruthlessly, led. Terror was a weapon Lenin was always prepared to use, but he operated through guile, acumen and sound judgement too. He had a clear goal and could inspire others towards reaching it. The Whites, as an American observer of the war put it, 'seldom rose above anarchic warlordism'. Kerensky agreed. He said in the summer of 1919, 'there is no crime the . . . [White armies] would not commit. Executions and torture have been committed in Siberia . . . and elsewhere and often the populations of whole villages have been flogged, including the teachers and intellectuals.'

In one village, Lezhanka, near Rostov, officers slaughtered sixty peasants in cold blood, including old men and women, in reprisal for an earlier attack on White Guards by the Reds. Hundreds of villagers were stripped and whipped while other groups of Volunteer Army officers stood by and watched, many of them laughing. It was a routine attack; there were scores of incidents like it. 'We had not brought pardon and peace with us, but only the cruel sword of vengeance,' admitted Pyotr Wrangel, one of the most senior White commanders.[7]

As so often in Russian history, it was the Jews who were directly targeted. As Denikin's army retreated from Moscow it launched an orgy of bloody pogroms. The commander did nothing to stop them while his political officers spewed out anti-Semitic propaganda: all Communists were Jews, it was the Jews who murdered the Tsar. Trotsky – 'real name Bronstein, the Jewish mass killer' – was singled out as the arch criminal.* Bolshevism was blamed on Jews so it was entirely legitimate to slaughter them, the White propaganda seemed to argue.

There were hundreds of pogroms and Volunteer Army officers were enthusiastic participants. Between 1 and 5 October 1919 Cossack soldiers attacked the Jewish quarter of Kiev, demanding money and killing and raping while their officers urged them on; 'Yids are killing our people and they all support the Bolsheviks,' one officer told his men.

Even Vasily Shulgin, the anti-Semitic Duma member who witnessed the Tsar's execution, was shocked. 'At night the streets of Kiev are in the grip of medieval terror. In the midst of silence and deserted streets

---

* When Trotsky said that while racially, yes, he was a Jew, he hated Judaism and was an internationalist, the Chief Rabbi of Moscow, Yakov Mazeh, observed: 'It was the Trotskys who made the Revolution, but the Bronsteins who paid the bills.'

suddenly there begins a wail that breaks the heart . . . whole streets, seized with fear howl.' An eyewitness described the horror: 'The Cossacks divided into separate groups, each of three or four men. A group would break into a Jewish home and their first word would be "money" . . . They would demand the head of the household and put a rope around his neck. A Cossack would take one end of the rope and another take the other end and begin to choke him. If there was a beam in the ceiling they would begin to hang him. If anyone burst into tears or begged for mercy – even a child – they beat him to death. Of course the family handed over every last kopeck. When there was no money the Cossacks choked the victim until he lost consciousness and they loosened the rope. The victim would fall to the floor, then the Cossacks would . . . pour cold water on him and bring him back to his senses. Then they would start again. Sometimes this would be repeated five or six times.'

In Chernobyl Jews were herded into the synagogue and the building was set on fire. In Charkan they raped hundreds of girls and forced their families to watch. As they were being defeated by the Bolsheviks, the Whites slaughtered about 150,000 civilians.

There were a few pogroms by the Reds, though an almost insignificant number compared to the Volunteer Army's orchestrated savagery. Reports reached Lenin in early 1920 that in Zhytomyr, capital of Volyn Province, 'a new wave of pogroms has swept the district . . . Divisions of the First Cavalry Army [a Bolshevik corps] have been attacking the Jewish population, killing and looting.' He received news from Ukraine that Red detachments had killed 'in Rogachov more than thirty Jews, in Barakopva fourteen. The district of Berdichev has been sacked . . . Gorashki and Cherniakov have been completely plundered.'

Lenin ordered a full investigation and tried to speak out against anti-Semitism, though he knew that would probably do the Bolshevik cause little good. When he made sixteen three-minute propaganda gramophone records to be played in villages and town halls he chose as one of them 'On Pogroms' and another 'The Persecution of the Jews'. 'It is not the Jews who are the workers' enemies,' he said. 'It is the capitalists of all the countries. The great majority of Jews are themselves workers . . . They are our brothers being oppressed by the capitalists, our comrades in the struggle for socialism. The Jews have their kulaks, their exploiters and their capitalists, just like the Russians. Just like all nations . . . It is the capitalists who inflame hatred against the Jews.'[8]

One leading figure among the Allies was honest enough to admit that the West was helping the White forces – and wanted to support them more effectively. Winston Churchill, the Secretary of State for War, said Bolshevism 'should be strangled in its cradle' and he continually urged for a full-scale military intervention alongside the Whites to oust Lenin. To him, Communism 'was not a creed, it is a pestilence. Bolsheviks are the enemies of the human race and must be put down at any cost.' Never one to exaggerate, he said that Russia 'is being reduced . . . to an animal form of barbarism. Civilisation is being extinguished over gigantic areas while Bolsheviks hop and caper like . . . ferocious baboons.'

He had slightly increased the number of British troops in Murmansk and Archangel to 3,000, though the Cabinet decided they should not take part in combat operations. But he upped the supply of weapons to the Whites. At his instigation, amid much secrecy, a consignment of M Weapons, poison gas canisters, was despatched to Russia to be used by White forces. Fifty thousand were sent, along with the equipment to fire them. A total of 2,717 were used against Bolshevik forces, though civilians became collateral damage too. 'Fullest use is now to be made of gas shell with your forces or supplied by us to [White] forces,' Churchill wrote to the commander of British forces in Russia.

Some senior officers were worried that information about the deployment of British chemical weapons would become public, but Churchill remained convinced that gas was a reasonable weapon. He said he would 'very much like the Bolsheviks to have it [a chemical attack] if we can afford the disclosure'. He thought it would be the most effective means to crush the Bolsheviks before it was too late.* When other Cabinet members objected he accused them of 'squeamishness'. He said: 'Gas is a

---

* He had the same attitude to gassing rebellious tribes in northern India and Afghanistan. He was frequently told by Lloyd George to tone down his rhetoric against the Bolsheviks. After one outburst in Cabinet, the PM wrote asking him to shut up about Russia. 'I wonder whether it is any use my making one last effort to induce you to throw off this obsession, which if you will forgive me for saying so, is upsetting your balance. I again ask you to let Russia be, at any rate for a few days.'

more merciful weapon than the high-explosive shell, and compels an enemy to accept a decision with less loss of life than any other agency of war.' Throughout 1918 there were scores of chemical attacks against the Bolsheviks, but they were less effective than Churchill and his generals had hoped.

Churchill wrote repeatedly to Woodrow Wilson urging a far more committed intervention, but the President was wary. He tried diplomacy instead. He proposed a peace conference in early 1919 between the Reds and the Whites, on one of the Princes Islands in the Sea of Marmara near Constantinople. Lenin was willing at least to talk about talks. He thought that with the war against Germany won, the Allies would not stop at supporting the Whites, but would combine forces to destroy the Soviet regime. He was willing to discuss a deal that would leave the Bolsheviks in power over most of Greater Russia. And he told the commissars that he would be prepared to negotiate repaying historic loans from the West and compensating foreigners for confiscated property. It was always unlikely that a deal would be struck, but Lenin said he would send a delegation to the talks anyway. Kolchak and the Whites refused: they wouldn't discuss a settlement that involved granting independence to the nationalities.

Wilson tried once again. He sent the author and millionaire diplomat William Bullitt as a peace envoy, but his efforts came to nothing. By late summer 1919 the Reds were on the way towards winning the Civil War and Lenin was less inclined to compromise. The Whites would not budge on independence for the other nations in the empire. Their position exasperated Wilson, at a time during the Versailles Conference when he was proposing to give self-determination to dozens of new countries from the ashes of the Austrian and Ottoman empires. The Americans and the British ditched the Whites. 'We cannot afford to continue with such a costly intervention in an interminable Civil War,' said Lloyd George in autumn 1919. 'Other methods must be found to restore peace.'

It was a devastating blow for the Whites, whose defeat was accompanied by a mass migration from Russia. Between 1.5 and two million people left the country within two years of the Revolution, most of them educated, professional people, the intelligentsia. Many would have agreed with Zinaida Gippius, in French exile, who mused bitterly: 'We know why the White movement perished . . . the leaders miscalculated the strength of the enemy . . . but the main reason was that it was totally abandoned, both internally and externally. It was abandoned not only by the Russians, but also by its perfidious allies of yesterday.'

By the end of 1919 Lenin no longer feared outside attack, though there was still a 'cordon sanitaire' around Russia and an economic blockade: his regime was not recognised internationally. He was confident he would not be ousted by an invading army. He still faced opposition internally, but it could be charmed, deceived, intimidated or, finally, terrorised into submission. It was from the end of the Civil War that Lenin can be said to be Russia's dictator, the first Red Tsar.[9]

47

FUNERAL IN MOSCOW

'For romantics, love holds the first place in a person's life – higher than anything else. And until recently I was nearer to believing that than I am now. True, for me love was never the only thing . . . There was also public activity . . . there were times in the past . . . where I've sacrificed myself for the good of the cause . . . In my life, love still occupies a big place, it makes me suffer a lot, and takes up a lot of my thoughts. But still, not for a minute do I cease to recognise that, however painful for me, love and personal relationships are nothing compared to the needs of the struggle.' Inessa Armand, 11 September 1920

As dawn was breaking in Moscow on 11 October 1920 a train formed of just two railcars drew into Kazan Station. Waiting on the platform were an honour guard standing to attention, a solemn-looking welcoming committee of twenty comrades dressed in black, and a catafalque with two white horses. A team of sentries climbed up to the rear car of the train, and reappeared carrying a coffin covered by a black cloth with a red overlay. They placed the coffin on the carriage and the cortège marched slowly a kilometre and a half through the centre of the city to the giant House of Unions,* a big neo-classical building in the Tverskoy district close to the Kremlin. An early-morning funeral procession of evident celebrities was a strange sight in Moscow, so many people at the start of their working day stopped to stare. Soon a buzz went around among the onlookers: wasn't Lenin among the mourners? Hundreds of people joined in, without at first knowing whose coffin they were following.

The closed casket was placed on a raised platform in the centre of the

---

* The magnificent building was built as the Assembly of Nobles in the mid-eighteenth century and later, during Stalin's Great Purge, would be where the big show trials took place.

House of Unions, where the body would lie in state for one day, guarded overnight by four Red Army officers and groups of Bolshevik Party workers in hour-long shifts.

The funeral procession on a sunny and crisp autumn morning the next day was far bigger. Thousands of people turned out to pay their respects as the catafalque was driven the short distance to Red Square, where the body would be buried by the East Wall of the Kremlin.

While the Bolshoi Theatre Orchestra played Chopin, Mozart and Beethoven, most of the Communist Party magnates arrived at the burial place, including Lenin, 'his head bare, in an autumn coat'. As the body was lowered into the grave the crowd sang the 'Internationale'. There were dozens of wreaths neatly placed by the side of the wall. One, of white hyacinths with a red ribbon, was simply inscribed, 'To Comrade Inessa, from V. I. Lenin'.

No one had ever seen him so overcome by emotion in public. Kollontai said he 'was unrecognisable at Inessa's funeral. He walked with his eyes closed and at every moment we thought he might fall to the ground.' Nadya was weeping openly, but gripped Lenin by the arm as strongly as she could to prop him up.

'I never saw such torment. I never saw another human being so completely absorbed by sorrow,' Balabanova remembered. 'At one point I found myself in the immediate vicinity of Lenin. Not only his face but his whole body expressed so much sorrow that I dared not greet him, not even with the slightest gesture. It was clear he wanted to be alone with his grief. He seemed to have shrunk . . . his eyes seemed drowned in tears held back with effort.'[1]

She had been feeling ill for months, exhausted, overworked and complaining of fevers. In March 1919, at the height of the Civil War, Inessa had gone on a tricky diplomatic mission to France as head of a Red Cross delegation to negotiate the return of 45,000 Russian POWs on the Western Front. She had a premonition that she would die before Lenin. The day before she went she wrote to her daughter Inna: 'I'm enclosing a letter for Sasha and Fedya [her sons] and a third one for Ilyich. *Only you* are to know about the third one . . . keep it to yourself for the time being. When we get back I'll tear it up. If something happens to me . . . then you must give the letter personally to V. I. The way to do it is to go to *Pravda* where Maria Ilyinichna works. Give her the letter and say it's from me and personal only for him . . . Meanwhile, hang onto it.'

The mission lasted two months. When she returned she looked painfully thin, almost haggard, and every bit her now forty-five years of age. Lenin saw a lot of her – she came to the Kremlin often, as did her children, and he sometimes visited her nearby flat. He worried about her health. When she came down with a series of ailments in the winter of 1919–20 he sent physicians to check on her, English and French newspapers for her and numerous notes along the lines of one in February 1920: 'Dearest Friend, I wanted to telephone you . . . when I heard you were ill, but the phone doesn't work . . . I'll tell them to repair it.'

A few weeks later: 'Please say what's wrong with you. These are appalling times: there's typhus, influenza, Spanish flu, cholera. I've just got up and I'm not going out. Nadya has a temperature of nearly 39 and wants to see you. What's your temperature? Don't you need some medicine? Tell me frankly.'

He ordered his office to send round a doctor, and hours later wrote, 'Has the doctor been? I beg you earnestly not to go out and tell your daughter from me that I want them to watch you and not to let you out 1) until your temperature is back to normal and 2) with the doctor's permission.'

The letters may not have been as passionate as they had been but he was still always calling her '*ty*' and he was showing care for her. 'Inessa, I rang to find out what size galoshes you take? I hope you get hold of some. Write and tell me how you are. Has the doctor been?'

In August 1920 she told him she was feeling exhausted, as though her 'lungs were collapsing', she was depressed about her work, and she needed a complete rest. She had always loved the sea and she wanted to go to the South of France where the air was clear. He convinced her against France, in his last letter to her dated 20 August: 'Can't I do something for you . . . get you into a sanatorium? I'll do anything with great pleasure. If you go to France I will, of course, help with that, too. I'm a bit concerned, in fact I am afraid, I'm really afraid, that you'll get into trouble there. They will arrest you and keep you there a long time. You must be careful. Wouldn't it be better to go to Norway . . . or Holland. Or Germany? . . . Best not to go to France, where they could put you inside . . . If you don't fancy a sanatorium, why not go to the south? To Sergo [Ordzhonikidze] in the Caucasus. Sergo will arrange rest, sunshine . . . he can fix it all up. Think about it.'

On the same day he wrote as head of the government a 'to whom it may concern' note. 'I request that you help in every way possible to arrange the best accommodation and treatment for the writer, Comrade Inessa Armand, and her son. I request that you give complete trust and all possible assistance to these Party comrades, with whom I am personally acquainted.' He also called Ordzhonikidze, asking him to put himself out over Inessa's safety and accommodation in Kislovodsk, and told his secretaries to help see her off and make sure she was comfortable on her journey south.[2]

Almost immediately she fell victim to a cholera epidemic sweeping through the southern Caucasus. Her final illness was ghastly. She drifted in and out of consciousness, but in her lucid moments she kept a harrowing account of her disease and a painfully honest, moving diary full of revelations about her feelings for Lenin.

On 1 September 1920 she wrote in her diary: 'Now I have time I'm going to write every day, although my head is heavy and I feel as if I've been turned into a stomach that craves food the whole time . . . I also feel a wild desire to be alone. It exhausts me even when people around me are speaking, never mind if I have to speak myself . . . I hardly ever laugh or smile because I'm prompted to by a feeling of joy, but just because one should smile sometimes. I'm also struck by my present indifference to nature. I used to be so moved by it. And I find I like people less now. I used to approach everyone with a warm feeling. Now I am indifferent to everyone . . . I'm bored with almost everyone. I have warm feelings left only for the children and V. I. In all other respects it's as if my heart has died. As if, having given up all my strength, all my passion to V. I. and the work, all the springs of love have dried up in me, all my sympathy for people, which I used to have so much of. I have none left, except for V. I. and my children and a few personal relations . . . And people can feel this deadness in me, and they pay me back in the same coin of indifference or even antipathy (and people used to love me) . . . I'm a living corpse and it's dreadful!'

From her last diary entry on 11 September it is clear she knew she would soon die. Lenin would have wholeheartedly approved of her last words. 'For romantics, love holds the first place in a person's life – higher than anything else. And until recently I was nearer to believing that than I am now. True, for me love was never the only thing . . . There was also public activity . . . there were times in the past, not a few instances, where I've sacrificed myself for the good of the cause. But the importance of love, compared to the cause, has become altogether less, it cannot be compared. In my life love still occupies a big place, it makes me suffer a lot, and takes up a lot of my thoughts. But still, not for a minute do I cease to recognise that, however painful for me, love and personal relationships are nothing compared to the needs of the struggle.'

Lenin knew that she was seriously ill, and was wracked with guilt that he had sent her to the Caucasus where diseases were rife and there was still occasional fighting and post-Civil War chaos. Early on the morning of 25 September he had heard that she was much improved and that both she and her son André were well. Later that same afternoon he received a telegram. 'Top Priority and Personal. To Lenin. Unable to save Comrade Inessa Armand sick with cholera. She died on 24 September. Sending body back to Moscow. Signed Nazarov.'

Lenin insisted that the body be sent back to Moscow and insisted on a state funeral, but it was two weeks before it was returned. Lenin was infuriated by the delays and wrote a string of cables to officials demanding speedier action. With famine and disease throughout southern Russia, it was no easy matter to secure a railway car and a coffin from outlying regions. Almost everyone was being buried without coffins. When Inessa lay in state she was in a lead-lined coffin, closed, as she had been dead for some time in the heat of late summer.[3]

After Inessa died her younger children spent long periods at the Kremlin and summers at Gorki. Nadya and Lenin unofficially adopted them. 'Vladimir Ilyich and Nadezhda Konstantinovna became the guardians of my sister, my youngest brother and me,' said Inna. The childless couple seemed to enjoy the role.

Varvara stayed in the Kremlin apartment for many months after the funeral. Nadya wrote to the girls often, usually beginning the letters 'My beloved daughter', and constantly fussed over their health and diet. They returned the affection. Years later, whenever either of them lived in Moscow they visited her every Sunday.

When in July 1921 Varvara and Alexander went to Tehran, Lenin ordered Theodore Rothstein, the Russian Ambassador to Iran, to keep an eye on them: 'I hope you will manage to devote some little time to Inessa's children.' Lenin wrote to the boys regularly, sending André annotated chess puzzles he had set himself.*

Both of them tried to keep Inessa's memory alive. He wrote to Kamenev, Chairman of the Moscow Soviet, on 24 April 1921, asking if there could be a permanent memorial to her in Red Square and flowers planted around her grave. She was given a simple granite gravestone. Soon after she died a collection of essays was published about her life as a socialist and her achievements. The warmest and longest was by Nadya, who for the rest of her life kept a picture of Inessa on her desk. The only other photographs were of her mother and Lenin.[4]

---

* Varvara graduated from the Art Institute in Moscow in 1927. She worked in a textile factory for seven years, then became a teacher of graphic design and an artist in her own right – named an 'Honoured Artist' of the USSR after the Second World War. There was a retrospective of her work, in the socialist-realist tradition, in 1977. She died in 1987. Inna lived in Berlin, where she worked in the Comintern, and married Hugo Eberlein, a leading German Communist. They had a daughter, Inessa. They left Germany in 1933. But even Nadya's protection couldn't save Eberlein from Stalin's terror. At one point, after the Hitler/Stalin pact, he came near to being handed over to the Gestapo. He escaped that fate but succumbed to one as ghastly: he died in the Gulag in 1941. Until her retirement in 1961 Inna worked at the Institute of Marxism-Leninism, editing sections of Lenin's collected works. She wrote a memoir in 1971 which contained letters between Inessa and her children. Her son Fyodor joined the air force as an instructor – the only one of Inessa's children not to join the Communist Party. He died (naturally) in 1936. André joined the Moscow Militia; he died at the Front in 1944. Alexander was a minor diplomat and remained a Stalin apologist until his death in the 1960s.

48

THE 'INTERNATIONALE'

'The policy and practice of the Russian government has always been
to push forward its encroachments as fast and as far as the apathy and
want of firmness of other governments would allow it to go, but always to stop and retire when it met with decided resistance and then
to wait for the next favourable opportunity to make another spring on
its intended victim.'

Henry John Temple, 3rd Viscount Palmerston (1784–1865)

'No nation that enslaves another nation can be free.'

Vladimir Lenin, *Imperialism: The Highest Stage of Capitalism*, 1917

In November 1920, a month after Inessa's funeral, the grande dame of
German socialism Clara Zetkin, a good friend of Nadya's, visited Moscow and had a long interview with Lenin. 'As we spoke, his face shrank
before my eyes,' she told a Berlin comrade. 'Furrows great and small en-
graved themselves deeply on it. And every furrow was drawn by a grave
trouble or a gnawing pain. An expression of unspoken and unspeakable
suffering was on his face.' Zetkin thought his appearance had something
to do with Inessa Armand's death – but he had a more pressing immediate concern, she pointed out. The Soviet regime was losing a war against
Poland and Russia was being humiliated.[1]

The newly independent Poles started the war. With England and
France's backing, they invaded Ukraine in spring 1920.* The Poles

---

* Though not all the Allied leaders supported the Poles. The former British Prime
Minister Herbert Asquith wondered why one of the first things a desperately poor
country – dependent on food aid from America – should do is to provoke a war. He said
in August 1920: 'There . . . [Poland] was six months ago, a population stricken with
disease and famine, and it is no exaggeration to say on the verge of national bankruptcy,
and it was under these circumstances, that she started the campaign . . . it was a purely
aggressive adventure, a wanton enterprise.'

and Ukrainians had had complicated territorial and religious conflicts over many centuries; but now a brash and confident Polish leader, Marshal Józef Piłsudski, renewed historic claims to lands that had formed the Polish empire of the seventeenth century. Piłsudski had been involved with Lenin's brother in the plot to murder Tsar Alexander III – he spent five years in exile in Siberia – but he was a Polish nationalist, not a socialist, and he had no sympathy with Lenin or the Bolsheviks.

By early 1920 the Civil War in Russia was won by the Reds, though there were still some mopping-up operations to complete. Within eighteen months of Poland's new independence, Piłsudski took his opportunity. He led an army of 70,000 Poles eastwards, and seized much of Byelorussia and Lithuania. He captured Kiev on 7 May, promising 'to liberate Ukraine from Russia'.

Lenin the great Marxist internationalist appealed to patriotism and the Right: 'We shall teach the Poles a lesson they will never forget,' he said. Thousands of former soldiers from the Tsarist army volunteered in a force to counter-attack the Poles and beat them back in a defensive war to recapture Ukraine. It was led by a new young war hero, Mikhail Tukhachevsky, aged just twenty-seven. The glamorous new poster boy of the Revolution could not claim unimpeachable proletarian roots: he was from an aristocratic house that could trace its ancestry back to a twelfth-century noble clan of the Holy Roman Empire which had served the rulers of Kievan Rus'. But his mother had been a servant girl. He was hugely popular with the men in the Red Army, and when he pledged fealty to the Communist Party the magnates in the Kremlin came to rely on him as a military saviour. His army rolled back the Poles, who appealed to the West for help to reach a peace settlement.[1]

Lenin always believed that world revolution was just around the corner. There had been short-lived socialist coups in Berlin and Munich in 1919, suppressed by the German army and a militia of anti-Communists, the Freikorps. For five months in Hungary a Soviet government under Béla Kun had modelled itself on Lenin's regime, until it was defeated in August 1919 by an authoritarian figure on the Right, Admiral Miklós Horthy.

Lenin's faith was undimmed: the worldwide revolution was taking rather longer than he thought, but it was coming. The uprisings in Germany failed, yet 'only a blind man can fail to see the ferment in Germany' he said in June 1919, a week or so after Rosa Luxemburg, inspiration for the Berlin rising, had been killed. In March 1920 he believed that 'the day is not far off when we shall march hand in hand with a German Soviet government'. He told the British journalist Arthur Ransome at around the same time, 'You would have to be a fool not to realise that socialist revolution is looming in Britain.' Ransome shook his head and suggested that perhaps the British were not a revolutionary people. Lenin told him severely that he wasn't looking at things in a 'broad and objective' way.

For the first two years after his coup Lenin was convinced that his regime could not survive unless there was revolution elsewhere in the West. The Soviet government would 'be encircled and we will be snuffed out', he told Trotsky. He had helped the Hungarian Communists with money and though endless messages to Kun offering advice, though there was little he could do directly to aid other revolutionaries.

But he took the establishment of the Comintern (Communist International) seriously. This was to be the group of socialist parties throughout Western Europe and the US that would spark the revolutions – as the Bolsheviks had done in Russia. The idea was based on his version of a Marxist principle: 'The interests of socialism, of world socialism, are superior to national interests, the interests of the State.' But, as so often, Lenin's need to control organisations, centralise them and dominate them turned the principle on its head. The Comintern was run from Moscow and soon became a branch of Soviet foreign policy. Its founding rules stated that if members wanted to be considered Communist Parties, if they wanted any help or support from Russia, all had to be Leninist-type organisations run like the Bolsheviks. They must expel from their ranks 'moderates and centrists'; they had to try to take over trade unions; and they had to toe the Moscow line on almost everything. In the long term this did immense harm to the idea of world revolution and set back Lenin and his successors' dreams of spreading socialism. Portraying the far-Left parties elsewhere as stooges of the Russians played into the hands of the Right.[2]

*

With the Poles back behind their own border, most of the other Kremlin chieftains assumed that would be the end of the war and they could exact a good price from Piłsudski. The British Foreign Secretary had tried to negotiate a peace deal and drew a new border between Russia and Poland: the Curzon Line.* The Poles felt forced to accept it – for now. But Lenin was determined to press on and turn the defensive war into an aggressive one and capture Warsaw. Trotsky was against the idea: 'this is the worst mistake you will ever make', he told Lenin. Stalin opposed it to begin with (though he would soon change his mind and support the leader). Dzerzhinsky, who had been at the same school as Piłsudski, warned that Poles would fight hard, and the Russians could never seize Warsaw. 'Poland is not ripe for a revolutionary war.' Karl Radek, another Pole, looked at Lenin and said simply, 'You will be beaten . . . and badly.' But Lenin would not listen. On 22 July he ordered Tukhachevsky to cross into Poland 'and take Warsaw within a month'. It was a foolish gamble – 'a flight of fancy', as one of his Sovnarkom critics put it.

At first the invasion went well and it was a popular war. Lenin might have had an aim of exporting revolution, but the newspapers, the Communist press, were full of nationalist venom against 'the Jesuitical Poles' and the 'wicked betrayal' that had to be avenged. Symbolically, Brest-Litovsk was captured within days. Tukhachevsky's army of 140,000 was advancing at twenty kilometres a day. Another war hero emerged, a swashbuckling, bewhiskered, thirty-seven-year-old cavalry officer, Semyon Budyonny, who took all before him for two weeks as he swept through Western Ukraine and into Poland. But the army's supplies ran low, ammunition was scarce, and when the Polish forces regrouped outside Warsaw the Russian army was routed. Forced into retreat over the late summer and autumn of 1920, the Russians lost 30,000 dead and 20,000 seriously wounded. Lenin had not thought the Red Army could invade Germany or Hungary, or even hold on to a Sovietised Poland. But he wanted to change the post-Versailles European balance and pierce the cordon sanitaire the West had established around Russia. If Lenin had made a deal in July 1920, he could have held all of Ukraine,

---

* Actually, it was very similar to an old border established in the 1780s. Neither side liked it, and the Curzon Line would be a major issue of conflict from 1920 until the end of the Second World War, when Stalin – together with the Yalta and Potsdam agreements – carved up Poland again.

Lithuania, Byelorussia and parts of eastern Poland. When he signed the Riga Treaty in March 1921 he had lost them all.

He admitted his mistakes privately, to Trotsky, Dzerzhinsky and Radek. But he used weasel words in public, either to fool himself or his Party. 'Without having gained an international victory . . . a sure victory, we have won the ability to exist side by side with the capitalist powers.' When he met Zetkin, he told her that he was surprised that 'the Poles thought and acted, not in a social, revolutionary manner, but as nationalists and imperialists. In the Red Army, they saw an enemy and not brothers, liberators. Budyonny and the other army leaders were brilliant . . . but they could not make up for our political mistakes.'[3]

After the Polish War, Lenin abandoned thoughts of sending troops to fight on foreign soil: 'we can't make revolution abroad at the point of a bayonet', he told Kamenev. But he did not give up spreading revolutionary ideas in an attempt to destroy the capitalist powers. It had always been his intention to spark uprisings elsewhere. Now he could justify doing so on the grounds that the Allies had helped the Whites against his regime; it was legitimate for the Soviets to interfere in the West. It may have been a weak, hypocritical argument, but it was one he used regularly.

He spared no expense on propaganda in Western Europe and in the US and on subsidies for Communist Parties and trade unions. He helped to establish leftist parties in colonies ruled by Western powers as a way to destabilise their empires, for example in British India. In China he gave large sums of money to the Chinese Communists – and, to begin with, hedging his bets, to the more moderate socialists.

Lenin installed Angelica Balabanova as the first Secretary of the Comintern in 1919 and sent her to Stockholm to establish links with leftist groups in the West. 'Ships arrived from Russia every Saturday,' she recalled. 'They brought me . . . huge amounts of money, which I deposited in a bank. My office didn't need such large sums and the purpose of these transfers was incomprehensible to me. I felt ill at ease about the money and I took every opportunity to ask Lenin for explanations and instructions. I received the following letter from Lenin. "Dear Comrade Balabanova. Excellent. *Excellent* [underlined] . . . you are our most capable and deserving collaborator. But I beg you, don't economise. Spend millions. Many many, millions." And that is what the Comintern did.'

Lenin was intimately involved with the selection of Comintern agents and interfered in minute details. As they were matters that had potential diplomatic consequences, he made the decisions himself – on broad policy, budgets, tactics. During one fortnight at the end of 1919 he was asked whether it was time to form a new Communist Party in Afghanistan (the answer was yes), whether an Indian branch of the Party should be established in Soviet Turkestan (maybe) and how much money should be given to the Communists in Bengal (a lot, up to five million rubles).* He received a request from the senior Finnish Communist Eino Rakhia, who had been his guide and bodyguard in 1917, for ten million rubles, to aid the Party in Helsingfors. It was granted. He supported a subsidy of US$1 million for John Reed, the American journalist, to spend on propaganda in the US. He approved a proposal of 200,000 rubles to pay 'agitators and propagandists in Asian labour organisations . . . the cost of each one, plus bonuses when he returns, would be . . . Korea 10,000 rubles, South China 20,000 . . . similar missions are envisaged for Persia and India'. He would handle Comintern issues personally in close detail every day.

Lenin's ability pragmatically to change direction when it seemed tactically sensible shocked true believers abroad, as it had his own Bolsheviks in exile before 1917. He told British Communists at the end of 1919 that they should enter the Labour Party and work for the cause that way rather than remain an irrelevant sect. The idea bewildered CP members, who had hitherto been instructed to do the exact opposite. Now Lenin said, 'You must support Labour, like the noose supports a hanged man.' The suffragette leader Sylvia Pankhurst, in Moscow at the time at a Comintern conference, was outraged. It took a brave woman to lecture Lenin on how to be a revolutionary, but she tried. 'On the contrary . . . we should be more "Left" than we have been. In England especially, there are not enough courageous people. Though I am a

---

* Lenin took great interest in attempts to weaken the British empire. As Bruce Lockhart said, 'this didn't seem so dissimilar to the Great Game of the Victorian/Edwardian era, only the ideological language was different'.

socialist, I participated a long time in the struggle of the Suffragettes and I could see the importance of radicalism and personal bravery in the defence of our ideas.' Lenin despised Pankhurst as 'boring and bourgeois' and expected the British Communist Party to obey his instructions if they wanted any recognition and support from Moscow.*

Lenin gave the subsidies from the Soviet regime to dozens of Communist Parties abroad which were to continue under his successors well into the 1980s. In the first full year after the Comintern was formed, according to the accounts presented at a budget meeting he attended, Lenin approved: '1. Budget to the German CP a grant . . . of 446,592 gold rubles [forty-two million German marks]. 2. Budget for French CP, a unanimous vote for 100,000 gold rubles. 3. For Italian CP, 360,842 gold rubles. 4. Budget for Czechoslovak Party, 250,000. For English CP, a unanimous vote for 200,000 gold rubles.' Money was sent to the US, Austria, Holland, Greece and many more countries – altogether more than five million rubles, an immense sum at a time of starvation in Russia, and more than Lenin awarded for famine relief programmes.[4]

---

* As so often, the most famous revolutionary leader in the world could spend inordinate time on trivial matters. For example, in August 1921 he wrote a long letter to Thomas Bell, who was about to launch a leftist journal for miners in South Wales: 'You should at first be very careful. In the beginning the paper should not be too revolutionary. If you have three editors, two should not be Communists . . . they should be real workers.'

49

REBELS AT SEA AND ON LAND

'The Kronstadt sailors . . . the pride and joy of the Revolution.'
Leon Trotsky, 26 October 1917

'Believe me. There can only be two kinds of government in Russia.
Tsarism or the Soviets.' Lenin, 3 March 1921

For many older, idealistic socialists in Russia and abroad, the event that
did most to shatter hopes and dreams for freedom under the Revolution
was the brutal suppression of the sailors at the naval base of Kronstadt.
They had played a major role in Bolshevik propaganda as the vanguard
of the vanguard which had won power for Lenin. Sailors from Kronstadt formed the crew of the cruiser *Aurora*, which shelled the Winter
Palace. Scores of them had become Red Guards during the Civil War.
They were considered the radical hard men of the Bolshevik Party,
totally loyal to the cause and to the leadership. Trotsky called them 'the
pride and joy of the Revolution'. Lenin said that when the Revolution
was in danger, 'we can't fail because we have the sailors with us'.

When these sailors showed dissent, it is obvious why they had to be
forced to submit. And after the savagery of the treatment they received,
few people would be under any illusions that Lenin would brook serious
opposition.

Inside the Communist Party, even into the winter of 1920 when he
was dictator in all but name, he would listen to some criticism about
internal Party issues. The old Bolshevik Timofei Sapronov was heard
politely when at a large Party meeting he accused Lenin of turning
members into 'recording machines who repeat one line . . . if you insist
on blind obedience the Revolution will be lost'. As was Nikolai Osinsky: 'There was a time when the important decisions in the Party were
taken by elected bodies . . . now it is in the hands of a small clique. Or

an individual.' But criticism was rare; the older Lenin became, the more intolerant and the more furious were his rages. Senior Party critics weren't purged, tried and executed – yet. That began later under Stalin. But usually they were sent well away out of Lenin's sight. After a series of clashes over workers' rights, Alexandra Kollontai was demoted from the Sovnarkom, sidelined and later made Ambassador to Norway.* After the defeat of the Whites, the 'class enemies', all opposition was suppressed, including former heroes of the Revolution like the men from Kronstadt.

Their complaints began with economic demands for higher rations and action on relieving food shortages for their families in the villages and in working-class areas of the cities. Nothing happened to them at that point: this was just about acceptable criticism. It was when they began to make political demands that they clashed with the regime.

On 28 February 1921 a mass meeting of sailors on two battleships, the *Petropavlovsk* and the *Sevastopol*, drew up a resolution demanding free elections to a new parliament, free trade unions independent of the Communist Party, a free press, the abolition of the Cheka – and a range of other broadly democratic reforms. The next day there was a demonstration of 16,000 sailors in the centre of the Kronstadt barracks town, where the demands were read out again by the young man who became the sailors' leader, a twenty-one-year-old petty officer on the *Sevastopol*, Stepan Petrichenko.

A small group of ratings seized the printing plant, peacefully, and started publishing a newspaper, the Kronstadt *Izvestia*. At no stage did they threaten violence or move in any way against Petrograd, which they could have shelled from their gun batteries or blockaded if they had chosen to. They had planned no uprising; theirs was a spontaneous expression of disappointment and anger. Immediately Lenin saw them as a threat and demanded they climb down 'or face destruction'. The sailors continued to publish their paper and Lenin put Trotsky in charge of smashing them. 'This is a rebellion and they must be shown no mercy. They must be destroyed. There will be no compromise,' Lenin told

---

* Shlyapnikov lost his job but turned to writing, and some others were given minor diplomatic postings. After the purges, following Stalin's death, being sent abroad – away from the power centre – was a routine 'punishment' for troublesome officials up to the collapse of the USSR.

him. Trotsky replied that if the sailors didn't climb down 'they will be shot like partridges'.[1]

Trotsky arrived in Kronstadt on 4 March, with Tukhachevsky in command of a unit of 20,000 Red Army troops. The following morning they issued an ultimatum authorised by Lenin. 'Kronstadt and the rebellious ships must immediately submit to the authority of the Soviet Republic. Only those who surrender unconditionally may count on the mercy of the Republic.'

There was no reply from Petrichenko. Two days later the shore batteries opened fire and Tukhachevsky's white-caped soldiers attacked the naval base in a snowstorm. 'The first shot was fired by Trotsky . . . standing up to his knees in the blood of workers . . . he opened fire against revolutionary Kronstadt, which has risen against the autocracy of the Communists,' said Petrichenko.

The young sailor made one last emotional appeal to the magnates in the Kremlin. 'Barely three years ago, you – Lenin, Trotsky, Zinoviev and all of you – were denounced as traitors and German spies. We, the workers and sailors, had to come to your rescue and saved your skins from the Kerensky government. It is we who placed you in power. Have you forgotten that? Now you threaten us with the sword. You are playing with fire. You are repeating the blunders and crimes of Kerensky. Beware that a similar fate doesn't overtake you.'

The troops were repulsed for a few days but in the end it was a massacre. They were outnumbered and outgunned. Even Tukhachevsky was appalled by the carnage and surprised by the sailors' determination to fight against hopeless odds. 'It wasn't a battle, but an inferno,' he said later. 'They fought like wild beasts. I cannot understand where they found the strength for such furious rage. Every house had to be taken by storm.' Nearly all the sailors who survived the final assault on 16 March were summarily executed. Petrichenko and around a hundred others managed to escape to Finland. But thousands died on the frozen lake around Kronstadt. When it was over the Finnish government demanded that the Soviets remove the bodies from the ice. Otherwise the dead would have been swept to Finland's shores when the thaw came.[2]

*

The terror became so routine that some people were slaughtered by ghastly mistake. At a Sovnarkom meeting in October 1919 commissars were discussing investment in railways. Halfway through, Lenin wrote a note to Dzerzhinsky asking: 'How many dangerous counter-revolutionaries do we have in prison?' The Cheka boss scribbled a reply, 'around 1,500', and returned the note to Lenin who read it, placed an X by the answer and returned it to Dzerzhinsky. That night hundreds of prisoners in Moscow were executed. Lenin had not ordered them to be shot, as his secretary, Fotieva, explained later. Sometimes he placed a cross by documents he had seen merely to show that he had read the information and taken note of it. So casual had the imposition of revolutionary justice become that this appalling error barely caused a stir of any kind.

Lenin would always justify the terror on principle, but occasionally relented when he was made aware of individual cases. Gorky's relationship with Lenin survived even though *Novaya Zhizn* had been closed down in summer 1918. He criticised Lenin relentlessly – one of the very few Russians allowed to do so. Yet they met frequently as friends and he was given special leeway as the most famous living Russian writer.[*]

He intervened often, mostly on behalf of other authors, artists or academics. He loathed Lenin's intolerance, which he had seen often in the past. In June 1919 he protested about the searches and arrests of members of the Petrograd intelligentsia. 'They are the same people who helped you personally, hid you in their homes,' Gorky told him. Lenin replied characteristically: 'Yes of course they are excellent, good people and that is precisely why their homes have to be searched. Precisely because of this one has sometimes *a contre coeur* to arrest them. Of course they are excellent and good, of course their sympathy goes always to

---

[*] Until he emigrated in autumn 1921. The Lenin-Gorky friendship is fascinating and has merited at least one book on its own. Gorky was a vociferous critic yet could write, a few months before leaving the country: 'Lenin's mistakes are the mistakes of an honest person, and no reformer in the world has ever operated without making mistakes . . . He always speaks of one thing – getting rid of social inequality. His faith in this is the faith of a fanatic, but an educated fanatic, not a metaphysical or mystical one . . . In a religious era, Lenin would have been considered a saint. A stern realist, a shrewd politician, Lenin is gradually becoming a legendary figure. This is good.' And when Lenin died in 1924 Gorky wrote an extraordinary paean of praise to him. The strangest thing about Gorky, though, was his willingness to return to Stalin's Russia in 1932, where he died four years later.

the oppressed, of course they are always against persecution. And what do they see around them? The persecutor – our Cheka; the oppressed – the Kadets, and the SRs who flee from it. Obviously their duty, as they conceive it, tells them to ally themselves . . . against us.' His principle was simple: it is better that 100 innocent people are killed than that one person who is a danger to the Revolution remains free and a potential threat. And the Cheka put this principle into bloody practice. 'Whoever does not understand the need for any revolutionary class to secure its victory understands nothing of the history of revolution,' he said. 'The dictatorship means – take note of this once and for all – unrestrained power and the use of force, not of law.'[3]

Gorky saved scores of people from death or prison by directly appealing to Lenin. After bringing up one case, on 12 April 1919 Lenin told officials of the Orel Soviet: 'Writer Ivan Volny has been arrested. His friend Gorky earnestly requests the greatest caution and impartiality in the investigation. Can he be set free under strict surveillance?' Volny was released soon afterwards. In the same month Gorky asked him to release the Left SR Nina Shklovskaya, Alexander Blok's secretary. In March 1920 Gorky wrote to Lenin asking for the release of the chemist Alexei Sapozhnikov from jail 'so that he can continue his valuable work on cures for various diseases'. Three days later he was freed. 'And also it is necessary to give [the physician Ivan] Manukhin the possibility of doing his research on an anti-typhus serum,' Gorky wrote as a postscript. Manukhin was released within a week.*

Somehow, on 3 September 1920 a letter reached Lenin from Nadezhda Nikulia, a seventy-four-year-old former actress from the Maly Theatre in Moscow. She said she had happily given up several rooms in her apartment to help the poor. Now she was threatened with jail if she didn't 'surrender my last passageway'. Lenin forwarded a note on the margin to Dzerzhinsky: 'Investigate and telephone her. Leave her

---

* One person whom Gorky couldn't save was the former Tsar's elderly cousin, Grand Duke Nikolai Mikhailovich, an academic historian who had never held any official post or court functions. He wanted to retire to write. Gorky met Lenin in Moscow; Lenin said he would send a letter to the Petrograd Soviet telling them to reopen the case against him. By the time Gorky returned to Petrograd the Grand Duke had been executed. Gorky maintained that Lenin must have known about the execution at the time they had their meeting.

in peace.' But these cases were like appeals to the sovereign in imperial times. Justice was arbitrary. For the millions who had no access to Gorky or to the Kremlin there was no protection against corrupt, vicious and cowardly officials, or the Cheka. Lenin's Russia was a state effectively without law.

The Mensheviks were banned in spring 1921. To begin with they were not being killed. The days of random mass purges of Communists were yet to come. But thousands were arrested and Lenin was happy to see them leave the country. When Sovnarkom met on 5 January to discuss 'the Menshevik question' they ordered Josef Unshlikht, the deputy chief of the Cheka, to find two or three towns – 'not excluding those on a railway' – where Mensheviks could be settled. Lenin told him 'not to obstruct' Mensheviks who wanted to emigrate abroad and if a 'subsidy for fares' was required, finance was available from Party funds to send them into exile.*[4]

* * *

In July 1921 Henry Fisher, a voluntary aid worker, described conditions at the railway station in Simbirsk, the town where Lenin was born and raised. 'Imagine a compact mass of sordid rags, among which are visible here and there lean, naked arms, faces already stamped with the seal of death. Above all one is conscious of a poisonous odour. It is impossible to pass. The waiting room, the corridor, every foot thickly covered with people . . . in every imaginable position. If one looks closely, one sees these filthy rags are swarming with vermin. Nursing babies have lost their voices and are no longer able to cry. Every day more than twenty dead are carried away, but it is not possible to remove

---

* In October 1920 Lenin gave permission for Yuli Martov to leave Russia. He spent his last years in Berlin, an exile again and a seriously ill man. He launched the Menshevik paper, *Socialist Messenger*, and disputed with Lenin to the end. One of his last pieces of journalism accused Lenin of conducting 'bloody debauchery . . . in Russia, which is being carried out in the name of socialism, in the name of the teaching which proclaimed the brotherhood of people labouring for the highest goal of humanity . . . A party of death penalties is as much an enemy of the working class as is a party of pogroms.' Lenin seldom expressed any regrets, but once, in summer 1921, he did wistfully say it was 'a pity Martov is not with us. What an amazing comrade he was . . . such a pure man.' He died in April 1923. When Lenin heard the news, near death himself and unable to speak, 'he looked desperately sad', said Nadya.

all of them. Sometimes corpses remain among the living for more than five days . . . A woman tries to soothe a small child lying in her lap. The child cries . . . For some time the mother goes on rocking it in her arms. Then suddenly she strikes it. The child screams anew. This seems to drive the woman mad. She begins to beat it furiously, her face distorted with rage. She rains blows with her fist on its little face, on its head, and at last she throws it upon the floor and kicks it with her foot. A murmur of horror rises around her. The child is lifted from the ground, curses are hurled at the mother, who, after her furious excitement has subsided, has again become herself, utterly indifferent to everything around her. Her eyes are fixed, but are apparently sightless.'

Starvation was not uncommon in Russia. There had been famines in 1906 and again in the year before the war. But the great Volga famine in 1921 was by far the worst since the horror which the young Vladimir Ulyanov had witnessed in 1891–2. A crop failure in 1920, followed by a heavy frost and a swelteringly hot summer, were serious natural disasters. However, the catastrophe the following year was caused more by man than by nature.

The main reason was Lenin's continued policy of grain requisitioning. Peasants had been used to maintaining stocks to see themselves through times of bad harvests. Now they grew just enough for subsistence, to feed their livestock and to keep sufficient seed to sow the next harvest. What was the point of producing more if the Bolsheviks took it all? By 1920 the sown area of the Volga region had declined by 25 per cent in three years. When a poor harvest came there were no reserves of stock.

The Volga region was the worst hit but there was mass starvation in Ukraine, the Urals and Kazakhstan. In Samara Province it was estimated that two million people were dying of hunger, more than two-thirds of the population: around 700,000 died over the next two years. A quarter of the peasantry in Russia were starving.

Vast numbers of people went to train stations along the Russian rail network, where they imagined there might be food or a means of catching a train somewhere else – hence the scene in Simbirsk described by Fisher. Cannibalism was common. People were storing corpses as food. One woman was caught with her child eating pieces of her dead husband. When police interviewed her she said, 'We won't give him up . . . he is our own family and no one has the right to take him away from us.'

There were several cases of mothers killing one of their children in order to feed the others.

Until July 1921 the Soviet government refused to admit there was a disaster happening, as the Tsar had done in the 1890s: the words 'famine' and 'starvation' were banned in the press on Lenin's orders. It was left to a few individuals to begin relief efforts – as in the 1890s when Tolstoy and Chekhov raised money for soup kitchens and hospitals. Gorky appealed for international help. Herbert Hoover offered aid from the American Relief Administration, which was feeding millions of people in Western Europe.

Initially Lenin rejected aid of any kind and furiously declared, 'one must punish Hoover, one must publicly slap his face so the whole world sees'. But he was talked round by comrades in the Kremlin, principally Litvinov, Foreign Commissar Chicherin and Zinoviev, who argued that continuing to refuse help would look bad internationally.

Lenin showed no gratitude and ordered the Cheka to spy on the ARA teams. He wrote to Vyacheslav Molotov, then a high-ranking official in the Sovnarkom secretariat: 'We can expect the arrival of a lot of Americans. We must take care of surveillance and intelligence . . . the main thing is to identify and mobilise the maximum number of Communists who know English to introduce them into the Hoover Commission and for other forms of surveillance.' Hoover's aid workers fed twenty-five million people in the Volga region alone and saved hundreds of thousands of lives before the ARA closed down its Russian efforts – prematurely. When it was revealed that the Soviets were taking foreign aid but at the same time selling its cereals for hard currency, it caused a scandal that forced the ARA teams to leave Russia, amid bitterness.[5]

The famine was accompanied by peasants' revolts throughout the country – the last major opposition to the regime before rural Russia was cowed into submission by the Soviets. The Red Army was used to suppress dozens of rebellions throughout 1921,* but Lenin was most

---

* Between March and November 1921 there was hardly a day when somewhere in Russia a Red Army detachment was not on duty linked to 'internal disorders' against peasants. According to the government's own records, in thirty-six provinces during 1921 there were 171,185 army casualties, the vast majority minor injuries, but the numbers show how serious the fighting was.

concerned about the rising in Tambov Province, south-east of Moscow, news of which was spreading to Russian cities and abroad. Thousands of food-requisitioning brigades had been attacked and Communist officials had been murdered. Lenin resorted to all means at his disposal to crush the rebels, including weapons of mass destruction. He said that the peasant wars 'were far more dangerous to us than all the Denikins, Kolchaks and Yudeniches put together'.

Tukhachevsky had no qualms about putting down the Kronstadt rising. A month later he was given four weeks to defeat the Tambov villagers, led by a Socialist Revolutionary, Alexander Antonov, who had taken part in Maria Spiridovlova's revolt three years earlier. An order approved by Lenin personally authorised Tukhachevsky to use poisoned gas against a band of peasants armed with a few hundred rifles. 'The remnants of [Antonov's] . . . bandits are gathering in a forest and carrying out raids on peaceful inhabitants. These forests where the bandits are hiding must be cleared with poison gas. Careful calculations must be made to ensure that the cloud of asphyxiating gas spreads throughout the forest and exterminates everything hidden there. The artillery inspector must immediately release the required number of poison gas . . . [shells] and necessary specialists to the localities. Signed Lenin.'

Even after these attacks some villagers fought on. Tukhachevsky had 50,000 troops, three armed trains, several mobile machine-gun units, seventy field guns and a squadron of fighter planes. They burned whole villages when they faced resistance and took no prisoners. Tukhachevsky could not keep to his deadline of one month but the rebellion was crushed – as were all the others.[*6]

The one institution that continued to resist Lenin's will was the Orthodox Church. Christianity and Lenin's brand of Communism were bound to collide, eventually. Lenin had always intended to campaign against religion and, if he could, destroy the Church, but he bided his time. For the first three years he was careful and relied on propaganda. After the Whites were defeated and the rebel peasants pacified, Lenin

---

* Alexander Antonov escaped and tried to form another rebel band near Voronezh, 350 kilometres from Tambov. He was located by the Cheka in June 1922 and killed, alongside his brother Dmitry.

seized his moment to strike at the Church – with an issue on which he hoped to find popular support.

Under the Tsars the Church had a unique position of immense temporal as well as spiritual power. The Orthodox faith alone had the right to proselytise; it received generous state subsidies which paid most of the salaries of 45,000 parish priests and financed 100,000 monasteries. It was one of the biggest landowners in Russia. Church attendance had been falling sharply for a decade before the February Revolution, but Russia was still a predominantly Orthodox country. Orthodoxy and Tsardom were united in an inseparable link: the Church was effectively a department of state with its own minister. Historically its politics were ultra-reactionary.

One of Lenin's first decrees separated Church and State, recognised civil marriages, banned the teaching of religion in state schools and took away all the Church's state funding – fairly moderate in a revolution led by diehard atheists. A new Patriarch, the Metropolitan of Moscow, Tikhon, had a reputation as a 'pious and unsophisticated man . . . with more than a touch of Russian fatalism about him'. He chose to clash with the Bolsheviks from the start. He deplored 'these monsters of the human race . . . the open and concealed enemies . . . of Christ who have begun to persecute the Church and are striving to destroy Christ's cause by sowing everywhere . . . the seeds of malice, hatred and fraudulent strife'.

There were a few isolated attacks on some priests, but they were not official policy at this stage. Lenin was quite specific in his instructions to the Cheka and the Red Guards to leave the Church alone, for now. 'Be very careful in handling the Church. Do nothing hasty. There will come a time for this battle, but wait,' he wrote to Dzerzhinsky. When he and the other Communist leaders were 'anathematised' by Tikhon, Lenin ignored the Patriarch.

In 1919 the government began to seize Church land and property, as it had already done from all the big landowners. This included factories, apartment blocks, dairies, hospitals, shops, as well as monasteries with large farms. The regime introduced tougher rules against teaching religion anywhere outside churches, including 'in public places such as parks'. Tikhon complained that 'this aims to make impossible the very existence of churches, Church institutions and the clergy'. He was put under house arrest for a few months and a hundred or so priests were arrested.

Then the famine came and Lenin saw the opportunity for a full-scale attack on faiths other than Communism. Tikhon offered to give the State a substantial amount of money and 'Church treasure – except for holy consecrated vessels'. In summer 1921 Lenin launched a propaganda campaign throughout the press, saying the Church was 'hoarding its treasures' and demanding that it hand over more of its 'hidden wealth . . . so we can turn gold into bread'. If it refused, the property would be confiscated.

When Tikhon replied that it would be sacrilege to use consecrated items for secular purposes, Lenin sent Cheka officers to loot the churches. In the small town of Shuya, 300 kilometres north-east of Moscow, early in 1922 fifteen devout townspeople were killed when they tried to stop soldiers seizing valuables from the church. In Lenin's absence, the Party's ruling Politburo decided to delay future confiscations, at least for a short while. When he was told about the decision he went into one of his rages. To him, this was the best time for a showdown with the clergy and comrades shouldn't shy away from one.

Lenin's response to his fellow Kremlin magnates – only available recently, some considerable time after the collapse of the USSR – still has the power to shock in its cynical brutality. It reveals Lenin at his worst, and it is hardly a surprise that his successors carefully hid the letter for decades. It is worth quoting at some length. Lenin deliberately used the famine as an excuse to launch an assault on the clergy: 'The enemy [he meant the Church] is committing an enormous strategic mistake in trying to drag us into battle at this time . . . for us this is the moment when we can with ninety-nine chances out of a hundred smash them and secure for ourselves an unassailable position for many decades to come. It is precisely now, when in the starving regions people are eating human flesh, and thousands of corpses are littering the roads . . . that we must carry out the confiscation of Church valuables, with the most merciless energy and crush any resistance. It is now, and only now, that the peasant mass will be for us, or at any rate will not be in a condition to support the clergy . . . We must seize the valuables now speedily; we will be unable to do so later because no other moment except that of desperate hunger will give us support among the masses. The confiscations must be conducted with merciless determination ... the greater the number of clergy and reactionary bourgeoisie we succeed in executing for this reason ... [i.e. resisting church looting] the better. We must teach these people a lesson so they will not dare even to think of resistance for decades.'[7]

This was the violent beginning of the suppression of religion, which over the next fifteen years or so saw more than 97 per cent of the Soviet Union's churches, synagogues and mosques closed down. Within two years of Lenin's edict more than thirty bishops and 1,200 priests had been killed and thousands more jailed. In Perm, witnesses said they saw Archbishop Andronik's eyes had been gouged out, his cheeks hollowed and his ears cut off before he was shot. Bishop Hermogenes of Tobolsk was tied to a rock and thrown into the river.

On the other hand, the Bolsheviks raised a huge amount of booty from robbing the churches. In November 1921 alone, according to a report to Lenin, they seized 500 kilos of gold, 400,000 of silver, 35,670 of diamonds, 265 of assorted gemstones 'and 964 other antique objects that will be weighed'.[8]

50

INTIMATIONS OF MORTALITY

'Lenin's health seemed to be one of the indestructible pillars of the Revolution . . . It seemed as if . . . [he] would never wear out.'

Leon Trotsky, 1924

For two years after the attempt on his life in August 1918, it seemed as though Lenin had fully recovered. He showed no obvious visible health problems to outsiders. But he was eating poorly, sleeping badly and taking none of the regular holidays that used to restore his energy levels – and keep his temper in check. He was under relentless pressure. A few occasional hunting trips and Sundays in Gorki were not enough.

He noticed a potential problem himself. Having always been fit, he was accustomed in the country to outwalk almost anyone who went with him. No longer. He was suffering from shortness of breath and pains in the chest and in his legs.* He would find some excuse to sit down and rest. He never mentioned the symptoms to anyone – not to Nadya, nor his physician brother Dmitry. He had been prone to hypochondria on small health issues, though now he didn't complain to a doctor. But alone, he consulted medical textbooks. His health worried him, and he had a sense that his life would not be long. He occasionally remarked that his father had died at fifty-four, and when it seemed as if a sentence would follow he remained silent. He appeared to grow even more impatient to complete the work he could in the time he had remaining – and that made him more irritable, impatient and more susceptible to 'the rages'.

From early 1921 the effects of insomnia, headaches and general

---

* Symptoms which doctors nowadays would speedily test for ischaemic heart disease and/or arteriosclerosis.

lassitude were evident to those close to him. He was unable to concentrate on work for long periods, infuriating for a man as controlled and driven as he was. Until then, those around him would have agreed with Trotsky that 'Lenin was considered a man of robust health, he was always active, alert . . . Only occasionally did I notice alarming symptoms. During the first Congress of . . . [the Comintern, in 1919] he surprised me with his tired look, the unevenness of his voice and his sick man's smile. More than once I told him that he was spending himself on matters of secondary importance. He agreed but said that he couldn't do otherwise. Sometimes he complained of headaches, always casually and with a little embarrassment. But two or three weeks of rest sufficed to restore him. It seemed as if Lenin would never wear out.'[1]

From early 1921 he was looking like an ill man, and he recognised it himself. 'Unfortunately I am very unwell, my nerves are kaput,' he wrote to Clara Zetkin, during the crisis of the revolt in Tambov Province. A team of doctors – from Russia and abroad – examined him but reached no consensus about what was wrong with him. Most of them diagnosed a neurological condition of some kind, but they were unsure what treatment to offer, apart from rest and a reduction of his workload.

On 8 July he formally asked for a month's holiday and went to Gorki. But the rest and recuperation were not having their usual effect. Early in August he wrote to Maxim Gorky: 'I am so tired that I am unable to do a thing.' He took the rest of the month off, on the orders of his comrades in the Kremlin.

He complained increasingly about noise in his office. He demanded that the bells be removed from the telephones on his desk as the sound put his nerves on edge. They were replaced by lights on the handset. When minor refurbishments were being done on his Kremlin apartment, he ordered that the partition walls between the rooms be made 'absolutely sound-proof, and the floors absolutely free of squeaks'.

He returned to the Kremlin, with a reduced workload, though still enough to exhaust a well man. In October he blacked out a few times – briefly, and when he recovered he seemed alert. But by the beginning of December he was utterly exhausted and asked for more sick leave. On 7 December, as he left for Gorki, he wrote a memo to his fellow commissars. 'I am going away today. Despite the reduction in my share of work and the increase of my time for rest in recent days, insomnia has increased devilishly.'

He was feeling no better in the new year and his leave was extended. It was the headaches that troubled him the most. Two eminent German professors – a physician, Georg Klemperer, and a general surgeon, Julius Borchardt – were summoned to Moscow. Both thought the headaches were caused by lead poisoning from the bullets still inside his body after the assassination attempt. The Russian doctors who had been treating him regularly had major doubts about the diagnosis: Lenin had been suffering from bad headaches for some years before he had been shot and there was no evidence that the bullets were causing any bother. But Lenin and the Commissar for Health, Nikolai Semashko, a practising doctor before the Revolution, argued there was no point bringing the German professors to Russia at considerable expense and then ignoring their advice. It was decided that the bullet in his neck could easily be removed with fairly minor surgery under a local anaesthetic; but the other was lodged deep within Lenin's left shoulder and demanded a tricky and potentially dangerous operation. 'Oh well, let's get rid of the one so people don't pester me and worry,' said Lenin. On the morning of 23 April 1922 Professor Borchardt extracted the bullet 'resting under the right sternoclavicular joint'. The procedure took fifteen minutes and Lenin seemed well. The following afternoon he was back at his desk.[2]

While in exile Lenin possessed around him a kind of 'court', a clique of loyal followers, the closest thing he had to friends. Though he had kept himself distant as 'the leader', for periods in Switzerland and Poland he and Nadya had lived with the Zinovievs and the Kamenevs. Nadya was intimate friends with their wives. Dozens of other Bolsheviks and leftists drifted into their lives. He had dined with them regularly, conspired in cafés, gone on expeditions with them, walked in the Alps with them. In the Kremlin he had practically no social life at all. Possibly this can be said of all dictators. However, Lenin was by any standards remote – not because he had flunkeys outside his doors protecting him from other people: he demanded none of those things; but he made himself more private. He loathed formality, parties and large dinners, which were common among the other magnates. He and Nadya and occasionally Maria had lunch together or an early supper that she had prepared (still woefully badly). The rest of the time he snacked. Even at Gorki he seldom saw people outside of business meetings. Decisions in the early Soviet years were not made, as they would be later under Stalin, late at night with other Communist chieftains over long, elaborate dinners with plenty of vodka and wine. Business was conducted in the Cabinet room – or in secret cabal in his office.

He was not frosty when he met strangers, but he seldom made a fuss of them either. A stream of foreign visitors wanted to meet the man who was building the first Communist state, a new society. He tried to win them over and often he succeeded: 'I have seen the future and it works,' the American journalist Lincoln Steffens famously said after a few days in Moscow which included an hour-long interview with Lenin. He didn't always charm, though. H. G. Wells, at that point one of the most famous authors in the world, and certainly one of the most self-important, came away unimpressed – as did Lenin, who loathed Wells and thought him pompous. The philosopher Bertrand Russell admired him: 'Lenin is entirely without a trace of *hauteur*. If one met him without knowing who he was, one would not guess that he is possessed of great power, or even that he is in any way very eminent. I have never met a personage so destitute of self-importance.' But he was appalled by Bolshevism and was disturbed by Lenin's laugh, 'which at first seems friendly and jolly, but gradually I came to feel it rather grim'.*

Lenin made little effort with his appearance. 'He always wore the same dark-coloured suit, with pipe-like trousers that always seemed a trifle too short for his legs, with a similarly abbreviated, single-breasted jacket, a soft white collar and an old tie. The necktie, in my opinion, was for years the same: black with little white flowers, one particular spot showing wear. When, sitting at his desk, he received visitors, one could notice that the heels of his shoes were somewhat higher than the

---

* Russell wrote in 1919: 'I went to Russia a Communist; but contact with those who have no doubts has intensified a thousandfold my own doubts . . . as to the wisdom of holding a creed so firmly that for its sake men are willing to inflict widespread misery . . . The price mankind must pay to achieve Communism by Bolshevik methods is too terrible . . . and even after paying the price I do not believe the result would be what the Bolsheviks profess to desire.' However, after meeting Lenin he wrote to one of his lovers, Lady Ottoline Morrell, that Communism was probably right for Russia – 'If you ask yourself how Dostoyevsky's characters should be governed you will understand.'

ordinary size,' said Simon Liberman, an old comrade who knew him from the 1890s.

He made few concessions even when he was posing for an artist. In October 1920 Kamenev persuaded him to sit for the sculptor Clare Consuelo Sheridan, a cousin of Winston Churchill. She was a great beauty and several leading Communist officials fell under her charms, Trotsky included. The rumour was that after he sat for her, they began an affair. Not Lenin, who barely even spoke to her on either of the times they met.

'He has a genial manner and a kindly smile which puts one instantly at ease,' she said later. He sat at his desk, working, for the first sitting. The next time, a few days later, she persuaded him to pose on a revolving stand. Again they hardly spoke. At one point she asked whether Churchill was the most hated man in Russia. Lenin 'shrugged his shoulders and said something about Churchill being the man with all the fire of the capitalists behind him'. Lenin told her, smiling, that on the revolving stand 'I have never sat up so high'. She kneeled before him to study his face from another angle. Putting on her most seductive smile, she asked, 'Are you accustomed to this attitude in women?' At this point a (female) secretary appeared and her moment was lost. She said, 'Give me a message to take back to Winston?', to which he replied: 'I have already sent him a message through the [British Labour] delegation and he answered it not directly but through a bitter newspaper article in which he said I was a most horrible creature.'[*3]

Lenin's chief fixer Bonch-Bruevich told a story that three weeks after he was shot by Fanny Kaplan, Lenin 'became very agitated one day, after he spent half an hour looking at the newspapers. He turned to me reproachfully. "What is this garbage? How could you have allowed this? See what they write . . . It's shameful. They call me a genius, a kind of extraordinary man . . . there is an element of mysticism in all this . . . they will end up by offering prayers for my health. This is terrible. All our lives we fought against exalting the individual, against the elevation of a single person, and long ago we were over and done with the business of an individual hero, and here it comes up again: the glorification of one

---

* Lenin, though it seems unlikely, insisted he had not seen the finished piece. But Lidia Fotieva said the sculpture was 'quite good'.

personality. This is not good at all that they single me out in such a way."

'When he had finished I said quietly that people really were devoted . . . that his office and I personally received an unending flood of enquiries, letters, telephone calls, telegrams wanting to know the state of his health. "All this is extremely moving . . . I did not know that I gave rise to so much apprehension and anxiety everywhere. But now one should put a halt to all this. It is superfluous and harmful." Vladimir Ilyich thought it went against our convictions about the role of personality.'[4]

The story was probably true. Yet Lenin didn't put a stop to the 'cult' surrounding his name and image, which started in his lifetime and lasted throughout the Soviet years. In an altered form it continues, while his embalmed body remains in Red Square. The idea of leadership cult, so alien to Marx's or Lenin's theories, defined the living practice of Communism. Whatever Lenin said he thought about the collective praise of him at parades or the millions of column inches devoted to his genius, he did little to discourage it. The more embarrassed he may have been privately, the deeper it entered into the soul of the Soviet state.

For his fiftieth birthday in April 1920 the celebrations were extraordinary in their scale and vulgarity. The newspapers spewed out articles applauding his personal qualities of courage, wisdom and sagacity. Posters of him began appearing in public places for the first time, postcards were printed of his face, badges were minted. In schools children were taught to refer to 'Dyedushka Lenin'. Two official biographies were published for general readers. Mayakovsky wrote a sycophantic birthday ode, even though he knew how much Lenin loathed his work:

> But who can constrain himself
> And not sing
> of the glory of Ilyich?
> Kindling the lands with fire everywhere,
> where people are imprisoned,
> like a bomb
> the name
> explodes:
> Lenin!
> Lenin!
> Lenin! . . .

I glorify
in Lenin
world faith
and glorify
my faith.

There is no record of Lenin making any comment about the poem.

The Party organised a huge commemorative meeting to honour him. One after the other his old comrades Zinoviev, Kamenev, Lunacharsky, Bukharin, Trotsky and Stalin spoke of his greatness. Lenin was not there. When the tributes were over he put in an appearance to make some brief remarks, not of personal reminiscence but a lecture about the history of the revolutionary movement. He ended by warning the Party against 'complacency and conceit, which could turn it into something stupid, shameful and ridiculous'. He could have chosen instead to have a simple birthday celebration at home, had he wished.

51

REVOLUTION – AGAIN

'We are making economic concessions now, in order to avoid having to make political ones.' Nikolai Bukharin, 14 April 1922

'Lenin repudiated what he had slaughtered so many for not believing. They were right, it seemed, all along. They were unlucky in that he did not find it out before.' Winston Churchill (1874–1965)

For a fanatical ideologue who dedicated most of his life to one set of socialist goals, Lenin possessed a remarkably pragmatic ability to bend with the wind. After the Kronstadt rebellion and the peasants' revolts he changed policy 180 degrees and abandoned most of the economic measures he had introduced since the coup. Factories had stopped producing, money was worthless, there was mass starvation, Russia was exporting nothing. He admitted that 'War Communism', as he called it, had not worked and big changes were needed – revolutionary changes, though of course he would never have considered using such a term.

He ditched the major economic experiments of the previous three years: the ban on private manufacturing, wholesale nationalisation, the seizure of peasant 'surpluses', the replacement of private trade with barter and the partial attempt to abolish money. Lenin now planned a 'tactical retreat' that would become known as the New Economic Policy. The requisitioning of grain was to be replaced by a 'tax in kind', and soon by a relatively straightforward money tax. Peasants would be allowed to dispose of any surpluses as they wanted to, implying a return to the private trade of farm produce on the open market. The 'commanding heights' of the economy would remain in State hands – banking, foreign trade, large-scale industry. But the remaining small enterprises could be leased to the State and run as co-operatives. People were allowed to employ labour once again, which had been banned since

1918. Money made a return and wages were paid in cash, not in kind as had been the custom in many enterprises for the past few years. Public services and utilities would no longer be free – even investment by 'foreign capitalists' was to be encouraged. The biggest concession of all was to the peasants, to try to keep them relatively content – or at least keep them from open rebellion. That was the main point of the NEP. 'We are making economic concessions now, in order to avoid having to make political ones,' as Bukharin, one of the brains behind the new policy, admitted.[1]

At first Lenin faced uproar within the Communist Party; thousands of people tore up their Party cards. To the idealist true believers – and there were still some left – the NEP sounded like a return to capitalism and an acknowledgement that all their efforts since October 1917 had been in vain. To the careerists – of which there were many more – it was a massive risk which they believed would not work and would reduce their direct authority over people's lives. For Lenin it was all about staying in power. He was prepared to give some economic handouts for political survival. He forced the NEP through an unwilling Party – his last big campaigning effort.

He admitted it was a retreat, 'but the whole army has to make this retreat, united', he told the Party Central Committee in summer 1921. 'Let us make things clear. The peasants are dissatisfied with their present relationship to the State – so it cannot continue . . . we are sufficient realists to say straight out "Let us revise our policy." We must give the smallholder some stimulus, a push.'

He admitted that introducing this element of 'State capitalism' – his words – was political rather than economic. 'I appeal to . . . [the Party] that if they don't want the Russian masses to do to them what they did to the Tsar's people, they must throw overboard impracticable daydreams and they must be prepared to face economic laws.'[2]

The NEP stimulated the economy quickly, but it distorted the socialist experiment. In the cities, a new kind of 'Soviet entrepreneur' emerged, extremely rich and brash and showy, but loyal to the Communist Party, nicknamed NEPmen. On the land farmers were producing again and were – for now – less fearful that their stock would be seized by the government.

In Moscow everything was available again, for a price. 'Shops and stores sprang up overnight, mysteriously stocked with delicacies Russians had not seen for years,' recalled Emma Goldman, who had spent two decades in the US. 'Large quantities of butter, cheese and meat were displayed for sale; pastry, rare fruit and sweets of every variety were to be purchased. Men, women and children with pinched faces and hungry eyes stood about gazing into the windows and discussing the great miracle: what was but yesterday considered a heinous offence was now flaunted before them in an open and legal manner.'

When Lenin was asked how long the 'tactical retreat' would last he would say, 'For a while, I think . . . probably not less than ten years.' From now, in the time left to him, when Lenin talked about the economy he would urge modernisation and industrialisation as quickly as possible, and if that meant elements of capitalism, so be it. His new definition of Communism would be 'Soviet power, plus electrification'.

And he would slam bureaucracy, which had grown exponentially under Communism. No matter that he had created most of it. In his Soviet system each government job, from low- to mid-level upwards, would have a Party shadow, so the number of officials doubled. In the Soviet Union this remained more or less intact until the 1980s. Lenin saw the problem: 'We should all be hanged for creating all this unnecessary red tape,' he told Alexander Tsyurupa on 21 February 1922. 'Everything around us is drowned in a filthy swamp of bureaucracy. Over-administration – madness. All these decrees: lunacy. Search for the right people, ensure that the work is properly done – that's all that's necessary.'

He saw that this hydra head of bureaucracy was run by people who on the whole were not up to the job. 'All the evils and hardships we are suffering from . . . are due to the fact that the Communist Party consists of ten per cent of convinced idealists, ready to die for the cause, but incapable of living for it, and ninety per cent of unscrupulous time-servers who have simply joined the Party to get jobs.' Many of the leftist critics of the Soviet state over the following decades said pretty much the same thing.[3]

While he was freeing the economy, Lenin made it plain he would allow no political reforms. If he was going to force the NEP through an unwilling Party there had to be discipline, order and restraints – Leninist principles from the time of *What Is To Be Done?* in 1902 onwards. 'We cannot have arguments about deviations and disagreements . . . we must put a stop to that,' he told Bukharin. He wrote a resolution On Party Unity, kept secret for many years. It banned all independent factions and groupings in the Communist Party which the Kremlin magnates did not recognise, on pain of immediate expulsion from the Party, with no appeal. 'No faction of any sort will be tolerated,' it said. This was to have the gravest consequences for millions of loyal Communists over the coming decades. It was the principal weapon that Stalin would use against 'deviationists' or anyone he perceived to be an opponent.

After the Reds won the Civil War there began a thaw in the Cold War between Russia and the West.* The Allied nations said they would end the trade blockade if Russia agreed to pay her pre-1914 debts – an important issue for Britain, especially, which was owed nearly £600 million. Lenin, reluctantly, agreed, though he continued to complain privately that he didn't see 'why a nation should be obliged to pay for the chains it has worn for ages'. He prevaricated for a long time before a deal about the loan repayments was approved. The blockade was lifted in the winter of 1920. 'We have failed to restore Russia to sanity by force. I believe we can save her by trade. Commerce has a sobering influence in its operations,' Lloyd George said.†

Lenin hoped that it would mean a boom in trade and he tried to attract American and British companies to invest in Russia. He wrote letters to some of the companies which used to do business there before the Revolution, imploring them to return. But few responded. He offered what he thought would be generous 'concessions' on access for exploring and developing Siberia's immense natural resources. It didn't

---

* British Labour politican and peace activist Ethel Snowden, on a Party delegation visit to Moscow in 1920, told Lenin that he must do something about the Allied economic blockade: 'there has to be an end to the Iron Curtain between Russia and the West', she said. This was the earliest use of the phrase Iron Curtain in reference to the Soviets.
† Lloyd George loathed Communism but had a high opinion of Lenin. In private he called Lenin 'the biggest man in politics', according to his crony Lord (George) Riddell, the newspaper proprietor. A year before the NEP was launched, Lloyd George prophesied that Lenin 'was a big enough man to confess the truth and face it when his big experiment of Communism failed . . . he will change his plans and govern Russia by other methods'.

quite turn out that way. He began talks with Singer, Westinghouse and General Electric, none of whom would invest in any significant way. He wooed millionaires like the oil magnate Armand Hammer, one of the few who took the bait. He became a Soviet apologist for the rest of his long life. Dealing with the Soviet regime in the early years was a risky business: assets could again be seized overnight in an unstable environment. Profits were uncertain. But the principal reason was that however much Lenin wanted foreign trade and needed foreign capital, he would never enter into any agreement that might weaken the regime's grip on economic life in Russia.

52

THE LAST BATTLE

'If one cannot work for the Party any longer one must be able to look the truth in the face and die . . .' Lenin to Nadya, 8 December 1911

For a month, Lenin seemed to be recovering well from the operation to remove the bullet from his shoulder. He was sleeping relatively soundly, for him, and he wasn't complaining of headaches. But on the morning of 26 May 1922 he had a relapse. He fell as he was getting out of bed in the dacha at Gorki and he began to vomit violently. At 10 a.m. his sister Maria, in a highly agitated state, rang the physician he liked the most, Dr Vladimir Rozanov. 'Doctor, I beg you, you must come at once.' He arrived with Nikolai Semashko, the Health Commissar, Lenin's brother Dmitry and a prominent Moscow general practitioner, Dr Leonid Levin. They could see straight away that he had suffered a serious stroke. He was paralysed along his right side and his speech was impeded.*

Lenin looked in great pain, according to Maria. He asked one of the doctors, 'Is it paralysis? Tell me. If it is paralysis it might as well be the end.' Rozanov tried to reassure him: 'Vladimir Ilyich you will be well again soon.' But he replied, 'This is the first alarm signal, for sure.' He looked at Nadya and said, 'This is the warning bell.'

Over the next few days, teams of distinguished professors from Russia and abroad examined him and performed a series of tests – including

---

* According to the neuropathologist Professor Viktor Kramer, in a report to the Kremlin kept secret until 1935, it was only now that doctors diagnosed what was really wrong with him. Lenin's terminal illness lasted all in all about two and a half years, and its general characteristics 'harboured signs that all the neurologists, whether Russian or foreign, dwelled on as something that did not conform to general disease of the central nervous system'. He said that 'the basis of his illness is not the overstrain of his brain . . . but severe disorder of the blood vessels in his brain'.

for syphilis (which came back negative, though doctors had already giv-en him the standard prophylactic treatment at that time of a mild arsenic dose).*

The doctors insisted to Lenin's family, and to the Kremlin magnates, that he had retained his mental powers, though the claim seemed to con-tain a logical inconsistency. Neuropathologist Professor Kramer noted that 'he is unable to perform the simplest arithmetical functions, and he has lost the ability to recall even a few short phrases, while retaining his intellect in full'. A depressing diagnosis.

Lenin's sister Maria recalled that three days after the stroke, doctors asked him to multiply twelve by seven. 'He could not do it and he was very depressed. But then his old stubbornness reasserted itself. When the doctors had gone, he struggled for three hours over the problem and solved it by addition instead (12+12=24, 24+12=36) and so on.' Pains-takingly, Nadya was teaching him how to write – for a few weeks he was filling pages of paper with illegible scrawls. In a depressed state, the idea of ending his life took hold of Lenin.[1]

In 1911 he had spoken at the funeral in Paris of Paul Lafargue and his wife Laura. His powerful eulogy had been translated into French for him by Inessa. When Lafargue reached seventy he decided that his social usefulness was over, he could no longer contribute anything sig-nificant to the Cause, and he made a suicide pact with his wife. After the ceremony Lenin told Nadya how much he approved. 'If one cannot work for the Party any longer one must be able to look the truth in the

---

* There remain historians who are convinced that Lenin's last illness was caused by syphilis he may have contracted from a prostitute, perhaps in Paris, and that a series of eminent doctors, along with the Soviet apparat for obvious reasons, tried to hide it. Why else, they argue, would he have been tested at this point? The answer is that some on his medical team believed he might have a degenerative brain disease caused by syphilis. But the test results were clear. As were the results of his post-mortem, and there is no alternative evidence that the autopsy was faked. Syphilis over a long period would have caused changes in the smaller vessels at the base of his brain. It was his larger blood vessels that were badly damaged, which almost certainly caused the series of strokes he suffered. Another clear sign of his arteriosclerosis was the narrow-ing of the blood vessels in his heart and aorta. It is nowhere near as interesting as the conspiracy theories, but it seems most likely that he had an inherited predisposition to arteriosclerosis, which was the main cause of his relatively early death. His father died from the same cause at roughly the same age, and his sisters and brother suffered from the same problem.

face and die like the Lafargues.'

According to Maria, Lenin asked Nadya to get him some poison. She tried to give him cyanide, but couldn't go through with it. It was Lenin who suggested asking Stalin, and his wife agreed. 'He is a firm and steady man devoid of sentimentality,' said Maria. Three days after his stroke, on the day he failed the doctors' arithmetic test, Lenin 'determined that it was all over for him . . . he asked us to send for Stalin', said Maria.

Stalin arrived at Gorki the following morning, 30 May. The two of them were left alone for just over five minutes and it is not known exactly what was said. Stalin definitely promised Lenin that he would carry out his wish 'if it becomes necessary'. But according to Maria and Bukharin, who was also at Gorki at the time, Stalin seemed to be 'sceptical' about the idea. Stalin reported back to the Kremlin that Lenin had asked for poison, but he was unwilling to give it personally – and the moment wasn't right. He was told he had done absolutely the right thing. There would be a time when Stalin wanted Lenin dead. But not yet. It was too early for him to take full advantage.[2]

From the moment of his first stroke until the day he died the true state of Lenin's health was a closely guarded secret. The public was systematically misinformed. His personal authority was considered by the comrades so crucial to the Bolshevik regime that anything that might have weakened it was considered a risk. Trotsky explained their thinking: 'We asked ourselves with genuine alarm how those outside the Party would receive the news – they believed above all in Lenin.'

On his sickbed, Lenin himself knew the lies being told. When, a week after the stroke, a bulletin was issued from the Kremlin saying he was suffering from a stomach ailment, he said: 'I thought the best diplomats were at The Hague, but it seems they are in Moscow – they are the doctors who have composed the statements about my health.' Throughout the summer newspapers were full of articles signed by Kamenev, Bukharin and Stalin about how Lenin was recuperating quickly, and in a slightly limited capacity was working as hard as ever before he returned to normal soon. There were no recent pictures of him, though.

Lenin's last great battle was with his doctors and the clique of Bolsheviks around him who he was convinced – rightly – were plotting to take over from him after his death. He was determined to keep control of the regime for as long as he possibly could.

He recovered, slowly. His speech improved, and he could just about walk and move his right arm within a few weeks. He tried to return to work, but managed only two or three hours a day before he exhausted himself. He could not maintain concentration and his thoughts drifted off at tangents. Yet nominally he was still running the country. He had wanted to go to the Genoa Conference, the first big international meeting Soviet Russia was invited to attend, which he hoped would alter his regime's pariah status. But he was too ill.

As a sick man he was still issuing orders to Dzerzhinsky and the 'organs'.* 'On the question of banishing abroad the writers and professors who help the counter-revolution. This should be done more thoroughly,' he wrote on 22 July, with a copy to Stalin. 'A commission . . . should submit a list of several hundred . . . who must be deported abroad. We will purge Russia for a long time to come.' Around the same time he was rewriting much of the new penal code, with the Justice Commissar Dmitry Kursky. It was his idea to make it a crime 'not to recognise the right of the Communist system of ownership to replace capitalism and attempt its overthrow'. This became the basis for the notorious Article 58 of the Soviet Penal Code under which millions of people were killed, jailed or sent into the great maw of the Gulag over the following decades.[3]

But the other magnates were starting to sideline him and Lenin knew what was happening. Nobody understood power and how it operated better than he. Big decisions were taken at meetings without him; a 'triumvirate' was forming of Stalin, Kamenev and Zinoviev – without Trotsky – which gathered before official government and Party meetings to agree a line. He thought they would remove him before too long. He was sent papers, but often the important documents were at the bottom of the pile, which the officials thought he might not reach before he got too tired.

Before the stroke he wrote important letters himself and he hated

---

* In February 1922, as a public relations initiative the Cheka had changed its name to the GPU, State Political Administration, in the faint hope that Russians would be fooled into imagining the terror was over. It still reported directly to Lenin, however, and later his successors. The only real difference was that the Chekists' trademark leather uniforms were replaced by bright-blue ones.

dictating to a secretary. Now, when he became overtired, he had little choice. 'He used to say that he was accustomed to seeing what he had written in front of him and was finding dictation difficult,' Fotieva said. 'He disliked the sight of a stenographer sitting there with pencil poised waiting for him to go on while he took a few moments to think what he wanted to say next. He had to adjust himself to it, however, and thought it would help if the stenographer had a book to read in the pauses, but that was not much good either. In the end, the stenographer was placed in the adjoining room and given earphones so that Vladimir Ilyich could dictate to her over the phone.'

By October he had rallied enough to make a few public appearances. The press and Kremlin officials talked him up, but he was a sad sight for those who had known him at all well. On 13 November, after a short speech to the Fourth Comintern Congress, he was drenched in sweat and admitted to Nadya afterwards, 'I forgot what I had already said . . . and what I already had to stay.'

A week later, after a speech at the Bolshoi he received rapturous applause for several minutes, but his performance fooled few people. The French Communist Alfred Messmer, who had known Lenin since his days in Paris, said sadly: 'Those who saw him for the first time might have said "this is the same old Lenin". But for others no such illusion was possible. Instead of the alert Lenin they had known, the man before them now was badly affected by paralysis, his features remained frozen and his general appearance was that of an automaton. His habitually simple, rapid, confident speech was replaced by a hesitant, jerky delivery. Sometimes words eluded him.'[4]

On 13 December he suffered two strokes, and from then onwards his life 'became a patchwork record of fluctuating illness and recovery', as one of his team of doctors said. Two days later he had another major stroke; 'his condition is much worse', recorded Professor Kramer. 'He can write only with difficulty, but what he writes is illegible, the letters overlapping with each other. He could not touch the top of his nose with the tip of his finger.' He would never write with his own hand again.

On 22 December Lenin dictated a frantic letter to Stalin begging him to keep his word and give him poison 'as a humanitarian gesture'. Stalin said no and told his senior comrades of his refusal. 'I do not have the strength to fulfil the request of Vladimir Ilyich,' he said.

Two days later his doctors,* along with Stalin, Kamenev, Bukharin and Zinoviev, imposed a set of rules on Lenin to keep him isolated from everyone except his family, the staff at Gorki and themselves as, now, the rulers of Russia. They passed a resolution kept secret until the 1950s that 'Vladimir Ilyich may dictate every day for five to ten minutes, but this cannot have the character of correspondence and . . . [he] may not expect to receive any answers. It is forbidden for him to have any political visitors . . . nobody around him is allowed to tell Vladimir Ilyich any political news.' Stalin was placed directly in charge of Lenin's health regime. In his way Lenin was a political prisoner of the Bolsheviks, and his chief jailer was Stalin. But he had no grounds for complaint that the Bolshevik leadership were interfering with his health regime. He had said many times that a revolutionary's health was a Party concern and 'public property'.[5]

One of Lenin's biggest mistakes was that he made no provisions for his succession. Like so many dominant, powerful leaders, he thought no one capable of taking over from him. Nobody knows exactly what he had in mind for the Soviet leadership after his death. It is clear he didn't think about it seriously until it was far too late. It is probable that Lenin wanted some form of collective leadership, but he laid down no procedure for successors to emerge.

Little in Soviet history remains so obscure as the truth behind Lenin's so-called 'Last Testament' – a few fragments of wishes for the post-Lenin era which he dictated, as secretly as he could, in the last months of his life. If it was supposed to settle the rivalry between Trotsky and Stalin, which he realised could split the Party, he was deluded. It reads more like a document by a sick, and somewhat confused, angry man.

---

* A team of doctors, twenty-six in all, were involved in treating Lenin over the last two and a half years of his life, including at least fifteen professors and a host of distinguished physicians from abroad. Obviously, the foreigners had to be paid – and in hard currency. The cost was vast, as a highly secret report, not revealed until after the Soviet Union collapsed, showed. They charged enormous fees, all of which the Soviets paid promptly: £11,900 in British money (a huge sum in those days) to Professor Otfrid Foerster, £4,400 to Oskar Minkowski, 220,000 German marks to Borchardt, US$29,000 to Professor Oswald Bumke, $9,500 to Klemperer and £4,500 to Adolph Strümpfel, demanded upfront, which the comrades paid without complaint.

Lenin didn't want either of the two likely candidates to assume supreme power. He had continued to play Trotsky and Stalin against each other, thinking both in their different ways were highly talented. In the last eighteen months or so, since the Civil War was won, he had promoted Stalin to the top position in the Party, creating the post of General Secretary specifically for him. Stalin had been prepared to perform the mundane, unexciting tasks which were necessary.

Trotsky remained a chief government fixer, and Lenin relied on him. He admired his intelligence and organising ability. But he wasn't a 'comradely' figure. Often he couldn't be bothered to turn up at either government or Party meetings. He had no post within the Communist Party and had made enemies of most of the magnates at one time or another because of his arrogance.

Stalin's new position gave him an enormous power base within the Party, from which he could dispense patronage and buy loyalty – and he remained Commissar for Nationalities, which gave him power in the CPs throughout the empire.

After Lenin became bedridden and isolated from politics he dictated the Testament, mostly to one of the duty secretaries, Maria Volodicheva, between 22 December 1922 and 4 January 1923. He returned to his conspiratorial past to make sure that the document would remain secret until he died.* 'At his request there were five copies typed,' she said. 'One . . . he kept himself, three copies [were] to be given to Nadezhda Konstantinovna and one to the secretariat marked "strictly secret". His copy was retyped fair with all his final corrections and was passed on to Maria Ilyinichna. The three copies that NK had received were also corrected. The rough copies were burned by me. He asked that the sealed envelopes in which the copies . . . were kept should be marked to the effect that they could only be opened by V. I. Lenin, or after his death by Nadezhda Konstantinovna.'

The first segment was dictated on 24 December: 'Comrade Stalin, having become General Secretary, has concentrated immeasurable power in his hands, and I am not sure that he always knows how to use that power with sufficient caution. On the other hand Comrade Trotsky . . .

---

* Though it is likely that Stalin knew all about the Testament. Technically he was in charge of Lenin's care, and all the secretaries ended up working for him later. It is clear the secretaries were reporting directly to him.

is distinguished not only by his exceptional abilities – personally, to be sure, he is perhaps the most able man of the present Central Committee [of the Party] – but also by his excessive self-assurance and excessive enthusiasm for the purely administrative aspect of his work. These two qualities of the two most eminent leaders of the present CC might, quite innocently, lead to a split, and if our Party does not take steps to prevent it, a split might arise unexpectedly.

'I will not further characterise the other members of the CC as to their personal qualities. I will only remind you that the October episode of Zinoviev and Kamenev was not, of course, accidental but neither can it be used against them any more than the non-Bolshevism of Trotsky.' He continued over the next few days to look at some of the lesser-known leadership figures – dismissing all of them – and made general points about Party management.

Then, on 4 January, he summoned Fotieva to add an explosive post-script to the Testament: 'Stalin is too rude and this defect, although quite tolerable in our midst and in dealings among we Communists, becomes intolerable in a General Secretary. That is why I suggest that comrades think about a way of removing Stalin from the post and appointing an-other man in his stead who in all other respects differs from Comrade Stalin in having only one advantage, namely that of being more tolerant, more loyal, more polite and more considerate to other comrades, less capricious.'[6]

The final row between Lenin and Stalin was personal, not political. Lenin did not suddenly discover, as he was dying, Stalin's true nature. He knew all along, and had not been too bothered by 'the wonderful' Georgian's ruthless immorality. Lenin created the monster, and it was his greatest crime that he was now leaving Stalin with good prospects of becoming the Soviet dictator.

At the beginning of March 1923 the Party Secretariat limited the amount of official papers they were sending to Gorki – which must have been on orders from Stalin, though no record exists. However incapaci-tated, Lenin still tried desperately to cling on to remnants of power and influence. He wanted to resolve the 'national question': what kind of state would the Soviet Union be? Towards the end of his life Lenin want-ed a federal union, with some autonomy for each of the nationalities.

Stalin wanted a highly centralised state with all power in Moscow. The battleground between them would be Stalin's home region, Georgia.

Lenin had heard that Ordzhonikidze, now leader of the Georgian Communist Party and one of Stalin's henchmen, had mounted a campaign to crack down on Georgian nationalism and had sent in troops to crush any dissent. It had led to fisticuffs among top officials at a Party meeting in Tbilisi. Lenin chose to back Stalin's opponents, and in mid-January 1923 he dictated a note via Nadya – not one of his secretaries – asking Trotsky to intervene in 'this Georgian affair'. Trotsky refused, but Stalin heard about the letter. He rang Nadya on 25 January and swore down the phone at her, accusing her of breaking doctors' orders by allowing Lenin to write a 'political letter' and warning her there would be severe disciplinary consequences within the Party. 'She burst into tears . . . totally hysterical,' said Maria, who overheard some of the conversation. But Nadya didn't tell Lenin about the incident until six weeks later.

She wrote to Kamenev instead: 'Lev Borisovich! Stalin subjected me to a storm of the coarsest abuse yesterday. About a brief note that Lenin dictated to me, with the permission of the doctors. I didn't join the Party yesterday. In the whole of the last thirty years I have never heard a single coarse word from a comrade. The interests of the Party and of Ilyich are no less dear to me than to Stalin . . . I know better than all the doctors what can and what cannot be said to Ilyich, for I know what disturbs him and what doesn't, and in any case I know this better than Stalin does.'

When Nadya eventually told Lenin about Stalin's behaviour her husband reacted more like an aristocratic hero from a Pushkin tale than a radical Bolshevik. On 5 March he summoned Volodicheva and dictated a 'Top Secret and Personal' note to Stalin, with copies to Zinoviev and Kamenev. 'You have been so rude as to summon my wife to the telephone and use bad language to her,' it began. 'Although she told you that she was prepared to forget this . . . I have no intention of forgetting so easily what has been done against me, and it goes without saying that what has been done against my wife I consider having been done against me as well. I ask you, therefore, to think it over whether you are prepared to withdraw what you have said and to make your apologies, or whether you prefer that relations between us should be broken off.' In an earlier age, and if he had not been bedridden, Lenin might have been in a mood to challenge Stalin to a duel.

By this stage Stalin was openly telling the other magnates 'Lenin – kaput', and was frequently rude about him to others. But he kept his cool and apologised, if in a mealy-mouthed way. Two days later he sent a note to Lenin saying, 'there is nothing here, other than a trivial misunderstanding. Still, if you consider that in order to maintain "relations" I must take back the words I said . . . I can take them back, but I refuse to understand what it was about, where my "guilt" lies and what is really wanted of me.'

Early in the morning of 10 March, three days after receiving Stalin's note, Lenin suffered another massive stroke. His right arm and leg were paralysed, he could not speak and doctors reported 'a cloudy consciousness . . . He kept trying to say something but only disjointed sounds emerged,' Professor Kramer said.[7]

Lenin's last nine months were agonising – for him and for those around him. Nadya patiently tried to teach him to speak again, but after the stroke in March he never managed to say more than a handful of words. With the help of special orthopaedic shoes he was able – just – to walk again, on good days. On the others he was in a wheelchair. Occasionally he would show some signs of improvement; on 19 June Nadya wrote to Clara Zetkin, saying that 'there are days when I begin to hope that recovery is not impossible'.

Her mood changed each day depending on Lenin's condition, as her letters to Inessa Armand's daughters – especially the eldest, Inna – reveal more clearly than in the sanitised memoir she wrote about the last months of his life. She told Inna on 23 May 1923: 'I'm kept alive only by the fact that Volodya is glad to see me in the mornings; he takes my hand, and sometimes we talk without words about different things which anyway have no names.' On 2 September: 'I spend whole days now with Volodya, who is improving rapidly, then in the evenings I go mad and am quite unable to write letters.' Ten days later she tells Inna that Lenin's 'improvement grows, but it's all going devilishly slowly'. On 28 October she sounds exhausted and defeated: 'Every day he makes a conquest but they're all microscopic, and we are still hanging between life and death. The doctors say that all the facts indicate that he's recovering, but I now know for sure that they don't know a damned thing, they can't possibly.'

Sometimes he showed some interest in newspapers. But on bad days he seemed in a vegetative state. His nephew Gora was desperately upset after a visit in July. 'I found him sitting in a wheelchair in a white summer shirt with an open collar . . . a rather old cap covered his head and his right arm lay somewhat unnaturally on his lap. He hardly noticed me even though I stood quite plainly in the middle of the clearing.'

The artist Yuri Annenkov had painted a portrait of Lenin in 1921. He saw him again in December 1923. 'Kamenev took me to Gorki to do a portrait, or rather a sketch, of the sick Lenin. Nadezhda Konstantinovna greeted us. She said there was no question of a portrait. And, indeed, reclining on a chaise-longue, wrapped in a blanket and looking past us with the helpless, twisted, babyish smile of a man in his second infancy, Lenin was not to model for a portrait.'[8]

In the new year doctors were giving favourable prognoses,* but Nadya knew better than to believe them. 'Starting on Thursday 17 January I began to feel something . . . [very bad] was coming,' she wrote. 'He looked horribly tired and tormented. He was closing his eyes frequently and went pale, but the main thing was that somehow the expression on his face changed, his gaze became somehow blind.'

She continued reading to him every day and he was usually attentive. Early in the evening of 19 January 1924 she read a Jack London story written in 1905, *Love of Life*, about a gold prospector in the Canadian wilderness who fights to stay alive, which he does by strangling a wolf and feeding on the animal's blood. Nadya said he liked the story.

While she was at his bedside that evening reading, a few miles away in Moscow the Soviet leaders were appearing at a Central Committee meeting and reporting optimistically about Lenin's health, suggesting he would be back in harness, leading the nation soon. The official Soviet

---

* Some doctors who read the notes of Lenin's post-mortem and examined his brain after his death were surprised he had lived as long as he had. Health Commissar Semashko reported: 'the sclerosis of the blood vessels of Vladimir Ilyich's brain had gone so far that . . . [they] were calcified. When struck with a tweezer they sounded like stone. The walls of many blood vessels were so thickened and the blood vessels so overgrown that not even a hair could be inserted into the openings. Thus, whole sections of the brain were deprived of fresh blood.'

head of state, Mikhail Kalinin, declared that Lenin was winning a 'grave battle with disease'. The delegates rose and applauded. 'Long live the leader of the world proletariat, Comrade Lenin.'

Two days later it was crisp, sunny and bright, if freezing cold. His doctors thought Lenin would benefit from some air. Bukharin, who was visiting, described how Lenin 'was propped up on pillows in a sleigh and watched while a group of workers on the estate went out hunting. He was in good spirits, clearly enjoying himself. There were few things he enjoyed more than a hunt. When a retriever brought back a bird to one of the workers near the sleigh Lenin raised his good hand and managed to say, "*Vot sobaka*" [Good dog].'

He returned to his room mid-afternoon, evidently tired, but he drank some vegetable bouillon. 'He drank thirstily and he felt slightly better, but then . . . [I heard] gurgling in his chest,' Nadya wrote. 'His eyes looked less and less conscious . . . he occasionally moaned quietly and then a tremor ran through his body. At first I held his hot, damp hand, but then just watched as the towel . . . [underneath him] turned red with blood and the stamp of death settled on his face. Professor Foerster and Doctor Yelistratov sprayed camphor and tried to give him artificial respiration, but in vain, it was not possible to save him.' He was pronounced dead at 6.50 p.m. on 21 January 1924.[9]

53

'AN EXPLOSION OF NOISE'

We are burying
the most earthy
Of all the men
Who ever walked
the earth
He was like you
And like me
The tears of snow
are falling
From the eyelids of flags red with weeping

Vladimir Mayakovsky, 'Poem on Lenin's Funeral', January 1924

At rest, Lenin's body, in a dark-brown jacket and black tie, bore a calm expression, a man at peace – not a face contorted by pain and illness as Nadya had feared. His hands rested on his chest, one clenched tight, the other relaxed, fingers slightly bent. He was lying in a crimson coffin.

On the morning of 23 January, during one of the coldest Russian winters on record, he was taken to Moscow. For four kilometres men carried the bier on their shoulders from the dacha in Gorki through the snow-covered woods to the nearest railway station. At train stops all along the way thousands of people gathered to pay their respects.

At about 1 p.m. the train arrived at Paveletsky Station in a southern suburb of Moscow. Lenin's body was placed on a catafalque and a long procession of dignitaries, headed by Lenin's family, marched the six and a half kilometres through the city to the House of Trade Unions, where he would lie in state, as Inessa had three years ago. Throughout the long walk Nadya looked exhausted and grief-stricken, but dignified.

Soldiers stood shoulder to shoulder along the entire length of the procession – along snowbound streets at temperatures of 20 degrees below
zero. 'Moscow became an armed camp,' recalled the American correspondent William Reswick. 'I sleighed to the railway station through
streets lined on both sides with solid ranks of infantry.' Red flags waved
and black-trimmed sashes hung from windows. Banners proclaimed
'Lenin is dead . . . his work lives on'. As the procession crossed the River
Moskva a formation of airplanes flew overhead scattering leaflets proclaiming 'Lenin's grave is a cradle for the freedom of humanity'.

There was genuine grief at Lenin's death, though how spontaneous
it was and how much was hijacked by the regime remains a matter of
argument. Hundreds of thousands of people – perhaps as many as a million – waited in the freezing cold and driving snow to catch a glimpse
of his body. For the entire four days he lay in state there was an honour
guard attending him. At first there were eight soldiers, replaced every
ten minutes. But so many people wanted to serve – Party workers, GPU
officers as well as troops – that the guard was doubled to sixteen and
later trebled to twenty-four and was changed every five minutes.

The death of Tsars was traditionally attended by large-scale public displays of mourning. But none were as large as this. The Soviet
magnates did all they could to encourage it: Lenin's leadership, his
personality, had legitimised their regime. But without a doubt Lenin
inspired real respect. Nikolai Valentinov, who fell out with him, went
to 'bid farewell to him', as so many of his compatriots did. 'There was
a frost that was unbearable. People . . . caught colds, yet they somehow
waited for hours for their turn to see the coffin . . . [perhaps] the Russian people have a far greater mystical curiosity than some others, some
kind of pull to look upon a corpse, especially if the deceased person is
above the common rank. In the pilgrimage to Lenin's coffin there was
this curiosity, but undoubtedly there was another impulse as well; an
enormous proportion of the population reacted to Lenin's death with
unmistakable grief.'[1]

There was a week of national mourning. All theatres and other places of
amusement were closed, as were the shops, except bakeries or those selling portraits of Lenin and black and red mourning cloth. For six days
the newspapers carried almost nothing except stories about Lenin.

On Sunday 27 January the temperature in Moscow had fallen to minus 33 degrees – 'beards, collars and eyebrows were white with the snow'. Hundreds of thousands of people had clogged Red Square, 'their congealed breath forming a fog in the icy air', as one mourner recalled. In the surrounding streets there were tens of thousands more, lined up under mourning banners. At the corners of the square, soldiers built log fires, around which each squad, relieved hourly, stamped and beat their arms against their bodies in an attempt to keep warm.

The funeral arrangements had been made by Stalin and Zinoviev, who had given their eulogies the night before at a special Congress of Soviets session to pay tribute to the departed leader. The only notable absentee was Trotsky, in the Caucasus convalescing from an illness when Lenin had died.*

At 10 a.m. Lenin's body was carried from the Hall of Columns at the House of Unions to Red Square, a kilometre away. Teams of soldiers, Party workers, Soviet representatives and peasant delegates had volunteered for the honour of bearing the coffin part of the way. The procession was again led by Nadya and Lenin's sisters and brother. It took almost an hour and a half to reach the East Wall of the Kremlin, where a wooden mausoleum had hastily been erected: Lenin's last place of rest. Bands played the 'Internationale', Chopin's Funeral March and martial music throughout. The speeches were interminable, but the multitude remained in Red Square.

At precisely 4 p.m. the pallbearers – Kamenev, Zinoviev, Stalin, Molotov, Bukharin, (Mihkail) Tomsky, Dzerzhinsky and Lenin's hunting companion Jan Rudzutak – carried the coffin down four steps to the shallow vault. Above ground, eerily moving, an extraordinary sound reverberated around Red Square, Moscow and other major cities in Russia. Every machine and apparatus that could be located was turned on – the sirens in thousands of factories, steam whistles of locomotives, foghorns, alarms and salvo after salvo of guns erupted into an explosion of noise.[2]

---

* Trotsky always maintained that he had been deliberately misinformed – by Stalin – about the date of the funeral. But he had time to get back if he had genuinely wanted to. He wrote a powerful eulogy in a newspaper, though. His absence was carefully noted, and was a major miscalculation on his part. Without a doubt it counted against his succession claims.

54

LENIN LIVES

'Do not let your grief for Ilyich spend itself in an outward veneration of his person. Do not build monuments and memorials to him,
palaces in his name. Do not organise splendid celebrations in his
memory. In his life he attached little importance to these things.'

Nadezhda Krupskaya, 29 January 1924

'For Russians, their worst misfortune was Lenin's birth; their next
worst, his death.'

Winston Churchill, *The World Crisis*, Volume Two, 1929

Lenin had wished to be buried next to his mother and sister Olga at
the Volkovo Cemetery in Petrograd. Nadya and the rest of his family
assumed that is what would happen, in a private ceremony, soon after
the state funeral. They wanted a plain and simple headstone at his grave.

But behind the scenes, in the Kremlin, an argument began about
Lenin's remains. It is not exactly clear who first suggested the extraordinary idea of preserving Lenin's body and displaying him like the relics
of a saint. Several of the magnates subsequently claimed credit, but Stalin and Dzerzhinsky steamrollered the plan through – against the wishes
of Nadya, Lenin's sisters and brother Dmitry.

Originally Dr Alexei Abrikosov, the pathologist who carried out the
autopsy the day after Lenin died, embalmed the body to preserve it for
six days, until the funeral. On 24 January, though, the Funeral Commission co-chaired by Stalin ordered the pathologist to embalm it for
forty days – not such an unusual wish in Orthodox Russia, where tradition was that prayers for the dead were said, often by the body, for
forty days. At first Nadya flatly refused to allow it but relented when
Zinoviev told her that if she agreed they could discuss the idea again in
a month.

But by this time the magnates had decided that if possible they would keep the body, preserved in the Red Square mausoleum, 'indefinitely . . . for ever if we can'. Dzerzhinsky, who had briefly trained for the Catholic priesthood before converting to Marxism, said: 'If science can preserve a human body for a long time then why not do it? The tsars were embalmed just because they were tsars. We will do it because Lenin was a great person, unlike any other.' Stalin, once an Orthodox seminarian, muttered at one Cabinet meeting, 'We must show that Lenin lives.'

Many of the old comrades were appalled, including Kamenev and Bukharin. Vladimir Bonch-Bruevich, the man probably closest to Lenin in his later years, said he knew that Lenin himself would have been horrified by the idea. Trotsky remarked that embalming Lenin's body was similar to the medieval religious cults: 'Earlier there were the relics of Sergius of Radonezh and Seraphim of Sarov; now they want to replace these with the relics of Vladimir Ilyich.' But the decision was made: the Bolsheviks needed a shrine for the cult of Lenin, and his embalmed body, immune from corruption, resting by the Kremlin, would be the place of pilgrimage.

Nadya did not know until the day after the funeral that the comrades were to take the decisions about Lenin's remains, and not his widow. On the morning of 28 January she wrote to Inna Armand: 'My beloved daughter . . . Right now they have not closed up his grave yet, so it is still possible to look upon Volodya,' so at that point she clearly thought that he would be properly buried. She heard later in the day about the discussions in the Kremlin, and the steps already taken by senior officials.

She tried to protest. On the following day *Pravda* published a prominent 'Message from Nadezhda Krupskaya. Comrades, workers and peasants, men and women . . . I have a great request to make. Do not let your grief for Ilyich spend itself in an outward veneration of his person. Do not build monuments and memorials to him, palaces in his name. Do not organise splendid celebrations in his memory. In his life he attached little importance to these things. Such things oppressed him. He found them trying. Remember how much poverty and disorder we still have in our country. If you want to honour the name of Vladimir Ilyich, build day-care centres, kindergartens, homes, schools, and – most importantly – fulfil his legacy.'

She failed to carry her point. On 26 February 1924, five weeks after

Lenin's funeral, the Marxist atheists in charge of Soviet Russia established, with no irony intended, the grandiloquently named Commission of Immortalisation.[*][1]

The 'Troika' of Stalin, Kamenev and Zinoviev, now in charge of Russia, made sure that one of Lenin's legacies 'would never be immortalised', as one of the old Bolsheviks remarked wistfully. They conspired to bury the 'Testament' about the succession which Lenin had dictated in the last few months of his life. Nadya possessed four copies and Maria Ulyanova had one, but most of the Party chieftains knew its potentially explosive contents. Nadya wanted the document circulated as widely as possible, within the Communist Party and throughout the country, in the hope of humiliating Stalin. She campaigned to ensure that Lenin's will would be implemented. But she lacked the power.

In fact all the leadership contenders had something to lose if the Testament became public, though Stalin obviously had the most. It showed that Lenin had no real faith in any of the comrades around him. The Politburo and newly formed Council of Elders – senior Party men – fixed things to ensure the least damage to the leadership. The Troika had been formed as a cabal against Trotsky, but it wasn't in his interests to see the Testament published either, as it was not exactly a wholehearted endorsement of his leadership qualities. Between them they stitched up the vote to prevent, as far as they could, the details of Lenin's will leaking out.

When the Party Congress met two weeks after Lenin's funeral, excerpts of the Testament – but not Lenin's postscript urging the removal of Stalin as General Secretary – were read out by Kamenev. Nobody was allowed to take notes. Nobody was allowed to tell anyone outside the hall what was in the document. There was a vote – carried unanimously – to 'approve' its contents.

Later at the Central Committee the rules were the same, though this time the whole of the Testament was read out. There was silence for a few moments and then Zinoviev rose. 'Every word of Ilyich is law to us. We have sworn to fulfil anything the dying Lenin ordered us to do. You

---

[*] The full title is the Commission for the Immortalisation of the Memory of V. I. Ulyanov (Lenin).

know we shall keep that vow. But we are happy to say that on one point Lenin's fears have proved baseless. I have in mind the point about our General Secretary. You have all witnessed our harmonious co-operation in the last few months.' Kamenev proposed that Stalin stay in the post, unanimously agreed. Trotsky voted in favour.*

It would be another seven or so years before Stalin possessed the power of a dictator, though this was the beginning of the end of Trotsky's role in front-line politics. Nobody knows who Lenin wanted to lead the Soviet Union after he was gone. But this was certainly not the outcome he had in mind.[2]

Of all the nonsense and hyperbole written in the hero-worship of Lenin little can match Anatoly Lunacharsky's claim that his genius can be explained by the shape of his head: 'The structure of . . . [Lenin's] skull is truly striking. One has to study him for a little while to appreciate its physical power, the contours of the colossal dome of the forehead, and to sense something that I can only describe as a physical emanation of light from its surface.'

Painstaking science over the following decades proved that there was nothing abnormal about his cranium – or what was inside it. Two years after Lenin died the Soviets established the Institute of the Brain, to unlock through reason and research the secrets of the master's brilliance. The pioneering German neurologist Dr Oskar Vogt was put in charge, and he began the process of comparing Lenin's brain with those of 'ordinary people', as one of his assistants explained, as well as the brains of other high achievers like Mayakovsky, Lenin's former sparring partner, the one-time 'God-builder' and rival Alexander Bogdanov, the novelist Andrei Bely and the French writer Henri Barbusse.†

Lenin's brain was preserved in a solution of formaldehyde and alcohol. One side was chopped into four parts, each sliced into 7,500 tiny slivers, which were microscopically analysed on the basis of Vogt's

---

* The contents of the Testament appeared in the *New York Times* in 1926. It was suggested at the time that Nadya may have leaked it out, but this theory has been discounted. In Russia details did not appear until 1956, at the 'secret speech' by Nikita Khrushchev that denounced Stalin.

† It was never clear whether their families approved, or even knew that their loved ones' brains were being used for this purpose.

theory (discredited in the 1930s) that the structure of the brain contributed to intelligence. It took ten years of study before Stalin was sent a 'top-secret' report of 153 pages with more than 700 illustrations by Vogt's successor, Dr Semyon Sassikov, stating that Lenin's brain 'is vastly superior to others because it had an exceptionally high degree of organisation', which supposedly explained his genius.*

Why the report was kept secret until the collapse of the Soviet Union is a mystery; it was always unlikely that at the time of Stalin's purges a doctor would come up with any other finding than 'Lenin's brain was extraordinary'. The reason might have been because tucked away inside the report was the fact that Lenin's brain was fairly ordinary. An average male brain weighs between 1,300 and 1,400 grams; Lenin's was 1,340 grams. Size doesn't matter in the context of intelligence. But it would not have done at all for the Soviets to admit that Lenin's brain was of only average dimensions. Lenin himself might have liked to know that his brain was much smaller than that of his great literary hero, whom he enjoyed reading all his life: Turgenev's brain weighed a mighty two kilos. Lenin's was just a normal brain.[3]

At first the Immortalisation Commission was told by Dr Abrikosov that Lenin's body could be preserved 'for many, many years' by refrigeration, if it was kept in the crypt, in a specially designed sarcophagus, at a carefully controlled temperature. But despite the most expensive and sophisticated freezing equipment bought from Germany, within two months there were already dark spots on Lenin's face and torso and his eye sockets were deformed. The magnates were worried their plan would not work out, particularly as the weather was becoming warmer.

Towards the end of March 1924 two prominent chemists, Vladimir Vorobyov and Boris Zbarsky, suggested re-embalming the body with a chemical mixture that they said 'could last hundreds of years'. They had studied the ancient Egyptian techniques of mummification but they

---

* The curious thing about Lenin's brain was just how diseased it was. The artist Yuri Annenkov, invited a few months after Lenin's death to select photographs and drawings for a memorial volume, was shown a glass jar. 'In it was Lenin's brain preserved in alcohol. One hemisphere was healthy and full-sized, with clearly defined convolutions. The other, which hung as it were with a ribbon, was wrinkled, crumpled, crushed and no larger than a walnut.'

could do a lot better 'and keep Vladimir Ilyich's body looking natural'. They worked day and night whitening Lenin's skin and devising the correct embalming fluid, under intense pressure, reporting directly to Stalin and Zinoviev. They experimented on several cadavers of fifty-ish-year-old men brought to them from morgues and scientific institutes in Moscow. After four months they found the correct formula of glycerin, alcohol, potassium acetate, quinine chlorate and another ingredient still strictly secret at the time of writing.

On 1 August the mausoleum opened for visitors. 'The body is in a perfect state of preservation,' one of the first people to see it said. The scientists boasted that they had managed to do what the Egyptians couldn't for Tutankhamun: 'the embalmers have even contrived to impart a smile'.[*4]

Nadya had always worshipped her own Lenin cult, but hated the public display everywhere around her. She particularly loathed the idea of Lenin's embalmed body resting half a kilometre from her home. She went once to view the mausoleum a few months before she died in 1939 and she was visibly upset. She looked at the body for a short while and told Ilya Zbarsky, the first curator of the mummy, who was showing her around, 'He's just the same . . . but look how I have aged.' She said she felt no wish to go again. She disapproved strongly when, five days after her husband died, Petrograd was renamed Leningrad. She continued to call the city 'Peter' as she always had.

Her declining years were sad. She continued to live in the Kremlin, sharing an apartment with Maria, who predeceased her by two years, but in a different apartment, further away from the government offices. After she failed to get Lenin's Testament circulated she continued to work at the Enlightenment Commissariat for four years, ridding Russia's libraries of dangerous books, such as those of Kant and Spengler.

She became a puppet of Stalin, whom she had always hated. She was told that she of all people with her devotion to the cause, and to the legacy of her husband, should think of Party loyalty first, and Stalin was

---

* Over the last ninety years many hundreds of scientists have worked on Lenin's body, which needs constant maintenance. In 2016 there were a dozen employed part-time, and three or four full-time, responsible for maintaining Lenin's body as part shrine, part tourist trap.

the unchallenged leader. During the purges in the 1930s she was fond of saying, 'if Volodya was alive now . . . he'd be in prison', but that was as far as her dissent took her.

She knew what her husband's view of the mausoleum would have been and she would occasionally remind people of the opening passages of *The State and Revolution*: 'During the lifetimes of great revolutionaries, the oppressive classes constantly hounded them and . . . treated them with the most furious hatred, the most unscrupulous campaigns of lies and slander. After their deaths attempts are made to convert them into harmless icons, as it were to canonise them, and surround their *names* with a certain halo . . . with the object of duping the masses, while at the same time emasculating and blunting the *real essence* of their revolutionary teachings, reducing them to vulgarity.'

For the Kremlin magnates the embalmed body and the overblown Lenin cult sent various messages beyond the bizarre fusion of religious and political ritual. Lenin was acclaimed as a secular saint, whom it was the people's duty to worship. But the crypt in Red Square was not merely a shrine. It was a physical reminder that even after Lenin's death Russians were not free of him. They would still be required to obey his commandments – through his anointed successors.

The wooden mausoleum was replaced in 1930 by the marble and granite building that remains a hundred years after Lenin's Revolution. It was his old friend Leonid Krasin who devised the idea of including a podium from which, on the high days and holidays of the Soviet Union, the next generations of Communist tsars addressed the masses. An estimated twenty million people visited the mausoleum and saw the embalmed, eerily wax-like Lenin in the eighty-five years after the crypt was opened for tourists.

The Soviet chieftains who succeeded him believed that Lenin's achievements legitimised their rule. A century later Lenin was used by a new breed of autocrats, is being extreme nationalists who may have dispensed with Communism but nevertheless respect him as a strongman in the Russian tradition.

PRINCIPAL CHARACTERS

Antonov-Ovseyenko, Vladimir (1884–1939)
First World War officer in Tsarist army who threw in his lot with Lenin. One of the military planners of the Bolshevik coup. He led the Red Guards who entered the Winter Palace at the climax of the Revolution and arrested the surviving members of the Provisional Government. Later became one of Lenin's most ruthless hatchet men, suppressing revolts by peasants in 1920–21. Was shot following a show trial during Stalin's Great Purge.

Armand, Inessa (1874–1920)
One of the best-known Bolshevik feminists until Lenin's death, when she was written out of the official Soviet histories because of her relationship with Lenin. She was his mistress in an on-off love affair – and a close working relationship – that continued from 1910 until she died. The only time Lenin was seen to break down in public was at her funeral. She had four children by her husband, whom she had left for her brother-in-law. Was on the 'sealed train' from Zurich to Petrograd in 1917. After she died, Lenin and his wife became guardians of Inessa's daughters Inna and Varvara.

Balabanova, Angelica (1878–1965)
Bolshevik supporter and admirer of Lenin, who grew disenchanted with him. In exile together during the 1900s. After the Revolution she was the first Secretary of the Communist International (Comintern), established to encourage Communist Parties throughout the world and plot Marxist revolutions. Wrote one of the first (and best) accounts of Lenin and his character.

Bogdanov, Alexander (1873–1928)
Doctor, philosopher, journalist and early Marxist. Supported Lenin in

the Bolshevik-Menshevik split, but broke with him over philosophical disputes about religion. Lenin in the early 1900s saw him as a rival as leader of the Bolsheviks and expelled him from the Party. Opposed the 1917 Revolution, but took senior posts afterwards in the arts establishment and medicine. Founded the Soviet Blood Transfusion Service; died following a medical experiment on himself.

Bonch-Bruevich, Vladimir (1873–1955)

Bolshevik activist in Petrograd and an old friend of Lenin's family. A publisher until the Revolution, when he became Lenin's personal secretary and head of his private office until 1920. Thereafter an official at the Soviet Academy of Science and Director of the State Literary Museum.

Bukharin, Nikolai (1888–1938)

Bolshevik activist and the leading Communist ideologist after Lenin, who mentored him as a gifted journalist and speaker. Took a series of leading positions in the Communist Party after the Revolution, including editor of the Party newspaper *Pravda* for many years. The last of the Soviet magnates to see Lenin, whom he visited on the day of his death. Fell out with Stalin in the 1930s, tried and shot in the purges.

Chernyshevsky, Nikolai (1828–89)

Writer and political activist who spent twenty-five years in jail, penal servitude and Siberian exile. Lenin's literary hero. Lenin admitted that Chernyshevsky's novel *What Is To Be Done?*, written when he was in prison, was as big an influence on his socialist politics as any of the works by Marx. Lenin carried a picture of Chernyshevsky in his wallet for most of his adult life.

Dzerzhinsky, Felix (1877–1926)

The first head of the Cheka, the Communist Party's secret police, which later morphed into the NKVD and eventually the KGB. An extreme ascetic. Offspring of minor Polish nobility, he was known as the Iron Count or Iron Felix. Spent years in Tsarist jails for offences ranging from speaking Polish at school to forming a Communist Party in Poland. Tortured severely and lived with scarring on his ankles and arms. Established the Cheka as the 'sword and shield' of the Communist Party, operating outside the law from the first and answerable only to Lenin.

Fotieva, Lidia (1881–1971)
Bolshevik exile with Lenin in Paris and Switzerland in the 1900s. Lenin's private secretary in Petrograd after the Revolution and in Moscow later. Wrote extensively about Lenin's life and working habits and worked in the Lenin Museum from the 1930s.

Gorky, Maxim (real name Alexei Peshkov, 1868–1936)
Playwright, novelist, socialist political activist. Became the best-known writer – and the highest-paid – for his books on his orphaned childhood and life in extreme poverty. Exiled after the failed Revolution of 1905, lived in Capri and the US. A supporter and generous financial backer of Lenin and the Bolsheviks. A severe critic of Lenin after the Revolution, though he remained a personal friend. Helped many writers and artists who faced persecution. Left Russia but returned under Stalin's dictatorship.

Kamenev, Lev (real name LevRozenfeld, 1882–1936)
Revolutionary conspirator with Lenin for many years in exile. Married to Trotsky's sister, Olga. Opposed the Bolshevik coup but took senior positions in the Party after the Revolution. Lenin sent him on a series of personal ultra-secret and diplomatic missions after the coup. One of the 'troika' – with Stalin and Zinoviev – who took power after Lenin's health collapsed in 1922. Stalin had him purged in a show trial and executed.

Kerensky, Alexander (1881–1971)
Lawyer, journalist, moderate socialist. A famously melodramatic orator who attracted huge crowds to his speeches. The leading figure in the Provisional Government that took power in Russia after the February 1917 Revolution and the abdication of Tsar Nicholas II, but proved a weak and indecisive Prime Minister. Overthrown by Lenin in the October Revolution. Exiled to France and then the US, where he spent the last four decades of his life.

Kollontai, Alexandra (1872–1952)
Revolutionary feminist whose first campaign was for education of

women workers. Talented novelist and author. In exile the leading Bolshevik in Scandinavia, trusted by Lenin. Rival of Inessa Armand as feminist propagandist. After Revolution, the first Commissar for Social Welfare. Clashed with Lenin on workers' rights, removed from senior Party positions and sent as Soviet Ambassador to Norway. Her book *A Great Love* was said to be based on the affair between Lenin and Inessa Armand. Had a series of love affairs of her own with leading Bolshevik revolutionaries.

Krasin, Leonid (1870–1926)

Electrical engineer and one of the few Bolsheviks who had ever worked in a business. Chief fundraiser for the Party, who managed to persuade millionaires to give money to the revolutionary cause. Head of the 'technical department' of the Party which organised bank robberies within Russia. After the Revolution, had high positions in Soviet trade and economic commissariats.

Krupskaya, Nadezhda (1869–1939)

Daughter of army officer and schoolteacher, both from minor nobility. Qualified as a teacher and taught workers to read and write. A passionately committed revolutionary socialist. Lenin's wife from 1898 – they married when both were exiled to Siberia for political offences. Lived with Lenin for nearly twenty years in exile and held senior posts in the Bolshevik Party, organising clandestine networks and handling agents. After the Revolution held senior post at the Commissariat of Public Enlightenment. Objected to the idea of embalming Lenin's body after he died and displaying it, but lost the battle. Opposed Stalin after Lenin died for a few years but turned into a reluctant Stalin loyalist for the last dozen years of her life.

Lunacharsky, Anatoly (1875–1933)

A revolutionary from school days and a supporter of Lenin after the Bolshevik- Menshevik split in 1903. A prolific and gifted writer of literary criticism, a close friend of Gorky. Broke with Lenin briefly but joined the Bolsheviks again. Was on the 'sealed train' from Switzerland to Russia. Became the first Commissar for Enlightenment after the Revolution, responsible for Soviet culture and education. Removed from office by Stalin after Lenin died and despatched to diplomatic posts away from Russia.

Malinovsky, Roman (1876–1918)

A metalworker, jailed for theft and charged with attempted rape. Released from prison, became active in trade unions and the Social Democratic Party. Caught the eye of Lenin in 1909 as a highly intelligent, authentic working-class leader. Lenin promoted him to be the most important Bolshevik inside Russia. A double agent for the Tsarist secret police, the Okhrana, for whom he was the most highly paid agent provocateur and spy they had ever employed. He betrayed scores of Bolshevik activists, who were arrested and exiled – including Stalin, Sverdlov and Bukharin. Despite the evidence Lenin refused to believe he was a traitor. At the start of the First World War he absconded to Germany and after the February Revolution Okhrana files revealed his double life. He returned to Russia in 1918 and was shot.

Martov, Yuli (born Julius Tsederbaum, 1873–1923)

Founder and leading thinker of the Mensheviks. Exiled to Siberia and Western Europe for two decades. Had been Lenin's closest male friend and they were inseparable when they launched Russia's first Marxist party, the Social Democrats, together and began the newspaper *Iskra*. But they fell out in a vicious dispute that split the Party irrevocably in 1903. A highly popular man, fine writer and witty speaker, he returned to Russia in 1917, but objected to Lenin's seizure of power. Lenin allowed him to leave Russia and he went into exile again in 1920, to Berlin, where he died of TB.

Plekhanov, Georgy (1856–1918)

The 'father' of Russian Marxism. Escaped from Russia in 1880, just before the police were about to arrest him. His books *Our Differences* (1885) and, despite its title, *The Development of a Monist View of History*, became classic Marxist texts, famous throughout Europe. Established the Social Democratic Party and *Iskra* with Lenin but repeatedly clashed with him. Supported the First World War, against Lenin. Returned to Russia in 1917 and objected to the Bolshevik coup. Went into hiding shortly afterwards, fearing for his life. Died from a natural illness.

Stolypin, Pyotr (1862–1911)

The most able statesman and administrator of the late Tsarist period. Launched a series of agrarian and economic reforms – but also draconian measures against 'subversives' in which thousands of people were killed. Lenin admired him as a clever politician and opponent. Assassinated in Kiev by a Socialist Revolutionary, but the evidence suggested that the murder was planned by rivals in the Tsarist police and royal court.

Sverdlov, Yakov (1885–1919)

Arrested first aged barely eighteen and jailed numerous times before 1917. A staunch Lenin loyalist and number two in the administrative machine after the Bolshevik Revolution. Lenin said it 'would need six men to replace Sverdlov'. He was the chief organiser and fixer in the regime, who carried out much of the secret dirty work Lenin would delegate to nobody else, such as organising the murder of the Tsar and his family. When Lenin was shot and, briefly, out of action after an assassination attempt, Sverdlov took over the reins. Died in the post-war influenza epidemic.

Trotsky, Leon (born Lev Bronstein, 1879–1940)

Marxist thinker and prolific writer. Originally a supporter of Lenin and contributor to *Iskra*, but sided with the Mensheviks in the Party split and then was neutral. Venomous disagreements with Lenin for a dozen years afterwards. A sparkling speaker who became famous in the failed 1905 Revolution when he led the Petrograd Soviet. In 1917 he made peace and sided with Lenin and became the public face of the Revolution – much better known than Lenin. He organised the Bolshevik coup and was head of the Red Army during the Civil War. Sidelined by Stalin after Lenin's death and forced into exile. Murdered on Stalin's orders.

Ulyanov, Alexander (1866–87)

Lenin's older brother (by three years). Gifted natural science student at St Petersburg University. Involved in a bungled plot by the People's Will revolutionary group to assassinate Tsar Alexandra III. Arrested, tried in secret and hanged six weeks after his twenty-first birthday.

Ulyanov, Ilya (1831–86)
Lenin's father. Leading Tsarist civil servant, an inspector of schools, who rose to the status of nobility because of his official rank as an administrator. Moderate liberal in politics. Died of a stroke when his son Vladimir was fifteen.

Ulyanova-Elizarova, Anna (1864–1935)
Lenin's older sister, a revolutionary socialist, who was arrested, jailed and exiled several times for her radical political activities. Married shipping agent Mark Elizarov and adopted a son, Gora. Wrote an Ulyanov family history in the 1930s detailing, among other things, her mother's Jewish background, which Stalin censored.

Ulyanova, Maria Alexandrovna (1835–1916)
Lenin's mother, whom he often described as 'a saint – pure and simple'. She was never a Marxist or any kind of socialist, but subsidised his revolutionary politics, and was a constant support to all her radical children. Throughout his two decades of exile he wrote her a constant stream of letters.

Ulyanova, Maria Ilyinichna (1878–1937)
Lenin's younger sister. Jailed and exiled regularly for her political activities. Occasionally lived with Lenin and Nadya in Switzerland and Poland – and shared an apartment with them in the Kremlin after the Revolution. Was given a senior post in the Communist Party after the Revolution by her brother, and a high-level job on the Party newspaper, *Pravda*.

Zinoviev, Grigory (born Hirsch Apfelbaum, 1883–1936)
Lenin's most faithful sidekick and aide during his years of exile from 1903, in Paris, Geneva, Poland and Zurich. Returned to Russia with Lenin on the 'sealed train'. Opposed the October coup and, initially, the establishment of a one-party state, but took leading jobs after the Revolution – as head of the Bolshevik Party in Petrograd and later Secretary of the Comintern. A popular speaker and after Lenin's death the

chief cheerleader of the 'Lenin cult' of mass hero worship. One of the 'troika' of leaders who succeeded Lenin but fell foul of Stalin, who drove him out of the Communist Party. Tried with Kamenev in the first of the show trials in Stalin's Great Terror and shot.

NOTES

PROLOGUE: THE COUP D'ETAT

The best accounts of the October Revolution remain the eyewitness reporting of Nikolai Sukhanov, *The Russian Revolution 1917: A Personal Record*, London, 1955 (from the Russian *Zapitski o Revolutsii*, originally published in 1922), John Reed, *Ten Days That Shook the World*, New York, 1919, and despite, in places, its manifest *parti pris* distortions, Leon Trotsky, *The History of the Russian Revolution*, London, 1934. The best modern account in English is Orlando Figes, *A People's Tragedy: The Russian Revolution 1891–1924*, London, 1996. I have drawn on all these works here.

[1] Lenin's *Collected Works* – around 9.5 million words of them – were published in the former USSR in various editions, the latest of them in 45 volumes between 1965–1973. I shall refer to them here, throughout, as CW. Lenin's letters to Fofanova and the Bolshevik Central Committee: CW, Vol. 44, pp. 68–72. The danger on Petrograd streets, Reed, p. 83.

[2] Lenin's arrival at Smolny: Harrison Salisbury, *Black Night, White Snow: Russia's Revolutions 1905–1917*, New York, 1978, pp. 434–42; Trotsky, *History of the Russian Revolution*, p. 288.

[3] Disorganisation of the October coup: Figes, pp. 484–90; Nikolai Podvoisky, 'Lenin in October', *Krasnaya Gazeta*, 6 November 1927.

[4] Lenin's furious pace of work: Podvoisky. Choosing the title People's Commissars: Trotsky, *My Life*, New York, 1930, pp. 427–31.

[5] Lenin's anger: Podvoisky; ministers in Winter Palace: Salisbury, pp. 440–6, Figes, pp. 495–497, Richard Pipes, *The Russian Revolution 1899–1919*, London, 1990, pp. 514–16.

[6] Lenin's statement at Soviet Congress: CW, Vol. 44, p. 83.

[7] Provisional Government in Winter Palace: Pipes, pp. 515–17.

[8] Petrograd during the coup: Sukhanov, pp. 392–4; Reed, pp. 195–7.

[9] Storming of the Winter Palace: Podvoisky; Figes, pp. 515–17; Trotsky, *History of the Russian Revolution*, pp. 313–15; Sukhanov, pp. 396–9.

[10] Trotsky's speech at Congress of Soviets: Isaac Deutscher, *The Prophet Armed: 1879–1921*, New York, 1954, p. 397; Lenin's speech: Reed, p. 213.

1: A NEST OF GENTLEFOLK

The best accounts of Lenin's family and childhood are by his two sisters – Anna Ulyanova-Elizarova, *Vospominaniya ob Il'iche*, published in Moscow in 1934 and translated into English as *The Childhood and School Years of Vladimir Ulyanov*, Moscow, 1988; and Maria Ulyanova, *O lenine i sem'ye Ulyanovikh: vospominaniya ocherki pisma*, Moscow 1978. Robert Service, *Lenin: A Biography*, London, 2000; Dmitry Volkogonov (trans. Harold Shukman), *Lenin: Life and Legacy*, London, 1994; Louis Fischer, *The Life of Lenin*, London, 1995; and Ronald Clark, *Lenin: The Man Behind the Mask*, London, 1988.

[1] Men had to agree with him, Mikhail Silvin: quoted in Adam Ulam, *Lenin and the Bolsheviks*, London, 1966.

[2] Lenin's mother and Blank family background: Volkogonov, pp. 45–9.

[3] Children's love for mother: Anna Ulyanova-Elizarova, p. 33.

[4] Maria Alexandrovna's charm: cited in Clark, p. 64.

[5] Ilya Ulyanov, Lenin's father, background and politics: Anna Ulyanova- Elizarova, p. 21, and Maria Ulyanova, p. 17. Gorky on Lenin's 'traits of a nobleman': 'Untimely Thoughts' column, *Novaya Zhizn*, 17 November 1917.

2: A CHILDHOOD IDYLL

[1] Lenin as a child: Anna Ulyanova-Elizarova, pp. 2–41, and Maria Ulyanova, pp. 5–17; Robert Service, pp. 33–41; Clark, pp. 21–30.

[2] Simbirsk described by Ivan Goncharov, *Oblomov*, London, 1989. Lenin's early reading and playing games: Service, pp. 37–42; Richard Abraham, *Kerensky: The First Love of the Revolution*, London, 1987; Lenin and chess: Fischer, pp. 98–101.

[3] The Ulyanovs at Kokushkino: Anna Ulyanova-Elizarova, pp. 31–3.

[4] Lenin's education: Service, pp. 36–7; Fischer, pp. 45–51.

[5] Memories from classmates at school: Clark, pp. 61–3.

[6] Lenin not interested in politics in adolescence: Anna Ulyanova-Elizarova, p. 26.

[7] Death of Lenin's father: Maria Ulyanov, pp. 29–31.

3: THE HANGED MAN

[1] Sasha's execution: Salisbury, pp. 5–9; Bertram Wolfe, *Three Who Made a Revolution*, Boston, 1955, pp. 72–4; Philip Pomper, *Lenin's Brother: The Origins of the October Revolution*, New York, 2010, pp. 173–9.

[2] Sasha's childhood and youth: Anna Ulyanova-Elizarova, pp. 26–8.

[3] Lenin's hatred for bourgeois liberals who snubbed his mother: Leon Trotsky, *The Young Lenin*, New York, 1972, pp. 43–4; Isaac Deutscher, *Lenin's Childhood*, London, 1970, pp. 123–5.

[4] Sasha's assassination plot: Pomper, pp. 103–9. Trial: Wolfe, pp. 62–4. Meetings in jail with his mother: Fischer, p. 124.

[5] Vladimir's reaction to death: Maria Ulyanova, p. 32, and quoted in Clark, pp. 86–8.

[6] The bourgeois 'traitors and cowards': Nikolai Valentinov, *Encounters With Lenin*, London, 1968, and letter to sisters Anna and Maria, 13 July 1901, CW, Vol. 43, p. 126.

4: THE POLICE STATE

[1] Pyotr Struve, *Collected Works: Vol. 9*, Ann Arbor, 1970.

[2] Count von Aehrenthal, quoted in Pipes, *The Russian Revolution*, p. 137.

[3] Zasulich trial: Anna Hillyar and Jane McDermid, *Revolutionary Women in Russia, 1870–1917*, London, 2000, p. 136.

[4] Women revolutionaries and Vera Figner: quoted in Hillyar and McDermid, pp. 35–55.

[5] Tsarist autocracy: Figes, pp. 73–84; Pobedonostev quoted in Pipes, *The Russian Revolution*, p. 89; Trotsky, *The History of the Russian Revolution*, pp. 65–74.

[6] Censorship and the Tsars: Pipes, *The Russian Revolution*, pp. 85–7; Fischer, pp. 73–5.

[7] Radical movements: Figes, pp. 130–6; Wolfe, pp. 73–9; Maxim Gorky, *My Universities*, New York, 1938, pp. 130–5.

8 Sergei Nechayev, *The Revolutionary Catechism*, www.marxists.org/subject/anar-chism/nechayev/catechism.htm

5: A REVOLUTIONARY EDUCATION

1 Fyodor Kerensky on Lenin, quoted in Fischer, p. 73.
2 Expulsion from university: Volkogonov, p. 68.
3 Lenin and smoking: Maria Ulyanova, p. 39.
4 Ministers' refusal to allow Lenin to study: Maria Ulyanova, p. 46. Lenin on his mother's courage: Valentinov, p. 61.
5 Lenin on Chernyshevsky: Valentinov, p. 81–2.
6 Lenin on landed estates: Valentinov, p. 148. On hunting: Anna Ulyanova-Elizarova, p. 47.
7 Lenin on discovering Marx: Maria Ulyanova, p. 43.
8 On farming: Nadezhda Krupskaya, *Reminiscences of Lenin*, New York, 1970, pp. 67–8.
9 Lenin's law exams: Ulam, p. 89.

6: VLADIMIR ILYICH – ATTORNEY AT LAW

1 Lenin's legal case against Arefev: Service, pp. 91–2 and Anna Ulyanova-Elizarova, p. 49.
2 Volga famine: Maria Ulyanova, p. 57 and Leon Trotsky, *On Lenin: Notes Towards a Biography*, London, 1971, p. 86.
3 Descriptions of Lenin: Valentinov, p. 46; Alexander Potresov, *Posmertinyi sbornik proizvednyii* (ed. B. Nikolayevsy), Paris, 1937; and quoted in Clark, p. 73. Alexander Kuprin quoted in Fischer, p. 85.
4 Lenin's character: Potresov, p. 63, and quoted in Clark, p. 72.
5 Lenin, *What the Friends of the People Are*, CW, Vol. 2, pp. 47–57.
6 Lenin lecturing to St Petersburg workers: Clark, pp. 82–4.

7: NADYA – A MARXIST COURTSHIP

1 Nadya's first meeting with Lenin: Krupskaya, *Reminiscences*, pp. 42–4.
2 Nadya's family and background: ibid., pp. 10–18; Robert McNeal, *Bride of the Revolution: Krupskaya and Lenin*, London, 1973, pp. 13–19; and Mary Hamilton-Dann, *Vladimir and Nadya*, New York, 1998 .
3 Nadya's idealism: quoted in Fischer, p. 95.
4 Work as railway clerk: Fischer, p. 73.
5 Nadya's friendship with Yakubova: McNeal, p. 89.

8: LANGUAGE, TRUTH AND LOGIC

1 Lenin uses argument to 'wipe him off the face of the earth': CW, Vol. 6, p. 156.
2 Moishe Olgin: quoted in Clark, p. 145.
3 Voitinsky: quoted in Salisbury, p. 126.
4 Lenin as a speaker: Maxim Gorky, *Days with Lenin*, New York, 1933, also as *Memories of Lenin* at the Marxists internet archive, www.marxists.org/archive/gorky-maxim/1924/01/x01.htm
5 Lenin as speaker: Trotsky, *On Lenin*, pp. 197–9.
6 Martov quote, see Israel Getzler, *Martov: A Political Biography of a Russian Social Democrat*, Cambridge, 1967.

9: FOREIGN PARTS

1 'Important mission': CW, Vol. 44, p. 265.
2 Lenin and Okhrana: quoted in Helen Rappaport, *Conspirator: Lenin in Exile*, London, 2009, p. 7; bad at languages: letter to his mother, 29 April 1895, CW, Vol. 44, p. 266.
3 First sight of Alps: letter to his mother, 2 May 1895, CW, Vol. 44, p. 261.
4 Meeting Plekhanov: CW, Vol. 9, p. 145; letter to Maria Ulyanova, 24 May 1895, CW, Vol. 44, p. 302.
5 Axelrod's letter to Plekhanov: quoted in Fischer, p. 173.
6 Asking mother for money: CW, Vol. 44, pp. 283 and 298.
7 On invisible ink: Lenin to Axelrod, CW, Vol. 44, p. 485.

10: PRISON AND SIBERIA

1 First interrogation: Clark, p. 83.
2 Keeping fit in jail: Letter to Maria Ulyanova, 13 February 1896, CW, Vol. 44, p. 532, and to his mother, 10 February 1896, CW, Vol. 44, p. 519.
3 Visitors to prison: letter to Anna and Maria Ulyanova, 3 March 1896, CW, Vol. 44, p. 546.
4 Letters in code: ibid.
5 Kzhizhanovsky: quoted in Fischer, p. 134.
6 Lenin in Siberia: letter to his mother, 14 March 1897, CW, Vol. 44, p. 527.
7 Arrival at Shushenskoye: letter to his mother, 28 May 1897, CW, Vol. 44, p. 539. Hunting: letter to Maria Ulyanova and Dmitry Ulyanov, 29 June, CW, Vol. 44, p. 556. Lonely: letter to Anna Ulyanova, 25 July 1897, CW, Vol. 44, p. 583.
8 Family sending supplies: letter to his mother, 6 September 1897, CW, Vol. 44, p. 573.
9 Nadya on her early married life: quoted in McNeal, p. 197.
10 Nadya's letters to Lenin's mother and sisters on hunting: 9 September and 11 October 1898, CW, Vol. 44, pp. 587 and 593 respectively; on being pregnant: 12 October 1899, CW, Vol. 44, p. 616.
11 Arrest at Tsarkoe Selo: Service, p. 156 and Fischer, p. 133; Nadya's illness: letter to his mother, 6 April 1900, CW, Vol. 44, p. 637.

11: LENIN IS BORN

1 Plekhanov's letters to Lenin about liberals: quoted in Ulam, p. 176. Lenin's replies: CW, Vol. 44, p. 312.
2 Letter from Lenin to Nadya from Munich, 12 December 1900, CW, Vol. 44, p. 456.
3 Lonely in Munich: letter to his mother, 3 January 1901, CW, Vol. 44, p. 487.
4 Nadya meeting Lenin in Munich: Krupskaya, *Reminiscences*, pp. 93–6.
5 *Iskra* as the 'collective agitator': CW, Vol. 5, p. 115.
6 Clash between Plekhanov and Lenin over *Iskra*, Lenin's quotes: *How the 'Spark' was nearly extinguished*, CW, Vol. 5, pp. 197–8.
7 Letter to Plekhanov on editing *Iskra*: 4 January 1901, CW, Vol. 44, pp. 276–7. Launch issue article by Lenin: 11 December 1900, CW, Vol. 5, pp. 276–81.
8 Smuggling *Iskra*: Service, pp. 132–6, and Rappaport, pp. 152–6.
9 Deciphering letters: Krupskaya, *Reminiscences*, pp. 179–81 and Rappaport, pp. 162–5.

[10] Lenin as editor: Krupskaya, *Reminiscences*, p. 183. Friendship with Martov: Fischer, pp. 133–7; Krupskaya, *Reminiscences*, pp. 180–3; Sukhanov, pp. 85–93; and Israel Getzler, *Martov: A Political Biography of a Russian Social Democrat*, Cambridge, 1967. Potresov on Martov quoted in Ulam, p. 135.

12: UNDERGROUND LIVES

[1] Mikhail Silvin: quoted in Ulam, p. 133.
[2] Conspiratorial life underground: Rappaport, pp. 133–40; Figes, pp. 242–9; and Krupskaya, *Reminiscences*, pp. 146–9.
[3] Elena Stasova: quoted in Rappaport, p. 139.
[4] Women conspirators: Rappaport, pp. 136–9.
[5] Lenin on organising underground networks: letter to Leonid Krasin, CW, Vol. 44, p. 253.
[6] Okhrana penetration of underground cells: Krupskaya, *Reminiscences*, p. 117.

13: ENGLAND, THEIR ENGLAND

[1] London, 'hideous' letter to Axelrod: 16 April 1902, CW, Vol. 44, p. 233. Lenin and Nadya hated English food: Krupskaya, *Reminscences*, p. 135. Landlady: quoted in Rappaport, p. 197. Letter from Lenin's mother about lodgings: quoted in Clark, p. 129.
[2] Lenin loathed communes and wanted his own space: Valentinov, pp. 196–7.
[3] British police relaxed about Russian radicals: Rappaport, pp. 194–5.
[4] Publishing *Iskra* and the British Museum Reading Room: Andrew Rothstein, *Lenin in Britain*, London, 1970, p. 76 and p. 92. Lenin aloof but cheerful: Valentinov, p. 199.
[5] Lenin taking walks and excursions outside London: Rothstein, pp. 78–81 and Rappaport, pp. 193–5.
[6] Country walks: letter to his mother, 2 July 1902, CW, Vol. 44, p. 598.
[7] Trotsky arrives in London and meets Lenin: Trotsky, *On Lenin*, p. 37.
[8] Leaving London, miserable and ill: Krupskaya, *Reminiscences*, p. 137.

14: WHAT IS TO BE DONE?

[1] *What Is To Be Done?* in the original *Leninski sbornik* (collected writings), Moscow, Vol. 7 of 50 published between 1927 and 1960. The best English version was translated by S. V. and Patricia Utechin, Oxford, 1963.
[2] Valentinov, p. 146.
[3] Krupskaya, *Reminiscences*, p. 104.
[4] 'Theory is only a hypothesis', said to Potresov: quoted in Clark, p. 138. Plekhanov quote 'Lenin could veer and prevaricate': letter to Angelica Balabonova, p. 159.

15: THE GREAT SCHISM – BOLSHEVIKS AND MENSHEVIKS

[1] Zelikson Bobrovskaya: quoted in Clark, p. 142.
[2] Martov in Geneva: Krupskaya, *Reminiscences*, p. 128.
[3] Lenin disliked boring people: Valentinov, p. 173.
[4] Lenin singing revolutionary songs: quoted in Clark, p. 144.
[5] Lenin divided himself from other exiles: Valentinov, p. 181.
[6] The 1903 Congress is described well by Rappaport, pp. 165–71, Service, pp. 156–62 and Ulam, pp. 173–9. Quote to Gleb Krzhizhanovsky: letter, 11 October 1903, CW, Vol. 44, p. 128. Lenin on 'a splendid Congress': quoted in Clark, p. 149.

[7] The Party splits are superbly recounted by Valentinov, pp. 178–81; Service, pp. 160–6; Fischer, pp. 197–201; and Rappaport, pp. 173–6.
[8] Lenin's 'rages': Valentinov, p. 189.

16: PEAKS AND TROUGHS

[1] Walking in the Alps: Lenin to his mother, 6 September 1903, CW, Vol. 44, p. 372.
[2] Reconciliation attempts in Party: Krzhizhanovsky in Ulam, p. 204.
[3] Walking holiday, 1903, and Lenin's need for holidays: Krupskaya, *Reminiscences*, p. 149.
[4] Climb of Rochers de Naye with Maria Essen: quoted in Fischer, pp. 169–71.

17: AN AUTOCRACY WITHOUT AN AUTOCRAT

Of the vast number of books about the last Tsar and his wife – and the late stages of the Romanov dynasty – the best are Simon Sebag Montefiore, *The Romanovs 1613–1918*, London, 2016; Dominic Lieven, *Nicholas II: Emperor of all the Russians*, London, 1993 and Edvard Radzinsky, *The Last Tsar*, London, 1992. The letters of Nicholas II and Alexandra, 1914–1918, are invaluable source material, available online at www.alexanderpalace.org/letters. There is excellent background on the Tsar and the 1905 Revolution in Figes, *A People's Tragedy*, and Pipes, *The Russian Revolution*.

[1] Nicholas absorbed in picking his nose: Figes, p. 172.
[2] 'Best-bred . . . yet tremendous parochialism', Sebag Montefiore, *The Romanovs*, p. 526.
[3] War with Japan: Pipes, *The Russian Revolution*, pp. 188–93.
[4] Lenin reaction to 1905 Revolution: Krupskaya, *Reminiscences*, p. 184.
[5] Bloody Sunday description: Figes, pp. 246–8.
[6] Gorky at Bloody Sunday: cited in Figes, p. 249.
[7] US Ambassador McCormick, Foreign Relations of the United States (FRUS), http://digital.library.wisc.edu/1711.dl/FRUS.FRUS1905.
[8] Lenin on Japan War: CW, Vol. 6, p. 274.
[9] Lenin's letters on street fighting: CW, Vol. 44, pp. 337–8.
[10] Lenin on arming the masses, 'an immediate task': CW, Vol. 6, p. 328.
[11] 'Victory . . . is not the point': quoted in Ulam, p. 253.
[12] Leonid Krasin on rich people's gifts to Bolsheviks: quoted in Roy Medvedev, *Let History Judge*, London, 1972. Putilov, 'Tsarism is lost': quoted in Ulam, p. 259.
[13] Landlords fear attacks: Figes, pp. 282–4.

18: BACK HOME

[1] Stalin's first meeting with Lenin: quoted in Simon Sebag Montefiore, *The Young Stalin*, London, 2007, p. 213.
[2] Gorky's relationship with Lenin: Gorky, *My Days with Lenin*, London, 1933, pp. 27–9 and Figes, pp. 257–9.
[3] Lenin speaking at Countess Panina's *soirée*: Krupskaya, *Reminiscences*, p. 195.
[4] Terror after 1905 Revolution: Pipes, *The Russian Revolution*, pp. 217–20; Salisbury, pp. 191–4; Sebag Montefiore, *The Romanovs*, pp. 493–5. Tsar Nicholas wanted harsh measures: Salisbury, p. 195.
[5] Tsar's anti-Semitism and support for Union of the Russian People: Sebag Montefiore, *The Romanovs*, pp. 497–8 and *Letters of Tsar Nicholas to* [his mother] *Empress Marie*, (ed. Edward Bing), London, 1930. Pogroms: Figes, pp. 271–3.
[6] Lenin's physical cowardice: Pipes, *The Russian Revolution*, p. 283.

19: 'EXPROPRIATE THE EXPROPRIATORS'

[1] 'Revolution is not a finishing school,' Lenin to Martov: 12 March 1902, CW, Vol. 44, p. 278 and to Valentinov, p. 196.

[2] *Record of Fifth Russian Social Democratic Congress*, London 1907, Service, p. 219. Gorky: quotes from *Days with Lenin*, p. 48. Lenin's concern for Gorky's comfort: quoted in Wolfe, p. 237. Maxim Litvinov: quotes on Rothschilds from John Holroyd-Doveton, *Maxim Litvinov: A Biography*, London, 2013, p. 135.

[3] 1907 Congress: Rappaport, pp. 204–10. Bank robbery in Tiflis: Sebag Montefiore, *The Young Stalin*, pp. 22–8. Schmidt inheritance: Volkogonov, pp. 194–201 and Fischer pp. 216–19. Lenin admits he could not have carried off the deception: Service, p. 182. 'A scoundrel . . . might be what we need': Lenin to Vladimir Bonch-Bruevich, 8 March 1909, CW, Vol. 44, p. 137.

[4] The 'trustees' of the Schmidt money: Volkogonov, p. 202.

[5] Lenin's money from Party: Volkogonov, pp. 238–40. Nadya admits they were not in penury: Krupskaya, *Reminiscences*, p. 198.

[6] Lenin needs rest: Nadya's letter to his mother, 22 June 1907, CW, Vol. 44, p. 423, and Lenin to his mother, 24 June 1907, CW, Vol. 44, p. 425.

[7] Lidia Dan: quoted in Boris Sapir (ed.), *Fyodor Ilyich Dan Prisma [Letters] 1899–1947*, Amsterdam, 1985, p. 137.

[8] Clara Zetkin, *Reminiscences of Lenin*, www.marxists.org/archive/zetkin/1924/reminiscences-of-lenin.htm.

[9] Walter Borg's quote about Lenin's freezing feet: Salisbury, p. 213.

[10] Krupskaya, *Reminiscences*, p. 194.

20: GENEVA – 'AN AWFUL HOLE'

[1] Lenin, 'I've come back to Geneva to be buried': Krupskaya, *Reminiscences*, p. 196.

[2] Ibid. p. 202.

[3] 'shall I live to see another Revolution': letter to Maria Ulyanova, 3 March 1909, CW, Vol. 44, p. 496.

[4] Plekhanov, *My i oni* ['*Us and Them*'], Moscow 1907, p. 32 and quoted in Samuel Baron, *Plekhanov: The Father of Russian Marxism*, Stanford, 1963. August Bebel to Lenin: quoted by Martov in Getzler, p. 136.

[5] Lenin and Bogdanov: letter to Gorky, CW, Vol. 44, p. 263.

[6] Lenin on religion: letter to Gorky, CW, Vol. 44, p. 186.

[7] Gorky on Lenin's charm and vivacity: Gorky, *Days with Lenin*, p. 28.

[8] Okhrana informers: Krupskaya, *Reminiscences*, pp. 173–4.

[9] Zinoviev's background: Ulam, pp. 213–14; and quotes: Balabanova, p. 139. Kamenev, quotes: Valentinov, p. 149 and Trotsky, *My Life*, p. 274.

[10] On Dr Zhitomirsky: Yuri Felshtinsky, *Lenin and His Comrades: The Bolsheviks Take Over Russia, 1917–1924*, New York, 2010. 'A large city will cheer us up': Lenin to his mother, 13 December 1908, CW, Vol. 44, p. 497.

21: INESSA – LENIN IN LOVE

[1] Background of Inessa Armand: Michael Pearson, *Inessa: Lenin's Mistress*, London, 2001 and R. C. Elwood, *Inessa Armand: Revolutionary and Feminist*, Cambridge, 1992.

[2] 'Lenin was mesmerised': Jean Fréville, *Lénine à Paris*, Paris, 1958, p. 13.

[3] Elizabeth de K. and Lenin: Fischer, p. 192 and Felshtinsky, pp. 93–5.

[4] Reports from Okhrana: quoted in Ben Fischer, *Okhrana: The Paris Operations of the Russian Imperial Police*, Washington D.C., Center for the Study of Intelligence, 1997. Also a double agent: Valerian Agafonov, *Zagranichnaya Okhrana*, Petrograd, 1918, has good first-hand accounts of spying throughout Europe for the Tsar.

[5] Inessa's background: Pearson, Elwood, Freville, Louis Fischer and Polina Vinogradskaya, *Pamyati Inessy Armand* (ed. Nadezhda Krupskaya), Moscow, 1926.

[6] Krupskaya, *Reminiscences*, p. 195. Food parcels from Russia: Lenin to his mother, 5 June 1909, CW, Vol. 44, p. 479. Tidy Paris flat: Ilya Ehrenburg, *People and Life: Memoirs 1891–1917*, London, 1961.

[7] Lenin's stress and insomnia: Krupskaya, *Reminiscences*, p. 197.

[8] Nadya on cycling: letter to Lenin's mother, 19 September 1909, CW, Vol. 44, p. 485. Last time Lenin saw his mother: Krupskaya, *Reminiscences*, p. 201 and quoted in Katy Turton, *Forgotten Lives: The Role of Lenin's Sisters in the Russian Revolution, 1864–1937*, London, 2007.

[9] The long-censored letters between Inessa and Lenin became available after the collapse of the USSR in 1991 in various stages over the next decade, not all at once. Most are in the Russian State Archive of Social and Political History (RGASPI) fond 127, but a few others are in the Archives of the President of the Russian Federation (APRF). Most of the family records were moved to the RGASPI by 1991, including most of Inessa's letters to her children. This letter 'I wasn't in love with you then': RGASPI f. 127, op. 17, d. 12.

[10] Nadya in 'a state of utter melancholy': letter to Lenin's mother and sister Maria, 12 April 1910 and 3 May 1910, CW, Vol. 44, p. 496 and p. 513. Kollontai claims Nadya offered to leave Lenin: Marcel Body, 'Alexandra Kollontai', *Preuves*, No. 14, April 1952, Paris.

[11] 'Life . . . more cheerful when Inessa around': Krupskaya, *Reminiscences*, p. 198.

[12] 'a hot bonfire of revolution': quoted in Rappaport, p. 201. Inessa was 'pedantic . . . repeated Lenin verbatim': Balabanova, p. 185.

22: BETRAYALS

[1] 'Theory is not Holy Writ': quoted in Ulam, p. 235. Lenin in favour of parliaments, in *Nevskaya Zveda*: 13 May 1912, CW, Vol. 7, pp. 257–8.

[2] Roman Malinovsky an 'outstanding worker representing us': Lenin to Alexander Shlyapnikov, 16 October 1912, CW, Vol. 43, p. 186.

[3] Malinovsky's background: Service, pp. 220–8; Felshtinsky, pp. 25–7; Ulam, pp. 237–40; and Rappaport, pp. 225–9.

[4] Lenin didn't believe Malinovsky a double agent: Krupskaya, *Reminiscences*, p. 219.

[5] 'That bastard . . . fooled us for years': Lenin to Zinoviev, quoted in Rappaport, p. 228.

[6] Launch of *Pravda*: Louis Fischer, pp. 278–80.

[7] Lenin to Gorky on moving to Austria: 12 May 1912, CW, Vol. 44, p. 104.

[8] Climbing Babya in the Tatra Mountains: quoted in Clark, p. 219.

[9] Galicia is 'almost Russia': Lenin to his mother, 3 September 1912, CW, Vol. 44, p. 496. Homesickness: Krupskaya, *Reminiscences*, p. 198.

23: A LOVE TRIANGLE – TWO INTO THREE WILL GO

[1] Nadya ill and needing treatment for Graves' Disease: letter to Maria Ulyanova, quoted in Clark, p. 285.

[2] Nadya's operation in Berne: Louis Fischer, pp. 284–7. Lenin's row with surgeon: letter to Kamenev, 15 June 1913, CW, Vol. 44, p. 138.

[3] Nadya on operation: ibid., p. 213.

[4] Nadya on Inessa in Galicia: Krupskaya, *Reminiscences*, p. 219.

[5] Lenin's fondness of children: Zina (Zinoviev) Lilina, 'Tov: Lenin edet v Rossiyu', *Leningradskaya Pravda*, 16 April 1924.

[6] Lenin thanks Inessa for representing him in Brussels: RGASPI f. 127, opis. 16, delo. 19.

[7] Nadya on drawing close to Inessa: Krupskaya, *Reminiscences*, p. 223.

[8] Inessa's letter from Paris, 14 December 1913: RGASPI f. 127, op. 13, d. 15; Lenin's reply: RGASPI f. 127, op. 13, d. 18.

24: CATASTROPHE – THE WORLD AT WAR

[1] Lenin predicting war, *Vyperod*: October 1907, CW, Vol. 7, p. 142.

[2] Lenin tells his mother there won't be war: 13 November 1912, CW, Vol. 44, p. 499; and to Gorky, 9 December 1912, CW, Vol. 44, p. 178.

[3] Arrest in Galicia and help from Victor Adler: Lenin letter to Zinoiev, CW, Vol. 44, pp. 258–9 and Clark, p. 195.

[4] Move to Berne: Lenin to his sister Maria, 21 August 1914, CW, Vol. 44, p. 513.

[5] Russian Interior Minister Durnovo warning against war: Figes, p. 387.

[6] The most comprehensive works in English on Russia's disastrous First World War and the Eastern Front 1914–1918 are Dominic Lieven, *Towards the Flame: Empire, War and the End of Tsarist Russia*, London, 2015; Norman Stone, *The Eastern Front, 1914–1917*, London, 1975; and Max Hastings, *Catastrophe: Europe Goes to War 1914*, London, 2013. I have drawn from each of them.

[7] Brusilov quotes, an 'army of ignoramuses': Figes, p. 398.

[8] Low morale in army: Hastings, p. 277.

[9] Polianov, Minister of War, to Tsar: quoted in Figes, p. 400.

25: IN THE WILDERNESS

[1] Lenin's squabble with his sister Anna: Turton, p. 96.

[2] Lenin complains to Inessa about squabbles in Party: quoted in Service, p. 296.

[3] Nadya's mother dies and is cremated: Krupskaya, *Reminiscences*, p. 224.

[4] Nadya ill again and needs holiday: letter to Kollontai, www.marxists.org/kollontai

[5] Nadya, Inessa and Lenin holiday at Sörenberg: Krupskaya, *Reminiscences*, p. 231.

[6] Lenin's opposition to war: letter to Kollontai, 12 November 1914, CW, Vol. 44, p. 199.

[7] Zimmerwald Conference: Service, pp. 246–8. Martov on Lenin's anti-war stand: Getzler, p. 197.

[8] Inessa and Lenin dispute on 'free love': Rappaport, p. 236; Pearson, *Inessa Armand*, pp. 176–8; Service, p. 276; Inessa to Lenin, RGASPI f. 127, op. 17, d. 9 and Georges Bardawil, *Inès Armand*, Paris, 1993, p. 187.

[9] Lenin to Inessa, RGASPI f. 127, op. 15, d. 14.

[10] Background on Helphand. Zbyněk Zeman, *The Merchant of Revolution*, London, 1965.

26: THE LAST EXILE

[1] Lenin's money troubles: Nadya to Maria Ulyanova, 16 December 1916, and Lenin to Maria, 13 January 1917, CW, Vol. 44, p. 512.

[2] Modest lodgings in Zurich: Krupskaya, *Reminiscences*, p. 231.

[3] Titus Kammerer, 'We rented to the Lenins', *Partisan Review*, Vol. 6, No. 3, New York, 1939.

[4] Stefan Zweig quote: from Zweig, *The Tide of Fortune: Twelve Historical Miniatures*, London, 1927.

[5] Lenin's plan to hand over Bolshevik funds to Inessa: see Service, p. 270.

27: REVOLUTION – PART ONE

[1] Dmitry Merezhovsky quote: from the diaries of Zinaida Gippius, *Peterburgskie dnevniki 1914–1919*, New York, 1982, p. 45; and her claim that Russia is 'a large lunatic asylum', p. 49.

[2] Alexander Blok on promiscuity: quoted in Figes, p. 159.

[3] Officers going AWOL: Major-General Sir Alfred Knox, *With the Russian Army 1914–1917*, London, 1921.

[4] The revolution 'will be started by the army': quoted in Pipes, *The Russian Revolution*, p. 374.

[5] Meriel Buchanan: quote from M. Buchanan, *Ambassador's Daughter*, London, 1958. Lord Milner: quoted in Louis Fischer, p. 297.

[6] Okhrana reports: see Alexander Rabinowitch, *Prelude to Revolution: The Petrograd Bolsheviks and the July 1917 Uprising*, Bloomington, Ind., 1968.

[7] Gippius, p. 165.

[8] Lenin to Inessa, RGASPI f. 127, op. 17, d. 11.

[9] Lenin's instructions to Kollontai: 2 March 1917, CW, Vol. 12, p. 165.

[10] Plans to leave Zurich using disguises: Krupskaya, *Reminiscences*, p. 225.

[11] 'My nerves overstrung': Lenin to Inessa, RGASPI f. 127, op. 18, d. 19.

[12] Alexandra's letter describing revolutionaries 'a hooligan movement': www.alexanderpalace.org/letters

[13] 'That fat fellow Rodzianko': quoted in Sebag Montefiore, *The Romanovs*, p. 489.

[14] Mutiny by regiments and casualties in Revolution: Figes, pp. 486–92.

[15] Tsar's abdication: Sebag Montefiore, *The Romanovs*, pp. 528–9.

[16] Bolsheviks unprepared for Revolution and short of money: Rabinowitch, *Prelude to Revolution*, p. 129.

28: THE SEALED TRAIN

[1] Lenin approves Martov's 'sealed train' plan: letter to Radek, 7 March 1917, CW, Vol. 44, p. 216.

[2] Tells Inessa he has to operate secretly: letter, 8 March 1917, RGASPI f. 127, op. 18, d. 13.

[3] German Generals Ludendorff and Hoffmann: quoted in Clark, p. 269; also see Hastings, p. 253.

[4] German defence of using Lenin: Volkogonov, p. 216.

[5] Lenin desperate to reach Russia: letter to Inessa, 10 March 1917, RGASPI f. 127, op. 18, d. 13.

[6] Negotiations with Germans: Fritz Platten, *Lenin iz emigratsii v Rossiyu*, Moscow, 1925.

[7] Reaction in Zurich to sealed train: Rappaport, pp. 228–30; Michael Pearson, *The Sealed Train* (London, 1975), pp. 49–51; Catherine Merridale, *Lenin on the Train*, London, 2016, pp. 73–9; Karl Radek, 'Lenin's Sealed Train', *New York Times*, 19 February 1922; J. Ley, 'A Memorable Day in April', *New Statesman*, 19 April 1958; Olga Ravich, 'The Journey Across Germany', *Pravda*, 10 April 1922.

[8] Lenin felt justified in taking German help: Clark, p. 214.
[9] British tried to bribe Lenin: Clark, p. 217.
[10] Lenin's belongings when he left Zurich: Kammerer, 'We rented to the Lenins'. Rappaport, p. 229.
[11] Departure from station in Switzerland: Karl Radek, 'V plombirovannom vagone', *Pravda*, 20 April 1924; Platten, p. 19; and Rappaport, pp. 232–3.
[12] Lenin a martinet on the journey: Radek, 'Lenin's Sealed Train', Merridale, pp. 82–6; and Rappaport, pp. 231–4.
[13] Lenin to Zinoviev: quoted in Louis Fischer, p. 317, and in Radek, 'V plombirovannom vagone'.
[14] Lenin in Stockholm: Platten, p. 35; Radek, 'V plombirovannom vagone'; and Rappaport, pp. 236–7.
[15] Esmé Howard quote, 'let things take their course': Louis Fischer, p. 286.
[16] Lenin infuriated by articles in *Pravda* supporting the war: Krupskaya, *Reminiscences*, p. 239.
[17] Women strip-searched by British soldiers: Zina Linina, 'Tov: Lenin edet v Rossiyu', *Leningradskaya Pravda*, 16 April 1924. British agent Harry Gruner letting Lenin into Finland: Giles Milton, *Russian Roulette: How British Spies Thwarted Lenin's Global Plot*, London, 2013.

29: TO THE FINLAND STATION

[1] Finland looked familiar to Nadya and Lenin: Krupskaya, *Reminiscences*, p. 245.
[2] Kamenev's pro-war editorial: *Pravda*, 31 March 1917.
[3] Lenin's arrival at the Finland Station on Easter Monday 1917 is best described in Sukhanov, pp. 86–90 and Robert Payne, *The Life and Death of Lenin*, New York, 1965, pp. 288–92.
[4] Trotsky on Mathilde Kshesinskaya's mansion and background: quoted in Trotsky, *History of the Russian Revolution* and Barbara Allen, *Shlyapnikov: The Life of an Old Bolshevik*, Leiden, 2015.
[5] Lenin's speech to Bolsheviks at the Party headquarters: Sukhanov, pp. 91–3.

30: THE INTERREGNUM

[1] Lenin at his mother's grave: Vladimir Bonch-Bruevich, *Vospomonanii o Lenine*, Moscow, 1985, p. 43.
[2] Lenin at Tauride Palace: Sukhanov, p. 103.
[3] Lenin's 'extremism', quotes from Prince Lvov and Pavel Milyukov: Figes, p. 487.
[4] Gorky, 'this is no longer a capital; it is a cesspit': Gorky, 'Untimely Thoughts' column, *Novaya Zhizn*, 13 June 1917.
[5] Trotsky on anarchy: Trotsky, *My Life*, p. 183.
[6] 'For sheer political incompetence, history has few better examples': Zinoviev, The History of the Bolshevik Party, www.marxists.org/archive/zinoviev/. Chaos at meetings of Petrograd Soviet: Pipes, *The Russian Revolution*, pp. 448–9.
[7] 'Soon the government will not . . . preserve itself': Bonch-Bruevich, p. 63.
[8] Prince Lvov: quoted in Figes, p. 482.
[9] Kerensky speaking: Sukhanov, pp. 91–3 and Albert Rhys Williams, *Through the Russian Revolution*, New York, 1921.
[10] Gippius, p. 193.

31: 'PEACE, LAND AND BREAD'

[1] Lenin said experts were not needed: to Alexander Shotman in Shotman, 'Lenin na-kanune Oktyabrya', *O Lenine: Sbornik vospominaniy*, Leningrad, 1925.
[2] 'We must talk about peace, land and bread, these things': Lenin to Kamenev, 13 May 1917, CW, Vol. 44, p. 134.
[3] Rhys Williams, p. 74.
[4] 'A peaceful reconnaissance of our enemies' forces': Lenin to Zinoviev and Kamenev, 2 May 1917, CW, Vol. 44, p. 201.
[5] Indiscipline in army and quotes from generals: Baron Alexei Budberg papers, Hoover Institution, Stanford, California, Box 1, Knox, pp. 109–10 and in Louis Fischer, p. 284.
[6] Gorky in despair: Maxim Gorky archive, www.marxists.org/archive/gorky-maxim/
[7] Revolution on the land, estates vandalised: Figes, pp. 493–9; Pipes, *The Russian Revolution*, pp. 423–6; and Rabinowitch, *The Bolsheviks Come to Power: The Revolution of 1917 in Petrograd*, London, 1979, pp. 286–9.
[8] Landowners murdered: Figes, p. 498.

32: THE SPOILS OF WAR

[1] June All-Russian Congress of Soviets: Sukhanov, p. 186; Rabinowitch, *The Bolsheviks Come to Power*, p. 123; and Morgan Philips Price, *Manchester Guardian*, 19 June and 20 June 1917.
[2] German money to Lenin: Volkogonov, pp. 167–73, Zeman, Zbyněk (ed.), *Germany and the Revolution in Russia, 1915–1918*, Oxford, 1953, pp. 101–3; Merridale, pp. 106–15.
[3] Details of German payments to Bolsheviks: Volkogonov, pp. 170–5; Merridale, pp. 105–9; and Pearson, *The Sealed Train*, pp. 116–19. Long-censored reports detailing the cover-up: letter to Trotsky and Lenin, RGASPI f. 32, op. 14, d. 12.

33: A DESPERATE GAMBLE

[1] Andrew Curtis, *Somerset Maugham*, London, 1977 is good on Maugham's role as a spy in Petrograd, as is Maugham's own *Ashenden: Or the British Agent*, London, 1928. Robert Bruce Lockhart's *Memoirs of a British Agent*, London, 1932 and *Diaries: Volume 1*, London, 1973, are highly readable (if not always entirely reliable) about espionage in Russia between 1917 and 1921, as is Robert Service, *Spies and Commissars*, London, 2011.
[2] The disastrous June offensive: Hastings, pp. 293–7; Figes, pp. 483–6; and Budberg Papers, Box 1.
[3] Funds from Germany. Volkogonov, pp. 372–9; Merridale, pp. 94–7.

34: THE JULY DAYS

[1] Lenin insists on caution in demonstrations: Nikolai Podvoisky, 'Lenin in October'. 'Holiday' before the July Days: Bonch-Bruevich, p. 72.
[2] July Days description: Figes, pp. 472–4 and Rabinowitch, *Prelude to Revolution*.
[3] 'A little more than a demonstration, but less than a Revolution': Lenin to Trotsky, in Trotsky, *The History of the Russian Revolution*, p. 296.
[4] Lenin demands explanation from insurrection planners: Podvoisky, 'Lenin in October'.
[5] Lenin and Nadya embrace and say goodbye, witnessed by Zinoviev, Stasova and

Kamenev: Bonch-Bruevich, p. 84.

[6] Lenin goes underground into hiding: Trotsky, *On Lenin*. Shaving with Stalin's help: Service, *Lenin*, p. 272.

35: ON THE RUN

[1] Escape from Petrograd with Zinoviev: Service, *Lenin*, pp. 274–6; Bonch-Bruevich, p. 82; and Clark, pp. 296–8.

[2] Lenin, *The State and Revolution*, CW, Vol. 12.

[3] Journey from Gulf of Finland to Helsingfors: Shotman, 'Lenin nakanune Oktyabrya', p. 24.

[4] In hiding at Helsngfors police chief's apartment: Volkogonov, p. 274.

[5] Gustav Rovio, 'Kak Lenin skryvalsya u gel'sinngforskogo politseimeisteria', in N. L. Meshcheryakov (ed.), *O Lenine: Sbornik vospominanii*, Moscow, 1924.

36: REVOLUTION – PART TWO

[1] Trotsky speech: account in Sukhanov, p. 284.

[2] Lenin back in Petrograd: Margarita Fofanova, 'V. I. Lenin na Vyborrgskoi Sytorone vy 1917 godu', in *VoVIL* (*Vospominaniya o V. I. Lenin*), Vol. 4, Moscow, 1989–91.

[3] The 10 October meeting was recounted by several of the people who were there, but not by Lenin. The best account was Trotsky, *The History of the Revolution*, pp. 291–9, but Zinoviev's is lively (www.marxists.org/archive/zinoviev/), and later interesting versions are Sukhanov, pp. 331–5 (his wife was there), Louis Fischer, pp. 345–34, Figes, pp. 468–70 and Rabinowitch, *The Bolsheviks Come to Power*, pp. 286–90.

[4] Trotsky speech at Cirque Moderne: Sukhanov, p. 494. Putilov quote: 'Tsarism is dead', Reed, p. 113.

[5] 'Nobody wants the Bolsheviks': Gippius, p. 183.

37: POWER – AT LAST

[1] Revolution would not last: Gippius, p. 175 and Gorky, *Novaya Zhizn*, 26 October 1926. Vladimir Nabokov: quoted in Pipes, *The Russian Revolution*, p. 469. US Ambassador Francis: quoted in FRUS, digital.library.wisc.edu/1711.dl/FRUS.1917.

[2] Lunacharsky: quoted in Figes, p. 492.

[3] 'The bourgeois press is a weapon. Why place it in their hands': Lenin to Trotsky, in Trotsky, *On Lenin*, p. 158.

[4] Gorky, 'To Lenin the working class is like iron ore to a metal worker': *Novaya Zhizn*, 17 November 1917.

[5] Plekhanov attacked: Volkogonov, p. 248. Zasulich quote: Jay Bergman, *Vera Zasulich: A Biography*, Stanford, 1983, p. 249.

[6] Hughes wire exchange, 26 October: RGASPI f. 201, op. 21, d. 15.

[7] Trotsky quote: Trotsky, *My Life*, p. 325, but also in *The Trotsky Papers 1917–1922*, Vols 1–2, The Hague, 1967–1971: Vol. 1, p. 145.

[8] Trotsky's first day as Commissar of Foreign Affairs: Trotsky, *My Life*, p. 297.

[9] Raid on the Russian National Bank: Richard Pipes (ed.), *The Unknown Lenin: From the Secret Archives*, New Haven and London, 1996, p. 86; Louis Fischer, pp. 347–9; Alexander Rabinowitch, *The Bolsheviks in Power: The First Year of Soviet Rule in Petrograd*, Bloomington, Ind. 2007, pp. 92–4.

38: THE MAN IN CHARGE

1 Lenin neglected his health: Krupskaya, *Reminiscences*, p. 269.
2 Sovnarkom members still thought they were conspirators: Figes, p. 489.
3 Lenin at Sovnarkom meetings and punctuality: Trotsky, *On Lenin*, pp. 173–4. Lenin's orders to Smolny staff: RGASPI f. 301, op. 32, d. 9.
4 Nikolai Gorbunov: Clark, p. 324.
5 Adolph Joffe, quotes from unpublished diaries and memoirs: 'Kanun Oktyabbrya. Zasedanie v Lesnom', in *Izvestiya Tsetral'nogo Komiteta Kommunisticheskoi Parti Sovetskogo Soyuza (1989–1991)*, or *ITsKKPSS*, a cache of Soviet Party documents from the 1920s. Joffe's are in cache 4.
6 Lenin quote, 'Sverdlov is indispensable': letter to Maria Ulyanova, 19 April 1918, CW, Vol. 45, p. 134.
7 Lenin's Decree on Libraries, RGASPI f. 32, op. 3, d. 22.
8 Kamenev and Zinoviev, letter objecting to 'one-party state': *Izvestia*, 4 November 1917. Zinoviev recants: *Izvestia*, 1 December 1917.

39: THE SWORD AND SHIELD

1 Formation of Cheka and Dzerzhinsky, background: Rabinowitch, *The Bolsheviks in Power*, pp. 104–10. Joszef Piłsudski, quotes: Piłsudski, *Memoirs of a Polish Revolutionary and Soldier*, London, 1931. Isaac Steinberg, quotes: Ulam, p. 297.
2 Lenin's support for Cheka on first anniversary: CW, Vol. 26, p. 312; Pipes, *The Unknown Lenin*, p. 87; and Stephen Kotkin, *Stalin, Vol. 1: Paradoxes of Power 1878–1928*, London, 2014, p. 317.

40: WAR AND PEACE

1 Ambassador Francis to State Department, digital.library.wisc.edu/1711.dl/FRUS. FRUS1917. Allied anger at the Soviets: Figes, pp. 501–4; Margaret MacMillan, *Peacemakers: The Paris Peace Conference and its Attempt to End War*, London, 2001; and Lieven, *Towards the Flame*, pp. 201–9.
2 Lenin wanted Trotsky to delay Brest-Litovsk talks: Trotsky, *On Lenin*, p. 201. Background to the conference: John Wheeler-Bennett, *Brest-Litovsk: The Forgotten Peace, March 1918*, London, 1938. Trotsky's queries about evening dress, 'Go in a petticoat': *The Trotsky Papers*, Vol. 1. Lenin forcing the Treaty through the Communist Party: a good background can be found in Figes, pp. 573–5 and Rabinowitch, *The Bolsheviks Come to Power*, pp. 303–4 and pp. 109–18. Effect on Lenin: Krupskaya, *Reminiscences*, pp. 242–3.

41: THE ONE-PARTY STATE

1 Lenin to Petrograd Soviet, 17 November 1917, CW, Vol. 23, p. 217.
2 Lenin wanted to cancel elections: Rabinowitch, *The Bolsheviks in Power*, p. 186 and Trotsky, *On Lenin*, p. 199. Banning the Kadets as 'enemies of the people': RGASPI f. 11, op. 6, d. 23.
3 Lindhagen quote to Trotsky: *The Trotsky Papers*, Vol. 1, p. 188. Lenin meets American reporter at Assembly: Rhys Williams, p. 253.
4 Assembly closed down: Richard Pipes, *Russia Under the Bolshevik Regime 1919–1924*, London, 1994, pp. 97–100. Justifies the closure: Trotsky, *On Lenin*, p. 204.
5 Murder of Kadet ministers: Isaac Steinberg, *In the Workshop of the Revolution*, New York, 1955, p. 97 and Ulam, p. 374. Murderers allowed to go free: Rabinowitch, *The*

Bolsheviks in Power, p. 218. 'a war against the rich': *Pravda*, 8 December 1917, CW, Vol. 24, p. 163.

6 'Let there be blood', call by Lenin to Fourth All-Russian Congress of Soviets,16 March 1918, CW, Vol. 26, pp. 98–102; To Isaac Steinberg, 'we [can't] be victorious . . . without . . . terror': Steinberg, p. 175.

7 Move to Moscow: Figes, pp. 564–5; Arthur Ransome, *Six Weeks in Russia in 1919*, London, 1919; and Zinoviev in *Pravda*, 13 March 1918. Lenin complains about repairs to his Kremlin apartment: RGASPI f. 168, op. 10, d. 24.

42: THE BATTLE FOR GRAIN

1 Starvation in Petrograd, Gorky quotes: Torvah Yedlin, *Maxim Gorky: A Political Biography*, Westport, Conn., 1999 and Emma Goldman, *Living My Life*, London, 1932, p. 239. Some friends 'unrecognisable': Gippius, p. 225.

2 Lenin's article 'The Battle for Grain': *Pravda*, 11 June 1918;'The Socialist Fatherland in Danger', *Pravda*, 21 February 1918.

3 Requisition brigades: Pipes, *Russia Under the Bolshevik Regime*, pp. 189–92; Figes, pp. 583–5; and Rabinowitch, *The Bolsheviks in Power*, p. 208. Lenin order to Penza Province to 'hang 100 kulaks': RGASPI f. 14, op. 17, d. 19. Stalin tells Lenin that 'my hand will not tremble': Kotkin, p. 297.

4 Maria Spiridonova's background: Isaac Steinberg, *Maria Spiridonova: Revolutionary Terrorist*, London, 1935.

5 Left Socialist Revolutionaries' Rebellion: *The Trotsky Papers*, Vol. 1, pp. 298–301; Steinberg, *Maria Spiridonova*, pp. 195–7; Rabinowitch, *The Bolsheviks in Power*, pp. 251–4; and Louis Fischer, pp. 398–401.

43: REGICIDE

1 Lenin decides on execution on 12 July with Sverdlov: Sebag Montefiore, *The Romanovs*, p. 527 and Volkogonov, pp. 328–30. Sovnarkom meeting reporting on murders, 18 July 1918: RGASPI f. 177, op. 9, d. 13. Trotsky to Sverdlov: Trotsky, *On Lenin*, p. 203.

2 Goloshchekin, background; and Ekaterinburg Soviet: Sebag Montefiore, *The Romanovs*, pp. 571–3; Helen Rappaport, *Ekaterinburg: The Last Days of the Romanovs*, London, 2008, pp. 276–8; and Pipes, *Russia Under the Bolshevik Regime*, pp. 294–6.

3 Yurovsky, background: Sebag Montefiore, *The Romanovs*, pp. 530–2; Rappaport, *Ekaterinburg*, pp. 280–2; Radzinksy, pp. 387–90. Execution described: Sebag Montefiore, *The Romanovs*, pp. 530–3. Yurovsky, quotes: Rappaport, pp. 283–4.

4 Bruce Lockhart, *Memoirs of a British Agent*, p. 296. Kokovtsov, quote: Pipes, *Russia Under the Bolshevik Regime*, p. 301.

44: THE ASSASSINS' BULLETS

1 Uritsky, murder: Rabinowitch, *The Bolsheviks in Power*, p. 296. Lenin to Trotsky, 'applying the model of the French Revolution': RGASPI f. 377, op. 10, d. 16.

2 Lenin shot: Service, *Lenin*, pp. 388–9; Bonch-Bruevich, p. 266; Professor Vladimir Rozanov (ed.), 'Iz vospominaniya a Vladimire Ilyiche, in *Po Vospominayam perepeske i dokumentam*, Moscow, 1935; and Krupskaya, *Reminiscences*, p. 274. Inessa's letter to her daughter Inna: cited in Pearson, *Inessa*, p. 198.

3 Fanny Kaplan's background: Volkogonov, pp. 237–8 and Service, *Lenin*. Arrest and interrogation: Archives of the President of the Russian Federation (APRF) f. 9, op. 21, d. 170.

4 Execution of Kaplan: Pavel Malkov, *Zapiski komendata Kremlyna*, Moscow, 1987.
5 Launch of Red Terror, Sverdlov's statement on attempted murder: RGASPI f. 678, op. 11, d. 17; Rabinowitch, *The Bolsheviks in Power*, p. 21. Executions in Petrograd: *Pravda*, 2 September 1918; Stalin to Sverdlov, RGASPI f. 19, op. 11, d. 19. Cheka officials shoot clown Bim-Bom: Figes, p. 567. Cult of Lenin, Zinoviev's speech 'Lenin, leader by the Grace of God': *Pravda*, 5 September 1917.
6 Photographs and film of Lenin: Bonch-Bruevich, p. 193. Krasin to his wife: cited in Louis Fischer, p. 307.

45: THE SIMPLE LIFE

1 Lenin's apartment in Kremlin: Krupskaya, *Reminiscences*, p. 297 and Clara Zetkin, *Reminiscences of Lenin*, www.marxists.org/archive/zetkin/1924/reminiscences-of-lenin.htm.
2 Dacha in Gorki: Krupskaya, *Reminiscences*, p. 291. Spiridon Putin was Lenin's cook: Kotkin, p. 413.
3 Privileges for Party officials: Louis Fischer, p. 398. Lenin's justification: RGASPI f. 14, op. 9, d. 23.
4 Stalin refuses to investigate Zinoviev's luxury lifestyle: Kotkin, p. 354.
5 Joffe depressed by corruption: letter to Trotsky, 19 September 1919, *The Trotsky Papers*, Vol. 1, p. 276.
6 Lenin's office: personal visit by the author, May 1987. Work habits: Lidia Fotieva, *Pages from Lenin's Life*, Moscow, 1960, pp. 45–8. Lenin loved to laugh: Gorky, *Days with Lenin*, p. 58. Lenin appears dressed in Bokharan national costume: Fotieva, p. 63.
7 Lenin orders Lunacharsky to place busts in public places: RGASPI f. 637, op. 10, d. 7. Loses temper at Sovnarkom meeting over bust of Marx: Ulam, p. 388. Reprimands commandant of Kremlin about lift repairs: APRF f. 13, op. 7, d. 13. Wastes time on trivia: Trotsky, *On Lenin*, p. 173. Hunting trips with Krylenko, 'the fox too pretty to shoot': Louis Fischer, p. 397. Hunting with Rudzutak: Ralph Carter Elwood, *The Non-Geometric Lenin: Essays on the Development of the Bolshevik Party 1910–1914*, New York, 2011.
8 Visits to the theatre: Krupskaya, *Reminiscences*, pp. 301–3. Lunacharsky says Lenin is a philistine about art: Lunacharsky, *Revolutionary Silhouettes*, www.marxistsfr.org/archive/lunachar/works/silhouet/index.htm. Admits to Zetkin he is a 'barbarian': Zetkin, p. 62.
9 Lenin on Tolstoy: 'Lev Tolstoy as the Mirror of the Russian Revolution', CW, Vol. 8, 1908, pp. 103–8. On Dostoyevsky to Valentinov, p. 232. Loathed Mayakovsky and wanted his poems published in smaller print runs: RGASPI f. 19, op. 11, d. 21.

46: REDS AND WHITES

1 Whites 'the last dream of the old world': Marina Tsvetayeva (ed. Jamey Gambrell), *Earthly Signs: Moscow Diaries, 1917–1921*, London and New Haven, 2002. The Whites' 'old regime psychology': Pyotr Struve, *The End Results and the Essence of the Communist Enterprise*, Paris 1921, CW, Vol. 11.
2 Trotsky as Commander of Red Army: Pipes, *Russia Under the Bolshevik Regime*, pp. 178–81; Robert Service, *Trotsky: A Biography*, London, 2009, pp. 285–91; and Evan Mawdsley, *The Russian Civil War*, Edinburgh, 2008. Trotsky recruits Tsarist officers: Figes, pp. 513–15 and Gippius, p. 135. Holding Tsarist officers hostage: Order Number 30, RGASPI f. 24, op. 8, d. 12. Lenin supports Trotsky: RGASPI f. 17, op. 8 1, d. 18.

[3] Whites' strategy and leaders: Mawdsley, pp. 73–80; Pipes, *Russia Under the Bolshevik Regime*, pp. 179–88; Anton Denikin, *The Russian Turmoil*, Berlin, 1922; and Alexander Kerensky, *The Kerensky Memoirs*, New York, 1965, pp. 297–301

[4] Western aid to the Whites: Mawdsley, pp. 186–92; British Cabinet discussion on support for Whites: Figes, p. 597 and David Lloyd George, *War Diaries*, London, 1938; American Secretary of State: quotes from FRUS 1918, Russia, Chapter 13, digital.library.wisc.edu/1711.dl/FRUS.FRUS1918

[5] Lenin, war telegrams, to Trotsky, Simbirsk: RGASPI f. 567, op. 13, d. 9; to Party leaders, Saratov: RGASPI f. 16, op. 9 1, d. 21; to Baku: RGASPI f. 16, op. 9 1, d. 10. Orders hostage-taking: Pipes, *The Unknown Lenin*, pp. 44–5 and document 20 from RGASPI f. 16, op. 9 1, d. 18.

[6] Rivalry between Trotsky and Stalin, who see Kollontai with her lover Dybenko: cited in Sebag Montefiore, *The Young Stalin*, p. 319. Stalin wants Trotsky removed as Red Amy chief: RGASPI f. 18, op. 6 1, d. 17. Trotsky demands Stalin recalled from Tsaritsyn: *The Trotsky Papers*, Vol. 1, p. 399. Lenin needed both of them: Kotkin, p. 376.

[7] Whites' atrocities: Kerensky, p. 347. Wrangel quote: Peter Wrangel, *Always with Honour*, New York, 1957.

[8] Pogroms by Whites: Figes, pp. 638–44 and Volkogonov, pp. 337–41. Red pogroms: Volkogonov, p. 242. Reports by Reds to Lenin: RGASPI f. 15, op. 9 1, d. 12. Lenin's gramophone recording, 'On Pogroms' and 'The Persecution of the Jews': CW, Vol. 40, pp. 287–9.

[9] British use chemical weapons against Reds: Milton, pp. 186–8 and Mawdsley, pp. 157–8. Lloyd George asks Churchill to keep quiet about Russia: Louis Fischer, p. 398. Woodrow Wilson's peace initiative: William Bullitt, *The Bullitt Mission to Russia*, New York, 1919 and Figes, pp. 609–10. Why the Whites lost: Gippius, p. 188.

47: FUNERAL IN MOSCOW

[1] Lenin overcome with emotion at Inessa's funeral: Alexandra Kollontai, quoted in Body, p. 34 and Balabanova, p. 135.

[2] Lenin's letters to Inessa before her final illness: RGASPI f. 127. Letter to Inès, 'give the letter personally to VI': quoted in Bardawil. Inessa's last letter to Lenin: RGASPI f. 127, op. 13, d. 19.

[3] Inessa's last journey to Caucasus: Lenin to Ordzhonikidze, RGASPI f. 127, op. 13, d. 12. Inessa's diary of her illness: RGASPI f. 127, op. 6, d. 12. Details of illness: Polina Vinogradskaya, *Sobytiya i pamiatnye vstrechi*, Moscow, 1926.

[4] Lenins unofficial guardians to Inessa's daughters: Varvara Armand, 'Zhivaya nit', *Novyi Mir*, No. 4, 1967; Polina Vinogradskaya, in Nadezhda Krupskaya (ed.), *Pamyati Inessy Armand*, Moscow, 1926; Pearson, *Inessa Armand*, pp. 213–15. Nadya's affection for Inessa: McNeal, p. 202. Grigory Kotov, in Kollontai, *Pamyati Inessy Armand*, p.36.

48: THE 'INTERNATIONALE'

[1] Clara Zetkin, 'his face shrank': Zetkin, p. 16.

[2] Creation of the Comintern: report of First Comintern Congress, APRF f. 23; Pipes, *The Unknown Lenin*, pp. 127–33; and Volkogonov, pp. 219–21.

[3] War with Poland, background: Service, *Lenin*, pp. 390–3; Figes, pp. 623–5; and Volkogonov, pp. 228–31. Lenin admits defeat at Tenth Communist Party Congress, 9 March 1921: CW, Vol. 38, pp. 239–42. Explains to Clara Zetkin: Zetkin, p. 28.

[4] Balabanova, first Secretary of Comintern, 'spend millions': Balabanova, p. 164. Lenin approves vast sums to foment revolution in Afghanistan: Volkogonov, pp.

391–7 and APRF f. 27, op. 3, d. 9; in Korea: APRF f. 27, op. 4, d. 8; in Finland: APRF f. 27, op. 4, d. 10. Approves money for John Reed: Central State special archive, TsGOA f. 4, d. 13.

49: REBELS AT SEA AND ON LAND

[1] Kronstadt rebellion, background: Louis Fischer, pp. 415–16; Emma Goldman, *My Disillusionment in Russia*, London, 1925, pp. 146–9; Pipes, *Russia Under the Bolshevik Regime*, pp. 213–16. Trotsky ordered to suppress uprising: *The Trotsky Papers*, Vol. 2, pp. 57–60.

[2] Petrichenko's last appeal to Trotsky, 4 March 1921, *Kronstadt Izvestia* and to Emma Goldman, p. 151. Tukachevsky, 'not a battle, an inferno': Russian State Military Archive, TsGASA f. 339986, op. 3, d. 56.

[3] Cheka killed suspect by accident: cited in Figes, p. 635. Lenin to Gorky, 'they are good people . . . that is why we must arrest them': Yedlin, p. 218. Lenin, 'dictatorship means use of force, not of law', to Zinoviev: RGASPI f. 16, op. 9, d 12.

[4] Gorky saves dissidents from prison, Lenin released Ivan Volny, 12 April 1919: RGASPI f. 18, op. 12, d. 34; asks Lenin for release of Blok's secretary, March 1920: RGASPI f. 19, op. 8, d. 13. Dzerzhinsky told to investigate case of actress Nadezhda Nikulia: RGASPI f. 19, op. 9, d. 114.

[5] Volga famine, background: Pipes, *Russia Under the Bolshevik Regime*, pp. 386–90 and Henry Fisher Report on American Relief Administration effort in Russia, ARA files, Hoover Foundation, Stanford, California. Lenin ordered Molotov to spy on Hoover's relief volunteers: APRF f. 20, op. 11, d. 9.

[6] Peasant revolt in Tambov Province: Volkogonov, pp. 345–7 and Pipes, *Russia Under the Bolshevik Regime*, pp. 281–3. Tukachevsky uses chemical weapons and burns down villages: TsGASA f. 339727, op. 2, d. 13.

[7] Lenin's campaign against Church, background: Pipes, *The Unknown Lenin*, pp. 119–23; Volkogonov, pp. 387–92; and Figes, pp. 624–7. Patriarch Tikhon excommunicates Bolsheviks: cited in Pipes, *Russia Under the Bolshevik Regime*. Lenin's note to Central Committee, 'we can smash the church': Volkogonov, pp. 381–3.

[8] Millions seized from Church: APRF f. 18, op. 9, d. 11.

50: INTIMATIONS OF MORTALITY

[1] Lenin had been considered 'of robust health': Trotsky, *On Lenin*, p. 201.

[2] 'I am unwell': letter to Zetkin, CW, Vol. 45, p. 167. Requests leave of absence from colleagues in July: RGASPI f. 11, op. 7, d. 9; again in December: RGASPI f. 11, op. 9, d. 4. Tells doctors to remove one of the bullets in his body left after Kaplan murder attempt: Rozanov, p. 3.

[3] Bertrand Russell meeting with Lenin: Russell, *The Practice and Theory of Bolshevism*, London, 1920. 'Lenin always wore the same tie': Simon Liberman, cited in Clark, p. 398. Sculptor Clare Sheridan makes a bust of Lenin: Sheridan, *Russian Portraits*, London, 1921.

51: REVOLUTION – AGAIN

[1] Bukharin explains the NEP, 'We are making economic concessions to avoid having to make political ones': APRF f. 12, op. 6, d. 9.

[2] Lenin defends NEP to Party Central Committee, 12 June 1921: CW, Vol. 45, p. 238. Speech to Tenth Party Congress, 16 March 1921: CW, Vol. 45, p. 217.

[3] Campaign against bureaucracy, 'We should be hanged for creating red tape': cited in Louis Fischer, p. 498.

52: THE LAST BATTLE

[1] Maria Ulyanova on Lenin's stroke: Maria Ulyanova, *Olerine i sem'ye Ulyanovikh*, RGASPI f. 16, op. 3, d. 6.
[2] Lenin wanted to kill himself and 'die like the Lafargues': ibid. Stalin saw Lenin and said he would give him cyanide 'if it becomes necessary': Kotkin, p. 313.
[3] He was still issuing orders to the Cheka: RGASPI f. 13, op. 9, d. 7; and to Justice Commissar about the new penal code: RGASPI f. 13, op. 8, d. 13.
[4] Was not like the old Lenin making speeches: French Communist, quoted in Clark, p. 493.
[5] Stalin refused to give him poison, 'I do not have the strength': Kotkin, p. 315.
[6] Lenin's 'Last Testament', background: Service, *Lenin*, pp. 450–2; Fotieva, *VoVIL*, Vol. 8, pp. 180–90; and Volkogonov, pp. 390–5.
[7] Lenin's last row with Stalin: Kotkin, pp. 320–2; Krupskaya, letter to Kamenev: RGASPI f. 12, op. 3, d. 9; Lenin's message to Stalin: RGASPI f. 12, op. 3, d. 11; Stalin's reply: RGASPI f. 12, op. 3, d. 12. March 1923 stroke and Professor Kramer quote: Moshe Lewin, *Lenin's Last Struggle*, New York, 1967.
[8] Nadya's letter to Zetkin: RGASPI f. 12, op. 9, d. 1; Nadya to Inna Armand, 23 May 1923: RGASPI f. 12, op. 9, d. 11; letter on 2 September: RGASPI f. 12, op. 9, d. 13. Lenin's nephew Gora's visit: record at RGASPI f. 13, op. 11, d. 17. Visit by artist Yuri Annenkov: cited by Volkogonov, p. 374.
[9] Lenin's last day remembered: Bukharin, *Pravda*, 30 January 1924; death described in Krupskaya, *Reminiscences*, pp. 301–2.

53: 'AN EXPLOSION OF NOISE'

[1] 'Unmistakable grief' after Lenin's death: Valentinov, p. 288.
[2] Funeral described: Walter Duranty, *New York Times*, 28 January 1924; Bukharin, *Pravda*, 29 January 1924; Balabanova, p. 215; and Lunacharsky, www.marxists.org/archive/lunachar.

54: LENIN LIVES

[1] Funeral Commission orders embalming the body for forty days: RGASPI f. 17, op. 9, d. 13. Dzherzhinsky, 'If science can preserve a human body': Politburo minutes, 25 January 1924, RGASPI f. 17, op. 17, op 8, d. 13. Trotsky objects to embalmment: *The Trotsky Papers*, Vol. 2, p. 59. Nadya's letter to Inna Armand: RGASPI f. 12, op. 13, d. 18.
[2] The 'Troika' ensure that Lenin's Testament is 'buried' at Politburo: RGASPI f. 17, op. 11, d. 13; and at Council of Elders: RGASPI f. 17, op. 11, d. 16 and Kotkin, pp. 424–6. Zinoviev's speech at Central Committee, 'Every word of Ilyich is law to us': RGASPI f. 17, op. 12, d. 116.
[3] Lunacharsky on the shape of Lenin's skull: *Pravda*, 3 September 1918. Studies by the Institute of the Brain: Volkogonov, pp. 400–2; post-mortem reports: Rozanov, p. 23; Service, *Lenin*, p. 463; and Louis Fischer, p. 483.
[4] Immortalisation Commission and embalming Lenin: Volkogonov, pp. 406–10; Ilya Zbarsky and Samuel Hutchinson, *Lenin's Embalmers*, London, 1998; Service, *Lenin*, pp. 453–4; and John Gray, *The Immortalisation Commission*, London, 2010.

SELECT BIBLIOGRAPHY

Abraham, Richard, *Alexander Kerensky: The First Love of the Revolution*, London, 1997

Alliluyev, Sergei, *Moyi vospominaniya, Krasnaya letopis*, Moscow, 1923

Archives of the President of the Russian Federation (APRF), Moscow

Armand, Varvara, 'Zhivaya nit', *Novy Mir*, No. 4, 1967

Ascher, Abraham, *The Revolution of 1905*, London, 1988

Ascher, Abraham, *P. A. Stolypin: The Search for Stability in Late Imperial Russia*, Stanford, 2001

Baedeker, Karl, *Baedeker's Russia*, London, 1914

Bagoczki, Sergiusz, 'V. I. Lenin v Krakove i Poronine', in *VoVIL*, Vol. 1, pp. 438–56

Balabanova, Angelica, *Impressions of Lenin*, Ann Arbor, 1964

Bardawil, Georges, *Inès Armand*, Paris, 1993

Baron, Samuel, *Plekhanov: The Father of Russian Marxism*, Stanford, 1963

Beer, Daniel, *The House of the Dead: Siberian Exile under the Tsars*, London, 2016

Bernov, Y. and Manusevich, A., *Lenin v Krakove*, Moscow, 1972

Blackstock, Paul and Hoselitz, Bert (eds), *The Russian Menace to Europe, Karl Marx and Friedrich Engels: A collection of articles, speeches, letters and news dispatches*, London, 1953

Bobrovskaya, Cecilia, *Twenty Years in Underground Russia*, San Francisco, 1934

Body, Marcel, 'Alexandra Kollontai', *Preuves*, No. 14, April 1952, pp. 12–24

Bonch-Bruevich, Vladimir, *Izbrannye Sochineniya*, Moscow, 1934

Bonch-Bruevich, Vladimir, *Vospomonaniya o Lenine*, Moscow, 1985

Brien, Alan, *Lenin: The Novel*, London, 1987

Brogan, Hugh (ed.), *Signalling from Mars: The Letters of Arthur Ransome*, London, 1998

Bryant, Louise, *Six Red Months in Russia*, New York, 1918

Buchanan, Sir George, *My Mission to Russia and Other Diplomatic Memories*, London, 1923

Buchanan, Meriel, *Ambassador's Daughter*, London, 1958

Bukharin, Nikolai, *The ABC of Communism*, Ann Arbor, 1966

Bukharin, Nikolai, *How It All Began*, New York, 1998

Carr, E. H., *The Bolshevik Revolution* (3 vols), London, 1950

Carrère d'Encausse, Hélène, *Lenin*, New York, 2001

Chernyshevsky, Nikolai, *Chto delat?*, St Petersburg, 1863; in English as Beraha, Laura (trans.), *What Is To Be Done?*, London, 1983

Churchill, Sir Winston, *The World Crisis, Vol. 2: The Aftermath*, London, 1929

Clark, Ronald W., *Lenin: The Man Behind the Mask*, London, 1988

Clements, Barbara, *Bolshevik Women*, Cambridge, 1997

Conquest, Robert, *Between Mars and Venus*, London, 1962

Conquest, Robert, *The Great Terror*, London, 1973

Conquest, Robert, *Tyrants and Typewriters*, London, 1989

Dan, L. O., *Iz Arkhiva Dan*, Amsterdam, 1957

Deutscher, Isaac, *The Prophet Armed: Trotsky 1879–1921*, New York, 1954

Deutscher, Isaac, *The Prophet Unarmed: Trotsky 1921–1929*, New York, 1959

Deutscher, Isaac, *Lenin's Childhood*, London, 1970

Deutscher, Tamara, *Not By Politics Alone: The Other Lenin*, London, 1973

Elwood, Ralph Carter, *Inessa Armand: Revolutionary and Feminist*, Cambridge, 1992

Elwood, Ralph Carter, *The Non-Geometric Lenin: Essays on the Development of the Bolshevik Party 1910–1914*, New York, 2011

Ehrenburg, Ilya, *People and Life: Memoirs of 1891–1917*, London, 1961

Engel, Barbara Alpen and Rosenthal, Clifford, *Five Sisters: Women against the Tsar*, London, 2013

Essen, Maria, 'Vstrechi s Leninym', in *VoVIL*, Vol. 1, pp. 244–62

Felshtinsky, Yuri, *Lenin and His Comrades: The Bolsheviks Take Over Russia 1917–1924*, New York, 2010

Figes, Orlando, *A People's Tragedy: The Russian Revolution 1891–1924*, London, 1996

Fischer, Ben, *Okhrana: The Paris Operations of the Russian Imperial Police*, Washington D.C., Center for the Study of Intelligence, 1997

Fischer, Louis, *The Life and Death of Stalin*, London, 1953

Fischer, Louis, *The Life of Lenin*, London, 1965

Fomicheva, L., *N. K. Krupskaya: Zhizn' i deyatelnost' v fotografiyakh i dokumentakh*, Moscow, 1988

Fotieva, Lidia, *Pages from Lenin's Life*, Moscow, 1960

Francis, David, *Russia from the American Embassy*, New York, 1921

Fréville, Jean, *Une grande figure de la révolution russe: Inessa Armand*, Paris, 1957

Fréville, Jean, *Lénine à Paris*, Paris, 1968

Ganecki, Yakub (von Vurstenberg), 'V. Lenin', *Voprosy istorii*, No. 3, Moscow, 1970, pp. 92–101

Geifman, Anna, *Thou Shalt Kill: Revolutionary Terrorism in Russia, 1894–1917*, Princeton, 1993

Geifman, Anna (ed.), *Russia Under the Last Tsar: Opposition and Subversion, 1894–1917*, Oxford, 1999

Getzler, Israel, *Martov: A Political Biography of a Russian Social Democrat*, Cambridge, 1967

Getzler, Israel, *Nikolai Sukhanov: Chronicler of the Russian Revolution*, Cambridge, 2011

Gil', Stepan, *Shest' let s V. I. Leninym: vospominaniya*, Moscow, 1957

Gippius, Zinaida, *Peterburgskie dnevniki 1914–1919*, New York, 1982

Goldman, Emma, *My Disillusionment in Russia*, London, 1925

Goldman, Emma, *Living My Life*, London, 1932

Golikov, Georgy, *Vospominaniya o V. I. Lenine* (5 vols), Moscow, 1968–1970

Golikov, Georgy, *V. I. Lenin: Biograficheskaya Khronika, 1870–1924* (12 vols), Moscow, 1970–1982

Gorky, Maxim, *My Days with Lenin*, London, 1933

Hasegawa, Tsuyoshi, *The February Revolution of Petrograd, 1917*, London, 1981

Hastings, Max, *Catastrophe: Europe Goes to War 1914*, London, 2013

Henderson, Robert, 'Lenin and the British Museum Library', *Solanus*, Vol. 4, London, 1990, pp. 3–15

Hillyar, Anna and McDermid, Jane, *Revolutionary Women in Russia, 1870–1917*, London, 2000

Hoffman, Max, *War Diaries and Other Papers*, London, 1929

Holroyd-Doveton, John, *Maxim Litvinov: A Biography*, London, 2013

Ivansky, A. I. (ed.), *Comet in the Night: The Story of Alexander Uly-anov's Heroic Life and Tragic Death as Told by his Contemporaries*, Honolulu, 2004

Joffe, Nadezhda A., *Back in Time: My Life, My Fate, My Epoch*, Oak Park, Mich., 1995

Kamenev, Lev, *Mezhdu dvumya revolyutsiyami; sbornik statey*, Moscow, 1923

Kennan, George, 'The Sisson Documents', *The Journal of Modern History*, Vol. 28, No. 2, June 1956, pp. 130–54

Kennan, George, *Russia and the West Under Lenin and Stalin*, Boston, 1961

Kerensky, Alexander, *The Crucifixion of Liberty*, New York, 1934

Kerensky, Alexander, *The Kerensky Memoirs: Russia and History's Turning Point*, New York, 1965

Knox, Major-General Sir Alfred, *With the Russian Army 1914–1917*, London, 1921

Kollontai, Alexandra, *Love of Worker Bees*, London, 1971

Kollontai, Alexandra, *A Great Love* (trans. Porter, Cathy), London, 1981

Kotkin, Stephen, *Stalin, Vol. 1: Paradoxes of Power 1878–1928*, London, 2014

Krupskaya, Nadezhda, *Reminiscences of Lenin*, New York, 1970

Krupskaya, Nadezhda, 'O Vladimire Ilyich', in *VoVIL*, Vol. 2, Moscow, 1975

Krzhizhanovsky, Gleb, 'O Vladimir Il'iche', in *VoVIL*, Vol. 2, Moscow, 1924

Lenin, Vladimir Ilyich, *Collected Works*, (45 vols) (in English), Moscow, 1963–1970

Lenin, Vladimir Ilyich, *Biograficheskaya khronika* (12 vols), Moscow, 1970–1982

Lenin, Vladimir Ilyich, *Neizvestnye Dokumenty 1891–1922* (ed. Amian-tov, Yuri), Moscow, 1999

Lepeshinskaya, Olga, *Vstrechi s Ilyichem*, Moscow, 1966

Lepeshinsky, Panteleimon, *Na povorot: ot kontsa 80-kh godov k 1905*, Moscow, 1922

Lih, Lars, *Lenin*, London, 2011

Liebman, Marcel, *Leninism under Lenin*, London, 1975

Lieven, Dominic, *Russia's Rulers Under the Old Regime*, London, 1989

Lieven, Dominic, *Nicholas II: Emperor of all the Russias*, London, 1993

Lieven, Dominic, *Towards the Flame: Empire, War and the end of Tsarist Russia*, London, 2015

Lilina, Zina (Zinovieva), 'Tov: Lenin edet v Rossiyu', *Leningradskaya Pravda*, 16 April 1924

Lunacharsky, Anatoly, *Revolutionary Silhouettes*, New York, 1968

Lyadov, M., *Iz zhizhni partii, Vospominaniya*, Moscow, 1926

McMeekin, Sean, *History's Greatest Heist: The Looting of Russia by the Bolsheviks*, New York, 2009

McMeekin, Sean, *The Russian Origins of the First World War*, Cambridge, Mass., 2011

McMeekin, Sean, *July 1914: Countdown to War*, London, 2014

McNeal, Robert, *Bride of the Revolution: Krupskaya and Lenin*, London, 1973

Maisky, Ivan, *Journey Into the Past*, London, 1960

Marcu, Valeriu, 'Lenin in Zurich: a Memoir', in *Foreign Affairs*, April 1943

Marxist Internet Archive, www.marxists.org

Mayakovsky, Vladimir, *And Other Poems,* London, 2016

Medvedev, Roy, *Let History Judge: The Origins and Consequences of Stalinism*, London, 1972

Mel'nichenko, Vladimir, *Ya tebya ochen' lyubila: Pravda o Lenine i Armand*, Moscow, 2002

Merridale, Catherine, *Lenin on the Train*, London, 2016

N. L. Meshcheryakov (ed.), *Po Vospominayam perepeske i dokumentam*, Moscow, 1935

Mikhailov, I. K., 'Vospominaniya o V. I. Lenin', in *VoVIL*, Vol. 3, Moscow, 1960, pp. 130–41

Milton, Giles, *Russian Roulette: How British Spies Thwarted Lenin's Global Plot*, London, 2013

Milyukov, Pavel, *The Russian Revolution*, New York, 1978

Muravyova, L. and Sivolap-Kaftanova, L., *Lenin in London: Memorial Places*, Moscow, 1983

Novikov, V., *Lenin i deyatel'nost' iskrovskikh grupp v Rossii 1900–1903*, Moscow, 1978

Ossendowski, Ferdinand, *Lenin: God of the Godless*, London, 1931

Payne, Robert, *The Life and Death of Lenin*, New York, 1965

Pearson, Michael, *The Sealed Train*, London, 1975

Pearson, Michael, *Inessa: Lenin's Mistress*, London, 2001

Pianzola, Maurice, *Lenine en Suisse*, Geneva, 1965

Piłsudski, Joseph, *The Memoirs of a Polish Revolutionary and Soldier*, London, 1931

Pipes, Richard, *The Russian Revolution 1899–1919*, London, 1990

Pipes, Richard, *Russia Under the Bolshevik Regime 1919–1924*, London, 1994

Pipes, Richard (ed.), *The Unknown Lenin: From the Secret Archives*, London and New Haven, 1996

Platten, Fritz, *Lenin iz emigratsii v Rossiyu*, Moscow, 1925

Podvoisky, Nikolai, 'V. I. Lenin v 1917 godu', in *VoVIL*, Vol. 4, Moscow, 1960

Pomper, Philip, *Lenin's Brother: The Origins of the October Revolution*, New York, 2010

Porter, Cathy, *Alexandra Kollontai: A Biography*, London, 2014

Possony, Stefan, *Lenin: The Compulsory Revolutionary*, London, 1966

Potresov, Alexander (ed. Nikolayevsky, B.), *Posmertny sbornik proizvedeniya*, Paris, 1937

Rabinowitch, Alexander, *Prelude to Revolution: The Petrograd Bolsheviks and the July 1917 Uprising*, Bloomington, Ind., 1968

Rabinowitch, Alexander, *The Bolsheviks Come to Power: The Revolution of 1917 in Petrograd*, London, 1979

Rabinowitch, Alexander, *The Bolsheviks in Power: The First Year of Soviet Rule in Petrograd*, Bloomington, Ind., 2007

Radek, Karl, 'Lenin's "Sealed Train"', *New York Times*, 19 February 1922

Radek, Karl, 'V plombirovannom vagone', *Pravda*, 20 April 1924

Radek, Karl, *Portrety i pamflety* (2 vols), Moscow, 1927

Rakhia, Eino, 'Moyi vospominaniya o Vladimir Ilyich', *Pravda*, 21 January 1927

Ransome, Arthur, *Six Weeks in Russia in 1919*, London, 1919

Ransome, Arthur, *The Autobiography of Arthur Ransome*, London, 1976

Rappaport, Helen, *Ekaterinburg: The Last Days of the Romanovs*, London, 2008

Rappaport, Helen, *Conspirator: Lenin in Exile: The Making of a Revolutionary*, London, 2009

Rappoport, Charles, 'Lénine à Paris', in *Russie d'aujourd'hui*, No. 70, January 1938

Raskolnikov, Fyodor, 'Priezd tov. Lenina v Rossiyu', *Proletarskaya revolutyutsiya*, No. 10, 1923, pp. 220–26

Reed, John, *Ten Days That Shook the World*, New York, 1919

Rothstein, Andrew, *Lenin in Britain*, London, 1970

Rozanov, Vladimir, 'Iz vospominaniya o Vladimire Ilyiche', in N. L. Meshcheryakov (ed.), *Po Vospominayam perepeske i dokumentam*, Moscow, 1935

Russell, Bertrand, *The Practice and Theory of Bolshevism*, London, 1920

Russian State Archive of Social and Political History (RGASPI), Moscow

Russian State Library (The Lenin Library), Moscow

Russian State Library of Literature and Arts (RGALI), Moscow

Russian State Military Archive (TsGASA), Moscow

Salisbury, Harrison, *Black Night, White Snow: Russia's Revolutions 1905–1917*, New York, 1978

Sanborn, Joshua, *Imperial Apocalypse: The Great War and the Destruction of the Russian Empire*, Oxford, 2014

Savinkov, Boris, *Memoirs of a Terrorist*, London, 1931

Sebag Montefiore, Simon, *The Romanovs 1613–1918*, London, 2016

Sebag Montefiore, Simon, *The Young Stalin*, London, 2007

Semashko, Nikolai, *Otchego bolel i umer V. I. Lenin*, Leningrad, 1924

Senn, Alfred, *The Russian Revolution in Switzerland 1914–1917*, London, 1975

Serge, Victor, *Memoirs of a Revolutionary*, London, 1963

Serge, Victor, *Year One of the Russian Revolution*, London, 1972

Service, Robert, *Lenin: A Political Life* (3 vols), London, 1985–95

Service, Robert, *Lenin: A Biography*, London, 2000

Service, Robert, *Stalin: A Biography*, London, 2004

Service, Robert, *Trotsky: A Biography*, London, 2009

Service, Robert, *Spies and Commissars*, London, 2011

Schapiro, Leonard, *The Communist Party of the Soviet Union*, New

York, 1970

Schapiro, Leonard, *The Russian Revolutions of 1917: The Origins of Modern Communism*, New York, 1984

Sheridan, Clare Consuelo, *Russian Portraits*, London, 1921

Shlyapnikov, Alexander, *On the Eve of 1917: Reminiscences from the Revolutionary Underground*, London, 1982

Shotman, A. V., 'Lenin nakanune Oktyabrya', in *O Lenine: Sbornik vospominaniy*, Leningrad, 1925

Shub, David, *Lenin*, London, 1966

Shukman, Harold, *Lenin and the Russian Revolution*, New York, 1981

Shukman, Harold (ed.), *The Blackwell Encyclopedia of the Russian Revolution*, Oxford, 1988

Smele, Jonathan, *Russian Revolution and Civil War 1917–1921: An Annotated Bibliography*, London, 2003

Solzhenitsyn, Alexander, *Lenin in Zürich*, London, 1975

Spengler, Tilman, *Lenin's Brain*, London, 1993

Stasova, Elena, *Vospominaniya*, Moscow, 1969

Steinberg, Isaac, *Maria Spiridonova: Revolutionary Terrorist*, London, 1935

Stone, Norman, *The Eastern Front 1914–1917*, London, 1975

Sukhanov, Nikolai, *Zapiski o Revolutsii*, Moscow, 1922; in English as *The Russian Revolution 1917: A Personal Record*, London, 1955

Sverdlova, Klavdia, *Yakov Mikhailovich Sverdlov*, Moscow, 1957

Tismaneanu, Vladimir, *The Devil in History: Communism, Fascism, and Some Lessons of the Twentieth Century*, Los Angeles, 2012

Trotsky, Leon, *My Life*, New York, 1930

Trotsky, Leon, *The History of the Russian Revolution*, London, 1934

Trotsky, Leon (ed. Meijer, M.), *The Trotsky Papers, 1917–1922* (2 vols), The Hague, 1964–1971

Trotsky, Leon, *On Lenin: Notes Towards a Biography*, London, 1971

Troyat, Henry, *Gorky*, London, 1989

Tsereteli, Irakli, *Vospominaniya o fevral'skom revolutsii*, Paris, 1963

Tsvetaeva, Marina and McDuff, David (trans.), *Selected Poems*, London, 1987

Tsvetaeva, Marina, *Earthly Signs: Moscow Diaries, 1917–1921*, London and New Haven, 2002

Tumarkin, Nina, *Lenin Lives!: The Lenin Cult in Soviet Russia*,

Cambridge, Mass., 1983

Turton, Katy, *Forgotten Lives: The Role of Lenin's Sisters in the Russian Revolution, 1864–1937*, London, 2007

Ulam, Adam, *Lenin and the Bolsheviks*, London, 1966

Ulam, Adam, *In the Name of the People*, New York, 1977

Ulyanova-Elizarova, Anna, *Vospominaniya ob Il'iche*, Moscow, 1934, in English as *The Childhood and School Years of Vladimir Ulyanov*, Moscow, 1988

Ulyanova, Maria, *O lenine i sem'ye Ulyanovikh: vospominaniya ocherki pisma*, Moscow, 1978

Valentinov, Nikolai, *Encounters With Lenin*, London, 1968

Vasilieva, Larissa and Porter, Cathy, *Kremlin Wives*, London, 1994

Vernadsky, George and Davis, Malcolm Warner (trans.), *Lenin: Red Dictator*, New Haven, 1931

Vinogradskaya, Polina and Krupskaya, Nadezhda (ed.), *Pamyati Inessy Armand*, Moscow, 1926

Volkogonov, Dmitri, *Stalin: Triumph and Tragedy*, London, 1988

Volkogonov, Dmitri and Shukman, Harold (trans.), *Lenin: Life and Legacy*, London, 1994

Wade, Rex, *The Russian Revolution, 1917*, London, 2000

Williams, Robert, *The Other Bolsheviks: Lenin and His Critics, 1904–1914*, Bloomington, Ind., 1986

Wilson, Edmund, *To the Finland Station: A Study in the Writing and Acting of History*, London, 1972

Wolfe, Bertram, *Three Who Made a Revolution*, Boston, Mass., 1955

Yedlin, Tovah, *Maxim Gorky: A Political Biography*, Westport, Conn., 1999

Zamoyski, Adam, *Warsaw 1920: Lenin's Failed Conquest of Europe*, London, 2008

Zbarsky, Ilya and Hutchinson, Samuel, *Lenin's Embalmers*, London, 1998

Zeman, Zbyněk (ed.), *Germany and the Revolution in Russia 1915–1918*, Oxford, 1953

Zeman, Zbyněk, *The Merchant of Revolution: The Life of Alexander Israel Helphand (Parvus), 1867–1924*, London, 1965

Zinoviev, Grigory, *History of the Bolshevik Party*, https://www.marxists.org/archive/zinoviev/works/history/ch01.htm

Zinoviev, Grigory, *Leninizm: vvedeniye v izuchenie*, Leningrad, 1925

Zuckerman, Frederic, *The Tsarist Secret Police in Russian Society, 1880–1917*, London, 1996

Zuckerman, Frederic, *The Tsarist Secret Police Abroad: Policing Europe in a Modernising World*, London, 2003

Zweig, Stefan, *The Tide of Fortune: Twelve Historical Miniatures*, London 1927

Zweig, Stefan, *The World of Yesterday: An Autobiography*, London 1943

ACKNOWLEDGEMENTS

I owe a major debt to the late, great Robert Conquest – always a source of encouragement – whose death in 2015, as I was halfway through researching this book, was such a blow to numerous historians of a later generation whom he inspired.

It is a measure of the tragedy that has befallen modern Russia that very few of the considerable number of people in Moscow and St Petersburg who helped me in this project wish their names to appear here. If I could write an 'anti-acknowledgement' it would be to the organs of state that the Russia of 2017 is building. Nevertheless, I owe an enormous and special debt to three people – they know who they are – who were invaluable research assistants and trawled through various archives for me and helped with advice and specialist knowledge about the early Bolsheviks. In Russia I am indebted to Pavel Gemenalov, Anna Nemtsova, Ilya Rhyzhkov, Nadezhda Semyenova, the staff at the Russian Presidential Archive (APRF) and of the Russian State Archive of Social and Political History (RGASPI) and Mikhail Rossokowksi, who kindly showed me around the Kremlin rooms occupied by Lenin. Many thanks to the staff at the Lenin Mausoleum, who gave me a private tour, and, some years ago, to the Gorbachev Foundation.

The Hoover Institution's Russia collection of material from the nineteenth century onwards – but particularly the Soviet years – has been invaluable, as always. I wish to thank the amazing staff at the London Library, where I wrote a large amount of this book (the back row of the art room is an inspiring place) and at the Bodleian Library. I am grateful to the staff at Wilton Park and at Chatham House.

Wonderfully generous friends have given me hugely appreciated emotional and practical support. Victoria Hislop organised a 'writers' retreat' at her beautiful house on Crete which was marvellous for getting work completed – and for companionship. Annalena

McAfee and Ian McEwan let me stay at their peaceful rural home when I was going through a difficult writing time. My thanks for seeing me through it.

I am grateful to ideas, advice and encouragement to a great many people: Richard Addis, Nina Adler, Anne Applebaum, Csaba Békés, Katalin Bogyay, Peta Brod, Archie Brown, Richard Burge, Sir Bryan Cartledge, Minderat Chauduri, Rollo Collins (for invaluable research on the First World War), Paul and Wendy Diggory, Hugo and Mark Dixon, Iain Fergusun, Helen and Lindsay Forbes, Danuta Galecka, Charles Gati, Miklós Haraszti, Barbara Kiss, Oleg Khlevniuk, Karsten Krenz, Ashkold Krushelnycky, Adam LeBor, Ben Lewis, Keith Lowe, Anne McElvoy, Boris Marelic, Annabel and Sasha Markova, Giles Milton, Anne-Elisabeth Moutet, Giuliana Nedelskaya, Christian Osterman, George Prochnik, Aram Radmoksi, László Rajk, Anna Reid, Andrew Roberts, Katya Rossokowski, Günter Schabowski (before his death in 2016), Dr Simon Sebag-Montefiore, Amanda Sebestyen, Damien Sharkov, Krassen Stanchev, Joanna Stein, George Szirtes, Stefan Tafrov, Vladimir Tismaneanu and John Walko.

Two books by scholars whose work has been inspirational and vastly helpful were Robert Service's *Lenin: A Biography* – a superb achievement – and Orlando Figes's *A People's Tragedy*. I have drawn ideas and knowledge from both.

I have been fortunate in so many things during my writing career. One above all is to have Georgina Capel as my agent. Her calm and unshakeable optimism are infectious.

This is a return to Weidenfeld and Nicolson as my publisher after a brief gap – and I am immensely glad I am back. Many thanks for the energy and enthusiasm of my editor, Alan Samson, and the super-efficiency of my assistant editor Lucinda McNeile, who have been working to the toughest of deadlines. Linden Lawson, the copy-editor, worked beyond the call of duty in a contest with time to bring the book out at speed. A great thank you to Bea Hemming, the editor who originally commissioned the book, saw it through the initial stages and had faith in it throughout.

None of my books would have been written without the constant support and loving encouragement of Jessica Pulay. She has always been a practical help with her sound judgment and clarity of thought and an inspiration for me to try harder and think deeper. It is impossible adequately to acknowledge all that I owe to her.

INDEX

Krupskaya, Nadezhda Konstantinovna
(Nadya)— *condt.*
life in London, 127–34; life in Paris,
207–10; life in Poland, 222–3; life
in Zurich, 254–7; lifestyle, 421–2;
and Malinovsky, 217, 219; marriage,
100–4; and Martov's death, 469n; and
Marxism, 88; meaning of 'Nadezhda',
77; meets Trotsky, 135–6; meets
Lenin, 76–7, 81; and mother's death,
242; and move of capital to Moscow,
388–90; organisational activity, 124–5,
198, 359; radicalisation, 79–81; returns
to Russia, 276–90; reunion with Lenin,
109–10; rows with Stalin, 495–7;
and Schmidt Affair, 186; and sexual
matters, 247–8n; walking holiday,
156–8; works at Enlightenment
Commissariat, 435, 508
Krupski, Konstantin Ignat'evich, 77–8
Krylenko, Nikolai, 429–30
Krylov, Ivan, 125
Krzhizhanovsky, Gleb, 71, 95, 99, 150–1,
155
Kshesinskaya, Mathilde, 288–9
Kshesinskaya Mansion, 288–9, 291, 323–
4, 326, 334
Kudrin, Mikhail, 405n
Kühlmann, Richard von, 314
kulaks, 66n, 392–7, 418, 429, 443, 447
Kun, Béla, 458–9
Kuprin, Alexander, 72
Kureiko, 219n
Kursky, Dmitry, 414, 491
Kuzhi, Kerensky prevents pogrom, 299

Labour Party, 462
Lac du Bré, 158
Lafargue, Laura, 89, 203n, 489–90
Lafargue, Paul, 89, 203n, 489–90
Land and Liberty (Zemlya y Volya), 55
land reform, 193n, 302
Landau, Dr Jan, 225
Lansing, Robert, 442
Las Wolski, 222
Lebedev, Pavel, 292
Léger, Fernand, 209
Lenin, Vladimir Ilyich; accused of
cowardice, 121, 177–8; adopts name
'Lenin', 107–8; and Alakayevka

property, 65–6; ancestry, 28–32;
appearance, 22–3, 30–1, 39, 71–2,
311n, 479–80; arrest and detention,
90–5; arrested in Poland, 232–4; and
bloodshed, 347, 388; and Bolshevik
government, 359–66; his brain, 506–
7; and brother Alexander, 44, 46–8,
58; his car stolen, 358n; childhood,
33–41; contracts food poisoning, 192;
conversation with tram conductress,
10; debating style, 74, 82–5; declares
himself a Communist, 232; description
of Russian army, 237; dislike of
Kerensky, 300; early journalism, 73–4;
education, 37–9, 58–9; embalming
of his body, 503–5, 507–9; emotional
control, 147–8; escape to Finland,
190–1; establishes Cheka, 367–71;
and 'expropriations', 179–81; faces
Kerensky at Congress of Soviets,
310–12; 'Farewell Address to Swiss
Workers', 277; and father's death,
40–1, 58, 347; fiftieth birthday
celebrations, 481–2; finances, 30, 60,
68, 184, 187–8, 253–4; first travels
abroad, 86–90; and First World War,
231–2, 239, 244–6; flight to Finland,
329–33, 336–8; and food shortages,
392–7; and foreign languages, 87, 93,
127, 133–4, 182, 203; friendship with
Martov, 119–20; German funding and
cover-up, 313–15, 325, 466; health
problems, 75, 86, 89, 136–7, 156, 188,
359, 430, 476–8, 488–99; importance
of holidays, 157n, 210–11; and Inessa's
children, 455–6; and Inessa's death,
451–6; infatuation with Plekhanov, 87–
9, 112–13; influence of Chernyshevsky,
61–3; interest in aeroplanes, 209–
10n; introduces economic reforms,
483–5; Jewish ancestry, 28n; Kaplan
assassination attempt, 410–20; last
illness, 488–99; last meeting with
mother, 211; his 'Last Testament',
493–4, 505–6, 508; and laughter, 427,
479; launches *Pravda*, 221–2; and
leadership, 32, 84, 138–9, 141; learns
of February Revolution, 262–3; leaves
Russia for Germany, 106; lectures to
workers, 74–5; legal career, 68–9, 71;